PRAYING
Like Fire & Water

סידור נוסח האר"י ז"ל

PRAYING
Like Fire & Water

SIDDUR WITH CHASIDIC MEDITATION
SHACHARIT — MORNING PRAYERS

ARRANGED WITH A COMMENTARY BY
RABBI DAVID STERNE

EDITING:
Ms. Uriela Sagiv

PROOFREADING:
Rabbi Avidan Shenhav

TYPESETTING:
Ms. Eden Chachamtzedek

COVER DESIGN:
R' Moshe Muchnik and Spotlight Graphics

Praying like Fire and Water,
the Siddur with Chassidic Meditation
and Commentary

First printing 2017

Paperback: ISBN 978-1-7321079-4-6
Hardcover color: ISBN 978-0-9855933-9-1
Hardcover B&W: ISBN 978-1-7321079-0-8

Copyright © 2020 by the author
POB 28186
Jerusalem, Israel
Jerconn1@gmail.com

All rights reserved.
No part of this publication may be translated, reproduced, stored in a retrieval system or transmitted, in any form or by any means, electronic or otherwise, without written permission from the publisher.

Dedicated to

My Friends and Students

the brave, intelligent, independent,
creative and resourceful immigrants
who uproot their lives and move
to Israel from all over the world,
giving up secure and comfortable
positions to take part in
the physical and spiritual
adventure that is called *Eretz Yisrael*,
transforming lives in the process.

To all of you and others
who have joined us,
and others who are yet to join us
in this adventure (God willing),
this siddur is dedicated to you.

ב"ה

RABBI MENACHEM M. GLUCKOWSKY
CHABAD RECHOVOT
12 HAGANA ST. RECHOVOT ISRAEL
Tel: 08-9493176 Fax: 08-9457620 Cel: 050-4145770

מנחם מענדל גלוכובסקי
רב קהילת חב"ד ברחובות
מען: רח' ההגנה 12/1 רחובות 76214
משרד 08-9493176. פקס 08-9457620. נייד 050-4145770

ב"ה

י"ח שבט ה'תשע"ז

To my good freind
Rabbi David Sterne שליט"א

It is not often that a new translation or summary of Chassidus is produced, that both pleases the eye and stimulates the mind and heart. The new siddur with Chassidus, "Praying Like Fire and Water," which you have written has both of these advantages

I can testify that the English reading population in Israel and elsewhere is thirsty for spiritual material that enables them to pray with more fervor and understanding. Many are the baal habatim who would like to spend more time learning Torah and praying, but whose busy schedules and demands on their time, prevent them from doing so. Many also are the "newcomers" to Torah and mitzvoth who have not yet developed their skills in Hebrew to be able to access this material in its original language. Your new work, providing excerpts of Chasidus on the words and phrases of the weekday morning prayers, allows the reader and davener to access Chasidus that would otherwise be beyond his or her reach. It does so by dividing each Chassidic excerpt into its Kaballistic elements, Chassidic elements, and finally by providing instructions about how to pray with this new information.

I can attest that you have invested a lot of time and labor into this siddur, with its translations, references and teachings.
I recommend this new siddur to anyone who is inclined to get involved and put effort into their personal prayers.

With blessing and much success,

RABBI MENACHEM M. GLUCKOWSKY

Rabbi L. Wineberg
Kollel Beit Mordechai
Hama'or Centre

The Saintly Ba'al Shem Tov famously interpreted the words of Hashem's instruction to Noah, "בא אל התיבה" ("enter the Ark"), as "enter the word". The word of *Tefillah* that carries a Jew safely through the floodwaters of life's disturbances — don't just recite it, *enter* it. Immerse yourself, let the word wash over you entirely.

To fulfil this, one must have a deep understanding and appreciation of the word, not just general sense of its meaning. Most of us lack that.

Rabbi Dovid Sterne of Jerusalem has done a remarkable job of making the depth of our prayers accessible to an English-speaking readership of non-scholars. He has painstakingly and expertly culled, from the richness of Chabad-Chassidic literature, a treasure of explanations of the prayers. He has additionally rendered them into a comprehensive and comprehensible English commentary, despite the sometimes abstruse and technical nature of the original, often difficult even for the initiated, Hebrew-reading student. And he has managed to convey this deep content without in any way attenuating the power of the sources. The Chabad Rebbes themselves stand, as it were, by the side of the prayer, as he prays with the meaning provided by their words.

I urge anyone wishing to "enter" his prayer and to come face-to-face with Hashem thereby, to avail himself of Rabbi Sterne's decades'-long labor of love — his love of the *Tefillah*, and the love of Hashem (פולחנא דרחימותא — 'service of love', as the Zohar terms it) that characterizes deep, immersive prayer.

Cheshvan 5777
Johannesburg

בס"ד

From the desk of
Rabbi Shneur Zalman Gafne

Aug 10, 2017   י"ט אב תשע"ז

During one of my personal (one-on-one interviews *beyechidus*) with the Rebbe, he informed me that his father-in-law the Rebbe *Rayatz* OBM was accustomed not to give *haskomos* ("agreements" or letters of recommendation) or acknowledgements to any *seforim*, which practice he (the Rebbe) followed implicitly. Thus I of *course*, am obliged, understandably, to adhere to this concept. However, since I know Rabbi David Sterne very well personally (well over 30 years ago he was a student of mine) and am aware of his work and gifted abilities, I wish to give him my encouragement. Even though I have not read the whole siddur, the portions I have studied carefully reveal remarkable control of, and sensitivity to, the messages and teachings of the *nesi'im* (Rebbeim) of Chabad — Lubavitch referring to *tefilo* (prayer). His *sefer* is the product of months and years of devoted toil and meticulous attention to detail. It is a significant achievement. I extend to him my warmest wishes for great success in all his efforts, together with my prayer that his *siddur* reaches all the thirsty seekers for cleavage to Divinity through prayer that it is meant to reach, throughout the world.

In his *sefer*, *Derech Mitzvoseicho* ("Path of the Commandments"), in the discourse *Shoresh Mitzvas HaTefilo* ("Roots of the commandment to pray"), the Rebbe the *Tzemach Tzedek* (third Lubavitcher Rebbe and grandson of the *Baal HaTanya*), brings a responsa from the "Questions and Answers of the *Rivash*" (the *Rivash* was a great *halachic* authority of the period of the *Rishonim* — medieval Jewish sages who lived roughly from 1000 through 1400) — in which the *Rivash* (albeit seriously and courteously) questions the need to be *mikaven* ("have intention") even correctly in prayer to the referring of Divine influence through the "holy *sefiros*" when, in simplicity based on our sages' declaration in the *Sifri* that prayer should be directed only "to Him (G-d), and not to his traits (*sefiros*). Therefore, according to the *Rivash*, it makes more sense to pray only directly to Him, relying on God to direct His holy infinite light through the right *sefiros* etc. In connection with this, the *Rivash* quotes a great contemporary sage of his period — Rabbi Shimshon de Kinon (who was also a Kabbalist) — who said that when he prays, he makes his prayer similar to the *da'as* (knowledge or inner level) of a *tinok* ("small child") and thus turns his prayer directly to God (rather than through the *sefirot*). The question arises — why does the *Tzemach Tzedek* mention this opinion or approach on the effectiveness (and necessity) of being *mekaven* ("having intention") to or through the *sefiros*? (see footnote of the Rebbe in *Likutei Sichos* Vol. 27 p. 318). This question is especially relevant since a *tinok* really has no *da'as*?

Moreover, toward the end of the above long *maamer* ("discourse"), the *Tzemach Tzedek* mentions the famous exclamation of the Alter Rebbe: "I don't want Your *Gan Eden*. I don't want Your *Oilam HaBa'a* ("world to come"). I want only to cleave to You Yourself," which seems further inappropriate to the whole theme of the *maamar*?

The Rebbe answers in the above footnote and in some of his *maamarim* (see *Parshas Poro* 5745, and elsewhere) that the very essence of *tefilo* ("prayer") is that our approach to *HaShem* lies in shaping ourselves *keda'as zeh hatinok* ("like the intention of the small child") by and through which we reach *HaShem's* Essential Being resulting from our having revealed the simplicity of the essence of ourselves beyond all reasoning and soul powers, which is the very expression of *zeh hatinok*. Realizing the *da'as zeh hatinok* ("intention of the small child") reveals the essential simplicity of the *pintele Yid* (essential, infinitesimal "point" of the Jewish soul.), thus elevating a Jew to linkage with *HaShem* beyond all the world's levels, to — "I want only You Yourself."

This is a form of application of the famous epigram of the *Sefer Yetziro*: "their beginning is fixed (or jammed literally) into their end-point (lowest level) and the end-point is fixed in their beginning." (see coming paragraphs). More simply, the highest point can (and does) reach the lowest and the lowest reaches the highest. This is prayer in its "reality" form.

In the above footnote, the Rebbe brings an example from the first night of *Pesach* (*seder* night) when we state that our eating of *matzo* derives from the revelation of "the King of Kings of Kings, the Holy One blessed be He," through which revelation he "swept" us into "redempton" (from all limitation). The Rebbe quotes from several discourses of the previous Rebbeim (based on or quoting from the *Ari zal*) that the *matzo* that we eat is the level of *katnus* (spiritual "immaturity" — similar to the *da'as zeh hatinok* — "intention of a small child") but precisely through that, the matzo elevates us to "You Yourself" — the essence of King of Kings etc.

In another discourse, (*Tu BeShevat,* 5746) the Rebbe, in light of the above, thus explains the conduct of the Baal Shem Tov who gave of his valuable time to visit villages and towns where simple (uneducated) Jews lived, and encouraged them to thank the *Eibishter* (the "One above" — "You Yourself") for good health, *parnosso* ("physical sustenance") — "praise be to the *Eibishter*" etc. etc. The Rebbe clarifies that their simple prayers (not knowing anything about *sefiros* and completely devoid of *da'as*), lifted them to the level of the "simplicity of Essential Divinity (to only "You Yourself").

Thus, the Rebbe introduces us to a fascinating fundament in the service of *tefilo* ("prayer").

In Volume 5 of the *Mamarim Melukatim*, in the discourse of *Lag B'Omer*, the Rebbe answers our question (that is, why did the Rebbe the *Tzemach Tzedek* bring at all the opinion of *da'as zeh hatinok* in a long discourse). The Rebbe states that even the *kavonos* ("intentions" during prayer) brought there at length, have to be based upon and illuminated by the simple intense *kavono* of *da'as zeh hatinok* ("intention of the small child"). That is, only fusion and unity of the two; child-like simplicity and brain power (*moichin*) lead to the ultimate ("You Yourself"). How this fusion is achieved is another theme to be dealt with elsewhere.

Perhaps we could illustrate this from the story in *Mishna* and *Gemoro* in tractate *Ta'anis* concerning the early *Mishnaic* sage, *Choni HaMa'agel* ("Choni the circle drawer"). During one heavy drought year when called on to pray for rain, *Choni* drew a circular shallow pit, and stood in it. He said to *HaShem*, "Your children have turned to me since I am a *ben bayis* ("part of the family")." He then declared he would not leave the circle until *HaShem* provided rain. And that in effect is what happened — rain descended (see the story for more details). The rabbi who was head of the rabbinic court (*Av Bais Din*) at the time, Rabbi *Shimon ben Shatach*, sent a message to *Choni* saying: "I should really penalize you for 'impropriety' towards *HaShem*, but what can I do, you are like a young son who, due to his father's great paternal love, grants his son's request, notwithstanding (and perhaps due to) the mischievousness of the son." *Choni* is the classic example of prayer as the medium for gaining Divine influence (as contrasted with *Rashbi* who brought rain through saying Torah) and here we see clearly the theme of *da'as zeh hatinok*, the child-like nuance with a rare touch of "mischief."

Perhaps we could step even further. It's well known the famous passage in the great *hemshech* (series of Chassidic *maamarim*, or "discourses") of *Ein Bais* (the year 5672, or 1912) of the Rebbe *Rashab* (Rabbi Shalom Dov Ber, fifth Lubavitcher Rebbe, grandson of the *Tzemach Tzedek*), in which he differentiates between the two concepts of *sof ma'aseh bemachashovo techilo* ("the final action arose in the original thought," from the poem of *Lecho Dodi* composed by Rabeinu Shlomo Alkabetz) and that of *noutz techilasan be soifan vesoifan be tichilasan* ("the beginning is wedged into the end, and the end in the beginning" — from *Sefer Yetziro* Chapter 1, Mishna 6). The Rebbe *Rashab* points out that despite the elevation of *noutz techilasan* ... wherein the thought and original purpose (or plan) of the Giver (*Mashpia* — HaShem) are expressed and realized (fulfilled) precisely in the final practical *ma'aseh* ("action") which occurs *b'soifan* — "at the end". However, there is still a recognizable connection between *techilo* ("beginning") and *sof* ("end") — that is, between the initial factors of the whole process and its finality of expression in *ma'aseh bepoel* ("ultimate action"). However, *soif ma'aseh bemachashovo techilo* implies that the ultimate practical conclusion rises much higher than the beginning of the process, reaching *machashovo techilo* ("initial beginning"), which is incomparably higher than the first or beginning *machashovo* ("thought"). In fact, *techilo* ("initial beginning") is a word in its own right, indicating the beginning or source of *machashovo* ("thought") itself, and not merely the first level or "top" of *machashovo*.

This is the level of *oneg* — "pleasure" in the fulfillment as well as the source of *machashovo* that produces and motivates it. The explanation reaches its peak by stressing that all this occurs only when the *sof ma'aseh* has been fully realized, by ideal reception and absorption in the "vessels" (*kelim*) of the receiver in this world. (See the series of *maamarim Ein Bais*, vol. 2, page one-thousand 1117).

Thus, we may be able to suggest that the *da'as zeh hatinok*, rooted as it is in the "simplicity" of the essence of the soul, beyond reasoning, from the essential point of a Jew, is indicative of the full realization and ideal state of the *mekabel* ("receiver") and thereby reaches the *oneg* of the Above (similar to the *ben bayis* of *Choni HaMa'agel* mentioned above) and that *oneg* is actually equivalent to "You Yourself" — higher and beyond. (This is briefly stated, and requires more development...)

This is the perfect fulfillment of the *Sifri* brought above — "To He Himself and not to His *midos*, attributes etc, mentioned above.

Rabbi Schneur Zalman Gafne

CONTENTS

Preface . . . . *xiii*

Foreword . . . . *xv*

Introduction . . . . *xix*

    Morning Blessings and *Korbanot* 2

    Hodu 72

    Verses of Praise 94

    Blessings of the *Shema* 190

    The *Shema* 238

    Shemonah Esreh — The *Amidah* 282

    Tachanun 334

    Torah Reading 356

    Remainder of Morning Prayers 364

Endnotes 429

Appendices

    APPENDIX 1: **Three Categories of Divine Love**
        (from the Rebbe Rayatz's *biurim* to *Sefer Maamorim*
        of his father, the Rebbe Rashab, 1906 – תרס״ו) 447

    APPENDIX 2: **Novel Themes in the *Chassidut***
        of the Rebbe Maharash 477

PREFACE

By way of preface: Prayer (*tefila*) is a labor of the heart. It is not merely an utterance of the mouth. In order to be successful in prayer, meditation on the "greatness of God and the lowliness of man" (*Rama, Shulchan Aruch Orech Haim* 98:1) is necessary. And therefore, it is necessary to learn Chassidus before prayers.

It is also important in general, and especially during prayers on *Shabbat Kodesh*, to contemplate the content of Chassidus before prayers. The more one does so, the better. And during prayers themselves, it is understood that in addition to paying attention to the simple meaning of the words (of *tefila*), we should also — wherever possible and even if briefly — think over the content of a Chassidic discourse. Doing so contributes greatly to the quality of our labor of the heart — *tefila*!

Even though when we pause in the middle of prayers in order to contemplate the content of a discourse that we studied before prayers, the Chassidic content usually bears no obvious connection to the section of prayers in which we are standing, nevertheless it is not considered to be an interruption in the middle of prayer at all, as explained in several places.

And therefore, at first glance it should not be necessary to provide Chassidus on every section of prayers in the siddur, since the main point is to learn Chassidus, in general.

However, practically speaking, the Alter Rebbe's siddur with Chassidus does provide us with Chassidus on all of our prayers. Moreover, it is obvious that as we pray, we often have questions regarding certain sections of prayers, and we want to delve deeper or to understand better, particular sections of the prayers. For example, "the *ofanim* ("lower angels") and *chayot* ("intermediate angels"), with great commotion, raise themselves up to the level of the *seraphim* ("higher angels")." What is this "commotion"? And what does it mean to "ascend to the level of the higher angels"? That is the great benefit of this *siddur* with excerpts of Chassidus provided by R' David Sterne — it makes it possible to immediately find Chassidic explanations on the words of prayer.

Moreover, there is a huge benefit for those who seek explanation — and especially deep and meaningful explanation according to Chassidus — on each and every section of *tefila*. By studying and absorbing this siddur with Chassidic explanations, they will become aroused to work even harder on their "labor of the heart" — the art of prayer.

And in our days — on the heels of Mashiach — during the last minutes of *galut*, it is incumbent upon us to conclude the final preparations and hasten the arrival of Mashiach (may he arrive very soon!) — every book that supports and encourages *avodat Hashem*, also hastens the arrival of redemption — may the Mashiach arrive and redeem us immediately!

My time constraints did not allow me to read this entire *siddur* with *Dach*. However, the sections that I did manage to read impressed me with the great amount of thought, preparation and care that went into this work. Moreover, the presentation, using symbols and concise wording, are sure to guide the reader in the right direction and aid him in the art of meaningful prayer.

I bless you with blessings of great success in spreading the well springs of Chassidus outward, in good health and expansiveness and happiness and a good heart!

R' Zalman Dubinsky שיח' HaCohen
Rosh Yeshiva, *Yeshivas Tiferes Bachurim*
Morristown, NJ
Lag B'Omer, 18 Iyar תשע"ו (May 26, 2016)

FOREWORD

When R. Shneur Zalman of Liadi, founder of Chabad Chassidism and known as the "Alter Rebbe," turned eighteen, he was already a renowned scholar with vast knowledge in all subjects of the Torah. Nonetheless, he felt a need for a special mentor. Considering several options, he decided on R. Dov Ber, known as the Maggid of Mezhirech, the major disciple of the Baal Shem Tov and his successor as leader of the Chassidic movement. At a number of occasions the Alter Rebbe explained this choice in slightly varying ways:

Proficiency in Torah-knowledge and methodology in the study of Talmud and Halachah study he had mastered already, but "as for *tefilah* I hardly knew anything."[1] At another time he expressed it in terms of "I was not aware how to serve G-d *(avodah).*"[2] And at a third occasion he said that elsewhere one learns how to master the Torah; in Mezhirech one learns how to let the Torah master you, i.e., "how the Torah teaches man to become a Torah himself."[3]

Torah-study is the comprehensive core of Jewish life: "*Talmud Torah keneged kulam* — Torah-study is equivalent to them all."[4] On the one hand it is a *mitzvah* on its own, thus a meritorious end by itself. On the other hand it is also a means towards another end: the practice of the Divine precepts and the spiritual perfection of man, which are impossible without prior study and knowledge of Torah — as Hillel taught: "A boor cannot be fearful of sin, nor can an unlearned person be a *chasid* (a person of scrupulous piety).[5] Torah-study, in spite of its unique and superior quality on its own,[6] may never be divorced from its application on the practical level. He who claims to have nothing but Torah - he has not even Torah, for one must be occupied with Torah and the performance of *chassadim*[7] (lit. acts of kindness, which include not only kindness to fellow-beings but also, as it were, to G-d, i.e., the performance of *mitzvot* and the worship of G-d[8]). The Torah is but the gateway to *yirat Shamayim* (the fear of, or reverence for, G-d).[9] The superiority of Torah, therefore, lies in the fact that "Torah-study leads to practical observance."[10]

Thus Torah must lead to *avodah*. It will do so when studied *lishmah*. *Lishmah* means (a) for its own sake, as opposed to ulterior motives of personal benefits (which include the objective of becoming a renowned scholar), as derived from the verse "to love G-d and to obey His voice and to cleave unto Him" (Deuteronomy 30:20).[11] (b) *Lishmah* also means literally "for its name's sake." The "name" Torah is an idiom of *hora'ah* — teaching, instruction, guidance.[12] This "name," then, implies that the Torah instructs, guides and counsels man to be wholehearted with his Maker and Master who, by means of revealing the Torah, "seeks to benefit man in this world and in the world-to-come."[13] In this sense, therefore, learning Torah *lishmah* means to absorb and internalize this guidance and counsel, to generate *ahavah veyirah*, love and fear (reverence) of G-d [14] "oneself to become a Torah."

Man was created to serve his Maker by means of Torah and *mitzvot*.[15] His mission on earth is to manifest to himself and others the concealed G-dliness that pervades all of creation - "I fill the heavens and the earth" Jeremiah 23:24) and there is no place devoid of His Presence even in the physical realm.[16] Thus one must breach the barriers of mundane illusions and bring about a full consciousness of the reality of Divine Presence.'[17] This *avodah*, service of G-d, cannot be perfunctory "as a commandment of men learned by rote" (Isaiah 29:13). Without *kavanah*, encompassing intent and concentration, the heart and the mind, it is lifeless, a "body without soul." Torah, *mitzvot* and *tefilah* that lack *ahavah veyirah* will not achieve their goal of ascending.[18] True *avodah* means the consciousness of "Now, Israel, what does G-d, your G-d, ask of you but to fear G-d, your G-d, to go in all His ways and to love Him, and to serve G-d, your G-d, with all your heart and with all your soul!" (Deuteronomy 10:12)

This fundamental principle is the major focus of Chassidism. It applies universally, equally to scholar and layman, to each according to his or her capacities. The Alter Rebbe once said: "I received from the Maggid of Mezhirech, and he had received that teaching from the Baal Shem Tov: the *mitzvah* of *ve'ahavta* (you shall love [G-d]) means to 'thrust' one's thought and mind (in Yiddish he said *men zol zich arajn tohn* - to immerse oneself) in those subject-matter that will stir that love,[19] while the resulting effects are not of the basic precept."[20]

Much has been taught by the Chassidic masters throughout the generations to emphasize this principle and to motivate its application. In this context, the fifth Rebbe of Chabad, R. Sholom Dov Ber of Lubavitch, known by the acronym "the Reshab," composed a special treatise *Kuntres Ha'avodah*, as a primer for those seeking guidance in *avodah* to explain "the principle of *avodah shebalev* (service of the heart), i.e., prayer, to draw near and cause one's soul to cleave unto G-dliness..."

This treatise touches upon many basic ideas of Chassidism, but its inspiration is not lessened by its profound scholarship. A proper study of its contents will most assuredly affect the student with new insights, a proper understanding of the issues, and above all result in the true and enhanced *avodah* it sets out to achieve.

Rabbi David Sterne deserves much credit for undertaking the arduous task of translating *Kuntres Ha'avodah,* thus making this treasure available and accessible to the English-speaking public. Moreover, he added numerous explanations for complex concepts as well as most helpful diagrams to ease the student's journey. His work is most certainly a tremendous achievement. Unfortunately, the restraints on my time did not allow me to review the translation. The few passages I did manage to scan, however, were sufficient to impress and to evoke admiration for the great effort Rabbi Sterne must have put into this labor of love, of which it may be said with confidence that he has the *zechut* that his work will cause many to attain merit. Hopefully he will use his blessed talents for further contributions.

Toronto, Tishrei 5766
J. Immanuel Schochet

1. Likkutei Diburim, III:p. 966
2. Ibid., IV:p. 1324
3. Ibid., II:II:p. 492
4. Pe'ah 1:1
5. Avot II:5
6. See Tanya, ch. 5-6
7. Yevamot 109b, and see there 105a. Note the Rebbe's glossary comment in Sefer Hama'amarim 5708, p. 266, note 7. Cf. Zohar III:119a, and the references cited there in Nitzutzei Zohar. Tanya, Igeret Hakodesh, sect. 5.
8. Zohar III:281a. See also Zohar II:214b and III:222b; Tikunei Zohar lb.
9. Shabbat 31b; Yoma 72b and Rashi ad loc.
10. Kidushin 40b
11. Sifre, Eikev, end of sect. 48. Nedarim 62a
12. Zohar III:53b. Redak on Psalms 19:8. Maharal, Gur Aryeh on Genesis1:1; Netivot Olam, Netiv Hatorah, ch. 1, and Netiv Ha'emunah, ch. 2.
13. Zohar II:82b. See also ibid. I:lla, II:96b. Cf. Avodah Zara 17b; Sifre, Ha'azinu, end of sect. 322. Rambam, Hilchot Shechitah 14:16, and Hilchot Temurah 4:13.
14. Maggid of Mezhirech, Or Torah, sect. 317. See there also sect. 453.

15. Kiduhin 82a
16. Tikunei Zohar 57:91b; ibid . 70:122b. Shemot Rabba 2:9. See Tanya, Igeret Hakodesh, sect. 25. Note also Tanya, ch. 41.
17. See Tanya, ch. 32
18. Zohar l:24a. Tikunei Zohar 10:25b. See also Zohar ll:121a.
19. See Rambam, Hilchot Yessodei Hatorah 2:2 and 4:12; Hilchot Teshuvah 10:6.
20. Keter Shem Tov, Hossafot, sect. 38. See the Rebbe's glossary comments n Sefer Hama'amari m 5701, p. 116.

INTRODUCTION

Ten years have passed since the publication (in 2010) of the first Siddur with Chassidut in English, then called *Daven Chabad (Mind over Heart)*, and eight years since its more complete iteration, *Meditation like Fire and Water*, was published in 2012 (see www.fireandwater.org). Feedback was generally positive, but some comments from readers indicated that a new and different kind of siddur with Chassidut was needed. *Meditation like Fire and Water* is an encyclopedia of Chassidut on the Siddur, and the accompanying commentary, intended to explain the Chabad technique of *hitbonenut*, is too verbose to be used as a "handbook of prayer." Therefore, we took upon ourselves to produce another version of the siddur with Chassidut, intended to be more manageable and easier for the reader to apply to the practice of *davening* ("praying"). The result is the current volume, *Praying like Fire and Water*, which also includes a commentary intended to accompany our translation of the Rebbe Rashab's *Kuntres Ha'avoda* (entitled *Love like Fire and Water*, published in 2005).

In the years since producing *Meditation like Fire and Water*, we strove to learn the Chassidut of the Rebbe Maharash (father of the Rebbe Rashab), and to add it to the Chassidut in English that is already present in the Siddur. As a result, *Praying like Fire and Water* includes not only much of the Chassidut of the Rebbe Rashab (and the other Chabad Rebbeim), but virtually all that his father, the Rebbe Maharash wrote about meditation and prayer. If *Meditation like Fire and Water* could be nicknamed, the "Rebbe Rashab's Siddur" (since it contains, in translation, virtually all that the Rashab wrote regarding prayer), *Praying like Fire and Water* could be called, "The Rebbe Maharash's Siddur," because it contains (in translation and summary form) nearly all that the Rebbe Maharash wrote regarding prayer. However, since their "styles" were very different from one another, it is also logical for the translations to take on different forms. The Chassidim of the Maharash tended to be *balabatim* ("workers" and "tradesmen") rather than rabbis and Torah scholars (although there were certainly many of the latter as well). Perhaps in recognition of his flocks, the Rebbe Maharash delivered Chasidic discourses that were brief and concise. The insights contained in his Chassidut are brilliant and luminous, without the lengthy and detailed explanations that are characteristic of the Chassidut of his Chabad predecessors. In contrast, the goal of the Rebbe Rashab was to introduce Chassidut into the educational setting — the yeshiva that he founded, *Tomchei Tmimim*. As a result, the Chassidut of the Rashab is didactic and approachable. It is the Chassidut of a consummate teacher and educator. His Chassidut is long and thorough, replete with explanations and examples meant to "deliver" his ideas into the minds and hearts of the young students, as well as to the accomplished *ovdei Hashem* and Chassidim of his era. Since the Chassidut of the Rebbe Rashab tends to "speak for itself," we translated his Chassidut "as is," in *Meditation like Fire and Water*. The same approach, though is not suitable when applied to the Chassidut of the Rebbe Maharash.

A story culled from the annals of the Rebbe Maharash will illustrate the contrast between the two Rebbeim (the story was heard from R' Yoseph Yitzhak Vilshansky שיח׳, Rosh Yeshiva of Tomchei Tmimim in Tzfat, who heard it from his father, R' Raphael Vilshansky ז״ל, who was a student in *Tomchei Tmimim* under the Rebbe Rayatz (son of the Rebbe Rashab) in the 1920's in Russia): Some Chassidim of the Rebbe Maharash approached him with the complaint that they could not connect the various intellectual themes contained in his Chassidut. The themes seemed disconnected, and the Chassidim felt "lost." The Rebbe Maharash answered them with a parable: 'Once a merchant went to the fair in order to buy some merchandise. After he chose what he wanted to buy, he requested "credit" from the sellers, in order to sell the merchandise elsewhere and then pay them at a later date. The sellers agreed, but then the merchant found that he did not have string or rope to tie the merchandise together to take it "home" with him. So, he asked the sellers for some string as well. They replied, "What kind of merchant are you? If you don't have money to buy, we can extend you credit, but do you also expect us to help you tie the merchandise together for you?" The parable is clear: The Rebbe Maharash was telling his Chassidim, "I can supply the merchandise (the Chassidut), but you have to do the work of putting it together and taking it home ("connecting the themes and internalizing them") yourselves."

Besides being a comment on the nature of the Rebbe Maharash's Chassidim, the story also illustrates the predicament facing a student of the Rebbe Maharash: His flashes of holy creative insight are tantalizing on the one hand, but on the other, how do we "take it home"? We feel like a spectator watching a brilliant magician, a holy tzaddik who produces pearls of wisdom that mesmerize, but who goes "offstage" before we can digest what we just saw. How do we "connect the strands" of what the Rebbe Maharash tried to teach us? In an attempt to "capture" the genius of his teaching, we decided to crystallize the learning in short "bytes" of information. Each "byte" is an attempt to summarize a creative component of the Maharash's Chassidut from a different angle: First of all, there is a quotation, followed by the kabalistic "byte," then a Chasidic summary, and finally an attempt to "take it home" by applying it to our *tefila*, or "prayers." Together, the four elements provide a complete summary of one particular Chasidic thought process (*mehalech*), or "meditation" culled from the Chassidut of the Rebbe Maharash. In this manner, we hope to accomplish that which the Maharash instructed his Chassidim, "it's up to you to provide the rope" in order to "tie the merchandise and take it home." The citation and endnote that is attached to the quote provide the "main" thrust of the meditation and from where it was sourced. Where other material intersected or enhanced the "meditation," the source was also quoted in the course of the four part summary. Taken together, each four part "summary" represents a "meditation" meant to aid the davener in contemplation of Chasidic concepts while praying.

While all of the meditations appearing in this siddur with Chassidut are approachable, some are clearly more advanced than others. They are intended for experienced meditators, people who have been praying and contemplating Chasidic concepts for years. Such, for example are meditations that employ *ohr chozer*, and those that apply the correct vowels to the name of God in each blessing of the *shemonah esreh*. No attempt was made to "edit out" or exclude any Chasidic concept, and therefore the included meditations cover all levels of difficulty. It is up to each person to decide what is in the realm of his or her intellectual and spiritual scope and work on that level, in conjunction with a Chasidic *mashpia*, or "mentor." *Aseh lecha Rav* — "make for yourself a *Rav*, or mentor" — applies in all walks of Jewish life, and especially when it comes to praying and meditating upon Chasidic concepts.

While compiling the material for *Praying like Fire and Water*, I happened to notice that the various stages of mental awareness described in *Love like Fire and Water* (*Kuntes Ha'avoda*) correspond rather precisely to all of the stages of *tefila* ("prayer"). That is, while climbing the "ladder" of prayer, we pass through all the stages of *kaballat ohl mlachut shamayim* ("acceptance of the yoke of heaven"), followed by *yirah tata'ah* ("lower fear") in all of its manifestations, and then by love of God, etc. Thus was born the idea of a commentary that not only "teaches" Jewish meditation, but also "pairs" it with *tefila* (in any case, Jewish meditation takes place before, during and after prayers, but it became clear that the stages of mental and emotional awareness developed during meditation correspond precisely to the stages of love and fear that we experience during prayer). Thus, the commentary ("Chasidic Insights") that appears in *Praying like Fire and Water* has a two-fold purpose. Number one, the goal is much the same as it was in *Meditation like Fire and Water* - to elucidate the Chabad technique of prayerful meditation, called *hitbonenut*. And number two, the goal is to point out how the principles of meditation taught in *Kuntres Ha'avoda* (*Love like Fire and Water*) also correspond to the *nusach*, or words, of the siddur.

Finally, it is impossible to launch a labor of love such as this, without noticing apparent contradictions in the material, interesting comparisons, and snippets of information in one place that illuminate matters in another place entirely. Words of Torah are "rich in one place and poor elsewhere." On the one hand, it was impossible and inappropriate to insert discussions and investigations of the material within the commentary or the summaries. On the other hand, at times it was so clear that there was a hand from Above guiding the discovery of material and illuminating it, that I could not omit it entirely from the project. The solution was to put such investigations at the end of the siddur, in the "endnotes." There, the reader will find occasional discussions of such topics as "constant re-creation of the universe," "two levels of *bina*," and other matters. The conclusions that I reached in these small "investigations" are part of an ongoing process of discovery, to clarify Chasidic concepts. Contributions and suggestions from readers are welcome.

The *Kuntres Ha'avoda* ("Essay on prayer," Ch. 6), of the Rebbe Rashab (1860–1920) mentions two styles of davening ("prayer"). While describing people who pray with only minimal preparation, and thereafter find themselves emotionally uninvolved during prayers, the Rebbe Rashab says that "it would be better for them to pray with the simple meaning of the words" (Page 183 and 185 in the translation, "Love like Fire and Water"). Elsewhere (Ch 6, page 166 in *Love like Fire and Water*), the Rashab says, "The main *avoda* of prayer is in detailed meditation, no matter what the subject of the meditation may be," and then continues to describe several topics for Chasidic meditation. The Rebbe Maharash delineates three types of davening: Those who daven with only the proper pronunciation of the words, those who pray with any kind of *pirush* ("explanation"), whether the "simple" translation of the words, or the Kaballistic intentions or with Chassidic interpretations, and finally, those who "look for the story" behind the words of prayers. Not mentioned explicitly, but implied in both the Rebbe Rashab's Chassidut as well as the Rebbe Maharash, is a style of prayer that was practiced in their days, and in prior generations as well. Called *davenen b'avoda* ("praying with meditation and self-investigation"), it seems that this manner of prayer was not formally taught or transmitted. Rather, it was handed down informally, from teacher to student, or from Rebbe to Chasid in each generation. Those who had the talent and sense for such a style of prayer, emulated and absorbed it, and then passed it on by way of example. The Rebbe Rashab perhaps does hint to this style of prayer, when he exhorts his Chassidim "not to worry about how much time it takes" to meditate and pray (Page 186 in "Love like Fire and Water"). And the Rebbe Maharash alludes to it with his description of those who "look for the story behind the prayers." For, *davenen b'avoda* demands total devotion and dedication, and it was common for the Chassidim practicing this style of prayer, to pray for hours on end. Unfortunately, like so many aspects of Torah and mitzvoth, the transmission was interrupted by the holocaust, and except for a few unique individuals (such as R' Shlomo Chaim Kesselman, *alov hashalom*, the Chabad *mashpia* in Tel Aviv, Lod and Kfar Chabad from 1947 until 1974), *davenen b'avoda* became a lost art. However, by delving into the Chassidut of the Chabad Rebbeim, as well as their letters and private communications, we can hope to re-construct *davenen b'avoda*. That is one of the goals of this siddur with Chassidut.

The three styles of prayer correspond to three kinds of people. The *amcha*, or common Jewish man (who is not "common" at all) who keeps Torah and mitzvoth, works and studies Torah at fixed hours, rarely has time to pray at length. He does well to pray with the simple meaning of the words. The *maskil*, or "intellectual," takes time to study Chassidut and thinks deeply into the Chasidic concepts, delving into the interpretations and struggling to understand them well enough to apply them to his prayers. He is the Jew who prays on the second level, with the Chasidic interpretation of the prayers. But, there is no guarantee that his prayers change him as a person. It is the *oved*, the Chasid who not only understands, but seeks to use Chassidut to transform his very personality, who practices the third level of prayer - *davenen b'avoda*. He prays at length, paying attention not only to the meaning of the concepts, but on how to internalize them and make the concepts a part of his very soul. As the Fredike Rebbe (the *Rayatz*) said, "The *oved* makes *keilim* ("vessels") to feel the concepts in his soul." As a result, he also grasps the concepts on a higher and deeper level than even the *maskil*.

The reader may wonder from where most of the material for this siddur with Chassidut was culled. The sources are many, including *Tanya*, *Torah Ohr* and *Likutei Torah*, Siddur with Chassidut and *maamorim* of the Alter Rebbe, *Imrei Bina, Pirush Hamilot, Torat Chaim, Sha'arei Teshuva* of the Mitteler Rebbe, *Ohr HaTorah* and *Derech Mitzvotecha* of the Tzemach Tzedek, *Meah Shearim* of all three Rebbeim (The Alter Rebbe, Mitteler Rebbe, and the Tzemach Tzedek), *Torat Shmuel* of the Rebbe Maharash, all of the *maamorim* of the Rebbe Rashab, as well as a few sources from the Fredike Rebbe and the Rebbe Mamash. In addition, there is some material from pre-Chasidic sources, such as the *Megaleh Amukot* (R' Nosson Nata Shapira, 1585–1633), when it applied directly to the subject of prayer. But most of all, special attention was paid to the Chassidut of the Rebbe Maharash and his son, the Rebbe Rashab, since it was during the Rashab's *nesiut* ("leadership") that *davenen b'avoda* reached its zenith. In future volumes, we hope to apply more material from the Chassidut of the Fredike Rebbe (the Rayatz) as well, God willing.

Old City of Jerusalem,
June 1, 2020

PRAYING
Like Fire & Water

ברכות השחר

מוֹדֶה אֲנִי לְפָנֶיךָ מֶלֶךְ חַי וְקַיָּם, שֶׁהֶחֱזַרְתָּ בִּי נִשְׁמָתִי בְּחֶמְלָה. רַבָּה אֱמוּנָתֶךָ:

נפש שבנפש
קבלת עול מלכות שמים
הודאה כללי
יראה תתאה
עולם העשיה (מלכות)

> **❝** We direct our *tefila* ('prayers') from below to above, as written, "a ladder placed on the earth with its head reaching into the heavens."[1] Prayer begins on the lowest levels and reaches the highest possible peaks..." (*Besha'ah Shehikdimu* 5672/1912 of the Rebbe Rashab, vol. 1, p. 619, *Kuntres Ha'Avoda* of the Rebbe Rashab, p. 1)[2]

When we awaken in the morning, we exist on the soul level of *nefesh,* in the World of *Asiya.* *Nefesh* is the lowest level of the soul, and *Asiya* is the lowest world.

Upon awakening, we are not capable of thinking or feeling anything spiritual. We merely acknowledge God's presence, and then we get dressed and say the morning blessings.

📖 Within the Words

The first thing we do upon awakening in the morning is say *Modeh Ani*—"I Acknowledge." With this simple statement we lay the spiritual foundation for our entire day.[3]

CHASSIDIC INSIGHTS

PRAYING LIKE FIRE AND WATER

Just as we need a map when setting out on a physical journey, we need a map when setting out on a spiritual journey. Another necessity for our journey is a vehicle, to take us from one place to another. The means of transportation on our Jewish spiritual journey is meditation, which, combined with the words of the Jewish prayer-book, or siddur take us to new spiritual levels. Our meditation and prayers traverse worlds, so it is a good idea to know in advance where we stand, and what awaits us, spiritually, as we travel. The map of Jewish prayer and

(continued on p. 4)

סידור עם חסידות – שחרית

MORNING BLESSINGS

Nefesh shb'nefesh
Yoke of Heaven
General Acknowledgment
Lower Fear
World of *Asiya* (*Malchut*)

I AM GRATEFUL TO YOU, ALIVE AND ETERNAL KING, for mercifully returning my soul within me, great is the faith that is due to You.

❝ Our acknowledgment is *lefanecha*—'before You'—before God Himself. Included within our acknowledgment are all the levels of *avoda*—'service of God.'" (*Besha'ah Shehikdimu* 5672/1912 of the Rebbe Rashab, vol. 1, p. 619)[4]

> The restoration of our soul within us comes from the divine aspect of *yesod* (*chai vekayam*—"living and eternal") as it unites with *malchut* ("sovereignty"). *Yesod* represents Godliness that transcends time and space—this is the realm of the soul. *Malchut* is the source of time and space, which is the realm of the body. The unity of *yesod* and *malchut* (as we recite *Melech Chai Vekayam*) facilitates the restoration of the soul to the body every morning.[5]

> Just as the One who dwells above faithfully restores our soul to our body every morning, even though we "owe" Him, so to speak—so should we faithfully return any lost objects to their rightful owners even if they are indebted to us. *Modeh Ani* also alludes to the resurrection of the dead, when God will faithfully return each soul to its resurrected body.[6]

📖 *Within the Words*

The second step after awakening is to wash our hands. As we sleep, our higher faculties are dormant and only our lower bodily functions are active. A spirit of impurity descends upon our body which is removed by washing our hands. As a matter of practical advice, we should arrange a container of water near the bedside to wash our hands as soon as possible upon awakening.[7]

סדר נטילת ידיים

בָּרוּךְ אַתָּה יְיָ אֱלֹהֵינוּ מֶלֶךְ הָעוֹלָם, אֲשֶׁר קִדְּשָׁנוּ בְּמִצְוֹתָיו, וְצִוָּנוּ עַל נְטִילַת יָדָיִם:

אחרי כל עשיית צרכים נוטלים ידיים ואומרים:

בָּרוּךְ אַתָּה יְיָ אֱלֹהֵינוּ מֶלֶךְ הָעוֹלָם, אֲשֶׁר יָצַר אֶת הָאָדָם בְּחָכְמָה, וּבָרָא בוֹ נְקָבִים נְקָבִים, חֲלוּלִים חֲלוּלִים, גָּלוּי וְיָדוּעַ לִפְנֵי כִסֵּא כְבוֹדֶךָ, שֶׁאִם יִסָּתֵם אֶחָד מֵהֶם, אוֹ אִם יִפָּתֵחַ אֶחָד מֵהֶם, אִי אֶפְשָׁר לְהִתְקַיֵּם אֲפִילוּ שָׁעָה אֶחָת. בָּרוּךְ אַתָּה יְיָ רוֹפֵא כָל בָּשָׂר וּמַפְלִיא לַעֲשׂוֹת:

נפש שבנפש
קבלת עול מלכות שמים
הודאה כללי
יראה תתאה
עולם העשיה
(מלכות)

> **"When we arise in the morning from sleep, our mind and heart are still blunt and dull…how can we recite the morning blessings at such a time?"** (*Besha'ah Shehikdimu 5672/1912* of the Rebbe Rashab, vol. 2, pp. 737-738)[8]

Even though we are still on the level of *nefesh*, incapable of clear thinking or feeling, our blessings access the highest Godly illumination. Simple water, lacking taste, color, or any other defining characteristic, represents *chochma*, the highest *sephira*. The divine influx from *chochma* also lacks definition and description. It needs a container to bring it down, which is why we wash with a vessel.[9]

After dressing, we again wash hands alternately, and say the blessing *Al Netilat Yadayim*. There are two reasons: 1) we are like a new creation in the morning, and the final step in manufacturing a new vessel is to rinse it, and 2) because the priests used to wash their hands before commencing their morning service in the Temple.[10]

--- CHASSIDIC INSIGHTS ---

(continued from p. 2)

meditation is symbolized by the ladder of which our forefather, Jacob, dreamt, as he lay his head down to sleep on that very holy place — the Temple Mount in Jerusalem. The Zohar (the seminal book of Jewish mysticism and kaballah, authored by R' Shimon bar Yohai) says

(continued on p. 6)

Nefesh shb'nefesh
Yoke of Heaven
General
   Acknowledgment
Lower Fear
World of *Asiya*
   (*Malchut*)

The Order of Ritual Washing of the Hands

BLESSED ARE YOU, LORD OUR GOD, KING OF THE universe, Who has sanctified us with His commandments, and commanded us regarding washing (lit. "taking") the hands.

After using the facilities and washing our hands ritually, we then say

Blessed are You, Lord our God, King of the universe, Who has formed man with wisdom, creating (him) with various openings and orifices, hollows and cavities. It is evident and apparent before the throne of Your glory, that if one of them is clogged, or another one is opened, then it is impossible to exist for even a moment. Blessed are You, God, Who heals all flesh and works wonders.

📖 *Within the Words*

With the word *Baruch* ("Blessed be"), we draw down God's infinite transcendent illumination. *Baruch* is from the word *berech*, meaning "knee." It indicates descent, as when we kneel. *Atah* means "You" directly addressing God. *Havaya* ("is, was and will be") is God's essential name, here associated with the *sephirah* of *chochmah*. The words *Baruch Atah Havaya* ("Blessed are You, Lord...") address God's very essence, and bring down revelation of His essential illumination. When mentioning God's four-letter name *Havaya*, we should recall that He always was, is and will be, and that He is Lord over all. When saying His name *Elokeinu*, we should have in mind that He has the power and force to do what He wants.[11] We conclude the blessing by saying "taking the hands," rather than "washing the hands," because in order to wash we must take a vessel called a *natla* in Aramaic.[12] It is also highly recommended to immerse in the *mikveh* before praying in the morning. Although immersion before prayers was a decree of the Prophet Ezra which was later cancelled, it still "helps."[13]

MORNING BLESSINGS

אֱ‍לֹהַי, נְשָׁמָה שֶׁנָּתַתָּ בִּי טְהוֹרָה (בנוסח תהילת ה':
הִיא), אַתָּה בְרָאתָהּ, אַתָּה יְצַרְתָּהּ, אַתָּה
נְפַחְתָּהּ בִּי, וְאַתָּה מְשַׁמְּרָהּ בְּקִרְבִּי, וְאַתָּה עָתִיד
לִטְּלָהּ מִמֶּנִּי, וּלְהַחֲזִירָהּ בִּי לֶעָתִיד לָבֹא. כָּל זְמַן

נפש שבנפש
קבלת עול מלכות שמים
הודאה כללי
יראה תתאה
עולם העשיה (מלכות)

> **Within the soul, we find two modes. The first is the soul as a creation [in the body] … the second is the soul prior to its creation [before entering the body]."** (*Sefer Maamorim 5672-6/1912-16* of the Rebbe Rashab, p. 137)[14]

> There are five levels to the soul. The three lowest levels—*nefesh, ruach* and *neshama*—are enclothed in our body (our lower anatomy, our heart and our mind, respectively.) The two highest levels—*chaya* and *yechida*—transcend our body. *Chaya* is in the immediate vicinity of the body, surrounding it, and *yechida* is said to be within the *dalet amot* ("four cubits," or roughly two meters) of the body.[15]

> The soul in the World of *Atzilut* is "pure" (*tehora*) and pristine. As it descends to the three lower worlds, it takes on their trappings of *chomer* ("substance"), *tzura* ("form") and *tikun* ("final status"). The World of *Bria* is associated with *chomer*, or mere possibility of

---

CHASSIDIC INSIGHTS

(continued from p. 4)

about Jacob's ladder, "This is prayer." The ladder had four rungs, corresponding to four "worlds," or realms of physical and spiritual creation through which we pass as we pray. And on the ladder, angels (spiritual beings) ascended and descended.

The angels are important, because elsewhere, the Jewish sages tell us that it is the angels who both elevate our prayers and who return to us with responses to our prayers from Above. We will get back to the angels, but for now it is important to realize that we undergo this ascent and descent of prayer and meditation every day. We usually undertake this journey in the morning, during the morning prayers (*shacharit*). The early sages of Judaism used to undertake the same journey three times a day, during the three prayers of the day (the

(continued on p. 7)

Nefesh shb'nefesh
Yoke of Heaven
General
   Acknowledgment
Lower Fear
World of *Asiya*
   (*Malchut*)

M Y GOD, THE SOUL THAT YOU PLACED WITHIN ME is pure; You created it, You formed it, and You blew it into me. And You preserve it within me, and you will remove it from me in the future, returning it within me in the future. The entire

existence. The World of *Yetzira* is associated with *tzura*, or general forms and templates of existence. Finally, the World of *Asiya* is associated with *Tikun*, or specific states of individual existence. Our goal during prayers is to bring down illumination from the highest levels of our soul, prior to its "existence" in a body (transcending creation), to within our soul as it "exists" within the body.[16]

> 📖 *Within the Words*
>
> Every creation, as it comes into existence in the Worlds of *Bria*, *Yetzira* and *Asiya* (*BY"A*), goes through the three stages — *chomer* ("substance"), *tzura* ("form") and *tikun* ("final status"). However, the soul maintains its essential nature even as it descends to the body. The words, *Atah barata* ("You created"), *Atah yatzarta* ("You formed") and *Atah nafachta bi* ("You blew it into me"), apply to the soul as it descends through the Worlds of *BY"A* to become enclothed within the body. The divine soul remains an "essential piece of Godliness from above" even when enclothed in the body.

─────── CHASSIDIC INSIGHTS ───────

(continued from p. 6)

other two are *mincha* — the afternoon prayers, and *ma'ariv* — the nighttime prayers). But we, not being on their high spiritual level, do well to attempt the journey once a day.

The sages also delineated four states of mind that we experience as we proceed on our journey. The Jewish spiritual journey is associated with emotions that develop as we think about, contemplate, and meditate on Godliness. The four states of mind are based upon two emotions — love and fear of God. We develop love as we learn to appreciate the harmony and beauty of God's creation, and we develop fear as we grow to appreciate His enormous and infinite power. Both

(continued on p. 10)

MORNING BLESSINGS

שֶׁהַנְּשָׁמָה בְּקִרְבִּי מוֹדֶה אֲנִי לְפָנֶיךָ יְיָ אֱלֹהַי וֵאלֹהֵי אֲבוֹתַי, רִבּוֹן כָּל הַמַּעֲשִׂים, אֲדוֹן כָּל הַנְּשָׁמוֹת: בָּרוּךְ אַתָּה יְיָ הַמַּחֲזִיר נְשָׁמוֹת לִפְגָרִים מֵתִים:

נפש שבנפש
קבלת עול מלכות שמים
הודאה כללי
יראה תתאה
עולם העשיה (מלכות)

> **Who says this: 'My Lord, the soul that you placed within me, is pure…'? The body without a soul is lifeless and inert; it certainly does not say anything. And how can the soul itself say, 'the soul that you placed within me'?"** (*Kovetz Meah She'arim*, letters of the *Tzemach Tzedek*, p. 90, *Ohr HaTorah, Inyanim*, p. 304)[17]

We possess two souls—an animal soul and a divine soul.[18] It is the animal soul that says, "My Lord, the soul that You placed within me…" and it says this about the divine soul that is enclothed within it. Just as the animal soul is enclothed within the limbs of the body to enliven it, so the divine soul is enclothed within the animal soul. The intellect of the divine soul is enclothed in the intellect of the animal soul, the emotions of the divine soul are enclothed in those of the animal soul, etc. The only way that Godliness can be expressed in this world is by being enclothed in the human intellect. But, the divine soul itself is pure and pristine. It descends through the Worlds of BY"A in order to illuminate the *nefesh, ruach* and *neshama*.

It is the animal soul that says, *Atah naphachta bi* ("You blew it into me") regarding the divine soul, meaning that "You did this for me," to en-clothe the divine soul within the animal soul. The nature of the divine soul is to rise above, to return to its spiritual source, like a flame always striving upward. That's why the saying of the animal soul continues, "and You preserve it within me," meaning that only with help from above does the divine soul remain enclothed within the animal soul—otherwise it would separate from the body. Moreover, it is important to guard the divine soul so that it does not become sullied by its sojourn within the animal soul.

📖 *Within the Words*

The animal soul continues its soliloquy, "And You will remove it from me in the future—and return it within me in the future." This is a proof that the reward in the future will apply to a soul in a body during the resurrection of the dead (in accordance with the

Nefesh shb'nefesh
Yoke of Heaven
General
 Acknowledgment
Lower Fear
World of *Asiya*
 (*Malchut*)

duration that the soul is within my innards, I am grateful before You, My God and the God of my fathers, Master of all deeds, Lord of all souls.

Blessed be You, Who returns souls to lifeless bodies.

📖 *Within the Words*

interpretation of Nachmanides/Ramban and not the interpretation of Maimonides/Rambam). The prayer ends with, "Blessed be You who returns souls to lifeless bodies," since sleep is considered to be like one sixtieth of death.

❝ **Divine revelation of kindness begins to illuminate after midnight…and descends mainly during the morning hours… That is what enables the rooster to discern between day and night."** (*Torat Chaim* of the Mittler Rebbe, *Shemot* p. 108 or p. 148 in the new edition)[19]

The Zohar[20] states, "A spirit of divine kindness strikes the wings of the rooster [in the morning]," causing an arousal of repentance to descend upon the Jewish people, stimulating them to do *teshuva* and return to the ways of God.[21]

Question: Why is it a significant achievement for the rooster to detect the light of daytime? And why does the Torah enjoin us to "choose life," when surely no one would choose the opposite? The answer is that we are presented with opportunities to choose between spiritual light and darkness, between a life of Torah or a life without it and its mitzvot, which is compared to the opposite of life. Not always are we clever enough to make the correct decision, but this blessing in the morning grants us the power to discern and decide.

📖 *Within the Words*

The rooster (sometimes called *gaver* in Hebrew[22]) originates from the angel Gabriel in the World of *Bria*, who comes from the emanation of *gevura* "("judgment, contraction") in the World of *Atzilut*. An arousal of *gevura* above signifies the midnight hour below, and causes the rooster to crow.[23] As a matter of practical advice, every Jew should own a rooster or hire someone to awaken him.[24]

MORNING BLESSINGS

PRAYING LIKE FIRE AND WATER

בָּרוּךְ אַתָּה יְיָ אֱלֹהֵינוּ מֶלֶךְ הָעוֹלָם, הַנּוֹתֵן לַשֶּׂכְוִי בִינָה לְהַבְחִין בֵּין יוֹם וּבֵין לָיְלָה:

בָּרוּךְ אַתָּה יְיָ אֱלֹהֵינוּ מֶלֶךְ הָעוֹלָם, פּוֹקֵחַ עִוְרִים:

נפש שבנפש
קבלת עול מלכות שמים
הודאה כללי
יראה תתאה
עולם העשיה (מלכות)

❝ All that descends to illuminate and provide revelation in our soul and body throughout the entire order of prayer comes from the power of illumination and revelation [of the morning blessings]." *(Besha'ah Shehikdimu 5672/1912, vol. 2, pp. 737-738)*[25]

The eighteen morning blessings correspond to the eighteen blessings of the *Amida (Shemonah Esreh)*. We are not aware of the illumination of the morning blessings, but we may be fully aware of the illumination of the eighteen blessing of the *Shemonah Esreh*.

To understand the morning blessings, consider the exodus from Egypt. We did nothing to deserve the exodus, but with a high spiritual illumination, God lifted us out of Egypt. The same applies to the morning blessings—we are tired and groggy in the morning but, with the illumination of the morning blessings, we are catapulted into prayers.

CHASSIDIC INSIGHTS
(continued from p. 7)

love and fear further sub-divide into basic and more advanced (mature) forms of emotion.

Furthermore, as we proceed on our journey, we activate various levels of our soul. We have two souls, a vitalizing "animal soul" that is mainly concerned with our physical wellbeing, and a divine "Godly soul" that is only concerned with Godly and spiritual matters. Both souls come into play during the process of prayer and meditation. As the Godly soul is "activated," it influences and transforms the animal soul. One of the goals of prayer and meditation is to persuade the animal soul, generally concerned with physical matters, that Godliness is good for it as well as for the divine soul. As this occurs, we activate four and sometimes five levels of both souls as we progress through our prayers.

(continued on p. 11)

Nefesh shb'nefesh
Yoke of Heaven
General Acknowledgment
Lower Fear
World of *Asiya* (*Malchut*)

Blessed are You, Lord our God, King of the universe, Who has given the rooster understanding to discern between day and night.

Blessed are You, Lord our God, King of the universe, Who opens the eyes of the blind.

> 📖 *Within the Words*
>
> The ability to distinguish between that which is holy and that which is not, resides in our spiritual eyesight. The soul is able to "see in the mind's eye"—that is, to detect the spiritual essence of creation, which is why the sages are called, the "eyes of the congregation." The soul is able to detect the essence as if it sees it with the naked eye. The side of unholiness is not capable of such spiritual vision—as it is written "they have eyes but they see not." And that is why, when we arise in the morning, we bless God that He should "open our eyes."[26]

--- CHASSIDIC INSIGHTS ---

(continued from p. 10)

In order to keep track of these correspondences and correlations, we will provide tables and explanations. It is also highly recommended to have on hand a copy of our translation of the Rebbe Rashab's *Kuntres Ha'avoda* ("Essay on Service of the Heart"), entitled "Love like Fire and Water." All of the soul levels and emotions of love and fear discussed here are also described in detail in "Love Like Fire and Water." The purpose of this volume is to apply those principles to the practice of prayer. Here is what we have so far, and we will add layers of correspondences and nuances as we proceed.

WORLD	MIND STATE	SOUL-LEVEL
1st rung — *Asiya*	Lower Fear	*Nefesh*
2nd rung — *Yetzira*	Lower Love	*Ruach*
3rd rung — *Bria*	Upper Love	*Neshama*
4th rung — *Atzilut*	Upper Fear	*Chaya-Yechida*

(continued on p. 12)

בָּרוּךְ אַתָּה יְיָ אֱלֹהֵינוּ מֶלֶךְ הָעוֹלָם, מַתִּיר אֲסוּרִים:

בָּרוּךְ אַתָּה יְיָ אֱלֹהֵינוּ מֶלֶךְ הָעוֹלָם, זוֹקֵף כְּפוּפִים:

בָּרוּךְ אַתָּה יְיָ אֱלֹהֵינוּ מֶלֶךְ הָעוֹלָם, מַלְבִּישׁ עֲרֻמִּים:

בָּרוּךְ אַתָּה יְיָ אֱלֹהֵינוּ מֶלֶךְ הָעוֹלָם, הַנּוֹתֵן לַיָּעֵף כֹּחַ:

נפש שבנפש
קבלת עול מלכות שמים
הודאה כללי
יראה תתאה
עולם העשיה
(מלכות)

> The main difference between humans and animals is that man walks upright, with his head up, and his heart beneath, and below that are his legs, which symbolize action." (*Kovetz Meah Shearim, Tzemach Tzedek*, p. 90)[27]

One who has not succeeded in activating his feelings of love and fear of God is as if he is tied and bound by his hands, which allude to our emotions. Therefore, before we launch into prayer, we bless God, who is *matir asurim* ("releases the imprisoned"). And then, since it is vitally important to maintain the primacy of intellect over emotions, we bless God who is *zokef kefufim* ("straightens up the bent over"). We strive to maintain the superiority of our intellect over our emotions so that our actions will always be appropriate and effective. Action is represented by our feet, which ensure that we move to avoid evil and pursue fulfillment of mitzvot.

When we arise in the morning, we are "naked" not only physically, but also spiritually. Since we have not yet performed any mitzvah that day, it is as if we have not yet clothed ourself. It is the mitzvot that give us a spiritual *levush* ("garment") which allows us to perceive Godliness, for we cannot perceive Godliness directly

─── CHASSIDIC INSIGHTS ───

(continued from p. 11)

Our morning journey begins as we awaken. Even before arising, we say the words *Modeh Ani Lefanecha* — "I am grateful/thankful to You." This we say even before washing our hands to rinse away the spiritual impurity that is associated with sleep. With this statement of abject submission and gratitude to God for returning our soul to us in

(continued on p. 13)

סידור עם חסידות – שחרית

סדר ברכות השחר

12

Nefesh shb'nefesh
Yoke of Heaven
General
  Acknowledgment
Lower Fear
World of *Asiya*
  (*Malchut*)

Blessed are You, Lord our God, King of the universe, Who releases the imprisoned.

Blessed are You, Lord our God, King of the universe, Who straightens the bent over.

Blessed are You, Lord our God, King of the universe, Who clothes the naked.

Blessed are You, Lord our God, King of the universe, Who gives strength to the weary.

---

anymore than we can look directly at the sun. The most important garment with which to start the day is *kabalat ohl malchut shamayim* ("acceptance of the yoke of heaven"). It is the basis for all the other mitzvot that we will perform that day, and it provides a spiritual garment that enclothes us completely, from head to foot, and therefore we bless God, who is *malbish arumim* ("clothes the naked").

📖 *Within the Words*

Even with the garment of *ohl malchut shamayim*, we sometimes just do not have the strength to activate our divine soul and persuade it to dominate our animal soul. That may occur at the beginning of the day, or during the course of the day, as our weekday activities and mundane commitments threaten to overwhelm and bury our spiritual instincts. And, therefore at the beginning of the day, we bless God, who "gives strength to the weary." Our intention is to request that He give us spiritual strength from above, to activate our divine soul with a transcendent light that will illuminate our animal soul.

CHASSIDIC INSIGHTS

(continued from p. 12)

the morning, we place ourselves squarely on the path to connection with Him. There are several types and expressions of submission and gratitude (*hoda'ah*), but this initial statement that we say in the morning carries no message of either emotion or understanding. Yet, it is

(continued on p. 16)

בָּרוּךְ אַתָּה יְיָ אֱלֹהֵינוּ מֶלֶךְ הָעוֹלָם,
רוֹקַע הָאָרֶץ עַל הַמָּיִם:

בָּרוּךְ אַתָּה יְיָ אֱלֹהֵינוּ מֶלֶךְ הָעוֹלָם,
הַמֵּכִין מִצְעֲדֵי גָבֶר:

בָּרוּךְ אַתָּה יְיָ אֱלֹהֵינוּ מֶלֶךְ הָעוֹלָם,
שֶׁעָשָׂה לִי כָּל צָרְכִּי:

בָּרוּךְ אַתָּה יְיָ אֱלֹהֵינוּ מֶלֶךְ הָעוֹלָם,
אוֹזֵר יִשְׂרָאֵל בִּגְבוּרָה:

בָּרוּךְ אַתָּה יְיָ אֱלֹהֵינוּ מֶלֶךְ הָעוֹלָם,
עוֹטֵר יִשְׂרָאֵל בְּתִפְאָרָה:

נפש שבנפש
קבלת עול מלכות שמים
הודאה כללי
יראה תתאה
עולם העשיה (מלכות)

> **It is not the steps of man alone, but the help and support of God… [that supplies] the arousal that we experience internally as the power of the divine soul…"** (*Kovetz Meah Shearim*, from the *Tzemach Tzedek*, pp. 91-92, *Ohr HaTorah, Inyanim*, pp. 306-307)[28]

There is far more water than land in the world, and if it weren't for God's benevolence, the water (which symbolizes the hidden spiritual worlds) would overwhelm the land. But, because He desires a place to dwell in the lower physical worlds, He caused the dry land to overwhelm the water. The fulfillment of mitzvot is a physical act, symbolized by the physical earth upon which we walk, and therefore we bless God as the One "who stretches the land over the water." However, it is not man's physical actions alone that lead to success, for spiritual arousal from above is also essential, and therefore we say the blessing, "He who guides the steps of man."

Man's initiative, coming from our desire for connection with God, stimulates a transcendent light (*ohr makif*) to descend, surround and aid us on all levels. About this transcendent illumination, we say three blessings. The first, *she'asah li kol tzorchi* ("He who provided all of my needs") is said about the shoes that we wear, that surround our lowest extremities — our feet (the symbols of action). The second

Nefesh shb'nefesh
Yoke of Heaven
General
   Acknowledgment
Lower Fear
World of *Asiya*
   (*Malchut*)

Blessed are You, Lord our God, King of the universe, Who stretches the land over the waters.

Blessed are You, Lord our God, King of the universe, Who guides the steps of man.

On Tisha b'Av and Yom Kippur the following blessing is omitted:

Blessed are You, Lord our God, King of the universe, Who has provided all of my needs.

Blessed are You, Lord our God, King of the universe, Who girds Israel with strength.

Blessed are You, Lord our God, King of the universe, Who crowns Israel with glory.

---

blessing, *ozer Yisrael b'gevura* ("He who girds Israel with strength") is said about the belt that surrounds our outer garment, binding it to our heart, or emotions. This blessing is said particularly about our heartfelt emotions of love and fear of God. And finally, we say *oter Yisrael b'tifara* ("He who crowns Israel with glory") regarding the hat that goes on our head. The hat represents the highest transcendent light, associated with our intellect. These are not mere physical garments — they are the physical representations of a high transcendent light that illuminates us as we pray and fulfill the mitzvot of the Torah.

📖 *Within the Words*

Concluding the morning blessings, we recite three blessings that each contain the words, *she'lo asani* ("He who did not make me…"). All of the previous blessings alluded to a positive need to bring down Godly illumination, both into our specific personality traits and as guidance and protection. But, it is also necessary to fend off negative influences that impinge upon us during the course of the day and knock us off of the track of Torah and mitzvot. That is the purpose of the final three blessings that we recite, containing the words, *sh'lo asani…* ("He who did not make me…")

בָּרוּךְ אַתָּה יְיָ אֱלֹהֵינוּ מֶלֶךְ הָעוֹלָם, שֶׁלֹּא עָשַׂנִי גּוֹי:

בָּרוּךְ אַתָּה יְיָ אֱלֹהֵינוּ מֶלֶךְ הָעוֹלָם, שֶׁלֹּא עָשַׂנִי עָבֶד:

בָּרוּךְ אַתָּה יְיָ אֱלֹהֵינוּ מֶלֶךְ הָעוֹלָם, שֶׁלֹּא עָשַׂנִי אִשָּׁה:

בָּרוּךְ אַתָּה יְיָ אֱלֹהֵינוּ מֶלֶךְ הָעוֹלָם, הַמַּעֲבִיר שֵׁנָה מֵעֵינָי וּתְנוּמָה מֵעַפְעַפָּי:

וִיהִי רָצוֹן מִלְּפָנֶיךָ יְיָ אֱלֹהֵינוּ וֵאלֹהֵי אֲבוֹתֵינוּ, שֶׁתַּרְגִּילֵנוּ בְּתוֹרָתֶךָ, וְתַדְבִּיקֵנוּ בְּמִצְוֹתֶיךָ, וְאַל תְּבִיאֵנוּ לֹא לִידֵי חֵטְא וְלֹא לִידֵי עֲבֵרָה וְעָוֹן וְלֹא לִידֵי נִסָּיוֹן וְלֹא לִידֵי בִזָּיוֹן, וְאַל יִשְׁלוֹט בָּנוּ יֵצֶר הָרָע, וְהַרְחִיקֵנוּ מֵאָדָם רָע, וּמֵחָבֵר רָע, וְדַבְּקֵנוּ בְּיֵצֶר טוֹב וּבְמַעֲשִׂים טוֹבִים, וְכוֹף אֶת יִצְרֵנוּ לְהִשְׁתַּעְבֶּד לָךְ, וּתְנֵנוּ הַיּוֹם וּבְכָל יוֹם לְחֵן וּלְחֶסֶד וּלְרַחֲמִים בְּעֵינֶיךָ וּבְעֵינֵי כָל רוֹאֵינוּ, וְתִגְמְלֵנוּ חֲסָדִים טוֹבִים. בָּרוּךְ אַתָּה יְיָ הַגּוֹמֵל חֲסָדִים טוֹבִים לְעַמּוֹ יִשְׂרָאֵל:

יְהִי רָצוֹן מִלְּפָנֶיךָ יְיָ אֱלֹהַי וֵאלֹהֵי אֲבוֹתַי שֶׁתַּצִּילֵנִי הַיּוֹם וּבְכָל יוֹם מֵעַזֵּי פָנִים, וּמֵעַזּוּת פָּנִים, מֵאָדָם רָע, וּמֵחָבֵר רָע, וּמִשָּׁכֵן רָע, וּמִפֶּגַע רָע, מֵעַיִן הָרָע, מִלָּשׁוֹן הָרָע, מִמַּלְשִׁינוּת, מֵעֵדוּת שֶׁקֶר מִשִּׂנְאַת הַבְּרִיּוֹת, מֵעֲלִילָה,

---

CHASSIDIC INSIGHTS

(continued from p. 13)

"to You" — to God Himself, the very essence of Godliness. When we arise in the morning, without any feeling or understanding of Godliness, we engage in "general submission" that has no emotional or intellectual component. Yet precisely because of that, we access the very

(continued on p. 18)

Nefesh shb'nefesh
Yoke of Heaven
General
 Acknowledgment
Lower Fear
World of *Asiya*
 (*Malchut*)

Blessed are You, Lord our God, King of the universe, Who has not made me a gentile.

Blessed are You, Lord our God, King of the universe, Who has not made me a servant.

Blessed are You, Lord our God, King of the universe, Who has not made me a woman.

Blessed are You, Lord our God, King of the universe, Who wipes away sleep from my eyes, and slumber from my eyelids.

And may it be Your will, Lord, my God and God of my fathers, to accustom us to Your Torah, and cause us to adhere to Your commandments. And do not bring us to sin, or to transgression or wrongdoing, nor to any test (of our resolve) or disgrace. And deflect the evil inclination from us and distance us from any evil man, as well as from any evil companion. Enable us to cling to the good inclination and to good deeds, and persuade our inclination to be subdued to You. And grant us today and every day, charm and kindness and mercy in Your eyes as well as the eyes of all who see us. And extend positive kindness to us. Blessed are You, Lord, Who grants positive kindnesses to His people, Israel.

And may it be Your will, Lord, our God and God of our fathers, to rescue us today, and every day from those who are insolent, as well as from insolence, from an evil person and from an evil companion, from a bad neighbor, or bad events, from the evil eye, and from evil speech, from evil reports, from false witness, from the

מְמִיתָה מִשְׁנָה, מֶחֱלָיִם רָעִים, מִמִּקְרִים רָעִים, וּמִשָּׂטָן הַמַּשְׁחִית מִדִּין קָשֶׁה, וּמִבַּעַל דִּין קָשֶׁה, בֵּין שֶׁהוּא בֶן בְּרִית, וּבֵין שֶׁאֵינוֹ בֶן בְּרִית. וּמִדִּינָהּ שֶׁל גֵּיהִנֹּם:

נפש שבנפש
קבלת עול מלכות שמים
הודאה כללי
יראה תתאה
עולם העשיה (מלכות)

ברכות התורה

בָּרוּךְ אַתָּה יְיָ אֱלֹהֵינוּ מֶלֶךְ הָעוֹלָם, אֲשֶׁר קִדְּשָׁנוּ בְּמִצְוֹתָיו, וְצִוָּנוּ עַל דִּבְרֵי תוֹרָה:

וְהַעֲרֶב נָא יְיָ אֱלֹהֵינוּ אֶת דִּבְרֵי תוֹרָתְךָ בְּפִינוּ, וּבְפִי כָל עַמְּךָ בֵּית יִשְׂרָאֵל. וְנִהְיֶה אֲנַחְנוּ וְצֶאֱצָאֵינוּ, וְצֶאֱצָאֵי כָל עַמְּךָ בֵּית יִשְׂרָאֵל, כֻּלָּנוּ יוֹדְעֵי שְׁמֶךָ וְלוֹמְדֵי תוֹרָתֶךָ לִשְׁמָהּ. בָּרוּךְ אַתָּה יְיָ הַמְלַמֵּד תּוֹרָה לְעַמּוֹ יִשְׂרָאֵל:

בָּרוּךְ אַתָּה יְיָ אֱלֹהֵינוּ מֶלֶךְ הָעוֹלָם, אֲשֶׁר בָּחַר בָּנוּ מִכָּל הָעַמִּים, וְנָתַן לָנוּ אֶת תּוֹרָתוֹ. בָּרוּךְ אַתָּה יְיָ נוֹתֵן הַתּוֹרָה:

וַיְדַבֵּר יְיָ אֶל מֹשֶׁה לֵּאמֹר: דַּבֵּר אֶל אַהֲרֹן וְאֶל בָּנָיו לֵאמֹר, כֹּה תְבָרְכוּ אֶת בְּנֵי יִשְׂרָאֵל אָמוֹר לָהֶם:

יְבָרֶכְךָ יְיָ וְיִשְׁמְרֶךָ:

יָאֵר יְיָ, פָּנָיו אֵלֶיךָ, וִיחֻנֶּךָּ:

יִשָּׂא יְיָ, פָּנָיו אֵלֶיךָ, וְיָשֵׂם לְךָ שָׁלוֹם:

--- **CHASSIDIC INSIGHTS** ---

(continued from p. 16)

essence of Godliness. He is not limited to our mind or emotions, and by approaching Him with neither, but from the very essence of our soul, we engage Him in the very essence of His being.

Our recital of *Modeh ani* is only the beginning of our morning

(continued on p. 22)

Nefesh shb'nefesh
Yoke of Heaven
General
  Acknowledgment
Lower Fear
World of *Asiya*
  (*Malchut*)

hatred of others, from false accusations, from unnatural demise, from harsh disease, from misfortune, from a destructive accuser, from severe judgment, and from a persistent adversary, whether he is Jewish or not, and from the judgment of gehinnom.

Blessings of the Torah

BLESSED ARE YOU, LORD OUR GOD, KING OF THE universe, who has sanctified us with His commandments, and commanded us regarding the words of Torah.

Lord, our God, please make the words of Torah sweet in our mouths, as well as in the mouths of all your nation, the House of Israel, so that we and our descendents, as well as the descendents of all of your nation, the House of Israel, will all be knowledgeable about Your name and learn Your Torah for its own sake. Blessed are You, Lord, Who teaches Torah to His people, Israel.

Blessed are You, Lord our God, King of the universe, Who chose us from among all the nations and granted us His Torah. Blessed are You, Lord, Who gives the Torah.

And the Lord spoke to Moses, saying: Speak to Aaron and to his sons, saying, 'So shall you bless the children of Israel — say to them:

"May the Lord bless you and keep you.
May the Lord shine His countenance upon you,
and give you grace.
May the Lord lift up His countenance to you,
and grant you peace."

וְשָׂמוּ אֶת שְׁמִי עַל בְּנֵי יִשְׂרָאֵל וַאֲנִי אֲבָרְכֵם:

אֵלּוּ דְבָרִים שֶׁאֵין לָהֶם שִׁעוּר, הַפֵּאָה, וְהַבִּכּוּרִים, וְהָרְאָיוֹן, וּגְמִילוּת חֲסָדִים, וְתַלְמוּד תּוֹרָה:

אֵלּוּ דְבָרִים שֶׁאָדָם אוֹכֵל פֵּרוֹתֵיהֶם בָּעוֹלָם הַזֶּה וְהַקֶּרֶן קַיֶּמֶת לָעוֹלָם הַבָּא, וְאֵלּוּ הֵן: כִּבּוּד אָב וָאֵם, וּגְמִילוּת חֲסָדִים, וְהַשְׁכָּמַת בֵּית הַמִּדְרָשׁ שַׁחֲרִית וְעַרְבִית, וְהַכְנָסַת אוֹרְחִים וּבִקּוּר חוֹלִים, וְהַכְנָסַת כַּלָּה, וּלְוָיַת הַמֵּת, וְעִיּוּן תְּפִלָּה, וַהֲבָאַת שָׁלוֹם שֶׁבֵּין אָדָם לַחֲבֵרוֹ, וּבֵין אִישׁ לְאִשְׁתּוֹ, וְתַלְמוּד תּוֹרָה כְּנֶגֶד כֻּלָּם:

נפש שבנפש
קבלת עול מלכות שמים
הודאה כללי
יראה תתאה
עולם העשיה (מלכות)

> **"These are the matters of which man enjoys the fruits (interest) in this world, and the principal in the world to come: Honoring one's father and mother, performing acts of kindness, attending the house of study early for both morning and evening prayers, accepting guests and tending the sick, arranging weddings and accompanying the dead, and prayer with intention..."** (From the Siddur, quoted in *Torat Shmuel* of the Rebbe Maharash, 5629/1869, pp. 71-72)[29]

Performance of "good deeds" is an activity that draws divine influx down from above to below, so how can we include "prayer with intention" in this category, since we know that the dynamic of prayer is from below to above? Some explain that prayer is an act of "pouring out the soul," which is healthy for the soul, and therefore it is in the category of "good deeds," from above to below. Nevertheless, our prayers were established in lieu of the sacrifices which took place from below to above. That brings us back to the original question — how can prayers be described as "good deeds"?

There is more than one kind of sacrifice. Our prayers were decreed specifically in lieu of the "regular burnt offering" (*olah*) that was brought every morning and every evening. These sacrifices provided spiritual "sustenance." Physical sustenance includes food, which joins the soul with the body. Spiritual sustenance links God with His

Nefesh shb'nefesh
Yoke of Heaven
General Acknowledgment
Lower Fear
World of *Asiya* (*Malchut*)

> And they shall place my name on the children of Israel, whereupon I will bless them.

These are the laws which have no fixed measure: peah ("corners of the fields" — left for the poor), bikurim ("first fruits" — for the priests), reayon (pilgrimage offering brought during the three festivals), deeds of kindness, and Torah learning.

These are the matters of which man enjoys the fruits (interest) in this world, and the principal in the world to come: Honoring one's father and mother, performing acts of kindness, attending the house of study early for both morning and evening prayers, accepting guests and tending the sick, arranging weddings and accompanying the dead, and prayer with intention and establishing peace between man and his companion, between husband and wife — and study of Torah is equivalent to all of them.

---

creation. The regular burnt offerings brought revelation of Godliness down to the creation. Our prayers were decreed specifically in place of these sacrifices to bring down Godliness from above to below. For this reason, our "prayers with intention" may also be included in the category of "good deeds," which draw down divine influx from above to below.

📖 *Within the Words*

The eighteen morning blessings bring down light that enables us to distinguish between good and bad, and to take our first steps of the day. The eighteen blessings of the *Shemonah Esreh* (*Amidah*) bring down new illumination that changes the world completely (*B'Sha'ah Shehikdimu 5672* (1912) of the Rebbe Rashab, vol. 2 pp. 737-739).

סדר לבישת טלית קטן

בָּרוּךְ אַתָּה יְיָ אֱלֹהֵינוּ מֶלֶךְ הָעוֹלָם, אֲשֶׁר קִדְּשָׁנוּ בְּמִצְוֹתָיו, וְצִוָּנוּ עַל מִצְוַת צִיצִית:

סדר לבישת טלית גדול

בָּרְכִי נַפְשִׁי אֶת יְיָ, יְיָ אֱלֹהַי גָּדַלְתָּ מְאֹד, הוֹד וְהָדָר לָבָשְׁתָּ: עֹטֶה אוֹר כַּשַּׂלְמָה, נוֹטֶה שָׁמַיִם כַּיְרִיעָה:

בָּרוּךְ אַתָּה יְיָ אֱלֹהֵינוּ מֶלֶךְ הָעוֹלָם, אֲשֶׁר קִדְּשָׁנוּ בְּמִצְוֹתָיו, וְצִוָּנוּ לְהִתְעַטֵּף בְּצִיצִית:

מַה יָּקָר חַסְדְּךָ אֱלֹהִים, וּבְנֵי אָדָם בְּצֵל כְּנָפֶיךָ יֶחֱסָיוּן: יִרְוְיֻן מִדֶּשֶׁן בֵּיתֶךָ וְנַחַל עֲדָנֶיךָ תַשְׁקֵם: כִּי עִמְּךָ מְקוֹר חַיִּים, בְּאוֹרְךָ נִרְאֶה אוֹר: מְשֹׁךְ חַסְדְּךָ לְיֹדְעֶיךָ וְצִדְקָתְךָ לְיִשְׁרֵי לֵב:

סדר הנחת תפילין

בָּרוּךְ אַתָּה יְיָ אֱלֹהֵינוּ מֶלֶךְ הָעוֹלָם, אֲשֶׁר קִדְּשָׁנוּ בְּמִצְוֹתָיו, וְצִוָּנוּ לְהָנִיחַ תְּפִלִּין:

בָּרוּךְ אַתָּה יְיָ אֱלֹהֵינוּ מֶלֶךְ הָעוֹלָם, אֲשֶׁר קִדְּשָׁנוּ בְּמִצְוֹתָיו, וְצִוָּנוּ עַל מִצְוַת תְּפִלִּין:

נפש שבנפש
קבלת עול מלכות שמים
הודאה כללי
יראה תתאה
עולם העשיה
(מלכות)

--- CHASSIDIC INSIGHTS ---

(continued from p. 18)

journey. However, it typifies the state of mind that we inhabit before we actually go to the synagogue in the morning and begin our prayers. That state of mind is called *yirah tata'ah*, or "lower fear." It is characterized by fundamental fear of He who is greater than us,

(continued on p. 24)

Nefesh shb'nefesh
Yoke of Heaven
General
  Acknowledgment
Lower Fear
World of *Asiya*
  (*Malchut*)

The Order of Putting on the Tallit Katan

BLESSED ARE YOU, LORD OUR GOD, KING OF THE universe, Who has sanctified us with His mitzvot, and commanded us regarding tzitzit.

The Order of Putting on the Tallit Gadol

Bless the Lord, my soul; Lord my God, You are greatly aggrandized, You are garbed in majesty and glory. You envelop Yourself with light as a cloak, Incline the heavens like a curtain.

BLESSED ARE YOU, LORD OUR GOD, KING OF THE universe, Who has sanctified us with His mitzvot, and commanded us to wrap (ourselves) in *tzitzit*.

How precious is Your kindness, God, men take refuge in the shadow of Your wings. They are satiated with the sweetness of Your house, and a stream of delight pours over them. For with You is the source of life, in Your illumination, we find light. Draw down Your kindness to those who know You, and Your righteousness upon the pure of heart.

The Order of Donning Tefillin

BLESSED ARE YOU, LORD OUR GOD, KING OF THE universe, Who has sanctified us with His mitzvot, and commanded us to don *tefillin*.

In case of interruption between the *tefillin* of the hand and of the head, recite the following blessing:

BLESSED BE YOU, LORD OUR GOD, KING OF THE universe, Who has sanctified us with His mitzvot, and commanded us regarding *tefillin*.

הֲרֵינִי מְקַבֵּל עָלַי מִצְוַת עֲשֵׂה שֶׁל וְאָהַבְתָּ לְרֵעֲךָ כָּמוֹךָ:

מַה טֹּבוּ אֹהָלֶיךָ יַעֲקֹב, מִשְׁכְּנֹתֶיךָ, יִשְׂרָאֵל:

וַאֲנִי בְּרֹב חַסְדְּךָ אָבֹא בֵיתֶךָ אֶשְׁתַּחֲוֶה אֶל הֵיכַל קָדְשְׁךָ בְּיִרְאָתֶךָ:

וַאֲנִי תְפִלָּתִי לְךָ יְיָ עֵת רָצוֹן, אֱלֹהִים בְּרָב חַסְדֶּךָ, עֲנֵנִי בֶּאֱמֶת יִשְׁעֶךָ:

אֲדוֹן עוֹלָם אֲשֶׁר מָלַךְ, בְּטֶרֶם כָּל יְצוּר נִבְרָא.
לְעֵת נַעֲשָׂה בְחֶפְצוֹ כֹּל, אֲזַי מֶלֶךְ שְׁמוֹ נִקְרָא.
וְאַחֲרֵי כִּכְלוֹת הַכֹּל. לְבַדּוֹ יִמְלוֹךְ נוֹרָא.
וְהוּא הָיָה וְהוּא הֹוֶה, וְהוּא יִהְיֶה בְּתִפְאָרָה.
וְהוּא אֶחָד וְאֵין שֵׁנִי, לְהַמְשִׁיל לוֹ לְהַחְבִּירָה.
בְּלִי רֵאשִׁית בְּלִי תַכְלִית, וְלוֹ הָעֹז וְהַמִּשְׂרָה.
וְהוּא אֵלִי וְחַי גֹּאֲלִי, וְצוּר חֶבְלִי בְּעֵת צָרָה.
וְהוּא נִסִּי וּמָנוֹס לִי, מְנָת כּוֹסִי בְּיוֹם אֶקְרָא.
בְּיָדוֹ אַפְקִיד רוּחִי, בְּעֵת אִישָׁן וְאָעִירָה.
וְעִם רוּחִי גְוִיָּתִי, יְיָ לִי וְלֹא אִירָא:

נפש שבנפש
קבלת עול מלכות שמים
הודאה כללי
יראה תתאה
עולם העשיה (מלכות)

CHASSIDIC INSIGHTS

(continued from p. 22)

who has control over us, and who can do whatever He wants with us. Therefore, we are afraid of Him, much as a child is afraid of the punishment that his parents can mete out. In the beginning, the child does not know why he is being told to do one thing and not to

(continued on p. 26)

Nefesh shb'nefesh
Yoke of Heaven
General
 Acknowledgment
Lower Fear
World of *Asiya*
 (*Malchut*)

I accept upon myself the positive commandment of, "And you shall love your neighbor as yourself."

HOW GOODLY ARE YOUR TENTS, JACOB, AND YOUR dwelling places, Israel!

And I, through Your magnanimous kindness, will enter Your House, (and) bow toward Your holy palace, in awe of You.

As for me, may my prayer to You be at an auspicious time; God in Your abundant kind-ness, respond to me with Your true salvation.

MASTER OF THE UNIVERSE, WHO REIGNED PRIOR to the creation of form,
When all was finished, with His will, then His name as King was coronated.
And after all will cease to be, He alone will awesomely reign,
He was and He is, and He will gloriously be.
He is one and there is no other, without comparison and without peer
He is without beginning, nor with end; His is the strength and the dominion.
He is my God and my living Redeemer,
 Refuge in times of my trouble and distress.
He is my banner and my protection, my drink of salvation on my day of reckoning.
Into His hand I place my spirit, as I slumber and as I awaken.
With my spirit, my body as well, the Lord is mine, I will not fear.

עקדה

אֱלֹהֵינוּ וֵאלֹהֵי אֲבוֹתֵינוּ, זָכְרֵנוּ בְּזִכָּרוֹן טוֹב לְפָנֶיךָ, וּפָקְדֵנוּ בִּפְקֻדַּת יְשׁוּעָה וְרַחֲמִים מִשְּׁמֵי שְׁמֵי קֶדֶם, וּזְכָר לָנוּ יְיָ אֱלֹהֵינוּ אַהֲבַת הַקַּדְמוֹנִים אַבְרָהָם יִצְחָק וְיִשְׂרָאֵל עֲבָדֶיךָ, אֶת הַבְּרִית וְאֶת הַחֶסֶד וְאֶת הַשְּׁבוּעָה שֶׁנִּשְׁבַּעְתָּ לְאַבְרָהָם אָבִינוּ בְּהַר הַמּוֹרִיָּה, וְאֶת הָעֲקֵדָה שֶׁעָקַד אֶת יִצְחָק בְּנוֹ עַל גַּבֵּי הַמִּזְבֵּחַ, כַּכָּתוּב בְּתוֹרָתֶךָ:

וַיְהִי אַחַר הַדְּבָרִים הָאֵלֶּה, וְהָאֱלֹהִים נִסָּה אֶת אַבְרָהָם וַיֹּאמֶר אֵלָיו, אַבְרָהָם, וַיֹּאמֶר הִנֵּנִי: וַיֹּאמֶר קַח נָא אֶת בִּנְךָ אֶת יְחִידְךָ אֲשֶׁר אָהַבְתָּ אֶת יִצְחָק, וְלֶךְ לְךָ אֶל אֶרֶץ הַמֹּרִיָּה, וְהַעֲלֵהוּ שָׁם לְעֹלָה עַל אַחַד הֶהָרִים, אֲשֶׁר אֹמַר אֵלֶיךָ: וַיַּשְׁכֵּם אַבְרָהָם בַּבֹּקֶר, וַיַּחֲבֹשׁ אֶת חֲמֹרוֹ, וַיִּקַּח אֶת שְׁנֵי נְעָרָיו אִתּוֹ וְאֵת יִצְחָק בְּנוֹ, וַיְבַקַּע עֲצֵי עֹלָה וַיָּקָם וַיֵּלֶךְ אֶל הַמָּקוֹם אֲשֶׁר אָמַר לוֹ הָאֱלֹהִים: בַּיּוֹם הַשְּׁלִישִׁי וַיִּשָּׂא אַבְרָהָם אֶת עֵינָיו וַיַּרְא אֶת הַמָּקוֹם מֵרָחֹק: וַיֹּאמֶר אַבְרָהָם אֶל נְעָרָיו שְׁבוּ לָכֶם פֹּה עִם הַחֲמוֹר, וַאֲנִי וְהַנַּעַר נֵלְכָה עַד כֹּה, וְנִשְׁתַּחֲוֶה וְנָשׁוּבָה אֲלֵיכֶם: וַיִּקַּח אַבְרָהָם אֶת עֲצֵי הָעֹלָה וַיָּשֶׂם עַל יִצְחָק בְּנוֹ וַיִּקַּח בְּיָדוֹ אֶת הָאֵשׁ וְאֶת הַמַּאֲכֶלֶת, וַיֵּלְכוּ שְׁנֵיהֶם יַחְדָּו: וַיֹּאמֶר יִצְחָק אֶל אַבְרָהָם אָבִיו וַיֹּאמֶר אָבִי, וַיֹּאמֶר, הִנֶּנִּי בְנִי, וַיֹּאמֶר, הִנֵּה הָאֵשׁ וְהָעֵצִים וְאַיֵּה הַשֶּׂה לְעֹלָה: וַיֹּאמֶר אַבְרָהָם אֱלֹהִים יִרְאֶה לּוֹ הַשֶּׂה לְעֹלָה בְּנִי, וַיֵּלְכוּ שְׁנֵיהֶם יַחְדָּו: וַיָּבֹאוּ אֶל הַמָּקוֹם אֲשֶׁר אָמַר לוֹ הָאֱלֹהִים, וַיִּבֶן שָׁם אַבְרָהָם אֶת הַמִּזְבֵּחַ, וַיַּעֲרֹךְ אֶת הָעֵצִים, וַיַּעֲקֹד אֶת יִצְחָק בְּנוֹ, וַיָּשֶׂם אֹתוֹ עַל הַמִּזְבֵּחַ מִמַּעַל

נפש שבנפש
קבלת עול מלכות שמים
הודאה כללי
יראה תתאה
עולם העשיה (מלכות)

CHASSIDIC INSIGHTS

(continued from p. 24)

do another. He only knows that he must listen to his parents. As he grows, he develops understanding of what he should and should not do, and then he also learns to appreciate parental guidance. But, to begin with, all he knows is that he must follow orders.

(continued on p. 32)

Nefesh shb'nefesh
Yoke of Heaven
General Acknowledgment
Lower Fear
World of *Asiya* (*Malchut*)

Akeidat Yitzhak

On Shabbat and Festivals, the following paragraph is omitted:

Our God and God of our fathers, remember us favorably before You, and bring down salvation and mercy upon us from the primordial supernal heavens. And recall on our behalf, Lord our God, Your love for our predecessors Avraham, Yitzhak and Yisrael Your servants, and the covenant, the kindness and the oath that You swore to Avraham our forefather on Mt. Moriah, and the binding with which he tied Yitzhak his son on the altar, as written in Your Torah.

And it happened after these events, that God tested Abraham, and said to him, "Abraham," and he answered, "I am here." And He said, "Take your son, your only beloved son, Isaac, and go to the land of Moriah, and elevate him there as an offering on one of the mountains, that I will tell you." And Abraham arose early in the morning, saddled his donkey, and took two young lads with him, as well as his son Isaac, and split wood for burning. And he arose and traveled to the place that God said to him. On the third day, Abraham raised his eyes, and saw the place from afar. And Abraham said to the young lads, "Remain here with the donkey, and I and the lad will go over there and bow down and return to you." And Abraham took the wood for the offering, and placed it upon Isaac his son, and carried the fire and the knife, and both of them journeyed together. And Isaac spoke to his father, saying, "Father," and he answered him, "Here I am, my son," and he said, "Here is the fire and the wood, and where is the sheep to offer?" And Abraham said, "God will show him the sheep to offer, my son," and both of them walked together. And they came to the place that God said to him, and there Abraham built the altar, and arranged the wood upon it, and bound his son Isaac, placing him on the altar on top of the wood. And

לָעֵצִים: וַיִּשְׁלַח אַבְרָהָם אֶת יָדוֹ וַיִּקַּח אֶת הַמַּאֲכֶלֶת, לִשְׁחֹט אֶת בְּנוֹ: וַיִּקְרָא אֵלָיו מַלְאַךְ יְיָ מִן הַשָּׁמַיִם וַיֹּאמֶר, אַבְרָהָם, אַבְרָהָם, וַיֹּאמֶר, הִנֵּנִי: וַיֹּאמֶר, אַל תִּשְׁלַח יָדְךָ אֶל הַנַּעַר, וְאַל תַּעַשׂ לוֹ מְאוּמָה, כִּי עַתָּה יָדַעְתִּי, כִּי יְרֵא אֱלֹהִים אַתָּה, וְלֹא חָשַׂכְתָּ אֶת בִּנְךָ אֶת יְחִידְךָ מִמֶּנִּי: וַיִּשָּׂא אַבְרָהָם אֶת עֵינָיו וַיַּרְא וְהִנֵּה אַיִל, אַחַר, נֶאֱחַז בַּסְּבַךְ בְּקַרְנָיו, וַיֵּלֶךְ אַבְרָהָם וַיִּקַּח אֶת הָאַיִל, וַיַּעֲלֵהוּ לְעֹלָה תַּחַת בְּנוֹ: וַיִּקְרָא אַבְרָהָם שֵׁם הַמָּקוֹם הַהוּא, יְיָ יִרְאֶה, אֲשֶׁר יֵאָמֵר הַיּוֹם, בְּהַר יְיָ יֵרָאֶה: וַיִּקְרָא מַלְאַךְ יְיָ אֶל אַבְרָהָם שֵׁנִית מִן הַשָּׁמַיִם: וַיֹּאמֶר, בִּי נִשְׁבַּעְתִּי נְאֻם יְיָ, כִּי יַעַן אֲשֶׁר עָשִׂיתָ אֶת הַדָּבָר הַזֶּה, וְלֹא חָשַׂכְתָּ אֶת בִּנְךָ אֶת

נפש שבנפש
קבלת עול מלכות שמים
הודאה כללי
יראה תתאה
עולם העשיה (מלכות)

> **After the angel instructed Avraham not to slaughter his son, the ram sought to be sacrificed in place of Yitzchak. But, the Satan prevented this from happening. 'What did the ram do? It stretched out its foot and touched the *tallit* of Avraham.'** (*Pirkei d'R'Eliezer*, ch. 31)[30]

Avraham symbolized the *kav* ("ray") of Godly energy that comes from the infinite light preceding the *tzimtzum* ("great contraction"). The task of the *kav* is to "allocate" Godly revelation to all spiritual creations, from the highest (*Adam Kadmon*) down to the lowest (our world, known as the World of *Asiya*). The *kav* is associated with *ohr pnimi*, or "immanent light" that we may feel and experience, each according to his own spiritual level. Avraham's *tallit* (which surrounded his body) symbolized the *makif hagadol,* or infinite light that preceded the *kav* and is beyond our experience. Therefore, the *tallit* represented *ohr makif,* or "transcendent illumination." This *ohr makif* is also the transcendant source of physical creation.[31]

When the ram reached out to touch the *tallit* of Avraham, it connected the pervasive light of *ohr pnimi* to the transcendant illumination of *ohr makif. Ohr pnimi* must always be in contact with *ohr makif,* so that creation may be constantly "renewed" from higher spiritual levels. Yitzchak's willingness to sacrifice his physical body put him in touch with his *ohr makif* and propelled him to even higher levels than his willingness to give up his soul. This is because the soul

Nefesh shb'nefesh
Yoke of Heaven
General
   Acknowledgment
Lower Fear
World of *Asiya*
   (*Malchut*)

Abraham extended his hand to take the knife in order to ritually slaughter his son. And an angel of God called out to him from the heavens, saying, "Abraham, Abraham," and he said, "I am here." And he said, "Do not lay your hand upon the lad, and do nothing to him, for now I know that you fear God, [so much so] that you would not withhold your son, your only son, from Me." And Abraham raised his eyes and saw, and behold, there was a ram caught in the thicket by its horns, and Abraham went and took the ram, and offered it up as a sacrifice in place of his son. And Abraham called this place, "God will see," and about this day will be said, "On the mountain of God, He will be seen." And an angel of God called a second time from the Heavens, saying, "I myself have sworn, the Lord says, that since you have done this deed, and did not withhold your son,

---

intrinsically yearns and strives for higher spiritual levels that are beyond the body, so it is natural for it to want to leave the body. But, to sacrifice our body requires us human beings to contradict our deepest nature. It requires that we act against our own physical well-being, and that is why Yitzchak's act of self-sacrifice touched the very essence of Godliness. In Chassidut, this is expressed by the statement: "the source of the *kelim* ('vessels') is higher than the source of the *orot* ('lights')." That is, the physical body has an even higher spiritual source than does the soul.

> 📖 *Within the Words*
>
> The prayer process requires us to join the lower levels of our soul with the upper levels of our soul which transcend our body. When we recite the *Akeida* in the morning, we prepare to join *memalle kol olmin* ("permeating, immanent illumination" that is characteristic of the lower levels of the soul) with *sovev kol olmin* ("surrounding, transcendent illumination" that is associated with the higher soul-levels). In addition, we recall the level of self sacrifice, even of the body, that was demonstrated by Yitzchak at the *Akeida*.

יְחִידְךָ: כִּי בָרֵךְ אֲבָרֶכְךָ, וְהַרְבָּה אַרְבֶּה אֶת זַרְעֲךָ כְּכוֹכְבֵי הַשָּׁמַיִם וְכַחוֹל אֲשֶׁר עַל שְׂפַת הַיָּם, וְיִרַשׁ זַרְעֲךָ אֵת שַׁעַר אֹיְבָיו:

נפש שבנפש
קבלת עול מלכות שמים
הודאה כללי
יראה תתאה
עולם העשיה (מלכות)

❝ In the merit of the *Akeida*, 'the ashes of Yitzchak were as if piled on top of the altar.'[32] The Talmud asks, 'How did they know where the altar of the second Temple was located?' [And answers,] 'They saw that the ashes of Yitzchak were placed there.'" (See *Likutei Sichot* of the Lubavitcher Rebbe, vol. 25, p. 131)[33]

Whether these were the ashes of the ram (which was considered "as if" it was Yitzchak) or the ashes of Yitzchak himself (as the Midrash indicates), we are faced with a question: Why were they not removed from the altar? After a burnt offering (*olah*), the priests were required to remove the ashes from the altar, in order to make room for the next sacrifice. If so, why did these ashes remain? According to *halacha*, this is not a difficulty. Since the *Akeida* occurred long before the Temple was built, the platform on which Yitzchak was bound did not have halachic status as an altar, and therefore it was permissible for the ashes to remain. However, from the Midrash it is apparent that it was not only permissible, but meritorious for his ashes to remain on the altar. Why was Yitzchak's self-sacrifice so "meritorious"? The Zohar tells us that even though Avraham did not actually slaughter his son, Yitzchak's soul left his body and another soul entered in its stead.[34] Thus, he underwent *techiyat hameitim* ("resurrection of the dead"). Yitzchak's willingness to be offered as a sacrifice was so great that it transformed him both physically and spiritually. Since the ram was considered to be in place of Yitzchak in every respect, so just as Yitzchak sanctified his body with his choice to allow himself to be sacrificed, so the ashes of the ram took on all the sanctification that Yitzchak took upon himself. And therefore, Yitzchak's near-sacrifice had an ongoing and continuous effect on these ashes as well, even after the event was over. His self-sacrifice raised the status of the ashes to a *cheftza shel mitzvah* (an article upon which a mitzvah has been performed) and therefore they retained their holiness even after the mitzvah (the near-sacrifice) had taken place.

Nefesh shb'nefesh
Yoke of Heaven
General
    Acknowledgment
Lower Fear
World of *Asiya*
    (*Malchut*)

your only son. Therefore I will bless, certainly bless you, and increase your seed tremendously, as the stars of the heavens and the sand on the shore of the sea, and your descendants will inherit the gates of their enemies. And

In general, ashes are what remain after an object has been incinerated. Upon burning, the more refined elements of the object — those which come from air, water and fire — are consumed and elevated to their spiritual source. All that remains are the ashes, coming from the most physical element — earth, which represents our most physical tendencies. These tendencies cannot be easily elevated to their spiritual source and, therefore, they must be removed from the altar and, eventually, from the surrounding camp. However, Yitzchak was a special case — his willingness to sacrifice his own body, the very essence of his physical self — had such a powerful effect that his ashes were not only permitted, but expected to remain on the altar, forever. Yitzchak's devotion and self-nullification to God were so great that they uplifted his entire body, so that even his physical matter was connected to Godliness.

Within the Words

We read the *Akeida* every morning before prayers, "in order to subdue our evil inclination and persuade it to serve God, just as Yitzchak gave himself up for God."[35] Although we focus "with all our soul" on God, after prayers we may have to go to work in a place that is not in the vicinity of the "holy altar" (i.e. the synagogue or study hall). The only reason that we are permitted to do so is to "make room for the next sacrifice" (the next order of prayers, which were decreed in lieu of the sacrifices). This is so that, the next time we pray, our prayers will take place on an even higher level. Although the natural place for a Jew is in the four cubits of Torah, studying, praying and serving God, sometimes this is not possible. Thus, we preface our prayers with recitation of the *Akeida* because it reminds us to pray with so much intensity and devotion that if we do have to leave the "altar" and the "camp" in order to support ourselves, we will nevertheless retain enough holiness to feel as if we are still "in the camp," actively serving God with all of our heart, soul and self.

וְהִתְבָּרֲכוּ בְזַרְעֲךָ כֹּל גּוֹיֵי הָאָרֶץ, עֵקֶב אֲשֶׁר שָׁמַעְתָּ בְּקֹלִי: וַיָּשָׁב אַבְרָהָם אֶל נְעָרָיו, וַיָּקֻמוּ וַיֵּלְכוּ יַחְדָּו אֶל בְּאֵר שָׁבַע, וַיֵּשֶׁב אַבְרָהָם בִּבְאֵר שָׁבַע:

רִבּוֹנוֹ שֶׁל עוֹלָם, כְּמוֹ שֶׁכָּבַשׁ אַבְרָהָם אָבִינוּ אֶת רַחֲמָיו מֵעַל בֶּן יְחִידוֹ לַעֲשׂוֹת רְצוֹנְךָ בְּלֵבָב שָׁלֵם, כֵּן יִכְבְּשׁוּ רַחֲמֶיךָ אֶת כַּעַסְךָ מֵעָלֵינוּ וְיִגֹּלּוּ רַחֲמֶיךָ עַל מִדּוֹתֶיךָ. וְתִתְנַהֵג עִמָּנוּ יְיָ אֱלֹהֵינוּ בְּמִדַּת הַחֶסֶד וּבְמִדַּת הָרַחֲמִים, וְתִכָּנֵס לָנוּ לִפְנִים מִשּׁוּרַת הַדִּין, וּבְטוּבְךָ הַגָּדוֹל יָשׁוּב חֲרוֹן אַפְּךָ מֵעַמְּךָ וּמֵעִירְךָ וּמֵאַרְצְךָ וּמִנַּחֲלָתֶךָ, וְקַיֵּם לָנוּ יְיָ אֱלֹהֵינוּ אֶת הַדָּבָר שֶׁהִבְטַחְתָּנוּ בְּתוֹרָתֶךָ, עַל יְדֵי מֹשֶׁה עַבְדֶּךָ מִפִּי כְבוֹדֶךָ כָּאָמוּר. וְזָכַרְתִּי אֶת בְּרִיתִי יַעֲקוֹב, וְאַף אֶת בְּרִיתִי יִצְחָק, וְאַף אֶת בְּרִיתִי אַבְרָהָם אֶזְכֹּר וְהָאָרֶץ אֶזְכֹּר: וְנֶאֱמַר, וְאַף גַּם זֹאת בִּהְיוֹתָם בְּאֶרֶץ אֹיְבֵיהֶם לֹא מְאַסְתִּים וְלֹא גְעַלְתִּים לְכַלּוֹתָם, לְהָפֵר בְּרִיתִי אִתָּם, כִּי אֲנִי יְיָ אֱלֹהֵיהֶם: וְנֶאֱמַר, וְזָכַרְתִּי לָהֶם בְּרִית רִאשֹׁנִים, אֲשֶׁר הוֹצֵאתִי אֹתָם מֵאֶרֶץ מִצְרַיִם, לְעֵינֵי הַגּוֹיִם, לִהְיוֹת לָהֶם לֵאלֹהִים, אֲנִי יְיָ: וְנֶאֱמַר, וְשָׁב יְיָ אֱלֹהֶיךָ אֶת שְׁבוּתְךָ וְרִחֲמֶךָ, וְשָׁב, וְקִבֶּצְךָ מִכָּל הָעַמִּים, אֲשֶׁר הֱפִיצְךָ יְיָ אֱלֹהֶיךָ שָׁמָּה: אִם יִהְיֶה נִדַּחֲךָ בִּקְצֵה הַשָּׁמָיִם, מִשָּׁם יְקַבֶּצְךָ יְיָ אֱלֹהֶיךָ וּמִשָּׁם

נפש שבנפש
קבלת עול מלכות שמים
הודאה כללי
יראה תתאה
עולם העשיה (מלכות)

CHASSIDIC INSIGHTS

(continued from p. 26)

Similarly, as the hour progresses, we recite passages from the siddur ("prayer book") that indicate that we are developing more understanding and more emotional appreciation of Godliness even before we make it to the synagogue to formally begin our prayers. And in fact, *yirah tata'ah* is sub-divided into three categories, as described in the third chapter of "Love like Fire and Water" (*Kuntres Ha'avoda*). So, even within this entry level state of consciousness there are categories and sub-divisions.

The subdivision of *yirah tata'ah* that we experience upon awakening in the morning is called *kabalat ohl malchut shamayim*, or "acceptance

(continued on p. 34)

Nefesh shb'nefesh
Yoke of Heaven
General
   Acknowledgment
Lower Fear
World of *Asiya*
   (*Malchut*)

through all of your descendants, the nations of the world will bless themselves, since you have listened to my voice. And Abraham returned to the lads, and they arose and traveled together to Beer Sheva, and Abraham dwelt in Beer Sheva.

On Shabbat and Festivals, the following paragraph is omitted:

Master of the universe, just as Avraham our forefather overcame the compassion that he felt for his only son in order to fulfill Your Will with a full heart, so let Your mercy overwhelm Your anger at us, and allow Your mercy to prevail over all of Your attributes. And act with us, Lord our God, with the attribute of kindness and the attribute of mercy, and deal with us within the letter of the law. And in Your great goodness, quash Your wrath from over Your nation and from over Your city and from over Your land and from over Your inheritance. And fulfill for us, Lord our God, that which You promised to us in Your Torah, by way of Moshe Your servant in Your very Honor, saying, "And I will recall My covenant with Yakov, and even my covenant with Yitzhak, and even My covenant with Avraham I will remember, and the Land I will remember." And as it says, "Even as they are in the land of their enemies, I will not forsake them, and I will not abhor them in order to destroy them, nor renege upon My covenant with them, since I am the Lord, their God." And as it says, "I will remember the covenant of their ancestors, whom I brought out of the land of Egypt in plain sight of the nations in order to be their God, I am the Lord." And as it says, "And the Lord Your God will return your remnants and have mercy upon you, and return to gather you from all of the nations, where the Lord your God has scattered you. If some of you are dispersed to the edge of the heavens, from there He will gather you, the Lord your God, and from there He will take you. And the Lord your God will bring

יְקָחֶךָ: וֶהֱבִיאֲךָ יְיָ אֱלֹהֶיךָ אֶל הָאָרֶץ אֲשֶׁר יָרְשׁוּ אֲבֹתֶיךָ, וִירִשְׁתָּהּ וְהֵיטִבְךָ וְהִרְבְּךָ מֵאֲבֹתֶיךָ: וְנֶאֱמַר, יְיָ חָנֵּנוּ, לְךָ קִוִּינוּ הֱיֵה זְרֹעָם לַבְּקָרִים, אַף יְשׁוּעָתֵנוּ בְּעֵת צָרָה: וְנֶאֱמַר, וְעֵת צָרָה הִיא לְיַעֲקֹב, וּמִמֶּנָּה יִוָּשֵׁעַ: וְנֶאֱמַר, בְּכָל צָרָתָם לוֹ צָר, וּמַלְאַךְ פָּנָיו הוֹשִׁיעָם, בְּאַהֲבָתוֹ וּבְחֶמְלָתוֹ הוּא גְאָלָם, וַיְנַטְּלֵם וַיְנַשְּׂאֵם כָּל יְמֵי עוֹלָם: וְנֶאֱמַר, מִי אֵל כָּמוֹךָ נֹשֵׂא עָוֹן וְעֹבֵר עַל פֶּשַׁע, לִשְׁאֵרִית נַחֲלָתוֹ, לֹא הֶחֱזִיק לָעַד אַפּוֹ, כִּי חָפֵץ חֶסֶד הוּא: יָשׁוּב יְרַחֲמֵנוּ, יִכְבֹּשׁ עֲוֹנֹתֵינוּ, וְתַשְׁלִיךְ בִּמְצֻלוֹת יָם כָּל חַטֹּאתָם: תִּתֵּן אֱמֶת לְיַעֲקֹב, חֶסֶד לְאַבְרָהָם, אֲשֶׁר נִשְׁבַּעְתָּ לַאֲבֹתֵינוּ, מִימֵי קֶדֶם: וְנֶאֱמַר, וַהֲבִיאוֹתִים אֶל הַר קָדְשִׁי, וְשִׂמַּחְתִּים בְּבֵית תְּפִלָּתִי, עוֹלֹתֵיהֶם וְזִבְחֵיהֶם לְרָצוֹן עַל מִזְבְּחִי, כִּי בֵיתִי בֵּית תְּפִלָּה, יִקָּרֵא לְכָל הָעַמִּים:

לְעוֹלָם יְהֵא אָדָם יְרֵא שָׁמַיִם בְּסֵתֶר וּמוֹדֶה עַל הָאֱמֶת, וְדוֹבֵר אֱמֶת בִּלְבָבוֹ וְיַשְׁכֵּם וְיֹאמַר:

נפש שבנפש
קבלת עול מלכות שמים
הודאה כללי
יראה תתאה
עולם העשיה
(מלכות)

CHASSIDIC INSIGHTS

(continued from p. 32)

of the yoke of heaven." It is not a conscious attitude. It is, rather a subconscious state of mind that determines our approach to fulfilling the will of the One above. It is the state of mind that says, "whatever He says to do, that's what I'll take upon myself." Although this "yoke" sounds onerous, it is actually quite liberating because this state of mind frees us of ego and from following our own whims that can lead us in negative directions. (see pages 46-49 of "Love like Fire and Water").

Kabalat ohl malchut shamayim is the state of mind that accompanies us through the first few prayers of the siddur. After *modeh ani*, we recite the morning blessings, during which we thank God for all of the steps that we take as we get dressed and prepare for the day. We then say the prayer *Adon Olam* ("Master of the universe"). This prayer, according to most opinions authored during the late Gaonic period, summarizes the creed and theology of the Jews. We then proceed to

(continued on p. 35)

Nefesh shb'nefesh
Yoke of Heaven
General Acknowledgment
Lower Fear
World of *Asiya* (*Malchut*)

you to the land that your forefathers inherited and you will inherit it, and He will do well by you and multiply you, more than your forefathers." And it says, "Lord, be gracious to us, in You is our hope, be our strength in the mornings, our salvation at times of trouble." And it says, "It's a time of trouble for Yakov, from which he will be saved." And it says, "In all of their troubles, He is troubled, and an angel of the Lord saves them. In His love and His mercy He redeems them, and He uplifts them and bears them forever." And it says, "Who is a God like You, bearing our sins and forgiving the transgression of the remnants of His inheritance, He holds not on to His anger, for he desires kindness. He will return and have mercy upon us, will quash our sins; throw all of our transgression into the sea. Grant truth to Yakov and kindness to Avraham, as You swore to our forefathers in the days of yore." And as it says, "And I will bring them to My holy mountain, and cause them to rejoice in My house of prayers; their constant daily offerings and sacrifices will be accepted with favor upon My altar, for My house will be called a house of prayer, for all of the nations."

Man should always be God fearing, even in private, should concede the truth and speak the truth within his heart, arising in the morning to say:

MORNING BLESSINGS

CHASSIDIC INSIGHTS

(continued from p. 34)

recite the one passage in the Torah that most epitomizes acceptance of the yoke of heaven — the *akeida*, or "binding" of Isaac. In this passage, we recount how God commanded Abraham to take his one and only son, Isaac, bind him upon an altar, and offer him as a sacrifice. Of course, in the end this did not occur, since God "stayed Abraham's hand," but without doubt this incident is the greatest illustration of

(continued on p. 36)

נפש שבנפש
קבלת עול מלכות שמים
הודאה כללי
יראה תתאה
עולם העשיה (מלכות)

רִבּוֹן כָּל הָעוֹלָמִים, לֹא עַל צִדְקוֹתֵינוּ אֲנַחְנוּ מַפִּילִים תַּחֲנוּנֵינוּ לְפָנֶיךָ, כִּי עַל רַחֲמֶיךָ הָרַבִּים. מָה אָנוּ, מֶה חַיֵּינוּ, מֶה חַסְדֵּנוּ, מַה צִּדְקֵנוּ, מַה כֹּחֵנוּ, מַה גְּבוּרָתֵנוּ. מַה נֹּאמַר לְפָנֶיךָ יְיָ אֱלֹהֵינוּ וֵאלֹהֵי אֲבוֹתֵינוּ, הֲלֹא כָּל הַגִּבּוֹרִים כְּאַיִן לְפָנֶיךָ, וְאַנְשֵׁי הַשֵּׁם כְּלֹא הָיוּ, וַחֲכָמִים כִּבְלִי מַדָּע, וּנְבוֹנִים כִּבְלִי הַשְׂכֵּל, כִּי רוֹב מַעֲשֵׂיהֶם תֹּהוּ, וִימֵי חַיֵּיהֶם הֶבֶל לְפָנֶיךָ, וּמוֹתַר הָאָדָם מִן הַבְּהֵמָה אָיִן, כִּי הַכֹּל הָבֶל: לְבַד הַנְּשָׁמָה הַטְּהוֹרָה שֶׁהִיא עֲתִידָה לִתֵּן דִּין וְחֶשְׁבּוֹן לִפְנֵי כִסֵּא כְבוֹדֶךָ. וְכָל הַגּוֹיִם כְּאַיִן נֶגְדֶּךָ. שֶׁנֶּאֱמַר הֵן גּוֹיִם כְּמַר מִדְּלִי, וּכְשַׁחַק מֹאזְנַיִם נֶחְשָׁבוּ, הֵן אִיִּים כַּדַּק יִטּוֹל:

אֲבָל אֲנַחְנוּ עַמְּךָ בְּנֵי בְרִיתֶךָ, בְּנֵי אַבְרָהָם אֹהַבְךָ, שֶׁנִּשְׁבַּעְתָּ לּוֹ בְּהַר הַמֹּרִיָּה; זֶרַע יִצְחָק יְחִידוֹ, שֶׁנֶּעֱקַד עַל גַּבֵּי הַמִּזְבֵּחַ; עֲדַת יַעֲקֹב בִּנְךָ בְּכוֹרֶךָ, שֶׁמֵּאַהֲבָתְךָ שֶׁאָהַבְתָּ אוֹתוֹ וּמִשִּׂמְחָתְךָ שֶׁשָּׂמַחְתָּ בּוֹ, קָרָאתָ אֶת שְׁמוֹ יִשְׂרָאֵל וִישֻׁרוּן:

לְפִיכָךְ אֲנַחְנוּ חַיָּבִים לְהוֹדוֹת לָךְ, וּלְשַׁבֵּחֲךָ וּלְפָאֶרְךָ וּלְבָרֵךְ וּלְקַדֵּשׁ וְלִתֵּן שֶׁבַח וְהוֹדָיָה לִשְׁמֶךָ.

אַשְׁרֵינוּ, מַה טּוֹב חֶלְקֵנוּ, וּמַה נָּעִים גּוֹרָלֵנוּ, וּמַה יָּפָה יְרֻשָּׁתֵנוּ; אַשְׁרֵינוּ, שֶׁאָנוּ מַשְׁכִּימִים וּמַעֲרִיבִים עֶרֶב וָבֹקֶר וְאוֹמְרִים פַּעֲמַיִם בְּכָל יוֹם:

CHASSIDIC INSIGHTS

(continued from p. 35)

"accepting the yoke of heaven" that appears in the Torah. Up to and including the *akeida*, all of our prayers are permeated with an attitude of unquestioning acceptance of God's will.

Moving on to the next phase of prayers, we begin to develop

(continued on p. 38)

Nefesh shb'nefesh
Yoke of Heaven
General Acknowledgment
Lower Fear
World of *Asiya* (*Malchut*)

MORNING BLESSINGS

MASTER OF THE UNIVERSE, IT IS NOT UPON OUR righteousness that we depend, as we plead before You, but upon Your abundant mercy. What is our life, what is our kindness, what is our righteousness, what is our strength and what is our power? What can we say before You, Lord our God and God of our fathers; for all human heroes are like nothing before You, and men of fame are as if non-existent, and wise men as if without knowledge. And the smart are as if lacking intellect, since most of their deeds are meaningless. The days of their life are like "vapor" before You, and the advantage of man over the animals is negligible, for all is vanity — aside from the pure soul, which will make an accounting and judgment in the future before Your glorious throne. And all the nations of the world are like nothing before You, as it says: "The nations are like a drop from a bucket, like dust upon a scale, and the islands are like flying dust."

However, we are Your nation, members of Your covenant, descendants of Abraham Your beloved, to whom You swore on Mt. Moriah; [We are] the seed of Yitzhak his only son, who was tied upon the altar, And we are the congregation of Yakov, Your firstborn, whom out of the love and the happiness that You professed for him, You called his name Yisrael and Yeshuron.

Therefore, we are obligated to acknowledge You, to exalt and to extol You, and to bless and sanctify and give praise and gratitude to Your Name.

Happy are we, how good is our portion, and how pleasant our lot, and how beautiful is our inheritance. Fortunate are we who early in the morning and also at night, say twice every day:

שְׁמַע | יִשְׂרָאֵל, יְיָ | אֱלֹהֵינוּ, יְיָ | אֶחָד:

בָּרוּךְ שֵׁם כְּבוֹד מַלְכוּתוֹ לְעוֹלָם וָעֶד:

וְאָהַבְתָּ אֵת יְיָ אֱלֹהֶיךָ, בְּכָל לְבָבְךָ, וּבְכָל נַפְשְׁךָ, וּבְכָל מְאֹדֶךָ:

וְהָיוּ הַדְּבָרִים הָאֵלֶּה אֲשֶׁר אָנֹכִי מְצַוְּךָ הַיּוֹם עַל לְבָבֶךָ:

וְשִׁנַּנְתָּם לְבָנֶיךָ וְדִבַּרְתָּ בָּם, בְּשִׁבְתְּךָ בְּבֵיתֶךָ, וּבְלֶכְתְּךָ בַדֶּרֶךְ, וּבְשָׁכְבְּךָ, וּבְקוּמֶךָ:

וּקְשַׁרְתָּם לְאוֹת עַל יָדֶךָ, וְהָיוּ לְטֹטָפֹת בֵּין עֵינֶיךָ:

וּכְתַבְתָּם עַל מְזֻזוֹת בֵּיתֶךָ וּבִשְׁעָרֶיךָ:

אַתָּה הוּא עַד שֶׁלֹּא נִבְרָא הָעוֹלָם, אַתָּה הוּא מִשֶּׁנִּבְרָא הָעוֹלָם, אַתָּה הוּא בָּעוֹלָם הַזֶּה, וְאַתָּה הוּא לָעוֹלָם הַבָּא. קַדֵּשׁ אֶת שִׁמְךָ, בְּעוֹלָמֶךָ עַל עַם מַקְדִּישֵׁי שְׁמֶךָ וּבִישׁוּעָתְךָ מַלְכֵּנוּ תָּרוּם וְתַגְבִּיהַּ קַרְנֵנוּ, וְהוֹשִׁיעֵנוּ בְּקָרוֹב לְמַעַן שְׁמֶךָ, בָּרוּךְ הַמְקַדֵּשׁ שְׁמוֹ בָּרַבִּים:

נפש שבנפש
יראת חטא
יראה תתאה
עולם העשיה (נה"י)

CHASSIDIC INSIGHTS

(continued from p. 36)

conscious awareness of Godliness. This stage, still within the category of *yirah tata'ah*, is called *yirat chait*, or "fear of sin" (it is described in "Love like Fire and Water" on page 49-53). *Yirat chait* is the level of fear that motivates us to avoid transgressing His will. Our level of conscious emotion remains low during *yirat chait*, yet within this level of fear, we are well aware of the consequences of our actions. As a result, we strive to protect and guard ourselves against any thought, speech or action that may lead to transgression. This

(continued on p. 40)

Nefesh shb'nefesh
Fear of Sin
Lower Fear
World of *Asiya* (*Neh'i*)

HEAR, O ISRAEL, THE LORD IS OUR GOD, THE LORD is one.

Blessed be the the name of the glory of His Kingdom for ever and ever.

And you shall love the Lord your God with all your heart, with all your soul, and with all your means.

And these words that I am commanding you today, should be on your heart.

And you shall teach them to your children and speak of them, while sitting in your house and as you travel on the road, when you lie down, and when you arise.

And you shall tie them as a sign on your arm, and they shall be as compartments between your eyes.

And you shall write them on the doorposts of your house and upon your gates.

You were before the universe was created, You are [the same] since the universe was created. You exist in this world, and You exist in the world to come. Sanctify Your Name in Your world through Your nation who sanctify Your name. And in Your salvation, our King, raise and elevate our prestige, and save us soon for the sake of Your Name. Blessed is He Who sanctifies His name in public!

אַתָּה הוּא יְיָ אֱלֹהֵינוּ בַּשָּׁמַיִם וּבָאָרֶץ, וּבִשְׁמֵי הַשָּׁמַיִם הָעֶלְיוֹנִים, אֱמֶת אַתָּה הוּא רִאשׁוֹן, וְאַתָּה הוּא אַחֲרוֹן, וּמִבַּלְעָדֶיךָ אֵין אֱלֹהִים. קַבֵּץ נְפוּצוֹת קֹוֶיךָ מֵאַרְבַּע כַּנְפוֹת הָאָרֶץ, יַכִּירוּ וְיֵדְעוּ כָּל בָּאֵי עוֹלָם, כִּי אַתָּה הוּא הָאֱלֹהִים לְבַדְּךָ לְכֹל מַמְלְכוֹת הָאָרֶץ. אַתָּה עָשִׂיתָ אֶת הַשָּׁמַיִם וְאֶת הָאָרֶץ, אֶת הַיָּם וְאֶת כָּל אֲשֶׁר בָּם, וּמִי בְּכָל מַעֲשֵׂה יָדֶיךָ בָּעֶלְיוֹנִים וּבַתַּחְתּוֹנִים, שֶׁיֹּאמַר לְךָ מַה תַּעֲשֶׂה, וּמַה תִּפְעָל, אָבִינוּ שֶׁבַּשָּׁמַיִם, חַי וְקַיָּם, עֲשֵׂה עִמָּנוּ צְדָקָה וָחֶסֶד בַּעֲבוּר שִׁמְךָ הַגָּדוֹל הַגִּבּוֹר וְהַנּוֹרָא שֶׁנִּקְרָא עָלֵינוּ, וְקַיֶּם לָנוּ יְיָ אֱלֹהֵינוּ אֶת הַדָּבָר שֶׁהִבְטַחְתָּנוּ עַל יְדֵי צְפַנְיָה חוֹזָךְ כָּאָמוּר: בָּעֵת הַהִיא אָבִיא אֶתְכֶם, וּבָעֵת קַבְּצִי אֶתְכֶם, כִּי אֶתֵּן אֶתְכֶם לְשֵׁם וְלִתְהִלָּה בְּכֹל עַמֵּי הָאָרֶץ, בְּשׁוּבִי אֶת שְׁבוּתֵיכֶם לְעֵינֵיכֶם, אָמַר יְיָ:

נפש שבנפש
יראת חטא
יראה תתאה
עולם העשיה (נה"י)

CHASSIDIC INSIGHTS

(continued from p. 38)

level of "lower fear" is more conscious than acceptance of the yoke of heaven, but it is still little more than fear of punishment, which is a primitive form of emotion.

Possibly, the point in prayers at which we begin to experience *yirat chait* is after the *akeida*, as we recite the *Shema* in the morning for the first time. The sages told us that during the first paragraph of the *Shema* (*ve'ahavta...*), we accept upon ourselves the yoke of heaven, and during the second paragraph (*ve'haya im shamoah*), we accept upon ourselves the yoke of mitzvot. In any case, during the second paragraph, we mention what will occur if we do not follow His commandments. The Torah tells us that we will incur God's wrath, upon

(continued on p. 41)

Nefesh shb'nefesh
Fear of Sin
Lower Fear
World of *Asiya* (*Neh'i*)

You are the Lord, God in the heavens and the earth, and in the upper heavens above. It is true that You are the first, and You are the last, and aside from You there is no God. Gather together the scattered who long for You from the four corners of the earth, so that all of mankind will know and recognize that You alone are God, over all the kingdoms of the earth. You created the heavens and the earth, the sea and all that is in it. And who among all of the works of Your hands, spiritual and physical will tell You what to do, and what to cause to happen. Our Father in the heavens, alive and ever-lasting, perform justice and kindness for us for the sake of Your great Name, the powerful and awesome by which You are called, and fulfill for us, Lord Our God, that which You promised via Your prophet and visionary, Zephania, saying, "At that time I will bring you back, and at that time I will gather you, for I will make you renowned and praiseworthy among all of the nations of the earth, as I return your captured remnants before your very eyes, so saith the Lord."

CHASSIDIC INSIGHTS

(continued from p. 40)

which He will not provide for our basic needs. Moreover, the phrases that we recite before and after the *Shema* indicate a level of conscious awareness that was missing in the previous sections. Therefore, it may be appropriate to say that we first experience *yirat chait* ("fear of sin") as we recite the *Shema* before prayers in the morning.

There is a third and final sub-division of *yirah tata'ah*, known

(continued on p. 42)

קרבנות

תרומת הדשן

וַיְדַבֵּר יְיָ אֶל מֹשֶׁה לֵּאמֹר: צַו אֶת אַהֲרֹן וְאֶת בָּנָיו לֵאמֹר, זֹאת תּוֹרַת הָעֹלָה, הִוא הָעֹלָה עַל מוֹקְדָה עַל הַמִּזְבֵּחַ כָּל הַלַּיְלָה עַד הַבֹּקֶר וְאֵשׁ הַמִּזְבֵּחַ תּוּקַד בּוֹ: וְלָבַשׁ הַכֹּהֵן מִדּוֹ בַד וּמִכְנְסֵי בַד יִלְבַּשׁ עַל בְּשָׂרוֹ וְהֵרִים אֶת הַדֶּשֶׁן אֲשֶׁר תֹּאכַל הָאֵשׁ אֶת הָעֹלָה עַל הַמִּזְבֵּחַ וְשָׂמוֹ אֵצֶל הַמִּזְבֵּחַ: וּפָשַׁט אֶת בְּגָדָיו וְלָבַשׁ בְּגָדִים אֲחֵרִים וְהוֹצִיא אֶת הַדֶּשֶׁן אֶל מִחוּץ לַמַּחֲנֶה אֶל מָקוֹם טָהוֹר: וְהָאֵשׁ עַל הַמִּזְבֵּחַ תּוּקַד בּוֹ לֹא תִכְבֶּה וּבִעֵר עָלֶיהָ הַכֹּהֵן עֵצִים בַּבֹּקֶר וְעָרַךְ עָלֶיהָ הָעֹלָה וְהִקְטִיר עָלֶיהָ חֶלְבֵי הַשְּׁלָמִים: אֵשׁ, תָּמִיד תּוּקַד עַל הַמִּזְבֵּחַ לֹא תִכְבֶּה:

נפש שבנפש
יראת חטא
יראה תתאה
עולם העשיה (נה"י)

"There are people who study Torah with great diligence…but who fail to receive any Godly illumination…the reason is that they put no effort into removing the concealment and blockage of the animal soul."
(*Sefer Maamorim* 5656/1896 of the Rebbe Rashab, p. 292)[36]

We have an animal soul that vitalizes our body, and a divine soul that is literally a piece of Godliness within us.[37] Both souls are composed of complete structures of ten *sephirot* and five soul levels.[38]

As much as we might desire to become conscious of our divine soul, we will not experience it unless we uplift and refine our animal soul. We should take some time before morning prayers to

--- CHASSIDIC INSIGHTS ---

(*continued from p. 41*)

as *yirat Elokim* ("fear of God"). This level (described on page 54 of "Love like Fire and Water"), sub-divides further into two levels. The first, which is simply *yirat Elokim*, goes beyond the *yirat chait* described earlier. Because it is fear of sin, *yirat chait* is mainly a means

(*continued on p. 50*)

Nefesh shb'nefesh
Fear of Sin
Lower Fear
World of *Asiya* (*Neh'i*)

Offerings

REMOVAL OF THE ASHES

And the Lord spoke to Moshe, saying, 'Command Aharon and his sons, saying, "This is the law of the burnt offering; which is the offering that is placed on the firewood of the altar all night long until the morning, while the fire of the altar is kept burning upon it. And the priest should wear his suit of linen and don pants of linen over his flesh. And he should raise the ashes resulting from the fire that consumed the burnt offering on the altar, and place them next to the altar. He should then remove his clothes and don other clothes, and take the ashes outside the encampment, to a pure location. And the fire on the altar should be kept burning, it should not extinguish; and the priest should burn wood upon it every morning. And he should arrange the offering upon it and smoke the fat of the peace-offerings upon it. It is an eternal fire, kept ignited upon the altar, not to be extinguished.

---

consider our negative character traits and how, because of them, we are far from anything spiritual or Godly. The best time to do this is during the midnight prayers (*tikun chatzot*) as well as during *Kriat Shema* before going to sleep.

> 📖 *Within the Words*
>
> Before morning prayers, it is imperative to take some time to consider the greatness of God and the lowliness of man; the early sages used to meditate on Godliness for an hour before and after each prayer service, reaching very high states of abstraction near to prophecy.[39] We should also spend as much time as is necessary to focus our minds on Godliness before praying in the morning.

קרבן התמיד

On Shabbat and Festivals, the following paragraph is omitted:

יְהִי רָצוֹן מִלְּפָנֶיךָ יְיָ אֱלֹהֵינוּ וֵאלֹהֵי אֲבוֹתֵינוּ, שֶׁתְּרַחֵם עָלֵינוּ וְתִמְחוֹל לָנוּ עַל כָּל חַטֹּאתֵינוּ, וּתְכַפֶּר לָנוּ עַל כָּל עֲוֹנוֹתֵינוּ, וְתִסְלַח לָנוּ עַל כָּל פְּשָׁעֵינוּ, וְשֶׁיִּבָּנֶה בֵּית הַמִּקְדָּשׁ בִּמְהֵרָה בְיָמֵינוּ, וְנַקְרִיב לְפָנֶיךָ קָרְבַּן הַתָּמִיד שֶׁיְּכַפֵּר בַּעֲדֵנוּ כְּמוֹ שֶׁכָּתַבְתָּ עָלֵינוּ בְּתוֹרָתֶךָ עַל יְדֵי מֹשֶׁה עַבְדֶּךָ מִפִּי כְבוֹדֶךָ כָּאָמוּר:

וַיְדַבֵּר יְיָ אֶל מֹשֶׁה לֵּאמֹר: צַו אֶת בְּנֵי יִשְׂרָאֵל וְאָמַרְתָּ אֲלֵהֶם, אֶת קָרְבָּנִי לַחְמִי לְאִשַּׁי, רֵיחַ נִיחֹחִי תִּשְׁמְרוּ לְהַקְרִיב לִי בְּמוֹעֲדוֹ: וְאָמַרְתָּ לָהֶם, זֶה הָאִשֶּׁה אֲשֶׁר תַּקְרִיבוּ לַיְיָ, כְּבָשִׂים בְּנֵי שָׁנָה תְמִימִם, שְׁנַיִם לַיּוֹם, עֹלָה תָמִיד: אֶת הַכֶּבֶשׂ אֶחָד תַּעֲשֶׂה בַבֹּקֶר, וְאֵת הַכֶּבֶשׂ הַשֵּׁנִי תַּעֲשֶׂה בֵּין הָעַרְבָּיִם: וַעֲשִׂירִית הָאֵיפָה סֹלֶת לְמִנְחָה, בְּלוּלָה בְּשֶׁמֶן כָּתִית רְבִיעִת הַהִין: עֹלַת תָּמִיד, הָעֲשֻׂיָה בְּהַר סִינַי לְרֵיחַ נִיחֹחַ אִשֶּׁה לַיְיָ: וְנִסְכּוֹ רְבִיעִת הַהִין

נפש שבנפש
יראת אלקים
יראה תתאה
עולם העשיה (חג"ת)

> **"A log that fails to catch on fire should be splintered... a body into which the light of the soul fails to penetrate should be crushed..."**
> (Zohar III 168A, quoted in *Tanya, Likutei Amarim* Ch. 29)[40]

The morning hours are a time of *mochin d'gadlut*, or "high-level spiritual revelation." It is an auspicious time for prayers and meditation, but since our divine soul is in a state of *katnut* (lacking Godly illumination), we must put in effort to arouse ourselves to meditate and pray in the morning.

Sometimes when we arise in the morning and meditate, we fail to arouse any emotions of love and fear of God. The advice at such a time is to "splinter the log" — minimize our ego in order to make room for Godly illumination.[41]

Nefesh shb'nefesh
Fear of God (*Elokim*)
Lower Fear
World of *Asiya*

THE CONTINUAL TAMID OFFERING

On Shabbat and Festivals, the following paragraph is omitted:

May it be Your Will, Lord our God and God of our forefathers, to have mercy on us and forgive us for all of our sins, and atone for all of our transgressions, and forgive and pardon all of our iniquity. And may the Beit Hamikdash be built speedily in our days, there to sacrifice before You the constant daily offerings in order to atone for us, as You wrote for us in Your Torah by way of Moshe your servant, in Your Honor, saying…"

And the Lord spoke to Moshe, saying, 'Command the children of Israel, and tell them, 'My sacrifices are sustenance for my servants, a pleasing aroma for Me, be careful to offer [them] to me at the appointed time. And tell them, this is the fire offering that you should sacrifice to the Lord: two one-year old sheep, free of blemishes, every day, for the regular burnt offering. One sheep in the morning, and the second sheep in the afternoon. And a tenth of an *epha* of refined wheat should be offered as a *mincha* offering, mixed with a quarter *hin* of oil, ground from olives. This is a regular burnt offering, as done on Mt. Sinai as a pleasing aroma, fire for the Lord. And its wine libation should be a quarter of a *hin*

📖 *Within the Words*

"And if [humility and fear of God] does not penetrate our awareness immediately, then we should delve further into the concept at length until we are able to actualize it…"[42] It may be necessary to meditate at length in order to uncover the Godly spark within and draw it into our conscious awareness.

לְכֶבֶשׂ הָאֶחָד, בַּקֹּדֶשׁ הַסֵּךְ נֶסֶךְ שֵׁכָר לַיְיָ: וְאֵת הַכֶּבֶשׂ הַשֵּׁנִי תַּעֲשֶׂה בֵּין הָעַרְבָּיִם, כְּמִנְחַת הַבֹּקֶר וּכְנִסְכּוֹ תַּעֲשֶׂה, אִשֵּׁה רֵיחַ נִיחֹחַ לַיְיָ:

וְשָׁחַט אֹתוֹ עַל יֶרֶךְ הַמִּזְבֵּחַ צָפֹנָה לִפְנֵי יְיָ, וְזָרְקוּ בְּנֵי אַהֲרֹן הַכֹּהֲנִים אֶת דָּמוֹ עַל הַמִּזְבֵּחַ סָבִיב:

קטרת

אַתָּה הוּא יְיָ אֱלֹהֵינוּ וֵאלֹהֵי אֲבוֹתֵינוּ, שֶׁהִקְטִירוּ אֲבוֹתֵינוּ לְפָנֶיךָ אֶת קְטֹרֶת הַסַּמִּים, בִּזְמַן שֶׁבֵּית הַמִּקְדָּשׁ קַיָּם, כַּאֲשֶׁר צִוִּיתָ אוֹתָם עַל יַד מֹשֶׁה נְבִיאֶךָ, כַּכָּתוּב בְּתוֹרָתֶךָ:

וַיֹּאמֶר יְיָ אֶל מֹשֶׁה, קַח לְךָ סַמִּים: נָטָף, וּשְׁחֵלֶת, וְחֶלְבְּנָה, סַמִּים, וּלְבֹנָה זַכָּה, בַּד בְּבַד יִהְיֶה: וְעָשִׂיתָ אֹתָהּ קְטֹרֶת, רֹקַח מַעֲשֵׂה רוֹקֵחַ, מְמֻלָּח טָהוֹר קֹדֶשׁ: וְשָׁחַקְתָּ מִמֶּנָּה הָדֵק, וְנָתַתָּה מִמֶּנָּה לִפְנֵי הָעֵדֻת בְּאֹהֶל

נפש שבנפש
יראת אלקים
יראה תתאה
עולם העשיה (חג"ת)

"The only way to approach prayer is with a contrite mind (lit: 'heavy head')...The only way to approach prayer is with joy." (Talmud, *Berachot* 32, *Shulchan Aruch*, *Orach Chaim* 93:2)[43]

If we are lacking anything in our personal lives, it is because there is a deficiency above, in the *sephira* of *malchut*, through which all spiritual influence descends to us. We must therefore pray on behalf of the "heavy head" (the *sephira* of *malchut*), which is lacking Godly influence, in order to correct this deficiency. This is the explanation of the Mezritcher Maggid.

The Alter Rebbe offers an alternative explanation: the "heavy head" is our own collective intellect, which sometimes fails to respond to Godly illumination. We must therefore request more Godly illumination that will enable us to pray in joy as well.[44]

Nefesh shb'nefesh
Fear of God (*Elokim*)
Lower Fear
World of *Asiya*

for each sheep, poured in holiness, a libation of drink for the Lord. And the second sheep in the afternoon, just as the *mincha* of the morning and its libation it should be done, as a pleasant odor for the Lord.

And it should be slaughtered at the northern side of the altar, before the Lord, and the sons of Aharon, the priests, should sprinkle its blood all around the altar.

INCENSE

You are the Lord, our God and the God of our forefathers, to Whom our forefathers offered incense before You; the incense of spices when the Temple stood, as you commanded them, through Moshe your prophet, as written in Your Torah:

"And the Lord said to Moshe, take for yourself spices, stacte, onycha and galbanum, fragrant spices, and pure frankincense; there should be an equal amount of each. And make it into incense, a pharmaceutical compound, the work of an expert, well mixed, pure and holy. You should take part of it and grind it up thoroughly, and place a portion of it before the Ark in the Tent of

---

📖 *Within the Words*

The time for contriteness is the midnight hour (*chatzot*), when we mourn the destruction of the Temple and lament our own distance from God. That clears away our resistance and blockages, allowing Godly light to enter and penetrate our mind. At that point, the tone of our prayers shifts from the bitterness (*merirut*) associated with the nighttime prayers (*tikun chatzot*) to the positive energy of the morning prayers. And that enables us to approach the morning prayers in joy.

מוֹעֵד, אֲשֶׁר אִוָּעֵד לְךָ שָׁמָּה, קֹדֶשׁ קָדָשִׁים תִּהְיֶה לָכֶם: וְנֶאֱמַר, וְהִקְטִיר עָלָיו אַהֲרֹן, קְטֹרֶת סַמִּים בַּבֹּקֶר בַּבֹּקֶר, בְּהֵיטִיבוֹ אֶת הַנֵּרֹת יַקְטִירֶנָּה: וּבְהַעֲלֹת אַהֲרֹן אֶת הַנֵּרֹת בֵּין הָעַרְבַּיִם יַקְטִירֶנָּה, קְטֹרֶת תָּמִיד לִפְנֵי יְיָ לְדֹרֹתֵיכֶם:

תָּנוּ רַבָּנָן, פִּטּוּם הַקְּטֹרֶת כֵּיצַד: שְׁלֹשׁ מֵאוֹת וְשִׁשִּׁים וּשְׁמוֹנָה מָנִים הָיוּ בָהּ. שְׁלֹשׁ מֵאוֹת וְשִׁשִּׁים וַחֲמִשָּׁה כְּמִנְיַן יְמוֹת הַחַמָּה, מָנֶה לְכָל יוֹם פְּרָס בְּשַׁחֲרִית, וּפְרָס בֵּין הָעַרְבַּיִם, וּשְׁלֹשָׁה מָנִים יְתֵרִים, שֶׁמֵּהֶם מַכְנִיס כֹּהֵן גָּדוֹל מְלֹא חָפְנָיו בְּיוֹם הַכִּפּוּרִים, וּמַחֲזִירָן לְמַכְתֶּשֶׁת בְּעֶרֶב יוֹם הַכִּפּוּרִים, וְשׁוֹחֲקָן יָפֶה יָפֶה כְּדֵי שֶׁתְּהֵא דַקָּה מִן הַדַּקָּה.

נפש שבנפש
יראת אלקים
יראה תתאה
עולם העשיה (חג"ת)

> **The incineration of the animal offering on the altar…corresponds to the excitement of our animal soul as we pray. The ashes that remain correspond to the full nullification of our ego…"** (Alter Rebbe's Siddur with Chassidut, p. ל"א)[45]

The letters *pei-reish* (spelling *par*, or "bull") indicate *din* or *gevurah*. (The sum of the five "ending letters" — *mem-nun-tzadik-peh-kof* — which separate between words and therefore allude to *gevura,* add up to 280 which is also the numerical value of *pei-reish,* or *par*). When a *par* ("bull") was burnt, the element of *ahfar* ("earth") was transformed into *aifar* ("ash"), indicating the oneness and unity of God (*aleph*) that combines with the *peh-reish,* to elevate and "sweeten" the judgment.[46]

The ashes left-over from the previous day's offerings were removed and placed next to the altar. Some of the ashes were absorbed into the ground — they represent our ego as it dissipates. Whatever ashes were not absorbed were removed from the area, since they allude to depression and sadness that are not useful in the service of God. Moreover, the ashes that were left after the

Nefesh shb'nefesh
Fear of God (*Elokim*)
Lower Fear
World of *Asiya*

meeting, where I will meet with you there, it should be holy of holies for you. And it is said, And Aharon should burn an incense [mixture] of spices upon the altar, every morning as he cleans the lamps [of the menorah], he should burn it. And as Aharon lights the lamps toward the evening, he should burn it, as a regular incense before the Lord, throughout your generations.

The Rabbis taught, How did the preparation of the incense take place? There were three hundred and sixty-eight portions in it. Three hundred and sixty-five corresponded to the number of days of the solar year, with one portion for each day, divided into part for the morning and part for the evening. And three portions were left over, from which the High Priest would fill up his hand on Yom Kippur [and take into the Holy of Holies]. On the day before Yom Kippur, these [three portions] were placed back into the grinder and ground very thoroughly to turn it into the finest of the fine.

---

animal was burnt correspond to the bitterness that we experience during prayers over our distance from God. There are two elements to this bitterness: 1) one is lowness (lack of ego), which is a positive trait, for with it we become *kelim* ("vessels") for Godly illumination; 2) the other element may be depression, which is a negative trait that must be removed from the scene.[47]

> 📖 *Within the Words*
>
> After it was consumed, all that was left of the sacrifice was *aifar* ("ash"). The original element of earth within the body was called *ahfar* (*eyn-pei-reish*, or "dust") but, after it was burned, it became *aifar* (*aleph-pei-reish*, or "ash"). Similarly, after proper prayer, we are reduced to "ashes" — lacking any ego. The entire process is likened to a fiery furnace that smelts metal, facilitating the removal of its impurities.

וְאֶחָד עָשָׂר סַמְמָנִים הָיוּ בָהּ. וְאֵלוּ הֵן: (א) הַצֳּרִי (ב) וְהַצִּפֹּרֶן (ג) הַחֶלְבְּנָה (ד) וְהַלְּבוֹנָה מִשְׁקַל שִׁבְעִים שִׁבְעִים מָנֶה, (ה) מוֹר (ו) וּקְצִיעָה (ז) שִׁבֹּלֶת נֵרְדְּ (ח) וְכַרְכֹּם מִשְׁקַל שִׁשָּׁה עָשָׂר שִׁשָּׁה עָשָׂר מָנֶה, (ט) הַקֹּשְׁטְ שְׁנֵים עָשָׂר, (י) קִלּוּפָה שְׁלֹשָׁה, (יא) וְקִנָּמוֹן תִּשְׁעָה. בֹּרִית כַּרְשִׁינָה תִּשְׁעָה קַבִּין, יֵין קַפְרִיסִין סְאִין תְּלָתָא וְקַבִּין תְּלָתָא, וְאִם אֵין לוֹ יֵין קַפְרִיסִין מֵבִיא חֲמַר חִוַּרְיָן עַתִּיק. מֶלַח סְדוֹמִית רוֹבַע, מַעֲלֶה עָשָׁן, כָּל שֶׁהוּא. רַבִּי נָתָן הַבַּבְלִי אוֹמֵר: אַף כִּפַּת הַיַּרְדֵּן כָּל שֶׁהִיא, וְאִם נָתַן בָּהּ דְּבַשׁ פְּסָלָהּ, וְאִם חִסַּר אֶחָד מִכָּל סַמְמָנֶיהָ חַיָּב מִיתָה:

נפש שבנפש
יראת אלקים
יראה תתאה
עולם העשיה (חג"ת)

❝ In general, the sacrifices corresponded to the four fundamental elements of fire, wind, water and earth. Earth corresponds to the inanimate mineral world…water to the vegetable world…fire to the animal world…and wind to man." (Alter Rebbe's Siddur with Chassidut, p. ל"ג)[48]

The purpose of the sacrifices was to elevate the world, which is composed of the four physical categories: mineral, vegetable, animal and man. The sacrifices included all of them — the salt that accompanied every sacrifice corresponded to the mineral world, the grain offering to the vegetable world, the offering itself to the animal world, and the person to the human world.

Even though the sacrifices included all the physical categories, the animal category, corresponding to fire, was predominant. Fire also corresponds to *gevura*, which is the power and discipline

--- CHASSIDIC INSIGHTS ---

(continued from p. 42)

of motivating us to avoid transgression. However, *yirat Elokim* injects a stronger element of conscious emotion into our experience. We begin to experience Godliness and as a result we become afraid, not only of transgression, but of God Himself.

(continued on p. 58)

Nefesh shb'nefesh
Fear of God (*Elokim*)
Lower Fear
World of *Asiya*

And there were eleven spices in [the incense]. And these are they: balm, onycha, galanum, frankincense — each of which weighed seventy units; there was myrrh, cassia, spikenard, and saffron, each of which weighed sixteen units. There was costus, weighing twelve units, and aromatic bark weighing three units, and cinnamon, which weighed nine units. There were nine *kavin* of lye from carshina used in the preparation, as well as three *kavin* and three *se'in* of Cypriot wine, and if there was no wine from Cyprus available, strong, white wine could be used instead. A quarter kab of sodomite salt went into the preparation, as well as a tiny bit of a herb for smoking. R' Natan the Babylonian said that a small amount of Jordan amber was used as well. If any honey was added, [the mixture] became invalid, and if any one of these spices were missing, the [person making the mixture] was liable for capital punishment.

---

within us to sacrifice and incinerate our own animal tendencies. Three animals (goats, sheep and cows) were acceptable as sacrifices, but the cow took precedence since it is directly related to the *pnei shor* ("face of the ox") in the *merkava*, or mystical "chariot" in the World of *Bria*.[49]

📖 *Within the Words*

When we fast for a few days, we become weak and feel like our soul could easily leave our body. When we then eat something, our soul is reconnected to our body, and we feel strong again. Similarly, the sacrifices are what links Godliness to the world. When we say, "My sacrifices are sustenance…" we realize that it is the sacrifices that connected the transcendent light of God with the limited world and infused the world with Godliness. Now, our prayers and mitzvot achieve the same goal.

רַבָּן שִׁמְעוֹן בֶּן גַּמְלִיאֵל אוֹמֵר: הַצֳּרִי אֵינוֹ אֶלָּא שְׂרָף הַנּוֹטֵף מֵעֲצֵי הַקְּטָף, בְּרִית כַּרְשִׁינָה שֶׁשָּׁפִין בָּהּ אֶת הַצִּפֹּרֶן, כְּדֵי שֶׁתְּהֵא נָאָה; יֵין קַפְרִיסִין שֶׁשּׁוֹרִין בּוֹ אֶת הַצִּפֹּרֶן, כְּדֵי שֶׁתְּהֵא עַזָּה, וַהֲלֹא מֵי רַגְלַיִם יָפִין לָהּ, אֶלָּא שֶׁאֵין מַכְנִיסִין מֵי רַגְלַיִם בַּמִּקְדָּשׁ מִפְּנֵי הַכָּבוֹד:

תַּנְיָא רַבִּי נָתָן אוֹמֵר: כְּשֶׁהוּא שׁוֹחֵק אוֹמֵר: הָדֵק הֵיטֵב, הֵיטֵב הָדֵק, מִפְּנֵי שֶׁהַקּוֹל יָפֶה לַבְּשָׂמִים. פִּטְּמָהּ לַחֲצָאִין כְּשֵׁרָה, לִשְׁלִישׁ וְלִרְבִיעַ, לֹא שָׁמַעְנוּ. אָמַר רַבִּי יְהוּדָה זֶה הַכְּלָל, אִם כְּמִדָּתָהּ כְּשֵׁרָה לַחֲצָאִין. וְאִם חִסַּר אַחַד מִכָּל סַמְמָנֶיהָ חַיָּב מִיתָה:

נפש שבנפש
יראת אלקים
יראה תתאה
עולם העשיה (חג"ת)

❝ Our morning and evening prayers correspond to the regular morning and evening sacrifices in the Temple." (Alter Rebbe's Siddur with Chassidut, p. ל"ג)[50]

Prayer, besides being a process of elevation, is a process of purification and rectification. We focus mightily on Godly concepts with the goal of understanding them thoroughly in order to ascend spiritually. This requires us to use our powers of *bina* (analytic understanding) and *gevura* (discipline). The resulting Godly light illuminates our animal soul, enabling us to root out the negative character traits that separate between us and God. The physical sacrifices were a paradigm of this process. The burning animal became included in its spiritual source above, in the *pnei shor* ("countenance of the ox" associated with the "left side" or *gevura*), and then a fire descended from above (from the *pnei aryeh*, the "countenance of the lion" associated with the "right side" or *chesed*) to consume the sacrifice.

The very existence of the worlds was dependent upon the proper offering of the sacrifices. The priests were required to act in a very precise manner and, if they failed to do so, no creative energy would descend to enliven the universe. The same is now true of our prayers which were established in lieu of the sacrifices. According to the Zohar, "the time of prayer is a time of war." It is the time for battle between the positive and negative forces within us. We fight

Nefesh shb'nefesh
Fear of God (*Elokim*)
Lower Fear
World of *Asiya*

Raban Shimon ben Gamliel says, balm is nothing more than sap that exudes from balsam trees. Lye of Carshina is used to massage the onycha and make it look nice, and Cypriot wine is used to marinate the onycha and make it stronger. Now, urine would also be good for this job, but we do not bring urine into the Temple out of respect.

It is taught that Rabi Natan said, as the priest would grind the incense, the overseer would recite, *hadek heitev, heitev hadek* ("grind it well, well it should be ground"), because his voice had a positive impact upon the spices. If only half of the required amount of incense was compounded, it was considered fit for use, but regarding a third or a fourth [of the required amount], we have not heard if it was fit. According to R' Yehuda, the general principle is that if all the spices were ground in the proper proportion, then the incense was fit even if only half the required amount was produced. And if any one of the spices were left out, the cohen was liable for capital punishment.

---

with our *yetzer harah* (negative inclination), which seeks to prevent revelation of Godly light. Our goal is to let the light of our divine soul shine through and illuminate us.

> 📖 *Within the Words*
>
> We are required to bring a "fire from below" — this is the excitement that we experience during meditation on Godliness while reciting the blessings preceding the *Shema*. This fire consumes our animal soul. It also ignites a fire from above that descends to us during the *Shemonah Esreh*. The entire process is a struggle within to remain focused on the goal of Godly illumination without becoming distracted by forces outside or inside of us. When we succeed, we bring down Godly illumination that rectifies the world.

PRAYING LIKE FIRE AND WATER

תַּנְיָא בַּר קַפָּרָא אוֹמֵר: אַחַת לְשִׁשִּׁים אוֹ לְשִׁבְעִים שָׁנָה הָיְתָה בָּאָה שֶׁל שִׁירַיִם לַחֲצָאִין: וְעוֹד תָּנֵי בַּר קַפָּרָא, אִלּוּ הָיָה נוֹתֵן בָּהּ קוֹרְטוֹב שֶׁל דְּבַשׁ, אֵין אָדָם יָכוֹל לַעֲמוֹד מִפְּנֵי רֵיחָהּ, וְלָמָה אֵין מְעָרְבִין בָּהּ דְּבַשׁ, מִפְּנֵי שֶׁהַתּוֹרָה אָמְרָה, כִּי כָל שְׂאֹר וְכָל דְּבַשׁ לֹא תַקְטִירוּ מִמֶּנּוּ אִשֶּׁה לַיְיָ:

יְיָ צְבָאוֹת עִמָּנוּ, מִשְׂגָּב לָנוּ אֱלֹהֵי יַעֲקֹב סֶלָה: (לומר שלום פימים)

יְיָ צְבָאוֹת, אַשְׁרֵי אָדָם בֹּטֵחַ בָּךְ: (לומר שלום פימים)

יְיָ הוֹשִׁיעָה, הַמֶּלֶךְ יַעֲנֵנוּ בְיוֹם קָרְאֵנוּ: (לומר שלום פימים)

"Animal sacrifices were offered upon the outer altar, and incense was offered upon the inner altar…the two altars correspond to the external and internal manifestations of the heart." (*Besha'ah Shehikdimu 5672/1912* of the Rebbe Rashab, Vol. 1, pp. 429-430)[51]

The outer altar is associated with the name *Ba'n* (the name of God spelled such that its *gematria* is 52, equal to *behama*, or "animal"). Animals were offered on the outer altar. The inner altar is associated with the name *Ma'h* (God's name spelled so that its *gematria* is 45, equal to *adam*, or "man"). Incense was burnt on the inner altar. The process of burning the incense corresponds to what transpires with our highest soul levels, that are bound in essential unity with God. To actualize these levels requires absolute self-nullification before the Divine.

The outer altar corresponds to immanent Godliness (*memalle kol olmin*). This is spirituality that we understand and experience. The inner altar corresponds to transcendent Godliness (*sovev kol olmin*). This is Godliness that is beyond our awareness and experience. On the outer altar, a fire was lit, corresponding to the work that we do within ourselves to bring down Godly revelation. On the inner altar, no fire was lit. Instead, whispering coals were brought from the outer altar to

Nefesh shb'nefesh
Fear of God (*Elokim*)
Lower Fear
World of *Asiya*

It is taught that Bar Kapara said, once in sixty or seventy years, half of the yearly quantity of incense came from the left-over portions of incense [from which the High Priest took into the Holy of Holies on Yom Kippur]. Moreover, Bar Kapara also taught that if one would add a bit of honey to the incense, that no-one would be able to resist the fragrance. So, why do we not mix in some honey? Because the Torah says, "No yeast and no honey may be burnt as a fire offering before the Lord."

"The Lord of Hosts is with us, the God of Jacob is our fortress forever." (Say three times).

"The Lord of hosts, happy is the man who relies upon You" (Three times)

"Lord save us, the King will answer us when we call to Him" (Three times)

---

burn the incense on the inner altar. Even though we cannot directly access the transcendent revelation of the inner altar, it becomes revealed to us when we fulfill the inner work that is required of us.

> 📖 *Within the Words*
>
> We should view the entire process of prayer as one long spiritual journey of elevation. Our prayers follow the path of lower fear of God (during *korbanot* and *Hodu*), followed by meditation leading to lower love of God ("love like water") during the *pesukei dezimra*. Lower love is based upon awareness of the spirituality that permeates and enlivens the world. This is followed by higher love of God ("love like fire") during *Birchot Kriat Shema* as well as during the *Shema* itself. Higher love is based upon awareness of God as He transcends creation. Finally, we achieve higher fear of God, or awe, based upon our perception of ourselves as null and void. This occurs during the *Shemonah Esreh*.

וְעָרְבָה לַיָי מִנְחַת יְהוּדָה וִירוּשָׁלָיִם, כִּימֵי עוֹלָם וּכְשָׁנִים קַדְמוֹנִיּוֹת:

אַבַּיֵי הֲוָה מְסַדֵּר סֵדֶר הַמַּעֲרָכָה מִשְּׁמָא דִגְמָרָא, וְאַלִּבָּא דְאַבָּא שָׁאוּל, מַעֲרָכָה גְדוֹלָה קוֹדֶמֶת לְמַעֲרָכָה שְׁנִיָּה שֶׁל קְטֹרֶת, וּמַעֲרָכָה שְׁנִיָּה שֶׁל קְטֹרֶת קוֹדֶמֶת לְסִדּוּר שְׁנֵי גִזְרֵי עֵצִים, וְסִדּוּר שְׁנֵי גִזְרֵי עֵצִים קוֹדֵם לְדִשּׁוּן מִזְבֵּחַ הַפְּנִימִי, וְדִשּׁוּן מִזְבֵּחַ הַפְּנִימִי קוֹדֵם לַהֲטָבַת חָמֵשׁ נֵרוֹת, וַהֲטָבַת חָמֵשׁ נֵרוֹת קוֹדֶמֶת לְדַם הַתָּמִיד, וְדַם הַתָּמִיד קוֹדֵם לַהֲטָבַת שְׁתֵּי נֵרוֹת, וַהֲטָבַת שְׁתֵּי נֵרוֹת קוֹדֶמֶת לִקְטֹרֶת, וּקְטֹרֶת קוֹדֶמֶת לְאֵבָרִים,

נפש שבנפש
יראת אלקים
יראה תתאה
עולם העשיה (חג"ת)

> **The Talmud tells us that without three groups (priests, Levites and Israelites) present at the sacrifices, the heavens and earth would cease to exist. This is why we are called an *am segula* (..).**" (*Sefer Maamorim 5643/1883*, p. 105)[52]

The ten *sephirot* are composed of three groups of three followed by one receptive *sephira* (*malchut*) that contains no intrinsic content of its own, but receives all of the influx of the preceding *sephirot* and transmits it to the lower worlds. The three triplets are intellectual (*chochma, bina* and *da'at*), emotional (*chesed, gevura* and *tiferet*) and instinctual (*netzach, hod* and *yesod*) in nature. In all three triplets, the *sephirot* follow the dialectical process of "thesis, antithesis and synthesis."

Many instances in Torah require three — the *Tanach* itself is tripartite (composed of the *Torah* or the Five Books of Moshe, the *Neviim* or Prophets, and the *Ketuvim* or Writings). The Torah was given at Mt. Sinai in the third month (*Sivan*) following the Exodus to a tripartite people (composed of priests, Levites and Israelites). Among the priests, there was a high priest, his second in command, and all the other priests. The Levites serving in the Sanctuary/Temple were composed of three families: Kehot, Gershon and Merari. And the Israelites were called by three names: Yaakov, Yisrael and Yeshurun.

Nefesh shb'nefesh
Fear of God (*Elokim*)
Lower Fear
World of *Asiya*

The gifts of Yehuda and Yerushalayim will be sweet for the Lord, as in the days of yore and in bygone years.

Abbaye systematized the offering of the sacrifices according to the process outlined in the Talmud, according to the opinion of Aba Shaul. First, the main pile of wood was set up before the secondary pile, [from which was lit] the incense offering. The secondary pile for the incense offering was set up prior to placing the two logs of wood on the main pile. The placing of the two logs of wood preceded the removal of ashes from the inner [incense] altar. The removal of ashes preceded the cleaning of the five candelabra [of the menorah]. The cleaning of the five candelabra preceded the sprinkling of the blood of the daily burnt-offering. The sprinkling of the blood of the burnt-offering took place prior to the cleaning of the remaining two candelabra. The cleaning of the two candelabra preceded the lighting of the incense, the lighting of the incense took place before burning the innards of the daily burnt-offering. The burning of the innards took place before the meal offering [of

---

📖 *Within the Words*

Groups of three function together to bring Godly influence into the world. When all the Jews (Priests, Levites and Israelites) camped at Mt. Sinai as one, we received the Torah. When all three groups of Jews were present at the sacrifices, Godly illumination shone in the Temple in a revealed way. Now that our prayers take the place of the sacrifices, our three Godly emotions — love of God, fear of God and mercy on the Godly soul within us — function together, in order to bring down revealed Godly illumination from above. Three represents the unity of disparate elements; this unity is called *echad*, and it differs from the simple unity of one element, which is called *yachid*.

נפש שבנפש
יראת אלקים
יראה תתאה
עולם העשיה (חג"ת)

וְאֵבָרִים לְמִנְחָה וּמִנְחָה לַחֲבִתִּין, וַחֲבִתִּין לִנְסָכִין, וּנְסָכִין לְמוּסָפִין, וּמוּסָפִין לְבָזִיכִין, וּבָזִיכִין קוֹדְמִין לְתָמִיד שֶׁל בֵּין הָעַרְבָּיִם. שֶׁנֶּאֱמַר, וְעָרַךְ עָלֶיהָ הָעֹלָה וְהִקְטִיר עָלֶיהָ חֶלְבֵי הַשְּׁלָמִים, עָלֶיהָ הַשְׁלֵם כָּל הַקָּרְבָּנוֹת כֻּלָּם:

אנא בכח

אָנָּא בְּכֹחַ גְּדֻלַּת יְמִינְךָ תַּתִּיר צְרוּרָה׃ אב"ג ית"ץ

קַבֵּל רִנַּת עַמְּךָ שַׂגְּבֵנוּ טַהֲרֵנוּ נוֹרָא׃ קר"ע שט"ן

נָא גִבּוֹר, דּוֹרְשֵׁי יִחוּדְךָ, כְּבָבַת שָׁמְרֵם׃ נג"ד יכ"ש

בָּרְכֵם טַהֲרֵם, רַחֲמֵי צִדְקָתְךָ, תָּמִיד גָּמְלֵם׃ בט"ר צת"ג

חֲסִין קָדוֹשׁ, בְּרֹב טוּבְךָ, נַהֵל עֲדָתֶךָ׃ חק"ב טנ"ע

יָחִיד גֵּאֶה, לְעַמְּךָ פְּנֵה, זוֹכְרֵי קְדֻשָּׁתֶךָ׃ יג"ל פז"ק

שַׁוְעָתֵנוּ קַבֵּל, וּשְׁמַע צַעֲקָתֵנוּ, יוֹדֵעַ תַּעֲלוּמוֹת׃ שק"ו צי"ת

בָּרוּךְ שֵׁם כְּבוֹד מַלְכוּתוֹ לְעוֹלָם וָעֶד׃

CHASSIDIC INSIGHTS

(continued from p. 50)

Within prayers, *yirat Elokim* is most closely associated with the *korbanot*, or list of sacrifices that we recite after the *Kriat Shema* in the *siddur*. The Cohanim, or priests serving in the Temple, certainly needed to maintain a high level of Godly awareness. Their Temple service required great precision on all levels — when offering sacrifices, they had to know exactly what was the purpose of the particular offering and where and what time it was to be offered. Failure to do so, in some cases (for example, during the *olah* "burnt offering" that was sacrificed every morning and evening) meant failure of the divine *shefa*, or divine influx, to descend to enliven the physical universe. Therefore,

(continued on p. 62)

Nefesh shb'nefesh
Fear of God (*Elokim*)
Lower Fear
World of *Asiya*

grain], the meal offering [of grain] took place before the pancakes, the pancakes took place before the libations of wine, the libations before the additional offerings (musaf) [of Shabbat and Yom tov]. The additional musaf offering took place prior to placing the containers [of frankincense], and the containers prior to the afternoon burnt-offering, as it is said, "And [the Cohen] will arrange for You a daily offering, and burn it upon the altar and smoke the fat of the peace-offering upon it; with this, all of the offerings are concluded."

Ana bekoach

WE BESEECH YOU, BY THE POWER OF YOUR RIGHT hand, free the bound.

Accept the song of Your nation, grant us strength, purify us, Awesome One.

Please, Mighty One, guard as the "apple of Your eye," those who seek Your unity.

Bless them, purify them, always bestow upon them the mercy of Your righteousness.

Powerful One, holy One, out of Your bountiful goodness guide Your congregation.

Unique One, lofty One, turn to Your people, who recall Your holiness.

Accept our prayer and heed our cries, You Who knows hidden matters.

Blessed be the Name of the glory of His kingdom forever and ever.

איזהו מקומן

נפש שבנפש
יראת אלקים
יראה תתאה
עולם העשיה (חג"ת)

רִבּוֹן הָעוֹלָמִים, אַתָּה צִוִּיתָנוּ, לְהַקְרִיב קָרְבַּן הַתָּמִיד בְּמוֹעֲדוֹ, וּלְהַקְטִיר הַקְּטֹרֶת בִּזְמַנָּהּ, וְלִהְיוֹת כֹּהֲנִים בַּעֲבוֹדָתָם, וּלְוִיִּים בְּדוּכָנָם, וְיִשְׂרָאֵל בְּמַעֲמָדָם, וְעַתָּה בַּעֲוֹנוֹתֵינוּ, חָרַב בֵּית הַמִּקְדָּשׁ וּבָטַל הַתָּמִיד וְהַקְּטֹרֶת, וְאֵין לָנוּ לֹא כֹהֵן בַּעֲבוֹדָתוֹ וְלֹא לֵוִי בְּדוּכָנוֹ, וְלֹא יִשְׂרָאֵל בְּמַעֲמָדוֹ: לָכֵן יְהִי רָצוֹן מִלְּפָנֶיךָ יְיָ אֱלֹהֵינוּ וֵאלֹהֵי אֲבוֹתֵינוּ שֶׁיְּהֵא שִׂיחַ שִׂפְתוֹתֵינוּ חָשׁוּב וּמְקֻבָּל לְפָנֶיךָ כְּאִלּוּ הִקְרַבְנוּ קָרְבַּן הַתָּמִיד בְּמוֹעֲדוֹ עַל מַעֲמָדוֹ, וְהִקְטַרְנוּ הַקְּטֹרֶת בִּזְמַנּוֹ, כְּמָה שֶׁנֶּאֱמַר, וּנְשַׁלְּמָה פָרִים שְׂפָתֵינוּ: וְנֶאֱמַר, זֹאת הַתּוֹרָה לָעֹלָה לַמִּנְחָה, וְלַחַטָּאת וְלָאָשָׁם וְלַמִּלּוּאִים וּלְזֶבַח הַשְּׁלָמִים:

[א] אֵיזֶהוּ מְקוֹמָן שֶׁל זְבָחִים, קָדְשֵׁי קָדָשִׁים שְׁחִיטָתָן בַּצָּפוֹן. פַּר וְשָׂעִיר שֶׁל יוֹם הַכִּפּוּרִים שְׁחִיטָתָן בַּצָּפוֹן, וְקִבּוּל דָּמָן בִּכְלִי שָׁרֵת בַּצָּפוֹן, וְדָמָן טָעוּן הַזָּיָה עַל בֵּין הַבַּדִּים, וְעַל הַפָּרֹכֶת, וְעַל מִזְבַּח הַזָּהָב. מַתָּנָה אַחַת מֵהֶן מְעַכֶּבֶת. שְׁיָרֵי הַדָּם הָיָה שׁוֹפֵךְ עַל יְסוֹד מַעֲרָבִי שֶׁל מִזְבֵּחַ הַחִיצוֹן, אִם לֹא נָתַן לֹא עִכֵּב:

[ב] פָּרִים הַנִּשְׂרָפִים וּשְׂעִירִים הַנִּשְׂרָפִים שְׁחִיטָתָן בַּצָּפוֹן, וְקִבּוּל דָּמָן בִּכְלִי שָׁרֵת בַּצָּפוֹן, וְדָמָן טָעוּן הַזָּיָה עַל הַפָּרֹכֶת, וְעַל מִזְבַּח הַזָּהָב. מַתָּנָה אַחַת

Aizehu Mekoman

Nefesh shb'nefesh
Fear of God (*Elokim*)
Lower Fear
World of *Asiya*

MASTER OF THE UNIVERSE, YOU HAVE COMMANDED US to offer the constant daily sacrifice at its appointed time, and to burn the incense at its time, with the Cohanim performing their service, and the Levites chanting, and the Israelites standing at attention. And now, because of our sins, the Temple has been destroyed and the regular daily offering and the incense discontinued. We have neither the Cohanim performing their service, nor the Levites chanting, nor the Israelites standing at attention. Therefore, may it by Your Will, Lord our God and God of our fathers, that the speech of our lips should be considered and accepted before You, as if we offered the regular daily sacrifice at its time and stood at attention and burned the incense at its appropriate time, as said, "[The prayers of] our lips in lieu of the animals [sacrifices]." And as it says, "This is the law of the regular daily sacrifice, the grain offering and the sin offering and the guilt offering, the inauguration offering and the peace offering."

[1] Where were the places [in the holy Temple where the offerings were sacrificed]? The holiest sacrifices (kodshei kodshim) were slaughtered on the north [side of the altar]. The bull and the goat of Yom Kippur were slaughtered on the north side, and their blood was gathered in a special service vessel. It was necessary to sprinkle their blood between the poles of the ark, and toward the curtain in front of the ark, and on the golden altar. If even one [of these sprinklings] did not take place, the entire sacrifice was invalid. The [priest] poured the remainder of the blood on the western side of the base of the outer altar, but if he failed to do so, the offering remained valid.

[2] Bulls which were meant to be burnt, and goats meant to be burnt were sacrificed on the north side of the altar, and their blood was gathered in a service vessel in the north, and their blood was to be sprinkled on the curtain in front of the ark,

נפש שבנפש
יראת אלקים
יראה תתאה
עולם העשיה (חג"ת)

מֵהֶן מְעַכֶּבֶת, שְׁיָרֵי הַדָּם, הָיָה שׁוֹפֵךְ עַל יְסוֹד מַעֲרָבִי שֶׁל מִזְבֵּחַ הַחִיצוֹן, אִם לֹא נָתַן לֹא עִכֵּב, אֵלּוּ וָאֵלּוּ נִשְׂרָפִין בְּבֵית הַדֶּשֶׁן:

[ג] חַטָּאות הַצִּבּוּר וְהַיָּחִיד, אֵלּוּ הֵן חַטֹּאות הַצִּבּוּר: שְׂעִירֵי רָאשֵׁי חֳדָשִׁים וְשֶׁל מוֹעֲדוֹת, שְׁחִיטָתָן בַּצָּפוֹן, וְקִבּוּל דָּמָן בִּכְלִי שָׁרֵת בַּצָּפוֹן, וְדָמָן טָעוּן אַרְבַּע מַתָּנוֹת עַל אַרְבַּע קְרָנוֹת, כֵּיצַד: עָלָה בַּכֶּבֶשׁ וּפָנָה לַסּוֹבֵב, וּבָא לוֹ לְקֶרֶן דְּרוֹמִית מִזְרָחִית, מִזְרָחִית צְפוֹנִית, צְפוֹנִית מַעֲרָבִית, מַעֲרָבִית דְּרוֹמִית. שְׁיָרֵי הַדָּם הָיָה שׁוֹפֵךְ עַל יְסוֹד דְּרוֹמִי, וְנֶאֱכָלִין לִפְנִים מִן הַקְּלָעִים לְזִכְרֵי כְהֻנָּה בְּכָל מַאֲכָל, לְיוֹם וָלַיְלָה עַד חֲצוֹת:

[ד] הָעוֹלָה, קֹדֶשׁ קָדָשִׁים, שְׁחִיטָתָהּ בַּצָּפוֹן, וְקִבּוּל דָּמָהּ בִּכְלִי שָׁרֵת בַּצָּפוֹן, וְדָמָהּ טָעוּן שְׁתֵּי מַתָּנוֹת שֶׁהֵן אַרְבַּע, וּטְעוּנָה הֶפְשֵׁט וְנִתּוּחַ, וְכָלִיל לָאִשִּׁים:

[ה] זִבְחֵי שַׁלְמֵי צִבּוּר וַאֲשָׁמוֹת, אֵלּוּ הֵן אֲשָׁמוֹת: אֲשַׁם גְּזֵלוֹת, אֲשַׁם מְעִילוֹת, אֲשַׁם שִׁפְחָה חֲרוּפָה, אֲשַׁם נָזִיר, אֲשַׁם מְצוֹרָע, אָשָׁם תָּלוּי. שְׁחִיטָתָן

--- CHASSIDIC INSIGHTS ---

(continued from p. 58)

in addition to fear of sin, the priests must have experienced a judicious measure of emotional fear of God as well. If so, it is plausible that this level of *yirat Elokim* is associated with the *korbanot*, or sacrifices, that we recite before prayers in the morning.

(continued on p. 76)

Nefesh shb'nefesh
Fear of God (*Elokim*)
Lower Fear
World of *Asiya*

and on the golden altar. If either one of these sprinklings did not take place, the offering was invalid. The [priest] poured the remainder of the blood on the western side of the base of the outer altar, but if he failed to do so, the offering remained valid. All of these offerings were burnt at the place where the ashes were deposited.

[3] Public sin-offerings and individual sin-offerings: these were the public sin offerings: the goats offered on Rosh Chodesh and on the festivals were slaughtered on the north side of the altar, their blood was gathered in a service vessel in the north, and of this blood it was necessary to do four sprinklings, one on each of the four corners of the altar. How? The priest ascended the ramp next to the altar and turned to go around, coming to the southeastern corner, then the northeastern corner, followed by the north western corner and the southwestern corner. He would pour the remainder of the blood on the southern base of the altar. These offerings were eaten within the courtyard of the Temple by male priests, prepared in any fashion, on the day of offering and the subsequent evening, until midnight.

[4] The burnt offering — which is a most holy offering — is sacrificed on the north side of the altar, and its blood is gathered in a service vessel on the north side, and its blood requires two sprinklings that constitute four [because the priest stands at one corner and simultaneously sprinkles the blood on it and on the opposite, diagonal corner]. And it requires the skin to be removed and the body cut up, and it is totally incinerated.

[5] Public peace offerings and guilt offerings: these are the guilt offerings. The guilt-offering for theft, the guilt-offering for misusing sacred objects, the guilt-offering for violating a betrothed maidservant, the guilt-offering of a *nazir*, and of one who is plague-ridden, and of one who is in doubt whether the act that he committed requires a sin-offering —

בַּצָּפוֹן, וְקִבּוּל דָּמָן בִּכְלִי שָׁרֵת בַּצָּפוֹן, וְדָמָן טָעוּן שְׁתֵּי מַתָּנוֹת שֶׁהֵן אַרְבַּע, וְנֶאֱכָלִין לִפְנִים מִן הַקְּלָעִים לְזִכְרֵי כְהֻנָּה, בְּכָל מַאֲכָל, לְיוֹם וָלַיְלָה עַד חֲצוֹת:

[ו] הַתּוֹדָה וְאֵיל נָזִיר, קָדָשִׁים קַלִּים, שְׁחִיטָתָן בְּכָל מָקוֹם בָּעֲזָרָה, וְדָמָן טָעוּן שְׁתֵּי מַתָּנוֹת שֶׁהֵן אַרְבַּע, וְנֶאֱכָלִין בְּכָל הָעִיר, לְכָל אָדָם, בְּכָל מַאֲכָל, לְיוֹם וָלַיְלָה עַד חֲצוֹת: הַמּוּרָם מֵהֶם כַּיּוֹצֵא בָהֶם, אֶלָּא שֶׁהַמּוּרָם נֶאֱכָל לַכֹּהֲנִים לִנְשֵׁיהֶם וְלִבְנֵיהֶם וּלְעַבְדֵיהֶם:

[ז] שְׁלָמִים, קָדָשִׁים קַלִּים, שְׁחִיטָתָן בְּכָל מָקוֹם בָּעֲזָרָה, וְדָמָן טָעוּן שְׁתֵּי מַתָּנוֹת שֶׁהֵן אַרְבַּע, וְנֶאֱכָלִין בְּכָל הָעִיר, לְכָל אָדָם, בְּכָל מַאֲכָל, לִשְׁנֵי יָמִים וְלַיְלָה אֶחָד. הַמּוּרָם מֵהֶם, כַּיּוֹצֵא בָהֶם, אֶלָּא, שֶׁהַמּוּרָם נֶאֱכָל לַכֹּהֲנִים לִנְשֵׁיהֶם וְלִבְנֵיהֶם וּלְעַבְדֵיהֶם:

Nefesh shb'nefesh
Fear of God (*Elokim*)
Lower Fear
World of *Asiya*

all of them are slaughtered on the north side of the altar, their blood is gathered in a service vessel, and their blood requires two sprinklings that constitute four [because the priest stands at one corner and sprinkles the blood on that corner and the opposite, diagonal corner simultaneously]. They are eaten within the courtyard of the Temple, by male priests, prepared in any fashion, on the day of offering and the subsequent evening, until midnight.

[6] The thanksgiving offering, as well as the ram offering of the *nazir*, are holy offerings of lesser holiness (*kedoshim kalim*). Their slaughtering takes place anywhere in the courtyard, and their blood requires two sprinklings that constitute four [since the Cohen stands at one corner of the altar and sprinkles the blood so that some of it simultaneously falls upon the opposite, diagonal corner as well]. They are eaten anywhere within the city, and anyone may eat them, prepared in any fashion, on the day of offering and the subsequent evening, until midnight.

The portions that are separated from them [for the priests] are treated similar to [the sacrifices themselves], except that the separated portion is eaten by the priests, their wives and their children and their servants.

[7] Peace offerings are holy offerings of lesser holiness. Their slaughtering takes place anywhere in the courtyard, and their blood requires two sprinklings which constitute four [since the Cohen stands at one corner of the altar and sprinkles the blood so that some of it simultaneously falls upon the opposite, diagonal corner as well]. They are eaten anywhere in the city, by anyone, prepared in any fashion, for two days, including the night between them. And the portion that is separated from them [for the priests] is treated similar to [the peace offering itself], except that the separated portion is eaten by the priests, their wives, their children and their servants.

[ח] הַבְּכוֹר וְהַמַּעֲשֵׂר וְהַפֶּסַח, קָדָשִׁים קַלִּים שְׁחִיטָתָן בְּכָל מָקוֹם בָּעֲזָרָה, וְדָמָן טָעוּן מַתָּנָה אֶחָת, וּבִלְבַד שֶׁיִּתֵּן כְּנֶגֶד הַיְסוֹד. שָׁנָה בַּאֲכִילָתָן, הַבְּכוֹר נֶאֱכָל לַכֹּהֲנִים, וְהַמַּעֲשֵׂר לְכָל אָדָם, וְנֶאֱכָלִין בְּכָל הָעִיר, בְּכָל מַאֲכָל, לִשְׁנֵי יָמִים וְלַיְלָה אֶחָד. הַפֶּסַח אֵינוֹ נֶאֱכָל אֶלָּא בַלַּיְלָה, וְאֵינוֹ נֶאֱכָל אֶלָּא עַד חֲצוֹת, וְאֵינוֹ נֶאֱכָל אֶלָּא לִמְנוּיָו, וְאֵינוֹ נֶאֱכָל אֶלָּא צָלִי:

ברייתא –
שלוש עשרה מדות

רַבִּי יִשְׁמָעֵאל אוֹמֵר, בִּשְׁלֹשׁ עֶשְׂרֵה מִדּוֹת הַתּוֹרָה נִדְרֶשֶׁת:

[א] מִקַּל וָחֹמֶר.

[ב] וּמִגְּזֵרָה שָׁוָה.

[ג] מִבִּנְיַן אָב מִכָּתוּב אֶחָד, וּמִבִּנְיַן אָב מִשְּׁנֵי כְתוּבִים.

[ד] מִכְּלָל וּפְרָט.

[ה] וּמִפְּרָט וּכְלָל.

Nefesh shb'nefesh
Fear of God (*Elokim*)
Lower Fear
World of *Asiya*

[8] The sacrifice of the first-born animal, as well as the tithe and the Pesach offering are considered holy offerings of lesser holiness. Their slaughtering takes place anywhere within the courtyard, and their blood requires one sprinkling, which must take place above the base [of the altar]. They differ in how they may be eaten: The first born sacrifice is eaten by the priests, and the tithe may be eaten by anyone. They are eaten in the entire city, in any manner of preparation, over the course of two days including the night between them.

The Pesach offering is eaten only at night, and is eaten only up until midnight, and only by those who are appointed to the particular offering, and is eaten only roasted.

The Thirteen Principles of Interpretation

Rabbi Yishmael said, "The Torah may be interpreted using thirteen different methods:

1) By drawing a conclusion from a lenient premise and applying it to a stricter premise (and vice versa),

2) By applying the same law to two texts that carry identical Biblical expressions (when based upon tradition),

3) By assuming that a law that applies in one or in two Biblical texts applies to all similar texts [in general, but not necessarily in all of their details].

4) When the Torah posits a general principle, followed by specific details, the principle applies only to the specific details.

5) When the Torah lists specific details, followed by a general principle, the principle applies to all details [not only to those listed].

6) When a verse offers a general principle, followed by specific cases, and then returns to the general principle, then the principle applies only to cases which are similar to those listed.

[ו] כְּלָל וּפְרָט וּכְלָל, אִי אַתָּה דָן אֶלָּא כְּעֵין הַפְּרָט.

[ז] מִכְּלָל שֶׁהוּא צָרִיךְ לִפְרָט, וּמִפְּרָט שֶׁהוּא צָרִיךְ לִכְלָל.

[ח] כָּל דָּבָר שֶׁהָיָה בִּכְלָל וְיָצָא מִן הַכְּלָל לְלַמֵּד, לֹא לְלַמֵּד עַל עַצְמוֹ יָצָא, אֶלָּא לְלַמֵּד עַל הַכְּלָל כֻּלּוֹ יָצָא.

[ט] כָּל דָּבָר שֶׁהָיָה בִּכְלָל, וְיָצָא לִטְעוֹן טַעַן אֶחָד שֶׁהוּא כְעִנְיָנוֹ, יָצָא לְהָקֵל וְלֹא לְהַחֲמִיר.

[י] כָּל דָּבָר שֶׁהָיָה בִּכְלָל וְיָצָא לִטְעוֹן טַעַן אַחֵר שֶׁלֹּא כְעִנְיָנוֹ, יָצָא לְהָקֵל וּלְהַחֲמִיר.

[יא] כָּל דָּבָר שֶׁהָיָה בִּכְלָל וְיָצָא לִדּוֹן בַּדָּבָר חָדָשׁ, אִי אַתָּה יָכוֹל לְהַחֲזִירוֹ לִכְלָלוֹ, עַד שֶׁיַּחֲזִירֶנּוּ הַכָּתוּב לִכְלָלוֹ בְּפֵרוּשׁ.

[יב] דָּבָר הַלָּמֵד מֵעִנְיָנוֹ, וְדָבָר הַלָּמֵד מִסּוֹפוֹ.

[יג] וְכֵן (נ"א וְכַאן) שְׁנֵי כְתוּבִים הַמַּכְחִישִׁים זֶה אֶת זֶה, עַד שֶׁיָּבֹא הַכָּתוּב הַשְּׁלִישִׁי וְיַכְרִיעַ בֵּינֵיהֶם:

יְהִי רָצוֹן מִלְּפָנֶיךָ, יְיָ אֱלֹהֵינוּ וֵאלֹהֵי אֲבוֹתֵינוּ, שֶׁיִּבָּנֶה בֵּית הַמִּקְדָּשׁ בִּמְהֵרָה בְיָמֵינוּ, וְתֵן חֶלְקֵנוּ בְּתוֹרָתֶךָ:

Nefesh shb'nefesh
Fear of God (*Elokim*)
Lower Fear
World of *Asiya*

7) When a general principle becomes understood only through specifics cases [then the general principle is not limited to those cases, as in no. 4 above]. But, when specifics become clarified only within the context of the principle, [then the principle applies only to those details, and not to others, as in no. 5 above].

8) Any detail that was included within a general principle, and was then mentioned specifically on its own, was not singled out for the purpose of learning something about the detail, but rather to reflect upon the entire principle,

9) Any case that was part of a general principle, but was singled out to teach a matter related to the principle, was singled out to indicate leniency in the matter and not severity.

10) Any case that was part of a general principle, but was singled out to teach a matter unrelated to the principle, was singled out to indicate leniency in some aspects of the matter and severity in other aspects.

11) Any case that was part of a general principle, but was singled out in order to teach a new case, is not re-included in the general principle unless the Scripture explicitly designates it as such.

12) A scriptural matter may be interpreted according to its context, or it may interpreted based upon the subsequent passage.

13) Similarly, two verses which contradict one another, may be resolved by a third verse that reconciles both of them.

May it be Your will Lord our God and Lord of our fathers, that we build the holy Temple soon in our days, and grant us our portion in Your Torah.

קדיש דרבנן

יִתְגַּדַּל וְיִתְקַדַּשׁ שְׁמֵהּ רַבָּא. (עונים: אָמֵן)

בְּעָלְמָא דִּי בְרָא כִרְעוּתֵהּ וְיַמְלִיךְ מַלְכוּתֵהּ, וְיַצְמַח פֻּרְקָנֵהּ וִיקָרֵב מְשִׁיחֵהּ. (עונים: אָמֵן)

בְּחַיֵּיכוֹן וּבְיוֹמֵיכוֹן וּבְחַיֵּי דְכָל בֵּית יִשְׂרָאֵל, בַּעֲגָלָא וּבִזְמַן קָרִיב. וְאִמְרוּ אָמֵן:

(עונים: אָמֵן. יְהֵא שְׁמֵהּ רַבָּא מְבָרַךְ לְעָלַם וּלְעָלְמֵי עָלְמַיָּא, יִתְבָּרַךְ:)

יְהֵא שְׁמֵהּ רַבָּא מְבָרַךְ לְעָלַם וּלְעָלְמֵי עָלְמַיָּא.

יִתְבָּרַךְ, וְיִשְׁתַּבַּח, וְיִתְפָּאַר, וְיִתְרוֹמַם, וְיִתְנַשֵּׂא, וְיִתְהַדָּר, וְיִתְעַלֶּה, וְיִתְהַלָּל, שְׁמֵהּ דְּקֻדְשָׁא בְּרִיךְ הוּא. (עונים: אָמֵן) לְעֵלָּא מִן כָּל בִּרְכָתָא וְשִׁירָתָא, תֻּשְׁבְּחָתָא וְנֶחֱמָתָא, דַּאֲמִירָן בְּעָלְמָא, וְאִמְרוּ אָמֵן:

עַל יִשְׂרָאֵל וְעַל רַבָּנָן. וְעַל תַּלְמִידֵיהוֹן וְעַל כָּל תַּלְמִידֵי תַלְמִידֵיהוֹן. וְעַל כָּל מָאן דְּעָסְקִין בְּאוֹרַיְתָא דִּי בְאַתְרָא הָדֵין וְדִי בְכָל אֲתַר וַאֲתַר. יְהֵא לְהוֹן וּלְכוֹן שְׁלָמָא רַבָּא חִנָּא וְחִסְדָּא וְרַחֲמִין וְחַיִּין אֲרִיכִין וּמְזוֹנָא רְוִיחָא וּפוּרְקָנָא מִן קֳדָם אֲבוּהוֹן דְּבִשְׁמַיָּא וְאִמְרוּ אָמֵן:

יְהֵא שְׁלָמָה רַבָּא מִן שְׁמַיָּא וְחַיִּים טוֹבִים עָלֵינוּ וְעַל כָּל יִשְׂרָאֵל, וְאִמְרוּ אָמֵן:

עֹשֶׂה שָׁלוֹם (בעשרת ימי תשובה עומרים: הַשָּׁלוֹם) בִּמְרוֹמָיו הוּא יַעֲשֶׂה שָׁלוֹם עָלֵינוּ וְעַל כָּל יִשְׂרָאֵל, וְאִמְרוּ אָמֵן.

Nefesh shb'nefesh
Fear of God (*Elokim*)
Lower Fear
World of *Asiya*

The Rabbis' Kaddish

Yitgadal v'yitkadash sh'mayh raba

*B'almah di v'rah chirutay veyamlich malchutay,
veyatzmach purkanay vikorave meshichay.*

*Bechayaychon uveyomaychon uvechayay dekol bayt
Yisrael, ba'agoloh u'vizman koriv ve'imru amen.*

*Yehay shemay rabo mevorach l'olam
v'le'olmay olmayah.*

*Yitboraych, vehishtabach, veyitpa'er veyitromom
veyitnasay veyithadar, vehitaleh, veyit'halolo,
sh'may dekudsha brich hu.*

*L'aylo min kol birchahtah, veshiratah, tush bechatah
venechematah, da'amiron b'almah, v'imru amen.*

*Al Yisrael v'al rabanen, v'al talmidayhon, v'al kol talmi-
day talmidayhon, v'al kol mahn de'oskin be'roayto. Di
be'atrah hadayn, v'di bechol atar ve'atar. Yehay l'hon
u'lechon shlamah raba, chinah vechisday v'erachamin
vechayin arichin umezonah revichah ufurkanah min
kadahm avuhon de'bishmaya ve'imru amen.*

*Yehay shlahmah raba min shemaya vechayim
tovim aleinu ve'al kol Yisrael v'im ru amen.*

Take three steps back, and bow to the right when saying "*Oseh shalom bimrovov*," bow forward when saying "*hu*," bow to the left when saying "*ya'aseh shalom aleinu*," and bow forward when saying "*ve'al kol Yisrael*"

*Oseh shalom bimrovov, hu ya'aseh shalom aleinu
ve'al kol Yisrael ve'imru amen.*

הודו

הוֹדוּ לַיָי קִרְאוּ בִשְׁמוֹ, הוֹדִיעוּ בָעַמִּים עֲלִילוֹתָיו:
שִׁירוּ לוֹ זַמְּרוּ לוֹ, שִׂיחוּ בְּכָל נִפְלְאֹתָיו:
הִתְהַלְלוּ בְּשֵׁם קָדְשׁוֹ, יִשְׂמַח לֵב מְבַקְשֵׁי יְיָ:
דִּרְשׁוּ יְיָ וְעֻזּוֹ, בַּקְּשׁוּ פָנָיו תָּמִיד:
זִכְרוּ נִפְלְאֹתָיו אֲשֶׁר עָשָׂה, מֹפְתָיו וּמִשְׁפְּטֵי פִיהוּ:
זֶרַע יִשְׂרָאֵל עַבְדּוֹ, בְּנֵי יַעֲקֹב בְּחִירָיו:
הוּא יְיָ אֱלֹהֵינוּ, בְּכָל הָאָרֶץ מִשְׁפָּטָיו:

רוח שבנפש
הודאה פרטי
יראת אלקים
יראה תתאה
עולם העשיה (חב״ד)

> **There is a difference between general acknowledgment of God, as when we arise in the morning and say** *Modeh Ani* **"(I acknowledge)… [and specific acknowledgment of God]."** (*Kuntres Ha'Avoda* of the Rebbe Rashab, first page)[53]

General acknowledgment corresponds to the soul level of *nefesh she'b'nefesh*. Specific acknowledgment occurs as our soul level of *nefesh* ascends to become included in the soul-level of *ruach*. When we acknowledge God's presence and greatness without any understanding or feeling for Him, we activate our *nefesh she'b'nefesh*. When we begin to develop a feeling for Godliness and acknowledge Him with our emotions, we rise to the level of *ruach sh'b'nefesh*.

General acknowledgment occurs as we express gratitude from the totality of our being and acknowledge His presence from our very essence. Our gratitude and acknowledgment is not limited to any specific soul faculty such as intellect or emotions. Specific acknowledgment occurs as we give thanks to God utilizing particular soul faculties, such as our mind or our heart. Specific acknowledgment is a stage of spiritual ascent during prayer, while general acknowledgment is not a stage but the foundation and basis of all prayer.

HODU

Ruach shb'nefesh
Particular
   Acknowledgment
Fear (Reverence)
Lower Fear
World of *Asiya*

GIVE THANKS TO THE LORD, PROCLAIM HIS NAME, INFORM the nations of His deeds.

Sing to Him, resonate with Him, speak of all His wonders.

Exalt in His holy name, those who seek Him rejoice in their hearts.

Search for the Lord and His might, seek His countenance at all times.

Recall the wonders that He performed, His signs and laws from His mouth.

The descendants of Israel are His servants, the sons of Jacob His chosen.

He is the Lord our God, His laws apply to all of the earth!

📖 Within the Words

When we awaken in the morning and recite *Modeh Ani*, we are operating on the level of *nefesh she'b'nefesh*, without any feeling or understanding, but from the essence of our soul, while accessing the very essence of Godliness. When we begin our prayers in the morning with *Hodu*, we are operating on the level of *ruach she'b'nefesh*, expressing emotional gratefulness to God.

Word Sparks

We give thanks (הודו) from the essence of our soul, but we call (קראו) to Him from a particular attribute of our self (Torat Shmuel 5640/1880 of the Rebbe Maharash, page 799).

Why do we mention the "nations" here? After reciting the verses of the ketoret, which arouse divine revelation that transforms our intellect, we next mention the "nations," who will undergo transformation in the future, when God calls to them "with a clear language." (Torat Shmuel 5642/1882, page 66).

We "sing" (שירו) to Him with our Godly soul, and "play" (זמרו) musical instruments for Him with our animal soul (Torat Shmuel 5635/1875 vol 1, page 181-182)

Why do we use the reflexive form of the verb התהללו, "cause to praise," rather than the more conventional form הללו, "praise"? Because we are required to meditate, which then causes us to sincerely praise God. (Torat Shmuel 5640/1880, Page 131-132).

זִכְרוּ לְעוֹלָם בְּרִיתוֹ, דָּבָר צִוָּה לְאֶלֶף דּוֹר:

אֲשֶׁר כָּרַת אֶת אַבְרָהָם וּשְׁבוּעָתוֹ לְיִצְחָק:

וַיַּעֲמִידֶהָ לְיַעֲקֹב לְחֹק, לְיִשְׂרָאֵל בְּרִית עוֹלָם:

לֵאמֹר: לְךָ אֶתֵּן אֶרֶץ כְּנָעַן, חֶבֶל נַחֲלַתְכֶם:

בִּהְיוֹתְכֶם מְתֵי מִסְפָּר, כִּמְעַט וְגָרִים בָּהּ:

וַיִּתְהַלְּכוּ מִגּוֹי אֶל גּוֹי, וּמִמַּמְלָכָה אֶל עַם אַחֵר:

לֹא הִנִּיחַ לְאִישׁ לְעָשְׁקָם, וַיּוֹכַח עֲלֵיהֶם מְלָכִים:

אַל תִּגְּעוּ בִמְשִׁיחָי וּבִנְבִיאַי אַל תָּרֵעוּ:

רוח שבנפש
הודאה פרטי
יראת אלקים
יראה תתאה
עולם העשיה (חב״ד)

❝ There are two kinds of acknowledgment. The first takes place when, after having thought about and meditated on the subject, we acknowledge that He exists…[the second] occurs when it is totally beyond our ability to grasp and recognize His greatness and wisdom for what it is, and all we can do is concede, admit and praise His greatness." (The Alter Rebbe's Siddur with Chassidut, p. 606, 303c)[54]

Within the admission (after meditating upon the topic) that God is beyond our ability to grasp and understand, shines a very high spiritual illumination (*chochma sh'b'malchut*). The highest spiritual levels that are beyond our grasp shine within the lowest levels of mere gratitude. This is because, "The beginning is wedged within the end."

According to the Ari, we recite *Hodu* in honor of the Ten Martyrs, who were executed by the Romans for teaching Torah. If so, *Hodu* was not part of the original order of prayers that was established much earlier than the time of the martyrs.[55]

Ruach shb'nefesh
Particular
   Acknowledgment
Fear (Reverence)
Lower Fear
World of *Asiya*

Remember His covenant forever,
His command for a thousand generations.

That He established with Abraham,
and His oath to Isaac.

He set it up as law with Jacob,
and a permanent covenant with Israel.

Saying, "To you I have given the land of
Canaan," as your inheritance.

When you were still few in numbers,
a minority living there.

Journeying from nation to nation,
from a kingdom to a different people.

He permitted no man to bother them,
and rebuked kings over them.

"Do not touch my anointed ones,
nor harm my prophets!"

📖 Within the Words

As we begin our prayers, saying *Hodu la'shem*, we express acknowledgment of God on specific levels, at first emotional, and later (after *Barchu*), intellectual. Ultimately, during the *Shemonah Esreh*, we come to the realization that even after all of our intellectual and emotional achievements, we still cannot grasp how great God is, and we are as naught before Him. We then say *Modim anachnu lach*. This is called *Modim d'Rabonen* and indicates that even the greatest wisdom cannot fathom God.

Word Sparks — *The first fifteen verses of Hodu were recited during the morning offering (עולה של שחרית) while the second fifteen verses were recited during the evening offering (עולה של בין הערבים) (Torat Shmuel 5639/1879, vol 2, Page 388).*

HODU

שִׁירוּ לַיָי כָּל הָאָרֶץ, בַּשְּׂרוּ מִיּוֹם אֶל יוֹם יְשׁוּעָתוֹ:

סַפְּרוּ בַגּוֹיִם אֶת כְּבוֹדוֹ, בְּכָל הָעַמִּים נִפְלְאֹתָיו:

כִּי גָדוֹל יְיָ וּמְהֻלָּל מְאֹד, וְנוֹרָא הוּא עַל כָּל אֱלֹהִים:

כִּי כָּל אֱלֹהֵי הָעַמִּים אֱלִילִים וַיְיָ שָׁמַיִם עָשָׂה:

הוֹד וְהָדָר לְפָנָיו, עֹז וְחֶדְוָה בִּמְקֹמוֹ:

הָבוּ לַיָי מִשְׁפְּחוֹת עַמִּים, הָבוּ לַיָי כָּבוֹד וָעֹז:

רוח שבנפש
הודאה פרטי
יראת אלקים
יראה תתאה
עולם העשיה (חב"ד)

" The oxen sang while walking, turning their heads toward the ark and uttering a song. Which song? R' Eliezer said it was *Hodu lashem kir'u bishmo...*" (Midrash Rabba Vayera 54)[56]

In the days of King David, the Philistines captured the Ark of the Covenant, with the Tablets of the Ten Commandments within, but many Philistines died upon contact with the Ark, and so they relinquished it. The oxen that drew the ark brought it back of their own accord to Beit Shemesh, singing *Hodu* as they walked. As they carried the Ark, the oxen were a physical representation of the spiritual "Face of the Ox" above, which carried the "throne" in the vision of Yehezkel. Because they were nullified to their spiritual source above in the chariot of Yehezkel, the oxen received the power to "sing" — to resonate with Godliness. The same is true of us humans as well during prayer; when we nullify our egos to make room for Godliness, He gives us the power and strength to "sing" and pray to Him.[57]

CHASSIDIC INSIGHTS

(continued from p. 62)

A second and more elevated level of *yirat Elokim* emerges from meditation not only upon God's power and omnipotence, but upon His creation. When we pay attention to the sheer number of creations, and their size and shape, and we pause to reflect upon the infinite details and beauty and harmony of creation, we experience reverence

(continued on p. 78)

Ruach shb'nefesh
Particular
    Acknowledgment
Fear (Reverence)
Lower Fear
World of *Asiya*

> Let the entire earth sing to the Lord,
> announce His salvation daily!
>
> Tell of His honor to the nations,
> His wonders to all peoples.
>
> For, great is the Lord, and very praiseworthy,
> awesome over all gods.
>
> For, the gods of the nations are all as naught…
> but the Lord made the heavens.
>
> Glory and honor precede Him,
> might and happiness exist where He is.
>
> Approach the Lord, families of the nations,
> approach the Lord with honor and might.

The *shemesh* ("sun") symbolizes the essential name of God, *Havaya*. *Beit Shemesh* ("House of the Sun") symbolizes *Elokim*, which is the name for Godliness enclothed in nature. The name *Havaya* is too high to illuminate our lives directly; instead, its light is refracted through the name *Elokim* within nature. The Ark and the Tablets also symbolized the two names *Havaya* and *Elokim* and that is why the oxen brought them to *Beit Shemesh*. [58]

Within the Words

The Zohar states, "When the Jews say *Hodu*, the sun also sings."[59] This is because the verse alludes to all ten *sephirot*, as follows: *Hodu Lashem* alludes to *Keter*; *Kir'u bishmo* — *chochma*; *Hodiyu ba'amim alilotov* — *bina*; *Shiru lo* — *chesed*; *Zamru lo* — *gevurah*; *Sichu b'kol niflotav* — *tiferet*; *Hithaleleu beshem kadsho* — *netzach*; *Yismach lev mevakshei Hashem* — *hod*; *Dirshu Hashem* — *yesod*; *Ve'uzo* — *malchut*.[60]

HODU

הָבוּ לַיָי כְּבוֹד שְׁמוֹ, שְׂאוּ מִנְחָה וּבֹאוּ לְפָנָיו, הִשְׁתַּחֲווּ לַיָי בְּהַדְרַת קֹדֶשׁ:
חִילוּ מִלְּפָנָיו כָּל הָאָרֶץ, אַף תִּכּוֹן תֵּבֵל בַּל תִּמּוֹט:
יִשְׂמְחוּ הַשָּׁמַיִם וְתָגֵל הָאָרֶץ, וְיֹאמְרוּ בַגּוֹיִם יְיָ מָלָךְ:
יִרְעַם הַיָּם וּמְלֹאוֹ יַעֲלֹץ הַשָּׂדֶה וְכָל אֲשֶׁר בּוֹ:
אָז יְרַנְּנוּ עֲצֵי הַיָּעַר מִלִּפְנֵי יְיָ, כִּי בָא לִשְׁפּוֹט אֶת הָאָרֶץ:
הוֹדוּ לַיָי כִּי טוֹב, כִּי לְעוֹלָם חַסְדּוֹ:

רוח שבנפש
הודאה פרטי
יראת אלקים
יראה תתאה
עולם העשיה (חב״ד)

❝ It is written [in the Book of Psalms]: 'At night, sing with me…'[61] — The sages said[62] that this applies to the Torah, and that 'all who learn Torah at night experience *chesed* ("kindness") during the day.' If so, why was King David punished for calling the Torah a 'melody'? What is the difference between a 'melody' and a 'song'?" (*Torat Shmuel* 5635/1875 of the Rebbe Maharash, pp. 178-182)[63]

The Torah possesses internal as well as external dimensions. In general when we study the Talmud and *halacha*, we are engaged in the external elements of the Torah. They are external because they deal with matters that are limited and physical. Even so, the entire universe is dependent upon the physical details that the Torah discusses. But, the Torah itself is the "soul of God" and, as such, it is infinite and essential.

A "melody" (*zmira*) is played with a musical instrument, while a "song" (*shir*) is sung by the human voice. A "song" is therefore more personal, more intimate, and more internally motivated than

──────── CHASSIDIC INSIGHTS ────────

(continued from p. 76)

for Him. This is the sort of mature appreciation that a scientist, for example, may experience as he deepens his knowledge of creation. It is the highest level of *yirah tata'ah*, and it corresponds to the beginning of our prayers, as we recite *Hodu*. This set of verses speaks of the

(continued on p. 80)

Ruach shb'nefesh
Particular
   Acknowledgment
Fear (Reverence)
Lower Fear
World of *Asiya*

Approach the Lord in honor of His name,
raise an offering and come before Him,
Bow to the Lord in holy splendor.

Tremble before Him, entire earth,
even the globe must be firm to avoid faltering.

Be happy, heavens and rejoice, earth,
and the nations shall say, "God reigns!"

The sea and all that fills it roars,
the field and all that is in it exults.

Then, all the trees of the field sing before the Lord, as He comes to judge the earth.

Give thanks to the Lord, for He is good,
His kindness is forever!

---

a "melody." When King David called the Torah a *zmira* ("melody"), he forgot, for the moment, the deeper, more intimate aspects of the Torah that are infinite and essential. He was so absorbed in the intricate power of the Torah to affect the physical universe that he lost focus, temporarily, of the inner dimensions of the Torah as the "soul of God." The punishment was that he temporarily forgot the proper manner of transporting the holy ark (containing the Torah).

> 📖 *Within the Words*
>
> When we say, *shiru* and *zamru* during *Hodu*, our intention is to engage God on both levels, the inner dimensions of *shir*, and the external dimensions of *zimra*. In fact, our intention is to bring the infinite, internal dimension down to permeate and pervade the physical and external. The same is true of the following verse, *Sichu bechol niflotav* ("Speak of all His wonders"); here our intention is to draw down awareness of His miracles and wonders into our experience of the mundane, everyday world.

HODU

וְאִמְרוּ הוֹשִׁיעֵנוּ אֱלֹהֵי יִשְׁעֵנוּ, וְקַבְּצֵנוּ וְהַצִּילֵנוּ מִן הַגּוֹיִם לְהֹדוֹת לְשֵׁם קָדְשֶׁךָ, לְהִשְׁתַּבֵּחַ בִּתְהִלָּתֶךָ:
בָּרוּךְ יְיָ אֱלֹהֵי יִשְׂרָאֵל מִן הָעוֹלָם וְעַד הָעוֹלָם, וַיֹּאמְרוּ כָל הָעָם אָמֵן וְהַלֵּל לַיְיָ:
רוֹמְמוּ יְיָ אֱלֹהֵינוּ וְהִשְׁתַּחֲווּ לַהֲדֹם רַגְלָיו, קָדוֹשׁ הוּא:
רוֹמְמוּ יְיָ אֱלֹהֵינוּ וְהִשְׁתַּחֲווּ לְהַר קָדְשׁוֹ, כִּי קָדוֹשׁ יְיָ אֱלֹהֵינוּ:
וְהוּא רַחוּם יְכַפֵּר עָוֹן וְלֹא יַשְׁחִית, וְהִרְבָּה לְהָשִׁיב אַפּוֹ וְלֹא יָעִיר כָּל חֲמָתוֹ:
אַתָּה יְיָ לֹא תִכְלָא רַחֲמֶיךָ מִמֶּנִּי, חַסְדְּךָ וַאֲמִתְּךָ תָּמִיד יִצְּרוּנִי:

רוח שבנפש
הודאה פרטי
יראת אלקים
יראה תתאה
עולם העשיה (חב"ד)

> **Consider the verse, 'And then all the trees of the forest will sing.' At first glance, how are we supposed to understand this verse, since trees have no voice whatsoever?"** (*Torat Shmuel* 5635/1875 of the Rebbe Maharash, p. 338)[64]

Elsewhere, the sages tell us that, "There is no blade of grass down here that is without a spiritual counterpart above that strikes it, telling it to grow." Every physical creation has a spiritual counterpart above that influences the creation below, providing its needs and aiding it to fulfill its purpose in creation. As we ascend higher in the spiritual worlds, there are more elevated spiritual beings, each with its own sphere of influence that it protects and guides below. These are angels — messengers of Godly influence — that operate with logic and with intellect.

────── **CHASSIDIC INSIGHTS** ──────

(continued from p. 78)

dawn of Jewish history as well as the greatness of creation, and instills within us a feeling of reverence for God's creative power.

In general, *yirah tata'ah* is associated with the lowest level of our soul — the level called *nefesh*, or "action consciousness." On this level,

(continued on p. 84)

Ruach shb'nefesh
Particular
  Acknowledgment
Fear (Reverence)
Lower Fear
World of *Asiya*

And let it be said, "Save us, God our savior, gather
and rescue us from the nations,
in order to acknowledge Your holy name,
to exult in Your praises.

Blessed is the Lord, God of Israel, for all
eternity," and then the entire nation will
say "Amen" and praise the Lord.

Exalt the Lord our God, and bow down
at his foot rest, for He is holy.

Exalt the Lord our God and bow down at His
holy mountain, for the Lord our God is holy.

And He, being merciful, atones for our sins
and refrains from destroying us,
He repeatedly quashes His anger,
and avoids arousing all of His wrath.

Lord, may You never withhold Your mercy
from me, and may Your kindness and
truth always surround me.

We may deduce, then, that it is not the physical trees, but rather their spiritual counterparts that "sing." These counterparts are angels, possessing Godly comprehension. They "sing" as they fulfill their purpose, conveying spiritual influence down to the physical creation. The Hebrew word for "trees" (עצים) — recalls the word for "advice" (עצה) — which is what the "trees" (angels) pass on to their spiritual counterparts below (*Torat Shmuel* 5633/1873, Vol 1, p. 177). Thus, they resonate with Godliness.

Within the Words

It was not uncommon for the early Chassidim to softly sing to themselves during davening. Singing is a spontaneous expression of our desire to connect with God, and there is no reason to avoid it.[65]

HODU

זְכֹר רַחֲמֶיךָ יְיָ וַחֲסָדֶיךָ, כִּי מֵעוֹלָם הֵמָּה:

תְּנוּ עֹז לֵאלֹהִים עַל יִשְׂרָאֵל גַּאֲוָתוֹ, וְעֻזּוֹ בַּשְּׁחָקִים:

נוֹרָא אֱלֹהִים מִמִּקְדָּשֶׁיךָ. אֵל יִשְׂרָאֵל, הוּא נוֹתֵן עֹז וְתַעֲצֻמוֹת לָעָם, בָּרוּךְ אֱלֹהִים:

אֵל נְקָמוֹת יְיָ, אֵל נְקָמוֹת הוֹפִיעַ:

הִנָּשֵׂא שֹׁפֵט הָאָרֶץ הָשֵׁב גְּמוּל עַל גֵּאִים:

לַיְיָ הַיְשׁוּעָה, עַל עַמְּךָ בִרְכָתֶךָ סֶּלָה:

יְיָ צְבָאוֹת עִמָּנוּ, מִשְׂגָּב לָנוּ אֱלֹהֵי יַעֲקֹב סֶלָה:

יְיָ צְבָאוֹת, אַשְׁרֵי אָדָם בֹּטֵחַ בָּךְ:

רוח שבנפש
הודאה פרטי
יראת אלקים
יראה תתאה
עולם העשיה (חב״ד)

> **When we meditate on Godliness…contemplating the creation of worlds, the wonders involved in the process of creation, the order contained in creation, and the praises uttered by all of creation…we ourselves sing praises…We meditate upon the unity of God [during the *Shema*], upon the Godly light that illuminates our soul, and we develop love and fear of God.** (*Sefer Maamorim* 5659/1899 of the Rebbe Rashab, pp. 5–6) 66

> It is our voice, more than meditation, that fans the fires of emotion in our heart. Our speech amplifies and enhances our emotions (love and fear of God). This is due to *ohr chozer* ("reflected illumination") from above that filters down from our mind to our speech as we pray. Just as sunlight is most intense when it strikes the earth, so Godly illumination is intensified when we express our innermost desires and feelings with words and song as we pray.

> We possess natural wells of fear and love of God in our heart, bequeathed to us by the forefathers. By meditating before prayers, we bring those natural wells of love and fear to the forefront of our consciousness. And then, as we say the words of prayer, the natural love and fear is amplified.

Ruach shb'nefesh
Particular
   Acknowledgment
Fear (Reverence)
Lower Fear
World of *Asiya*

> Recall Your mercy and Your kindness,
> for they are eternal.
>
> Ascribe strength to God regarding His people, Israel,
> His pride, and might to the heavens.
>
> God, You are awesome from Your sanctuary, the
> God of Israel grants might and power
> to the nation, blessed is God.
>
> The Lord is a vengeful God,
> God of revenge appear!
>
> Arise, Judge of the earth,
> give to the arrogant their just deserts.
>
> To the Lord belongs salvation,
> let Your blessing be on Your nation forever.
>
> The Lord of Hosts is among us,
> the God of Jacob is a fortress for us forever.
>
> Oh Lord of Hosts,
> happy is the man who trusts in You.

📖 *Within the Words*

As we pray, we need no longer focus on the subject of our meditation. Instead, we should focus on the simple meaning of the words (especially if we know some of their deeper meanings as well, according to Chassidut). Or, we should focus on the simple desire of our heart (*reuta deliba*) to connect with God. Following our meditation, vocalizing the words of prayer will fan the flames of Godly love and fear within us.

Word Sparks
"One who fails to think deeply, delving into Godly concepts, is like an animal. In truth, he is worse than an animal, since an animal does not possess intellect. Man, who possesses intellect but fails to meditate in depth, is lower than an animal. Deep meditation leads to complete divine service, about which it is said, 'And you shall cleave to the Lord your God'..." (Torat Shmuel 5636/1876 of the Rebbe Maharash, in the summaries of the Rebbe Rashab, pp. 415-6)

HODU

יְיָ הוֹשִׁיעָה, הַמֶּלֶךְ יַעֲנֵנוּ בְיוֹם קָרְאֵנוּ:

הוֹשִׁיעָה אֶת עַמֶּךָ וּבָרֵךְ אֶת נַחֲלָתֶךָ, וּרְעֵם וְנַשְּׂאֵם עַד הָעוֹלָם:

נַפְשֵׁנוּ חִכְּתָה לַיְיָ, עֶזְרֵנוּ וּמָגִנֵּנוּ הוּא:

כִּי בוֹ יִשְׂמַח לִבֵּנוּ, כִּי בְשֵׁם קָדְשׁוֹ בָטָחְנוּ:

יְהִי חַסְדְּךָ יְיָ עָלֵינוּ, כַּאֲשֶׁר יִחַלְנוּ לָךְ:

הַרְאֵנוּ יְיָ חַסְדֶּךָ, וְיֶשְׁעֲךָ תִּתֶּן לָנוּ:

קוּמָה עֶזְרָתָה לָנוּ, וּפְדֵנוּ לְמַעַן חַסְדֶּךָ:

רוח שבנפש
הודאה פרטי
יראת אלקים
יראה תתאה
עולם העשיה (חב"ד)

> "There are three distinct souls that inhabit the body of every Jew (although, in the *Tanya*, only two souls are mentioned, in truth there are three). They are, the divine soul, the animal soul, and the intellectual soul (which serves as an intermediary between the divine soul and the animal soul). The three souls are intertwined, such that the maintenance of the higher soul is dependent upon the lower soul in which it is enclothed." (*Sefer Maamorim 5659*/1899 of the Rebbe Rashab, p. 106. See also *Torat Shmuel 5630* of the Rebbe Maharsh, p. 140)[67]

> Kabbalah mentions only two souls — the divine soul and the animal soul.[68] The divine soul needs no rectification, since it is a spark of Godliness from above. However, the animal soul, while neutral, is naturally drawn toward the mundane tasks of feeding and maintaining the body. Therefore, it tends toward the physical rather than the spiritual. Yet, there is nothing that brings as much joy, even to the animal soul, as the discovery and understanding of Godly

---

CHASSIDIC INSIGHTS

(continued from p. 80)

we function without emotion or intellect. *Nefesh* is the instinctual level that energizes and motivates us to persist and persevere. But, as described above, there are various levels within *yirah tata'ah*, just as there are different levels within each world. *Yirah tata'ah* corresponds to the world of *Asiya*. Entry-level acceptance of the "yoke of heaven" (*kabalat*

(continued on p. 92)

Ruach shb'nefesh
Particular
  Acknowledgment
Fear (Reverence)
Lower Fear
World of *Asiya*

> The Lord saves,
> the King will answer us on the day that we call.
>
> Rescue Your nation and bless Your inheritance, care
> for and elevate them forever.
>
> Our soul longs for the Lord,
> He is our help and our shield.
>
> For, in Him our heart rejoices,
> and in His holy name we are secure.
>
> May Your kindness, Lord be upon us,
> as we have placed our hope in You.
>
> Show us Your kindness, Lord,
> and grant Your salvation to us.
>
> Arise, assist us,
> and save us for the sake of Your kindness.

---

concepts. Proper comprehension of Godliness elicits love and fear of God from the recesses of our heart. When that occurs, we are happy.

A third, intellectual soul is mentioned in the *Tanya*,[69] but is discussed at greater length elsewhere in Chassidut. The task of the intellectual soul is to "explain" Godliness and spirituality to the animal soul, in order to persuade it of the importance of Godliness. When the animal soul begins to grasp this through proper meditation upon Godly topics, happiness ensues. The joy that we experience during meditation is even more effective than the meditation itself.[70]

📖 *Within the Words*

We must make sure to meditate properly on Godly concept, until they penetrate our awareness before prayers. This enables us to pray in joy.[71]

Word Sparks — And the meditation leading to this divine love corresponds to Vayiven — "they built" (ויבן), from the verse 'They built the altar' — which is related to the word hitbonenut, or "meditation." (Torat Shmuel 5633/1873, Vol 1, p. 294)

HODU

PRAYING LIKE FIRE AND WATER

אָנֹכִי יְיָ אֱלֹהֶיךָ הַמַּעַלְךָ מֵאֶרֶץ מִצְרָיִם,
הַרְחֶב פִּיךָ וַאֲמַלְאֵהוּ:
אַשְׁרֵי הָעָם שֶׁכָּכָה־לּוֹ, אַשְׁרֵי הָעָם שֶׁיְיָ אֱלֹהָיו:
וַאֲנִי בְּחַסְדְּךָ בָטַחְתִּי יָגֵל לִבִּי בִּישׁוּעָתֶךָ,
אָשִׁירָה לַיְיָ כִּי גָמַל עָלָי:

מִזְמוֹר שִׁיר חֲנֻכַּת הַבַּיִת לְדָוִד:
אֲרוֹמִמְךָ יְיָ כִּי דִלִּיתָנִי, וְלֹא שִׂמַּחְתָּ אֹיְבַי לִי:
יְיָ אֱלֹהָי, שִׁוַּעְתִּי אֵלֶיךָ וַתִּרְפָּאֵנִי:
יְיָ הֶעֱלִיתָ מִן שְׁאוֹל נַפְשִׁי, חִיִּיתַנִי מִיָּרְדִי בוֹר:
זַמְּרוּ לַיְיָ חֲסִידָיו, וְהוֹדוּ לְזֵכֶר קָדְשׁוֹ:

רוח שבנפש
הודאה פרטי
יראת אלקים
יראה תתאה
עולם העשיה (חב"ד)

❝ There are two types of refinement of the soul. The first occurs with a struggle — similar to a fight between two wrestlers until one is victorious. The second takes place peacefully, as happened to King Solomon...who did not need to fight wars at all." (Sefer Maamorim 5655/1895 of the Rebbe Rashab, pp. 105-107)[72]

> The divine soul is enclothed within the animal soul in order to refine it. This entails a struggle, as the divine soul makes contact with the positive elements of the animal soul and strives to elevate them. At the same time, the negative elements of the animal soul put up a struggle in order to remain relevant. That is why the Zohar declares, "The hour of prayer is an hour of battle."

> The struggle to refine the animal soul reaches its apex during prayer. This is when we are able to illuminate the animal soul and expose it to Godly concepts through meditation. The positive elements of the animal soul then ascend above, but the negative elements put up a fight for survival. We experience this struggle when coarse or negative thoughts arise, disturbing our concentration as we are praying.

Ruach shb'nefesh
Particular
   Acknowledgment
Fear (Reverence)
Lower Fear
World of *Asiya*

I am the Lord, Your God, Who has raised you up out of the land of Egypt, open your mouth wide [state your requests] and I will fulfill them.
Happy is the nation that so exists, happy is the nation that the Lord is their God.
And I will feel secure in Your kindness, my heart rejoices in Your salvation, I sing to the Lord since He has been kind to me.

A PSALM, A SONG OF DEDICATION OF THE TEMPLE, by David.
I exalt You, Lord, for You uplifted me, and did not permit my enemies to rejoice over me.
Lord, I cried out to You, and You healed me.
Lord, You have elevated my soul from the grave, enlivened me to keep me from falling into the pit.
Sing to the Lord, all His pious ones, and acknowledge His holy name.

📖 *Within the Words*

During meditation, we should strive to shine as much Godly illumination upon our animal soul as possible. Ideally, intense levels of Godly illumination should totally overwhelm any resistance coming from the animal soul. But, if not, we need not be overly concerned if the animal soul puts up a fight, sending coarse thoughts to disturb our concentration during prayers. If that occurs, we should ignore such thoughts and continue our meditation with even more intensity.[73]

Word Sparks
"Know the God of your fathers, and serve Him with a complete heart." When we delve in depth into Torah and prayer, 'to see the Godliness in the word,' since we ourselves are also created from Godliness, we are therefore empowered to detect it in the creation...this leads to perfected Godly service..." (Torat Shmuel 5636/1876 of the Rebbe Maharash, pp. 415-416 in the summaries of the Rebbe Rashab).

HODU

כִּי רֶגַע בְּאַפּוֹ, חַיִּים בִּרְצוֹנוֹ, בָּעֶרֶב יָלִין בֶּכִי, וְלַבֹּקֶר רִנָּה:
וַאֲנִי אָמַרְתִּי בְשַׁלְוִי, בַּל אֶמּוֹט לְעוֹלָם:
יְיָ בִּרְצוֹנְךָ הֶעֱמַדְתָּה לְהַרְרִי עֹז,
הִסְתַּרְתָּ פָנֶיךָ הָיִיתִי נִבְהָל:
אֵלֶיךָ יְיָ אֶקְרָא, וְאֶל אֲדֹנָי אֶתְחַנָּן:
מַה בֶּצַע בְּדָמִי בְּרִדְתִּי אֶל שָׁחַת,
הֲיוֹדְךָ עָפָר הֲיַגִּיד אֲמִתֶּךָ:
שְׁמַע יְיָ וְחָנֵּנִי, יְיָ הֱיֵה עֹזֵר לִי:
הָפַכְתָּ מִסְפְּדִי לְמָחוֹל לִי, פִּתַּחְתָּ שַׂקִּי וַתְּאַזְּרֵנִי שִׂמְחָה:

רוח שבנפש
הודאה פרטי
יראת אלקים
יראה תתאה
עולם העשיה (חב״ד)

"The ladder of prayer, which stands on the ground while its head reaches into the heavens, has four rungs." (*Sefer Hasichot 5706-10/1946-50* of the *Rebbe Rayatz*, pp. 143-145)[74]

The four rungs of the ladder correspond to the four worlds — *Asiya*, *Yetzira*, *Bria* and *Atzilut*. *Asiya* is the world of action, in which physical creation conceals Godliness. *Yetzira* is the world of formation, of spiritual archetypes and general templates of creation, also known as "angels." *Bria* is the world of "possibility of creation," or pure substance, before it adopts any form. All these three worlds seem detached from Godliness, existing as if disconnected from His infinite light (however, this is only in our perception, but not in reality). *Atzilut* is the world of the ten emanations of Godliness, also known as the *sephirot*, which are like ten rays of light connected to their source in His infinite light.

The World of *Asiya* corresponds to the beginning of our prayers, from before *Hodu* until (but not including) *Baruch She'Amar*. The World of *Yetzira* corresponds to the *pesukei dezimra*, from *Baruch She'Amar* through *Yishtabach*. The World of *Bria* extends from *Barchu* up to the *Shemonah Esreh*. The World of *Atzilut* (where we are one and united with Godliness) corresponds to the *Shemonah Esreh*.

Ruach shb'nefesh
Particular
   Acknowledgment
Fear (Reverence)
Lower Fear
World of *Asiya*

His wrath lasts but a moment,
He wishes long life for us; we fall asleep
in tears and awaken with rejoicing.

And I in my self-satisfaction said, "I will never falter."

Lord, by Your will, You established mountains of strength, then You concealed Your countenance, and I was taken aback.

To You, Lord, I call,
and to the Lord I supplicate.

What profit is there in my blood; in my descent to the grave? Can the dust acknowledge You, can it tell of Your truth?

Listen to me, Lord, and be gracious to me;
Lord, come to my aid.

You have transformed my eulogy into a dance for me, You loosened my sackcloth and girded me with happiness.

📖 *Within the Words*

The four rungs of prayer also correspond to the four soul levels and to the four meditative states. During the prayers prior to *Baruch She'Amar*, we exist on the soul level of *nefesh*, corresponding to "lower fear" of God (based upon awareness of divine reward and punishment). Then, during *pesukei dezimra*, from *Baruch She'Amar* through *Yishtabach*, we are on the level of *ruach*, corresponding to the lower love of God (based on awareness of Godliness with creation). From *Barchu* through the *Shema*, we are on the soul level of *neshama* and we experience a higher love (based upon Godliness that transcends creation). And during *Shemonah Esreh*, we are on the level of *chaya* and at times *yechida*, as we experience higher fear or awe of God.

HODU

לְמַעַן יְזַמֶּרְךָ כָבוֹד וְלֹא יִדֹּם, יְיָ אֱלֹהַי לְעוֹלָם אוֹדֶךָּ:

יְיָ מֶלֶךְ, יְיָ מָלָךְ, יְיָ יִמְלֹךְ לְעוֹלָם וָעֶד

יְיָ מֶלֶךְ, יְיָ מָלָךְ, יְיָ יִמְלֹךְ לְעוֹלָם וָעֶד

וְהָיָה יְיָ לְמֶלֶךְ עַל כָּל הָאָרֶץ

בַּיּוֹם הַהוּא יִהְיֶה יְיָ אֶחָד וּשְׁמוֹ אֶחָד:

הוֹשִׁיעֵנוּ יְיָ אֱלֹהֵינוּ, וְקַבְּצֵנוּ מִן הַגּוֹיִם לְהֹדוֹת לְשֵׁם קָדְשֶׁךָ לְהִשְׁתַּבֵּחַ בִּתְהִלָּתֶךָ:

בָּרוּךְ יְיָ אֱלֹהֵי יִשְׂרָאֵל מִן הָעוֹלָם וְעַד הָעוֹלָם וְאָמַר כָּל הָעָם אָמֵן. הַלְלוּיָהּ:

כֹּל הַנְּשָׁמָה תְּהַלֵּל יָהּ הַלְלוּיָהּ:

רוח שבנפש
הודאה פרטי
יראת אלקים
יראה תתאה
עולם העשיה (חב״ד)

❝ **And there was a great and strong wind, [capable of] disintegrating mountains and shattering rocks...[but]** *Havaya* **was not in the wind. And after the wind there was a noise but** *Havaya* **was not in the noise, and after the noise, there was fire, but** *Havaya* **was not in the fire, and after the fire there was a still small voice."** (1 *Melachim* 19:11-12)[75]

As we ascend the ladder of prayer, we pass through various levels of concealment, called *klipot* ("shells") which are so called because they hide the Godliness within them. They conceal levels of spirituality that we are not yet ready to experience. These *klipot* are described as "wind, noise, and fire." Ultimately our prayers bring us to the "still small voice" of the *Shemonah Esreh*.

On our journey up the ladder of prayer, we encounter various forms of resistance. While reciting the *pesukei dezimra*, we run into "wind" — these are the extraneous thoughts that distract us from focusing upon Godliness as we meditate upon creation from nothing to something. After *Barchu*, we encounter "noise," which is the inner turmoil that we experience when we know there is something beyond us, but we are unable to come to terms with it. During the blessings prior to the *Shema* as well as during the *Shema*, we experience "fire"

Ruach shb'nefesh
Particular
 Acknowledgment
Fear (Reverence)
Lower Fear
World of *Asiya*

So that Your glory will sing Your praise and not be silent, Lord, my God, I will praise You forever…

Rise and remain standing until יְהִי כָבוֹד

The Lord reigns, the Lord reigned,
the Lord will reign forever and ever.

The Lord reigns, the Lord reigned,
the Lord will reign forever and ever.

And the Lord will be King over all the earth; on that day, the Lord will be one and His name one.

Save us, Lord, our God and gather us from among the nations, in order to praise Your holy name and to revel in Your praises.

Blessed is the Lord, God of Israel, forever and ever.
And let the entire nation say
"Amen, praise the Lord."

Let every soul praise the Lord. Praise the Lord.

---

as we grasp the nature of Godliness both within and beyond us, and ignite with love and fear of God. "Noise" and "fire" affect us internally, before we break through to the full experience of cleaving to God during the *Shemonah Esreh* (when we hear the "still small voice"). (*Sefer Maamorim* 5668/1908 of the Rebbe Rashab, p. 116-117, *Besha'ah Shehikdimu* 5672/1912 of the Rashab, Vol 2, p. 819 (Ch 398)[76]

> 📖 *Within the Words*
>
> It is recommended to prepare for meditation in the morning by first learning a Chassidic discourse. We should take time to ponder the concepts contained in the discourse, and integrate them into our intellectual and emotional awareness. Only afterward should we begin to pray. The words of the Siddur come alive with meaning as we pass through the various stages of prayer described above.

HODU

לַמְנַצֵּחַ בִּנְגִינֹת מִזְמוֹר שִׁיר:

אֱלֹהִים, יְחָנֵּנוּ וִיבָרְכֵנוּ, יָאֵר פָּנָיו אִתָּנוּ סֶלָה:

לָדַעַת בָּאָרֶץ דַּרְכֶּךָ, לְדַעַת בְּכָל גּוֹיִם יְשׁוּעָתֶךָ:

יוֹדוּךָ עַמִּים אֱלֹהִים. יוֹדוּךָ עַמִּים כֻּלָּם:

יִשְׂמְחוּ וִירַנְּנוּ לְאֻמִּים, כִּי תִשְׁפֹּט עַמִּים מִישׁוֹר, וּלְאֻמִּים בָּאָרֶץ תַּנְחֵם סֶלָה:

יוֹדוּךָ עַמִּים אֱלֹהִים, יוֹדוּךָ עַמִּים כֻּלָּם:

אֶרֶץ נָתְנָה יְבוּלָהּ, יְבָרְכֵנוּ אֱלֹהִים אֱלֹהֵינוּ:

יְבָרְכֵנוּ אֱלֹהִים, וְיִירְאוּ אוֹתוֹ כָּל אַפְסֵי אָרֶץ:

רוח שבנפש
הודאה פרטי
יראת אלקים
יראה תתאה
עולם העשיה (חב״ד)

CHASSIDIC INSIGHTS

(continued from p. 84)

STATE OF MIND (within *yirah tata'ah*/ "lower fear")	SOUL — LEVEL	WORLD	PRAYER SEGMENT
Kabalat ohl malchut shamayim ("acceptance of the yoke of Heaven")	Nefesh	Malchut of Asiya	Modeh Ani, morning blessings, Adon Olam, the Akeida
Yirat chait ("Fear of Transgression")	Nefesh	Netzach and Hod of Asiya	Kriat Shema (prior to *tefila*)
Yirat Elokim ("Fear of God")	Nefesh	Gevura of Asiya	Korbanot ("sacrifices")
Yirat Elokim ("Reverence")	Nefesh	Chabad of Asiya	Hodu

(continued on p. 93)

Ruach shb'nefesh
Particular
 Acknowledgment
Fear (Reverence)
Lower Fear
World of *Asiya*

F OR THE ORCHESTRAL CONDUCTOR, A SONG WITH instruments, a psalm.

God, grant us grace and bless us,
shine Your countenance among us forever.

To inform the earth of Your ways,
and the nations of Your salvations.

People submit to You, God,
all peoples submit to You.

The nations will rejoice and sing,
for You will judge the people justly
and guide the nations of earth forever.

People accede to You, God,
all peoples accede to You.

The earth gave its produce, may God,
our God bless us.

God bless us, and may people from all corners
of the globe be in awe of Him.

CHASSIDIC INSIGHTS

(continued from p. 92)

ohl malchut shamayim) corresponds to the *sephira* of *malchut* within *Asiya*. Fear of transgression (*yirat chait*) is associated with the *sephirot* of *netzach* and *hod* of *Asiya*. Fear of God (*yirat Elokim*) is associated with *gevura* of *Asiya*, and reverence of God is associated with *chabad* within *Asiya*. On the facing page is a table summarizing the elements associated with *Yirah Tata'ah* ("Lower Fear"):

(continued on p. 94)

HODU

PRAYING LIKE FIRE AND WATER

פסוקי דזמרה

לְשֵׁם יִחוּד קֻדְשָׁא בְּרִיךְ הוּא וּשְׁכִינְתֵּהּ לְיַחֲדָא שֵׁם י"ה בו"ה בְּיִחוּדָא שְׁלִים בְּשֵׁם כָּל יִשְׂרָאֵל:

בָּרוּךְ שֶׁאָמַר וְהָיָה הָעוֹלָם:

אר"י: רדל"א דאצילות ממלא כל עולמים אהבת עולם (כמים) רוח (חיות העולם) עולם היצירה

> **(Meditation #1)** In order to encourage ascent from below, it is necessary to provide stimulus from above — this is the general purpose of *Baruch She'Amar...*" (*Maamorei Admor Hazaken* on *Maamorei rz"l*, p. 349)[77]

Spiritual stimulation comes in the form of high illumination from above, from prior to the *tzimtzum* ("great contraction") of His infinite light. This spirituality is so high that it is capable of illuminating even our physical world. Even though prayer is a process of ascent from below to above, it is necessary to initiate the process by shining a high illumination from above. The initial illumination shows us what to strive for and encourages us to continue the process of elevation during the *pesukei dezimra*.

Before prayers is a good time to meditate on the entire *seder hishtalshelut* ("chain or hierarchy of creation"), in order to gain a sense of the extremely high levels of spiritual illumination that are available to us during prayers.[78]

📖 *Within the Words*

We should recite *Baruch She'Amar* while softly singing to ourselves…it was composed by the *Anshei Knesset Hagedola* ("Men of the Great Assembly") during the early part of the second Temple period, according to a "note that fell from above" with the words of the prayer written upon it.[79]

--- CHASSIDIC INSIGHTS ---

(continued from p. 93)

Next in our prayers, we come to the section called *pesukei dezimra* ("verses of song"). This section begins with the prayer *Baruch She'Amar* and continues through to *Yishtabach*, just before *Barchu*. During this

(continued on p. 96)

Ari: Radl'a (A"K)
Immanent Godliness
Lower love (water)
Ruach (vitality of creation)
World of Yetzira

VERSES OF PRAISE

For the sake of unity of the Holy One with His holy presence (the *Shechina*), in order to join the name *yud-kay* with the *vav-kay* [of His name] in total unity in the name of all Israel.

BLESSED BE HE WHO SAID, AND THE UNIVERSE CAME into being,

> **(Meditation #2) Within the word *Baruch*, we find two meanings. One is passive, as when something is "blessed" from its source…the other is active, as when we offer our blessings to another person…"**
> (*Pirush Hamilot* of the Mitteler Rebbe, ch. 98, p. 62c)[80]

Baruch She'Amar alludes to the highest spiritual level — A"K — wherein all of creation (time and space) exists in one creative point. Following *Baruch*, the next words of the prayer — *She'Amar vehaya haolam* ("He who said and the universe came into being") — form the acrostic *shaveh* ("equal"). On this spiritual level, all is equal, and all is both blessed and capable of extending its blessing to the levels below it.

By taking the end of a plant and bending it into the ground, a farmer may increase vegetation on his farm. This process is called *lehavrich*, a term which shares its Hebrew root with *baruch* ("blessed"). Since the original plant was successful ("blessed"), it is capable of extending its success ("blessings") to the new plant as well. In the same vein, if we dig near the source of a well and create a new source of water (*breicha*, or "pool"), it is both blessed from its original source and capable of supplying water ("blessings") to others. This occurs on all spiritual levels alluded to in *Baruch She'Amar*. All are both "blessed" from above and capable of extending blessing to levels below.

📖 *Within the Words*

Each of the thirteen times that we mention the word *baruch* during *Baruch She'Amar*, we are both blessed from a specific spiritual level and capable of passing the blessing on to lower levels.

בָּרוּךְ הוּא,

אר"י: גלגלתא
דא"א
ממלא כל עולמים
אהבת עולם
(כמים)
רוח (חיות העולם)
עולם היצירה

❝ **(Meditation #3) The mind has the power to grasp wisdom or illumination in many forms. All intellectual revelation has a source and origin in the level that we call** *maskil* **("creative thought") that is the source of intellect and initiates all intellectual activity."** (Alter Rebbe's Siddur with Chassidut, Page 78)[81]

> Our minds work on many different levels, some of which we are aware of and others of which we are not. Our unconscious thought processes are comparable to the level of *Keter* ("crown"). Our conscious thought processes begin at the level of *chochma* ("wisdom"). We know that *Keter* must exist because as we experience conscious thought, we also sense that it comes from somewhere — it has a source. As the source of consciousness, *Keter* is called *maskil*. There is yet a third level, of which we have no awareness whatsoever. It is called *radla* ("the unknown and unknowable head").

CHASSIDIC INSIGHTS

(continued from p. 94)

section of prayers, our state of mind progresses from lower fear of God (*yirah tata'ah*) to lower "entry level" love of God. Upon reciting the first prayer — *Baruch She'Amar* — we begin to meditate upon the nature of creation from "nothing to something." *Baruch She'Amar* itself is said to be a prayer that "fell" from the heavens (see *Shulchan Aruch Harav 51:2*). Since it comes from such a high place, it is a good introduction to the rest of our prayers, which require much labor and effort on our part, from below. The best way to inspire us to labor from below during prayers is with a high revelation from above, and that is what *Baruch She'Amar* provides. The main topic of *Baruch She'Amar* is how the universe was created, spontaneously and effortlessly by God (*Baruch She'Amar* — "Blessed be He Who said and the universe came into being"). Nevertheless, the rest of *pesukei dezimra* also alludes to the details of creation from nothing to something and requires that we invest time and effort in focusing on creation ex-nihilo. There are

(continued on p. 97)

B LESSED BE HE.

Ari: Gulgulta (Keter of Arich)
Immanent Godliness
Lower love (water)
Ruach (vitality of creation)
World of Yetzira

🐇 Meditation is an ongoing process of bringing the unconscious into our conscious awareness. We are blessed with a divine soul that is connected to the highest, most essential levels of Godliness — it is up to us to refine our awareness to bring these levels down into our consciousness.

📖 *Within the Words*

Near the beginning of *Baruch She'Amar*, we say *Baruch Hu*, "Blessed be He…" (in third person) as if referring to one who is not present or listening as we speak. This corresponds to *maskil* (within *Keter*) — the hidden source of intellect. We know it exists, but we do not experience it directly. As we progress through the prayer, we finally say *Baruch Atah* — "Blessed are You" (in second person) referring to Godliness that has descended so that we experience it directly.

CHASSIDIC INSIGHTS

(continued from p. 96)

many details in this meditation. The meditation must be applied to specific objects and must not remain in the realm of theoretic principles. As applied to this section of prayers, this means that we should meditate upon the principles of creation from nothing to something as we consider specific objects and classes of created objects.

The category of divine love associated with the *pesukei dezimra* is called "love like water." It is a soothing and calm sort of love (like water that "flows" over and around us) that results from meditation upon *memalle kol olmin*, or immanent Godliness that permeates and fills the creation. It is comparable to the love that siblings have for one another, or that children possess for their parents and vice versa. It is a love that is always present, but not always conscious. We may go for extended periods of time without "missing" or thinking consciously of our brothers or sisters, for example, but the minute that we are back together with our siblings, or parents and children, there is a

(continued on p. 98)

בָּרוּךְ אוֹמֵר וְעוֹשֶׂה,

אר"י: מוחא סתימאה
דא"א
ממלא כל עולמים
אהבת עולם (כמים)
רוח (חיות העולם)
עולם היצירה

> **(Meditation #4)** The sages determined that we should say *Baruch She'Amar* before *pesukei dezimra* so that we should become aware of the concept of 'He Who spoke and the universe came into being' … and we should become excited by it." (*Likutei Torah* of the Alter Rebbe, *Ve'etchanan* 2a)[82]

The thirteen times that we say the word *Baruch* in this prayer correspond to the "thirteen strands of the beard," which signify Godly illumination that descends to us from *Keter* (above *Atzilut*) to *chochma* (of *Atzilut*). Since the divine illumination from this level is so high, it can only descend to us in a contracted form, which we call "hairs." Hair is external compared to the brain, but it is attached to the head, which imparts a high spiritual level.

--- **CHASSIDIC INSIGHTS** ---

(continued from p. 97)

warm and relaxed familiarity that permeates the relationship. This is the kind of love that results from contemplation upon how God fills and permeates the creation. We may not be consciously aware of it at all times, but when we return to focus on it, we are filled with a warm and familiar love of God. This is also the natural love that is associated with the soul level of *ruach*, or "spirit consciousness." Here is what the *Kuntres Ha'avoda* (Page 13-15 in "Love like Fire and Water") has to say about it:

""The love and fear that become revealed in the heart as a result of meditation on the greatness of God and which cause us to truly cleave to Him with heartfelt desire, are called *ruach*. The meditation that leads to *ruach* focuses upon Godliness that can be readily grasped with the intellect. That is, this meditation focuses on the Godly light and energy that is en-clothed in the universe to create and maintain it. In general, it is called *ohr memalle* ("immanent light'), which is well grasped by the human intellect…*avoda* (service of God in meditation and prayer) on this level requires "labor of the soul and labor of the flesh." It necessitates intellectual acumen in order to properly grasp

(continued on p. 99)

סידור עם חסידות – שחרית

Ari: Mocha Stima (Chochma of Arich)

Immanent Godliness

Lower love (water)

Ruach (vitality of creation)

World of *Yetzira*

BLESSED BE HE WHO SAYS AND ACCOMPLISHES,

Hair is not vitally important to the head or the body (indeed, when we cut our hair, we do not feel it). Similarly, the divine influence that descends to us from above, creating our awareness of transcendent spirituality, is in the form of a mere ray or reflection ("hair") of its spiritual source. The essential divine source of revelation is not in any way changed when it becomes revealed below.

> *Within the Words*
>
> That God merely "spoke" and the entire universe came into existence should be a source of true amazement. Each of the twelve times that we say the word *Baruch* is associated with a special spiritual level that brings this concept down to our awareness, and the thirteenth time brings down a general form of all the previous levels.

CHASSIDIC INSIGHTS

(continued from p. 98)

and internalize Godly concepts through meditation. We must not be satisfied with general superficial knowledge alone. Rather, we must develop a deep and comprehensive knowledge of the details of these concepts. For this, we must focus our concentration on the subject until it is clear in our minds and experienced in our hearts. By so doing, we arouse true love of God within and then we will develop a strong desire to cling to the One above."

It is worthwhile to note that even though the goal is to develop conscious feelings of love and fear in our heart, nevertheless the path that leads to such emotions is intellectual. We must think, in order to feel. The path of *ruach* meditation requires us to meditate on Godly concepts in order to develop feelings for Godliness and spirituality within our heart. In truth, the emotions are already present, latent in our hearts. They were implanted in our "genes" by our forefathers; Abraham implanted love of God, Yitzhak bequeathed us fear of God, and Yaakov granted us *rachamim*, or mercy upon our soul that came from such a high place to become enclothed in a physical

(continued on p. 100)

בָּרוּךְ גּוֹזֵר וּמְקַיֵּם,

אר"י: חכמה דאצילות
ממלא כל עולמים
אהבת עולם (כמים)
רוח (חיות העולם)
עולם היצירה

❝ (Meditation #5) The main factor [contributing to our spiritual illumination] comes from the ten *sephirot* of the four worlds and descends via the twelve tribes." (*Sefer Maamorim 5673* in the book *Maamorim 5672-6/1912-16* of the Rebbe Rashab, pp. 80-81)[83]

The twelve tribes correspond to the twelve *alexonim* ("diagonal lines") connecting the *sephirot* of *Atzilut* with one another. The tribes are like a "chariot" — a vehicle "transporting" Godliness — from the World of *Atzilut* down to the lower three worlds of *Bria, Yetzira* and *Asiya*. The twelve times that we mention the word *Baruch* during *Baruch She'Amar* correspond to the twelve tribes, and the thirteenth corresponds to the tribe of Levi [who lived dispersed among all of the other tribes].

--- CHASSIDIC INSIGHTS ---

(continued from p. 99)

body. Nevertheless, it is our intense meditation that induces these latent emotions to become conscious and revealed in our mind and heart.

Within the soul level of *ruach* and the prayers of *pesukei dezimra*, there is a second, more elevated path that is called "gazing upon the glory of the King." Here is what it says about this meditative path in "Love like Fire and Water" (Page 26-27): "Elsewhere, it is explained that the *pesukei d'zimra* consists of exaltations of matters beyond intellect. This is like the person who praises a king in his majesty, even though he has no grasp whatsoever of the king's true greatness. Nevertheless the sheer act of praying on this level creates an "impression from without" on the person praying that uplifts and elevates his soul to a higher level. This does not contradict what was explained previously, that *ruach* corresponds to love of God based upon intellectual meditation revealed in the heart. There are several approaches to the soul level of *ruach*, and even the approach described above ("Gazing on the glory of the King") does not imply a total lack of intellect during meditation during the *pesukei dezimra*. Rather, the general topic of meditation associated with *pesukei dezimra* is creation from nothing

(continued on p. 101)

BLESSED BE HE WHO DECREES AND FULFILLS,

Ari: Chochma of Atzilut
Immanent Godliness
Lower love (water)
Ruach (vitality of creation)
World of Yetzira

While our three patriarchs (and four matriarchs) bequeathed to us our natural emotions of love, fear and mercy, the tribes transmitted all of the myriad nuances of spiritual awareness and revelation that have descended to the Jewish people since their time. From them, we have inherited the entire spectrum of spirituality. The influence of the tribes is comparable to the power of germination in the soil, giving rise to all kinds of herbs and grains, etc.

Within the Words

Just as with meditation #2, the point of this meditation is to gain awareness of the amazing nature of God's creative power. We should be "blessed" with such awareness — that is, it should become part of our consciousness. Each time that we say *Baruch* corresponds to a specific level of awareness as well as to one of the tribes, from where the awareness descends to us.

CHASSIDIC INSIGHTS

(continued from p. 100)

to something, and this is a process that is in essence beyond the ability of mortal man to grasp. Even awareness of the existence of this process is beyond us. Nonetheless, within the process are to be found several ideas, in particular those concerning the Godly light and energy that en-clothe themselves in creation in order to enliven it. This is the *avoda* of "coming to love the Lord your God because He is your life…"

From this passage, we glean that while it is impossible to fully internalize the process of creation, nevertheless we can grasp some of the details that are involved. In a *sicha* ("talk"), the Lubavitcher Rebbe outlines the steps involved (from *Torat Menachem*, vol 16, page 4, also appearing in *Sha'arei Tefila* from *Heichal Menachem*, page 295):

1. We must first of all understand that the creation occurred from nothing to something. The "proofs" of this are that a) No object

(continued on p. 102)

VERSES OF PRAISE

בָּרוּךְ עוֹשֶׂה בְרֵאשִׁית,

אר"י: בינה דאצילות
ממלא כל עולמים
אהבת עולם (כמים)
רוח (חיות העולם)
עולם היצירה

> **(Meditation #6) With one utterance, God created the universe and in His goodness He constantly renews the creation every instant."**
> (*Likutei Torah* of the Alter Rebbe, *Shir HaShirim* 41d)[84]

There are two modes of information flow. In one mode, the information flows down from one level to the next, within range of each other. The receptive level has some awareness and cognizance of the giving side. This mode of transfer is called *ilah v'alul* (roughly translated, "cause and effect"). The second mode occurs when the transfer is between two levels that are out of range of one another. The receiver has no awareness nor concept of the giver. This mode is called *b'ein aroch* ("out of range").

--- CHASSIDIC INSIGHTS ---

(continued from p. 101)

can create itself, b) Creatures are compound entities, and therefore creation must have originated from an unlimited source that is capable of combining and maintaining opposing elements, and c) All creatures ultimately meet their demise, and this is a proof that they are limited, the product of an unlimited force that creates from nothing to something (all these "proofs" are found in the *Sefer Hachakira* of the *Tzemach Tzedek*).

2. Having been convinced that creation occurs from nothing to something, we need to next understand something about the nature of creation. First of all, creation is a result of the *tzimtzum,* or great contraction of God's infinite illumination. Only after the infinite light becomes greatly contracted, is it possible for the creation of the physical universe to occur.

3. Since ultimately, creation is a product of His contracted infinite light, it occurs from a spiritual "distance." That is, there is an infinite force working from afar in order to create the physical universe. At the same time, that force is invested in and permeates the physical objects that it creates. So, there is an inherent tension and contradiction — to the human mind at any rate — regarding the

(continued on p. 103)

BLESSED BE HE WHO ACCOMPLISHES CREATION.

Ari: Bina of Atzilut
Immanent Godliness
Lower love (water)
Ruach (vitality of creation)
World of Yetzira

Meditation is not merely a progression from one logical step to the next, although linear reasoning also plays an important role. Meditation requires us to develop sensitivity to spiritual levels that are totally beyond us.

📖 Within the Words

When reciting the prayer, *Baruch She'Amar*, we might think that the descent of creative power occurred as in the first mode of transfer, between related levels. That is, we might entertain the notion that it occurred in a manner similar to a teacher educating a student, or a father educating a son. The words of the prayer, "Blessed be He who spoke and the universe came into existence" indicate otherwise. The universe "came into existence" spontaneously and automatically. Creation happened between two levels that are totally unrelated, and out of range of one another, since the created world is limited while He is unlimited.

CHASSIDIC INSIGHTS

(continued from p. 102)

process of creation. It is both impossibly distant (because God is transcendent) and yet unavoidably intimate (because God is everywhere in His creation). This inherent contradiction is what arouses our love and awe of God. It is impossible to reconcile according to human intellect, and yet it is unavoidably true.

4. Nevertheless, we may understand the process in human terms by way of an illustration. When we decide to move a limb, the decision is not taken by the limb itself. We think about it and make a decision, but our hand, for example, does not move merely because it decided to move itself. The decision is an act of will that occurs from our mind. And yet, without the local participation of our hand, it will not move. So, there is a "distant" (willful) component to movement, and yet, the actual movement will not occur without the "local" cooperation of the hand. Similarly, the Godly will to

(continued on p. 104)

בָּרוּךְ מְרַחֵם עַל הָאָרֶץ,

אר"י: ז"א דאצילות
ממלא כל עולמים
רוח (חיות העולם)
אהבת עולם (כמים)
עולם היצירה

❝ **(Meditation #7)** Only when we fulfill our ultimate desire in a concrete manner are we truly satisfied. Consequently, after we achieve satisfaction, and we revisit our original thesis to compare it with our final result, we ascend mentally by way of *ohr chozer* ('reflected illumination') to review the initial stages of our desire." (*Sha'ar Hatefila*, within *Sha'arei Tshuva* of the Mitteler Rebbe, p. 53, sec. 9)[85]

There are two sets of ten *sephirot* — there are the ten *sephirot* of "direct illumination" (*ohr yashar*) and the ten *sephirot* of "reflected illumination" (*ohr chozer*). That is because divine revelation arrives via one of these two possible paths. When it arrives as a result of meditation, as we contemplate God's creation and excitement pervades our mind and heart, this is the path of *ohr yashar*, or "direct illumination." But, when we are not successful, and we pause and return to our original desire to access Godliness, we may suddenly attain clarity. This is the path of *ohr chozer*, or "reflected illumination."[86]

The primal "scream" of the soul in distress, desiring Godliness, has the power to bring us directly in contact with the soul's source. This is the path of *ohr chozer*, or "reflected illumination."[87] To illustrate, the air temperature close to the earth is hotter than in the upper atmosphere. This is strange, since the upper atmosphere is closer to the sun and should therefore be hotter. But, as sun rays strike the earth, they "bounce," and the resulting energy radiates extra warmth. This parable helps illustrates *ohr chozer*. At times it is

--- **CHASSIDIC INSIGHTS** ---

(continued from p. 103)

create acts from afar, yet simultaneously, every specific creature is dependent upon the Godliness that is invested in it.

5. We are aware of the energy invested within ourselves. We are conscious of the vitality that courses through our veins and enlivens us. But, we are not usually aware that this vitality is Godly. It is only through avid meditation that we become aware of the divine origins of the vitality within, and this is the goal of meditation

(continued on p. 105)

Ari: Z"a of Atzilut
Immanent Godliness
Ruach (vitality of creation)
Lower love (water)
World of *Yetzira*

Blessed be he who has compassion on the earth,

more effective to stop, pause and even "scream" (mentally) after we reach a "dead end" during meditation and re-establish contact with our original goals. Then we may attain clarity.

> 📖 *Within the Words*
>
> (This is an advanced meditation — for definitions of soul levels, see ch. 1 of *Love like Fire and Water*). The first five times that we say *Baruch* during *Baruch She'Amar* represent *ohr yashar* descending to us through the five different soul levels. As we say *Baruch She'Amar*, the *yechida* descends to us. As we say *Baruch Hu*, the *chaya* descends. During *Baruch omer v'oseh*, the *neshama* descends to us. During *Baruch gozer u'mekayem*, the *ruach* descends. And during *Boruch oseh bereishit*, *nefesh* descends. These are all revelations of *memalle kol olmin* ("immanent spirituality"). The next five times that we say *Baruch* represent transcendent levels of the soul, with which we ascend via *ohr chozer* ("reflected illumination"). First, we say *Baruch merachem al ha'aretz*, representing the transcendent illumination of *nefesh*. Then, *Baruch merachem al habriyot*, representing the transcendent level of *ruach*. *Baruch meshalem sachar tov* represents *neshama*, *Baruch chai la'ad* represents the *chaya*, and finally *Baruch podeh u'matzil* represents *yechida*. These are all revelations of *sovev kol olmin* ("transcendent illumination") that arrive via *ohr chozer*. Following these ten utterances, *Baruch Shemo* is an all-inclusive, supremely transcendent level of illumination.

VERSES OF PRAISE

CHASSIDIC INSIGHTS

(continued from p. 104)

throughout *pesukei dezimra*. Awareness of the divine origins of creation and of our own selves is what arouses our innate love of God.

Looking more in detail at how we may achieve this level of love of God, we find in the beginning of Ch. 4 of "Love like Fire and Water" (Page 86-87), the Rebbe Rashab says, "Love like water is associated

(continued on p. 106)

בָּרוּךְ מְרַחֵם עַל הַבְּרִיּוֹת,

אר"י: מלכות
דאצילות
ממלא כל עולמים
אהבת עולם (כמים)
רוח (חיות העולם)
עולם היצירה

> **(Meditation #8)** When we meditate on Godly topics ... our ultimate goal is the arousal of conscious love and fear of God in our heart ... And this is the entire purpose of man in the world, and the reason for the descent of his soul into his body." (*Besha'ah Shehikdimu 5672/1912* of the Rebbe Rashab, vol. 1, pp. 129-132, 293)[88]

Just as there are four specific worlds of *Atzilut, Bria, Yetzira,* and *Asiya (ABY"A)* culminating in creation, so there are four "general" worlds of *ABY"A*, that culminate in the emanation of the ten *sephirot*. "Specific worlds" lead to the creation of the physical world, while the higher "general worlds" lead to the emanation of the ten *sephirot* in *Atzilut*. The infinite light that precedes the *tzimtzum* ("great contraction) corresponds to the "general" World of *Atzilut*. The contracted light that shines after the *tzimtzum* (*A'K* — all ten *sephirot* in one point) corresponds to the "general" World of *Bria*. The next spiritual level (*Tohu*, or *Keter* of *Atzilut* — ten *sephirot* in ten vessels) corresponds to the "general world of *Yetzira*. Finally, the ten *sephirot* in ten interacting vessels in the world of *Atzilut*, correspond to the general world of *Asiya*.

———— **CHASSIDIC INSIGHTS** ————

(continued from p. 105)

with closeness to Godliness. It results from meditation on the Godly light and energy en-clothed in the worlds, as written "And You enliven them all..." (*Nehemia* 9:6). Within each and every specific aspect of creation is to be found a Godly light and energy that enlivens it, as it says, "From my flesh, I grasp/see God" (*Job* 19:26). We all experience within ourselves a life-force that vitalizes us. And so it is in the world at large, which is called a macrocosm, as known. By meditating properly, with intellectual understanding, while concentrating deeply, we feel and perceive within ourselves how the world receives its vitality from a Godly light. When we concentrate and focus our attention on this Godly light enlivening the universe, we begin to experience the preciousness and spiritual elevation of Godliness (that is, that Godliness in itself is very desirable and uplifting). This motivates us to unite

(continued on p. 107)

B LESSED BE HE WHO HAS COMPASSION ON THE creatures,

Ar"i: Malchut of Atzilut
Immanent Godliness
Lower love (water)
Ruach (vitality of creation)
World of Yetzira

"Blessed is He who spoke…" — speech comes from the heart, which is the seat of our emotions, rooted in our will. God willed to create something that appeared "outside" and "separate" from Himself — "and the universe came into existence." In Hebrew, this phrase (*vehaya haolam*) begins with the second two letters (*vav-hey*) of God's name, which are often associated with happiness (since the letters represents the achievement of the goal of bringing light down to illuminate the creation). The happiness will take place in the future upon purification of all the holy sparks of this physical world.

Within the Words

(Advanced meditation) The phrase, *Baruch she'amar vehaya haolam* ("Blessed be He who said and the universe came into being") alludes to the very essence of God, who alone has the power to create from nothing to something. Just as the lower spiritual realms are divided into four specific worlds, so the higher realms above *Atzilut* are divided into four "general worlds." *Baruch Hu* ("Blessed be He") refers to His infinite light before the *tzimtzum*, or "general *Atzilut*." *Baruch omer v'oseh* ("Blessed be He who says and accomplishes") refers to A"K, or "general *Bria*" *Baruch gozer u'mekayam* ("Blessed be He who decrees and fulfills") refers to *Keter* of *Atzilut*, or "general *Yetzira*," and *Baruch oseh bereishit* ("Blessed be He who accomplishes the creation") refers to *Atzilut* itself, or "general *Asiya*."

CHASSIDIC INSIGHTS

(continued from p. 106)

our souls with Godliness, such that our entire will and desire is focused on God and nothing else. This love grows stronger when we meditate on the fact that Godliness constitutes the life-force of the universe in general and of our own soul in particular."

At first glance, this seems to be a general meditation upon the divine source that permeates the world. It necessitates a "feel" or sense of Godliness in order to experience its preciousness and desirability.

(continued on p. 108)

בָּרוּךְ מְשַׁלֵּם שָׂכָר טוֹב לִירֵאָיו,
בָּרוּךְ חַי לָעַד וְקַיָּם לָנֶצַח,
בָּרוּךְ פּוֹדֶה וּמַצִּיל,

אר"י: חכמה, ובינה
דבריאה
ממלא כל עולמים
אהבת עולם (כמים)
רוח (חיות העולם)
עולם היצירה

> **(Meditation #9)** The *Radah* (R' David Abudrahram) writes that the prayer *Baruch She'Amar* corresponds to the first of the ten creative utterances with which the world was created — "In the beginning, God created the heavens and the earth." *(Ohel Yoseph Yitzchak on Tehilim, from the Tzemach Tzedek, p. 652)*[89]

> The prayer *Mizmor Letoda*, which follows *Baruch She'Amar*, corresponds to the second creative utterance, "Let there be light." The following psalm, *Yehi kevod* corresponds to the utterance, "Let there be a firmament." Possibly, the reason why many of our morning prayers begin with *Yehi* ("Let there be…") is because they correspond to the ten creative utterances that also begin with *Yehi*. *Yehi* contains the first two letters (*yud-hey*) of God's essential name *Havaya*. Most of the psalms of *pesukei dezimra* also begin with *yud-hey*, found in the word *Halleluyah*. So, there is a correspondence between the ten original creative utterances and the *pesukei dezimra*, beginning with *Baruch She'Amar*. The *yud-hey* alludes to the two highest *sephirot* of *chochma* and *bina*, which provide the added spiritual influence that we seek to bring down to the creation with our prayers.

CHASSIDIC INSIGHTS

(continued from p. 107)

The Rebbe Rashab expands on this (on page 91-93), "There is, though a certain advantage to meditation on Godliness as found in the world. In such meditation, our attachment is to the Godliness within physical objects and not to the physical as such…Therefore, the *avoda* of the One above begins with this love and closeness [based upon meditation on the Godly ray invested in the world], which brings us as well to involvement in Torah and fulfillment of its mitzvot, since in general we desire Godly matters. And in particular, we desire to learn Torah and fulfill its mitzvot, since they are precious to us and we derive vitality from them, since they are Godly."

(continued on p. 109)

Ar"i: Keter, Chochma and *Bina* of *Bria*
Immanent Godliness
Lower love (water)
Ruach (vitality of creation)
World of *Yetzira*

BLESSED BE HE WHO COMPENSATES WELL THOSE who fear Him.

Blessed be He Who lives forever and exists eternally,

Blessed be He Who redeems and rescues,

The words, *Baruch She'Amar* ("Blessed be He who spoke") are all-inclusive and correspond to the first creative utterance (*Bereishit bara*), which is also all-inclusive. That utterance contains the details of all the following nine utterances of creation. (*A"K* — ten *orot* in one *keli*.) The next phrase of the prayer — *Baruch omer ve'oseh* ("Blessed is He Who says and accomplishes...") — alludes to the unfolding details of creation in the remaining nine utterances, each one as stated in the Torah (corresponding to *Keter* — ten *orot* in ten *kelim*). Finally, the phrase, *Baruch oseh bereishit* ("Blessed is He Who makes the creation") alludes to the actual creation, each on its own day (*Atzilut*) — the creation of light on the first day, the creation of land on the second day, etc.[90]

> *Within the Words*
>
> Based upon the *Radah*, the *pesukei dezimra* follow the path of the ten creative utterances, as well as of the ten *sephirot*. If *Baruch She'Amar* corresponds to the first creative utterance, (*Bereishit bara*...), then Psalm 150 (the last of the *pesukei dezimra*)[91] corresponds to the final creative utterance. In terms of the *sephirot*, Psalm 150 then corresponds to *malchut*, the tenth and final *sephira*, which is also the source of creation.

VERSES OF PRAISE

CHASSIDIC INSIGHTS

(continued from p. 108)

Here, we see that the goal of meditation is not only elevation of the soul during prayers, but also connection with God after prayers. The *Kuntres Ha'avoda* tells us that there is an added benefit to meditation that accrues even after our prayers — and that is the desire to connect

(continued on p. 110)

בָּרוּךְ שְׁמוֹ.

אר"י: ז"א דבריאה
ממלא כל עולמים
אהבת עולם (כמים)
רוח (חיות העולם)
עולם היצירה

> **(Meditation #10)** From *Baruch Hu* until *Baruch Shemo*, we say the word *Baruch* ten times, corresponding to the ten *sephirot*. This corresponds to all of *seder hishtalshelut*, about which we say, *Baruch Shemo* ('Blessed be His name.')" (*Torat Menachem* of the Rebbe, vol. 12, p. 166)[92]

> *Baruch Hu* corresponds to *keter*; *Baruch omer v'oseh* to *chochma*; *Baruch gozer u'mekayam* to *bina*; *Baruch oseh bereishit* to *chesed*; *Baruch merachem al ha'aretz* to *gevurah*; *Baruch merachem al ha'briyot* to *tiferet*; *Baruch meshalem sachar tov* to *netzach*; *Baruch chai la'ad* to *hod*; *Baruch podeh u'matzil* to *yesod*; *Baruch Shemo* to *malchut*. (Alternatively, counting *da'at* and excluding *keter*, the first three correspondences would be: *Baruch Hu* to *chochma*; *Baruch omer v'oseh* to *bina*; *Baruch gozer u'mekayam* to *da'at*, and the rest would be as above.)

CHASSIDIC INSIGHTS

(continued from p. 109)

with God by learning Torah and fulfilling the mitzvot. Let us look at meditation even more in detail...(from page 119 in "Love like Fire and Water"):

"The main focus of our effort during 'service of the heart,' which is prayer, should be to approach and unite our soul with Godliness through meditation on the Godly light en-clothed in the worlds. This may be a meditation on the lower world, on the Godly light and energy infusing each and every aspect of creation and every specific detail. This meditation in itself is enough to bring our soul to an experience of Godliness and good and the preciousness associated with it. Or, we may also throw ourselves into this meditation with more energy and focus on how the main point is Godliness, as in the verse, "See, I have placed in front of you the life and the good." Or, we may focus on how the Godly light is garbed and revealed in the higher worlds, each one of us according to our own intellectual level and in our level of *avoda*. All of these meditations produce a significant weakening of the animal soul, such that it is no longer attracted by physical matters and no

(continued on p. 111)

Ar"i: *Z"a* of *Bria*
Immanent Godliness
Lower love (water)
Ruach (vitality of creation)
World of *Yetzira*

BLESSED BE HIS NAME.

Since the ten *sephirot* of *Atzilut* are intermediaries, serving as conduits to channel the infinite light of God down to the lower worlds of creation, they correspond to the entire chain of spiritual creation. Ultimately, creation emerges from the final *sephira*, *malchut*, also known as *Shemo* ("His Name"). A name has no substance and yet we respond with our whole being when someone calls our name. Similarly, God did not exert Himself to create the universe, and yet the entire creation reflects back on His very essence.

> *Within the Words*
>
> During *Baruch She'Amar*, we refer to *Shemo* ("His Name"). During *Yishtabach*, we say *Shimcha* ("Your name"). The path of *pesukei dezimra* leads from "His Name" which is beyond our awareness, to "Your name" as we become conscious of God's presence within nature. After reciting *pesukei dezimra*, we finally conclude that creation comes from a mere reflection of "Your Name," and therefore, *Yishtabach Shimcha* (May Your Name be blessed…").

CHASSIDIC INSIGHTS

(continued from p. 110)

longer engages our will for physicality. We should strive to bring our animal soul as well to an understanding of Godly matters, such that it will also be aroused by closeness to God. Throughout all this, we will become stronger in our Torah learning and fulfillment of the mitzvot, since they are Godly, as previously mentioned."

Here we see that there is more than one path of meditation leading to "love like water." What all of the paths have in common is that they are based upon meditation upon Godliness in the world, permeating and penetrating the creation. In the first instance ("on the lower world"), the emphasis is upon the amazing nature of the physical creation and its harmony and how such a beautiful and harmonious creation could only have been created by God. In the second meditation ("with more energy and focus on how the main point is

(continued on p. 112)

VERSES OF PRAISE

בָּרוּךְ אַתָּה יְיָ אֱלֹהֵינוּ מֶלֶךְ הָעוֹלָם, הָאֵל, אָב הָרַחֲמָן, הַמְהֻלָּל בְּפֶה עַמּוֹ, מְשֻׁבָּח וּמְפֹאָר בִּלְשׁוֹן חֲסִידָיו וַעֲבָדָיו, וּבְשִׁירֵי דָוִד עַבְדֶּךָ.

אר"י: עולם היצירה
ממלא כל עולמים
אהבת עולם (כמים)
רוח (חיות העולם)
עולם היצירה

> **(Meditation #11)** From [the beginning] of *Baruch She'Amar* until we say, *Baruch Shemo* ("Blessed is His Name"), all spiritual levels are essentially equivalent, until we say *Baruch Atah Hashem* ("Blessed are You, Lord..."). (*Pirush Hamilot* of the Mitteler Rebbe, ch. 108, p. 69a)[93]

Even after the *tzimtzum* ("great contraction") of God's infinite light, all spiritual levels are imbued with His infinite light. But, a more limited version of His infinite light shines into the ten *sephirot*, or emanations of the World of *Atzilut*. The *sephirot* are connected to God's infinite illumination like a ray is connected with the sun. Below the world of *Atzilut*, His divine light shines in a truncated and nearly invisible fashion, in order to "allow room" for the three created worlds that to us seem detached from Godliness — *Bria*, *Yetzira* and *Asiya*..

─── **CHASSIDIC INSIGHTS** ───

(continued from p. 111)

Godliness..."), we focus more upon the Godly energy invested in the physical creation. We place less emphasis upon the physical world per se, and more upon the Godliness that enlivens it. This is also a more advanced meditation since it requires focus on a more abstract topic. Finally, we may shift our attention to the "higher worlds" ("how the Godly light is garbed and revealed in the higher worlds..."), in which exist the spiritual creatures known as angels. This, of course is an advanced meditation, since it demands that we shift our attention away from physical creatures that we can see, touch and feel, to spiritual creatures that are beyond our mundane experience. Interestingly, Chassidut does not give us explicit instructions in how to perform this mental shift from physical to spiritual. Nevertheless, it does generate enough "hints" and information for us to construct a "method" that takes us up to the higher worlds...

Possibly, the three meditations suggested here correspond to the

(continued on p. 113)

Ar"i: Yetzira
Immanent Godliness
Lower love (water)
Ruach (vitality of creation)
World of *Yetzira*

BLESSED ARE YOU, LORD, OUR GOD, KING OF THE universe, the [all-powerful] God, merciful Father, extolled in the mouth of His people, praised and glorified by the tongue of those who fear Him and those who serve Him, and in the songs of David, Your servant;

The blessing (within *Baruch She'Amar*), *Baruch Atah HaShem* signifies the end of the World of *Bria*. This is where the universe emerges as a creation, which is why the following words are *Melech HaOlam* ("King of the Universe"). The spiritual energy that descends prior to this point provides us with the stimulus to recite the *pesukei dezimra* (associated with *Yetzira*) and arouse further revelation of Godliness later in the prayers.

> *Within the Words*
>
> The Worlds of *Bria* and *Yetzira* are spiritual worlds, inhabited by spiritual creatures (angels). By contrast, the World of *Asiya* is physical, which is why it is called the World of Action. Because of this distinction between the higher spiritual worlds and the physical World of *Asiya*, the word referring to *Asiya* — *Nehalelcha* ("We extol You") — is separated by a colon from the words preceding it. We say, *Nehalelcha* on our level in *Asiya*, much lower than "the spiritual creatures" who praise God in the higher worlds of *Yetzira* and *Bria*.[94]

VERSES OF PRAISE

——— CHASSIDIC INSIGHTS ———

(continued from p. 112)

three worlds of *Asiya*, *Yetzira* and *Bria*. The emphasis upon the physical creation that is characteristic of the first meditation ("on the lower world") corresponds to the physical world of *Asiya*. Next, by concentrating upon the Godliness within the creation ("on how the main point is Godliness"), we arrive to a higher concept of creation, based upon the unity of physical objects in their source. The source of all physical creation is spiritual, corresponding to the angels of the world

(continued on p. 114)

נְהַלֶּלְךָ יְיָ אֱלֹהֵינוּ בִּשְׁבָחוֹת וּבִזְמִירוֹת. וּנְגַדֶּלְךָ וּנְשַׁבֵּחֲךָ וּנְפָאֶרְךָ, וְנַמְלִיכְךָ וְנַזְכִּיר שִׁמְךָ מַלְכֵּנוּ אֱלֹהֵינוּ,

אר"י: עולם העשיה
ממלא כל עולמים
אהבת עולם (כמים)
רוח (חיות העולם)
עולם היצירה

❝ (Meditation #12) The thirteen times that we mention *Baruch* in the prayer *Baruch She'Amar* correspond to the thirteen strands of the beard...which are also known as the thirteen attributes of divine mercy...the thirteen times that we mention *Baruch* all allude to the trascendant illumination known as *makifim*.❞ (Besha'ah Shehikdimu 5672/1912 of the Rebbe Rashab, vol.1, p. 136)[95]

> The "thirteen strands of the beard" as well as the "thirteen attributes of mercy" are paths of descent that bring divine influence down from *keter* into *chochma*. They are described as "strands" because just as a strand of hair is very thin and resembles a contracted "ray" from our head, so these "rays" of mercy come from a very high origin down to a very contracted spiritual level. Specifically, they descend from *keter*, which is transcendent (*ohr makif*) down to *chochma*, which is immanent (*ohr p'nimi*).

— **CHASSIDIC INSIGHTS** —

(continued from p. 113)

of *Yetzira*, which include angels such as the *chayot*, which are spiritual archetypes and "general" templates for the creation of the physical world. About them, the sages said, "There is no blade of grass that is without a spiritual constellation (*mazal*) that 'strikes it' and tells it to grow." Finally, we lift our meditation to consider how "the Godly light is garbed in the higher worlds..." This may be an allusion to the world of *Bria*, which is the rarefied world of "possibility of existence." Here, no creation exists in a specific or even general sense. Instead, there is only the potential and "possibility of existence." This requires advanced meditation, which may be why the Rebbe adds the qualifier, "each according to his intellectual level..." But, what all of these meditations have in common is that they are focused upon Godliness permeating the creation, whether on a physical or spiritual plane. Whether

(continued on p. 115)

Ar"i: Asiya
Immanent Godliness
Lower love (water)
Ruach (vitality of creation)
World of *Yetzira*

> We will extol You, Lord our God, with praises and psalms, we will adulate You and praise You and glorify You, and we will coronate You and mention Your name, our King our Lord.

Mercy is always a product of *ohr makif*, or transcendent illumination. This is because one who has mercy is in a position of relative strength regarding the beneficiary of his mercy. Generally, the greater the distance between benefactor and beneficiary, the greater the mercy. The greatest possible distance is that between God and man, and therefore we constantly ask for His mercy.

📖 Within the Words

As we say *Baruch She'Amar*, we should realize that each time we say the word *Baruch*, we access a different level of transcendent light that brings mercy down to us and to the world from above. Although each "strand" represents a specific spiritual level, that is only its "external" manifestation. Internally, each strand/level contains the infinite light of God.

CHASSIDIC INSIGHTS

(continued from p. 114)

entry-level beginning meditation, or more advanced meditation, all of these methods lead to "love like water," which is the calm, soothing love that accompanies our meditation during the *pesukei dezimra*.

It is important that our meditation be focused upon details. It will not help to contemplate vague ideas and semi-understood concepts. Such "general" meditation will only give us a brief and passing "high" that is not the goal of meditation before and during prayers. The only way to achieve true elevation and to approach Godliness is through ongoing and strenuous meditation focused upon the details of creation from nothing to something. As the *Kuntres Ha'avoda* itself says ("Love like Fire and Water," Page 166-168): "Therefore, the main *avoda* of prayer is in detailed meditation, no matter what the subject of

(continued on p. 116)

VERSES OF PRAISE

יָחִיד, חֵי הָעוֹלָמִים מֶלֶךְ.

אר"י: עולם העשיה
ממלא כל עולמים
אהבת עולם (כמים)
רוח (חיות העולם)
עולם היצירה

❝ **(Meditation #13) Just as all that is required to rule the kingdom is the Name of the King alone, even though His Name is not His essence, so it is in the divine world above."** *(Sefer Maamorim 5672-5676/1912-1916 of the Rebbe Rashab, p. 139)*[96]

 A ray of who we are is reflected in our name. The essence of any creature is also contained in the Hebrew word that identifies it. It is not the entire essence, but a mere reflection thereof. Similarly, the aspect of *malchut* that creates and enlivens the universe is a mere ray and reflection of Godliness.

We can understand a little about how creation takes place by studying the conduct of an earthly ruler. The king is not required

---
CHASSIDIC INSIGHTS

(continued from p. 115)

the meditation may be. It may be upon the details of creation ex nihilo (from nothing). Or, it may be a meditation on the greatness of God as expressed in the tremendous variety of creations and their size. Or, it may be on how each individual creation receives its own spiritual energy according to its character and nature, as written, "He who takes out by number the heavenly hosts," and "He counts each one...and to each He calls its own name" (Isaiah 40:26). About this it is written, "Great is our Lord, and tremendously powerful..." in the creation and spontaneous existence of the creations. Regarding this verse, the Sages said that the "measure of height" of the "creative power is...[236 *parsaot*]." This is also the topic of the verse (in Isaiah above), "Raise your eyes to the heights...from immense strength and with great power, no individual goes missing..." This verse refers to the Godly power inherent in the very act of creation itself. It also indicates that creations were made to endure, both as species and as individuals...and in this as well is revealed the infinite power of God in the world. We should meditate as well on how all creations praise and extol God (as the Rambam wrote in *Hilchot Yesodei HaTorah* — that they (the higher abstract creatures) know and recognize themselves and their

(continued on p. 117)

The Singular One, life of the worlds, is King.

Yesod of Ohr Chozer
Immanent Godliness
Lower love (water)
Ruach (vitality of creation)
World of *Yetzira*

to be in every corner of his kingdom in order to rule. He merely issues decrees, and it is his edict that rules his kingdom. So, too, God creates from a distance so to speak, using His "word" (in the ten utterances of *Bereishit*). Nevertheless, He is present in every corner of His universe.

> 📖 *Within the Words*
>
> As we say the words, *yachid chei haolamim melech* ("the singular one, vitality of the universe, is King"), we keep in mind that He is one, singular in essence, and it is only a ray of His essence that creates. That ray is His name.

--- CHASSIDIC INSIGHTS ---

(continued from p. 116)

source and they recognize "He who 'said' and the world came into being'…). Within this meditation are to be found many levels and varieties of praise of the higher creatures, each according to its perception and understanding, and each according to the Godly light and energy invested in it in order to enliven it…All of this constitutes a narrative of praise of the One above. Via meditation and excitement over these topics, an "impression is made from the outside," causing us to relinquish our previous spiritual station and to ascend to a higher and more elevated status, approaching Godliness." (from "Love like Fire and Water" Page 166-168).

Given the distinct advantage of detailed meditation over general and vague contemplation of Godly concepts, here is the place to suggest a detailed meditation based upon a *sicha* of the Lubavitcher Rebbe (*Likutei Sichot*, Vol 6 on *parshat Yitro*). A full translation of the *sicha* appears in the commentary of "Love Like Fire and Water," (Ch. 6, page 169-202). This detailed meditation is based upon the four categories of creation: mineral, vegetable, animal and man, which in turn correspond to the four letters of His holy name, *Yud-Hey-Vav-Hey*. The final *Hey* corresponds to the mineral world, which is purely physical and expresses no evidence of any life or vitality whatsoever. The *Vav* of His name corresponds to the vegetable kingdom, which

(continued on p. 118)

VERSES OF PRAISE

מְשֻׁבָּח וּמְפֹאָר עֲדֵי עַד שְׁמוֹ הַגָּדוֹל:

אר"י: מלכות דא"ס
ממלא כל עולמים
אהבת עולם (כמים)
רוח (חיות העולם)
עולם היצירה

❝ **(Meditation #14) There are three levels [of spiritual progress] — standing, walking, and jumping."** (*Sefer Maamorim 5671/1911* of the Rebbe Rashab, pp. 69-70)[97]

Angels are created from letters of "speech." Souls are created from a higher, more intimate source, from the letters of divine "thought." Speech normally occurs in an orderly fashion, as we proceed from one topic to the next in order to make ourselves understood. Speech corresponds to *memalle kol olmin* — limited, immanent light that creates and enlivens the world in an organized fashion. Meditation upon the light of *memalle* produces measured, step-by-step progress on the ladder of prayer. Thought, on the other hand, need not progress in an orderly fashion. Sometimes, we are able to grasp entire concepts that take us to utterly new realms of awareness. Thought corresponds to the mode of *sovev kol olmin* — transcendent light.

We must be able to stand before we can walk, and we must be able to walk before we can run. Meditation during prayers begins from a standing position. That's because the meditation that accompanies the beginning of prayers is upon creation. It occurs within a limited spiritual range, corresponding to the limited Godliness that

--- CHASSIDIC INSIGHTS ---

(continued from p. 117)

while immobile, nevertheless expresses a low level of vitality in that it "grows." The first *Hey* of His name corresponds to the animal kingdom, which not only grows, but moves, with purpose and with intelligence. Finally, the *Yud* of God's name corresponds to man, who is intelligent and who speaks. Thus, the four categories of creation correspond to the letters of God's essential name *Havaya*, which is the name that created the universe from afar.

For that reason, it makes sense to begin a detailed meditation of creation from nothing to something by selecting individual species from each of the four categories, as the objects of our detailed

(continued on p. 119)

סידור עם חסידות - שחרית

Praiseworthy and glorious until (and including) His great name forever and ever.

Malchut of *Ein Sof*
Immanent Godliness
Lower love (water)
Ruach (vitality of creation)
World of *Yetzira*

is present within creation. Angels are called "standers" for that very reason - their spiritual progress occurs precisely within this natural range. But, as souls, we are capable of grasping concepts that are beyond nature and beyond creation. We become "walkers," as we grasp concepts that transcend us. And, occasionally, we may even lose contact with the physical world and become "runners" and "jumpers," cleaving to the essence of Godliness.

> *Within the Words*
>
> "Walking," "standing" and "jumping" are expressed in the words *meshubach u'mefoar adei ad shemo hagadol* ("praiseworthy and glorious until His great name"). Sometimes, we "stand" (meditating upon Godliness in creation) and progress only "until" His great name. We know that He is the source of creation, but we do not experience Him within creation. Other times, we "walk" and even "jump" (focus on Godliness beyond creation), progressing "until" His great Name — when we not only know about but also experience Godliness on a transcendent level. It is at that point that we fulfill our true potential as meditators who are able to experience transcendent Godliness.

CHASSIDIC INSIGHTS

(continued from p. 118)

meditation. For example, the Torah mentions six types of metals (lead, tin, iron, copper, gold and silver) for various purposes, and our meditation could focus on the metals as creations from the mineral category. From the vegetable category, the Torah mentions at least four different kinds of trees (acacia (*eshel*), cypress (*erez*), oak (*alon*) and pine (*oren*) which we might choose as objects of meditation. And from the animal category, we might choose the species mentioned in the "chariots" of Yehezkel and of Isaiah: the eagle (*nesher*), the ox (*shor*) and the lion (*aryeh*). The important thing is to consider not the physical objects themselves, but the divine power that went into creating them from nothing to something, as well as the variety, the size and individual

(continued on p. 120)

בָּרוּךְ אַתָּה יְיָ, מֶלֶךְ מְהֻלָּל בַּתִּשְׁבָּחוֹת:

אר"י: ז"א דכללות
ממלא כל עולמים
אהבת עולם (כמים)
רוח (חיות העולם)
עולם היצירה

❝ (Meditation #15) When the king's troops are of one kind, even if they are as numerous as the sand of the sea, they do not express the "glory" of the king. But, if there are different kinds of troops — such as cavalry, infantry, archers, swordsmen — each serving the king in his own manner…this demonstrates the true glory (*hadar*) of the king."
(*Besha'ah Shehikdimu* 5672/1912 of the Rebbe Rashab, vol.1, p. 238)[98]

Not only souls, but also the angels above, are divided into myriad camps, each attached to God in its own way. There are those who serve Him in love, others in fear, and yet others who do nothing but stand at attention nullified to Him forever.

The myriad camps and groups and categories of angels and souls, each expressing its love or fear of God in its own way, express the "glory" of the king. This is an external manifestation that is manifested in both the quantity of the angels and souls, and in their variety. However, the "majesty" (*hod*) of the king emanates from within the king himself — it emerges from the very essence and personality of the king, rather than from the myriad ways in which His servants serve Him.

📖 *Within the Words*

As we say in the closing of *Baruch She'Amar*, "Blessed are You, Lord, King Who is lauded with praises," we may think of the myriad different ways in which angels and souls serve God and are nullified to Him, each in their own fashion.

CHASSIDIC INSIGHTS

(continued from p. 119)

nature of each creation, as indicated in the above quote from *Kuntres Ha'avoda*. It is important to use the Hebrew word for each object, since Hebrew is the original language of creation.

And then (from "Love like Fire and Water" Page 175-177), "…the beginning of our detailed meditation must be upon the influx of Godly energy drawn down from the spiritual constellations above

(continued on p. 124)

סידור עם חסידות – שחרית

ברוך שאמר

Z"a (all inclusive)
Immanent Godliness
Lower love (water)
Ruach (vitality of creation)
World of *Yetzira*

Blessed are You, Lord, King Who is lauded with praises.

❝ (Meditation #16) The entire framework of prayer and the verses of praise, beginning with 'Blessed be He who said and the universe came into being...' is organized around this principle..."
(*Torat Shmuel* 5636/1876 of the Rebbe Maharash, p. 322)

The thirteen instances that the word *Baruch* is mentioned in *Baruch She'amar* correspond to the thirteen attributes of mercy. The first mention corresponds to how with one utterance, God created the entire universe, as mentioned in *Pirkei Avot* (5:1) that God could have created the world with one utterance.

After several expressions beginning with the word *Baruch* and how it conveys spirituality down into to the creation, we arrive to, "Blessed be He who has compassion over the earth" — which represents *alma d'itgalia*, or the "revealed world" in which we live. "Blessed be He who well compensates those who fear Him" refers to the concealed world of *Gan Eden*, where God rewards souls by granting them spiritual revelation in proportion to their deeds in this world. "Blessed be He who lives forever and exists eternally" refers to fifty thousand Jubilee years, which symbolize the eternity of the infinite light of God, with its infinite number of spiritual elevations that the soul undergoes.

Within the Words

"Blessed be He who redeems and rescues" — The gemora (*Pesachim* 50A) tells us that, "Whatever the horse is able to run and rescue, becomes holy for God." The "horse" is an allusion to Hebrew letters, which carry a person who is praying or learning Torah, to exalted levels he would not otherwise have attained on his own. The word for "rescue" may also mean "shade." Shade symbolizes the very high illumination that we draw down to ourselves as *ohr makif*, or "transcendent light," that surrounds and protects us. Finally, "Blessed be His name," because all of these spiritual revelations and elevations come to us from His name alone, and do not affect His essence.

VERSES OF PRAISE

> **"Just as some people arrange a sofa, positioning each cushion in its proper place, so those who arrange their praises of God allocate a role to every aspect of creation, seeing it as an expression of God, created in His honor, so that [they might perceive] His greatness."** (*Likutei Torah* of the Alter Rebbe, *Beha'alotcha* p. 32d [64])[99]

אר"י: ז"א דכללות
ממלא כל עולמים
אהבת עולם (כמים)
רוח (חיות העולם)
עולם היצירה

There are seven paths of intellectual ascent from below to above, corresponding to the seven *midot*, or emotional character traits that we possess. They also correspond to the seven candelabra of the Menorah. Each of the seven also contains ten *sephirot*, for a total of seventy paths of intellectual ascent. They correspond as well to the original seventy Jewish souls who descended to Egypt.

It was not always necessary to pray at length. During the First Temple period, Jews who came to the Temple would immediately experience Godliness, and it was not necessary for them to say more than the *Kriat Shema* and a few words of supplication. But, with the passage of time, we became more attached to physical temptations and, as a result, the sages of the Second Temple period added the *pesukei dezimra* and the blessings before *Kriat Shema* to our prayers. During the *pesukei dezimra*, we meditate upon the nullification of the physical world to God. During the blessings preceding the *Kriat Shema*, we meditate upon the nullification of our own animal soul to its spiritual source above. Since we are souls within a body, our meditation occurs with "arousal and return" (*ratzoh v'shuv* — ascent of the soul followed by its return to the body).[100] That is why, "One should first organize his praises of God, and then pray."[101]

> *Within the Words*
>
> Love of God is compared to silver (*kesef* in Hebrew, related to the word, *lichsof,* meaning "to yearn"). Fear of God is associated with gold. We achieve love of God by meditating on His closeness in order to reveal the wells of love concealed in our heart. We achieve fear of God by considering His transcendent distance and how puny we are in relation to Him. The realization causes us to "ignite" with love like fire and with desire to unite with Him. However, this occurs only after our meditation has led us to a full and complete understanding of the concepts upon which we were meditating.

Z"a (all inclusive)
Immanent Godliness
Lower love (water)
Ruach (vitality of creation)
World of *Yetzira*

> Regarding angels, it is written, "And their feet were a straight leg" (Yehezkel 1:7). "Straight" (*yeshara*) carries the numerical value (gematria) of 515… With their "straight leg"…the angels draw down "fifteen," which represents intellect from beyond creation (*chochma* and *bina*) into "five hundred"…(*Torat Shmuel 5675/1875* of the Rebbe Maharash, Vol 2, pp. 363-4)

The *sephira* of *Yesod* is not counted in this calculation because it merely serves as a conduit. The remaining *sephirot* are five in number. Each one of them includes ten and each ten includes another ten for a total of five hundred. Souls do not "stand." They walk and progress, as in the verse, "I established you as walkers among these standers [the angels]" (Zacharia 3:7). Jewish souls are in a perpetual state of spiritual ascent. Nevertheless, they also possess the trait of steadfastness and persistence. They do not "fall," but perpetually ascend. There is another verse that says about souls, "My foot stands on an even plain…" (Psalms 26:12). This indicates that Jewish souls possess both advantages: They progress on the one hand but they are steady and persistent on the other.

The "progress" of Jewish souls is dependent upon meditation. The topics for meditation are based on the letters of the Torah. When we understand Torah topics via the letters of the Torah, they become the basis of our *hiluch*, or "progress" in Torah. There are other elements of the written Torah, such as "crowns, and vowels and incantations." Currently (before the advent of *mashiach*), it is only the letters that provide us with content for meditation. About the other elements – the crowns, vowels and incantations – we do not even grasp the nature of their existence. Nevertheless, by learning Torah via its letters, we access and bring down essential Godliness into the world.

📖 *Within the Words*

The form of the letters indicates their spiritual dynamic. For example, the *aleph* is formed by two lines and another line in the middle joining them together.…this [kind of analysis] is what is meant by "Know the God of your father and serve Him with a complete heart." By "knowing Him" via the letters, we become able to serve Him with a full heart. Since our own Godly souls are "a part of divinity," when we delve into Torah and *tefila* in order to "see the Godliness within the word," we are able to find it "in the *vort*"…by meditating in depth, we achieve full and complete *avoda*. (*Torat Shmuel 5636/1876* of the Rebbe Maharash, pp. 415-416, in the *hanachos* of the Rebbe Rashab).

VERSES OF PRAISE

מִזְמוֹר לְתוֹדָה: הָרִיעוּ לַיְיָ, כָּל-הָאָרֶץ:

ממלא כל עולמים
אהבת עולם (כמים)
כי הוא חיות העולם
רוח
עולם היצירה

> "Just as doves gaze upon each other and derive great pleasure as they prepare to unite, so Jewish souls find immense enjoyment when gazing upon the glory of the King." (*Likutei Torah* of the Alter Rebbe, *Shir HaShirim* p. ל"ט and p. 82, *Sefer Maamorim* 5662/1902 of the Rebbe Rashab, pp. 247-249)[102]

During *Kriat Shema*, we achieve *yichud av v'aim* ("unity of the father and mother"). We access a very high spiritual level that is beyond intellect and bring it down to unite our two intellectual faculties of *chochma* ("insight") and *bina* ("analysis"). This facilitates a new Godly revelation that permeates our awareness, ourselves and our environment. During the *Shemonah Esreh*, we accomplish *yichud z'un* ("unity of *Zeir Anpin* and *malchut*"), which channels the light of *Kriat Shema* into our specific requests during the eighteen blessings.

There are at least two paths in prayer. One utilizes our intellectual faculties as we meditate, contemplate and consider Godly concepts (as described above for the *Kriat Shema* and *Shemonah Esreh*). The other path is simply gazing upon His greatness, without utilizing our power of intellect. This takes place during the *pesukei dezimra*, as we recite/sing God's praises, mentioning His greatness. God hears our praises, and our prayers elicit His qualities, even without any intellectual involvement from us.

📖 *Within the Words*

Awareness of God's greatness affords far greater enjoyment than does intellectual understanding of Godly concepts. By repeating His praises, we elicit a divine response from the ten hidden *sephirot*, above the World of *Atzilut*. By first organizing our praise of God during the *pesukei dezimra*, we prepare ourselves to perceive Godliness on a far higher level during the *Kriat Shema* and *Shemonah Esreh*.

--- CHASSIDIC INSIGHTS ---

(continued from p. 120)

in order to enliven the physical creations below. This corresponds to the saying of the sages, "There is no blade of grass below without a

(continued on p. 126)

סידור עם חסידות - שחרית

Immanent Godliness
Lower love (water)
Love: vitality of the universe
Soul level: *Ruach*
World of *Yetzira*

VERSES OF PRAISE

The following Psalm not said on Erev Pesach, Chol HaMoed Pesach, or Erev Yom Kippur

A SONG OF GRATITUDE, LIFT YOUR VOICES TO THE Lord, all the land!

❝ When we carve something out from the inside, it becomes a receptacle. Nevertheless, we must also burnish it from the outside, for if we don't, it is of no use whatsoever..." (*Sefer Maamorim* 5657/1897 of the Rebbe Rashab, p. 122. See also *Torat Shmuel* 5630/1870 of the Rebbe Maharash, p. 151)[103]

Man and woman were created joined back to back. In order to come together face to face, they had to undergo a *nesira* ("separation"). Similarly, in order to become *keilim* ("vessels") and unite with His infinite light, we need to separate our Godly and animal souls from one another. This takes place as we "carve out" our animal soul while reciting the *pesukei dezimra*. (*Le'zamer* also means, "to cut away.") As we ascend in spiritual awareness, we become more sensitized to our negative traits and are able to "cut them away."

After minimizing our animal soul during the "carving from without," we carve out a "no-ego" zone within, in order to transform ourselves into a receptacle for Godly light. This process is called the "etching from within." At this point, our *avodat Hashem* ("service of God") becomes progressive and dynamic. When lacking the "etching from within," we "stand" like the angels, who remain within a particular spiritual range at all times. Our goal is to uncover the well of Godly love inside and let it flow, so that we are able to "walk," achieving the highest form of love — *bechol me'odecha* ("with all of your might").

📖 *Within the Words*

Pesukei dezimra recalls the phrase, *lezamer aritizim*, meaning "to cut away thorns." This is the process that we undergo during this segment of prayer. First, by organizing our praises of God and focusing on Godly illumination, we "carve out" our negative traits and free ourselves of negative influences. Then, during the blessings preceding *Kriat Shema*, we "etch out" a space within, to become a receptacle for Godliness. The *pesukei dezimra* "prune away" the spiritual obstructions, and the blessings before the *Shema* create a "vessel" to contain Godly illumination.

עִבְדוּ אֶת יְיָ בְּשִׂמְחָה; בֹּאוּ לְפָנָיו בִּרְנָנָה:

ממלא כל עולמים
אהבת עולם (כמים)
כי הוא חיות העולם
רוח
עולם היצירה

> **The animal soul is trapped — very trapped — and it is unable to ascend. It is necessary to extricate it from its environment, much as one might uproot a plant and transplant it to another locale and cultivate it there."** *(Besha'ah shehikdimu 5672/1912 of the Rebbe Rashab, vol. 2, ch. 392 [p. 806])*[104]

We extricate the animal soul from its predicament by meditating upon transcendent matters throughout the *pesukei dezimra*. This meditation influences the animal soul and persuades it of the importance of Godliness. The most important topic of meditation is creation from nothing to something, which has no rational explanation; we just know that it must be so because no object is capable of creating itself, or another object.

All of the psalms comprising the *pesukei dezimra* inspire meditations on the topic of creation from nothing to something. There are details within this meditation, such as that nothing can create something else without a void (*ayin*) between them, and that, while the Creator invests energy in the creation, He nevertheless remains essentially removed and beyond creation. This elicits great excitement from the animal soul, which then ascends to a higher, more refined level.

📖 Within the Words

Many of the words of *Baruch She'Amar*, such as the very beginning of the prayer, refer to creation that came into being through God's supernal speech. The same is true of *Baruch omer ve'oseh* ("Blessed is He who says and does"), and *Ki hu amar vayehi* ("He said and so it took place"[105]), and *Gadol Adoneinu…* ("Great is our Lord, immense in power…"[106]). Meditation on these words elevates the animal soul so that it can begin to meditate upon higher concepts during the *Birchot Kriat Shema* and the *Shema*. This process is called the "etching from within."

--- CHASSIDIC INSIGHTS ---

(continued from p. 124)

spiritual counterpart above, that strikes it and tells it to grow…" (*Bereishit Rabba* 10:6). Furthermore, the prophet declared, "I will answer

(continued on p. 130)

Immanent Godliness
Lower love (water)
Love: vitality of the universe
Soul level: *Ruach*
World of *Yetzira*

Serve the Lord in joy, come before Him in song.

"Everything in the lower world possesses a source and origin above, as it is written in the Zohar, 'God made the lower world similar to the upper world.' Every creature down here in the physical world is a parable of its corresponding level in the spiritual world."
(*Sefer Maamorim* 5679/1919 of the Rebbe Rashab, p. 315)[107]

The ultimate source of light and darkness in this world are the *orot* ("lights") and *kelim* ("vessels") of the World of *Atzilut*. The *orot* are Godly revelation, while the *kelim* conceal the illumination in order to contain and channel it. The *orot* and *kelim* have sources in the *kav* ("ray" from His infinite light) and the *tzimtzum* (contraction of His infinite light), respectively.

Examples of light and darkness include day and night, as well as the conscious and unconscious faculties of the soul. There is light and darkness of the intellect as well, such as when we understand or fail to understand a concept. Moshe, while on Mt. Sinai knew it was daytime when the angels said *Kadosh*, and he knew it was nighttime when they said *Baruch*. It was the intellectually enlightened angels (*Seraphim*) who said *Kadosh*, and it was the less enlightened (*Ofanim*) who said *Baruch*. Moshe also knew that it was daytime when they learned the written Torah (compared to light) with him, and that it was nighttime when they learned the oral Torah with him, since the dialectic nature of the oral Torah is compared to nighttime.[108]

> 📖 *Within the Words*
>
> The foundation of *hitbonenut* ("meditation") is that whatever exists in our physical world has a spiritual source above. Our task is to strip away the outer appearance of creation in order to find the Godly spark within it. We then contemplate the source of the Godly spark, following it up to the highest spiritual levels. This is the basis of spiritual ascent on the ladder of prayer of four rungs, symbolizing the four worlds. As the Rebbe Rashab says (*Kuntres Ha'avoda*, Ch 6), "If you are not performing this meditation, then what are you doing here in this world?"

דְּעוּ כִּי יְיָ הוּא אֱלֹהִים, הוּא עָשָׂנוּ, וְלוֹ אֲנַחְנוּ, עַמּוֹ, וְצֹאן מַרְעִיתוֹ:

בֹּאוּ שְׁעָרָיו בְּתוֹדָה, חֲצֵרֹתָיו בִּתְהִלָּה, הוֹדוּ לוֹ בָּרְכוּ שְׁמוֹ.

ממלא כל עולמים
אהבת עולם (כמים)
כי הוא חיות העולם
רוח
עולם היצירה

> "Every spiritual level serves as a "parable" in relation to the level above it. That is why the holy books say that King Solomon was capable of delivering three thousand parables. That is, he grasped three thousand spiritual levels, each serving as a parable in relation to the one above it." (*Sefer Maamorim* 5679/1919 of the Rebbe Rashab, pp. 315-317)[109]

King Solomon represented the *sephira* of *malchut* ("kingship") of *Atzilut*, which is the source of the lower three worlds of *BY"A*. Therefore, he grasped three thousand parables, corresponding to the lower three worlds, in order to explain Godliness. R' Meir was a *tanna* (teacher of *Mishna*) who was capable of delivering three hundred parables. He was associated with the World of *Bria*.

Let us consider the lion. The physical lion has a spiritual counterpart in the "face of the lion" in the prophetic vision of the "chariot" (*merkava*) above. Such a "chariot" exists in the World of *Yetzira*, in *Bria* and even in *Atzilut*. In *Atzilut*, the lion alludes to the *sephira* of *chesed*, which itself is a "parable" for the *sephira* of *chochma*. A clue is that *reiya* ("spiritual vision"), corresponding to *chochma*, is composed of the same letters as *aryeh* ("lion").

📖 *Within the Words*

The Torah compares man to a tree, and the Midrash compares the angels (*serafim*) to cypress trees, the tallest trees in the world. Just as trees grow from a thin sapling to a full tree, so both man and the angels "grow" emotionally. Our meditation during *pesukei dezimra* focuses upon finding the spiritual roots of physical objects. Although this is an intellectual pursuit, the objective is to "grow" and cultivate our emotions of love and fear of God. The love that we develop during the process is called "love like water," since it flows through us and motivates us.

סידור עם חסידות – שחרית

פסוקי דזמרה

Immanent Godliness
Lower love (water)
Love: vitality of the universe
Soul level: Ruach
World of Yetzira

> Know that the Lord is God, He made us; we are His, His nation and the sheep whom He shepherds.
>
> Approach His gates in gratitude, His courts in praise, give thanks to Him, bless His name.

❝ **Psalm 100 (*Mizmor LeToda*) corresponds to the one hundred blessings that we recite every day. And the first letters of the first four words form an acrostic — *halacha*...**" (*Yahel Ohr*, the *Tzemach Tzedek* on Psalms, p. 369, *ot beit*) [110]

The four words at the beginning of Psalm 100 correspond to the "four cubits of *halacha*," and to the four letters of God's name, *Havaya*. The remaining four verses of the psalm correspond to the four worlds of *ABY"A*.

The first phrase of the second verse, "Serve God in joy..." alludes to the service of the priests (Cohanim). The second part of the second verse — "Approach Him in song" — alludes to the Levites, who accompanied the sacrifices with their songs. The third verse — "Know that *Havaya* is *Elokim*" refers to all the Jews, as they all went to the Temple with their sacrifices.

📖 *Within the Words*

The beginning of the second verse ("Serve God in joy...") alludes to our morning prayers from the *Korbanot* ("Sacrifices") until *Baruch She'Amar*. And this is the World of *Asiya*. The end of the second verse ("Approach Him in song") corresponds to the *pesukei dezimra*, and this is the World of *Yetzira*. The third verse "Know that *Havaya* is *Elokim*" refers to the *Kriat Shema* and the World of *Bria*. The three sections of the fourth verse apply to the pinnacle of prayer, the *Shemonah Esreh* and the World of *Atzilut*. "Come to His gates with gratitude" refers to the first three blessings of the *Shemonah Esreh*; "to His court with praise" refers to the middle thirteen blessings; and finally "acknowledge Him and give thanks to His name" (together with the final verse) refer to the final blessings of the *Shemonah Esreh*.[111]

VERSES OF PRAISE

כִּי טוֹב יְיָ, לְעוֹלָם חַסְדּוֹ, וְעַד דֹּר וָדֹר, אֱמוּנָתוֹ:

ממלא כל עולמים
אהבת עולם (כמים)
כי הוא חיות העולם
רוח
עולם היצירה

"God above truly exists, and He is the source of all. The creation is nothing (*ayin*) — truly nothing..." (*Siddur* of the Alter Rebbe with Chassidut, p. מ"ד)[112]

From the perspective of above, God is real, and the creation questionable, since the existence of the universe is entirely dependent upon God's will. This awareness is called *yichuda ila'ah* ("supernal unity"), or *da'at elyon* ("supernal awareness"). But from our mundane perspective, the physical universe is real and we do not perceive the Godliness that permeates it. This is called *yichuda tata'ah* ("lower unity"), or *da'at tachton* ("lower awareness").

Since we live in a physical world, our perspective is that of *da'at tachton* ("lower awareness"). However, we must also acknowledge the higher perspective of *yichuda ila'ah* and *da'at elyon*. This is an act of "informed acknowledgement." That is, we acknowledge that He truly exists and that we are His creatures. This is the *hoda'ah* ("thankful acknowledgment") of *Mizmor LeToda*.

Within the Words

The name *Havaya* enclothed in nature is not apparent to creatures on our level, because we are unable to detect Godliness within nature without the packaging and "garments" associated with the name *Elokim*, which shrouds and hides the essential name *Havaya*. That is why we say, "Know that *Havaya* is *Elokim*" — to make it clear that the name *Havaya* is the important factor, moreso than the name *Elokim*. It is impossible for us to completely grasp this concept, since it is associated with the higher perspective of *da'at elyon* from above to below, but by admitting that it is so, we gain some grasp of the concept.

— CHASSIDIC INSIGHTS —

(continued from p. 126)

the heavens, and they will answer [the earth]" (*Hoshea* 2:23). This implies that the physical creation is nullified to the spiritual creation that is beyond it. The spiritual constellations themselves receive their vitality from the "leftovers" of the *ofanim* (lower angels of *Asiya*), who

(continued on p. 132)

Immanent Godliness
Lower love (water)
Love: vitality of the universe
Soul level: *Ruach*
World of *Yetzira*

For the Lord is good, His kindness is eternal, and His faith in us extends from generation to generation.

❝'Let the honor of the Lord last forever; may the Lord rejoice in His works' — this was said by the angel known as the 'Minister of the Universe' (*Metat*)." (Saying of the sages from Torat Chulin p. 60a, quoted in Torat Shmuel 5626/1866 of the Rebbe Maharash, p. 219)[113]

Metat is also the angel who elevates our prayers and uses them to "fashion crowns for His Creator." He exists in two modes — one in the World of *Yetzira* where he receives the prayers of the Jews, and the other in the World of *Bria*, to where he elevates the prayers. About him, a verse says, "I was a youngster and I also grew old"[114] — "youngster" in *Yetzira* and "old" in *Bria*.

Typically, our prayers are mixed with our own emotions, desires, and misguided ideas. We possess a divine soul that wants to cling to its source above, but our divine soul is enclothed in an animal soul and embedded in a physical body. Therefore, our prayers are tinged with the traits of the animal soul and body. Our prayers are comparable to rocks and stones, which *Metat* takes up to "polish" so that they "shine" like precious stones, fit for the crown of the Creator. That is what is meant by the description of *Metat*, as the one who "elevates our prayers."

📖 *Within the Words*

Here, it is *Metat* who says, *Yehi ch'vod* ("Let the honor...") Why? It is related in the Talmud[115] that he observed the newly created grass of the fields reasoning: "The trees, who naturally grow separately, were commanded to remain separate. We, who grow intertwined, should then also be careful to remain only among our own kind." Upon hearing this, he broke into praise ("Let the honor..."). But since when does grass and vegetation "reason?" The answer: "There is no blade of grass in this world that is without a spiritual counterpart above, who 'hits' it and tells it to grow." That is, every physical creature also possesses a spiritual counterpart above, and it is the spiritual counterpart, or the angel above, who "reasons," and then passes on the conclusions to the physical creation in this world.

VERSES OF PRAISE

יְהִי כְבוֹד יְיָ לְעוֹלָם, יִשְׂמַח יְיָ בְּמַעֲשָׂיו:

יְהִי שֵׁם יְיָ מְבֹרָךְ, מֵעַתָּה וְעַד עוֹלָם:

מִמִּזְרַח שֶׁמֶשׁ עַד מְבוֹאוֹ מְהֻלָּל שֵׁם יְיָ:

רָם עַל כָּל גּוֹיִם, יְיָ, עַל הַשָּׁמַיִם כְּבוֹדוֹ:

יְיָ שִׁמְךָ לְעוֹלָם, יְיָ זִכְרְךָ לְדֹר וָדֹר:

יְיָ בַּשָּׁמַיִם הֵכִין כִּסְאוֹ, וּמַלְכוּתוֹ בַּכֹּל מָשָׁלָה:

ממלא כל עולמים
אהבת עולם (כמים)
כי הוא חיות העולם
רוח
עולם היצירה

"Answer us on the day that we call..." — There are two ways [in which our prayers are answered]. Sometimes the answer is delayed... and at other times we are answered immediately, as on the day of our request... (*Pirush Hamilot* of the Mitteler Rebbe, ch. 158, p. ק)[116]

Sometimes when we make a request during prayers, we are not answered immediately because the arousal from below (*ma'an — mayin nukvin*) must be judged above. At other times, our requests are "fast-tracked" above and we receive answers immediately.

Our physical needs are meted out on Rosh Hashana. However, sometimes the blessings that we deserve remain in the spiritual realm where, either because of our transgressions or for other reasons, they do not descend to us. Our daily prayers, plus at times the intercession of a *tzaddik*, a "righteous person" who prays on our behalf, can "clean the pipes" and ensure that the channels are open and the blessings descend to meet our physical and other needs. The Hebrew word for "pipe" (*tzinor*) is spelled with the same letters as the word for "will" (*ratzon*), as in God's will.

CHASSIDIC INSIGHTS

(continued from p. 130)

in turn receive their influx from the *chayot* (higher level of angels in the world of *Yetzira*), and so forth, all the way up to the *sephira* of *malchut* of *Atzilut*...the nullification of each spiritual level to the level beyond it continues all the way up to the initial revelation of the ray of

(continued on p. 133)

Immanent Godliness
Lower love (water)
Love: vitality of the universe
Soul level: Ruach
World of Yetzira

Let the honor of the Lord be forever, let the Lord rejoice in His works.

Let the name of the Lord be blessed, from now and forever.

From sunrise in the east until sunset, the name of the Lord is praised.

The Lord is exalted over the nations, His honor transcends the heavens.

Lord, Your name is forever, Lord, Your memory for all generations.

The Lord established His throne in the heavens, and His reign in every domain.

> 📖 *Within the Words*
>
> When we receive immediate answers, such as on the very day of our prayers, it is the result of *yichud-beracha-kedusha* ("unity-blessing-holiness"). The acrostic in Hebrew is the name of the river (*Yabok*) that Yaakov crossed before wrestling with the angel of his brother Esau. It also emerges from the final verse of our psalm — *Ya'aneinu beyom kareinu* ("Answer us on the day of our call…") — *yud-beit-kuf*.

--- **CHASSIDIC INSIGHTS** ---

(continued from p. 132)

infinite light from God. This ray [the first revelation after the *tzimtzum*, or "great contraction"] is the source of all immanent, permeating light, which illuminates the worlds [and upon which we meditate]."

On a practical level, the above-mentioned *sicha* of the Rebbe suggests how we might put the advice of the *Kuntres Ha'avoda* ("Love like Fire and Water") into practice. The *sicha* discusses how the four categories of creation and the letters of His name also correspond to our inner world and the outer worlds above. The mineral world corresponds to "letters" within us. Letters, like inanimate objects of the

(continued on p. 134)

VERSES OF PRAISE

יִשְׂמְחוּ הַשָּׁמַיִם וְתָגֵל הָאָרֶץ, וְיֹאמְרוּ בַגּוֹיִם יְיָ מָלָךְ:
יְיָ מֶלֶךְ יְיָ מָלָךְ, יְיָ יִמְלֹךְ לְעֹלָם וָעֶד:
יְיָ מֶלֶךְ עוֹלָם וָעֶד, אָבְדוּ גוֹיִם מֵאַרְצוֹ:
יְיָ הֵפִיר עֲצַת גּוֹיִם, הֵנִיא מַחְשְׁבוֹת עַמִּים:
רַבּוֹת מַחֲשָׁבוֹת בְּלֶב אִישׁ, וַעֲצַת יְיָ הִיא תָקוּם:
עֲצַת יְיָ לְעוֹלָם תַּעֲמֹד, מַחְשְׁבוֹת לִבּוֹ לְדֹר וָדֹר:
כִּי הוּא אָמַר וַיֶּהִי, הוּא צִוָּה וַיַּעֲמֹד:
כִּי בָחַר יְיָ בְּצִיּוֹן, אִוָּהּ לְמוֹשָׁב לוֹ:
כִּי יַעֲקֹב בָּחַר לוֹ יָהּ, יִשְׂרָאֵל לִסְגֻלָּתוֹ:
כִּי, לֹא יִטֹּשׁ יְיָ עַמּוֹ, וְנַחֲלָתוֹ לֹא יַעֲזֹב:
וְהוּא רַחוּם יְכַפֵּר עָוֹן וְלֹא יַשְׁחִית,
וְהִרְבָּה לְהָשִׁיב אַפּוֹ, וְלֹא יָעִיר כָּל חֲמָתוֹ:
יְיָ הוֹשִׁיעָה, הַמֶּלֶךְ יַעֲנֵנוּ בְיוֹם קָרְאֵנוּ:

ממלא כל עולמים
אהבת עולם (כמים)
כי הוא חיות העולם
רוח
עולם היצירה

CHASSIDIC INSIGHTS

(continued from p. 133)

mineral class, have no vitality of their own. They have shape and form, and they convey meaning to those who know how to use them, but on their own, letters have no intrinsic content, and so they are comparable to the mineral kingdom in creation. The vegetable kingdom though, is similar to our emotions. Just as plants and trees grow, so our emotions develop. As we mature, our emotions also mature, and we value higher and more refined objects. As children, we may have valued candy and toys, but as we grow, we come to value money and nice physical objects. As we mature more, we begin to value wisdom and philosophy over any physical belongings. Ultimately, we should come to the level that we value and hold dear the wisdom of Godliness and belief in the Creator. All of this chronicles our emotional growth from youth to maturity, and demonstrates that, like the vegetable kingdom, our emotions grow and develop.

(continued on p. 136)

Immanent Godliness
Lower love (water)
Love: vitality of the universe
Soul level: Ruach
World of Yetzira

The heavens will rejoice and the earth be delighted, and the nations will proclaim, 'The Lord is King.'

The Lord reigns, the Lord reigned, and the Lord will reign forever and ever.

The Lord is King forever, the nations have vanished from His land.

The Lord foils the wiles of nations, annuls the schemes of peoples.

Many are the thoughts in the heart of man, and the plan of God is what endures.

The plan of God endures forever, and the thoughts of His heart from one generation to the next.

For, He said and it happened, He commanded and it took place.

For, the Lord chose Zion, desiring it as His place of dwelling.

For, God chose Jacob, [and] Israel as his treasure.

For, the Lord will not abandon His people, nor will He forsake His heritage.

And He, being merciful, atones for our sins and refrains from destroying us,

He repeatedly quashes His anger, and avoids arousing all of His wrath.

The Lord saves, the King answers us on the day that we call [Him].

אַשְׁרֵי יוֹשְׁבֵי בֵיתֶךָ, עוֹד יְהַלְלוּךָ סֶּלָה:

אַשְׁרֵי הָעָם שֶׁכָּכָה לוֹ, אַשְׁרֵי הָעָם שֶׁיְיָ אֱלֹהָיו:

תְּהִלָּה לְדָוִד,

אֲרוֹמִמְךָ אֱלוֹהַי הַמֶּלֶךְ, וַאֲבָרְכָה שִׁמְךָ לְעוֹלָם וָעֶד:

בְּכָל יוֹם אֲבָרְכֶךָּ, וַאֲהַלְלָה שִׁמְךָ לְעוֹלָם וָעֶד:

גָּדוֹל יְיָ וּמְהֻלָּל מְאֹד, וְלִגְדֻלָּתוֹ אֵין חֵקֶר:

ממלא כל עולמים
אהבת עולם (כמים)
כי הוא חיות העולם
רוח
עולם היצירה

> **"The Men of the Great Assembly (Anshei Knesset Hagedola) established [the first two verses of Ashrei] as preparation and introduction to the pesukei dezimra..."** (*Pirush Hamilot* of the Mitteler Rebbe, ch. 159)[117]

The prayer *Ashrei* represents all the subsequent praises of God, since it is organized according to the Hebrew alphabet. Those prayers (the *pesukei dezimra*) are characterized by the word *Halleluyah*, ("Praise God") which is composed of the words *Hallel* ("Praise") and *Y-ah*, the first two letters of God's holy name *Havaya*. These two letters correspond to *chochma* and *bina*, or the holy intellect that we wish to draw down into the creation.

The word *Ashrei* ("Happy") represents *Keter*, the source of all joy. From there, we seek to draw down holy influence into God's name *Havaya*, but especially into the first two letters of that name, *yud-hey*. The method of doing so is by praising Him, uttering the

———————— CHASSIDIC INSIGHTS ————————

(continued from p. 134)

Beyond the emotions, our intellect is comparable to the animal kingdom, that is characterized by the additional trait of movement. While emotions grow, they do so only within a given range. In order to go beyond that range, we need intellect. With our minds, we may govern over our emotions to take us to places that our emotions alone would not have allowed us to go. Emotionally, we always prefer

(continued on p. 138)

Immanent Godliness
Lower love (water)
Love: vitality of the universe
Soul level: Ruach
World of Yetzira

H APPY ARE THOSE WHO DWELL IN YOUR HOUSE, they will yet praise You forever.

Happy is the nation for whom this is their lot, happy is the nation whose God is the Lord.

A psalm of praise from David;

I will exalt You, my God the King, and I will bless Your name forever.

Every day, I will bless you, and I will praise Your name forever.

Great is the Lord, and very praiseworthy, there is no limit to His greatness.

---

word *Halelluyah*. *Hallel* comes from the word *Bahilu naro* ("Let His candle shine"). Calling upon His name, we seek to shine His holy light into the physical universe.

> 📖 *Within the Words*
>
> All of the *pesukei dezimra* begin and end with the word *Halleluyah*. The last two letters of *Halleluyah*, *yud-hey* are the first two letters God's holy name, *Havaya*. They correspond to the higher love (*ahava rabba*) and higher fear (*yirah ila'ah*) bequeathed to us by Aharon, the High Priest. However, while meditating, we focus upon the final two letters of His name, *vav-hey*, which correspond to lower love (*ahavat olam*) and lower fear (*yirah tata'ah*). Our task is to perfect our lower love and fear of God. Only then can we aspire to revelation of the higher spiritual levels. Nevertheless, we hope and pray that higher love and higher fear will be revealed to us, and therefore we repeat the word *Halleluyah*, and the two letters *yud-hey* associated with those higher levels, during prayer. The *gematria* of *yud-hey* is fifteen — and this number re-occurs regularly throughout our prayers (for example, fifteen praises in *Yishtabach*, fifteen "*vav's*" in *Emet veyatziv*).[118]

VERSES OF PRAISE

דּוֹר לְדוֹר יְשַׁבַּח מַעֲשֶׂיךָ. וּגְבוּרֹתֶיךָ יַגִּידוּ:

הֲדַר כְּבוֹד הוֹדֶךָ, וְדִבְרֵי נִפְלְאֹתֶיךָ אָשִׂיחָה:

וֶעֱזוּז נוֹרְאוֹתֶיךָ יֹאמֵרוּ, וּגְדֻלָּתְךָ אֲסַפְּרֶנָּה:

זֵכֶר רַב טוּבְךָ יַבִּיעוּ, וְצִדְקָתְךָ יְרַנֵּנוּ:

חַנּוּן וְרַחוּם יְיָ, אֶרֶךְ אַפַּיִם וּגְדָל חָסֶד:

טוֹב יְיָ לַכֹּל, וְרַחֲמָיו עַל כָּל מַעֲשָׂיו:

יוֹדוּךָ יְיָ כָּל מַעֲשֶׂיךָ, וַחֲסִידֶיךָ יְבָרְכוּכָה:

כְּבוֹד מַלְכוּתְךָ יֹאמֵרוּ, וּגְבוּרָתְךָ יְדַבֵּרוּ:

לְהוֹדִיעַ לִבְנֵי הָאָדָם גְּבוּרֹתָיו, וּכְבוֹד הֲדַר מַלְכוּתוֹ:

מַלְכוּתְךָ, מַלְכוּת כָּל עוֹלָמִים, וּמֶמְשַׁלְתְּךָ בְּכָל דּוֹר וָדֹר:

סוֹמֵךְ יְיָ לְכָל הַנֹּפְלִים, וְזוֹקֵף לְכָל הַכְּפוּפִים:

עֵינֵי כֹל אֵלֶיךָ יְשַׂבֵּרוּ, וְאַתָּה נוֹתֵן לָהֶם אֶת אָכְלָם בְּעִתּוֹ:

ממלא כל עולמים
אהבת עולם (כמים)
כי הוא חיות העולם
רוח
עולם היצירה

CHASSIDIC INSIGHTS

(continued from p. 136)

to remain "safe." However, to fully mature, we frequently need to override our emotions and our "need for safety," and allow ourselves to try "something new." In order to do so, we need our intellect. With the intellect, we can take calculated risks. With our minds, we can detect new horizons and new possibilities that go beyond our emotional need for safety. In this sense, we can "move," uprooting ourselves from our natural emotions and transporting ourselves to a totally new "environment," or state of mind, associated with our intellect. In this sense, then the intellect corresponds to the animal kingdom, that is characterized by "movement."

Finally, what characterizes humans, and takes us beyond the realm of intellect, is speech. With our power of speech (it is with divine

(continued on p. 140)

Immanent Godliness
Lower love (water)
Love: vitality of the universe
Soul level: Ruach
World of Yetzira

One generation to the next praises Your works, and tells of Your might.

Your majesty is glorious, and words of Your wonders I will speak.

They will talk of the boldness of Your awesome acts and of Your greatness I will tell.

Remembrance of Your great goodness will be expressed, and Your righteousness will be sung.

The Lord is gracious and compassionate, He is patient, and of great kindness.

The Lord is good to all, and compassionate over all of His works.

Lord, all of Your works will be grateful to You, Your pious ones will bless You.

They narrate the honor of Your reign, and speak of Your might.

In order to inform men of His might, and the honor of His glorious reign.

Your reign is the Kingship of all worlds, and Your dominion over all generations.

The Lord raises all who have fallen, and straightens all who are stooped.

The eyes of all gaze at You longingly, and You grant them their sustenance at the right time.

Word Sparks — *The three verses (Psalms 145:11-13), "They narrate the honor...In order to inform men...Your reign..." allude to three tzimtzumim ("contractions") as Godliness descends to relate to our world. The gevurot ("might, power" that enable contraction) mentioned in verse 11 form the conditions for creation of the universe ("Your reign"), which is mentioned in verse 13. But, what is the "might" mentioned in verse 12, and why is it expressed as "His might" rather than as "Your might" as in the previous verse? In answer, the gevurot mentioned in verse 12 refer not to creation of the world, but to the souls of men, which remain hidden until they descend to become enclothed in bodies in this world. This descent of the soul requires a much higher form of gevura ("might"), coming from the supremely high level of atik, which is hidden from us. Therefore, it requires "His might" (third person, concealed) and not "Your might" (second person, revealed). (Torat Shmuel 5637/1877 of the Rebbe Maharash, Vol 2, p. 572 and Torat Shmuel 5642/1882 p. 71)*

פּוֹתֵחַ אֶת יָדֶךָ, וּמַשְׂבִּיעַ לְכָל חַי רָצוֹן:
צַדִּיק יְיָ בְּכָל דְּרָכָיו, וְחָסִיד בְּכָל מַעֲשָׂיו:

ממלא כל עולמים
אהבת עולם (כמים)
כי הוא חיות העולם
רוח
עולם היצירה

❝ The great love (*ahava rabba*) embedded in the very root of our soul, emerging from the same source as the soul itself, knows no interruption." (*Torah Ohr* of the Alter Rebbe, מ"ז, col. 2)[119]

About *ahava rabba*, we say *poteach et yadecha* ("open Your hands"), which can also be read as "open up Your *yud*'s," referring to the two *yud*'s of God's name (the first letter of the name *Havaya* and the final letter of the name *Ado-nay*). The *yud* represents *chochma*, and when He opens the letter *yud* of His name, there is a flow of *chochma* from above, and we may experience *ahava rabba*. We may encourage this to occur by studying the secrets of the Torah.

There are at least two levels of love of God. The first, *ahavat olam* (*olam* meaning "world"), results from meditation pertaining to creation and the Godliness embedded in creation. While meditating on these topics, we may easily be distracted or tempted by other themes, and then the experience of love is interrupted. However, when we meditate upon higher transcendent Godliness that is beyond creation and achieve *ahava rabba*, we may experience uninterrupted love of God..

📖 *Within the Words*

It is important to think of the meaning of the words as we say, *Poteach et yadecha* ("Open Your hands...") — and if not, we are required to return and recite the words again.[120]

──── **CHASSIDIC INSIGHTS** ────

(continued from p. 138)

"speech" that God created the universe), we are able to manipulate and express all of our lower attributes (letters, emotions, intellect) in an organic whole that is more than the sum of its parts. It is speech that takes us out of the animal realm and puts us in a new category in

(continued on p. 142)

סידור עם חסידות – שחרית

Immanent Godliness
Lower love (water)
Love: vitality of the universe
Soul level: *Ruach*
World of *Yetzira*

> You open Your hands, and satisfy the desire of all living creatures.
>
> The Lord is righteous in all of His paths, and kind in all His deeds.

❝ 'And satisfy the desire of all living creatures...' with spiritual energy that descends and illuminates, expanding throughout the universe from the highest to the lowest levels..." (*Torah Ohr* of the Alter Rebbe, p. 94, col 1)[121]

This is the energy of the first two letters of His name, *Havaya*, that flows into the universe when He "opens His *yud*'s" as a result of our prayers. It flows into creation, and we become conscious of it as well, experiencing it as *ahava rabba*.

This *ahava rabba* is embedded in the soul and comes from the same place that the soul itself comes from. That is what enables the soul to tolerate such a great and infinite revelation of Godliness. It is expressed in our fulfillment of Torah and its mitzvot in thought, speech and action. Moreover, even when we are involved in other matters, this love remains wedged in our heart.

📖 *Within the Words*

The word *chai* ("life" or "living") applies to the *sephira* of *yesod*, which channels divine energy, or "life," from the upper nine *sephirot* into the lowest, *malchut*. For the same reason, *yesod* is also called *tov* ("good"), since the divine vitality that *yesod* channels from the higher *sephirot* of *Atzilut* into *malchut*, and from there to the lower worlds, is for the benefit of creation. Throughout the spiritual chain of creation (*seder hishtalshelut*) as well as within each world, there are fifteen such *yesodot* ("foundations") that channel Godly energy from above to below. After requesting that He "open His *yud*'s" and show His benevolence, we then request that He "satisfy the desires of all living..." — meaning that He provide goodness to all of the various levels of *yesod* that channel His goodness down to the lowest physical world...[122]

VERSES OF PRAISE

קָרוֹב יְיָ לְכָל קֹרְאָיו, לְכֹל אֲשֶׁר יִקְרָאֻהוּ בֶאֱמֶת:
רְצוֹן יְרֵאָיו יַעֲשֶׂה, וְאֶת שַׁוְעָתָם יִשְׁמַע וְיוֹשִׁיעֵם:

ממלא כל עולמים
אהבת עולם (כמים)
כי הוא חיות העולם
רוח
עולם היצירה

> **The 'hands'** [in *poteach et yadecha*] **are the left and right hands. They refer to** *ahavat olam* **("worldly love") and** *ahava rabba* **("great love").** (*Torat Chaim* of the Mitteler Rebbe, *Parshat Vayechi*, p. 100c, or p. 241a in the new printing)[123]

The right hand is the hand of *chesed* ("kindness") that descends to us as we meditate upon Godliness that transcends creation; that is how we develop *ahavah rabba*. The left hand imparts the willpower and discipline that is necessary to develop *ahavat olam* — love resulting from meditation upon Godliness embedded in nature.

As we meditate upon the Godliness embedded in the creation, we develop *ahavat olam* ("wordly/mundane love"). Then, we ascend and experience transcendent love from above, called *ahava rabba* ("great love").

📖 Within the Words

"Open Your hands" refers to the two letters *yud* and *vav* of God's name. With the "left hand," we minimize our egos and ascend. Our self-nullification is symbolized by the letter *yud* of God's name. As our love of God grows and develops, the *yud* "opens" into a *vav* from above to bestow upon us *ahava rabba* from His right hand. And then we say, "You satisfy the will of every living creature," for we are sated with the happiness and joy of divine revelation.

CHASSIDIC INSIGHTS

(continued from p. 140)

which we, like God, are creative (it is understood that we are not creative in the Godly sense, creating from nothing to something. However, human creativity contains an element of newness and originality that is beyond the intellect and is, indeed, imbued with a quality that is spiritual and transcendent).

From the *sicha* of the Rebbe (translated in "Love like Fire and Water"), we understand that these four elements — letters, emotions,

(continued on p. 144)

Immanent Godliness
Lower love (water)
Love: vitality of the universe
Soul level: Ruach
World of Yetzira

The Lord is near to all who call Him, to all who call upon Him in truth.

He fulfills the will of those who fear Him, hears their cry and saves them.

> **The expectation and yearning that is part of the human condition…is for Godly illumination of the heart…"** (*Sefer Maamorim* 5665/1905 of the Rebbe Rashab, p. 84)[124]

Two divine names illuminate the creation — the name *Havaya* (*yud-hey-vav-hey*) during the day and the name *Ado-nay* (*aleph-dalet-nun-yud*) during the night. The two names are enmeshed, so that the first letter of the combined names is the *yud* of the name *Havaya*, and the final letter is the *yud* of the name *Ado-nay*. Thus, the first and last letters of the intertwined names are *yud*'s. When we say *poteach et yadech*, we allude to *yudecha* — "Your *yud*'s" — the first and last letters of His names. We request that they "open" to allow physical and spiritual influx to descend to the world.

Godly illumination from His essential name *Havaya* does not shine directly into the creation. It arrives enclothed in the names *Elokim* and *Ado-nay*. Only a contracted and limited ray of spirituality illuminates the universe, enclothed in His name *Elokim*, and from there it descends to *Ado-nay*. Thus, it is like the *yud* of God's name, contracted and limited. Yet, we seek revelation of Godliness from beyond creation.

Within the Words

First, the verse tells us, "The eyes of everyone look to You expectantly…" "Everyone" (*kol* in Hebrew) carries the *gematria* of fifty, and represents the Fifty Gates of Understanding, from the mind to the heart.[125] This is our yearning for Godly revelation. And then, we pray, "Open Your hands…" and bestow Godly revelation upon us. We pray that God "open His *yud*'s," so that Godly revelation flows down to us. The contraction of the *yud* contains all of the details of Godliness within creation, but to perceive them, we must first request that He "open" to us.

VERSES OF PRAISE

שׁוֹמֵר יְיָ אֶת כָּל אֹהֲבָיו, וְאֵת כָּל הָרְשָׁעִים יַשְׁמִיד:
תְּהִלַּת יְיָ יְדַבֶּר פִּי, וִיבָרֵךְ כָּל בָּשָׂר שֵׁם קָדְשׁוֹ לְעוֹלָם וָעֶד:
וַאֲנַחְנוּ נְבָרֵךְ יָהּ, מֵעַתָּה וְעַד עוֹלָם, הַלְלוּיָהּ:

הַלְלוּיָהּ, הַלְלִי נַפְשִׁי אֶת יְיָ:
אֲהַלְלָה יְיָ בְּחַיָּי, אֲזַמְּרָה לֵאלֹהַי בְּעוֹדִי:
אַל תִּבְטְחוּ בִנְדִיבִים, בְּבֶן אָדָם שֶׁאֵין לוֹ תְשׁוּעָה:

ממלא כל עולמים
אהבת עולם (כמים)
כי הוא חיי נפשי
רוח
עולם היצירה

> "It is not a simple matter for man to draw upon revelation and illumination of the soul from the ten holy *sephirot*...but the opposite is true of the *klipa* and *sitra achra* which oppose and conceal holiness — from them, man is able to attain his needs relatively easily and free of cost..." (Alter Rebbe's Siddur, p. 112)[126]

> The world was created *zeh l'umat zeh* — with diametrically opposing forces. God created the ten holy *sephirot*, from which we attain divine inspiration and revelation. He also created negative forces that oppose and conceal holiness. The negative forces divide into two categories: *klipat noga* ("shining concealment") and *klipot t'meot* ("impure concealments"). *Klipat noga* contains sparks of good as well as evil, and our job is to purify and "remove" the good from the evil. But the *klipot t'meot* contain only evil and completely conceal Godliness; our task is to avoid them.

─── **CHASSIDIC INSIGHTS** ───

(continued from p. 142)

intellect and creativity — give us clues to understanding the four worlds. From our own flesh and being, we grasp Godliness. By meditating upon the letters of the physical objects that we chose from each of the four categories of creation, we activate the letters within us, corresponding to the world of *Asiya*. Our emotions correspond to the world of *Yetzira*, our intellect to *Bria*, and our power of speech to the world of *Atzilut*. In this manner, we are able to extrapolate from our

(continued on p. 146)

Immanent Godliness
Lower love (water)
Love: vitality of my soul
Soul level: Ruach
World of Yetzira

> The Lord guards over all who love Him,
> and destroys the wicked.
>
> My mouth speaks the praises of the Lord,
> and all flesh blesses His holy name forever.
>
> And we bless God, from now and forever, Halleluyah!
>
> HALLELUYAH, MY SOUL PRAISES THE LORD. I will praise the Lord with my life, I will sing to the Lord from the essence of my being.
>
> Do not rely upon gratuitous volunteers, upon man who brings no salvation.
>
> His spirit departs and returns to its dust, on that day all his plans dissipate.

When we lead a life of Torah and mitzvot, we are usually able to meet our physical needs, even though we may have to work hard to do so. However, those who do not lead a holy life are often "blessed" with more than they need, even though they put out little effort. This may occur when they access realms of spirituality that are not "clean," that require subjugation to impropriety or immorality. Sometimes such opportunities even come knocking on the door, so to speak, and offer their services for "free."

Within the Words

The psalm warns us, "Do no rely upon gratuitous volunteers (*nedivim*)..." — this is the realm of *klipat noga*, that supplies us upon request, but demands that we subjugate ourselves to the evil that is also mixed in with the good. "[Nor] upon man who brings no salvation" — this is the realm of the three totally impure *klipot*, which offer their "services" for free, but are accompanied by addictive and negative consequences from which it is difficult to extract ourselves. We should pray that Godly influence should descend to us only via "kosher" channels.

VERSES OF PRAISE

תֵּצֵא רוּחוֹ יָשֻׁב לְאַדְמָתוֹ, בַּיּוֹם הַהוּא אָבְדוּ עֶשְׁתֹּנֹתָיו:

אַשְׁרֵי שֶׁאֵל יַעֲקֹב בְּעֶזְרוֹ, שִׂבְרוֹ עַל יְיָ אֱלֹהָיו:

עֹשֶׂה שָׁמַיִם וָאָרֶץ, אֶת הַיָּם וְאֶת כָּל אֲשֶׁר בָּם, הַשֹּׁמֵר אֱמֶת לְעוֹלָם:

עֹשֶׂה מִשְׁפָּט לָעֲשׁוּקִים, נֹתֵן לֶחֶם לָרְעֵבִים, יְיָ מַתִּיר אֲסוּרִים:

יְיָ פֹּקֵחַ עִוְרִים, יְיָ זֹקֵף כְּפוּפִים, יְיָ אֹהֵב צַדִּיקִים:

ממלא כל עולמים
אהבת עולם (כמים)
כי הוא חיי נפשי
רוח
עולם היצירה

❝ [There are four categories of holy sparks: 1) *re'evim* (the "hungry"); 2) *asurim* (the "imprisoned"); 3) *ivrim* (the "blind"); and 4) *kefufim* (the "bent over"). They correspond to the four worlds of *ABY"A*. (Psalm 145:14, Alter Rebbe's Siddur with Chasidut, p. 114)[127]

Re'evim correspond to the World of *Atzilut*. *Asurim* correspond to the World of *Bria*. *Ivrim* correspond to the World of *Yetzira*. And *Asurim* correspond to the World of *Asiya*.

All of these descriptions fit "personality types" of Jews meditating and praying with various levels of success. First of all, there are those called *noflim* ("fallen"),[128] because they have fallen completely under the influence of negative forces and are unable to extract themselves. Above them are the *kefufim* — those who have not fallen but whom are bent over — their attention and thoughts are directed downward, toward the physical world and its temptations, and not toward Godliness and spirituality. Above them are the *asurim* — the

--- CHASSIDIC INSIGHTS ---

(continued from p. 144)

own inner experience in order to "taste" the Godliness that is present in higher worlds and on higher spiritual levels. This is the goal of meditation upon the Godly light that illuminates the world as *memalle kol olmin* (inner, permeating immanent light), and arouses us to "love like water."

(continued on p. 166)

Immanent Godliness
Lower love (water)
Love: vitality of my soul
Soul level: Ruach
World of Yetzira

> Happy is he who is aided by the God of Jacob, his hope rests upon the Lord, his God.
>
> Who creates the heavens and earth, the sea and all within it; Who guards the truth forever.
>
> He renders justice for the wronged, gives bread to the hungry, and frees the imprisoned.
>
> The Lord opens the eyes of the blind, the Lord straightens the stooped over, the Lord loves the righteous.

"imprisoned" — who do manage to meditate upon and understand Godliness, but are unable to withstand the temptations of their animal soul. All of these three types are in the category of *ashukim* — those who are "oppressed" because, in one way or another, they are unable to achieve conscious Godly revelation. Above all of the "oppressed," we find two kinds of Jews who do manage to attain some kind of Godly revelation. There are the *re'eivim* (the "hungry") who understand Godliness intellectually, but who are unable to feel and experience it in their heart; they grasp what it is, but since they are unable to attain it, they are "hungry." And then there are the *ivrim* — the "blind" — who glimpse Godliness, but from afar; they are aware of Godliness, but not clearly, and therefore they are called "blind."

📖 *Within the Words*

In response to the *noflim*, Psalm 145:16 says that God "supports all of the fallen." Regarding the *kefufim*, Psalm 146:8 says that God "straightens out all the bent-over." Regarding the *asurim*, the psalm (146) says that "He frees the imprisoned." About all of them, Psalm 146:7 tells us, "He renders justice for the *ashukim* ("oppressed")." And then, "He gives bread to the *re'eivim* ("hungry") and "opens the eyes of the *ivrim* ("blind"). Whatever their spiritual deficiencies, God resolves them, by elevating those trapped in the *klipot*, by opening the hearts of the "hungry" so that they experience Godliness, and by opening the eyes of the "blind" so that they become clearly aware of Godliness.

VERSES OF PRAISE

יְיָ שֹׁמֵר אֶת גֵּרִים, יָתוֹם וְאַלְמָנָה יְעוֹדֵד,
וְדֶרֶךְ רְשָׁעִים יְעַוֵּת:
יִמְלֹךְ יְיָ לְעוֹלָם, אֱלֹהַיִךְ צִיּוֹן לְדֹר וָדֹר הַלְלוּיָהּ:

ממלא כל עולמים
אהבת עולם (כמים)
כי הוא חיי נפשי
רוח
עולם היצירה

❝ [The reference to] *gerim* ("converts") alludes to sparks of holiness that fell into the realm of the seventy non-Jewish nations of the world and then entered the world of Judaism, under the wings of the *Shechina*." (Alter Rebbe's Siddur with Chassidut, p. נ"ח, col 2)[129]

The concept of *shevirat hakelim* ("shattering of the vessels") tells us that elements of *kedusha* "fell" from their initial holy status and found their way into the *klipot*, or various levels of concealment of Godliness. The fallen sparks might be souls, or they could be elements of the physical world. When they either convert to Judaism or are used for holy purposes, such as a mitzvah, they revert to the realm of *kedusha* and are called "converts."

Interestingly, one who converts to Judaism is considered retroactively to have always had a Jewish soul. However, before conversion, the soul was housed in a non-Jewish body, which becomes Jewish upon conversion. That is why we never refer to a convert as a "non-Jew who converted," but rather as a "convert who converted."

📖 *Within the Words*

Similar to *ba'alei teshuva* — those Jews who strayed off the path of Torah and mitzvot and returned — converts need special attention and protection so that they do not slip back to their previous lifestyles. Therefore, Psalm 146:9 tells us that God is *shomer et gerim* — "He guards the converts."

❝ Now in exile, the Jews are called an *almanah* ("widow")...about whom the sages said, "her husband went overseas." (Torat Shmuel 5630/1870 of the Rebbe Maharash, p. 232)[130]

There are two ways of counting the "fifty gates of *bina*," which are conduits connecting the intellect with the heart. One path is from below to above, as we seek to uplift our emotions so they become imbued with intellect, and ultimately subsumed in the infinite light Above. The other path is from Above to below, as we bring the infinite light from Above down to our intellect and from there into our divine emotions, during prayers.

סידור עם חסידות – שחרית

Immanent Godliness
Lower love (water)
Love: vitality of my soul
Soul level: *Ruach*
World of *Yetzira*

The Lord guards the proselytes, supports orphans and widows, and thwarts the path of the wicked.

May the Lord reign forever: Your God over Zion, from generation to generation, Halleluyah!

🕯️ The path of ascent is associated with the verse, "To You (*lecha* = fifty) Lord belongs the greatness, the might, the harmony, the victory and the majesty…" There are five attributes listed, each including all of the ten *sephirot* for a total of fifty. The path of descent is associated with the end of the verse; "…for all (*col* = fifty) that is in the heavens of the earth…" Together, the paths of ascent and descent add up to one hundred, as in the verse, "And Yitzhak sowed in the land and reaped one hundred gates that year." To the extent that we meditate, developing paths of spiritual ascent and descent, we become acquainted with the "husband" who is overseas, with God. "Her husband is known in the gates" — each according to his level of meditation.

> 📖 *Within the Words*
>
> The sages said, "One should always organize his praises of God, and then pray." When we praise God ("To You Lord belongs the greatness, the might…etc"), we bring out His attributes from a state of concealment to revelation. And then we pray ("…for all that is in the heavens and earth"), bringing down Godliness from Above to below. But in *galut* ("exile"), we are compared to an *almanah* ("widow"), whose wedding contract includes only one hundred coins (unlike the virgin who receives two hundred coins). Therefore, we are like a widow who is "lacking" one hundred (*al-manah* — "without one hundred"); that is, lacking the one hundred gates of spiritual ascent and descent. We are like an *almanah* in another sense as well, from the word *ilem* ("dumb") — we do not hear the "voice" of God in exile, since there are no revealed signs of Godliness. And therefore we are like an *ilem* — like one who is unable to speak. Godliness has departed, gone "overseas." Divine intellect is not shining into our emotions, and therefore His voice is not heard. But when we say one hundred blessings every day, we bring Godliness from Above into our lives. And therefore, we also request from God to "support the orphan and the widow," meaning to support our quest for Godly revelation to descend to us from Above.

VERSES OF PRAISE

הַלְלוּיָהּ, כִּי טוֹב זַמְּרָה אֱלֹהֵינוּ, כִּי נָעִים נָאוָה תְהִלָּה:

ממלא כל עולמים
אהבת עולם (כמים)
כי הוא חיי נפשי
רוח
עולם היצירה

> **The reason our praise is called *hillul*, from *yahel oro* ("let His light shine") is because a flash of illumination emerges as our praises elicit a divine trait from concealment to revealed light."**
> (Alter Rebbe's Siddur with Chasidut p. נ"ו, col. 2)[131]

The word *Halleluyah* ("Praise God") that occurs throughout the *pesukei dezimra* is composed of the words *Hallel* ("Praise") and *Yud-Hey*, the first two letters of God's holy name *Havaya*. These two letters represent divine intellect (*chochma* and *bina*) that penetrates our consciouness as we pray. As divine intellect permeates our awareness, it evolves into emotions of divine love and fear of God.

There are two types of intellect that we develop as we pray. One is the intellect that infuses our emotions as we pray the *pesukei dezimra*. This is intellect that we readily grasp and understand, and it is called *memalled kol olmin* ("immanent spirituality"). It descends to influence our emotions as we meditate upon how Godliness fills and permeates creation. The second type of intellect is experienced later in prayers, after *Barchu*, as we meditate upon Godly levels that surpass and transcend creation. This is "pure intellect" that does not descend to the emotions. It is called *sovev kol olmin* ("transcendent Godliness"), and it uplifts our emotions to the level of intellect so that we cleave to Godliness. This is what we experience on the soul level of *neshama* and *chaya*.

📖 *Within the Words*

When we praise somebody as kind or wise, he usually responds positively to our praise. In fact, he generally responds by demonstrating the very trait with which we praise him. Our praise brings out his latent potential to a state of revelation. In a similar way, our praise influences God's divine characteristics above. As we say *Halleluyah*, we elicit His divine trait of wisdom and understanding so that it flows down to us in the lower worlds of BY"A. This is how our prayers have the potential to influence creation.

Immanent Godliness
Lower love (water)
Love: vitality of my soul
Soul level: Ruach
World of Yetzira

HALLELUYAH, FOR IT IS GOOD TO SING (TO) OUR Lord, for He is pleasant and praise is befitting.

❝ **When we sing in front of a bride and groom, we seek to arouse joy and happiness in their heart with our singing…The songs and melodies [resonate in the] World of *Atzilut*.**❞ (Alter Rebbe's Siddur with Chasidut, p. נ"ט, col 1)[132]

The songs of the angels and souls above stimulate joy within *bina* of *malchut* of the World of *Atzilut*. The joy comes from a high concealed level within *Atik Yomin* (*Keter*) but it becomes revealed within *bina* (*Elokeinu*) of *malchut*.

During the recitation of the psalms of *pesukei dezimra*, our praises of God elicit His divine attributes to emerge from concealment into conscious revelation. Our joy during prayer also has an effect above — it resonates in the *sephira* of *malchut*, the final *sephira* of the World of *Atzilut*. There, our joy elicits revelation of Godliness from the highest sources — from the hidden recesses (*Atik Yomin*) of *Keter* — causing "singing" above in the celestial worlds as well.

📖 *Within the Words*

Here, the question is why does the first verse of Psalm 147 read, "Praise God for it is good to sing our Lord…"? Why doesn't the verse just say, "sing to our Lord"? The answer is that our "singing" during prayer has the effect of bringing down holy influx. It has the effect of arousing divine illumination from the highest levels (*Atik Yomin*) to shine within our intellect (*bina*). If the verse would have said, "sing to our Lord," it would have implied the opposite dynamic — pleading to God from below to above. And therefore, the verse states, "Praise God for it is good to sing our Lord" — to demonstrate that we stimulate singing in the celestial worlds to descend from above to below, to descend and permeate own consciousness. We do not merely sing in front of Him, but we stimulate song above.[133]

VERSES OF PRAISE

בּוֹנֵה יְרוּשָׁלַיִם יְיָ, נִדְחֵי יִשְׂרָאֵל יְכַנֵּס:
הָרוֹפֵא לִשְׁבוּרֵי לֵב, וּמְחַבֵּשׁ לְעַצְּבוֹתָם:
מוֹנֶה מִסְפָּר לַכּוֹכָבִים, לְכֻלָּם שֵׁמוֹת יִקְרָא:
גָּדוֹל אֲדוֹנֵינוּ וְרַב כֹּחַ, לִתְבוּנָתוֹ אֵין מִסְפָּר:
מְעוֹדֵד עֲנָוִים יְיָ, מַשְׁפִּיל רְשָׁעִים עֲדֵי אָרֶץ:
עֱנוּ לַיְיָ בְּתוֹדָה, זַמְּרוּ לֵאלֹהֵינוּ בְכִנּוֹר:
הַמְכַסֶּה שָׁמַיִם בְּעָבִים, הַמֵּכִין לָאָרֶץ מָטָר, הַמַּצְמִיחַ הָרִים חָצִיר:
נוֹתֵן לִבְהֵמָה לַחְמָהּ, לִבְנֵי עֹרֵב אֲשֶׁר יִקְרָאוּ:

ממלא כל עולמים
אהבת עולם (כמים)
כי הוא חיי נפשי
רוח
עולם היצירה

> **Since** *Tzion* is a greater spiritual level than *Yerushalayim*...why is *Yerushalayim* associated with the name *Havaya* (Psalm 147:2), while *Tzion* is associated with the name *Elokim* (Psalm 146:10)?" (*Torat Shmuel* 5627/1867 of the Rebbe Maharash, pp. 423-425)[134]

Tzion is such a high level that it draws down illumination from the infinite light of God (*ohr ein sof*). This light would be available to everyone, regardless of whether they deserve it, were it not limited by the name *Elokim*, which is associated with the *hey gevurot* ("five stringencies") that contract and limit His infinite light.

Psalm 147:13 states, "He has strengthened the bolts of your gates.." The purpose of a bolt is to lock a gate or door, to prevent the entrance of those who do not belong within the city. The name *Elokim* is like a bolt or lock, limiting the infinite light so that it does not become accessible to those who do not deserve it. And then, the verse continues: "He has blessed your children within." As a result of the "lock," only those who are within the "city" are "blessed" because the Godly illumination flows only to them.

📖 *Within the Words*

Psalm 147:14 states, "He establishes peace at your borders." Peace is attained when two opposites become joined and united. In the case

Immanent Godliness
Lower love (water)
Love: vitality of my soul
Soul level: Ruach
World of Yetzira

The Lord builds Jerusalem,
He will gather the dispersed Jews.

He heals the broken-hearted,
and treats all of their suffering.

He counts the number of stars,
calling them all by name.

Great is our Master, and abundantly powerful,
his intellect cannot be quantified.

The Lord supports the humble,
lowers the wicked down to the earth.

Respond to the Lord in gratitude,
sing to our God with a harp.

Who covers the heavens with clouds, prepares rain
for the earth, germinates pasture on the mountains.

He provides fodder for the cattle,
for the offspring of ravens who call.

> 📖 *Within the Words*
>
> of prayer and *avodat Hashem*, "peace" occurs when the animal soul acquiesces to the divine soul and accepts Godliness. At that point, our "borders" become "peaceful" — our thought, speech, and action (which are the "borders," or interfaces with which our soul interacts with the outside world) are no longer challenged. They become dedicated and devoted to God. And then the verse continues, "He satiates you with the cream of wheat." Wheat corresponds to Torah, since the numerical value of wheat (*chita* in Hebrew) is twenty-two, symbolizing the twenty-two letters of the Hebrew alphabet. When we guard our borders to allow in only *kedusha*, we deserve the "cream of wheat" — the secrets of the Torah.

לֹא בִגְבוּרַת הַסּוּס יֶחְפָּץ, לֹא בְשׁוֹקֵי הָאִישׁ יִרְצֶה:
רוֹצֶה יְיָ אֶת יְרֵאָיו, אֶת הַמְיַחֲלִים לְחַסְדּוֹ:
שַׁבְּחִי יְרוּשָׁלַיִם אֶת יְיָ, הַלְלִי אֱלֹהַיִךְ צִיּוֹן:
כִּי חִזַּק בְּרִיחֵי שְׁעָרָיִךְ, בֵּרַךְ בָּנַיִךְ בְּקִרְבֵּךְ:
הַשָּׂם גְּבוּלֵךְ שָׁלוֹם, חֵלֶב חִטִּים יַשְׂבִּיעֵךְ:
הַשֹּׁלֵחַ אִמְרָתוֹ אָרֶץ, עַד מְהֵרָה יָרוּץ דְּבָרוֹ:
הַנֹּתֵן שֶׁלֶג כַּצָּמֶר, כְּפוֹר כָּאֵפֶר יְפַזֵּר:
מַשְׁלִיךְ קַרְחוֹ כְפִתִּים, לִפְנֵי קָרָתוֹ מִי יַעֲמֹד:
יִשְׁלַח דְּבָרוֹ וְיַמְסֵם, יַשֵּׁב רוּחוֹ יִזְּלוּ מָיִם:

ממלא כל עולמים
אהבת עולם (כמים)
כי הוא חיי נפשי
רוח
עולם היצירה

"There are two ways in which Godliness descends to us — either slowly or rapidly…" (*Sefer Maamorim 5659/1899 of the Rebbe Rashab, p. 114*)[135]

"There is *chesed* and there is *chesed*," says the Zohar. There is the *chesed* that filters down to us through the various spiritual levels of the World of *Atzilut* and through the entire chain of creation. And there is *rav chesed* ("great kindness") that circumvents the entire of hierarchy of creation. Since *rav chesed* is connected to the very source and origin of *chesed* in *Keter*, it "skips" all the intermediary steps to arrive directly at our "doorstep."

Why must we request our needs, such as health and sustenance every day, during the *Shemonah Esreh*? Isn't it enough to pray for our annual physical needs on Rosh Hashana, when they are granted to us? The answer is that even though our needs are granted on Rosh Hashana, they may not descend to us exactly when we need them during the year, at the time that we need them most. They may be delayed or obstructed at any spiritual level. Therefore, we need to pray every day and request that our current needs be met on that day. The same is true of "judgment." We are judged for the entire year on Rosh Hashana, and yet our judgment is delayed in each

Immanent Godliness
Lower love (water)
Love: vitality of my soul
Soul level: Ruach
World of Yetzira

> He desires not the strength of the horse, nor does he want the legs of man.
>
> The Lord desires those who fear Him, those who yearn for His kindness.
>
> Praise the Lord, Jerusalem, praise your God, Zion!
>
> For He has strengthened the bolts of Your gates, [and] blessed Your children within.
>
> He establishes peace at your borders, He satiates you with the cream of wheat.
>
> He sends His utterance earthward, His word travels very quickly.
>
> He provides snow [soft] as wool, He scatters frost like ashes.
>
> He hurls His ice like crumbs, who can stand before His cold?
>
> He dispatches His word and [the ice] melts, He makes His wind blow and water flows.

world as it descends to us. For that reason, we must pray every day that what we need on that day should descend to us.

Within the Words

The words of Psalm 147:15, "He sends His utterance earthward..." refer to our physical needs and judgment that descend "slowly," stopping in each world and at each spiritual level while we pray for its descent. The end of the verse, "His word travels very quickly," refers to the divine response that descends rapidly from *rav chesed* ("great kindness"), circumventing the entire chain of spiritual and physical creation to arrive at our "doorstep" without delay.

מַגִּיד דְּבָרָיו לְיַעֲקֹב, חֻקָּיו וּמִשְׁפָּטָיו לְיִשְׂרָאֵל: לֹא עָשָׂה כֵן לְכָל גּוֹי, וּמִשְׁפָּטִים בַּל יְדָעוּם. הַלְלוּיָהּ:

הַלְלוּיָהּ, הַלְלוּ אֶת יְיָ מִן הַשָּׁמַיִם, הַלְלוּהוּ בַּמְּרוֹמִים: הַלְלוּהוּ כָל מַלְאָכָיו, הַלְלוּהוּ כָּל צְבָאָיו: הַלְלוּהוּ שֶׁמֶשׁ וְיָרֵחַ, הַלְלוּהוּ כָּל כּוֹכְבֵי אוֹר:

ממלא כל עולמים
אהבת עולם (כמים)
כי הוא חיי נפשי
רוח
עולם היצירה

> **God wraps the light of Torah around Himself like a robe…about this it is written, 'His garments are like white snow.'**[136] **So, there is such a thing as snow and ice above…"** (Sefer Maamorim 5655/1895 of the Rebbe Rashab, p. 3)[137]

Godly illumination is infinite. We are capable of perceiving it only when it descends enclothed in a "garment" that reduces its intensity, but reveals its illumination to people on our level. That "garment" is the Torah, which descends to us as from the *sephira* of *chochma* ("wisdom"). *Chochma* is the interface between ourselves and the infinite light of God. In turn, Godly illumination descends to the Torah from *Keter*, via the "thirteen strands of the beard," which also represent the "thirteen attributes of mercy" and correspond to the thirteen principles with which the Torah is interpreted.

Snow and ice are two paths of divine descent to our world. Godly light descends as "ice," which is hard and impenetrable, in order to create the world. As Godly energy descends from *Atzilut* to create the three lower worlds of *BY"A*, it "freezes" so that divine illumination becomes totally concealed in this world. But, the light of the Torah descends to us as "snow," which is soft and melts easily. Through the laws and secrets of the Torah, we are able to penetrate the concealment and more easily comprehend Godliness.

📖 *Within the Words*

Psalm 147:17 reads, "He hurls His ice like crumbs…" This refers to the creation of the universe, and therefore, "…who can stand before His cold?" That is, who is able to detect and experience Godliness by merely meditating upon the garments of nature, which are

Immanent Godliness
Lower love (water)
Love: vitality of my soul
Soul level: Ruach
World of Yetzira

He tells His words to Jacob, His laws and judgments to Israel.

He did not do so for any other nation,

[to them His] statutes are unknown. Halleluyah!

HALLELUYAH, PRAISED BE THE LORD FROM THE HEAVENS, praise Him on the heights.

Praise Him, all of His angels, praise Him, all of His hosts.

Praise Him, sun and the moon, praise Him,
all of the shining stars.

📖 *Within the Words*

comparable to "ice"? But the Book of Daniel says, "His garments are like white snow…" God's garment — the Torah — is compared to snow, which melts easily so those who learn and practice it may more easily detect and comprehend Godliness.

Word Sparks

"Praised be the Lord from the heavens" — we don't see the heavens themselves at all, because they are so high.

"Praise Him on the heights" — this is the world of bria, which reveals the color of the heavens but not heaven itself. There are angels here, but they are not "conduits of influence," since they are too high to convey influx to our world.

"Praise Him, all of His angels…" — this is the world of yetzira, "home" of angels who are conduits of influence and influx to the lower worlds including our own.

"All of His hosts…" these are the angels of asiya, known as His "hosts" who fulfill His will.

"Praise Him, sun and the moon…" — this is the world of asiya as it ascends to be included in yetzira; yetzira is the "sun" and asiya the "moon."

"All of the shining stars" — this is yetzira as it ascends to be included in bria.

"Praise be the name of the Lord…" — this refers to the creation of the world from the name Havaya, beyond creation. From this level, the universe was created "automatically," unlike in the creation narrative in Genesis in which the name Elokim was enclothed in nature in order to create it. (Torat Shmuel 5639/1879 of the Rebbe Maharash, pp. 170-172, based on the Ariz'l)

VERSES OF PRAISE

הַלְלוּהוּ שְׁמֵי הַשָּׁמָיִם, וְהַמַּיִם אֲשֶׁר מֵעַל הַשָּׁמָיִם:
יְהַלְלוּ אֶת שֵׁם יְיָ, כִּי הוּא צִוָּה וְנִבְרָאוּ:
וַיַּעֲמִידֵם לָעַד לְעוֹלָם, חָק נָתַן וְלֹא יַעֲבוֹר:
הַלְלוּ אֶת יְיָ מִן הָאָרֶץ, תַּנִּינִים וְכָל תְּהֹמוֹת:
אֵשׁ וּבָרָד, שֶׁלֶג וְקִיטוֹר, רוּחַ סְעָרָה עֹשָׂה דְבָרוֹ:
הֶהָרִים וְכָל גְּבָעוֹת, עֵץ פְּרִי וְכָל אֲרָזִים:
הַחַיָּה וְכָל בְּהֵמָה, רֶמֶשׂ וְצִפּוֹר כָּנָף:

ממלא כל עולמים
אהבת עולם (כמים)
כי הוא חיי נפשי
רוח
עולם היצירה

> **Psalms 148 and 150 are the most important psalms of the *pesukei dezimra*"**[138] **"This is because they mention all aspects of the heavens and the earth."** (*Torat Shmuel 5627/1867* of the Rebbe Maharash, p. 169)[139]

Psalm 148 begins by discussing *ohr yashar*, divine illumination descending from above to below. The opening verses of Psalm 148 tell us that God is praised in the *shamayim* ("heavens") — this refers to the World of *Atzilut*. Then, He is praised in *meromim* ("heights") — this refers to the World of *Bria*. Then, all of His *malachim* ("angels") praise Him in the World of *Yetzira*. The angels of *Yetzira* are like ministers before the King, ready to do His bidding when necessary. Finally, the *tzva'ot* ("hosts") are like foot soldiers, incapable of carrying out complicated or subtle missions, but ready to fight for the King at a moment's notice — they are the angels of the World of *Asiya*.

The psalm then proceeds to discuss *ohr chozer* — our efforts to uplift the creation from below to above through prayer. "Praised be the sun and the moon" alludes to the inclusion of the World of *Asiya* within *Yetzira*. "Praised be all of the shining stars" refers to the inclusion of *Yetzira* within *Bria*. "The heaven's heavens" refers to *Bria* ascending to *Atzilut*, and the "waters that are above the heaven" refers to the elevation of *Atzilut* to the essential Godly light that transcends *Atzilut*. The psalm then goes on to mention creations from the four elements of fire, water, air and earth, as well as the categories of mineral, vegetable, animal and human. Altogether, it mentions the word *Hallelu* ("Praise God") ten times, corresponding to the ten

> Immanent Godliness
> Lower love (water)
> Love: vitality of my soul
> Soul level: *Ruach*
> World of *Yetzira*

Praise Him, heaven's heavens, as well as the waters that transcend the heavens.

Praise be the name of the Lord, for He commanded and they were created.

And He established them forever, He issued a decree, not to be transgressed.

Praised be the Lord from the earth, the serpents and all of the depths.

Fire and hail, snow and mist, stormy winds all do His bidding.

The mountains and all of the hills, fruit trees and all the cedars.

The wild animals and all beasts, crawling creatures and winged fowl.

---

creative utterances of *Bereishit*, to indicate that the entire creation is nullified to God. Finally, the psalm closes by mentioning the elevation of the Jewish people.

📖 Within the Words

From the "heavens" (*Atzilut*), Godly influence descends to the "heights" (*Bria*). Looking upward, we are able to detect only a tiny portion of what exists above us. Beyond the blue sky and clouds that we are able to detect, there is the troposphere, stratosphere, ionosphere, mesosphere and finally outer space (exosphere). But, all that we are capable of seeing is the blue sky above. This is an analogy for Godliness as well — our awareness is limited to the physical world and, if we are lucky and diligent, to the higher spiritual worlds. However, the World of *Atzilut* is invisible to us. Only when it descends to the World of *Bria* do we begin to have any concept of Godliness in the world.

✨ Word Sparks

"Praised be the Lord from the earth..." In the following verses, we find the four elements (earth, wind, water and fire) of creation and the four categories of creation (mineral, vegetable, animal and human), before concluding, *"His majesty over the earth and the heavens."* (Torat Shmuel 5639/1879 of the Rebbe Maharash, pp. 170-172, based on the Ariz'l)

מַלְכֵי אֶרֶץ וְכָל לְאֻמִּים, שָׂרִים וְכָל שֹׁפְטֵי אָרֶץ:
בַּחוּרִים וְגַם בְּתוּלוֹת, זְקֵנִים עִם נְעָרִים:
יְהַלְלוּ אֶת שֵׁם יְיָ כִּי נִשְׂגָּב שְׁמוֹ לְבַדּוֹ,
הוֹדוֹ עַל אֶרֶץ וְשָׁמָיִם:
וַיָּרֶם קֶרֶן לְעַמּוֹ, תְּהִלָּה לְכָל חֲסִידָיו,
לִבְנֵי יִשְׂרָאֵל עַם קְרֹבוֹ הַלְלוּיָהּ:

ממלא כל עולמים
אהבת עולם (כמים)
כי הוא חיי נפשי
רוח
עולם היצירה

> **The corner (קרן)** between two walls has no surface area of its own whatsoever. It joins two opposites, one of which may be a wall to the east and the other a wall to the south...In the spiritual realm, this is understood to refer to the very origin of Jewish souls..." (Alter Rebbe's Siddur with Chassidut, p. ס"ז)[140]

When the priest ascended the altar in the Temple, he began at the southeastern corner. The Zohar says that "first he had to become a 'corner' and then he could proceed to the south" — in the direction representing divine love of God. During prayer, we must also become like a "corner." We must nullify our ego to become "non-existent," and only then may we hope to achieve divine elevation. Jewish souls (*Knesset Yisrael*) come from the "corner" — from *malchut* of *Atzilut*, which has nothing of its own. It is the "meeting place" where the light and illumination of *Atzilut* meet and descend to *Bria*. Jewish souls emerge from this *ayin* ("divine void"). Just as a corner occurs where two walls meet, *malchut* occurs where Godliness (*Atzilut*) meets creation.

Similarly, a Jewish king possesses no real existence of his own — he is totally dependent upon the nation and upon God. His sovereignty (*malchut*) occurs only at the "place" where he encounters his own people, so that without his people, he is not a king. In this sense, sovereignty is like a corner — it has no real existence of its own, since it is nothing more than the place where two entities "meet." The same is true of Jewish souls, which are nothing more than the place where the Godliness meets the creation in a human body. It is from this rendezvous that Jewish souls derive their trait of *kabalat ohl malchut shamayim* ("acceptance of the yoke of heaven").

Immanent Godliness
Lower love (water)
Love: vitality of my soul
Soul level: Ruach
World of Yetzira

> The kings of the earth and all the nations,
> ministers and all judges of the earth.
>
> Young men as well as maidens,
> the elderly with the youth.
>
> Praised the name of the Lord, for His name is exalted alone, His majesty over the land and the heavens.
>
> And He raises the status of His people, in praise of all His pious ones, the Jews, His close people, Halleluyah!

📖 *Within the Words*

The word *keren* has three meanings. It may mean "corner," it may mean "ray of light," or it may mean "sovereignty." Just as a corner joins two directions of the wall, but doesn't really "exist," so a Jewish king is entirely dependent upon his connection with the people. He "exists" as a person, but he is not a king unless he has a nation that coronates him. Similarly, a ray of light is entirely dependent upon its source; it is non-existent without its source. Within us, *keren* is the ability to nullify ourselves, to make ourselves "non-existent" in order to accept the yoke of heaven. And when we do so, "He raises the *keren* of His people" — He raises us up to the highest spiritual levels, from where we bring a new light down to the world.[141] Moreover, with intense devotion during the *Kriat Shema*, we ascend to the *Baal Haratzon* — to the "Master of All Wills," who is capable of bringing a new will and light down into the world. This is what is meant by, "And He raises the status (*keren*) of His people…"[142]

Word Sparks

"His majesty over the land and the heavens" — Here we mention the earth ("land") before the Heavens, because here, the heavens "receive" from the earth: The "majesty" mentioned in the verse is the "Torah," which was given to man on earth. The angels requested from God, "Give Your majesty to the heavens," but since God gave the Torah to man on earth, the verse informs us that the "heavens" (angels) requested it from the "land" (Jewish souls). (Torat Shmuel 5639/1879 of the Rebbe Maharash, pp. 170-172, based on the Ariz'l)

VERSES OF PRAISE

הַלְלוּיָהּ, שִׁירוּ לַיְיָ שִׁיר חָדָשׁ, תְּהִלָּתוֹ בִּקְהַל חֲסִידִים:
יִשְׂמַח יִשְׂרָאֵל בְּעֹשָׂיו, בְּנֵי צִיּוֹן יָגִילוּ בְמַלְכָּם:
יְהַלְלוּ שְׁמוֹ בְמָחוֹל, בְּתֹף וְכִנּוֹר יְזַמְּרוּ לוֹ:
כִּי רוֹצֶה יְיָ בְּעַמּוֹ, יְפָאֵר עֲנָוִים בִּישׁוּעָה:
יַעְלְזוּ חֲסִידִים בְּכָבוֹד, יְרַנְּנוּ עַל מִשְׁכְּבוֹתָם:
רוֹמְמוֹת אֵל בִּגְרוֹנָם, וְחֶרֶב פִּיפִיּוֹת בְּיָדָם:
לַעֲשׂוֹת נְקָמָה בַּגּוֹיִם, תּוֹכֵחוֹת בַּלְאֻמִּים:
לֶאְסֹר מַלְכֵיהֶם בְּזִקִּים, וְנִכְבְּדֵיהֶם בְּכַבְלֵי בַרְזֶל:
לַעֲשׂוֹת בָּהֶם מִשְׁפָּט כָּתוּב, הָדָר הוּא לְכָל חֲסִידָיו, הַלְלוּיָהּ:

ממלא כל עולמים
אהבת עולם (כמים)
כי הוא חיי נפשי
רוח
עולם היצירה

> **"The root of all song is ascent, from below to above. Wherever there is spiritual ascent, there is song…"** (Alter Rebbe's Siddur with Chassidut, p. ס"ז) [143]

Spiritual ascent occurs after a purification process, called *birur rishon* ("initial refinement"). The creation of the universe is associated with the *sephira* of *malchut* which, as the tenth and final *sephira,* receives all of its influx from the nine previous *sephirot*. Malchut "has nothing of its own," aside from what it receives from above. However, the initiative to "improve and ascend," to "return" to spiritual origins begins with the creation itself, from below to above, and takes place through the process of *birur* ("refinement/purification") from below to above. The initiative from below in order to return and receive from above, is described as a "female" process.

In Hebrew, there are two kinds of song. One is female (*shira*) and the other male (*shir*). They correspond to two processes of refinement. One process involves extracting good from bad. It occurs from below to above, as we work to refine ourselves. This is the *birur rishon* ("initial refinement") that the creation undergoes. The other process occurs when all the good has been extracted, and divine light descends from above to elevate the refined material (in this case, sparks of Godliness). This is called *birur sheni* ("advanced refinement").

> Immanent Godliness
> Lower love (water)
> Love: vitality of my soul
> Soul level: *Ruach*
> World of *Yetzira*

HALLELUYAH, SING A NEW SONG TO THE LORD, His praise among the pious ones.

The Jews rejoice in their Maker, the sons of Zion delight in their King.

They will praise His name in dance, with drums and harp they will sing to Him.

For, the Lord desires His people, He glorifies the humble with salvation.

The pious ones will revel in honor, they will sing upon their beds.

The greatness of God is in their throats, and a double-edged sword in their hands.

To take revenge among the nations, and rebuke the people.

To imprison their kings in chains, and their notables in iron cables.

To fulfill upon them the written judgment, this will be glory for all of His pious ones, Halleluyah.

📖 *Within the Words*

Psalm 149 mentions the male song (*shir chadash*). In the future, after the culmination of the worldly refinement process (*birur rishon*), it will no longer be necessary to extract Godly sparks from below. Only *birur sheini* ("advanced refinement") will take place, elevating the good. As the holy sparks ascend, the entire creation will "sing" as it arises to spiritual levels never before seen. This is why it is called a "new song." This is a "male" process, which is why it is called *shir chadash* (male) and not *shira chadasha* (female).[144]

הַלְלוּיָהּ, הַלְלוּ אֵל בְּקָדְשׁוֹ, הַלְלוּהוּ בִּרְקִיעַ עֻזּוֹ:
הַלְלוּהוּ בִגְבוּרֹתָיו. הַלְלוּהוּ כְּרֹב גֻּדְלוֹ:
הַלְלוּהוּ בְּתֵקַע שׁוֹפָר, הַלְלוּהוּ בְּנֵבֶל וְכִנּוֹר:
הַלְלוּהוּ בְתֹף וּמָחוֹל, הַלְלוּהוּ בְּמִנִּים וְעֻגָב:

ממלא כל עולמים
אהבת עולם (כמים)
כי הוא חיי נפשי
רוח
עולם היצירה

> **In general, ten types of musical instruments are mentioned here, corresponding to the ten *sephirot*. [Their purpose is] to bring the *sephirot* from total concealment in the recesses of the Emanator to full consciousness in all the four worlds…"** (Alter Rebbe's Siddur with Chassidut, p. 70D [140])[145]

This psalm discusses the descent of Godly light from *Atzilut* to *Bria*. In *Atzilut*, the light is a ray of Godly illumination, connected to its source. It is like a song that we sing with our own voice. But as it descends to the lower worlds, the light of *Atzilut* appears to become disconnected from its source. It takes on the characteristics of the lower worlds, which appear to be detached from their spiritual source. It is like music that we play with musical instruments, which are separate from us. The instruments are comparable to the *kelim* ("vessels") of the lower worlds, which also appear separate from God. The musical instruments named in this psalm express our song, in a detached manner.

Musical instruments symbolize the *kelim* or external dimensions of the World of *Yetzira*, and Jewish souls are like the *orot* ("Godly lights"). Souls are always associated with the inner spiritual dimensions of the world. The musical instruments express the external illumination of *Yetzira*, but souls express the inner essence of the world.

📖 *Within the Words*

The first verse of Psalm 150 alludes to *Keter*, and *chochma* of *Yetzira*, and the beginning of the second verse refers to *bina* of *Yetzira*. Then, "praise Him for all His greatness" refers to *chesed* of *Yetzira*. "Praise Him by blowing the shofar" symbolizes *gevura* of *Yetzira*, since the shofar with its loud blast causes everyone who hears it to tremble in

Immanent Godliness
Lower love (water)
Love: vitality of my soul
Soul level: *Ruach*
World of *Yetzira*

Halleluyah, praise God in His holiness, praise Him in the firmament of His strength.

Praise Him for His mighty deeds, praise Him for all of His greatness.

Praise Him with blowing of the shofar, praise Him with lyre and harp.

Praise Him with drums and dance, Praise Him with stringed instruments and flute.

> 📖 *Within the Words*
>
> fear. "Praise Him with lyre and harp" represents *tiferet* of *Yetzira*, since the lyre and harp are two instruments that play melodiously, combining different notes in harmony, just as the *sephira* of *tiferet* brings together disparate qualities in harmony. "Praise Him with drums and dance, praise Him with stringed instruments and flute" allude to *netzach* and *hod* of *Yetzira*. Drums do not carry a melody at all, but serve to encourage and support the listener. This is the quality of *netzach*. Stringed instruments and flutes play pleasing music as accompaniment in the background, similar to the *sephira* of *hod*, which is the underlying integrity that we maintain in order to persevere. "Praise Him with clanging cymbals…" Cymbals do not carry a tune, but they serve to amplify and convey the music to the listeners. Thus they correspond to *yesod*, which is the conduit through which all of the higher *sephirot* transfer their influx to the *sephira* of *malchut*. And finally, "Praise Him with resounding cymbals" refers to *malchut*, the lowest of the ten *sephirot*. *Malchut* possesses a resounding quality, like an echo, since it is in *malchut* that the infinite light from Above "strikes" (*truah*) its lowest level, before being distributed among the lower three worlds of BY"A. After all this, the psalm continues, "Let every soul praise God, *Halleluyah*." Souls convey the inner illumination (*orot*) of the world, which includes the expression of all ten *sephirot*. Since souls are all inclusive, it is not necessary for the psalm to list them in detail, so it says simply, "Let every soul praise Him…"

VERSES OF PRAISE

הַלְלוּהוּ בְּצִלְצְלֵי שָׁמַע, הַלְלוּהוּ בְּצִלְצְלֵי תְרוּעָה:

כֹּל הַנְּשָׁמָה תְּהַלֵּל יָהּ הַלְלוּיָהּ:

כֹּל הַנְּשָׁמָה תְּהַלֵּל יָהּ הַלְלוּיָהּ:

בָּרוּךְ יְיָ לְעוֹלָם אָמֵן וְאָמֵן:

בָּרוּךְ יְיָ מִצִּיּוֹן שֹׁכֵן יְרוּשָׁלָיִם הַלְלוּיָהּ:

בָּרוּךְ יְיָ אֱלֹהִים אֱלֹהֵי יִשְׂרָאֵל, עֹשֵׂה נִפְלָאוֹת לְבַדּוֹ:

וּבָרוּךְ שֵׁם כְּבוֹדוֹ לְעוֹלָם, וְיִמָּלֵא כְבוֹדוֹ אֶת כָּל הָאָרֶץ, אָמֵן וְאָמֵן:

וַיְבָרֶךְ דָּוִיד אֶת יְיָ לְעֵינֵי כָּל הַקָּהָל וַיֹּאמֶר דָּוִיד, בָּרוּךְ אַתָּה יְיָ אֱלֹהֵי יִשְׂרָאֵל אָבִינוּ, מֵעוֹלָם וְעַד עוֹלָם:

לְךָ יְיָ הַגְּדֻלָּה, וְהַגְּבוּרָה, וְהַתִּפְאֶרֶת, וְהַנֵּצַח, וְהַהוֹד, כִּי כֹל בַּשָּׁמַיִם וּבָאָרֶץ:

לְךָ יְיָ הַמַּמְלָכָה וְהַמִּתְנַשֵּׂא, לְכֹל לְרֹאשׁ:

וְהָעֹשֶׁר וְהַכָּבוֹד מִלְּפָנֶיךָ, וְאַתָּה מוֹשֵׁל בַּכֹּל, וּבְיָדְךָ כֹּחַ וּגְבוּרָה, וּבְיָדְךָ, לְגַדֵּל וּלְחַזֵּק לַכֹּל:

ממלא כל עולמים
אהבת עולם (כמים)
כמו בן המשתדל לאביו
רוח
עולם היצירה

CHASSIDIC INSIGHTS

(continued from p. 146)

There are several levels of "love like water" (described in *Kuntres Ha'avoda*/"Love like Fire and Water," page 102-105). Each seems to correspond to a particular section of the *pesukei dezimra*. The first level, described above, develops as the result of meditation upon creation from nothing to something. We discover the divine energy at the heart of

(continued on p. 174)

Immanent Godliness
Lower love (water)
Love as a son for his Father
Soul level: Ruach
World of Yetzira

Praise Him with resounding cymbals,
praise Him with amplifying cymbals.
Let every soul praise Y-H, Halleluyah,
Let every soul praise Y-H, Halleluyah!

Rise and remain standing until after בָּרְכוּ

B**LESSED BE THE LORD FOREVER, AMEN AND AMEN**
Blessed be the Lord from Zion, dwelling in Jerusalem, Halleluyah!

Blessed be the Lord, God Who is the God of Israel, Who alone performs wonders.

And blessed be His glorious name forever, and let the whole earth be filled with His glory, Amen and amen.

A**ND DAVID BLESSED THE LORD IN THE EYES OF** the entire congregation, and David said, "Blessed are You, Lord, God of Israel our father, in all realms.

To You, Lord belongs the greatness, the might, the harmony, the victory and the majesty, for all that is in the heavens and on the earth [is Yours].

The reign is Yours, Lord, and You are exalted over all other leaders.

The wealth and the honor come from You, and You govern over all, and in Your hand are power and might, and it is in Your hand to aggrandize and to strengthen everyone.

VERSES OF PRAISE

וְעַתָּה אֱלֹהֵינוּ מוֹדִים, אֲנַחְנוּ לָךְ וּמְהַלְלִים לְשֵׁם תִּפְאַרְתֶּךָ:

וִיבָרְכוּ שֵׁם כְּבוֹדֶךָ וּמְרוֹמַם עַל כָּל בְּרָכָה וּתְהִלָּה:

אַתָּה הוּא יְיָ לְבַדֶּךָ, אַתָּה עָשִׂיתָ אֶת הַשָּׁמַיִם שְׁמֵי הַשָּׁמַיִם וְכָל צְבָאָם, הָאָרֶץ וְכָל אֲשֶׁר עָלֶיהָ, הַיַּמִּים וְכָל אֲשֶׁר בָּהֶם, וְאַתָּה מְחַיֶּה אֶת כֻּלָּם, וּצְבָא הַשָּׁמַיִם לְךָ מִשְׁתַּחֲוִים:

אַתָּה הוּא יְיָ הָאֱלֹהִים אֲשֶׁר בָּחַרְתָּ בְּאַבְרָם וְהוֹצֵאתוֹ מֵאוּר כַּשְׂדִּים, וְשַׂמְתָּ שְׁמוֹ אַבְרָהָם:

וּמָצָאתָ אֶת לְבָבוֹ נֶאֱמָן לְפָנֶיךָ:

ממלא כל עולמים
אהבת עולם (כמים)
כמו בן המשתדל לאביו
רוח
עולם היצירה

> **God alone created the heavens and the earth...and He chose Abram because He found his heart to be "trustworthy," meaning capable of *ahava rabba*..."** (*Sefer Maamorim* 5655/1895 of the Rebbe Rashab, p. 126)[146]

As Avraham traversed the Land of Israel, God tested him. As he passed each spiritual test, Avraham grew in spiritual stature. His initial love of God (*ahavat olam*) was the fruit of his intellectual prowess, but it soon grew to include a great love (*ahava rabba*) that was beyond human intellect. As he approached full spiritual maturity, he attained awe of God (*yirah ila'ah*) as well as awareness of Godliness as the only real and true existence, compared to which the entire universe is as naught.

Avraham's journeys and spiritual growth laid the groundwork for all subsequent spiritual growth. We all begin meditation by contemplating God's "garments," the wonder of nature and creation from nothing to something. This is meditation upon *memalle kol olmin*, or how He fills the creation. The resulting love is called *ahavat olam* ("mundane love"). We then consider how God transcends the creation (*sovev kol olmin*). This leads us to *ahava rabba* ("great love"). Finally, we become so nullified to God that we recognize Him as the only really true existence. This is called *yirah ila'ah* ("higher fear").

Immanent Godliness
Lower love (water)
Love as a son for his Father
Soul level: Ruach
World of Yetzira

And now, our God, we acknowledge You, and we praise Your harmonious name.

And [Israel] will bless Your honorable name, and exalt it over all blessings and praise.

You, Lord, are alone, You made the heavens and the heaven's heavens, and all of their hosts, the earth and all that is upon it, the seas and all that is within them, and You enliven them all, and the hosts of the heavens bow down to You.

You, Lord are God, Who chose Avram, and took him out of the land of Ur Kasdim, and changed his name to Avraham.

And You found his heart to be true to You.

> 📖 *Within the Words*
>
> "You Lord are alone…" refers to God's very essence. "You created the heavens…" from nothing to something. "You chose Avram…You found his heart to be true…" — meaning that Avraham's heart was capable of containing the transcendent love called *ahava rabba*. "You formed a covenant with him…" in order to strengthen Avraham spiritually to attain the highest form of awe (*yirah ila'ah*). The purpose of the covenant was also to unite the two kinds of love that Avraham experienced, bringing down the transcendent love (*ahava rabba*) to permeate Avraham's mundane love (*ahavat olam*). This is what enabled Avraham to transform his seven negative character traits, eradicating them altogether. And then, "You kept Your promise" to deliver the Land of Israel to Avraham's offspring, by driving the seven Canaanite nations out before them.

VERSES OF PRAISE

וְכָרוֹת עִמּוֹ הַבְּרִית לָתֵת אֶת אֶרֶץ הַכְּנַעֲנִי.
הַחִתִּי הָאֱמֹרִי וְהַפְּרִזִּי וְהַיְבוּסִי וְהַגִּרְגָּשִׁי לָתֵת לְזַרְעוֹ,
וַתָּקֶם אֶת דְּבָרֶיךָ כִּי צַדִּיק אָתָּה:
וַתֵּרֶא אֶת עֳנִי אֲבוֹתֵינוּ בְּמִצְרָיִם,
וְאֶת זַעֲקָתָם שָׁמַעְתָּ עַל יַם סוּף:
וַתִּתֵּן אֹתֹת וּמֹפְתִים בְּפַרְעֹה וּבְכָל עֲבָדָיו וּבְכָל עַם אַרְצוֹ,

ממלא כל עולמים
אהבת עולם (כמים)
כמו בן המשתדל לאביו
רוח
עולם היצירה

❝ Why is it necessary for the verse to explain that God is righteous? In any case He must keep His word…but there is logical flow and continuity to these verses." (*Sefer Maamorim 5680*/1920 of the Rebbe Rashab, pp. 291-292)[147]

The soul is capable of comprehending spiritual levels beyond *bina* (analytic "understanding"), all the way up to the highest levels that transcend the *tzimtzum* ("great contraction"). This is because the soul is a "piece of Godliness" — it is rooted in God's very essence. This is what is meant by "You are He, Lord, who alone…" — "You" alludes to His very essence, also expressed in His Name *Havaya*; from His essence He contracts His light to become known to us. "You made the heavens and the heaven's heavens…" — these are transcendent levels called *makifim* (including *Keter* of *Atzilut*) that descend to impinge upon our consciousness. We cannot apprehend these levels clearly, and yet since we are rooted in Godly essence, we gain some awareness. "And the earth and all that is upon it" alludes to levels that we can understand well and experience (*tikun*). The "sea" refers to spiritual creatures, and the "land" refers to physical creatures.

Since he was aware of all these spiritual levels, Avraham developed tremendous love for God. He used his intellectual prowess to achieve recognition and love of God, who then "chose Avraham" and "brought him out of Ur Kasdim." This is an allusion to how God brought Avraham out of a negative spiritual milieu and helped him to escape negative spiritual forces. And then, "He changed his name to Avraham," adding a *hey* and enabling Avraham, to become the "father of many nations…" This allowed Avraham to purify and spiritually uplift whatever sparks of holiness ("converts") happened to remain

Immanent Godliness
Lower love (water)
Love as a son for his Father
Soul level: *Ruach*
World of *Yetzira*

And You formed a covenant with him, [promising] to give the land of the Canaanites, the Chitites, the Emorites, the Perizites and the Jebusites and the Girgashites to his descendants, and You fulfilled Your word, since You are just.

And You took note of the poverty of our ancestors in Egypt, and their cries, and you heard them at the edge of the Reed Sea.

And You delivered signs and wonders to Pharaoh and to all of his servants and all of his land,

---

among the seven Canaanite nations. God "found Avraham's heart trustworthy," because he was capable of purifying and uplifting the world, and therefore, He "formed a covenant" with him.

📖 *Within the Words*

Even though we were commanded not to leave any of the seven Canaanite nations alive, this applied to the generation of Joshua, eight generations after Avraham. In Avraham's generation, there were various sparks of holiness among the Canaanite nations. And therefore, "You fulfilled Your words." The word for "fulfilled" — *vatakem* — also means "and You raised," referring to the holy sparks that Avraham raised from the Canaanite nations, allowing them to ascend and become included in holiness. These souls may be the souls of converts, such as Shemaya and Avtalyon, as well as Rabbi Meir and others. And that is why we conclude by saying "…because You are righteous." It is the nature of good to do good, meaning to lower themselves to the lowest possible levels in order to rescue and extract sparks of holiness and return them to their rightful place above.

VERSES OF PRAISE

Word Sparks — "And You fulfill Your word" — When we pray and learn Torah, we cause revelation of the ten creative utterances of Bereishit (Genesis) in the physical world, thus confirming that "He fulfills His word." (Torat Shmuel 5633/1873 of the Rebbe Maharash, V 2, p. 398)

כִּי יָדַעְתָּ כִּי הֵזִידוּ עֲלֵיהֶם וַתַּעַשׂ לְךָ שֵׁם כְּהַיּוֹם הַזֶּה:

וְהַיָּם בָּקַעְתָּ לִפְנֵיהֶם וַיַּעַבְרוּ בְתוֹךְ הַיָּם בַּיַּבָּשָׁה, וְאֶת רֹדְפֵיהֶם הִשְׁלַכְתָּ בִמְצוֹלֹת כְּמוֹ אֶבֶן בְּמַיִם עַזִּים:

שירת הים

וַיּוֹשַׁע יְיָ בַּיּוֹם הַהוּא אֶת יִשְׂרָאֵל מִיַּד מִצְרָיִם, וַיַּרְא יִשְׂרָאֵל אֶת מִצְרַיִם מֵת עַל שְׂפַת הַיָּם:

וַיַּרְא יִשְׂרָאֵל אֶת הַיָּד הַגְּדֹלָה אֲשֶׁר עָשָׂה יְיָ בְּמִצְרַיִם וַיִּירְאוּ הָעָם אֶת יְיָ, וַיַּאֲמִינוּ בַּייָ וּבְמֹשֶׁה עַבְדּוֹ:

אָז יָשִׁיר מֹשֶׁה וּבְנֵי יִשְׂרָאֵל אֶת הַשִּׁירָה הַזֹּאת לַייָ וַיֹּאמְרוּ

ממלא כל עולמים
אהבת עולם (כמים)
כמו בן המשתדל לאביו
רוח
עולם היצירה

> **On the night of the seventh day of Pesach [when we commemorate the splitting of the sea], a great light shines from above, resulting in a tremendous and powerful revelation that transcends all spiritual levels.**" (*Likutei Torah* of the Alter Rebbe, *Parshat Tzav*, p. 14b)[148]

The tenth and final *sephira* of *Atzilut* — *malchut* — plays a crucial role. It "has nothing of its own," and yet it is the conduit for all influx and Godly revelation from above *Atzilut* down to the lower worlds, including our physical world. *Malchut* has two modes: in one mode it receives from the *sephirot* above it; in the second mode, it descends in order to create, influence and refine the worlds below.

In its capacity as receiver from above, *malchut* is called *alma de'itcasia* ("realm of hidden objects"). And in its capacity as mentor and benefactor to the worlds below, *malchut* is called *alma de'itgalia* ("realm of visible objects"). Whatever exists in the sea exists on land as well, but while in the sea, we are not aware of it. Everything physical possesses a spiritual source above, but while it is spiritual we cannot detect it, even though it is real and present.

Immanent Godliness
Lower love (water)
Love as a son for his Father
Soul level: Ruach
World of Yetzira

since You knew that they wronged the Jews, and You made a name for Yourself to this very day.

And You split the sea in front of them, and they passed through the sea on dry land, and You… hurled their pursuers down to the depths, like stones in raging waters.

Song of the Sea

And on that day, the Lord saved Israel from the hand of the Egyptians, and Israel saw the Egyptians dead at the edge of the sea.

And the Jews observed the powerful hand that the Lord deployed against the Egyptians, and the nation was in awe of the Lord, and they believed in the Lord and in Moses, His servant.

Then, Moses and the children of Israel sang this song to the Lord, saying,

---

📖 *Within the Words*

"And You split the sea in front of them…" This verse pertains to the seventh day of Passover, when the Reed Sea split, allowing the Jews to pass through to the other side. When the "sea" — the invisible spiritual world above — splits, then revelation descends from above, bypassing all of the usual intermediate channels. This occurs on the seventh day of Passover but we yearn for it all year long. When it occurs, all physical creatures are able to detect their spiritual source above and even higher — to the very essence of Godliness.

VERSES OF PRAISE

לֵאמֹר, אָשִׁירָה לַײָ כִּי גָאֹה גָּאָה, סוּס וְרֹכְבוֹ רָמָה בַיָּם:

עָזִּי וְזִמְרָת יָהּ וַיְהִי לִי לִישׁוּעָה,

זֶה אֵלִי וְאַנְוֵהוּ אֱלֹהֵי אָבִי וַאֲרֹמְמֶנְהוּ:

יְיָ אִישׁ מִלְחָמָה, יְיָ שְׁמוֹ:

מַרְכְּבֹת פַּרְעֹה וְחֵילוֹ יָרָה בַיָּם,

וּמִבְחַר שָׁלִשָׁיו טֻבְּעוּ בְיַם סוּף:

תְּהֹמֹת יְכַסְיֻמוּ, יָרְדוּ בִמְצוֹלֹת כְּמוֹ אָבֶן:

יְמִינְךָ יְיָ נֶאְדָּרִי בַּכֹּחַ, יְמִינְךָ יְיָ תִּרְעַץ אוֹיֵב:

וּבְרֹב גְּאוֹנְךָ תַּהֲרֹס קָמֶיךָ, תְּשַׁלַּח חֲרֹנְךָ יֹאכְלֵמוֹ כַּקַּשׁ:

וּבְרוּחַ אַפֶּיךָ נֶעֶרְמוּ מַיִם נִצְּבוּ כְמוֹ נֵד נֹזְלִים,

קָפְאוּ תְהֹמֹת בְּלֶב יָם:

אָמַר אוֹיֵב אֶרְדֹּף אַשִּׂיג אֲחַלֵּק שָׁלָל,

תִּמְלָאֵמוֹ נַפְשִׁי, אָרִיק חַרְבִּי, תּוֹרִישֵׁמוֹ יָדִי:

ממלא כל עולמים
אהבת עולם (כמים)
כמו בן המשתדל לאביו
רוח
עולם היצירה

CHASSIDIC INSIGHTS

(continued from p. 166)

creation, and that arouses our love for Godliness. Then, continuing to meditate, we realize that there is Godliness not only in the world, but within our soul as well. We now begin to develop love of God not only because of His ability to create, but because "He is the life of my soul." Not only does He enliven the world, but He enlivens our very soul. As described elsewhere in Chassidut (in *Besha'ah she'hikdimu 5672*, vol. 3, page 1310), we realize that we are "the ultimate intention" and that within us shines a "higher and more inner light and Godly energy." One of the benefits of this level of love is that it motivates us to learn more Torah. As a general rule, we are aware of the vitality and life-force coursing through our veins, but we are not aware that our life force is divine. When that awareness penetrates our consciousness, we are motivated to devote ourselves to the Torah, which is described as "God's soul."

(continued on p. 178)

Immanent Godliness
Lower love (water)
Love as a son for his Father
Soul level: Ruach
World of Yetzira

'I will sing to the Lord, because He is very exalted, He hurled the horse and its rider into the sea.

The might and vengeance of God was my salvation, this is my God and I will glorify Him, the God of my father and I will exalt Him.

The Lord is a man of war, Havaya is His name.

He tossed the chariots of Pharaoh and his troops into the sea, the best of his choice warriors He drowned in the Reed Sea.

The deep waters covered them over, they descended into the depths like stones.

Your right hand, Lord is enhanced with power, Your right hand shatters the enemy.

In Your immense grandeur, You crush those who rise against You, You unleash Your fury and it incinerates them like straw.

And with the wind of Your nostrils the waters piled up, the flowing streams stood erect as a wall, the deep fountains froze in the heart of the sea.

The enemy said, I will chase and I will overtake them, I will divide the spoils, they will satiate my lust, I will unsheathe my sword and my hand will inherit them.

VERSES OF PRAISE

Word Sparks

When the Jews saw the sea split and discovered that this was not only a physical miracle but also a spiritual miracle that revealed the hidden spiritual worlds beyond them, they sang, "I will sing to the Lord..." (Torat Shmuel 5637/1877 of the Rebbe Maharash, V 2, p. 706).

On the other hand, the Egyptians, representing the klipa ("negative forces") that normally syphon energy from such high transcendent illumination, were "thrust down" from those levels like a "stone" (א-בן) into the raging waters of the Reed Sea, where they churned and suffered but did not die. They did not die because they were "creatures of the water" (the "lower waters" that are the source of physical pleasure) who derive their vitality from the water. It was not until they were cast up on the opposite shore, out of the waters, that they died (Torat Shmuel 5642/1882 of the Rebbe Maharash, pp. 273-275)

PRAYING LIKE FIRE AND WATER

נָשַׁפְתָּ בְרוּחֲךָ כִּסָּמוֹ יָם צָלֲלוּ כַּעוֹפֶרֶת בְּמַיִם אַדִּירִים:

מִי כָמֹכָה בָּאֵלִם יְיָ, מִי כָּמֹכָה נֶאְדָּר בַּקֹּדֶשׁ, נוֹרָא תְהִלֹּת עֹשֵׂה פֶלֶא:

נָטִיתָ יְמִינְךָ תִּבְלָעֵמוֹ אָרֶץ:

נָחִיתָ בְחַסְדְּךָ עַם זוּ גָּאָלְתָּ, נֵהַלְתָּ בְעָזְּךָ אֶל נְוֵה קָדְשֶׁךָ:

ממלא כל עולמים
אהבת עולם (כמים)
כמו בן המשתדל
לאביו
רוח
עולם היצירה

> **When the Holy One decides to resurrect the dead, He will prepare Himself by inviting every [soul] to its place…at that time He will invite all of them to sing a song…what is the song? It is "Hashem, who is like You, rescuer of the poor…"** (Zohar, Parshat Ve'etchanan 267b)[149]

More from the Zohar: "This song (from *Nishmat*), 'Hashem, who is like You, rescuer of the poor…' is a greater song than what the Jews sang after the splitting of the sea ('Who is like You among all divinity, Lord, who is comparable to You, adorned in holiness'). There, the Jews did not mention God's name until after three other words ('who is like…'), whereas in this verse, God's name is mentioned first." This is similar to the Talmudic passage[150] describing the *Seraphim* who mention God's name *Havaya* after three words, while the lower *Ofanim* mention His name after only two words. This is because the *Ofanim* come from a higher spiritual source, from transcendent Godliness that is beyond us, while the *Seraphim* originate from immanent Godliness that we can understand and feel. Here as well, the verse "Who is like You, among all divinity, *Havaya*…" refers to the immanent Godliness that we saw and experienced at the splitting of the Reed Sea, while the verse "*Havaya*, who is like You, rescuer of the poor" refers to the transcendent illumination that will become evident at the resurrection of the dead.

We find two ways of describing God: 1) as He exists in essence (this perspective remains hidden), and 2) as He expresses Himself via His actions (from this perspective, He is recognizable to everyone, including fools). King David described the two perspectives in Psalm 103, wherein the phrase "Blessed is my soul," appears twice. Similarly,

Immanent Godliness
Lower love (water)
Love as a son for his Father
Soul level: Ruach
World of Yetzira

> You blew with Your wind and the sea overwhelmed them, they sank like lead in the mighty waters.
>
> Who is like You, among all divinity, Lord, who is comparable to You, adorned in holiness, too awesome for praises, working wonders?
>
> You extended your right hand, the earth swallowed them.
>
> You lead in kindness this nation that You redeemed, in Your strength, You guided them to Your holy abode.

---

during the Song at the Sea, the phrase, "Who is like You..." appears twice. The first time corresponds to God Himself, and the continuation of the verse describes God as "too awesome to praise." The second mention corresponds to God as He is evident in creation, and the verse continues, "performing wonders." Possibly, these two modes of praising God correspond to two levels of His ineffable name *Havaya*: 1) as He totally transcends creation (in which we describe Him as "too awesome to praise," because we have no grasp of His essential greatness), and 2) within the spiritual chain of creation (and then it applies to His wonders within creation).[151]

> 📖 *Within the Words*
>
> *Targum Yonatan* translates this verse as "Who is comparable to You, among the angels, dwelling in holiness, awesome in praise, performing wonders for His people, the Jews." *Rashi*, though translates it as "Who is like You, among the mighty of the land." The *Ohr Hachaim* explains that at the splitting of the Reed Sea, the Jews saw the angel of Egypt slain in front of them, and therefore they proclaimed, "Who is comparable to God among the powerful and mighty?"[152]

VERSES OF PRAISE

שָׁמְעוּ עַמִּים יִרְגָּזוּן, חִיל אָחַז יֹשְׁבֵי פְּלָשֶׁת:

אָז נִבְהֲלוּ אַלּוּפֵי אֱדוֹם, אֵילֵי מוֹאָב יֹאחֲזֵמוֹ רָעַד, נָמֹגוּ כֹּל יֹשְׁבֵי כְנָעַן:

תִּפֹּל עֲלֵיהֶם אֵימָתָה וָפַחַד, בִּגְדֹל זְרוֹעֲךָ יִדְּמוּ כָּאָבֶן, עַד יַעֲבֹר עַמְּךָ יְיָ, עַד יַעֲבֹר עַם זוּ קָנִיתָ:

תְּבִאֵמוֹ וְתִטָּעֵמוֹ בְּהַר נַחֲלָתְךָ, מָכוֹן לְשִׁבְתְּךָ פָּעַלְתָּ יְיָ, מִקְּדָשׁ אֲדֹנָי כּוֹנְנוּ יָדֶיךָ:

יְיָ יִמְלֹךְ לְעֹלָם וָעֶד:

יְיָ יִמְלֹךְ לְעֹלָם וָעֶד:

יְיָ מַלְכוּתֵהּ קָאֵם לְעָלַם וּלְעָלְמֵי עָלְמַיָּא:

כִּי בָא סוּס פַּרְעֹה בְּרִכְבּוֹ וּבְפָרָשָׁיו בַּיָּם וַיָּשֶׁב יְיָ עֲלֵיהֶם אֶת מֵי הַיָּם וּבְנֵי יִשְׂרָאֵל הָלְכוּ בַיַּבָּשָׁה בְּתוֹךְ הַיָּם:

CHASSIDIC INSIGHTS

(continued from p. 174)

Further meditation brings us to yet another level of "love like water," best described as love "like a son loves his father." The previously described love of God because "He is our soul" motivates us like a servant is motivated to serve his master. He seeks to fulfill his master's will in every way possible. Similarly, motivated by love "because He is our soul," we seek to fulfill God's will by learning Torah and fulfilling His commandments. However, once we realize that He also cares for us as a father cares for a son, we also want to understand the purpose behind His will. When we know not only what He wants, but why He wants it, we are able to go "behind the scenes" and "between the lines" to fulfill His will in ways that He did not even instruct us. This is the role of a son in relation to his father, described by the Zohar — "like a son who strives for the sake of his father and mother, whom he loves even more than his own body, soul and spirit…"

(continued on p. 179)

Immanent Godliness
Lower love (water)
Love as a son for his Father
Soul level: Ruach
World of Yetzira

Nations heard and trembled, waves of fear gripped the dwellers of Philistia.

Then the leaders of Edom were shocked, the strong men of Moab were gripped with trembling, all the inhabitants of Canaan melted away.

May fear and terror fall upon them, at the great might of Your arm let them become still like stones; until Your nation passes, Lord, until this nation of Yours passes through.

You will bring them and You will plant them upon the mountain of Your inheritance, the place of Your dwelling that You made, Lord, the sanctuary of God, that You prepared with Your hands.

The Lord will reign forever, eternal,

the Lord will reign forever, eternal.

Lord, Your Kingship lasts forever and ever.

For when the horses of Pharaoh, with his chariot and troops [went] into the sea, and the Lord overcame them with the waters of the sea, and the children of Israel walked on the dry land in the midst of the sea.

VERSES OF PRAISE

--- CHASSIDIC INSIGHTS ---

(continued from p. 178)

Examining the *nusach*, or words of the siddur during *pesukei dezimra*, we can actually detect these successive levels of "love like water" within the words. The initial prayer, *Baruch She'Amar* speaks explicitly of creation from nothing to something. The psalms (113 and

(continued on p. 180)

PRAYING LIKE FIRE AND WATER

כִּי לַיְיָ הַמְּלוּכָה וּמוֹשֵׁל בַּגּוֹיִם:

וְעָלוּ מוֹשִׁיעִים בְּהַר צִיּוֹן לִשְׁפֹּט אֶת הַר עֵשָׂו,
וְהָיְתָה לַיְיָ הַמְּלוּכָה:

וְהָיָה יְיָ לְמֶלֶךְ עַל כָּל הָאָרֶץ,
בַּיּוֹם הַהוּא יִהְיֶה יְיָ אֶחָד וּשְׁמוֹ אֶחָד:

ממלא כל עולמים
אהבת עולם (כמים)
כמו בן המשתדל
לאביו
רוח
עולם היצירה

> After their meeting, Yaakov said to Esau, "...until I arrive to [you] at Seir." R' Huna said, "We find nowhere that Yaakov went to Seir." R' Yudin said in the name of Rav, "It will occur in the future, as it says, 'And the saviors ascended Mt. Zion to judge Mt. Seir...'" (*Bereishit Rabba* 153, *Ovadia* 1:21)[153]

During the exile, the *klipot* gain energy that is not meant for them; their judgment will take place in the future. Why did that energy go to the *klipot* and not to the holy forces for whom it was intended? In the realm of *kedusha*, holy vitality is supposed to flow from the *sephira* of *yesod* to *malchut*, but during this long exile, it

─────────── CHASSIDIC INSIGHTS ───────────

(continued from p. 179)

145) that succeed *Baruch She'Amar* also speak of God's mastery and omnipotent presence in the creation. Thus, they seem to correspond to "entry level" love like water associated with meditation upon creation from nothing to something.

The following set of psalms (146-150) are clear expressions of the soul. The first psalm (146) opens with, "*Halleluyah,* my soul praises the Lord." Similar expressions appear throughout the following psalms. Thus, it is no stretch of the imagination to suggest that this section of *peshukei dezimra* corresponds to "love of God because He is the life of my soul." This may also explain why the Chasidic excerpts on the *pesukei dezimra*, taken from the Alter Rebbe's siddur, discusses the various spiritual postures which the soul may adopt toward God. For

(continued on p. 183)

Immanent Godliness
Lower love (water)
Love as a son for his Father
Soul level: Ruach
World of Yetzira

> For sovereignty is the Lord's,
> and He rules the nations.
>
> And the saviors ascended Mt. Zion to judge
> the mountain of Esau, and the Kingship
> will belong to the Lord.
>
> And the Lord will be the King over all the land,
> and on that day, the Lord will be one
> and His name one.

has flowed from *yesod* to *klipat noga*. He and His name will not be complete until Godly energy flows into *malchut*.

Parable (from *Midrash Tehillim*): "A man once set out on the road, lighting a candle for illumination. It went out, but he re-lit it and yet it went out again. He asked himself, 'Why bother, I'll wait until the morning.' Similarly, the Jews were subjugated and then freed by Moshe; and they were again subjugated and freed by Hanania, Mishael and Azaria; and again they were subjugated. They said, 'How many times will we be saved by man, let us wait until the future when God Himself will free us.'" Another parable (from *Midrash Rabba*): "Why is a pig called a *chazir*? Because it returns (*machzir*) the crown to whom it belongs." Esau is likened to a pig, and the final exile is associated with Esau, who torments and pressures the Jews until they return to God — thus this final exile is like a "pig" that returns the crown to its owner.

Within the Words

The main judgment that accompanies the end of exile will be over *avodat habirurim* — the process of refining and uplifting the remaining sparks of holiness that takes place as we fulfill Torah and mitzvot. In addition, we are required to "judge ourselves" regarding our physical needs — we must not become absorbed in extraneous physical matters that are unnecessary for our *avodat Hashem*. This self-control is what will lead to the end of the long exile of Esau.[154]

VERSES OF PRAISE

ישתבח

יִשְׁתַּבַּח שִׁמְךָ לָעַד מַלְכֵּנוּ, הָאֵל הַמֶּלֶךְ הַגָּדוֹל וְהַקָּדוֹשׁ, בַּשָּׁמַיִם וּבָאָרֶץ, כִּי לְךָ נָאֶה יְיָ אֱלֹהֵינוּ וֵאלֹהֵי אֲבוֹתֵינוּ, שִׁיר וּשְׁבָחָה, הַלֵּל וְזִמְרָה, עֹז וּמֶמְשָׁלָה, נֶצַח, גְּדֻלָּה וּגְבוּרָה, תְּהִלָּה, וְתִפְאֶרֶת, קְדֻשָּׁה, וּמַלְכוּת:

ממלא כל עולמים
אהבת עולם (כמים)
כמו בן המשתדל לאביו
רוח
עולם היצירה

> **Just as *Baruch She'Amar*, which opens the *pesukei dezimra*, mentions praise of God's essential name, so does *Yishtabach* (the closing blessing)...**" (*Sha'ar HaTefila* within *Sha'arei Teshuva* of the Mitteler Rebbe, p. ל"א)[155]

During *Baruch She'Amar*, we say *Baruch Shemo* ("Blessed is His name"), after reciting words that allude to levels of direct illumination (*ohr yashar*) and reflected illumination (*ohr chozer*). Then, we recite the *pesukei dezimra*, ending with *Yishtabach*, which elevates us to receive revealed levels of essential Godliness.

The point of *pesukei dezimra* is to elicit holy illumination from the One above. When we describe someone as "wise," we may elicit his wisdom, and when we describe him as "kind," we hope to elicit his kindness. By attributing to God all the positive traits that we mention during *pesukei dezimra*, we hope to elicit revelation and illumination of those traits. When we succeed, we are elevated and uplifted to higher spiritual levels.

> *Within the Words*
>
> *Shemo* ("His name") that we mention in *Baruch She'Amar* refers to God in the third person, in the same manner that we would speak of a person who is not present. Our purpose is to bring down His holy illumination during the *pesukei dezimra*. Having done so, we can now refer to Him directly, saying *Shimcha* ("Your name") during *Yishtabach*, as if He is now among us. The King is more exalted by praise coming from afar (from below, in the physical world) than by praise from nearby (from the spiritual worlds above).

Immanent Godliness
Lower love (water)
Love as a son for his Father
Soul level: Ruach
World of Yetzira

Yishtabach

MAY YOUR NAME BE PRAISED FOREVER, OUR King, the almighty God, the great and holy Sovereign in the heavens and upon the earth. For to You, Lord our God and the God of our fathers, it is forever appropriate [to offer]; Song and praise, admiration and melody, power and government, triumph, greatness and strength, adulation and harmony, holiness and reign:

--- CHASSIDIC INSIGHTS ---

(continued from p. 180)

example, the soul may have "fallen," or it may be "suppressed," or "imprisoned," all of which are discussed during Psalm 146 of the *Pesukei dezimra*. This allusion makes sense if the level of love associated with this section of prayer is "love of God because He is the life of my soul."

And finally, following Psalm 150, we close the *pesukei dezimra* with passages from Chronicles and from Exodus that tell of the relationship of the Jewish people to God as they developed from a family into a set of tribes and finally become a full fledged nation. It was upon leaving Egypt, described in the final section of *pesukei dezimra* (from Exodus, parshat *Beshalach*), that our sages described the Jewish people as the newborn "children of God." So, it is appropriate to associate this part of our prayers with the level of "love like water" known as "love like a child for his father."

Something else to take note of is the frequency with which we say the word *Halleluyah* during the *pesukei dezimra*. The word *Halleluyah* literally means, "Praise be the Lord," but it utilizes only the first two letters (*yud-hey*) of His four letter name. That is, the beginning of the word (*Hallel*) means "praise" (or "illumination" as in *Behilo naro* —

(continued on p. 186)

VERSES OF PRAISE

בְּרָכוֹת וְהוֹדָאוֹת, לְשִׁמְךָ הַגָּדוֹל וְהַקָּדוֹשׁ, וּמֵעוֹלָם עַד עוֹלָם אַתָּה אֵל:

בָּרוּךְ אַתָּה יְיָ, אֵל מֶלֶךְ גָּדוֹל וּמְהֻלָּל בַּתִּשְׁבָּחוֹת, אֵל הַהוֹדָאוֹת, אֲדוֹן הַנִּפְלָאוֹת, בּוֹרֵא כָּל הַנְּשָׁמוֹת, רִבּוֹן כָּל הַמַּעֲשִׂים, הַבּוֹחֵר בְּשִׁירֵי זִמְרָה, מֶלֶךְ יָחִיד, חֵי הָעוֹלָמִים:

ממלא כל עולמים
אהבת עולם (כמים)
כמו בן המשתדל לאביו
רוח
עולם היצירה

> "King Solomon attained his spiritual level because he was from the fifteenth generation after Avraham..." (*Sefer Maamorim 5662*/1902 of the Rebbe Rashab, p. 354)[156]

During *pesukei dezimra*, we attempt to bring *yud-hey*, the first two letters of God's name, into our prayers. These two letters, taken together, have the numerical value of fifteen. They represent the first two *sephirot* — *chochma* ("creative wisdom") and *bina* ("intellectual analysis"). In practical terms, this is spiritual illumination (*mochin*) that we seek to bring down from above.

Avraham was the first of our ancestors to "shine" — that is, he brought Godliness down from above and focused it onto this physical world. King Solomon was the fifteenth generation from Avraham. On the fifteenth day of the month, the "moon is at its fullest." During Solomon's generation, the Jewish people were settled in their land and the Temple was built. The entire world streamed to Jerusalem to see the Temple. It was the zenith of Jewish history.

Within the Words

During *Yishtabach*, we recite fifteen words of praise (from *shir u'shvacha* all the way to *berachot v'hodaot*). This we do in order to focus Godly illumination on *Shimcha* — on "Your name." This also corresponds to the fifteen words of the priestly blessing (*Yeverachecha...*), which bring holy illumination all the way down to the final *sephira* of *malchut*. They also correspond to the fifteen "Songs of Ascent" within Psalms (Psalm 120-134), as well as the fifteen steps that separated the *Ezrat Nashim* from the next higher level of the holy Temple.

Immanent Godliness
Lower love (water)
Love as a son for his Father
Soul level: Ruach
World of Yetzira

> Blessings and acknowledgement of Your great and holy Name, in all of the worlds, You are almighty God.
>
> Blessed are You, Lord, the almighty God, great Sovereign, extolled in praises, almighty God worthy of acknowledgment, Master of wonders, Creator of all the souls, Ruler of all events, Who chooses songs of praise, King, the One and Only, Life of the worlds.

❝ **Sometimes we say, 'One and Only, Life of the Worlds, King,' and other times we say, 'King, the One and Only, Life of the Worlds.'"** *(Sefer Maamorim 5680/1920 of the Rebbe Rashab, p. 134)*[157]

Malchut — His reign — exists on all levels. Our prayers mention those levels from the very highest to the very lowest. There is *malchut* within the infinite light that precedes the *tzimtzum*, and there is a *malchut* in all of the four worlds. The King of Kings reigns on all levels — *Chei Haolamim* ("Life of the Worlds") refers to the divine vitality that descends to create and enliven the universe. *Yachid* ("the One and Only") refers to the very essence of Godliness, which is simple and indivisible.

The difference between the words *yachid* ("singular, one and only") and *echad* ("one") is the difference between simple unity and unity of disparate parts and elements working together. During our prayers, we want to draw simple unity of *yachid* down to illuminate disparate elements of *echad* so that they become one.

📖 *Within the Words*

During *Baruch She'Amar*, we seek to bring down a powerful revelation of Godliness to inaugurate our prayers. Therefore, we first mention "One and Only" followed by "Life of the Worlds, King." In this way, we bring the very essence of Godliness (the "One and Only") down to *malchut* of *Atzilut*, the source of creation. But, following the *pesukei dezimra*, we ascend spiritually and become aware of His transcendent reign within *malchut* of *Atzilut*. Therefore, we reverse the order, first saying "King..." followed by "who is One and Only, Life of all the Worlds." Our elevation to this level allows us to bring the holy light of *yachid* from *malchut* of *Atzilut* down to the lower worlds of *BY"A* as well.[158]

VERSES OF PRAISE

מראש השנה עד יום הכיפורים מוסיפים:

שִׁיר הַמַּעֲלוֹת מִמַּעֲמַקִּים קְרָאתִיךָ יְיָ:

אֲדֹנָי שִׁמְעָה בְקוֹלִי תִּהְיֶינָה אָזְנֶיךָ קַשֻּׁבוֹת לְקוֹל תַּחֲנוּנָי:

אִם עֲוֹנוֹת תִּשְׁמָר יָהּ אֲדֹנָי מִי יַעֲמֹד:

כִּי עִמְּךָ הַסְּלִיחָה לְמַעַן תִּוָּרֵא:

קִוִּיתִי יְיָ קִוְּתָה נַפְשִׁי, וְלִדְבָרוֹ הוֹחָלְתִּי:

נַפְשִׁי לַאדֹנָי, מִשֹּׁמְרִים לַבֹּקֶר שֹׁמְרִים לַבֹּקֶר:

יַחֵל יִשְׂרָאֵל אֶל יְיָ כִּי עִם יְיָ הַחֶסֶד, וְהַרְבֵּה עִמּוֹ פְדוּת:

וְהוּא יִפְדֶּה אֶת יִשְׂרָאֵל, מִכֹּל עֲוֹנוֹתָיו:

ממלא כל עולמים
אהבת עולם (כמים)
כמו בן המשתדל לאביו
רוח
עולם היצירה

CHASSIDIC INSIGHTS

(continued from p. 183)

"may His candle shine") and the end of the word (*yud-hey*) is an abbreviated form of God's essential name, *Havaya*. From kaballah, we know that these two letters (*yud-hey*) are associated with the "intellectual" *sephirot* of *chochma* (creative insight) and *bina* (analytic understanding). While reciting the *pesukei dezimra*, we "fan" and encourage our emotional attachment to God, but at the same time, we seek intellectual enlightenment from *chochma* and *bina*. The word *Halleluyah* appears thirteen times in the *pesukei dezimra*, perhaps corresponding to the thirteen times that we say the word *baruch* during *Baruch She'Amar*. Within *Baruch She'Amar*, our intention is to bring Godly illumination down from above to below, whereas during *pesukei dezimra*, we strive to arouse illumination with our prayers from below to Above.

The path to arouse this intellectual enlightenment lies in praising God. When we praise a wise man for his wisdom and intelligence, for example, our praise elicits more of his wisdom. Similarly, when we praise God during the *pesukei dezimra*, we call upon Him to shine His enlightenment and wisdom upon us. In this context, it is logical that we mention the word *Halleluyah* most frequently during the "middle" section of *pesukei dezimra*, as we develop love for God "because He is our life." At this point, we serve Him as a servant, learning Torah and

(continued on p. 187)

Immanent Godliness
Lower love (water)
Love as a son for his Father
Soul level: *Ruach*
World of *Yetzira*

From Rosh HaShanah until Yom Kippur, the following is added:

Song of ascents: From the depths, I call to You, Lord.
Master, heed to my voice,
lend Your ears to the voice of my pleas.
If You take into account transgressions, God,
then who can stand [before You]?
It is Your prerogative to forgive, in order that You be feared.
I hope for the Lord, my soul hopes, and for His word, I await.
My soul is with the Master, more than the guard waits for
the morning, pining for daybreak.
Israel, wait for the Lord, for kindness is with the Lord, and
much redemption with Him.
And He will redeem Israel from all of his iniquities.

Word Sparks

The Rebbe Maharash offers a much higher interpretation of the closing lines, "King...life of the worlds." When we recite, "Singular One, life of the worlds, King" at the end of Baruch She'amar, we allude to the 'ten concealed sephirot' within His infinite light, that we bring down to reign within His malchut, or "kingship," via the "life of the worlds," an allusion to yesod (the sephira of "transmission" that is just above malchut). Yesod exists on many different levels and transmits His infinite light down through many contractions in order to enliven malchut which is the source of creation. And when we recite "King, Singular One, Life of the universe" at the end of the prayer, Yishtabach, immediately prior to Kaddish and Barchu, we allude to His supernal reign above the great Tzimtzum ("contraction") where all is in a state of simple unity within His infinite light." (Torat Shmuel 5634/1874, pp. 243-44).

——— CHASSIDIC INSIGHTS ———

(continued from p. 186)

fulfilling His commandments. However, we also seek spiritual enlightenment from Him in order to ascend to the next stage of love of God — love like a son for his father and mother.

We may also better understand "love like water" as well as the soul-level of *ruach* from the following quote: As Elijah the prophet

(continued on p. 188)

ממלא כל עולמים
אהבת עולם (כמים)
כמו בן המשתדל לאביו
רוח
עולם היצירה

חצי קדיש:

יִתְגַּדַּל וְיִתְקַדַּשׁ שְׁמֵהּ רַבָּא. (עונים: אָמֵן)

בְּעָלְמָא דִּי בְרָא כִרְעוּתֵהּ וְיַמְלִיךְ מַלְכוּתֵהּ, וְיַצְמַח פֻּרְקָנֵהּ וִיקָרֵב מְשִׁיחֵהּ. (עונים: אָמֵן)

בְּחַיֵּיכוֹן וּבְיוֹמֵיכוֹן וּבְחַיֵּי דְכָל בֵּית יִשְׂרָאֵל, בַּעֲגָלָא וּבִזְמַן קָרִיב. וְאִמְרוּ אָמֵן:

(עונים: אָמֵן. יְהֵא שְׁמֵהּ רַבָּא מְבָרַךְ לְעָלַם וּלְעָלְמֵי עָלְמַיָּא, יִתְבָּרֵךְ:)

יְהֵא שְׁמֵהּ רַבָּא מְבָרַךְ לְעָלַם וּלְעָלְמֵי עָלְמַיָּא, יִתְבָּרֵךְ, וְיִשְׁתַּבַּח, וְיִתְפָּאַר, וְיִתְרוֹמַם, וְיִתְנַשֵּׂא, וְיִתְהַדָּר, וְיִתְעַלֶּה, וְיִתְהַלָּל, שְׁמֵהּ דְּקֻדְשָׁא בְּרִיךְ הוּא. (עונים: אָמֵן)

לְעֵלָּא מִן כָּל בִּרְכָתָא וְשִׁירָתָא, תֻּשְׁבְּחָתָא וְנֶחֱמָתָא, דַּאֲמִירָן בְּעָלְמָא, וְאִמְרוּ אָמֵן: (עונים: אָמֵן)

CHASSIDIC INSIGHTS

(continued from p. 187)

ran away from Queen Jezebel and arrived at *Horeb*, he received instructions, "Go out and stand on the mountain before God. And behold, God passed before him and there was a great and strong wind [capable of] disintegrating mountains and shattering rocks…[but] God was not within the wind. And following the wind, there was a noise, but God was not in the noise. And after the noise, there was fire, but God was not in the fire. And after the fire, there was a still, small voice" (1 Kings 19:11-12)

Within these prophetic words, the sages tell us, are found the successive stages of prayer. These are the phases through which we have to pass in order to arrive to the essence of Godliness — to the "still small voice" within. We must first pass through "wind," followed by "noise and commotion" and then finally through "fire." In none of these stages do we find the deepest expression of spirituality. That only

(continued on p. 190)

Immanent Godliness
Lower love (water)
Love as a son for his Father
Soul level: *Ruach*
World of *Yetzira*

Chazzan recites the Half Kaddish:

Exalted and sanctified is His great Name.
(cong: "Amen")
In the universe that He created according to His Will, May He establish His reign, and sprout forth His redemption, and quickly bring His mashiach.
(cong: "Amen")
In your life and during your days and in the life of the entire house of Israel, speedily and soon, and say Amen!
(the congregation here says: "Amen, may His great Name be blessed forever and for eternity")
May His great Name be blessed forever and for eternity.
(cong: "Amen")
May He be blessed, may He be extolled, may He be glorified, may He be exalted, may He be elevated, may He be honored, may He be lauded, and may he be praised, the Name of the holy One, blessed be He.
(cong: "Amen")
Beyond all the blessings and the hymns, the praises and the consolations that are recited in the world, and let us say Amen.

VERSES OF PRAISE

Word Sparks

From Baruch She'amar until the blessings before Kriat Shema, all our prayers are in the world of yetzira. The main prayers/songs are Psalms 148 and 150, which are the songs of the creatures of heavens and the earth. Psalm 150 corresponds to Chabad (the "intellect") of yetzira. It alludes to all the ten sephirot and includes six verses, alluding to the six spiritual vectors (z'a) of yetzira, and representing their ascent from asiya to yetzira. The Kaddish before Barchu symbolizes the ascent from yetzira to bria, and from the blessing, "Who forms light..." begins the prayers of bria, during which the angels of bria say 'Kadosh' (Torat Shmuel 5637/1877 of the Rebbe Maharash, pp. 35-36).

ברכות קריאת שמע

סובב כל עולמים
אהבת עולם (כאש)
פנימיות המוחין
נשמה
עולם הבריאה

בָּרְכוּ אֶת יְיָ הַמְבֹרָךְ:

בָּרוּךְ יְיָ הַמְבֹרָךְ לְעוֹלָם וָעֶד:

CHASSIDIC INSIGHTS

(continued from p. 188)

appears in the "still small voice." But, first, we need to pass through the initial stage of "wind" (*ruach*)

We experience wind on our skin and clothes. It does not usually stop us from going where we need to go or doing what we want to do, neither does it interfere with our activities. What it does do is alter our mood — when there is wind, we find ourselves battening the hatches, placing weight holders, closing doors and windows — we go into a protective mode. Similarly, the "wind" of prayer puts us in a particular mode…the sages called it, "etching from without." Our prayers in this mode are meant to affect us so that we drop any occupation that we might have had with other topics, and focus on creation from nothing to something. We shuck off the last vestiges of sleep and sloth, and focus on how God enlivens the creation. This is also evident in the name of this section of prayers — *pesukei dezimra*. The obvious translation of *pesukei dezimra* is "verses of song," and yet the word *zimra* also comes from *lezamer aritizim* — to "prune away thorns." This stage of prayer is dedicated to fending off all distractions from outside and focusing on creating a mood of concentration within…concentration on the topic of creation from nothing to something.

STATE OF MIND (within *ahavat olam*/"worldly love")	SOUL-LEVEL	WORLD	PRAYER SEGMENT (within *pesukei dezimra*)
Love because He is the vitality of creation	Ruach ("wind"/emotion consciousness")	Nehy of Yetzira	Baruch She'Amar thru Ashrei
Love because He is the vitality of my soul	Ruach – "intellect within emotion – *Halleluyah*"	Chagat of Yetzira	Psalm 146 thru 150
Love like a son for his father	Ruach – "engraving from without"	Chabad of Yetzira	Psalm 89:13 thru *Yishtabach*

(continued on p. 191)

Transcendent Godliness
Lower love (fire)
Inner mindfulness
Soul level; Neshama
World of Bria

BLESSINGS OF THE SHEMA

B*ARCHU*: BLESSED BE THE LORD, WHO IS SANCTIFIED!
Bless the Lord, Who is sanctified
forever and ever!

CHASSIDIC INSIGHTS

(continued from p. 190)

BIRCHOT KRIAT SHEMA AND THE SHEMA

Upon reciting *Barchu* (after *Yishtabach*), we begin the section of prayers known as *Birchot Kriat Shema* ("Blessings associated with recital of the *Shema*"). The purpose of this section is to elevate our soul to a higher spiritual level (called *neshama*), as well as to prepare our vital, animal soul for the level of devotion that is necessary in order to recite the *Shema* with proper intention.[i]

In the previous section of prayers (the *pesukei dezimra*), we focused our attention on the Godliness that is embedded in nature, in order to creation and enliven it. We described three levels of meditation corresponding to the three worlds of *Asiya*, *Yetzira* and *Bria*. Our meditation brought us to the realization that the energy that is responsible for creating and maintaining all of existence is divine in nature, and therefore the entire creation is spiritual at heart. The universe is physical, but it is composed of Godly energy that enlivens it, without which it would not exist at all. Our meditation focused upon specific items of creation in the world of *Asiya*, on general templates and archetypes of creation ("angels") in the world of *Yetzira*, and upon the "possibility" and potential of creation in the world of *Bria*.

After *Barchu*, though, we shift our thought processes to higher levels. The Lubavitcher Rebbe enlightens us regarding meditation during *Birchot Kriat Shema*: "Overall, the difference between meditation during the *Birchot Kriat Shema* and meditation during the *pesukei dezimra*, is that the latter focuses upon the ray and reflection of Godliness that becomes en-clothed within the worlds. The meditation takes place with "external mindfulness" (*chitzoniut hamochin*), which is the intellect that is associated with emotions. And therefore, it takes

(continued on p. 192)

בָּרוּךְ אַתָּה יְיָ אֱלֹהֵינוּ מֶלֶךְ הָעוֹלָם, יוֹצֵר אוֹר וּבוֹרֵא חֹשֶׁךְ, עֹשֶׂה שָׁלוֹם וּבוֹרֵא אֶת הַכֹּל:

הַמֵּאִיר לָאָרֶץ וְלַדָּרִים עָלֶיהָ בְּרַחֲמִים, וּבְטוּבוֹ מְחַדֵּשׁ בְּכָל יוֹם תָּמִיד מַעֲשֵׂה בְרֵאשִׁית.

סובב כל עולמים
אהבת עולם (כאש)
פנימיות המוחין
נשמה
עולם הבריאה

> **"** The reason that the World of *Bria* is described as 'dark' is due to the large amount of illumination present. The brightness renders it 'invisible' to the spiritual levels below it." (*Sefer Maamorim 5666* /1906 of the Rebbe Rashab, p. 300 and p. 399 of the new printing)[159]

> Why is *Bria* called "darkness," even though it is higher than *Yetzira*, which is called "light"? This condition is comparable to one who cannot see because the protective layers of his eyes have desiccated, allowing too much light to enter. In Aramaic, he is called a *sagi nahor* (literally, "too much light"), or a blind person.

> In spiritual terms, revelation to "others" is called "speech." By "others," we mean independent, separate objects, created with God's "speech." Revelation to ourselves is called "thought." The creatures of *Bria* are a product of God's "thought," or revelation to Himself. Hence, they are nullified and united with Godliness. They are invisible to spiritual creatures below them, which is why *Bria* is "dark" (invisible) to the separate creatures of *Yetzira* and *Asiya*.

> ─ 📖 *Within the Words* ─
> Blessed are You, Lord our God, "who forms light" (this is the World of *Yetzira*) "and creates darkness" (this is the World of *Bria*).

─── **CHASSIDIC INSIGHTS** ───

(continued from p. 191)

place on the soul-level of *ruach* alone. However, the meditation associated with the *Birchot Kriat Shema* takes place with "mature mindfulness" (*pnimiyut hamochin*) which is beyond emotions. It takes place on the soul level of *neshama*, which implies grasp and meditation on the essence of God's infinite illumination that is beyond the created

(continued on p. 194)

סידור עם חסידות – שחרית

Transcendent Godliness
Lower love (fire)
Inner mindfulness
Soul level; *Neshama*
World of *Bria*

BLESSED ARE YOU, LORD, OUR GOD AND KING OF the universe, Who forms light and creates darkness, makes peace and creates everything.

He Who illuminates the earth and those who dwell upon it in mercy, and in His goodness constantly renews the act of creation, every day.

❝ *Mayim chaim* ('live waters') flow constantly without interruption or variation; every day new waters flow. Similarly, the infinite light of God is called *makor mayim chaim* ('source of live waters'), since it is renewed constantly, every day…" (*Sefer Maamorim 5655*/1895 of the Rebbe Rashab, p. 141)[160]

Creation and its constant renewal take place with the divine name *Havaya* enmeshed in the divine name *Ado-nay*. The two names work together to bring vitality into the world; the name *Havaya* is dominant during the day, while *Ado-nay* is dominant at night. There are twelve combinations of the four letters *Havaya*, and twelve of the four letters *Ado-nay*, corresponding to the twenty four hours of the day, and at every hour a new combination of letters brings new Godly vitality into the world.

In truth, God renews the world not only every "day," nor every "hour," but at every instant. There are 1,080 such "instants" in every "minute," and divine creative renewal takes place during each and every one of them. Since that is the case, why do we not pray, "He who in His goodness renews the act of creation, every instant"? Why do we say, "every day"?

📖 *Within the Words*

Within man's consciousness, we are much more aware of the passage of a "day" than we are of instants, minutes, or even hours. That is why the creation story says, "And there was evening and there was morning…" The Torah descends to our own level of consciousness, and that is also why we pray, "He who in His goodness renews… every day."

BLESSINGS OF THE SHEMA

מָה רַבּוּ מַעֲשֶׂיךָ יְיָ, כֻּלָּם בְּחָכְמָה עָשִׂיתָ,
מָלְאָה הָאָרֶץ קִנְיָנֶךָ.

סובב כל עולמים
אהבת עולם (כאש)
פנימיות המוחין
נשמה
עולם הבריאה

"The process of creation requires constant renewal, since created existence demands constant refreshing [of spiritual input]." (*Sefer Maamorim 5656/1896* of the Rebbe Rashab, pp. 293-294)[161]

> The renewal of creation comes from *yesod abba* (literally, "foundation of the father") referring to the *sephira* of *yesod* within A"K. This spiritual level is so high that it can even descend to the lowest of worlds, the physical world in which we dwell, in order to permeate it with Godly vitality and renewal. In layman's terms, *yesod* of A"K is the highest level after the *tzimtzum* that propels transcendent Godly light down to lower levels, and ultimately to creation

> The gulf between Creator and creation is so great that only constant energy from the Creator keeps the creation in existence. Left to its own, without spiritual input, creation would return to its spiritual source and cease to "exist." For that reason, His "word" — the speech with which He created the physical world — remains embedded in creation in order to constantly renew it.

Within the Words

It is the nature of good to do good, and thereby to benefit creation. It is only the kindness of God, who in His "goodness" constantly inputs energy into creation, that guarantees the continued existence of the physical world. The reason God created the world is so that there will be recipients of His goodness. That is why we say that He, "in His goodness constantly renews the act of creation, every day."

──────── **CHASSIDIC INSIGHTS** ────────

(continued from p. 192)

universe" (*Sha'arei Tefila* from *Heichal Menachem*, page 304). While our meditation during *pesukei dezimra* focused on spirituality that is embedded in creation (*ohr pnimi*, or *memalle kol olmin*), our meditation during *Birchot Kriat Shema* and the *Kriat Shema* itself focuses upon Godly light that transcends the creation (*ohr makif*, or *sovev kol olmin*).[ii]

(continued on p. 202)

Transcendent Godliness
Lower love (fire)
Inner mindfulness
Soul level; Neshama
World of Bria

> How many are Your works, Lord;
> You made them all in wisdom,
> the earth is full of Your acquisitions.

❝ Clearly, man becomes excited when he discovers something new.... the novelty of [the creation] process produces excitement and arousal within our soul, which is enthralled and enraptured with this phenomena..." (*Sefer Maamorim 5666*/1906 of the Rebbe Rashab, p. 136, [p. 180 in the new printing]¹⁶²

In the Holy Temple, it was necessary for the Jews to bring fire to the altar to burn their offerings. Similarly, we must bring fire to our prayers. We do so by meditating upon the creation from nothing to something. The process begins as we recite the *pesukei dezimra*, focusing upon how God creates from afar, and yet simultaneously permeates His creation with Godly vitality. His vitality is embedded in creation. The process culminates as we recite the blessings prior to the *Shema* and the *Shema* itself, with great focus and intention, stimulating love like fire within our soul.

Deep contemplation of the uniqueness and novelty of this creation process arouses love like fire within us. Awareness of creation at every instant generally elevates us, and then a corresponding fire from above descends (just as fire descended from above to burn the animal sacrifice on the altar). This is the fire from above that consumes the animal soul, which occurs during the blessings preceding the *Shema*.

📖 *Within the Words*

Continued awareness of the novelty of creation, based upon the verse, "He who in His goodness constantly renews the act of creation, every day," catalyzes fire from above of the divine soul to descend to us. This occurs as we recite the *Shema*, and "fire from above" descends to ignite our divine soul with love like fire. This is comparable to the lighting of the Menorah in the Temple, by Aharon the priest. Simultaneously, and during the *Shemonah Esreh* as well, we experience the reward for our *avoda* in the form of *ahava rabba* ("great love") from above.

BLESSINGS OF THE SHEMA

הַמֶּלֶךְ הַמְרוֹמָם לְבַדּוֹ מֵאָז, הַמְשֻׁבָּח וְהַמְפֹאָר וְהַמִּתְנַשֵּׂא מִימוֹת עוֹלָם.

סובב כל עולמים
אהבת עולם (כאש)
פנימיות המוחין
נשמה
עולם הבריאה

> **"**All of the variations and details occurring within all worlds…as well as variations in time, in the past, present and future, and various events that occur throughout history, all are the result of variation in the letters [of creation], all of which conduct divine vitality from His attributes…while God Himself remains unchanged…" (*Tanya, Igeret Hakodesh* #6)[163]

"Before the universe was created, all that existed was He and His name."[164] A name is nothing more than a ray and reflection of who we are, and so God's name is nothing more than a ray and reflection of His Godly essence. But, from this ray and reflection, the entire universe was created.

Before the creation, the ray was absorbed in the infinite light that illuminated His essence. Only a "contraction" (*tzimtzum*) of His infinite light allowed the ray to emerge, and from it, the universe was created. However, none of this changed God in any way whatsoever. He remained after the creation exactly as He was before creation took place. From the limited ray (*kav*) of His infinite light, emanated the *sephirot* of the World of *Atzilut*.

Within the Words

Hamelech hameromam levado me'az — "The King who is exalted, alone from primordial times…" — that is, just as before the creation, there was only God and God alone, so now as well there is only He alone. *Hamitnaseh miyemot olam* — "elevated above the days of creation" — He is elevated and transcendent, above and beyond time ("days of creation"). Time is a creation that requires creative input, just as does the rest of creation. The spiritual input that creates and vitalizes time comes from the King Himself. This concept should be the cause of great excitement within our soul, but it often fails to stimulate us because our soul is trapped in a physical body. For that reason, it is deserving of mercy, as indicated in the continuation of the prayers, *Elokei olam berachamecha harabim rachem aleinu* ("God of the universe, in Your great mercy have compassion upon us…")

Transcendent Godliness
Lower love (fire)
Inner mindfulness
Soul level; *Neshama*
World of *Bria*

The King Who is exalted, alone from primordial times, praiseworthy and extolled, elevated above the days of creation.

❝ The origin of Godly illumination is from within the ten *sephirot*, which emerged differentiated and minimized after the *tzimtzum*. [Only in this manner] was the infinite illumination able to become enclothed within the vessels of the World of *Atzilut*." (*Besha'ah Shehikdimu* 5672/1912 of the Rebbe Rashab, vol. 1, p. 49)[165]

> The ten *sephirot* come from the infinite light of God that precedes the *tzimtzum*, where they are concealed, known only to the Creator. They emerge from concealment as undifferentiated illumination in *Keter*, which precedes the World of *Atzilut*. Finally they descend to *Atzilut*, where they become the *orot* ("illumination") of the ten *sephirot*.

> All Godly illumination, from inception to its ultimate revelation, passes through three stages. Initially, it is included in its source. In the next stage, it emerges from its source as undifferentiated light. Finally, it descends to the specific spiritual level that it is intended to illuminate.

📖 *Within the Words*

Hamelech hameroman levado me'az — this refers to Godly illumination as it is concealed in its source, totally transcending the creation. *Hamitnasei miyamot olam* — this refers to the Godly light as it emerges from concealment, but before it becomes enclothed in the ten *sephirot* of *Atzilut*. At this stage, it is "elevated above the days of creation" — meaning that it is elevated above the *sephirot*. Finally, Godly illumination descends to the creation via the lower seven *sephirot* of *Atzilut*. They are called the "days of creation," since they are involved in the creation of the universe. The higher 'intellectual' *sephirot* are not involved in creation, but the lower seven *sephirot* are involved in creation.

BLESSINGS OF THE SHEMA

אֱלֹהֵי עוֹלָם, בְּרַחֲמֶיךָ הָרַבִּים רַחֵם עָלֵינוּ, אֲדוֹן עֻזֵּנוּ צוּר מִשְׂגַּבֵּנוּ, מָגֵן יִשְׁעֵנוּ מִשְׂגָּב בַּעֲדֵנוּ:

אֵל בָּרוּךְ גְּדוֹל דֵּעָה, הֵכִין וּפָעַל זָהֳרֵי חַמָּה, טוֹב יָצַר כָּבוֹד לִשְׁמוֹ, מְאוֹרוֹת נָתַן סְבִיבוֹת עֻזּוֹ, פִּנּוֹת צְבָאָיו קְדוֹשִׁים, רוֹמְמֵי שַׁדַּי, תָּמִיד מְסַפְּרִים, כְּבוֹד אֵל וּקְדֻשָּׁתוֹ:

תִּתְבָּרֵךְ יְיָ אֱלֹהֵינוּ בַּשָּׁמַיִם מִמַּעַל וְעַל הָאָרֶץ מִתָּחַת, עַל כָּל שֶׁבַח מַעֲשֵׂה יָדֶיךָ, וְעַל מְאוֹרֵי אוֹר שֶׁיָּצַרְתָּ יְפָאֲרוּךָ סֶּלָה:

סוֹבֵב כָּל עוֹלָמִים
אהבת עולם (כאש)
פְּנִימִיּוּת הַמּוֹחִין
נְשָׁמָה
עוֹלָם הַבְּרִיאָה

> **Elokei Olam** ('God of the Universe...') corresponds to the opening lines of *Baruch She'Amar* ('Blessed be He who said...')... This is the origin of all transcendent illumination (*makifim*), which descend to our five soul levels..." (*Sha'ar Hatefila* within *Sha'arei Teshuva* of the Mitteler Rebbe, p. 54)[166]

There are two types of transcendent illumination. There are *makifim* ("transcendent light") of *ohr yashar* ("direct illumination") that descend from *Keter* of each world. And there are *makifim* of *ohr chozer* ("reflected illumination").

Makifim exist on two levels. One is beyond us but reachable — this is called *makif hakarov* ("transcendent but nearby"). The other is transcendent light that is beyond us and unreachable — this is called *makif harachok* ("transcendent and far away"). The first category is also associated with *ohr yashar* ("direct illumination"), and the second is associated with *ohr chozer* ("reflected illumination"). Our prayers preceding the *Shema* involve *makif hakarov/ohr yashar*, while our prayers during *Baruch She'Amar* involve *makif harachok/ohr chozer*.

Within the Words

The words of *Elokei Olam* are associated with *makifim* of *ohr yashar*, or *makif hakarov* — transcendent light that is "nearby" and attainable. This illumination descends to the five levels of our soul as we say the words: *Rachem aleinu* ("have compassion upon us") brings the might") illuminationdown to our level of *yechida*; *Adon uzeinu* ("Master of our brings it down to our *chaya*; *Tzur misgabeinu* ("Rock of our fortress")

> Transcendent Godliness
> Lower love (fire)
> Inner mindfulness
> Soul level; *Neshama*
> World of *Bria*

God of the universe, in Your great mercy have compassion upon us, Master of our might, Rock of our fortress, Shield of our salvation, Refuge for us.

Blessed Almighty, of great knowledge, Who prepared and created the illumination of the sun, Who well-formed honor in His name, Who placed the luminaries around His majesty; leaders of His holy hosts, holy angels who exalt God, who constantly narrate the majesty of the Almighty and His holiness.

Be blessed, Lord, our God in the heavens above and on the earth below, for all the praiseworthy work of Your hands, and for the radiant luminaries that You formed, may they glorify You forever.

📖 *Within the Words*

bring its down to *neshama*; *Magen yisheinu* ("Shield of our salvation") bring it down to our *ruach*; and finally *Misgav ba'adeinu* ("Refuge for us") brings it down to our *Nefesh*.[167] Alternative interpretation: *Rachem aleinu* applies to A"K, which is the all-inclusive *Keter* of all of creation; *Adon uzeinu* is the divine will associated with *Atzilut*; *Tzur misgabeinu* is associated with *Bria*; *Magen yisheinu* is associated with *Yetzira*; and *Misgav ba'adeinu* is associated with *Asiya*.[168] In all cases, the words of *Elokei Olam* bring down *makifim* of mercy whose purpose is to reinforce and support the divine soul within us in the struggle against the temptations of the physical world.[169]

Word Sparks

רוממי שדי ("*elevated creatures associated with God's name, Shadai*") refers to seraphim, angels of bria. (Torat Shmuel 5641/1881, Page 361)

Our animal soul is illuminated by the ofanim and chayut during the blessing, *yotzar hameorot* ("He who forms the luminaries"). Our Godly soul is illuminated by the seraphim during the blessing, *Ahavat Olam* ("Everlasting love...") (Torat Shmuel 5633, Vol 1, Page 162)

BLESSINGS OF THE SHEMA

❝ **We request His great mercy on ourselves in order to become *kelim*, or "vessels" for His mercy. That is why we say, "In Your great mercy, have compassion upon us…"** (*Torat Shmuel* 5636/1876 of the Rebbe Maharash, p. 507)

סובב כל עולמים
אהבת עולם (כאש)
פנימיות המוחין
נשמה
עולם הבריאה

This section of the prayers involves the *makifim*, or transcendent parts of the soul, that are not ordinarily enclothed in the body, and which are not normally part of our everyday experience. With God's mercy, we strive to "bring down" the *makifim* to our own level of spiritual experience. However, the true mercy that we should feel toward our own soul is nearly impossible to experience, because we do not know the soul in its natural habitat, before it is enclothed in a body, when it simply gazes upon and enjoys Godliness. We only know of the soul as the enlivening source of our body, with all of its physical desires and temptations. And since we do not know the soul in its true habitat, we cannot experience true mercy on the soul after it has descended to become enclothed in our body. For that reason, we ask for "His great mercy," to make us into *kelim* for His compassion from Above.

When we meditate upon how the King is alone and exalted beyond us, removed from time and space just as before He created the universe, and yet He created the universe with a mere ray and reflection of His divinity, the result is that we feel His presence as *Adon Uzeinu* — "the Lord of power" who rules over us. He does so not in a manner that we feel and understand, but as a King who makes rules and decrees that we accept and strive to fulfill (*Torat Shmuel* 5639/1879 of the Rebbe Maharash, pp. 144-5).

📖 *Within the Words*

The words of prayer following *Rachem aleinu* ("Have mercy upon us") and *Adon Uzeinu* ("Lord of power") continue with three more transcendent levels of *makifim*: "Rock…Shield…Refuge" alluding to the three 'garments' that surround our soul as thought, speech and action. These three 'garments' of the soul enable us to fulfill God's mitzvoth in thought speech and action. They also en-clothe the lower three levels of the soul that are enmeshed in the body (the *nefesh*, *ruach* and *neshama*), and facilitate their inclusion in the infinite light of the One above.

Transcendent Godliness
Lower love (fire)
Inner mindfulness
Soul level; Neshama
World of Bria

> **❝ We find that angels sing, but we do not find that souls sing. Yet the truth is that souls sing all the time."** *(Torat Shmuel 5633/1873 of the Rebbe Maharash, p. 269)*

We mention the song of the angels during the blessings before *Kriat Shema* of the daytime (as we say *Kadosh* and *Baruch*) and the nighttime, as we recite a total of seven blessings ("With seven during the day I praise You" — Psalms 119:164). According to the *Ariz'l*, the blessings are associated with the "seven chambers of *bria*" ("chamber of love, chamber of merit, chamber of the holy of holies," etc), but according to the Zohar, they are associated with the "seven supernal levels" of Atzilut. By reciting the seven blessings in the world of *bria*, we merit to revelation from the world of Atzilut. The blessings during *birchot kriat shema* are preparation for receiving "seven supernal levels" (from *chesed* through *malchut*) during *Shemonah Esreh*.

Angels possess refined bodies from the ethereal elements of wind and fire. Since they have bodies, they have a voice. Prophets and refined beings can hear their song and even sometimes "see" angels. Souls are not enclothed in a body and therefore they have no voice. However, that does not mean that souls do not sing. The song of the soul is constant and ongoing, and takes place during the *Shemonah Esreh*, as we recite, "You are holy and Your Name is holy, and holy creatures praise You every day, forever…"

📖 *Within the Words*

In order to access the "seven supernal levels" of the world of Atzilut, we meditate on our own spiritual level. We are the *ani* ("I") of the *sephira* of *malchut*, lowest of the ten *sephirot*, created from a mere ray and reflection of Godly light. Nevertheless, we nullify ourselves and yearn for the ultimate connection with God Himself, and His infinite light. By purifying and refining the seven attributes of our animal soul, we elevate the seven chambers of *bria* (associated with the "animals" of the *merkava*) from below to above, and during *Shemonah Esreh*, we pray that He will reveal the seven supernal levels of *Atzilut* to us *(Torat Shmuel 5633/1873 of the Rebbe Maharash, p. 279 and pp. 308-9)*.

BLESSINGS OF THE SHEMA

תִּתְבָּרֵךְ לָנֶצַח צוּרֵנוּ מַלְכֵּנוּ וְגוֹאֲלֵנוּ בּוֹרֵא קְדוֹשִׁים,

סובב כל עולמים
אהבת עולם (כאש)
פנימיות המוחין
נשמה
עולם הבריאה

❝ During the blessings preceding the *Kriat Shema*, we speak of angels and of creatures of the lower three worlds of *Bria*, *Yetzira* and *Asiya*, which are called a "supernal army." (*Sefer Maamorim 5650*/1890 of the Rebbe Rashab, p. 297)[170]

> First of all, we bless the angels of *Bria*, with the words, *Titbarech lanetzach* ("Be eternally blessed...") since they are far higher than the angels of *Yetzira*.

> The "higher" angels of *Bria* are the ones who say *Kadosh* ("Holy") three times, since they have very high perception of Godliness and holiness. The lower angels say *Baruch Hashem mimkomo* ("Blessed be God from His place"). Although they lack the intellectual perception of the higher angels, they desire the holiness to descend to them.

📖 *Within the Words*

Borei kedoshim ("He who creates holy beings") alludes to the angels (*Seraphim*) of *Bria*. *Yotzar meshartim* ("who forms heavenly servants") refers to the angels (*Chayot*) of *Yetzira*. *Asher meshartav* ("And whose ministering servants...") refers to the angels (*Ofanim*) of *Asiya*.

—— CHASSIDIC INSIGHTS ——

(continued from p. 194)

The Rebbe expresses this concept even more clearly a bit later (*Shaarei Tefila*, Page 306): "...the difference between 'external mindfulness' and 'mature mindfulness' in personal *avoda*, is that 'external mindfulness' (associated with emotions) requires meditation that focuses upon the ray of Godliness enclothed within the worlds. 'Mature mindfulness' requires meditation on the illumination that transcends the worlds, as implied in the verse, 'there is no holiness like that of *Havaya*.'" This is especially true of the *Shema*, which is the "song of the soul." In short, then, the previous section of prayers (*pesukei dezimra*) focused our attention on the level of spirituality that we call *memalle*

(continued on p. 210)

Transcendent Godliness
Lower love (fire)
Inner mindfulness
Soul level; Neshama
World of Bria

Be blessed forever, our Rock, our King and our Redeemer, Who creates holy beings:

❝ The most numerous of all creations are the angels, who are also the most spiritual of all creatures. They are also called 'exalted intellects' (*sichlim nivdalim*) **in the language of the philosophers and mystics.**" (Alter Rebbe's Siddur, *Tefilot Rosh Hashana* p. 472)[171]

Creation is the result of the ten creative "utterances" at the beginning of Genesis. Godly speech comes from *malchut* of *Atzilut*, but has a source in *Z"a* of *Atzilut* and ultimately in *malchut* of the unlimited light of God (*ein sof*). That is why there are so many angels. Similar to other creations, they come from the speech of God, but they are closer to His infinite light than are other creations.

All speech emerges from a voice. In its inception, the voice is simple and undifferentiated. But, as it emerges from the breath of our heart, it takes on form and becomes sub-divided into the letters of speech. The original voice is infinite, but as it turns into speech, it takes on form and limitation. The angels who are highest (*Seraphim*) and closest to His infinite light are also closer to the original "breath" with which God created the universe. Therefore, they are more numerous than the lower angels. And angels in general, as spiritual creatures, are more numerous than physical creatures.

📖 *Within the Words*

We say *Titbarech lanetzach* ("Blessed be forever...") and continue, *borei kedoshim* ("who creates holy ones") because He creates innumerable angels — the "exalted intellects" of *Bria*. We continue, *bechol* ("with a voice"), because creation began with a simple, undifferentiated voice of the heart, and then became differentiated into the *divrei Elokim chaim* ("the words of the living God"). *Elokim* is the source of creation, after which point the undifferentiated voice became divided into the letters of speech, forming all of the lower creations. Finally, *u'Melech Olam* ("and King of the Universe") because with creation, He became King over all the creatures of the universe, the subjects of His creation.

BLESSINGS OF THE SHEMA

יִשְׁתַּבַּח שִׁמְךָ לָעַד מַלְכֵּנוּ יוֹצֵר מְשָׁרְתִים,
וַאֲשֶׁר מְשָׁרְתָיו, כֻּלָּם עוֹמְדִים בְּרוּם עוֹלָם, וּמַשְׁמִיעִים
בְּיִרְאָה יַחַד בְּקוֹל, דִּבְרֵי אֱלֹהִים חַיִּים וּמֶלֶךְ עוֹלָם:

סובב כל עולמים
אהבת עולם (כאש)
פנימיות המוחין
נשמה
עולם הבריאה

"As we become aware of the majesty of the king, and we perceive his retinue, his [army and his servants and ministers], we experience fear. About God, it is written [in the Book of Daniel],[172] 'there are one thousand thousand's serving before Him.' For this reason, the sages decreed that we should recite the blessing *Yotzar ohr*, which describes this level of fear." (*Likutei Torah* of the Alter Rebbe, *Parshat Re'eh*, p. 38)[173]

Initial fear of God (associated with *malchut*) develops into love of God as we proceed through the *pesukei dezimra* (associated with *chesed* of Z"a). There, we develop love of God based upon His presence in this world (*memalle kol olmin*, or "immanent Godliness"). After *Barchu*, we shift our attention to Godliness that transcends creation (*sovev kol olmin*). This is a far higher form of "great love" that develops as we recite the blessings prior to the *Shema*, as well as the *Shema* itself. Finally during the *Shemonah Esreh*, we achieve the total self-nullification associated with *chochma*. This is higher fear, or awe of God.

Regarding these levels of love and fear, it is said, "I consumed my forest with my honey…" The "forest" is full of trees, alluding to the angels called *Seraphim*, who stand upright in fear of God. And "honey" refers to the sweetness of love of God. The sweetness is experienced by Jewish souls, after meditation upon the angels. And the angels themselves receive spiritual elevation as the souls ascend.[174]

📖 *Within the Words*

Yotzer mesharetim va'asher mesharetov kulam omdim — "who forms heavenly servants and whose ministering servants all stand" — these are the standing angels. They are the source of our animal soul, and as we meditate upon their level, our animal soul becomes nullified to its source among these angels. As a result, we develop love of their spiritual level of Godliness, which they reflect down to us and we back to them. This is what is meant by "I consumed my forest with my honey…" — our main objective is the "honey" (love of God), but in order to achieve that, we need the "forest" (the angels).

Transcendent Godliness
Lower love (fire)
Inner mindfulness
Soul level; Neshama
World of Bria

> May His name blessed praised forever, our Sovereign, Who forms heavenly servants, and Whose ministering servants all stand at the heights of the universe, letting their voices be heard in awe [and] in unison, reciting the words of the living God and King of the universe.

❝ The creation of 'holy creatures' pertains to the two *sephirot* of *chochma* ('insightful wisdom') and *bina* ('analytic understanding') about which the prayer says that they…emerged from nothing to something…" (*Sefer Maamorim 5665* (1905) of the Rebbe Rashab, p. 261)[175]

Chochma is created "from nothing" — from a void that we cannot identify, since its origin in *Keter* is completely "out of range." We cannot say that *chochma* was "included" in its source prior to its creation, or that its source is embedded within it after its creation.

Therefore, the faculty of *chochma* is comparable to something that we "find." It occurs without our awareness of its source. It is not like a "gift," which we receive from a friend whom we know. There is a piece of the giver within such a gift, making it similar to a "cause and effect" relationship. Creation from nothing to something, though, is comparable to a "find."

📖 *Within the Words*

When saying *Borei kedoshim yishtabach shimcha* — "He who creates holy beings, blessed be Your name" — we think of the two *sephirot* of *chochma* and *bina*, which are created as if from "nothing to something." *Chochma* implies awareness of essential Godliness within prayer and that, without God, nothing exists whatsoever. *Bina* implies awareness that everything is Godly and that, within everything, there is a spark of Godliness.

BLESSINGS OF THE SHEMA

כֻּלָּם אֲהוּבִים, כֻּלָּם בְּרוּרִים, כֻּלָּם גִּבּוֹרִים, כֻּלָּם קְדוֹשִׁים, וְכֻלָּם עוֹשִׂים בְּאֵימָה וּבְיִרְאָה רְצוֹן קוֹנָם.

סובב כל עולמים
אהבת עולם (כאש)
פנימיות המוחין
נשמה
עולם הבריאה

> **All levels that are called *kedoshim* allude to 'holy creatures' who praise His name every day. They come from *chochma*…and [like *chochma*] they are also created from nothing to something. Their spiritual level is no higher than *shimcha* ('Your name'), which is associated with *malchut* of *Atzilut*.** (*Sefer Maamorim 5655* (1895) of the Rebbe Rashab, pp 13, 16-17)[176]

> *Chochma*, the first *sephira* of the World of *Atzilut*, is created from nothing to something, from the infinite light that precedes the World of *Atzilut*. However, all subsequent emanations (*sephirot*) of *Atzilut* come from *chochma* in a "cause and effect" relationship. There is a *merkava* ("chariot") in *Atzilut*, as well as in every world. The *merkava* contains four facets, which are the source of vitality of the four animal categories within each world. It is called a *merkava*, because like a chariot it transmits its "rider" (in this case, Godliness) from one place (or one spiritual level) to another, and also like a chariot, it is *butel* ("nullified") to its "driver" — to God above.

> The four "facets" of the *merkava* are the "face of the ox," from which come all of the domesticated animals, the "face of the lion," from which come all the wild animals, the "face of the eagle," from which come all of the fowl, and the "face of man," from which come all of the righteous gentiles. There is another element — the "supernal man" who resides above the *merkava* — and this is the source of Jewish souls. The animal soul also descends from the *merkava*, and there is a *merkava* in each of the three worlds of BY"A.

> 📖 *Within the Words*
>
> *Borei kedoshim* — "He Who creates holy beings" — refers to the *sephira* of *chochma* which is created from nothing to something, as are the physical bodies of all creatures. However, the souls of all creatures who come from *chochma* emerge in a "cause and effect" relationship from their source. They descend via the *merkava* of each world, but they recognize their source in the creative ray of Godliness emerging from *malchut* of *Atzilut*, which is also called *shimcha* ("Your name"). Therefore, they give thanks and praise His name.

סידור עם חסידות - שחרית

Transcendent Godliness
Lower love (fire)
Inner mindfulness
Soul level; Neshama
World of Bria

> All of them are beloved, all are clear, all of them mighty, all of them holy, and all of them fulfill the will of their Creator in fear and in awe.

❝ When the sages said that there are a large number (186,000) of angels in each 'batallion,' as well as an infinite number of battalions of angels, their intention was not to say that there are an infinite number, but rather that their number is beyond what we are capable of counting." *(Besha'ah Shehikdimu 5672/1912 of the Rebbe Rashab, vol. 2, p. 684 [Ch. 333])*[177]

The large number of angels indicated by the sages was true of the time when the Temple stood. However, with the destruction of the Temple, their number was reduced, so that now in essence they are quantifiable.

Angels are refined spiritual creatures, so refined that we are unaware of them. They are distinct from one another in their nature, intellectual grasp and spiritual content. However, the fact that they may be quantified indicates that they occupy "space." They possess refined physical "bodies," composed of the two refined categories of creation — fire and air.[178] And since they exist within space, they exist within time as well, since both are products of creation.

📖 *Within the Words*

When saying the words, *Borei kedoshim, yishtabach shimcha*, we should have in mind the angels, who are holy because they possess high perception and awareness of Godliness. Although when the Temple stood, the Jews experienced revealed Godliness directly from the *Shechina* (without angels as intermediaries), when we went into exile our spiritual level was greatly diminished. In exile, Godly revelation arrives through the spiritual prism of the angels of the *merkava*. That is one more reason why we focus upon the angels while reciting the blessings preceding the *Kriat Shema*, which mention the angels of the *merkava*.[179]

BLESSINGS OF THE SHEMA

וְכֻלָּם פּוֹתְחִים אֶת פִּיהֶם בִּקְדֻשָּׁה וּבְטָהֳרָה,
בְּשִׁירָה וּבְזִמְרָה, וּמְבָרְכִים וּמְשַׁבְּחִים,
וּמְפָאֲרִים וּמַעֲרִיצִים, וּמַקְדִּישִׁים וּמַמְלִיכִים:

אֶת שֵׁם הָאֵל, הַמֶּלֶךְ הַגָּדוֹל,
הַגִּבּוֹר וְהַנּוֹרָא קָדוֹשׁ הוּא:

סובב כל עולמים
אהבת עולם (כאש)
פנימיות המוחין
נשמה
עולם הבריאה

> There are two types of angels...those who are standing and currently serving (*yotzar mesharatim*) and those who were formed during the six days of creation and have been standing and serving since then (*asher mesharatav*)." (Besha'ah Shehikdimu 5672/1912 of the Rebbe Rashab, vol. 1, p. 288)[180]

There are angels created every day from the elevation of holy sparks that occurs as we uplift and refine the physical world. These sparks ascend to become included in *malchut*, the tenth and final *sephira* of *Atzilut*. The angels created from such sparks have limited capacity for spiritual illumination. Once included in *malchut*, they are called "fodder for the animal" (*chatzir la'behama*).[181] Fodder (grass) comes and goes, as do these angels, and *malchut* is sometimes called "animal" because of its association with the physical world.

The angels that are standing since creation are not nullified by the Godly light that shines upon them. Since they come from a higher spiritual source, they are able to absorb this holy illumination and say *Kadosh* ("holy"). These are angels of *Bria*, sometimes compared to "animals," and the lesser angels are of *Yetzira*, sometimes referred to as "vegetables."

Within the Words

As we say *yotzar mesharatim* ("who are serving"), we focus on the spiritual beings (angels) of *Yetzira*, created from our mitzvot and *avodat Hashem*. And as we say *v'asher mesharatav* ("and who have served"), we focus on the angels of *Bria*, which are so high that they can withstand intense spiritual illumination and intellectual revelation, and say *Kadosh*.

Transcendent Godliness
Lower love (fire)
Inner mindfulness
Soul level; Neshama
World of Bria

And all of them open their mouths in holiness and in purity, in song and in melody, and they bless and praise, and extol and laud, and sanctify and coronate:

The Name of the Almighty, the great King, the mighty and the awesome — He is holy.

❝ There is a 'higher chariot' and a 'lower chariot.' The 'lower chariot' is the vehicle of 'holy beasts,' named after the animals, such as the 'face of the lion' and the 'face of the oxe." (*Torat Shmuel* 5630/1870 of the Rebbe Maharash, p. 175)[182]

> The chariot (*merkava*) is a conduit for the flow of holy influx from upper worlds to the lower worlds. There is a "chariot" in every world and on every spiritual level. The "upper chariot" is in the world of Atzilut, and the "lower chariot" is between Atzilut and the lower worlds of *Bria*, *Yetzira* and *Asiya*. — The spiritual creatures (angels) associated with the "lower chariot" seek awareness of God's "name," associated with *malchut*, the lowest *sephira* of Atzilut.

> The angels have direct experience and intellectual grasp of the lower worlds, but not of the world of Atzilut. For them, the Godliness of Atzilut is *makif*, or, "transcendent." The same is true of lower souls, of the worlds of *Bria*, *Yetzira* and *Asiya*. However, souls of the world of Atzilut have direct comprehension of the "higher chariot" in the world of Atzilut.

> 📖 *Within the Words*
>
> When we say the words, "The Name of the Almighty, the great King..." we have in mind the angels of the "lower chariot," who are aware of Godliness in the world of Atzilut, even though it is beyond them. They strive for "His Name," which is *malchut* of Atzilut, because they wish to experience the pristine Godliness of Atzilut. Most of us are also souls of the lower worlds of *Bria*, *Yetzira* and *Asiya*, and all we can do is like the angels, strive for the higher levels of transcendent Godliness associated with God's Name in Atzilut.

BLESSINGS OF THE SHEMA

וְכֻלָּם מְקַבְּלִים עֲלֵיהֶם עֹל מַלְכוּת שָׁמַיִם זֶה מִזֶּה, וְנוֹתְנִים בְּאַהֲבָה רְשׁוּת זֶה לָזֶה, לְהַקְדִּישׁ לְיוֹצְרָם בְּנַחַת רוּחַ בְּשָׂפָה בְרוּרָה וּבִנְעִימָה קְדוֹשָׁה. כֻּלָּם כְּאֶחָד עוֹנִים בְּאֵימָה וְאוֹמְרִים בְּיִרְאָה:

קָדוֹשׁ | קָדוֹשׁ קָדוֹשׁ יְיָ צְבָאוֹת, מְלֹא כָל הָאָרֶץ כְּבוֹדוֹ:

סובב כל עולמים
אהבת עולם (כאש)
פנימיות המוחין
נשמה
עולם הבריאה

> **"** Why is it necessary for us to mention the angels who say *Kadosh*? Are we not already familiar with His praises and aware that He is exalted and holy? And why mention this praise in the name of the angels?... Need we become aroused with their excitement? Souls are higher than angels…so either our souls need not get excited over what arouses the angels, or if so, then why via the excitement of the angels?" (*Sefer Maamorim 5666*/1906 of the Rebbe Rashab, pp. 137-138 [pp. 182-3 in the new printing] [183]
>
>> There is a *merkava* in every world. It is composed of angels who conduct divine influence from above to below and vice versa. These angels have no free choice. Like animals, they are nullified to whatever is above them, and they serve as mere conduits to create and enliven the creatures below them. Among the angels of each *merkava* are those who serve as the source of our animal soul.[184]

---— CHASSIDIC INSIGHTS ———

(continued from p. 202)

kol olmin ("immanent spirituality" that is embedded in creation). But, during the *Birchot Kriat Shema* as well as the *Shema* itself, we focus upon *sovev kol olmin* ("transcendent Godliness" that is beyond the creation).

We can see the new elevated focus on transcendent Godliness in the *nusach hatefila* ("words of prayers") of *Birchot Kriat Shema*. In the first paragraph following *Barchu*, we mention several sentences that allude to *ohr makif* (transcendent illumination"), also known as *sovev kol olmin* ("transcending all worlds"). For example, "He Who illuminates the earth and all who dwell upon it in mercy…" According to Chasidut, the quality of mercy is always associated with transcendent illumination, since it requires a "higher" power to relate to a "lower"

(continued on p. 211)

Transcendent Godliness
Lower love (fire)
Inner mindfulness
Soul level; Neshama
World of Bria

And all of them accept upon themselves the yoke of the Kingship of heaven, each from the other, each lovingly granting permission to the other, to pleasantly sanctify their Maker, in a clear language and holy tone. All of them in unison, answer in awe and say in fear,

"Holy, holy, holy is the Lord of Hosts, the entire earth is filled with His glory."

When we meditate upon the source of our animal soul in the *merkava* above and realize that our animal soul is nullified to its source, it has an electrifying effect upon us. We ignite with love like fire to be included in His holiness. This is one reason that we recite the blessings preceding the *Kriat Shema*.

Within the Words

The purpose of the blessings preceding the *Shema* is to identify with and nullify our animal soul to the Godliness that is beyond it. That is why we recite *Kadosh, Kadosh, Kadosh* as we perceive the holy spiritual levels that are beyond us, into which our animal soul is subsumed. This prepares us to recite the *Shema* afterward. Yet another purpose of the blessings preceding the *Shema* is to provide us with the necessary level of *mesirut nefesh* ("self-sacrifice") in order to recite the *Shema* with total dedication.[185]

BLESSINGS OF THE SHEMA

CHASSIDIC INSIGHTS

(continued from p. 210)

level in order to invoke mercy. Two verses later, "The King Who is exalted, alone…" refers to God Himself, exalted and alone, transcendent and beyond His creation. "Elevated above the days of creation…" — Chasidic literature tells us that the "days of creation" refers to the *sephirot* of *Atzilut*, with which God created the universe. And yet, in our prayers He is "elevated above the days of creation," meaning that we are referring to Him as He is above, beyond creation. The prayer

(continued on p. 212)

❝ **The sages said, 'There are three groups of angels: One says *Kadosh*, one says *Kadosh Kadosh*, and one group says *Kadosh, Kadosh, Kadosh Hashem Tzevaot...*'"** (*Likutei Torah* of the Alter Rebbe, Parshat Emor p. 31a, quoting *Chulin* 91b)[186]

> The divine force that energizes the universe, creating it from nothing to something, comes from beyond the creation. It is unlike the vitality that enters the body and is distributed among different levels — the head, the heart and the extremities. Nevertheless, the sages taught, "Just as God fills the universe, so the soul fills the body,"[187] so there must be a parallel. Indeed, a transcendent light (*sovev kol olmin*) descends to enliven the world, but only a ray of that light (*memalle kol olmin*) descends to become enclothed in the creation. He Himself remains holy and removed, unaffected by the creation.

סובב כל עולמים
אהבת עולם (כאש)
פנימיות המוחין
נשמה
עולם הבריאה

CHASSIDIC INSIGHTS

(continued from p. 211)

continues, "God of the universe, in Your great mercy, have compassion..." The prayer continues with five descriptions of God, which according to Chasidic literature correspond to five levels of transcendent light associated with the five levels of the soul (see *Sha'ar Hatefila* within *Sha'arei Teshuva* of the Mitteler Rebbe, page 54). And the final sentence of this paragraph, containing the words "all the praiseworthy work of Your hands," is also a reference to transcendent illumination, since the entire creation comes from a mere ray and reflection of Godliness while God Himself remains unchanged. (See *Besha'ah Shehikdimu* 5672 of the Rebbe Rashab, vol. 1, Page 49).[iii]

During our previous *ruach* meditation (during the *pesukei dezimra*), it became clear that the objects of our meditation — the creations upon which we focused our attention — are like "garments" and "packages" that conceal the Godliness that is embedded within them. Whether meditating upon the "general archetypes" of the world of *Yetzira*, or upon the refined "possibility of creation," in the world of *Bria*, we access only the outer layers, or "shrouds" of creation that hide the Godly kernel that enlivens them. All of nature is only a "garment" that hides and conceals the true Godly nature of the universe. Once that becomes clear, our task becomes to "de-shroud" and "unpack" the objects of creation upon which we meditated, and to expose the Godly kernel within them. This takes place on the soul-level of

(continued on p. 213)

Transcendent Godliness
Lower love (fire)
Inner mindfulness
Soul level; Neshama
World of Bria

🕯 The first group of angels, who say *Kadosh* one time, seeks to ascend from below to above, and become aware of the Godliness that is beyond them (*sovev kol olmin*). The second group of angels wish not only to ascend, but also to bring Godliness down to them, from above to below. The third group is only aware that something is beyond them, but they have no concept of what it is. They seek to bring Godliness down to their lowest level.

📖 *Within the Words*

The first group of angels are the *Seraphim* of *Bria* — they say *kadosh* once since they have only one desire — to ascend and become included in transcendent Godliness (*sovev kol olmin*). Their love of God is *bechol levavcha* ("with all your heart") The second group are the *Chayot* of *Yetzira* — they say *kadosh* twice because they also wish to bring Godliness down to them. Their love is *bechol nafshecha* ("with all your soul"). Finally, the *Ofanim* of *Asiya* say *Kadosh* three times, bringing the holy illumination all the way down to their level in *Asiya*. Their love of God is *bechol meodecha* ("with all your might").

─────── CHASSIDIC INSIGHTS ───────

(continued from p. 212)

neshama, during which we penetrate to the very essence of the creation and find its spiritual core. Even though our meditation was focused upon the higher spiritual creatures (angels) of *Yetzira* and *Bria*, still such creatures are "en-clothed" in garments that hide their Godly essence. Their "garments" are refined and spiritual, but they remain "garments" nonetheless, and as such, they hide their spiritual core. As we meditate, searching for the kernel of Godliness within, we ultimately realize that the spiritual core has a source Above, in the transcendent illumination of Atzilut. The process that allows us to de-shroud and to un-package the "garments" is called *pnimiyut hamochin* ("mature mindfulness").

From the *Kuntres Ha'avoda*, we get a good description of the soul level of *neshama* and the process of *pnimiyut hamochin* that occurs as we pray the *Birchot Kriat Shema*, "The level known as *neshama* corresponds to *mochin* ("spiritual intellect"), as written, "The breath (*nishmat*) of God gives understanding." At this level, through meditation we are able to grasp the essential Godliness that is the "soul" of the

(continued on p. 214)

❝ It is known that there were angels who uttered *Kadosh* at the beginning of their creation and then stood utterly nullified for two thousand years, whereupon they once more uttered *Kadosh* and stood for another two thousand years in a state of abject nullification. And now they are in a state of nullification associated with uttering the word *Kadosh* for a third time..." (*Sefer Maamorim 5655*/1895 of the Rebbe Rashab, p. 223)[188]

סובב כל עולמים
אהבת עולם (כאש)
פנימיות המוחין
נשמה
עולם הבריאה

The first time that we say *Kadosh*, we consider how *tiferet* ascends to receive a ray of enlightenment from *chochma*. The second time, we consider how *tiferet* returns to its own level imbued with *chochma*...and the third time we consider how *tiferet* descends to illuminate *yesod* and *malchut* of *Atzilut*.[189] The three times that we say *Kadosh* correspond to the three levels of *nehi* (*netzach*, *hod* and *yesod*), *chagat* (*chesed*, *gevura* and *tiferet*), and *chabad* (*chochma*, *bina* and *da'at*). And the letter *vav* within each word *Kadosh* represents a "vector," or channel of direction — this can be either to the right side tending toward kindness, or the left tending toward strictness, or the middle, combining the right and left.[190] The three times that we say *Kadosh* also correspond to the first three letters, *yud-hey-vav* of God's holy four letter name.[191] The three times that we say *Kadosh* also correspond to the three worlds, BY"A.[192]

--- **CHASSIDIC INSIGHTS** ---

(continued from p. 213)

concept, stripped of its outer garments. What is left is essential Godliness, and it becomes revealed in our mind. It shines with a tremendous light, riveting our attention and causing us to cleave mightily to this illumination in our mind. (The sign of this occurring is that we completely lose awareness of anything physical because of our intense connection to the Godly light revealed in our mind.) This level of intellectual understanding is beyond anything emotional." (From Love like Fire and Water, Page 17)

How, then, do we attain this state of mindful consciousness, known as *neshama*? Again, the *Kuntres Ha'avoda* comes to our aid: "We have explained that the path of "mature mindfulness" (*pnimiyut hamochin*), involving meditation on the spiritual essence of Godliness, constitutes the level of *neshama*. Within this path, several approaches exist. One

(continued on p. 215)

סידור עם חסידות - שחרית

Transcendent Godliness
Lower love (fire)
Inner mindfulness
Soul level; Neshama
World of Bria

The first time that we say *Kadosh* corresponds to the Godliness that He reveals and grants to souls as they exist above, before they are enclothed in a body. The second time that we say *Kadosh* corresponds to Godliness that descends to the angels. And the third time that we say *Kadosh* corresponds to Godliness that descends to souls enclothed within bodies in this physical world. (*Sefer Maamorim 5678/1918 of the Rebbe Rashab, pp. 214-215*)[193]

> 📖 *Within the Words*
>
> The multiple Chassidic and Kabbalistic interpretations of *Kadosh, Kadosh, Kadosh* indicate a number of possible meditations during the blessings preceding the recital of the *Shema*. Those who are capable of meditating on the World of *Atzilut* may focus on the *sephirot* and *partzufim* of *Atzilut*. Those who have achieved the intellectually-informed love of God ("love like fire") associated with the World of *Bria* may focus on the refined angels who comprehend the transcendent light that is beyond them and say *Kadosh*. Those who are limited to the natural love within the soul ("love like water") may focus upon the process of creation from nothing to something and upon the celestial beings of *Yetzira*. These creatures perceive the immanent spirituality that permeates and enlivens the universe. It is most important to achieve complete grasp and understanding of the Godliness that pervades the world (*memalle kol olmin*), in order to ascend and contemplate the Godliness that transcends the creation (*sovev kol olmin*).

CHASSIDIC INSIGHTS

(continued from p. 214)

may arrive at the "soul" (*neshama*) of the concept only after a lengthy meditation on its outer garments. This approach can be used when it is beyond our ability to directly grasp the inherent Godliness of the concept, without first en-clothing it in outer garments. We are capable of grasping the inner spiritual "kernel" only when it comes "packaged" in images and examples that we understand. The packaging enables us to understand the Godly concept with all its details. For, it is impossible to grasp the concept without its details. This understanding comes as a result of the explanations and analogies, through which the concept becomes clear. Afterward [upon achieving intellectual understanding], we must negate, abstract and strip away all of the

(continued on p. 216)

❝ There are two types of angels. There are 'benefactor angels,' serving as intermediaries providing all that is necessary in this world…and there are 'beneficiary angels,' who 'receive from one another' but do not provide anything for the worlds below them."
(*Likutei Torah* of the Alter Rebbe, *Shir HaShirim*, p. 5, col 2)[194]

סובב כל עולמים
אהבת עולם
(כאש)
פנימיות המוחין
נשמה
עולם הבריאה

The *Seraphim* in the World of *Bria* grasp how the infinite light of God is truly beyond them. Their only desire is to become included in that illumination. The *Chayot* and *Ofanim* are in *Yetzira* and *Asiya*. They lack perception of the transcendent holiness of *Bria*, of which they are aware only via the *Seraphim* above them.

When the *Ofanim* hear the *Seraphim* saying *Kadosh*, they enter a state of great commotion. They realize that there is something "new," far beyond their comprehension, and they nullify themselves to the infinite light that is beyond them. They forsake their previous spiritual level, intellect and nature, and attempt to rise to the new spiritual level that is beyond them.

Within the Words

The *Seraphim* say *Kadosh*, acknowledging the Godliness that is beyond them, holy and removed. They are "receiving" angels, who provide nothing for the worlds below them. Nevertheless, they say *Kadosh* three times, corresponding to BY"A. The *Ofanim* say *Baruch*, since they are "benefactors" whose task is to convey Godly influence to the worlds below them. *Baruch* is associated with *malchut*, since it is *malchut* that descends to conduct Godliness to the lower worlds.

--- CHASSIDIC INSIGHTS ---

(*continued from p. 215*)

packaging, through which we initially understood the concept, in order to penetrate to the spiritual essence. In this way, we arrive at the essence of the Godly concept to whatever extent we are able to grasp it, using the "tools" mentioned above. We remove the concept from its physical shrouds (the image which enabled us to comprehend it). We then come to understand that this is a Godly concept, whose essence cannot be depicted by the image that we had formerly evoked. After we realize that, in general, Godliness is beyond anything that we can grasp, we can come to terms with the concept on its own Godly terms."

(*continued on p. 218*)

Transcendent
Godliness

Lower love
(like fire)

Inner mindfulness

Soul level; *Neshama*

World of *Bria*

> **"** The angels called *Ofanim* become excited with a great commotion as they grasp that He is the diametric opposite of what appears...while creatures appear to exist, in truth they are totally nullified, as if naught..." (*Sefer Maamorim* 5661/1901 of the Rebbe Rashab, p. 198)[195]

The *Ofanim* are aware of the power of *malchut* of *Atzilut*, which is invested in the lower worlds in order to create from nothing to something. The power within *malchut* to create comes from its source in *malchut* of the infinite light of God prior to the *tzimtzum*. The *Ofanim* grasp that this power is invested in the lower creatures of BY"A. That is why the *ofanim* have four wings, corresponding to the four facets of the *merkava*, and to the four "camps" of the *shechina*, and to the four rivers — "And from there the waters parted into four headwaters...." Furthermore, the four wings of the *ofanim* were separated, alluding to the lower "worlds of separation," whose source is in the four letters of the name *Adny*, associated with malchut and creation of the lower worlds."[196]

The angels of *Bria* (*Seraphim*) grasp the infinite light of God and how it is holy and lofty, and that therefore the creation is "as naught" in comparison to God. The *seraphim* have six wings, alluding to the letter *vav* (numerical value of 6) in the word *kadosh*, meaning "holy and removed." But, the *ofanim* grasp how God is great and praiseworthy within creation, within the creatures that He enlivens from nothing to something. Thus they detect the essence of Godliness in the creation itself.

Within the Words

The awareness that the world is not what it seems to be — that the creatures of the lower worlds only appear to exist but their existence is impermanent and illusory since they are nullified to God — sends the *Ofanim* into a state of great excitement. This is a "new" concept for them and it generates commotion. They say, *Baruch kevod Hashem mimekomo* — "Blessed be the glory of the Lord from His place." His "place" is *malchut* of *Atzilut*, which creates the worlds of BY"A. As His glory is manifest above, so should it become revealed in the lower worlds.

וְהָאוֹפַנִּים וְחַיּוֹת הַקֹּדֶשׁ בְּרַעַשׁ גָּדוֹל מִתְנַשְּׂאִים לְעֻמַּת הַשְּׂרָפִים, לְעֻמָּתָם מְשַׁבְּחִים וְאוֹמְרִים:

בָּרוּךְ כְּבוֹד יְיָ מִמְּקוֹמוֹ:

סובב כל עולמים
אהבת עולם (כאש)
פנימיות המוחין
נשמה
עולם הבריאה

> **Noise is not a praiseworthy quality, for noise implies feeling [oneself and one's ego] and this is a negative trait....So, why is it necessary to mention that the path of worship [of the *Chayot* and *Ofanim*] takes place with great noise? This is not a [praiseworthy] quality."** (*Sefer Maamorim 5663*/1903 (vol. 2) of the Rebbe Rashab, pp. 314-316)[197]

The *Ofanim* (lower angels of *Asiya*) mention God's name *Havaya* after only two words (*Baruch kevod*), while the *Seraphim* (higher angels of *Bria*) must mention three words before saying God's holy name. The implication is that the *Ofanim* are on a higher level, but how can this be, since they are in *Asiya*, while the *Seraphim* are in *Bria*?

The highest form of *avoda* (divine service) occurs when we abandon our personal limitations and achieve a wholly new spiritual level. The *Seraphim* never accomplish this, because their *avoda* is intellectual. They always remain within the boundaries of wisdom, understanding and knowledge. However, the *Ofanim* lack intellectual grasp. They hear the *Seraphim* proclaiming *Kadosh*, and they raise

---
CHASSIDIC INSIGHTS

(continued from p. 216)

The *Kuntres Ha'avoda* further elaborates:

"When the approach of the "outer garments" is used, there must be a feeling that, as we are meditating, we are involved in a divine process. That is, we are delving into a Godly matter [which cannot be compared with] something that we seek to learn intellectually. Even as we strive to grasp the concept with our minds in such a way that we can understand well and are able to internalize, we must never lose the awareness (in our consciousness) that the concept is a Godly one, and that we have no real understanding of the essential Godliness except through the intellectual garments that correspond to our own

(continued on p. 219)

Transcendent Godliness
Lower love (fire)
Inner mindfulness
Soul level; Neshama
World of Bria

> And the *ofanim* and the holy *chayot*, with a great tumult, ascend to the *seraphim*, and facing them, utter praises and say,
>
> "Blessed is the glory of the Lord from His place."

themselves in an attempt to grasp what the *Seraphim* are describing. By "uplifting themselves" to the level of *Seraphim*, the *Ofanim* forsake their previous spiritual level. They abandon their own limitations, and this causes them great excitement, which is why they make noise. Because they completely forsake their own limitations, their *avoda* is higher than that of the *Seraphim*.

📖 Within the Words

The *Seraphim* perceive the very high level of holiness of the World of *Atzilut*. This level is so high that it does not descend to us. It is called *kodesh* (קדש), spelled without the letter *vav*. However, they utter the word *kadosh* (קדוש), containing the letter *vav*, three times. The *vav*, in the form of a straight line, represents connection and descent of holiness from above to below and vice versa. The holiness of *Atzilut* is above and beyond comprehension and is therefore *kodesh*. But, through the *Seraphim* who say *kadosh*, the holiness of *Bria* descends to the *Ofanim* and creatures below.[198]

— CHASSIDIC INSIGHTS —

(continued from p. 218)

avoda of the One above. This, as we mentioned before, constitutes the "service of the heart," and it is demanded of every Jew. What is being established here is that intellect — through a process of negation and abstraction — leads us to comprehend the Godliness at the very core of the concept. We gain an awareness of just what it is and how it exists. (It is understood that this is not referring [to the *avoda* of God that is called] *yediat hashlila* [negated, or circumscribed knowledge couched in negative terms, since positive terms are inapplicable when

(continued on p. 220)

לָאֵל בָּרוּךְ נְעִימוֹת יִתֵּנוּ, לַמֶּלֶךְ אֵל חַי וְקַיָּם, זְמִירוֹת יֹאמֵרוּ וְתִשְׁבָּחוֹת יַשְׁמִיעוּ, כִּי הוּא לְבַדּוֹ מָרוֹם וְקָדוֹשׁ, פּוֹעֵל גְּבוּרוֹת, עוֹשֶׂה חֲדָשׁוֹת, בַּעַל מִלְחָמוֹת,

סובב כל עולמים
אהבת עולם (כאש)
פנימיות המוחין
נשמה
עולם הבריאה

❝ As for [this] phrase — 'He is alone, exalted and holy, He performs mighty deeds, etc...' — the *Pardes Rimonim* (by R' Moshe Cordovero) explains that there are ten spiritual levels counted from 'exalted and holy' through 'Master of Wonders' (*Adon Haniflaot*)." (*Ohr HaTorah* of the *Tzemach Tzedek*, *Shemot*, vol. 8 (*Parshat Bo*), p. 2937)[199]

Within the prayer, *Yotzar ohr*, there are ten levels from *marom ve'kadosh* ("exalted and holy") through *Adon Haniflaot* ("Master of Wonders"), corresponding to the ten *sephirot*. *Marom* ("exalted") corresponds to *Keter*; *kadosh* ("holy") to *chochma*...*Adon Haniflaot* ("Master of Wonders") to *malchut*. It is possible that *malchut* is associated with *niflaot* ["wonders" which would normally be connected with *Keter*] because it receives the thirty-two paths of wondrous (*niflah*) wisdom and reveals them to the lower worlds.[200]

Unlike King Saul, King David's reign was "forever," since he was anointed with oil poured from the most elevated level, called *ramah* ("heights"), which is beyond *chochma*. Therefore King David's reign was very exalted, from the level of *Keter*, which is called *ram*

─── CHASSIDIC INSIGHTS ───

(continued from p. 219)

used to describe God, as explained by the Rambam]) ("Love like Fire and Water" page 20-22)."

From this passage, we may glean that the path of meditation during the *Birchot Kriat Shema* is a path of abstraction and negation. The *Kuntres Ha'avoda* gives us examples: "For example, when we want to understand the kabbalistic concept of *zeir anpin*, we associate it with emotions that we feel. We describe *chochma* and *bina* as "wisdom" and "understanding." To explain *memalle kol olmin*, or "immanent Godliness," we use the simile "as the soul permeates the body. And to explain *sovav kol olmin*, or "transcendent Godliness," we use the example

(continued on p. 221)

Transcendent Godliness
Lower love (fire)
Inner mindfulness
Soul level; Neshama
World of Bria

> To the Blessed One, they offer pleasant tones;
> to the almighty King, living and everlasting,
> they express melodies and utter praises, because He alone
> is exalted and holy — He performs mighty deeds, does
> new things, is a master of war,

and *marom*, meaning "exalted." Since his reign came from the exalted level of *Keter*, it is eternal. That is why we say, "Because He alone is exalted (*marom*) and holy, performing mighty deeds…"… mentioning ten levels, corresponding to the ten *sephirot*. (*Torat Shmuel 5639/1879* of the Rebbe Maharash, vol. 1, pp. 141-142)[201]

📖 *Within the Words*

While reciting the paragraph, "To the Almighty, they offer pleasant tones" (*la'El baruch neimot yiteinu*), we concentrate on the ten phrases beginning with, "because He alone is exalted and holy" (*Ki hu levado marom ve'kadosh*), as follows: "Because He alone" corresponds to the essential infinite light of God. "Exalted" (*marom*) corresponds to *Keter*. "And holy" (*ve'kadosh*) corresponds to *chochma*. "He performs mighty deeds" (*poel gevurot*) corresponds to *bina*. "Does new things" (*oseh chadashot*) corresponds to *chesed*. "Is a Master of War" (*Baal Milchamot*) corresponds to *gevurah*. "Who sows acts of righteousness" (*zoreah tzedakot*) corresponds to *tiferet*. "Germinates salvation" (*matzmiach yeshuot*) corresponds to *netzach*. "Creates healing" (*borei refuot*) corresponds to *hod*. "Awesome in praises" (*norah tehilot*) corresponds to *yesod*. And "Master of Wonders" (*Adon Haniflaot*) corresponds to *malchut*.[202]

--- CHASSIDIC INSIGHTS ---

(continued from p. 220)

of human will or general knowledge, and so forth…" ("Love Like Fire and Water," page 20). The use of "feelings," and of "wisdom" and "understanding" is a kind of packaging that we must strip away in order to arrive to the true kernel of Godly comprehension. This is the process of *pnimiyut hamochin* that occurs during *neshama* meditation.

We come to realize that the tools that we developed for penetrating

(continued on p. 222)

BLESSINGS OF THE SHEMA

זוֹרֵעַ צְדָקוֹת, מַצְמִיחַ יְשׁוּעוֹת, בּוֹרֵא רְפוּאוֹת, נוֹרָא תְהִלּוֹת, אֲדוֹן הַנִּפְלָאוֹת, הַמְחַדֵּשׁ בְּטוּבוֹ בְּכָל יוֹם

סובב כל עולמים
אהבת עולם (כאש)
פנימיות המוחין
נשמה
עולם הבריאה

> There is a thread running between the three themes: *Norah tehilot* ('awesome in praises'), *Adon Haniflaot* ('Master of Wonders'), and *hamechadesh betuvo…* ('Who in His goodness…')" *(Sefer Maamorim 5679/1919 of the Rebbe Rashab, p. 375)*[203]

There are two levels within the infinite light of God. The first is the very essence of Godliness, for which we have no name or description. The phrase, *Norah tehilot* ("awesome in praises") describes this level as it descends to become revealed (but before it is revealed). *Adon Haniflaot* ("Master of Wonders") describes transcendent Godliness that becomes revealed after the *tzimtzum* ("contraction") of His infinite light.

Three stages of spirituality are sufficient to encompass the entire spectrum of spirituality. The first is the very essence of Godliness, and it cannot be named, expressed, described or limited. Yet, everything emerges from this level because as essence, it includes everything. Then, there is transcendent Godliness, that we can feel

--- **CHASSIDIC INSIGHTS** ---

(continued from p. 221)

to the Godly essence of creation during the *pesukei dezimra*, only "opened the door" for us to begin to understand Godliness. Now that we understand that all of creation is nothing more than the "garments" of the Creator, the King of Kings, we set about stripping away the garments to get to the "soul," or essence of the creation. This process is called *pnimiyut hamochin* ("mature mindfulness"), and it leads us to the most abstract spirituality that rivets our attention and transfixes us, so that we become entirely unaware of our surroundings. In fact, the effect of *neshama* upon our emotions is very different than the effect that *ruach* meditation has upon us. Meditation on the level of *neshama* lifts our emotions to the same level as our intellect, so that they become one and the same (which is why during *neshama* meditation

(continued on p. 223)

Transcendent Godliness
Lower love (fire)
Inner mindfulness
Soul level; Neshama
World of Bria

> Who sows acts of righteousness, germinates salvation, creates healing, is awesome in praises, Master of wonders, Who in His goodness constantly renews the creation, every day.

but not grasp — it is called *sovev kol olmin* ("surrounding all worlds"). We know that it is present, but we cannot grasp it intellectually or emotionally for the very reason that it is beyond us. Finally, there is immanent Godliness that fills and permeates the universe. We can understand, grasp and feel this level of Godliness — it is called *memalle kol olmin* ("permeating all worlds").

📖 *Within the Words*

Norah tehilot represents the essence of Godliness. *Adon Haniflaot* represents transcendent Godliness (*sovev kol olmin*) that we are aware of but is beyond us. *Hamechadesh b'tuvo* represents immanent spirituality (*memalle kol olmin*) that is accessible and available to us.

CHASSIDIC INSIGHTS

(continued from p. 222)

we are as if in a trance, unaware of our surroundings). During meditation on the level of *ruach*, the intellect descends to engage and permeate the emotions. Our emotions are uplifted in this process but nonetheless the intellect and the emotions remain two distinct entities.

We may wonder, if so, then why the next stage of our prayers speaks of angels and celestial beings on all kinds of spiritual levels? If our objective is to focus on God's transcendent illumination while also stripping away the layers of "packaging and shrouds" that conceal Godliness, and to detect the Godliness at the core of creation coming from the world of Atzilut, then we should be focused on *sephirot* or other concepts of divine illumination associated with the world of Atzilut. Why then are the prayers about creatures of *BY"A*, such as angels, as spiritual as they may be?

(continued on p. 224)

BLESSINGS OF THE SHEMA

PRAYING LIKE FIRE AND WATER

תָּמִיד מַעֲשֵׂה בְרֵאשִׁית. כָּאָמוּר, לְעֹשֵׂה אוֹרִים גְּדֹלִים, כִּי לְעוֹלָם חַסְדּוֹ. (בנוסח הדרכי חיים ושלום ממונקטש: אוֹר חָדָשׁ עַל צִיּוֹן תָּאִיר וְנִזְכֶּה כֻלָּנוּ בִּמְהֵרָה לְאוֹרוֹ:)

בָּרוּךְ אַתָּה יְיָ יוֹצֵר הַמְּאוֹרוֹת: (אָמֵן)

סובב כל עולמים
אהבת עולם (כאש)
פנימיות המוחין
נשמה
עולם הבריאה

> There are two categories of divine descent — 'basic' and 'enriched.' There is a category of divine descent that is constant and homogenous…and there is a much different category of divine descent that consists of 'enriched' illumination. And whatever comes from God that is 'enriched' far outstrips the 'basic' influx…" (*Sefer Maamorim 5658*/1898 of the Rebbe Rashab, p. 167)[204]

"Basic" influx of divine descent comes from *yesod abba* ("foundation of wisdom") in the World of *Atzilut*. As such, it is the illumination that exists within the spiritual hierarchy of creation (*seder hishtalshelut*). "Enriched" divine influx stems from *yesod abba* within the infinite light of God that precedes the *tzimtzum*. It is illumination that arrives as a "gift" from beyond *seder hishtalshelut*.

A certain amount of spiritual energy is required to maintain the status quo of creation. The rhythm of existence that we observe — the passing of days and weeks and seasons, the waxing and waning of the moon — are all the product of a system that requires regular

— CHASSIDIC INSIGHTS —

(*continued from p. 223*)

The answer is that we have a second goal during the *Birchot Kriat Shema*, beyond our own spiritual elevation. Our second goal is not only to penetrate to the spiritual essence of creation, but also to influence and uplift our animal soul. Our meditation during *pesukei dezimra* had the effect of weakening our animal soul by inducing it to consider Godly concepts and to cease obstructing our spiritual path. However, in order to entirely "convert" and "transform" the animal

(*continued on p. 226*)

Transcendent Godliness
Lower love (fire)
Inner mindfulness
Soul level; Neshama
World of Bria

As is said, [thanks to Him, Who] makes the great luminaries, for His kindness is everlasting. (*Nusach Munkatsch* adds: A new light will shine over Zion, to which we will all soon merit):

"Blessed are You, Lord,
Who forms the luminaries."

input of energy. This is the energy that "He in His goodness constantly renews, everyday." It is not new energy — it is the same level of energy that was always required to maintain the universe in "working order." However, we are capable of bringing down a far higher level of energy that augments, enhances and adds to the quality of life in the universe. This may occur as we 1) acknowledge God from the depth of our heart,[205] or 2) attain revelation of *yichuda ila'ah* during prayer,[206] or 3) achieve fulfillment of the Torah and its mitzvot.[207]

📖 Within the Words

The words *Hamechadesh b'tuvo bechol yom* appear twice during the recital of the blessings preceding the *Shema*; first after *Barchu*, and a second time immediately before the conclusion of the blessing, *yotzar hame'orot*. Perhaps the two correspond to the two types of divine influx that the blessing brings into the world: the first mention corresponds to the descent of influx that merely "renews" the creation with "basic" input; and the second mention corresponds to the "enhanced" influx that descends from far above *seder hishtalsheut*. Support for this interpretation may be derived from the Rebbe Rashab who describes the second, "enhanced" influx with the phrase, "a new light will shine upon Zion."[208] These words appear in the *Nusach Ashkenaz* version of the Siddur just prior to the second time that we say *hamechadesh*, at the conclusion of *yotzar hame'orot*. However, it might be argued that since the phrase "a new light will shine…" was omitted from *Nusach Ari* and from *Nusach Tehilas Hashem*, it may be that this level of illumination is not associated with our prayers at all, but descends as a "gift" from above.

אַהֲבַת עוֹלָם אֲהַבְתָּנוּ יְיָ אֱלֹהֵינוּ, חֶמְלָה גְדוֹלָה וִיתֵרָה חָמַלְתָּ עָלֵינוּ.

סוֹבֵב כָּל עוֹלָמִים
אהבת עולם
(נצחיית), כמים
אהבה בתענוגים
נשמה-חיה
עולם הבריאה

> **"What is the connection between the blessings preceding the *Shema* and the *Shema* itself?"** (*Tanya, Likutei Amarim* ch. 49, also found in *Rishonim*)[209]

The World of *Atzilut* is truly Godly. In order to create the World of *Bria*, which is inhabited by souls and supernal angels whose Godly service is intellectual, a tremendous contraction was necessary. The same is true from *Bria* to *Yetzira*, because the illumination of *Bria* is infinite in comparison to that of *Yetzira*. And the same is true from *Yetzira* to *Asiya*.

The *Kriat Shema* calls upon us to dedicate ourselves entirely to love of God, with all our heart, soul and might. This is not a simple matter. But, when we recite the blessings preceding the *Shema* and become aware of the dedication and devotion of the angels and heavenly hosts, despite the fact that these souls and angels have far higher perception of Godliness than we do, this "rubs off" and prepares us to devote our own energy to the love of God. And when we realize that He undertook all of these spiritual contractions only in order to reach out to us in the physical world, we return the love with greater intensity, called *ahavat olam*. This is also the level known as *ahavah beta'anugim* ("love with delight").[210]

─── **CHASSIDIC INSIGHTS** ───

(continued from p. 224)

soul, it is necessary to focus upon its spiritual root, which is from the angels above. The way to fight fire is with fire. The animal soul burns with physical lusts and temptations, and the way to combat physical temptation is to demonstrate to the animal soul that it can be equally attracted to spiritual matters.

Therefore, our prayers focus our animal soul on its spiritual source above, amongst the various levels of angels, all the up to the *seraphim*, or "burning" angels of the world of *Bria*, who are totally focused upon and overwhelmed by their awareness of God's

(continued on p. 227)

- Transcendent Godliness
- Great love (water)
- Love like delight
- Soul level: *Neshama-Chaya*
- World of *Bria*

WITH AN EVERLASTING LOVE YOU HAVE LOVED us, Lord our God, [and] great and extra mercy You have bestowed upon us.

> 📖 *Within the Words*
>
> *Olam* may mean either "worldly" or "everlasting." By meditating upon the Godliness permeating the world, we eventually achieve recognition of God as He transcends the creation as well. From there, He reaches "down" to arouse us to strive for awareness of Him. When that occurs, then "like a face peering into the water," we experience eternal love of God. In the prayers, the phrase "great and extra mercy" refers to the great love that He extends toward us, over and beyond what He extends toward the angels. "And You chose us" refers to our souls in physical bodies…"And You drew us close" refers to acknowledgment of God, as discussed elsewhere. "And to unite" alludes to our ultimate inclusion in God's unity.

CHASSIDIC INSIGHTS

(continued from p. 226)

transcendent illumination in the world of *Atzilut*. Their transcendent awareness bring them to recite the words, *Kadosh, kadosh, kadosh* ("holy, holy, holy," as we recite in the prayer service). The lower angels of *Yetzira* (*chayot hakodesh*) and of *Asiya* (*ofanim*) do not have as high a perception of Godliness as do the *seraphim*, but nevertheless they create a great commotion because they are aware of something beyond themselves, even if they do not know what it is. Their diminished awareness is also acknowledged during our prayers, as we say *Baruch Havaya mimkomo* ("Blessed is the glory of the Lord from His place"). That is, the lower angels do not have the same awareness as the *seraphim*, but they plead that such awareness should descend (*baruch*) to them "from His place."

During this meditation, we ignite with a new form of divine love, one that is different from the "love like water" that we experienced during the *pesukei dezimra*. "Love like water" is calm and soothing,

(continued on p. 228)

אָבִינוּ מַלְכֵּנוּ. בַּעֲבוּר שִׁמְךָ הַגָּדוֹל וּבַעֲבוּר אֲבוֹתֵינוּ שֶׁבָּטְחוּ בְךָ, וַתְּלַמְּדֵם חֻקֵּי חַיִּים, לַעֲשׂוֹת רְצוֹנְךָ בְּלֵבָב שָׁלֵם, כֵּן תְּחָנֵּנוּ וּתְלַמְּדֵנוּ.

סובב כל עולמים
אהבת עולם
(נצחיות), כמים
אהבה בתענוגים
נשמה-חיה
עולם הבריאה

❝ In the path of worship...within the soul of man, there are two elements...an external layer that is derived from meditation upon the angels — the *Seraphim*, the *Chayot* and the *Ofanim*...[and an] internal layer of the heart that is activated by the infinite light of His very essence..." (*Sefer Maamorim* 5656/1896 of the Rebbe Rashab, pp. 297-298)[211]

> The external and internal layers of the heart are associated with both *chochma* and *bina*. The external layers correspond to our conscious thought processes with which we actively seek out and contemplate Godliness within creation. This occurs during the *pesukei dezimra* and the *Yotzar ohr,* when we reason that, if the angels above are nullified to God, then we as well should be like nothing before Him.

─── **CHASSIDIC INSIGHTS** ───

(continued from p. 227)

but as we contemplate the higher realms of *Atzilut* and the "burning angels" (*seraphim*) of *Bria*, we ignite with a new form of love, known as "love like fire." Unlike "love like water," "love like fire" has an immediate objective — similar to intimate love between husband and wife. This is not the cool, calm and collected "love like water" that exists between siblings or between parents and children, who can emotionally afford to be distant from one another for extended periods of time. This is more similar to the mature love between husband and wife that brings them together in intimacy. It will not rest until it establishes unity, in this case unity between man and Creator. It is a burning and insistent love that knows no limitations, and that is the emotion that accompanies us as we pray the *Birchot Kriat Shema*.

From the *Kuntres Avoda*, we learn how to achieve "love like fire": "In *Likutei Torah*, in the discourse entitled *Levaer inyan Yom*

(continued on p. 229)

Transcendent Godliness
Great love (water)
Love like delight
Soul level: *Neshama-Chaya*
World of *Bria*

Our Father, our King, for the sake of Your great name and for the sake of our fathers who trusted in You, and to whom you taught living laws regarding how to do Your will with a complete heart, so should You grace us and teach us.

However, the inner levels of the heart are not activated by any conscious level of logical meditation. They are activated by our simple will and desire to connect with God. This will and desire is not associated with any particular spiritual level, but rather with our innate yearning to connect with the very essence of God. When it is activated, it is called *reuta deliba* ("will of the heart") and it comes from the very essence of our soul.

📖 Within the Words

Veyached levaveinu ("Unite our hearts") refers to the two levels of our heart. With our work on the external layers of our consciousness, we prepare to receive the infinite light within. When we properly dig the well, removing all of the unwanted debris, the fresh spring waters flow in automatically. The outer layers of our heart become a receptacle for the "living waters" of the inner recesses of our heart.

CHASSIDIC INSIGHTS

(continued from p. 228)

Hakippurim, it is explained that the excitement of "love like flames of fire" comes from a sense of newness, a sense of renewal in creation at every instant, "new every morning." When we "see" with our own "eyes" (here it is appropriate to speak of the physical sense of vision, as in the verse "See Who created these...' — Isaiah 40:26), and our heart understands, it also catches on fire, as written (*Eicha* 2:18), "their heart cried out...' This involves revelation of the divine soul, as well."

The *Kuntres Ha'avoda* continues: "But, on the average, we who

(continued on p. 230)

PRAYING LIKE FIRE AND WATER

אָבִינוּ אָב הָרַחֲמָן, הַמְרַחֵם, רַחֵם (בנוסח תהילת ה':
נָא) עָלֵינוּ, וְתֵן בְּלִבֵּנוּ בִּינָה לְהָבִין וּלְהַשְׂכִּיל, לִשְׁמֹעַ
לִלְמֹד וּלְלַמֵּד, לִשְׁמֹר וְלַעֲשׂוֹת, וּלְקַיֵּם אֶת כָּל דִּבְרֵי
תַלְמוּד תּוֹרָתֶךָ בְּאַהֲבָה:

סובב כל עולמים
אהבת עולם
(נצחיות), כמים
אהבה בתענוגים
נשמה-חיה
עולם הבריאה

❝ [This is the *avoda*] of desire to be included and nullified within the infinite light of the One above...which is not commensurate with intellect, but rather comes from the essence of the soul, which stands unfaltering with a determination to be included and nullified to the Infinite One..." (*Sefer Maamorim 5663*/1903 of the Rebbe Rashab, vol. 2, pp. 305, 309)[212]

About the outer levels of the heart, we say, "*bina* is the heart, and with it the heart understands." This level of intellect corresponds to the emotions in our heart, which we cultivate via intellect and meditation. In this case, the intellect covers matters that are readily grasped and understood. The meditation may be, for example, on how God is our very life, or upon how all of the worlds are nothing more than a ray and reflection of Godliness, out of range of His essence. And the emotions that we develop are in proportion to our level of intellectual grasp.

--- CHASSIDIC INSIGHTS ---

(continued from p. 229)

would achieve love "like flames of fire" require meditation on our distance from the One above. That is, we must think about how far away we are from anything Godly. We must, first of all, undergo the meditation explained earlier in which we think about the Godliness inherent in the physical creation , or the nature of the spiritual light and illumination in the upper worlds, and we must feel the preciousness and elevation of Godliness. We must then combine this with contemplation of our own situation — how far we are from anything Godly, not only in our soul in general, but even in the garments of our soul: in our thought, speech and action. This leads us to a state of great bitterness, as a result of which our soul is motivated to catch

(continued on p. 231)

Sidenote:
Transcendent Godliness
Great love (water)
Love like delight
Soul level: *Neshama-Chaya*
World of *Bria*

Our Father, merciful Father, Who has compassion, have mercy upon us, and place in our heart [the] understanding [necessary] to grasp and to analyze, to perceive, to learn and to teach, to observe and to do, and to fulfill all the words of Your Talmud Torah, with love.

The inner dimensions of the heart though are not proportionate to intellect. They come from the very essence of the soul — the *yechida*, which is the highest level of the soul. The *yechida* is the simple desire to be included in and united with the infinite light of God above. This desire is called *reuta deliba*. (Elsewhere in Chassidut, *reuta deliba* is associated with the soul level of *chaya*.)

Within the Words

The plea *veyached levaveinu* ("unite our hearts") refers to our desire to unite the external dimensions of our heart with the internal layers. We begin by meditating upon the subjects that we can readily grasp and understand, using our conscious soul powers. Eventually this leads us to the realization that all of creation is but a ray and reflection of Godliness, from which we are distant. Our meditation turns to the gulf between ourselves and the Creator, and this is what ultimately unites the two levels of the heart. We join that which is beyond intellect with our intellectual faculties, and this is the entire purpose of the descent of our soul to this world.

CHASSIDIC INSIGHTS

(continued from p. 230)

on fire, flaming like a torch with thirst and desire to be close to the One above and to abandon all matters that separate and distance it from God...These flames of fire eradicate and nullify the ego of the animal soul, causing it to become totally incinerated and consumed, unlike "love like water" which brings about only a weakening of the

(continued on p. 234)

❝ **We say, 'Our Father, merciful Father, Who has compassion, have mercy on us…" Since we already mentioned that He is merciful, why is it necessary to add, "Who has compassion"?** (*Torat Shmuel 5640*/1880 of the Rebbe Maharash, V 1, p. 285)

סובב כל עולמים
אהבת עולם
(נצחיות), כמים
אהבה בתענוגים
נשמה-חיה
עולם הבריאה

There are two categories of mercy: One category is the mercy that is built into *seder hishtalshelut* (the "chain of spiritual evolution," including the ten *sephirot* and the four worlds). This mercy is associated with Yaakov our forefather. But, there is another level of mercy that surpasses the "chain of spiritual evolution." It descends to us from the transcendent level of *keter*. Our first request ("merciful Father") for mercy flows through our father Yaakov Avinu ("merciful father"), with whom is associated the mercy of the "chain of creation." But, our second request ("Who has compassion, have mercy…") is a direct request from God that bypasses *seder hishtalshelut*. We ask God directly for "His mercy." With the words, "Have mercy," we request 'simple' mercy from Him, from beyond creation (*Keter*).

A similar quandary faces us earlier in the blessings before the *Kriat Shema*, when we say, "God of the universe, in Your great mercy have compassion upon us…" Having already stated that He is a God of "great mercy," why do we proceed to request from Him to have compassion upon us? Are we not capable of asking Him in our own merit, regardless of 'His compassion'? But, since our human intellect is limited, and we cannot truly grasp the nature of our soul even after it became enclothed in the body (indeed we know of no one who has ever "seen" a soul and we only know that the soul exists because there must be something that enlivens the body), therefore we cannot request "mercy" on our soul. We are not aware of the state of the soul before it descended to become enclothed in the body and therefore we have nothing to which to compare its current state. And therefore, we cannot arouse "great mercy" on our own. For these reasons, we request that He, God, shine His unlimited mercy upon us. (*Torat Shmuel 5636*/1876 of the Rebbe Maharash, p. 438).

📖 *Within the Words*

With the blessing, "With an everlasting love…" (*Ahavat Olam*), we request mercy from God in order to motivate our learning and to facilitate fulfillment of His commandments. His mercy ("Our Father, merciful Father…") is the factor that produces the *bina* ("understanding") in our heart, with which we then go on to learn and fulfill His mitzvoth. It is the *bina* that He plants in us that catalyzes meditation and understanding, and ultimately leads to learning and fulfillment of the Torah. (*Torat Shmuel 5638*/1878 of the Rebbe Maharash, p. 220)

Transcendent Godliness
Great love (water)
Love like delight
Soul level: Neshama-Chaya
World of Bria

❝ R' Elazar would give a coin to a poor person, and then pray (Baba Batra 10B)." One who gives a coin receives six blessings, one who [not only gives but] comforts the poor person receives eleven blessings" (Baba Batra 9B). (*Torat Shmuel* 5633/1873 of the Rebbe Maharash, V 2, pp. 464-466)

When we give *tzedaka* in this world, God gives *tzedaka*, so to speak, in the upper spiritual realms. His *tzedaka* filters down to our world as well. Just as the *tzedaka* that we give provides life and vitality for the poor person who is in need, so when God "gives *tzedaka*," He provides life and vitality to the "lower worlds" of *bria*, *yetzira* and *asiya* in which we live. The "six" blessings that accrue to one who gives a coin correspond to the letter "*vov*" of His name *Havaya*, that connects with holiness and influx on the highest spiritual levels and conveys it down to our world, the realm of the "poor person." When we not only give but also comfort the poor person, we "activate" the first *hey* of His name as well as the *vov*. The first *hey* of God's name is associated with intellect and understanding (*bina*). When we comfort with words as well as give, we merit to eleven (the *vov* is six, and the *hey* is five) blessings.

The order of prayers (of the blessings preceding *kriat shema* as well as *kriat shema* and *shemonah esreh*) was fixed according to spiritual structures above known as *heichalot* ("chambers" — from the *Ariz'l*). The physical chambers within the Temple were built to correspond to the spiritual chambers (*heichalot*) above. Our prayers correspond to the *heichalot* above, and when we utter the words of the prayers, the illumination of the *heichalot* descends to us. The result is that just as the name of God illuminated in the Temple, so it illuminates our *tefila*. This takes place when we pray from the depths of our heart (*pnimiyut*) and also give *tzedaka*, as the verse says, "With *tzedek* (*tzedaka*), I behold Your countenance (*panecha*)" (Psalms 17:15).

> 📖 *Within the Words*
>
> Normally, *tefila* is a process that is *acharei* — from "behind." From "behind," we look for evidence of God and follow His footsteps to reach greater understanding and spiritual levels. However, the experience in the Temple was *lifnei* — an experience of direct revelation of His *p'nim*, or "countenance." This is called "seeing." What brings us now to this state is giving *tzedaka*, and *piyus* ("appeasing" or "comforting") which is the same Hebrew letters as Yoseph. Yoseph (whose name means "to add") brings additional Godly influence into the world that "appeases" and enhances our lowly spiritual status. (*Torat Shmuel* 5642/1882, p. 89).

BLESSINGS OF THE SHEMA

וְהָאֵר עֵינֵינוּ בְּתוֹרָתֶךָ, וְדַבֵּק לִבֵּנוּ בְּמִצְוֹתֶיךָ, וְיַחֵד לְבָבֵנוּ לְאַהֲבָה וּלְיִרְאָה אֶת שְׁמֶךָ, וְלֹא נֵבוֹשׁ וְלֹא נִכָּלֵם, וְלֹא נִכָּשֵׁל, לְעוֹלָם וָעֶד:

כִּי בְשֵׁם קָדְשְׁךָ הַגָּדוֹל וְהַנּוֹרָא בָּטָחְנוּ, נָגִילָה וְנִשְׂמְחָה בִּישׁוּעָתֶךָ:

וְרַחֲמֶיךָ יְיָ אֱלֹהֵינוּ וַחֲסָדֶיךָ הָרַבִּים אַל יַעַזְבוּנוּ נֶצַח סֶלָה וָעֶד:

סובב כל עולמים
אהבת עולם
(נצחיות), כמים
אהבה בתענוגים
נשמה-חיה
עולם הבריאה

CHASSIDIC INSIGHTS

(continued from p. 231)

animal soul. This is because our involvement [in love like water] is only with the Godly concept as we strive to understand that Godly concept and feel the Godliness and how it is good and elevated. In so doing, we truly come closer to God, and our animal soul becomes weakened. However, this is only weakness and not nullification... However, when it comes to "love like fire," the ego of the animal soul becomes incinerated, consumed and nullified. This is because our distress over our distance from God brings about the onset of fiery flames and excitement [of love of God] which in turn causes the nullification of the animal soul." (from "Love like Fire and Water," pp. 110-113).

To sum up, then, thorough and complete understanding of Godly concepts, in tandem with meditation on our personal distance from God, leads to "love like fire" during the *Birchot Kriat Shema*. When, through meditation, we achieve thorough intellectual grasp of the Godly concept upon which we are focused, and we suddenly grasp that we are far from Him, our calm, sedate love can turn into a fiery desire to unite with Him. This happens when we meditate so thoroughly on the topic that it becomes crystal clear in our mind's eye, and yet we experience a huge gulf between our understanding and God Himself. Then, our emotion of love becomes so strong that it is comparable to the love between a husband and wife. This is "love like fire."

The Rebbe Rashab does not suffice with the mere possibility of

(continued on p. 235)

Transcendent Godliness
Great love (water)
Love like delight
Soul level: Neshama-Chaya
World of Bria

And light up our eyes with Your Torah, and cause our hearts to cleave to Your commandments, and unite our hearts to love and to fear Your name, without shame, without failure, and without stumbling, forever.

For, in Your great and holy and awesome name we trust, [therefore] will rejoice and be happy in Your deliverance.

And in Your mercy and great kindness, Lord our God, do not forsake us, eternally, forever and everlasting.

--- CHASSIDIC INSIGHTS ---

(continued from p. 234)

achieving love like fire. He insists that it is a necessity: "(We must of necessity achieve this level since only [this level] strongly reveals the light of the divine soul, and also because it is the main expression of the desire and yearning for Godliness). This we do by meditating upon our own status and situation and how far we are [from God]…But the truest expression of this love comes about through meditation on His greatness. The Godly fire burns and consumes the alien fire of the animal soul — and elevates it as well to be included in Godliness — with excitement and flames of fire ("Love like Fire and Water" page 120-121). From this passage, it is evident that meditation upon "God's greatness," which is also meditation upon *sovev kol olmin* — transcendent Godliness — is an important component in achieving "love like fire."

However, even at this advanced stage of meditation to achieve "love like fire," we are not yet finished with "love like water." For, the next section of prayers, beginning with the paragraph, *Ahavat olam*, is associated not with love like fire, but with a higher form of love like water called *ahava be'taanugim*, or "love with delight" (See *Torat Shmuel 5626*, of the Rebbe Maharash, page 217.)[iv] This is a very high form of

(continued on p. 236)

מַהֵר וְהָבֵא עָלֵינוּ בְּרָכָה וְשָׁלוֹם מְהֵרָה, וַהֲבִיאֵנוּ לְשָׁלוֹם מֵאַרְבַּע כַּנְפוֹת הָאָרֶץ, וּשְׁבוֹר עֹל הַגּוֹיִם מֵעַל צַוָּארֵנוּ, וְתוֹלִיכֵנוּ מְהֵרָה קוֹמְמִיּוּת לְאַרְצֵנוּ, כִּי אֵל פּוֹעֵל יְשׁוּעוֹת אָתָּה, וּבָנוּ בָחַרְתָּ מִכָּל עַם וְלָשׁוֹן, וְקֵרַבְתָּנוּ מַלְכֵּנוּ לְשִׁמְךָ הַגָּדוֹל בְּאַהֲבָה לְהוֹדוֹת לְךָ וּלְיַחֶדְךָ וּלְאַהֲבָה אֶת שְׁמֶךָ:

בָּרוּךְ אַתָּה יְיָ הַבּוֹחֵר בְּעַמּוֹ יִשְׂרָאֵל בְּאַהֲבָה:

סובב כל עולמים
אהבת עולם
(נצחיות), כמים
אהבה בתענוגים
נשמה-חיה
עולם הבריאה

CHASSIDIC INSIGHTS

(continued from p. 235)

spiritual awareness for which it is impossible to prepare, but which may occur spontaneously to one who is well versed in meditation of love like water during *pesukei dezimra* and love like fire during the *Birchot Kriat Shema*. *Ahava be'taanugim* is a "gift from above," during which the meditator finds himself united with and basking in Godliness. It is a form of love like water because it "washes" over the meditator, and leaves him cleaving with the highest delight and pleasure in Godliness.

If so, then why is it called *ahavat olam* during our prayers? *Ahavat olam* literally means "love derived from the universe," which bears more in common with the love like water that we experienced during the *pesukei dezimra*. However, the word *olam* has a second connotation, which is "everlasting." The *Tana d'bei Eliyahu* says, "You might have thought, three years, or ten years, or one hundred years …but I mean love without any interruption whatsoever, because *olam* means forever." The Rebbe Maharash (*Torat Shmuel 5630*, page 275) suggests that "three years" alludes to *netzach*, *hod* and *yesod* of *Atzilut*, "ten years" refers to the *midot* and *chochma*, and "one hundred years" to *keter*. Yet, *ahavat olam* is above the ten *sephirot*. The Rebbe Maharash concludes that this level of *ahavat olam* is even higher than *ahava rabba*. And indeed, the person who experiences this level of divine love is changed forever — he realizes that he has been gifted from Above and he is no longer the same person as he was previously — he feels that he has been gifted

(continued on p. 237)

Transcendent Godliness
Great love (water)
Love like delight
Soul level: Neshama-Chaya
World of Bria

Hasten and speedily bring upon us blessings and peace, and bring us in peace from the four corners of the earth, and break the yoke of the nations from around our necks, and lead us quickly, upright to our land, because You are an almighty God of salvation, and You chose us from among all the nations and tongues, and drew us close to our King for the sake of Your great name, in love and in order to acknowledge You and to unite and to love Your name:

Blessed are You, Lord, Who chooses His people, Israel, in love.

--- CHASSIDIC INSIGHTS ---

(continued from p. 236)

with something lasting and eternal. About this love, R' Akiva said, "When you arrive to the slabs of marble, do not cry 'water, water...'" In Chasidut (*B'sha'ah shehikdimu 5672* (1912) of the Rebbe Rashab, vol 2, pp 972-4), it is explained that the meditator who reaches this unspeakably high level should not think that there is anything separating him from God. If he does experience some sort of resistance or spiritual obstacle, it is only the resistance that he discovers within himself, but in essence he is united with the One above. The *Kuntres Ha'avoda* adds; "Although love which is beyond logic and reason is generally "love like fire," — the exception is *ahavah beta'anugim*, or cleaving to the One above, within which there are two levels — *ohr yashar* ("direct illumination" from transcendent light that is beyond, but accessible to us) and *ohr chozer* ("reflected illumination," associated with transcendent light that is not only beyond but generally inaccessible to us) (from "Love like Fire and Water" page 135). We should not expect to experience this level of love for God, but if we do, it is associated with the prayer, *ahavat olam*, just prior to the *Kriat Shema*.

(continued on p. 238)

סדר קריאת שמע

שְׁמַע | יִשְׂרָאֵל, יְיָ | אֱלֹהֵינוּ, יְיָ | אֶחָד:

סובב כל עולמים
אהבה רבה (כאש)
יחודא עילאה
(דעת עליון)
חיה
עולם האצילות
בתוך בריאה

> **"** When a Jew enters a synagogue or house of study and answers the *Kaddish* (*Yehei shmei rabba mevarach* — 'May His great name be blessed'), God nods His head..." (*Gemora Berachot* 50a, quoted in *Derech Mitzvotecha* of the Tzemach Tzedek p. קכ"ד)²¹³

The head is composed of a skull and the brains within it. According to Kabbalah, the skull represents our will, while the brains symbolize the hidden reasoning behind our will. God "willed" the world into existence, and the hidden reason behind His creation is the Jewish people, with whom God "consulted" before creating the universe.

Therefore, the Jewish people are comparable to a "head" in divine terms. The head includes all aspects of the body, and the head controls the body. The Hebrew letters of *Yisrael* may be re-combined to obtain the two words, *li rosh* — "a head for Me." Thus, God says about the Jewish people, *Li Rosh* — "they are like a 'head' for Me."

Within the Words
The first two words of the *Shema* — *Shema Yisrael* — allude to the divine "head" (*gulgolta*) that brings Godly influence down into the creation. God admonishes the Jewish people, telling them "Hear O Israel" — upon you the world is dependent for divine revelation of His infinite light. The Jews bring Godly focus and intellect to bear upon the creation, and to this, God "nods His head" in agreement with the prayers of the Jews.

— **CHASSIDIC INSIGHTS** —

(continued from p. 237)

Finally, we arrive to the *Kriat Shema*, and with it the attendant state of mind known as *ahava rabba* ("great love"). According to *Kuntres Ha'avoda*, *ahavah rabba* is a form of love like fire (see "Love like Fire and Water," page 135, mentioned above). Unlike the love like water

(continued on p. 239)

סדר קריאת שמע

סידור עם חסידות – שחרית

Transcendent Godliness
Great love (fire)
Supernal unity
Soul Level: Chaya
World of Atzilut within Bria

THE SHEMA

H EAR, O ISRAEL, THE LORD IS OUR GOD, THE LORD is one.

❝ The infinite light of God shines within *chochma*…from there it becomes enclothed in *bina*…and from there derives the origin of… both man and the angels…" (*Derech Mitzvotecha* of the Tzemach Tzedek, p קכ״ד)[214]

> The two names of God, *Havaya* and *Elokeinu* correspond to the first two *sephirot* of *chochma* and *bina*. *Havaya* is the name that channels the infinite light into *chochma* of *Atzilut*, and *Elokim* channels the light of *chochma* into *bina*. These two *sephirot* are called "two fast friends who never part company." They always function in tandem to bring the infinite light of God down to us.

> The infinite light of God can only filter down to our intellect and emotions after a process of *tzimtzum* ("contraction"). As it enters the *sephira* of *chochma*, the infinite light impinges on our consciousness as a "flash" of insight or inspiration. As it enters *bina*, the divine light becomes illumination that we can analyze and absorb.

Within the Words

As the light descends to us, coming within range of our intellect, it becomes "ours." And thus, the name *Elokim* becomes *Elokeinu*, "our God." We do not say this about any other name of God — only the name *Elokim* becomes *Elokeinu* in *bina*, as it contracts and descends to our awareness. As we say *Havaya Elokeinu*, the infinite light descends from *chochma* to *bina* and from there to us as well.

CHASSIDIC INSIGHTS

(continued from p. 238)

that we experienced during *pseukei dezimra*, that is localized in our minds and heart, *ahavah rabba* is an all-consuming love of God that causes us to devote ourselves to *avodat Hashem* with all of our heart(s) (both the good and the evil inclinations).[v] Chasidut equates "love like

(continued on p. 240)

❝ [Here], the intention is to declare that He is one and the universe, together with all that is within it, is nullified, as if it does not exist at all, and only God Himself exists." (*Derech Mitzvotecha* of the Tzemach Tzedek, p. קכ״ד)²¹⁵

סובב כל עולמים
אהבה רבה (כאש)
יחודא עילאה
(דעת עליון)
חיה
עולם האצילות
בתוך בריאה

Since we have already mentioned the unity of *chochma* and *bina* for the purpose of bringing down infinite light into creation, why is it necessary to mention His name *Havaya* a second time, saying *Havaya echad* ("the Lord is one")? And why do we describe Him as *echad* ("one") and not *yachid* ("unique"), which is more accurate?

While the word *yachid* better describes God's unique status as the "only One," without peer, it does not fit our perception of reality, which is plural and changing. We recognize myriads of creatures in the universe, so how could they all be from one Creator? Therefore, after stating His uniqueness as the source of the infinite illumination that precedes creation, we also need to declare His oneness in light of creation. This is better described by the word *echad* — "one." He is "one" in the seven heavens and the earth, as well as the four directions of the universe.

📖 *Within the Words*

As we say the word *echad*, we may meditate upon His unity (symbolized by the letter *aleph* of *echad*) in the seven heavens and the earth (symbolized by the letter *chet* of *echad*, with *gematria* of eight) and in the four directions (symbolized by the letter *dalet* of *echad*, with *gematria* of four). This is a meditation upon how not only physical space, but also the spiritual origin of space in the *sephirot* of *Atzilut*, is "nullified" to God, as the Torah states, "Behold, space is with Me."²¹⁶

CHASSIDIC INSIGHTS

(continued from p. 239)

fire" and *ahava rabba* that accompanies the *Kriat Shema*, with the fire of the Menorah, kindled by Aharon the High Priest.ᵛⁱ

Our intense meditation, first on Godliness en-clothed in the world, and then on transcendent Godliness that transcends creation, uplifts us to high, transcendent spiritual levels during the *Kriat Shema*. Such spiritual elevation occurs after exercise of what the Rambam calls the highest form of meditation, called — *yediat hashlilah*, "knowledge through negation." During meditation upon divine concepts,

(continued on p. 241)

סידור עם חסידות – שחרית

Transcendent Godliness
Great love (fire)
Supernal unity
Soul Level: Chaya
World of Atzilut within Bria

❝ The first letter [of the word *echad*], *aleph*, symbolizes the very essence of God Himself, the One and only 'Being' of the universe who truly 'exists'…[The three letters of *echad*] allude to the entire process of creation…starting from the simple unity of God." (*Derech Mitzvotecha* of the Tzemach Tzedek, p. 248 at the bottom)[217]

The *aleph* of *echad* symbolizes the infinite light of God, associated with *Keter*, which transcends the ten *sephirot* of *Atzilut*. The letter *chet* of *echad* symbolizes the *sephira* of *chochma*, while the *dalet* alludes to *dibur* (divine "speech") which emerges from the *sephira* of *malchut*. Thus, the three letters of *echad* allude to the entire process of creation.

In order to create the universe, God had to first diminish and contract His infinite illumination to become within range of the ten *sephirot* of *Atzilut*. The contracted light then entered the *sephira* of *chochma* and descended to the lowest *sephira*, *malchut*, which is the source of the ten creative utterances of Genesis. To cite a parable: A king rules not by personally visiting every corner of his kingdom, but by issuing decrees. His "word," communicated by messengers, is what makes it possible for him to reign. That is why creation is associated with *malchut* ("kingship") from which divine speech (God's "word") emerges. But even after creation, the world remains "one" since its ultimate origin is the infinite light of God, which is simple and undifferentiated.

📖 *Within the Words*

The previous meditation, upon the "seven heavens and the earth," comes from the Talmud. The meditation on the three letters of *echad* comes from the Zohar. The two meditations are equivalent, but the Talmudic interpretation alludes to the spiritual origin of space within the lower seven *sephirot* of *Atzilut*, while the Zohar meditation alludes to the source of creation within the highest *sephira* — *chochma* of *Atzilut*. For this reason, the Aramaic translation (*Targum Yerushalmi*) of "In the beginning *Elokim* created" is "With *chochma*, He created…"[218]

─── CHASSIDIC INSIGHTS ───

(continued from p. 240)

we realize that whatever descriptions, definitions, or categories we apply to God, are necessarily deficient. Since they originate from our own human frame of reference, they cannot possibly describe God, who is infinite and omniscient. Is our meditation, then worthless?

(continued on p. 246)

❝ The word *echad* ("one") may be broken down to *ach* (אח)— *dalet* (ד). The word *ach* means "brother," so *echad* may be interpreted as "brother of the *dalet*". We find the word *ach* in the verse, "If only you were my *ach* ("brother")..." (*Shir Hashirim* 8:1). "Brother" is an allusion to God, and the *dalet* is the Jewish people. As a letter, the *dalet* represents an "opening" or gate, as in "Open for me, *achoti* ("my sister" — *Shir Hashirim*), and the opening allows God and the Jews to become "one." (*Torat Shmuel* 5633/1873 of the Rebbe Maharash, p. 289)

סובב כל עולמים
אהבה רבה (כאש)
יחודא עילאה
(דעת עליון)
חיה
עולם האצילות
בתוך בריאה

The first time that we say the name *Havaya* during the *Kriat Shema* alludes to *sovev kol olamim*, or "transcendant Godliness" that is beyond our grasp. The second time alludes to *memalle kol olamim*, or "immanent spirituality" that we can internalize and grasp (*Torat Shmuel* 5639/ 1879 of the Rebbe Maharash, p. 444). We say *kriat shema* twice a day in order to reach the spiritual state known as *reuta deliba* — strong "desire of the heart" and yearning for God, by meditating and contemplating on the unity of God (*Torat Shmuel* 5639/1879 of the Rebbe Maharash, p. 75).

The three words, *shem k'vod malchuto* — "Name of the honor of His Kingdom" — allude to the three lower worlds of *bria, yetzira* and *asiya* (*Torat Shmuel* 5640/1880 of the Rebbe Maharash, p. 39). The six words of the two verses of *kriat shema* — beginning with *Shema Yisrael* and with *Baruch Shem* — correspond to a verse that describes the *avoda* (divine service) of a Jew: "To You, Lord, is the kindness, the strength, the harmony, the initiative, and the glory, for all that is in the heavens and the earth")Chronicles 1, 29:11). The six words, "kindness, strength, etc" correspond to the six words of each of the first two lines of the *kriat shema*. (*Torat Shmuel* 5636/1876 of the Rebbe Maharash, p. 85).

📖 *Within the Words*

It is necessary to mention God's unity during the *Kriat Shema*, because otherwise a question might arise: Is He then our God, but not God over the entire universe? Therefore, we must mention not only that He is our God, but that He is "One," God over the entire universe. (*Torat Shmuel* 5640/1980 of the Rebbe Maharash, pp. 233-4).

Transcendent Godliness
Great love (fire)
Supernal unity
Soul Level: Chaya
World of Atzilut within Bria

❝ The Midrash on the verse, "And Noach built an altar," tells us that the word for "built" (*vayiben*) is from the same root as *hitbonenut*, or "meditation." And what exactly is the meditation that leads to divine love? (*Torat Shmuel* 5633/1873 of the Rebbe Maharash, V 1, p. 294)

Prayer is like a house, as we see from the verse, "For My house is called a house of prayer" (Isaiah 56:7). Specifically, a house of prayer is associated with the very high level of divine love called *bekol meodecha* ("with all of my might"), which we strive to achieve during *kriat shema* and maintain during the *Shemonah esreh*. Whle praying the *Shemonah esreh* with its eighteen blessings, we access *makifim* (transcendent illumination) that descend to protect us. But to get to the house (the *shemonah esreh*), we must first traverse two courtyards, as in the verse, "Happy is he chooses and dwells in Your courtyards" (Psalms 65:5). (*Torat Shmuel* 5638/1878, pp. 240-2)

Although courtyards and houses are both built with stones, there is a difference. Houses are covered, while courtyards are not. All manner of items can enter the courtyard, such as birds, rain, etc. In our personal service, this occurs when we pray with attention to the words, but without thinking (meditating) on their deeper meaning. When we pray with attention to pronunciation and grammar, for example, but without contemplating the concepts that lay behind the words, then all kinds of foreign "thoughts" can find their way into our prayers. Neither courtyard — not the outer nor the inner — is covered, but the inner courtyard (*kriat shema*) is at least close enough to the house to feel the presence and protection of the King. To enter the house of the King during *Shemonah esreh*, our thoughts must be focused and protected.

📖 *Within the Words*

Our prayers are established in lieu of the *korbanot* ("sacrifices"). During prayers, we "pour out our soul" (as in the verse, "I pour out my soul before God" — Shmuel 1, 1:15). The only analogue found in the Torah for "pouring" (*sh'ficha*) is associated with blood, as in the injunction against murder, "He who spills the blood of man, by man" (Gen 9:6). The equivalent during prayers is "pouring out our soul." (*Torat Shmuel* 5640/1880 of the Rebbe Maharash, p. 613 and p. 796).

THE SHEMA

בָּרוּךְ שֵׁם כְּבוֹד מַלְכוּתוֹ לְעוֹלָם וָעֶד:

סובב כל עולמים
אהבה רבה (כאש)
יחודא תתאה
(דעת תחתון)
חיה
עולם האצילות
בתוך בריאה

> **This [advanced meditation] is known as the 'secret of one.' It demands nullification of the ego...This is what is meant by 'all who meditate at length upon *echad*' — all who comprehend that the *echad* of *yichuda ila'ah* should become revealed within *yichuda tata'ah*..."** (*Sefer Maamorim* 5678/1918 of the Rebbe Rashab, pp. 386-395)[219]

The *aleph* of *echad* alludes to *chochma stima* (*chochma* within *Keter*). The *chet* symbolizes *chochma* of *Atzilut*, and the *dalet* symbolizes *malchut* of *Atzilut*, which is also the source of divine *dibur*. However, *dibur* exists on two levels: 1) in *Atzilut* (represented by an enlarged letter *dalet*), and 2) as it descends to BY"A. The word *va'ed* (*vav-eyn-dalet*) indicates the descent of *dibur* to BY"A. The *vav* symbolizes vertical descent. The *eyn* again represents *chochma*, but this time it is a lower form of *chochma* that is "received" from *Atzilut*. The final *dalet* of *va'ed* represents the power of divine speech to create the lower creatures of the worlds BY"A.[220]

The *aleph* of *echad* may be rewritten as *peleh*, meaning "wonder," since it represents a high spiritual level — *chochma stima* within *Keter* above *Atzilut*. It may also take on the meaning, "I will teach," as in *a'alephcha chochma* ("I will teach you wisdom").[221] The *chet* of *echad* is also *chochma*, but it represents the *sephira* of *chochma* within *Atzilut*, unlike the *aleph* of *chochma stima* which is above *Atzilut*. The large *dalet* of *malchut* of *Atzilut* represents the divine speech with which God created the universe. All this is in *Atzilut*, where the perspective is of *yichuda ila'ah* — God in the foreground while creation is secondary.

> 📖 *Within the Words*
>
> The "secret of one" is the descent of Godliness from *Atzilut* into the lower worlds of BY"A. This takes place with the *vav* of *va'ed*, symbolizing the long descent from the highest transcendent spiritual levels down to our mundane awareness (*yichuda tata'ah*). The *chet* of *echad* is exchanged for the *eyn* of *va'ed*, which symbolizes the wisdom of the sages, who are called *eynei ha'eida* ("the eyes of the congregation").[222] The large *dalet* of *echad* becomes a normally sized *dalet* in *va'ed*, indicating the divine speech that animates the lower worlds of BY"A. In this manner, all of the spiritual unity of the upper worlds descends to become revealed to those who meditate upon it at length in the lower worlds of BY"A.

Transcendent Godliness
Great love (fire)
Lower unity
Soul Level: Chaya
World of Atzilut within Bria

Blessed be the Name of His glorious kingdom forever and ever.

> **The verse 'Blessed be the Name of the glory of His Kingdom forever and ever' alludes to the state of consciousness called *yichuda tata'ah* [wherein the physical world is in the foreground of our awareness and God is in the background...]"** (*Derech Mitzvotecha* of the Tzemach Tzedek, p. קכ"ז)[223]

The word *va'ed* ("forever") is equivalent to *echad* ("one") through an exchange of the Hebrew letters. Letters of the same enunciators (the lips, the tongue, the palate, the teeth and the throat) are considered to be equivalent. The *aleph* of *echad* and the *vav* of *va'ed* are both "source letters" (there are four such letters: *aleph, hey, vav* and *yud*) from which all other letters derive, so they are exchangeable. The *chet* of *echad* and the *eyn* of *va'ed* are both throat letters. And of course both final letters are *dalet's*, so no exchange is necessary.

The first two verses (*Shema Yisrael* and *Baruch shem*) of the *Shema* represent two different perspectives. The perspective of *Shema Yisrael* is from above to below. This is the awareness of *yichuda ila'ah*, wherein we are primarily conscious of God, while creation is in the background. The perspective of *Baruch shem* is from below to above. This is the awareness of *yichuda tata'ah*, wherein our primary focus is on the created physical world, while God is in the background of our awareness.

> *Within the Words*
>
> While reciting *Shema Yisrael* we should focus on bringing the unity of *yichuda ila'ah* down into our lower awareness of *yichuda tata'ah*. The awareness of oneness and unity that we cultivate as we say *echad* during the *Shema* should also apply to our consciousness as we say *va'ed* during *Baruch shem*... We must draw that spiritual awareness of unity down into our mundane consciousness of *yichuda tata'ah*. These two verses teach us that the supernal unity of the *Shema* should be brought to bear upon and experienced within the context of *Baruch shem* as well.

THE SHEMA

> **Why do we mention the name *Havaya* twice? At first glance, it would have been sufficient to simply say, *Shema Yisrael, Havaya Elokeinu echad* ('The Lord our God is one').**" (*Sefer Maamorim 5680/1920* of the Rebbe Rashab, p. 266)²²⁴

סובב כל עולמים
אהבה רבה (כאש)
יחודא תתאה
(דעת תחתון)
חיה
עולם האצילות
בתוך בריאה

The first name *Havaya* corresponds to the divine source of Jewish souls that arose in God's thought. And the second name *Havaya* alludes to the creation of the universe, which is associated with the final letter *hey* of His name. The *dalet* of *echad* also hints at the divine speech which created the universe.

Speech is separate from the speaker, which is why we say that the creation of our world, which seems "detached" from God, took place with speech. Thought, though is always united with the thinker's soul, and hence Jewish souls which arose in God's thought, are always united with the Creator. Divine speech produces creatures of the "revealed worlds," and Divine thought produces creatures of the "hidden world."

--- **CHASSIDIC INSIGHTS** ---

(continued from p. 241)

Does it have no value whatsoever in attaining some sort of awareness and consciousness of God? The Rambam answers "no" to this question. Our meditation does have value, but we must develop a meditation of "negation," during which we say to ourselves that while God is "not this" (meaning, "not" the positive description that we wished to apply to Him), He is also not the opposite of that description. We may not be able to describe God as "wise," for example, in human terms, but neither is He lacking wisdom. We may not be able to describe Him accurately by saying that He is merciful (in human terms), but He is certainly not the opposite of merciful. In this manner, we may attribute whatever traits or definition that we want to God, while keeping in mind that our descriptions do not accurately portray Him.

But if so, what have we achieved? If we cannot accurately describe, define or categorize Godliness, then what does our *avoda* of *yediat hashlilah* contribute? The answer is that it provides us with meditative approximations that allow us to gain a concept of His greatness.

(continued on p. 247)

סידור עם חסידות – שחרית

Transcendent Godliness
Great love (fire)
Lower unity
Soul Level: *Chaya*
World of *Atzilut* within *Bria*

> 📖 *Within the Words*
>
> Elsewhere,[225] the Rebbe Rashab states that the first name *Havaya* is the name of God enclothed in creation, while the second *Havaya* represents God as He transcends creation. That is why the first *Havaya* is paired with *Elokeinu* — "our God" in nature (*Elokim* has the same *gematria* as *hateva*, or "nature") — while the second is *Havaya* alone, above creation. The two names also symbolize *da'at tachton* ("lower consciousness," in which we are primarily aware of creation) and *da'at elyon* ("higher consciousness," in which we are primarily aware of God). However, here (in the meditation described above), the Rebbe Rashab suggests that we first concentrate on how He is "our God" — God of the Jews who arose in His thought (transcendent, above *Atzilut*) — and how from there He descends to become God within creation.

--- CHASSIDIC INSIGHTS ---

(continued from p. 246)

Such meditative approximations are more accurate than mundane positive descriptions when we strive for awareness of transcendent Godly levels. Our spiritual awareness based upon *yediat hashlilah* does not result in clear perception of transcendent spiritual levels, but it nevertheless propels us to levels that our beyond our conventional cognitive abilities.

As we approach the *Kriat Shema*, we apply the technique of *yediat hashlilah* in order to meditate upon Godliness that transcends the creation. Previously, during the *pesukei dezimra* and *Birchot Kriat Shema*, we focused upon Godliness that permeates and transcends creation. We sought to "tear away the shrouds and packaging" to penetrate to the Godliness within creation, and then to focus upon the infinite light that transcends creation. However, as we recite the *Kriat Shema*, we become aware that ultimately God is "not" whatever spirituality we were able to detect at the core of creation. He is above and beyond that. Our new approximations do not give us a "clear" perception of Godliness beyond nature, since that is beyond human capacity. However, this technique will give us a better approximation than if we employ mere positive meditative techniques alone. *Yediat hashlilah* affords us awareness of spiritual levels that

(continued on p. 248)

THE SHEMA

וְאָהַבְתָּ אֵת יְיָ אֱלֹהֶיךָ, בְּכָל לְבָבְךָ, וּבְכָל נַפְשְׁךָ, וּבְכָל מְאֹדֶךָ:

סובב כל עולמים
אהבה רבה (כאש)
יחודא תתאה
(דעת תחתון)
חיה
עולם האצילות
בתוך בריאה

> 'And you shall love the Lord your God' — this means that your actions should cause other people to love God." *(Talmud Yoma* 86a discussed in *Torat Shmuel 5631/1871,* vol. 1, p. 70 of the Rebbe Maharash) **226**

In the opening lines of the *Shemonah Esreh*, we address "our God and the God of our fathers." But shouldn't the order be reversed? Shouldn't we give precedence to our forefathers, and only afterward mention ourselves? But the reason we first mention "our God" is because in order for Godliness to descend to the *sephirot* at all, He must first contract His infinite light. When we say "our God," we imply that His infinite light has contracted and descended to come within range of the ten *sephirot*. Only after His illumination enters the ten *sephirot* can He become "God of our fathers" — that is, God of the holy *sephirot* of *chochma* and *bina*, which are called the "father and the mother." Once the Godly light has entered *chochma* and *bina*, it can then descend to the rest of the *sephirot* and to creation.

"And you shall love..." is a command. And yet, how can we be commanded regarding an emotion in our heart? The standard answer is that we are commanded to meditate and contemplate Godliness in order to develop spontaneous love of God. And yet, what is spontaneous about a command? If love develops automatically upon meditation, then why does the Torah issue a command "to love"? But the command is to love God "in this world," as a soul in a body, and not to strive for abstract levels that take us out of this world, such the love of Ben Azai, who "peeked at God and died," or the love

--- CHASSIDIC INSIGHTS ---

(continued from p. 247)

cannot be put into precise words and descriptions, but are nonetheless accurate.

The *Kuntres Ha'avoda* is careful to distinguish between the process of *p'nimiyut hamochin* ("mature mindfulness") that we employ

(continued on p. 249)

Transcendent Godliness
Great love (fire)
Lower unity
Soul Level: Chaya
World of Atzilut within Bria

AND YOU SHALL LOVE THE LORD YOUR GOD WITH all your heart, with all your soul, and with all your means.

of Aharon's sons, who offered a "strange incense and died as they got near to God."[227] Love of God develops automatically with proper meditation, but the command (*v'ahavta* — "and you shall love") is to develop love of God in this world in a manner that uplifts creation and influences others to love God as well.

📖 Within the Words

The famous Chabad Chassid, R' Yitzchak of Humel, who was a student of the Alter Rebbe, the Mittler Rebbe and the Tzemach Tzedek, wrote about the command to love God in his book, *Shnei Hameorot*.[228] There, he writes that he "heard directly from the Alter Rebbe who heard from the Maggid of Mezritch, who received from the Baal Shem Tov, that the command is to focus our mind and thoughts on topics that arouse our love of God. Whatever occurs afterward, as a result of our meditation is not an integral part of the mitzvah." However, according to the Rebbe Rashab, our meditation while reciting *Shema Yisrael* should bring us to transcendent love of God (*ratzoh*), but the command *v'ahavta* during the first paragraph leads to a settled love of God (*shuv*). About this second love of God (*shuv*), the Talmud (*Yoma* 86a) tells us that the command is to cause others to love God. Just as during the *Shemonah Esreh*, when the infinite light becomes contracted to become "ours," so must the *ratzoh* of *Shema Yisrael* become a love of *shuv* during *v'ahavta*.

CHASSIDIC INSIGHTS

(continued from p. 248)

during the *Birchot Kriat Shema*, and the meditative technique of *avodat hashlilah* that occurs during *Kriat Shema* itself. The negation of "shrouds and packaging" (*pnimiyut hamochin*) that we employ during *Birchot Kriat Shema* is not negation of knowledge, but rather negation of "packaging." By tearing away the "packaging," we hope to arrive at

(continued on p. 250)

❝ **The command, *v'ahavta* ("and you shall love…") has two explanations. One is that it is a commandment, and the other is that it is a promise…"** *(Torat Shmuel 5630/1870 of the Rebbe Maharash, p. 121)*[229]

סובב כל עולמים
אהבה רבה (כאש)
יחודא תתאה
(דעת תחתון)
חיה
עולם האצילות
בתוך בריאה

The highest qualities of divine love that we experience descend to us from the spiritual level called *Arich Anpin* (literally, "the long countenance"). This is the external dimension of *Keter*, beyond the ten *sephirot* of *Atzilut*. It is about this level that the sages said that "all who meditate at length on the unity of God, experience long days and years."[230]

We cannot hope to attain the level of love (*ahavah rabba*) coming from *Keter* by meditation alone. However, our meditation does uncover the natural love that is within us, bequeathed to every Jew by our forefather, Avraham. This is the meaning of the command to love God — that is, to meditate deeply upon His unity until we activate the innate love of God that is present within us. And then, we are promised that a commensurate revelation of Godliness will descend from above in the form of "great love" (*ahava rabba*), from the level of *Keter*. It is conveyed to us by Aharon, the High Priest, during the Priestly Blessing.

📖 *Within the Words*

We are commanded to meditate at length upon the unity of God as expressed in the *Shema*. And, if we do so, we are promised that we will attain "length of days" — that is, an additional level of love of God (*chesed*) that radically improves the quality, if not the quantity, of our years. This is the level of Godly revelation from above, called *ahavah rabba* ("great love") that descends to us from *Arich Anpin* (the "long countenance" of *Keter*), to "lengthen our days and years." However, from the words of the Rebbe Maharash, it may be possible to infer that "lengthened days and years" means to literally lengthen our lives.…[231]

— **CHASSIDIC INSIGHTS** —

(continued from p. 249)

the true nature of Godliness within the creation (*memalle kol olmin*). However, *yediat hashlilah* negates our very concept of Godliness. It demands that we temporarily forsake our dearly attained awareness and use it as a springboard to achieve higher levels of awareness (*sovev kol olmin*). Chassidut calls this *lehavin davar mitoch davar* — "to gain awareness of something (*sovev* — transcendent illumination) from

(continued on p. 252)

Transcendent Godliness
Great love (fire)
Lower unity
Soul Level: Chaya
World of Atzilut within Bria

❝ In the verse, 'You shall love the Lord your God with all your heart(s), with all your soul and with all your might,' we find three levels. They correspond to the three levels of love...1) love born of logic and intellect, 2) natural love hidden within us that is beyond logic, and 3) 'great love' that descends from above..." (*Torat Chaim* of the Mittler Rebbe, *Parshat Tezaveh*, p. 364, col. 3)[232]

There are three categories of Godliness: 1) *memalle kol olmin* ("immanent spirituality" that permeates the universe), 2) *sovev kol olmin* ("transcendent Godliness" that surpasses creation), and 3) essential infinite Godliness that is beyond both immanent and transcendent Godliness. These three correspond to the three kinds of love, "with all your heart(s), with all your soul and with all your might."[233]

Love "with all your heart" is the result of meditation on the divine light enclothed within creation to enliven it, which is of the category of *memalle kol olmin*. When we consider that the divine light of *memalle kol olmin* is but a ray alone, nullified to the infinite light of God that transcends the creation — *sovev kol olmin* — we achieve love "with all your soul." And when there occurs revelation of the essential, infinite light that is totally beyond the category of creation, we achieve love "with all your might," beyond any measure or limitation whatsoever.[234]

― 📖 *Within the Words* ―

Love "with all your heart(s)" results from meditation on Godliness enclothed within creation. This level of meditation speaks to our animal soul as well, which is capable of comprehending Godliness enclothed within nature. The next step, love "with all your soul" is the result of a process of "negation" — as we grasp a spiritual concept, we simultaneously realize that our concept cannot completely describe God, who is infinite and inscrutable. Therefore, we negate our understanding and attempt to transcend it. That which we grasp is in the category of *memalle kol olmin*, but when we negate it and arrive to a higher more elevated concept, we meditate on *sovev kol olmin*. We realize that God also operates on creation from "beyond," without being enclothed in creation. And love "with all your might" is yet a third level, a gift from above, that arrives to those who have achieved all that is possible utilizing meditation on the lower levels of love of God, both *memalle* and *sovev*.

THE SHEMA

❝ Since our physical world was created from God's speech, as are the upper spiritual worlds, why is our world so spiritually opaque and dark? No ray of Godly light shines into our world as it does in the higher spiritual worlds, in the higher and lower *Gan Eden*. If so, what is the source of creation of our physical world, with its four categories of physical creation; mineral, vegetable, animal and human?"
(*Torah Shmuel 5630*/1870 of the Rebbe Maharash, p. 40)[235]

סובב כל עולמים
אהבה רבה (כאש)
יחודא תתאה
(דעת תחתון)
חיה
עולם האצילות
בתוך בריאה

The universe was created from the ten creative utterances of *Bereishit*. However, there are far more than ten creations in the universe, so how did the myriad of creations of all types, shapes and sizes emerge from the ten creative utterances? The answer is that the letters of the ten utterances re-combined and re-formed on successive occasions, so that myriad new creations were formed from the combinations and permutations of the ten utterances as they descended.[236] Nevertheless, all of the re-combinations of divine "speech" were not sufficient to create the physical world. For physical creation to occur, the letters of creation underwent another process — known as "shattering of the vessels" (*shvirat hakelim*).

In the language of Chassidut, *shvirat hakelim* is described as *heelam v'hester gamur* — "complete and total concealment." While creation from divine speech does reveal a certain level of Godliness (since the "letters" of speech form "words"), the creations of our physical world do not reveal any Godliness whatsoever. They are

——— CHASSIDIC INSIGHTS ———

(continued from p. 250)

within something (*pnimi* — immanent illumination)". It is the process of meditation that is associated with the *Kriat Shema* and leads us to *ahava rabba* as we recite the *Kriat Shema*.[vii]

Our association with the soul level of *neshama* and the world of *Bria* begins with the *Birchot Kriat Shema* and continues with the *Kriat Shema* itself. We recite the *Kriat Shema* with the utmost devotion and dedication, with determination to give up our lives if necessary for the unity of God. That dedication takes place on two levels. First of all as we say, "Hear o Israel the Lord your God, the Lord is One," we must be ready to give up our Godly soul and "deliver" it into His hands, so

(continued on p. 253)

Transcendent Godliness
Great love (fire)
Lower unity
Soul Level: Chaya
World of Atzilut within Bria

compared to detached and isolated letters that have no meaning of their own. For example, the word *baruch*, spelt *beit-reish-vav-caf*, means "blessed." But, if we were to separate the letters from one another, the word *baruch* would no longer exist, and the letters on their own would have no meaning. This is an analogy to help us understand the "shattering of the vessels" that accompanied the creation of our physical world. As a result of *shvirat hakelim*, separate objects that seem completely detached from Godliness were created. It is our job to return them to their Godly source by our fulfillment of the Torah and its mitzvot.

> **Within the Words**
>
> Our job is to elevate the fallen letters ("sparks") and return them to their spiritual source, thus enhancing the unity and oneness of the world. We do this by meditating during the *Kriat Shema* on various topics — for example, how all of creation is as naught before God, or how all of creation took place from a mere ray and reflection of His light. This leads us to love of God with all our heart, soul and might. Love with all our heart corresponds to the blood of the animal offered on the altar. Love with all our soul corresponds to the candelabra of the menorah, which Aharon lit in order to elevate Jewish souls. And love with all our might corresponds to the service of the *ketoret* ("incense") in the holy Temple. The process of uplifting and unifying the fallen letters also enables us to understand what is written later in the *Shema* — "And you shall gather your grain…" There are two main grain crops: wheat and barley. Wheat (*chitah*) has the *gematria* of twenty-two, alluding to the twenty-two letters of the Hebrew alphabet. Barley (*se'or*, similar to *shiur*, meaning "measure") alludes to our ability to analyze and understand Godly concepts during meditation.

CHASSIDIC INSIGHTS

(continued from p. 252)

to speak. This is *mesirut nefesh*, or "self-sacrifice" of the Godly soul within us. Then, as we recite the first paragraph succeeding the *Shema*, we say, "You shall love the Lord your God with all your heart(s), with all your soul, and with all of your might." Here again, we are required to give up our soul as we say *bechol nafshecha* — "with all your soul."

(continued on p. 254)

וְהָיוּ הַדְּבָרִים הָאֵלֶּה אֲשֶׁר אָנֹכִי מְצַוְּךָ הַיּוֹם עַל לְבָבֶךָ: וְשִׁנַּנְתָּם לְבָנֶיךָ וְדִבַּרְתָּ בָּם, בְּשִׁבְתְּךָ בְּבֵיתֶךָ, וּבְלֶכְתְּךָ בַדֶּרֶךְ, וּבְשָׁכְבְּךָ, וּבְקוּמֶךָ:

סובב כל עולמים
אהבה רבה (כאש)
יחודא תתאה
(דעת תחתון)
חיה
עולם האצילות
בתוך בריאה

> **"** The Zohar says…that we achieve *mesirut nefesh* ('self-sacrifice') as we say the word *echad*…but if so, what did the sages mean when they said that to love God 'with all your soul' means, 'even as He takes away your soul'?" *(Sefer Maamorim 5664/1904 of the Rebbe Rashab, p. 191) (Sefer Maamorim 5664/1904 of the Rebbe Rashab, p. 191)*[237]

> We have, within us, two souls competing for prominence. We have an animal soul that animates our body. Since it is associated with the body, it is attracted to all of the physical temptations that characterize the body, such as eating, drinking and procreating. And we have a divine soul that resides in our mind and heart and seeks to persuade our animal soul to forsake physical temptations and join in its quest for Godliness and spirituality.[238]

> Rabbi Akiva, "father of the Talmud," asked, "When will I achieve love of God *bechol nafshecha*?" As he was tortured by the Romans, he passed away while meditating upon the word *echad*, which occurs even before we say *bechol nafshecha*…so did he achieve his

─── **CHASSIDIC INSIGHTS** ───

(continued from p. 253)

But, in this case, the *mesiras nefesh* is of the animal soul, not the Godly soul. What process allows us to achieve such a lofty spiritual level that we are willing to give up our soul?

The answer is that our meditation and focus on His unity must take place on such a deep and exacting level that it leads to a form of vision. Our powers of analysis and recognition lead us to such a powerful experience of spirituality that it is similar to real eyesight and vision. This is hinted to in the letters of the *Kriat Shema* itself. In the first verse, as it is written in the Torah, we find two enlarged letters — one is the large letter *eyn* of the first word *shema*, and the second is the large letter

(continued on p. 255)

סידור עם חסידות – שחרית

Transcendent Godliness
Great love (fire)
Lower unity
Soul Level: *Chaya*
World of *Atzilut* within *Bria*

> And these words that I am commanding you today, should be on your heart.
>
> And you shall teach them to your children and speak of them, while sitting in your house and as you travel on the road, when you lie down, and when you arise.

aim? In order to answer that question we need to be reminded that there are two types of *mesirut nefesh:* 1) sacrificing our soul, and 2) sacrificing our body. Rabbi Akiva's *mesirut nefesh* was of his soul as he said *echad*, but at the same time, his meditation brought him to *mesirut nefesh* of the body (*bechol nafshecha*) as well.

📖 *Within the Words*

We must meditate to achieve *mesirut nefesh* of the divine soul as we say the word *echad* during the *Kriat Shema*. Our divine soul wants to return to its natural source and be one with God. However, we must also meditate in a manner that has influence upon our animal soul as well. This occurs as we "explain" Godly concepts, using words and symbolism that the animal soul understands. As our animal soul grasps Godly concepts, we develop love of God *bechol nafshecha*. At that point, the animal soul is ready to forsake physical temptation and devote itself to spirituality — and that is the *mesirut nefesh* of the animal soul.

─────────── **CHASSIDIC INSIGHTS** ───────────

(continued from p. 254)

dalet of the final word *echad*. Together, the two enlarged letters spell the word *eid*, or "witness." A witness must have seen the event about which he bears testimony; if he merely heard about it, his testimony is not accepted, for he is not a proper witness. Apparently, within the process of meditation leading to recognition of the oneness and unity of God, is embedded the concept of eyesight and vision as well. That

(continued on p. 256)

THE SHEMA

PRAYING LIKE FIRE AND WATER

וּקְשַׁרְתָּם לְאוֹת עַל יָדֶךָ, וְהָיוּ לְטֹטָפֹת בֵּין עֵינֶיךָ: וּכְתַבְתָּם עַל מְזֻזוֹת בֵּיתֶךָ וּבִשְׁעָרֶיךָ:

סובב כל עולמים
אהבה רבה (כאש)
יחודא תתאה
(דעת תחתון)
חיה
עולם האצילות
בתוך בריאה

❝ Why do we not mention love 'with all your might' in the second paragraph of the *Shema*?" (*Remzei Torah* of the Mezricher Maggid, #166)²³⁹

The first two levels of love ("with all your hearts" and "all your soul") mentioned in the *Kriat Shema* require effort and labor in meditation. But, the third level ("with all your might") requires that we abandon intellect and throw ourselves with all of our being and dedication into divine love and devotion. The effort that we exert in achieving the first two levels of love is necessary to overcome the resistance of our animal soul and also to uplift the Godly sparks that are our "portion" in this world. They correspond to the first two wells that Yitzchak dug which were contested by the Philistines; these two wells were *esek* ("fight") and *sitna* ("accusation"). But, when we achieve love "with all your might" — beyond limitation — the holy sparks that are our "portion" emerge spontaneously, without exertion. Therefore, the third level of love corresponds to the third well — *rehovot* ("expansiveness") — from which flowed "living waters" which were not contested at all by the "other side."²⁴⁰

──────── **CHASSIDIC INSIGHTS** ────────

(continued from p. 255)

is intriguing, because the plain meaning of the word, *shema*, is "Hear, Israel…" On a basic level, it is a commandment to gather our powers of concentration and focus on the oneness of God. This process is synonymous with "hearing." Within this process, though, we are expected to achieve some form of immediate and direct experience of Godliness, that is called "seeing."

In Chasidic terminology, this is called *re'iya d'chochma b'eyn ha-sechel* — "vision of *chochma* with the eye of the mind." It is the meditative level that is associated with *ahava rabba* and *yediat hashlilah*. It is not the same eyesight that is associated with our physical power of vision. Rather, our meditation during *Birchot Kriat Shema*

(continued on p. 257)

סידור עם חסידות - שחרית

סדר קריאת שמע

256

Transcendent Godliness
Great love (fire)
Lower unity
Soul Level: Chaya
World of Atzilut within Bria

> And you shall tie them as a sign on your arm, and they shall be as compartments between your eyes.
>
> And you shall write them on the doorposts of your house and upon your gates.

The three levels of love of God mentioned in the first paragraph correspond to three levels of meditation. Meditation upon *memalle kol olmin* ("immanent Godliness") results in love "with all your heart." Meditation upon *sovev kol olmin* ("transcendent Godliness") leads to love "with all your soul." Finally, desire to connect with God Himself, beyond any levels that we can comprehend, leads to love "with all your might." The first two levels are mentioned again in the second paragraph, but the third is omitted.

Within the Words

Another distinction between the first and second paragraphs of the *Shema* is that the first paragraph does not mention physical work, but the second paragraph mentions working the land, planting and harvesting crops. When we achieve the highest level of love of God, from the very essence of our soul, our physical sustenance is provided from above, and we need not exert any effort for it. However, when we fail to totally commit ourselves "with all our might" to God, then we have to work for our physical sustenance. Thus, the first paragraph, which mentions love "with all your might," omits any reference to physical work. However, the second paragraph that does not mention love "with all your might," mentions the need to work the land for our physical sustenance.

CHASSIDIC INSIGHTS

(continued from p. 256)

ultimately leads to an even higher level of cognition during the *Kriat Shema*. That level of spiritual cognition is so clear that it is "like seeing." This is the level of "seeing with the mind's eye" that

(continued on p. 258)

וְהָיָה אִם שָׁמֹעַ תִּשְׁמְעוּ אֶל מִצְוֹתַי אֲשֶׁר אָנֹכִי מְצַוֶּה אֶתְכֶם הַיּוֹם, לְאַהֲבָה אֶת יְיָ אֱלֹהֵיכֶם וּלְעָבְדוֹ בְּכָל לְבַבְכֶם וּבְכָל נַפְשְׁכֶם:

סובב כל עולמים
אהבה רבה (כאש)
יחודא תתאה
(דעת תחתון)
חיה
עולם האצילות
בתוך בריאה

> "The first paragraph of the *Shema* corresponds to *chesed* ('kindness'), since it mentions that, 'You shall love the Lord your God…' Love is the 'vessel,' but the illumination of the paragraph comes from *gevura* ('strict judgment')…The second paragraph is the opposite…since it says, 'Guard yourselves…' and 'His anger will be kindled….' therefore [the 'vessel' is judgment while the illumination is love…]" (*Likutei Torah* of the Alter Rebbe, *Parshat V'etchanan*, p. י"ג, col 2.)[241]

> Within the first paragraph of the *Shema*, there are forty-two words from *v'ahavta* ("you shall love…") until *bisharecha* ("in your gates"). They correspond to the divine name with the *gematria* of 42, which is associated with spiritual ascent… The first paragraph mentions love that is "with all your might," describing a love that is so powerful that our soul wishes to leave our body and ascend above. Thus, the vessel of the first paragraph is associated with *gevura*, but the illumination comes from *chesed*, since we mention the words, "and you shall love." The inverse is true of the second paragraph. The vessel is defined by the seventy-two words from the beginning of the paragraph until *v'samtem*, corresponding to the divine name with the *gematria* of 72, which is associated with *chesed* (gematria 72) and spiritual revelation from above to below. However, the illumination is associated with *gevura*, since the words mention the "anger" of God and how He will punish the Jews if they do not fulfill His will. Moreover, here we do not mention the love that is "with all your might" that we mention in the first paragraph.[242]

────── CHASSIDIC INSIGHTS ──────

(continued from p. 257)

we experience during *ahava rabba* ("great love"), associated with the Kriat Shema.[viii]

Yet, even "seeing with the mind's eye" and *ahava rabba* are not sufficient for us. We long for direct perception of Godliness. We

(continued on p. 259)

Transcendent Godliness
Great love (fire)
Lower unity
Soul Level: *Chaya*
World of *Atzilut* within *Bria*

> And now, if you will heed My commandments which I am commanding you today, to love the Lord your God and to serve Him, with all of your heart and all of your soul.

It is strange that the first and second paragraphs of the *Kriat Shema* are associated with the divine names of *gematria* of 42 (*gevura*) and 72 (*chesed*), respectively, when their content is the opposite — the first paragraph mentions love and the second mentions strict judgment. The explanation is that the content of the two paragraphs "switched places," so that the illumination of *gevura* entered the vessel of *chesed* in the first paragraph, while the illumination of *chesed* entered the vessel of *gevura* in the second paragraph [see endnote regarding apparent contradiction].[243]

Within the Words

As we say the first and second paragraphs of the *Shema*, we should be aware that the words of the first paragraph form a vessel of *gevura*, associated with the name of God with the *gematria* of 42, which facilitates spiritual ascent. And the content of the first paragraph brings down light of *chesed* to illuminate the vessel. The opposite is true of the second paragraph; the words form a vessel of *chesed* and the content brings down illumination associated with *gevura* into the vessel. This "place-switching" occurs when, with our intense concentration, we access a high infinite light from above that transcends both *chesed* and *gevura* and causes them to interact.[244]

--- CHASSIDIC INSIGHTS ---

(continued from p. 258)

become "love sick" for God as we progress through the *Kriat Shema*, and intellectual vision "in the mind's eye" does not satiate us — it only whets our appetite for more revelation. We yearn for real vision of spirituality, with the naked eye. However, that is not to occur until the *mashiach* — the Jewish messiah — arrives. At that time, Chasidic literature tells us, we will detect Godliness within nature with the naked eye — the dichotomy of "spiritual-physical" will no longer

(continued on p. 260)

וְנָתַתִּי מְטַר אַרְצְכֶם בְּעִתּוֹ יוֹרֶה וּמַלְקוֹשׁ,
וְאָסַפְתָּ דְגָנֶךָ, וְתִירֹשְׁךָ וְיִצְהָרֶךָ:

סובב כל עולמים
אהבה רבה (כאש)
יחודא תתאה
(דעת תחתון)
חיה
עולם האצילות
בתוך בריאה

❝ In Tractate *Ta'anit*, there are two rainy seasons mentioned — *yoreh* and *malkosh*. *Yoreh* occurs in the month of *Cheshvan* (November) as we sow the seeds…And *malkosh* is the rain that descends in *Nissan* (April) as the crops conclude their growth and ripen." (*Imrei Bina* of the Mitteler Rebbe, ch. 58, p. נ"ה)[245]

Rain has a spiritual source in the *mazalot* of *Keter*, above the chain of spiritual creation. These spiritual sources flow down to our world like water descending from above. The descent is described in the "Thirteen Attributes of Mercy" as *notzer chesed* ("forming kindness") and ending with *v'nakeh* ("and cleanses"). *Notzer* is the source of *chochma*, which descends to our world as the November rains (*yoreh*), while *v'nakeh* is the source of *bina*, which descends to us as the April rains (*malkosh*).

The two rains have opposite effects on the creation. The November rains (*yoreh*) soften the earth while the seed decays, decomposing from something to nothing (*m'yesh l'ayn*). However, the April rains (*malkosh*) arrive when the grain is grown, but not yet mature. *Malkosh* has the effect of fattening and improving the quality of the grain. In other words, it takes the grain from a state of relative "nothing to something" (*m'ayn l'yesh*).

──────── CHASSIDIC INSIGHTS ────────

(continued from p. 259)

exist because we will be directly aware of divinity penetrating and permeating the physical world.

In the meantime, as we recite the second verse of the *Kriat Shema* (*Baruch shem k'vod malchuto leolam va'ed*), we experience yet another spiritual stage, known as *hacara*, or "recognition." *Hacara* is the inner dimension of *da'at*, or visceral knowledge of the subject of our meditation. We achieve *hacara* when we have so internalized a concept that it becomes "second nature" for us to think about it, and we recognize it even without utilizing conscious thought processes. At that point, we have actualized our faculty of *hacara*, or "recognition." The standard mentioned in the Talmud (*Berachot* 9B, *Shulchan Aruch HaRav* 58:2)

(continued on p. 261)

Transcendent Godliness
Great love (fire)
Lower unity
Soul Level: *Chaya*
World of *Atzilut* within *Bria*

Then I will provide the rain of your land in its season, in the fall and in the spring, and you will gather your grain and your wine and your oil.

📖 *Within the Words*

Yoreh and *malkosh* are associated with the two *sephirot* of *chochma* and *bina*. *Chochma* within *Keter* is the experience of the essence of Godliness and the realization that, without God, nothing whatsoever exists. It corresponds to *yoreh*, the rain that turns the seeds from "something to nothing." *Bina* within *Keter* provides the realization that Godliness is in everything, and that every object that exists is Godly. It corresponds to *malkosh*, the rain that ripens the grain from "nothing to something." As we become aware of these feelings, they descend from *Keter* to produce conscious awareness of *chochma* ("insight") and *bina* ("understanding") within our soul. Conscious *chochma* is the ability to sense the unifying principle among details, while *bina* is the ability to apply the unifying principle to the details of our meditation.[246] The two words, *tiroshcha v'yitzharecha* ("your wine and your oil") that appear later in the verse also allude to *chochma* and *bina* (in Atzilut). "Your oil" is an allusion to *chochma*, and "your wine" is an allusion to *bina*.[247]

CHASSIDIC INSIGHTS

(continued from p. 260)

to determine when it is light enough in the morning to recite the *Kriat Shema*, is when we can "recognize a friend" from a distance of four cubits (roughly two meters). At that distance, and at that level of daylight, it is unlikely that we can detect all of the features of our friend. Nevertheless, we can detect enough features to "recognize" him beyond any doubt. That is because we have mentally processed enough of his shape, size and appearance to put together exactly who he is. This is the state known as *hacara*, or "recognition." Just as "recognition of a friend from a distance of four cubits" is the physical criteria for the earliest hour to recite the *Shema*, so spiritual *hacara* of transcendent

(continued on p. 266)

THE SHEMA

PRAYING LIKE FIRE AND WATER

וְנָתַתִּי עֵשֶׂב בְּשָׂדְךָ לִבְהֶמְתֶּךָ, וְאָכַלְתָּ וְשָׂבָעְתָּ:

הִשָּׁמְרוּ לָכֶם פֶּן יִפְתֶּה לְבַבְכֶם, וְסַרְתֶּם וַעֲבַדְתֶּם אֱלֹהִים אֲחֵרִים וְהִשְׁתַּחֲוִיתֶם לָהֶם:

וְחָרָה אַף יְיָ בָּכֶם וְעָצַר אֶת הַשָּׁמַיִם וְלֹא יִהְיֶה מָטָר וְהָאֲדָמָה לֹא תִתֵּן אֶת יְבוּלָהּ, וַאֲבַדְתֶּם מְהֵרָה מֵעַל הָאָרֶץ הַטֹּבָה אֲשֶׁר יְיָ נֹתֵן לָכֶם:

וְשַׂמְתֶּם אֶת דְּבָרַי אֵלֶּה עַל לְבַבְכֶם וְעַל נַפְשְׁכֶם, וּקְשַׁרְתֶּם אֹתָם לְאוֹת עַל יֶדְכֶם וְהָיוּ לְטוֹטָפֹת בֵּין עֵינֵיכֶם: וְלִמַּדְתֶּם אֹתָם אֶת בְּנֵיכֶם לְדַבֵּר בָּם, בְּשִׁבְתְּךָ בְּבֵיתֶךָ וּבְלֶכְתְּךָ בַדֶּרֶךְ וּבְשָׁכְבְּךָ וּבְקוּמֶךָ: וּכְתַבְתָּם עַל מְזוּזוֹת בֵּיתֶךָ וּבִשְׁעָרֶיךָ:

לְמַעַן יִרְבּוּ יְמֵיכֶם וִימֵי בְנֵיכֶם עַל הָאֲדָמָה אֲשֶׁר נִשְׁבַּע יְיָ לַאֲבֹתֵיכֶם לָתֵת לָהֶם, כִּימֵי הַשָּׁמַיִם עַל הָאָרֶץ:

סובב כל עולמים
אהבה רבה (כאש)
יחודא תתאה
(דעת תחתון)
חיה
עולם האצילות
בתוך בריאה

"All year long, during the *Kriat Shema*, we say, 'And I will provide grass in your fields for your animals…'" (*Likutei Torah* of the Alter Rebbe, *Parshat Re'eh*, p. 66 [33b])[248]

The Hebrew word for "grass" — *esev* — is comprised of the letters *ayin-beit-sin*. *Ayin-beit* has the numerical value of 72, which is the *gematria* of *chesed*. The letter *sin* is composed of three *vav*'s, which represent the descent of *chesed*, *gevura* and *tiferet* into *malchut* as we say *Kadosh, Kadosh, Kadosh*.[249] This transcendent kindness occurs "in your fields" where we harvest the grain (God's kindness). The field is where a Jew "does his work," refining sparks of holiness, separating them and elevating them to their source above. The "field" is also *klipat noga*, the realm of mixed good and bad, which it is the job of the Jew to refine and elevate.[250]

"Animals" is an allusion to the angels of *Bria*. With our daily *avoda*, we elevate sparks to their source in the higher spiritual worlds, from where they respond with an influx of kindness and spirituality down to the lowest worlds. Our *avoda* elevates sparks from the realm of *klipat noga* to create angels in the World of *Yetzira* ("He who forms…" every day), and from there to the higher angels of *Bria* ("and those who serve Him…" standing since the six days of creation),

Transcendent Godliness
Great love (fire)
Lower unity
Soul Level: Chaya
World of Atzilut within Bria

And I will provide grass in your field for your animals, and you will eat and be satisfied.

Take care amongst yourselves lest you be seduced by your hearts, and you turn away and serve foreign deities and bow down to them.

And then the wrath of the Lord will flare up on you and He will close up the heavens, and there will be no rain and the land will fail to provide its produce, and you will be quickly banished from the good earth that the Lord has given you.

And you shall place these words of Mine upon your heart and upon your soul, and tie them as a sign upon your hands and as compartments between your eyes. And you should teach them to your children, speaking of them as you sit in your house and as you travel on the road, and when you lie down and when you arise. And you should write them on the doorposts of your houses and on your gates.

In order to prolong your days and the days of your children upon the land that the Lord swore to give to your fathers, for as long as the heavens are over the earth.

---

which are called *behamot* ("animals"). They, in turn, influence the animal and intellectual soul of man.[251]

> 📖 *Within the Words*
>
> In the second paragraph of the *Kriat Shema*, we first mention human food, followed by animal food. Finally, the verse returns to human food. We must first "feed the animals" — perform the divine service of refining our animal soul and elevating sparks to their divine source above — and then we ourselves may "eat," that is, bask in the spiritual pleasure that descends from above. All of this takes place during our daily *avoda*. Just as grass grows spontaneously and must be constantly mowed, so sparks of holiness rise spontaneously to the surface to be elevated. Similarly, converts (a form of holy spark) emerge of their own volition from the non-Jewish nations and convert to Judaism.[252]

וַיֹּאמֶר יְיָ אֶל מֹשֶׁה לֵּאמֹר: דַּבֵּר אֶל בְּנֵי יִשְׂרָאֵל וְאָמַרְתָּ אֲלֵהֶם וְעָשׂוּ לָהֶם צִיצִת עַל כַּנְפֵי בִגְדֵיהֶם לְדֹרֹתָם, וְנָתְנוּ עַל צִיצִת הַכָּנָף פְּתִיל תְּכֵלֶת:
וְהָיָה לָכֶם לְצִיצִת וּרְאִיתֶם אֹתוֹ וּזְכַרְתֶּם אֶת כָּל מִצְוֹת יְיָ וַעֲשִׂיתֶם אֹתָם, וְלֹא תָתוּרוּ אַחֲרֵי לְבַבְכֶם וְאַחֲרֵי עֵינֵיכֶם אֲשֶׁר אַתֶּם זֹנִים אַחֲרֵיהֶם: לְמַעַן תִּזְכְּרוּ וַעֲשִׂיתֶם אֶת כָּל מִצְוֹתָי, וִהְיִיתֶם קְדֹשִׁים לֵאלֹהֵיכֶם:
אֲנִי יְיָ אֱלֹהֵיכֶם אֲשֶׁר הוֹצֵאתִי אֶתְכֶם מֵאֶרֶץ מִצְרַיִם לִהְיוֹת לָכֶם לֵאלֹהִים, אֲנִי יְיָ אֱלֹהֵיכֶם

סובב כל עולמים
אהבה רבה (כאש)
יחודא תתאה
(דעת תחתון)
חיה
עולם האצילות
בתוך בריאה

> **"** ...we must bring down *HaKadosh Baruch Hu* to become enclothed within the garments of Torah... in this manner we join the secrets of the Torah with the revealed Torah...it is the Jews who cause this to happen... the Torah is the garment, and on this garment, we must make *tzitzit*..."
> (*Torah Shmuel* 5630/1870 of the Rebbe Maharash, p. 359)[253]

The four corners of the *tzitzit* allude to the four *chayot* ("angels") and the four strings also hint to the four *chayot*. The *gematria* of *chut* ("string") is the same as that of *chaya*. The 4 *knafayim* ("wings") of the *chayot* hint at the 4 *kanfot* ("corners") of the garment and the *p'nai* ("face") of the *chayot* hints at the *p'nim* ("internal dimension") of the *chayot*). Divine power streams from the higher *merkava* ("chariot") in the world of *Atzilut* (Avraham, Yitzhak and Yaakov) down to the "lower *merkava*" of *chayot* (a class of angels), in the world of *Bria*. The divine power descends via the *chut*, imparting power to the lower *merkava* to uplift the "throne of glory" that is above it. The descent from *Atzilut* to *Bria* is symbolized by the *tzitzit*.

The "face of the lion" (*pnei aryeh*) represents our love of God. The "face of the oxe" (*pnei shor*) represents our fear of God. The "face of the eagle" (*pnei nesher*) is the mercy that we bring down when we recall how the soul has come down from a high spiritual level to be trapped in our physical body. And the "face of man" (*pnei adam*) alludes to our thought, speech and action (*aleph* is thought, *dalet* is *dibur*, or "speech" and *mem* is *maaseh* or "deed"). The goal is to attach our thought, speech and action to God — this is the purpose of the *merkava* of "four corners."

Transcendent Godliness
Great love (fire)
Lower unity
Soul Level: Chaya
World of Atzilut within Bria

And the Lord spoke to Moshe, saying:
Speak to the children of Israel and tell them, 'Make fringes on the corners of their garments throughout their generations, and place a thread of blue-green within the fringes of the corners.'

And they should be fringes for you, and you shall look at them, and remember all the commandments of the Lord, and fulfill them, without straying after your hearts and after your eyes, that you lust after them. So that you recall and fulfill all of My commandments, and you shall be holy to your God.

I am the Lord, your God, I am He Who brought you out of the land of Egypt in order to be your God, I am the Lord your God.

> 📖 *Within the Words*
>
> Both *tzitzit* and *tzitz* are derived from a word meaning "to gaze." But, while *tzitzit* allude to a spiritual gaze from below to Above ("to gaze upon the glory of the King"), *tzitz* represents gazing from Above to below (in response and in proportion to our meditation below, as we develop "love like fire," we receive a response from Above). However, we cannot make *tzitzit* (achieve love of God via "gazing") until we possess a garment (of Torah and mitzvot). Hair is also called *tzitzit* in the Torah, and holiness is associated with the hair. There are three kinds of hair mentioned in the Torah — white, black and red — each with its own level of holiness. They correspond to the three times that *tzitzit* are mentioned in this paragraph, as well as to the three times that we say *kadosh* in *Birchot Kriat Shema*. The third time that *tzitzit* are mentioned in this paragraph, as *letzitzit* carries the *gematria* of 620, or *Keter*, alluding to the 613 mitzvot of the Torah plus seven from the rabbis.

Word Sparks

The tzitzit are also called gedilim ("enlargements, enhancements"), as in the verse (Deut 22:12), "Place gedilim on the four corners of your garment..." since the four corners of the garment correspond to the four animals of the merkava . And, as the sages said about R' Yohanan ben Zakai, "There was no matter, neither large or small, that he neglected." "Large matter" refers to his study of the merkava . And when we don the large tallit (prayer shawl) in the morning, we recite, "My Lord, You have enlarged/enhanced me greatly." This mitzvah brings down gedula, or "greatness" from Above, as well. (Torat Shmuel 5633/1873 of the Rebbe Maharash, V 1, pp. 170-1)

אֱמֶת, וְיַצִּיב, וְנָכוֹן, וְקַיָּם, וְיָשָׁר, וְנֶאֱמָן: וְאָהוּב וְחָבִיב, וְנֶחְמָד וְנָעִים, וְנוֹרָא וְאַדִּיר, וּמְתֻקָּן וּמְקֻבָּל, וְטוֹב וְיָפֶה, הַדָּבָר הַזֶּה עָלֵינוּ לְעוֹלָם וָעֶד:

סובב בתוך ממלא
התאמתות, ראיה
דחכמה בעין השכל

יחודא עילאה תוך יחודא תתאה

חיה

עולם האצילות בתוך בריאה

> **Following the *Kriat Shema*,** we say [15 words beginning with the letter *vav*], all of which corroborate and confirm the nullification of the soul that we achieve during *Kriat Shema*. What is the necessity of mentioning this confirmation so many times?" (*Sefer Maamorim 5679/1919* of the Rebbe Rashab, p. 639)[254]

> The nullification associated with *Kriat Shema* occurs within our divine soul. But our goal is to experience Godliness within our animal soul as well. This occurs during *Emet v'yatziv*, as we repeat the 15 words all beginning with *vav*. The 15 *vav's* connect the divine soul with the animal soul, so that we experience Godliness within our animal soul. Moreover, the 15 *vav's* confirm and repeat the experience of Godliness that occurred during *Kriat Shema*. Man himself is like a *vav*, connecting Godliness (*yud-hey*, the first two letters of *Havaya*) with the world (the final *hey*, with which the world was created).[255]

> Godliness descends from above in four stages of evolution. The first is a point of contraction, similar to the mentor who minimizes his own intellect in order to find the point that is possible to transmit to his student. But this is not sufficient, since even after the mentor finds this point, it is too concentrated for the student to absorb. The mentor must further contract his intellect in order to discern the details that are appropriate to convey to his student. All of this occurs within "thought." A further two-step contraction is necessary to present the details to the student. The mentor must weigh

─── **CHASSIDIC INSIGHTS** ───

(continued from p. 261)

divine levels is what enables us to achieve *ahava rabba* during the *Kriat Shema*. Just as we cannot make out the full details of our "friend" at that hour, and yet we recognize him, so we are unable to fathom the full details of spirituality at this point in prayers (because we at this

(continued on p. 267)

Transcendent within Immanent

Confirmation, Vision in the mind's eye

Higher unity within Lower

Soul Level: Chaya

World of Atzilut within Bria

> **True; and certain and established and lasting; and straightforward and trustworthy and beloved; and endearing and delightful and pleasant; and awesome and mighty and correct, and acceptable and good and beautiful, is this thing for us forever and ever.**

which words to choose in order to successfully relay his ideas, so that ultimately his speech will communicate his ideas to his student. These four contractions correspond to the four letters of God's name. The contractions occur as we say *Emet v'yatziv*, conveying Godly illumination from above to below.[256]

📖 *Within the Words*

The name *Havaya* is involved in the descent of Godliness as we pray — the first letter *yud* represents the descent of Godliness from before the *tzimtzum* down to the world of *A"K*. The *hey* itself is *A"K*, which contains all of the details of creation in time and space, in one point. The descent of the *yud-hey* of His name occurs during the *pesukei dezimra*, as we pray *Baruch She'Amar* and all the psalms containing the word *Halleluyah*. The *vav* represents the descent of the *kav* through the realm of *Keter* (or *Tohu*) and the final *hey* represents the World of *Atzilut*. This descent takes place during *Emet v'yatziv* (as we recite the 15 words beginning with the letter *vav*) and during the *Shemonah Esreh* (as we say the introductory praises beginning with the letter *hey* — *Hagadol, Hagibur v'Hanorah*). And there is a higher interpretation of the name *Havaya* in which all four letters represent spiritual levels that precede the *tzimtzum*.

THE SHEMA

——————— CHASSIDIC INSIGHTS ———————

(continued from p. 266)

point we are using the technique of *yediat hashlilah* — "negative" or circumscribed knowledge — that gives us only approximations of a Godly reality that is beyond our awareness). Yet with our faculty of *hacara*, we grasp Him fully and we are ready to say the *Shema*. *Hacara*

(continued on p. 276)

❝ **The first two paragraphs of the *Kriat Shema*, and the fourth paragraph, *Emet v'yatziv* are associated with the tribes of Reuven, Shimon and Levi. But, about Yehuda, Leah said, 'This time I will thank (*odeh*) God'**[257] **...We express this thankfulness while bowing during the *Shemonah Esreh*...**" (*Sefer Maamorim 5680*/1920 of the Rebbe Rashab, p. 220)[258]

סובב בתוך ממלא
התאמתות, ראיה
דחכמה בעין
השכל
יחודא עילאה תוך
יחודא תתאה
חיה
עולם האצילות
בתוך בריאה

The sages of the Talmud[259] say that if one causes his fellow to go deaf, he must pay him damages worth his full value, but if he blinds him in one eye, he need only pay him for that eye. This does not seem to make sense, for eyesight is far more valuable the hearing. Why then should he pay more for making him go deaf than for blinding him in one eye?

Reuven embodies the style of *avodat Hashem* that utilizes vision. When we meditate on a concept so intensely that it becomes as if we "see" it in our mind's eye, we have adopted the path of Reuven (*Reu–ben*, "see — a son"). This is the intense *avoda* of the first paragraph of the *Shema*. Shimon embodies the analysis and grasp of Godly concepts that is associated with "hearing" (*Shimon* — "hearing"). This path requires that we deduce one idea from another and achieve ever greater understanding of Godliness. This is the path associated with the second paragraph of the *Shema*. Although "seeing" brings us to higher spiritual levels, it is not as "accurate" and "clear" as "hearing." Prophecy, which is a form of "vision," ceased in the time of the Second Temple, and thereafter, "a sage is preferable to a prophet"[260] since the intellectual grasp of a sage extends further and is more accurate than spiritual revelation. For that reason, one who destroys the "hearing" of his fellow must pay full damages, while if he blinds him, he need only pay for the eye.

📖 *Within the Words*

The "vision" of the first paragraph of the *Shema* empowers us to love God, while the "hearing" of the second paragraph causes us to fear Him. But, who are we to experience such "highs" and "lows" in our *avodat Hashem*? It is only because He chooses to lower Himself to relate to us that we have any experience of Godliness whatsoever. This "lowering" occurs during *emet v'yatziv*, as we recite the fifteen words each beginning with a *vav* (a letter which is a "hook" or "connector"). This is the paragraph of Levi *(livui* — "accompaniment,

Transcendent within Immanent
Confirmation, Vision in the mind's eye
Higher unity within Lower
Soul Level: Chaya
World of Atzilut within Bria

> 📖 *Within the Words*
>
> joining"), who connects and joins Godliness from above with Jewish souls below. To benefit from Levi's path of worship, we must be in a state of abject *bitul* ("nullification") and that leads us into the *Shemonah Esreh*, wherein we bow in deference and respect to God. This is the approach of Yehuda: "I will acknowledge, give thanks, to God."²⁶¹

❝ **The purpose of *pesukei dezimra* and the *Kriat Shema* is to transform our physical nature and animal soul....And then, as we recite *Emet v'yatziv*, we begin to serve God with our Godly soul. The Godly soul is elevated as reward for its service..."** (Yom Tov shel Rosh Hashana 5666/1906 of the Rebbe Rashab, p. 145 or p. 191 in the new version)²⁶²

The 15 words of *Emet v'yatziv*, all beginning with the letter *vav*, connect us to the *heichal haratzon* (the "chamber of His divine will"). As the phrase states, "with the *vav*'s you are connected." The previous blessing of *Ahavat olam* and the first paragraphs of the *Kriat Shema* are associated with His "chamber of love," but with the advent of *Emet v'yatziv*, we are connected with the very will of the One above, beyond logic and intellect, and that is why at this point, as we recite *Emet v'yatziv*, we are in a state of cleaving to God.²⁶³

Our *avoda* (meditation and prayer) from below takes place during the *pesukei dezimra* and the *Kriat Shema*, as we recite the prayers loudly in order to involve our animal soul enclothed in our physical body. This section of *avoda* is associated with the second two letters of God's name, *vav-hey*. And then as we recite *Emet v'yatziv*, the Godly soul "takes over," receiving its reward from above via the 15 words of the prayer. We cling to God in a state of *reuta deliba* — the fiery "will of the heart" to cleave to God. This part of *avoda*, through the *Shemonah Esreh*, is associated with the first two letters of His name, *yud-hey*.²⁶⁴

> 📖 *Within the Words*
>
> According to the *Radah*, the fifteen words of *Emet v'yatziv*, all beginning with the letter *vav*, correspond to the fifteen "Songs of Ascent" (Psalms 120-134). They also correspond to the first two letters *yud-hey* of God's name, which together have the *gematria* of 15. And that is why the festivals, Pesach and Succot, occur on the 15th day of the month.²⁶⁵

THE SHEMA

אֱמֶת, אֱלֹהֵי עוֹלָם מַלְכֵּנוּ צוּר יַעֲקֹב מָגֵן יִשְׁעֵנוּ, לְדֹר וָדֹר הוּא קַיָּם, וּשְׁמוֹ קַיָּם, וְכִסְאוֹ נָכוֹן. וּמַלְכוּתוֹ וֶאֱמוּנָתוֹ לָעַד קַיָּמֶת.

וּדְבָרָיו חָיִים וְקַיָּמִים, נֶאֱמָנִים וְנֶחֱמָדִים לָעַד וּלְעוֹלְמֵי עוֹלָמִים עַל אֲבוֹתֵינוּ וְעָלֵינוּ, עַל בָּנֵינוּ וְעַל דּוֹרוֹתֵינוּ, וְעַל כָּל דּוֹרוֹת זֶרַע יִשְׂרָאֵל עֲבָדֶיךָ:

סוֹבֵב בְּתוֹךְ מְמַלֵּא
הִתְאַמְּתוּת, רְאִיָּה
דְחָכְמָה בְּעֵין
הַשֵּׂכֶל
יִחוּדָא עִילָּאָה תּוֹךְ
יִחוּדָא תַּתָּאָה
חַיָּה
עוֹלָם הָאֲצִילוּת
בְּתוֹךְ בְּרִיאָה

> **There are many levels of good (*tov*)...corresponding to the 15 levels of *yesod* within the five structures (*partzufim*) of *sephirot* in every world. They also correspond to the 15 *vav*'s of *Emet v'yatziv*..."** (*Besha'ah Sh'hikdimu* 5672/1912 of the Rebbe Rashab, vol. 2, p. 1031)[266]

The *sephira* of *yesod* is called "good" because it channels the positive divine influence from above into *malchut* and from there down to the lower worlds. The descent begins with *bina* (via the "49 gates of *bina*"), and from there it continues down to the lower *sephirot*. As the intellectual influx descends and becomes "emotional" (applicable to creation), it passes through three stages, each of them called a *yesod*. There are five sets of *sephirot* in every world, for a total of 15 *yesodot*, or passageways in each world. They correspond to the 15 words of *Emet v'yatziv*, each beginning with a *vav* — "with *vav*'s you will be connected." (from a Shabbat song composed by the *Ari z'l*)

Initially, intellect exists in *bina* in a pure pristine form, unrelated to any emotion or to anything practical that may later emerge from it. However, the more we consider a concept, and contemplate upon it, the more it has an effect upon us. We may accept the idea, we may reject it, we may feel warmed and attracted by it, or we may want to have nothing to do with it. But, the more we think about it, the more we begin to "relate" to the concept. At first, this is no more than an intellectual inclination within our mind. It is not a clear and conscious experience of the intellect; it is a mere inclination or tendency. Next, it develops into a full-fledged emotion within the mind, as we gain a clear picture of how we would like to proceed to concretize the concept. Finally, the intellect filters down to the heart and becomes a full-fledged emotion of fear, love or otherwise. Thus, there are three "transitions" that the initial intellectual concept undergoes as it transforms into an

Transcendent within Immanent

Confirmation, Vision in the mind's eye

Higher unity within Lower

Soul Level: Chaya

World of Atzilut within Bria

True, God of the universe is our King, the Rock of Jacob is the shield of our salvation, from generation to generation He endures, and His name endures, and His throne is established, and His reign and His faith last forever.

And His words live and last, they are dependable and delightful forever and for all eternity, for our forefathers and for us, for our children and for our generations, and upon all generations of the seed of Israel, Your servants.

---

emotion. Each "transition" is called a *yesod*, and since there are five sets of *sephirot*, there are a total of 15 such *yesodot* in each world.

> 📖 *Within the Words*
>
> The above process may be illustrated by way of an example. We may have read about a new trade or skill that appeals to us. But, we have no way of approaching the trade or skill, so the thought remains no more than an inclination within our mind. Then, we begin looking into it and make a plan of approach. This is comparable to the emotions within intellect. Finally, we actually go out and buy the books or materials that enable us to learn the skill. At that point, we have developed a full-fledged emotion in the heart. There are three points of transition (*yesodot*) — from pure intellect to inclination, from inclination to emotion in the mind, and finally to full-fledged emotion of the heart. In our prayers, since the 15 *yesodot* correspond to the 15 initial words of *Emet v'yatziv*, we can focus our intention on each set of three as we pray. The first three words correspond to the three *yesodot* within *Keter* (the super-conscious awareness that is beyond our normal mundane consciousness). The second set of three words corresponds to the three *yesodot* within *chochma* (our creative thought process). The third set corresponds to *bina* (our analytic ability). The fourth set corresponds to *Z"a* (our emotions). And finally the fifth set corresponds to *malchut* (our practical abilities). All of this takes place in the World of *Atzilut*. This completes the transition from intellect (*yud-hey*) to emotions (*vav-hey*) within the World of *Atzilut*. The same process takes place in all of the lower worlds as well, as we conclude our prayers.

THE SHEMA

PRAYING LIKE FIRE AND WATER

עַל הָרִאשׁוֹנִים וְעַל הָאַחֲרוֹנִים דָּבָר טוֹב וְקַיָּם בֶּאֱמֶת וּבֶאֱמוּנָה חוֹק וְלֹא יַעֲבֹר.

אֱמֶת, שָׁאַתָּה הוּא יְיָ אֱלֹהֵינוּ וֵאלֹהֵי אֲבוֹתֵינוּ, מַלְכֵּנוּ מֶלֶךְ אֲבוֹתֵינוּ, גּוֹאֲלֵנוּ גּוֹאֵל אֲבוֹתֵינוּ, צוּרֵנוּ, צוּר יְשׁוּעָתֵנוּ, פּוֹדֵנוּ וּמַצִּילֵנוּ מֵעוֹלָם הוּא שְׁמֶךָ, וְאֵין לָנוּ עוֹד אֱלֹהִים זוּלָתֶךָ סֶלָה:

עֶזְרַת אֲבוֹתֵינוּ אַתָּה הוּא מֵעוֹלָם, מָגֵן וּמוֹשִׁיעַ לָהֶם וְלִבְנֵיהֶם אַחֲרֵיהֶם בְּכָל דּוֹר וָדוֹר:

סובב בתוך ממלא
התאמתות, ראיה דחכמה בעין השכל
יחודא עילאה תוך יחודא תתאה
חיה
עולם האצילות בתוך בריאה

> **The word** *emet* ('truth') is associated with *geula* ('redemption')... And God's name *Havaya* is also called *emet*...This, then explains the four times that we say *emet*, corresponding to the four letters of the name *Havaya*..." (Sefer Maamorim 5654/1894 of the Rebbe Rashab, pp. 110 and 116)[267]

Why do we say the word *emet* four times in the prayer *Emet v'yatziv* followed by another four times in the next paragraph, *Ezrat avoteinu* ("help of our fathers")? The Zohar says that the four times we mention *emet* correspond to the four terms of redemption mentioned in Exodus: "I brought you out," "I rescued you," "I redeemed you," and "I took you out." And regarding the future redemption, it is written, "As in the days of your departure from Egypt, I will show you wonders."[268] This implies that the future redemption will also involve the four terms of redemption mentioned in the Exodus from Egypt. Therefore, the sages established that we should say *emet* another four times in *Ezrat avoteinu*, corresponding to the redemption of the future.

Truth is absolute, but its expression is relative. In Egypt, the Jews knew about Godliness through the name *Shaddai* (*dai* — "enough," implying limited Godliness for the limited world). But God told Moshe that *Shaddai* was not His "true" name. His "true" name is *Havaya* ("is, was and will be" — beyond time and space), which is the name that accompanied Moshe as he took the Jews out of Egypt and received the Torah. This name *Havaya* transcends the creation

Transcendent within Immanent
Confirmation, Vision in the mind's eye
Higher unity within Lower
Soul Level: Chaya
World of Atzilut within Bria

For the original [generations] and for the recent [generations], [Your] word is good and lasting in truth and in faith, an immutable law that cannot be violated.

True, You, Lord, are our God and the God of our fathers, our King and the King of our forefathers, our Redeemer, the Redeemer of our forefathers, our Fortress and the Fortress of our salvation, our Redeemer and Rescuer You were always named; and we have no other God aside from You, forever.

You have always been the help of our fathers, the shield and salvation for them and for their offspring after them, in each and every generation.

---

but at the same time it is related to it. In the future, God will reveal a yet higher level of His holy name *Havaya* which is completely beyond creation. This higher name *Havaya* is associated with the secrets of the Torah that will become revealed in the future with the arrival of Mashiach.

> 📖 *Within the Words*
>
> The first four times that we say *emet* are associated with "lower awareness" (*da'at tachton*), in which we are mainly aware of the physical world and God is in the background. The second four times are associated with "higher consciousness" (*da'at elyon*) in which we are mainly aware of God, while creation remains in the background. We mention *emet* now, before the *Shemonah Esreh* because the *Kriat Shema* is an act of *mesirut nefesh* ("self-sacrifice"). It raises us to the higher level that we need in order to bring Godly influence down with our blessings during the *Shemonah Esreh*.

THE SHEMA

בְּרוּם עוֹלָם מוֹשָׁבֶךָ, וּמִשְׁפָּטֶיךָ וְצִדְקָתְךָ עַד אַפְסֵי אָרֶץ.

אֱמֶת, אַשְׁרֵי אִישׁ שֶׁיִּשְׁמַע לְמִצְוֹתֶיךָ, וְתוֹרָתְךָ וּדְבָרְךָ יָשִׂים עַל לִבּוֹ.

אֱמֶת, אַתָּה הוּא אָדוֹן לְעַמֶּךָ, וּמֶלֶךְ גִּבּוֹר לָרִיב רִיבָם, לְאָבוֹת וּבָנִים.

❝ The four times that *emet* is mentioned correspond to the four [stages of] redemption from Egypt, [and] the four redemptions correspond to the four letters of the name *Havaya*, which is called *emet*… thus the four times that *emet* is mentioned correspond to the four letters of *Havaya*, since there are four levels of truth…" (*Sefer Maamorim 5658*/1898 of the Rebbe Rashab, pp. 87, 93)[269]

Since the spiritual illumination of the name *Havaya* is very high, it must undergo contraction in order to descend to this world. The contraction is reflected in the four letters of His name, corresponding to the verse in Scripture alluding to the giving the Torah, "Then he saw, and told, prepared and investigated, and then He spoke to man."[270] "He saw" refers to the first letter *yud*, associated with the *sephira* of *chochma*, which involves vision. "Told" refers to the second letter *hey*, associated with *bina*, corresponding to hearing. "Prepared and investigated" is an allusion to the letter *vav*, corresponding to the six *sephirot* of Z"a, through which the divine illumination passes during its descent. Finally, "And He said to man" alludes to the final letter *hey* of His name, associated with *malchut* and speech.

When the Torah mentions the name *Havaya* twice in one verse, it does so with an interruption between the two names, indicating that they are two different levels of His name. One is the name *Havaya* that descended to free the Jews from Egypt and to give them the Torah; the other is associated with the future redemption. Currently, we do not pronounce the name *Havaya* as it is written — we pronounce it as *Ado-nay* — indicating that His name is enclothed in

Transcendent within Immanent
Confirmation, Vision in the mind's eye
Higher unity within Lower
Soul Level: *Chaya*
World of *Atzilut* within *Bria*

In the heights of the universe is Your dwelling place, and Your laws and Your justice reach the very ends of the earth.

True, happy is the man who heeds Your commandments, and who places Your Torah and Your word upon his heart.

True, You are the Lord of Your nation, and mighty King, fighting their fights for both fathers and children.

---

a lower name (*Ado-nay*) in order to descend to this world. In the future though, His higher name *Havaya* will shine without contraction, and then it will be pronounced as written. The higher name *Havaya* will shine within the lower name, and creation will be uplifted.

> 📖 *Within the Words*
>
> The Midrash gives two explanations for the four terms of redemption from Egypt ("brought out," "rescued," "redeemed" and "took out"). One is that they correspond to the four decrees of Pharaoh, and the other is that they correspond to the four exiles that the Jews suffered. The explanation of the Zohar — that the four terms of redemption refer to the four words *emet* in our prayers — allows us to accept both Midrashic explanations. The four times that we say *emet* during *Emet v'yatziv* correspond to the four decrees of Pharaoh and, by extension, to the four stages with which the redemption took place and the four letters of the lower name *Havaya*. The four times that we say *emet* in *Ezrat avoteinu* ("help of our fathers") correspond to the redemption from the four exiles — including the fourth and final redemption which will occur in the future — and by extension to the four letters of the higher name *Havaya*.

THE SHEMA

PRAYING LIKE FIRE AND WATER

אֱמֶת, אַתָּה הוּא רִאשׁוֹן, וְאַתָּה הוּא אַחֲרוֹן, וּמִבַּלְעָדֶיךָ אֵין לָנוּ מֶלֶךְ גּוֹאֵל וּמוֹשִׁיעַ.

אֱמֶת, מִמִּצְרַיִם גְּאַלְתָּנוּ יְיָ אֱלֹהֵינוּ, וּמִבֵּית עֲבָדִים פְּדִיתָנוּ.

כָּל בְּכוֹרֵיהֶם הָרָגְתָּ, וּבְכוֹרְךָ יִשְׂרָאֵל גָּאָלְתָּ, וְיַם סוּף לָהֶם בָּקַעְתָּ, וְזֵדִים טִבַּעְתָּ, וִידִידִים הֶעֱבַרְתָּ, וַיְכַסּוּ מַיִם צָרֵיהֶם. אֶחָד מֵהֶם לֹא נוֹתָר.

עַל זֹאת שִׁבְּחוּ אֲהוּבִים, וְרוֹמְמוּ לָאֵל, וְנָתְנוּ יְדִידִים זְמִירוֹת שִׁירוֹת וְתִשְׁבָּחוֹת, בְּרָכוֹת וְהוֹדָאוֹת לַמֶּלֶךְ אֵל חַי וְקַיָּם:

רָם וְנִשָּׂא גָּדוֹל וְנוֹרָא, מַשְׁפִּיל גֵּאִים עֲדֵי אָרֶץ, וּמַגְבִּיהַּ שְׁפָלִים עַד מָרוֹם, מוֹצִיא אֲסִירִים, פּוֹדֶה עֲנָוִים, עוֹזֵר דַּלִּים, הָעוֹנֶה לְעַמּוֹ יִשְׂרָאֵל בְּעֵת שַׁוְּעָם אֵלָיו.

סובב בתוך ממלא
התאמתות, ראיה דחכמה בעין השכל
יחודא עילאה תוך יחודא תתאה
חיה
עולם האצילות בתוך בריאה

CHASSIDIC INSIGHTS

(continued from p. 267)

occurs as we join the high spiritual levels that we perceived during the first verse of the *Shema* with our routine perception of the world. At that point, we have so internalized transcendent awareness of Godliness that it becomes part of our routine awareness as well. This is also called joining *yichuda ila'ah* ("higher unity," in which God is the focus of intention) with *yichuda tata'ah* ("lower unity," in which the creation is the focus of attention).[ix]

There is one more stage that we experience before reaching the *Shemonah Esreh*, the pinnacle of prayer. As we conclude the first three paragraphs of the *Shema*, and begin the final prayers before

(continued on p. 278)

Transcendent within Immanent
Confirmation, Vision in the mind's eye
Higher unity within Lower
Soul Level: Chaya
World of Atzilut within Bria

True, You are the original, and Your are the final, and aside from You, we have no King, Redeemer and Savior.

True, You redeemed us from Egypt, Lord our God, and from the house of bondage You rescued us.

All of their first-born You slew, and the first-born of the Jews You saved, and You split the Reed Sea for them, and their wicked ones you drowned, You brought Your beloved intimates over and You covered their tormentors over with water, leaving not one of them [alive].

For this, the beloved ones praised God and exalted God, and the dear ones offered songs and melodies and praises, blessings and thanks to the King, the everlasting and living God.

He is exalted and transcendent, great and awesome, lowering the proud to the very earth, and raising the low to the heights, He frees the captives, redeems the humble, aids the impoverished, He Who answers His people the Jews when they turn to Him.

THE SHEMA

תְּהִלּוֹת לְאֵל עֶלְיוֹן גֹּאֲלָם, בָּרוּךְ הוּא וּמְבֹרָךְ, מֹשֶׁה וּבְנֵי יִשְׂרָאֵל לְךָ עָנוּ שִׁירָה בְּשִׂמְחָה רַבָּה, וְאָמְרוּ כֻלָּם:

מִי כָמֹכָה בָּאֵלִים יְיָ,
מִי כָּמֹכָה נֶאְדָּר בַּקֹּדֶשׁ,
נוֹרָא תְהִלֹּת עֹשֵׂה פֶלֶא:

סובב בתוך ממלא
התאמתות, ראיה
דחכמה בעין
השכל

יחודא עילאה תוך
יחודא תתאה

חיה

עולם האצילות
בתוך בריאה

CHASSIDIC INSIGHTS

(continued from p. 276)

the *Shemonah Esreh*, we say the words, *emet veyatziv*…("true and established…"). Here, we experience confirmation and corroboration of our meditation. That is, all that we have mentally deduced and even envisioned (in our mind's eye) undergoes a stage of independent confirmation and verification from another angle. That occurs as we "lose" the shackles of our animal soul, and our Godly soul "takes over" with its own powers of ascent and elevation (leading to the *Shemonah Esreh*). The process of meditation during *Birchot Kriat Shema* and the process of *mesirut nefesh* during the *Shema* itself totally uproot and eradicate the animal soul. At that point, our divine soul takes over as we recite the prayer *emet veyatziv* (which contain fifteen words, recalling the *Halleluyah's* of *pesukei dezimra*, which were also for the sake of bringing down divine intellect to infuse our love for God. There, it was the letters *yud-hey* — of gematria fifteen — within the word *Halleluyah* that provide the illumination. Here, it is the fifteen words beginning with the letter *vav*, meaning "connection," that provide the illumination of divine intellect leading into the *Shemonah Esreh*). During *emet veyatziv*, it is the divine, Godly soul that perceives spirituality in the form of angels and other divine beings. In fact, the divine soul is much more capable of detecting Godliness than is the animal soul, since Godliness is its natural "habitat" and environment. Therefore, during *emet veyatziv*, we receive "verification" and "confirmation" of what was previously the experience of our animal soul. Now, our Godly experience verifies and confirms the experience of our animal soul. This occurs as we say the prayer, *emet veyatziv*.

(continued on p. 279)

Transcendent within Immanent

Confirmation, Vision in the mind's eye

Higher unity within Lower

Soul Level: Chaya

World of Atzilut within Bria

Praise to sublime God Who is their redeemer,
Blessed is He and he is blessed,
Moshe and the children of Israel answered
you in song and in great joy,
and all of them proclaimed:

Who is like You among the deities, Lord,
Who is like You, mighty and holy,
awesome in praise, performing wonders:

─── CHASSIDIC INSIGHTS ───

(continued from p. 278)

Here are the correspondences with the world of *Bria*, on the soul level of *neshama*…

STATE OF MIND	SOUL-LEVEL	WORLD	PRAYER SEGMENT
P'nimiyut hamochin — "mature mindfulness" and *reuta deliba* ("desire of the heart")	Neshama	Bria	From Barchu to *yotzar hameorot*
Ahavah B'taanugim ("Love with Delight")	Yechida	Atzmut Ohr Eyn Sof	Ahavat Olam
Ahava Rabba ("Great Love"), *Reiya b'eyn hasechel* — ("vision in the mind's eye") *Hacara* ("Recognition"),	Neshama	Bria	Shema Yisrael
Hitamtut ("verification, confirmation")	Neshama/Chaya	Bria	Emet veyatziv

(continued on p. 282)

THE SHEMA

שִׁירָה חֲדָשָׁה שִׁבְּחוּ גְאוּלִים לְשִׁמְךָ הַגָּדוֹל עַל שְׂפַת הַיָּם, יַחַד כֻּלָּם הוֹדוּ וְהִמְלִיכוּ וְאָמְרוּ:

יְיָ יִמְלֹךְ לְעוֹלָם וָעֶד:

וְנֶאֱמַר. גֹּאֲלֵנוּ יְיָ צְבָאוֹת שְׁמוֹ קְדוֹשׁ יִשְׂרָאֵל:

בָּרוּךְ אַתָּה יְיָ גָּאַל יִשְׂרָאֵל:

סובב בתוך ממלא
התאמתות, ראיה דחכמה בעין השכל
יחודא עילאה תוך יחודא תתאה
חיה
עולם האצילות בתוך בריאה

> **We mention** *geula* ('redemption') immediately before the *Shemonah Esreh* in order to impart momentum to the elevation that occurs during the *Shemonah Esreh*…" (*Sefer Maamorim* 5680/1920 of the Rebbe Rashab, pp. 153, 155)[271]

The concept of *geula* ("redemption") is also associated with *emet* ("truth"). And both are associated with *tov* ("good") and with *chai* ("life"). All of these terms are associated with the *sephira* of *yesod*, which gathers divine illumination from above and channels it down into *malchut*. Thus, *yesod* is always paired with *malchut*. We recite *Emet v'yatziv*, mentioning *emet* and alluding to *yesod*, and we then launch into the *Shemonah Esreh* (also called *tefila*), which is associated with *malchut*, since we must nullify ourselves completely in order to pray properly. This process is called *smichat geula letefila* — "proximity of redemption to prayer" — and it is personified by the two brothers, Yoseph (representing *yesod*, or *geula*) and Yehuda (representing *malchut*, or *tefila*).

According to the sages, "three pairs are always found in proximity to one another."[272] The pairs are: *Semicha* and *Shechita* (placing of hands on the animal followed by slaughtering it in the Temple), *geula* and *tefila* (reciting the *Shema* followed by praying the *Shemonah Esreh*), and washing and blessing (reciting the blessing immediately after washing our hands for bread). Prayer is in lieu of the offerings in the Temple, and its goal is to "sacrifice" our animal soul. This begins during the *Kriat Shema*, as we say the words *echad* and dedicate our animal soul, and culminates in the *Shemonah Esreh*, as we totally nullify our animal soul. The two steps in this process

Transcendent within Immanent

Confirmation, Vision in the mind's eye

Higher unity within Lower

Soul Level: Chaya

World of Atzilut within Bria

With a new song, those who You redeemed praised Your great name on the edge of the sea, together they all acknowledged and coronated You, saying;

The Lord reigns forever and ever.

And as is stated, our Savior, the Lord of Hosts is His name, the holy One of Israel.

Blessed are You, Lord, who redeemed Israel.

— 1) the initial nullification in which the animal still exists (*geula* during *Emet v'yatziv*, and placing hands on the animal), followed by 2) its total nullification from existence (during *tefila* — i.e. *Shemonah Esreh*, and sacrificing the animal) — must take place in proximity to one another. The initial nullification of the animal soul during *Kriat Shema* lends it the ability to become completely nullified during the *Shemonah Esreh*.

📖 *Within the Words*

The "laying of hands" upon the animal before it was sacrificed called for the use of both hands. This symbolized the two kinds of nullification that occur during *Kriat Shema*. First, there is nullification of the soul (*echad*), followed by nullification of the body (*bechol naphshecha*). The "laying of hands" was performed by the priest, using all of his power. It was a forceful act because such dedication requires our highest and innermost powers to achieve the spiritual levels associated with *Kriat Shema* and *Shemonah Esreh*, during which we activate our *chaya* and *yechida*. In fact, the word for power — *koach* — alludes to the two transcendent levels of the soul. The *caf* of *koach* symbolizes *Keter* (the spiritual level of *yechida*) and the *chet* symbolizes *chochma* (the spiritual level of *chaya*). The total nullification of the animal soul adds momentum to our spiritual ascent during *Shemonah Esreh*. See also *Torat Shmuel 5640/1980* of the Rebbe Maharash, p. 111, and *Torat Shmuel 5641/1881*, p. 30.

שמונה עשרה – עמידה

אֲדֹנָי, שְׂפָתַי תִּפְתָּח וּפִי יַגִּיד תְּהִלָּתֶךָ:

סובב בתוך ממלא
דביקות באלקות
יראה עילאה
חיה-יחידה
עולם האצילות

> **The *Shema* is associated with the World of *Atzilut* within *Bria*. However, the *Shemonah Esreh* is associated with *Atzilut* itself."** (*Sefer Maamorim* 5659/1899 of the Rebbe Rashab, p. 200)[273]

The *Zohar* tells us that "*bina* nests in *Bria*." That means that in the World of *Bria* shines intellect of the highest order — the intense experience of *pnimiyut bina*, with which we grasp the essential kernel at the core of a spiritual concept. This is the world that we inhabit while reciting the *Shema*. However, "*chochma* nests in *Atzilut*." That is, the total psychological nullification associated with *chochma* is what illuminates *Atzilut*. And this is what we experience during the *Shemonah Esreh*.

--- CHASSIDIC INSIGHTS ---

(continued from p. 279)

YIRAH ILA'AH — SUPERNAL FEAR, OR "AWE"

Upon completing the *Kriat Shema* and *emet veyatziv*, we are ready to enter the highest section of the prayers, the *Shemonah Esreh*. The *Shemonah Esreh* is associated with *yirah ila'ah*, or "awe." At this point, we are so overwhelmed by our experience of Godliness that we virtually lose all sense of self in His Presence. That is why we precede the *Shemonah Esreh* by quietly beseeching, "Lord, open my lips..." We are so overcome that we have trouble praying without requesting His assistance. The best way to understand what occurs during the *Shemonah Esreh* is to contrast it with the *Kriat Shema* that precedes it.

The sages of Kaballah describe what occurs during the *Kriat Shema* as *yichud av v'aim* — "unity of the father and mother." With our intense devotion and dedication during *Kriat Shema*, we transcend our normal awareness and access realms that are beyond us. In fact, we access the infinite light and illumination that transcends creation. At that point we wish to bring it down to influence and

(continued on p. 283)

SHEMONAH ESREH — THE AMIDAH

Transcendent within Immanent
Cleaving to Godliness
Higher Fear – Awe
Haya and *Yechida*
World of *Atzilut*

Lord, open my lips and
let my mouth tell Your praise...

The recitation of the *Shema* is accompanied by keen intellectual analysis and meditation, leading to internal illumination of the soul. It takes place with great inner excitement, producing commotion within the soul. However, our experience during *Shemonah Esreh* is of direct recognition and cleaving to Godliness, and that is why we are still and quiet.

> *Within the Words*
>
> The recitation of the *Shema* is called *Kriat Shema* because when we read/recite, we organize and pay attention to our words. The words are the product of deep intellectual effort. However, the direct experience of Godliness — of the name *Ma'ah* (signifying *bitul* within us), which verifies and confirms Godliness within — takes place quietly during the *Shemonah Esreh*. We do not put conscious effort into speech during the *Shemonah Esreh*, but nevertheless our words emerge spontaneously and unintentionally. And they express the "truth" of our inner conviction. That is why we preface the *Shemonah Esreh* by saying *Ado-nay sfatai tifatch* ("Lord open my lips"). Since our experience is beyond intellect, our lips open up automatically and spontaneously.

CHASSIDIC INSIGHTS

(continued from p. 282)

improve the quality of our everyday life. However, since it is infinite illumination, we can only bring it down to a level that is accessible, but not particularly useful for our mundane purposes. That level is called *chochma* ("wisdom"), and it is the first (highest) of the ten *sephirot*. Within *chochma*, His infinite light becomes channeled, and yet it remains spiritual and ethereal. On this level, we are aware of His presence, but do not directly experience Godliness. Even when

(continued on p. 284)

בָּרוּךְ אַתָּה יְיָ אֱלֹהֵינוּ וֵאלֹהֵי אֲבוֹתֵינוּ, אֱלֹהֵי אַבְרָהָם, אֱלֹהֵי יִצְחָק, וֵאלֹהֵי יַעֲקֹב, הָאֵל הַגָּדוֹל הַגִּבּוֹר וְהַנּוֹרָא אֵל עֶלְיוֹן, גּוֹמֵל חֲסָדִים טוֹבִים, קוֹנֵה הַכֹּל, וְזוֹכֵר חַסְדֵי אָבוֹת, וּמֵבִיא גוֹאֵל לִבְנֵי בְנֵיהֶם לְמַעַן שְׁמוֹ בְּאַהֲבָה:

סובב בתוך ממלא
דביקות באלקות
יראה עילאה
חיה-יחידה
עולם האצילות

❝ During the *Shemonah Esreh*, we pray in the merit of 'Our God and the God of our fathers.' Why do we first mention 'our God,' and only afterward, 'the God of our fathers?' Wouldn't it be more appropriate to preface 'our God' with 'the God of our fathers?'" (*Torat Shmuel 5631/1871* of the Rebbe Maharash, p. 70)[274]

The word *Elokeinu* ("our God") alludes to God's infinite illumination after it has contracted to connect with the intellectual *sephirot* of *chochma* and *bina* (the two highest *sephirot*). Only after His infinite light has become contracted, so that we become aware of it intellectually, can it descend to our emotions (represented by the forefathers). First, He must become "our God" (descend to our range, our intellect), and thereafter He may become "the God of our fathers" (descend to our emotions). With our intellect, we become aware of Godly illumination, which then filters down to join with our emotions of love and fear of God.

Upon their descent from our intellect, our emotions are diametrically opposed to one another. How can we feel tremendous love for God, which motivates us to want to approach Him, while simultaneously feeling tremendous fear of Him, which motivates us to

──── CHASSIDIC INSIGHTS ────

(continued from p. 283)

it filters down to the next *sephira* — *bina* — the spirituality that we access during *Kriat Shema* remains intellectual. The sages called this act (the joining of *chochma* and *bina*), "unity of the father and

(continued on p. 287)

Transcendent within Immanent
Cleaving to Godliness
Higher Fear — Awe
Haya and Yechida
World of Atzilut

BLESSED ARE YOU, LORD, OUR GOD AND GOD OF our forefathers, the God of Abraham, the God of Isaac, and the God of Jacob, the great, mighty and awesome God, supernal God, Who performs good deeds of kindness, creates everything, and recalls the good deeds of the forefathers, and brings a redeemer to the offspring of their descendants, for the sake of His name, with love.

---

keep our distance? The answer is that there is a third, much higher influx of divine illumination that descends from the highest levels of Godliness to enable us to transcend our emotions and attach ourselves directly to the One above. This extremely high level is called awe, and it is associated with the third of the forefathers — Yaakov Avinu. It includes elements of both love and fear of God. [275]

> 📖 *Within the Words*
>
> As we say the words, *Elokeinu* ("our God") we focus on the contraction of His infinite light that descends to the intellect (*chochma* and *bina*). As we say *Elokei avoteinu* ("the God of our fathers"), the illumination descends to our emotions of love and fear of God. Upon mentioning the forefathers (Avraham and Yitzchak), we experience contradictory emotions of love and fear, which we transcend upon mentioning the third forefather — "and Yaakov." The *vav* of "and Yaakov" (*v'Yaakov*) creates a direct connection between God and man, transcending both emotions and eliciting a third transcendent emotion of awe. Avraham represents *chesed* (love of God), Yitzchak represents *gevura* (fear of God), and Yaakov represents *tiferet* (mercy), which is the "middle vector" that descends from *Keter* (transcendent Godliness) to elicit awe within us. The same is true of the subsequent words — *hagadol* ("great"), *hagibor* ("powerful") *v'hanorah* ("and awesome") — the *vav* of *v'hanorah* is a "connector" that joins *Kel elyon* ("God above") with our emotions, enabling us to transcend the contradictory elements of love and fear and connect directly with the One above during the *Shemonah Esreh*.

❝ **The word *hakol* ('everything') that we recite during *Shemonah Esreh* (*koneh hakol* — 'God acquires everything') carries the gematria fifty-five, seventeen less than concealed *chesed* ('kindness').**" (Torat Shmuel 5635/1875, V 1, p. 69)

סובב בתוך ממלא
דביקות באלקות
יראה עילאה
חיה-ויחידה
עולם האצילות

Seventeen is the gematria of *tov* ("good"), and we know that there are two levels of "good" — the hidden good that is the source of all blessings that descend indiscriminately to the world, and revealed good that is meted out to those who actively seek God and try to bring Him into their lives through fulfillment of mitzvoth, learning Torah and praying. "Good" descends to us through the beneficence of Yoseph, the archetypal *tzaddik* ("righteous person"), associated with the *sephira* of *yesod*, through which all blessings and beneficence (*Tov*) flow down to the world. Yoseph was brought down to Egypt when he was seventeen years old. (*Torat Shmuel 5637/1877* of the Rebbe Maharash, V 1, p. 169-70). Yoseph "softened" the Egyptians with his love of God. Moshe was also called *Tov;* and he later "broke" the Egyptians with fear (the plagues) (*Torat Shmuel 5642/1882* of the Rebbe Maharash, p. 92).

During the Shabbat morning prayers (*Shacharit*), we mention "*koneh shamayim va'aretz* — "He who acquires the heavens and earth." This seems to be the opposite of what we know to be true, that He "created" the heavens and earth. Creation occurs from His infinite light, from which He creates ex nihilo, from nothing to something. But *kinyan*, or "acquisition" implies the opposite dynamic, as if He draws the creation to Him. The resolution is that indeed, on Shabbat, creation "returns" so to speak to its source, to God Himself. The entire creation undergoes a spiritual elevation and ascends to the world of *Atzilut* (*Torat Shmuel 5638/1876* of the Rebbe Maharash, p. 51). Perhaps when we say *koneh hakol* ("everything"), the reference is to the lower worlds of *Bria*, *Yetzira* and *Asiya* (as in the blessing after Barchu, when we mention *hakol* to include even the negativity present in the universe). If so, perhaps when we mention *koneh hakol*, the lower worlds return to their origin in *Tov*, His desire to benefit the world. And then, *hakol* (55) plus *tov* (17) equals *chesed* (72).

Transcendent within Immanent
Cleaving to Godliness
Higher Fear – Awe
Haya and *Yechida*
World of *Atzilut*

📖 *Within the Words*

In the introductory section of *Shemonah esreh*, we say, "You are forever mighty, Lord, You enliven the dead…" The sages (Pesachim 87B) tell us, "The Jews were exiled in order to add converts to their numbers." Yet, we see that very few converts were actually made in the course of two millennia that the Jews have been in exile? The answer is that "converts" does not mean merely proselytes, those people who convert to Judaism. Rather, "converts" are sparks of holiness that fell from a high spiritual source to become entrapped in the physical objects that we elevate during the course of fulfillment of mitzvoth, prayer and Torah study. The words, *Mechayeh Hameitim* ("Enliven the dead") refers to our ability to free these trapped sparks that were "dead" to spirituality, and return them to their spiritual source. However, the power to free and elevate the holy sparks comes from Above, which is why we first say, *Atah Gibur* ("You are mighty…"). That is, He in His might gives us the strength and power to uplift and free entrapped sparks, and that is what is meant by "add converts." That also explains the following words that we recite, *rav lehoshiah* — "capable of saving." The word *rav* indicates multiplicity and division, but with the aid of His power of elevation and uplifting, we are enabled to provide *yeshuah* — "redemption" — for the fallen sparks of holiness (*Torat Shmuel* 5639/1879 of the Rebbe Maharash, V 1, pp. 335-6).

Word Sparks

"קונה הכל" — "creates everything" — the word *hakol* carries gematria of 55, seventeen less than the word *chesed* (72 – "kindness"). Seventeen is the gematria of the *tov* ("good") that remains hidden until the advent of *meshiach*. *Hakol* plus *Tov* equals *Chesed* (*Torat Shmuel* 5635/1875 of the Rebbe Maharash, V 1, p. 69").

—— CHASSIDIC INSIGHTS ——

(continued from p. 284)

mother," and perhaps we can understand this by reference to our own parents. Part of the task of parenting is to make new realms accessible to our children. One of the vital things that parents do for their children is provide opportunities and open up possibilities. However,

(continued on p. 288)

בעשי"ת יש להוסיף:

זָכְרֵנוּ לְחַיִּים, מֶלֶךְ חָפֵץ בַּחַיִּים,
וְכָתְבֵנוּ בְּסֵפֶר הַחַיִּים, לְמַעַנְךָ אֱלֹהִים חַיִּים:

מֶלֶךְ, עוֹזֵר וּמוֹשִׁיעַ וּמָגֵן.

בָּרוּךְ אַתָּה יְיָ, מָגֵן אַבְרָהָם:

סובב בתוך ממלא
דביקות באלקות
יראה עילאה
חיה-יחידה
עולם האצילות

❝ In truth, God (*Elokim*) deserves praise because He is the God of Avraham, who was so incredibly important that, on account of him, God is praised…*Elokim* is praiseworthy as God precisely because of Avraham…" (*Maamorei Admor Hazaken* [*Maamorei R'zl*] on *Tefila*, page 443)[276]

The source of creation is *chesed* of *Atzilut*, which "accompanies" the rest of the *sephirot* as they descend to create the lower worlds of *BY"A*. The "light" of *chesed* descends as we say *Baruch* ("Blessed be…") at the very beginning of the *Shemonah Esreh*. As we mention the forefathers (Avraham, Yitzchak and Yaakov), the light of *chesed* "enters" the *kelim* ("vessels") of *chesed*. Since the forefathers were the *merkava* ("vehicle") through which the divine light descended to create and maintain the worlds, they themselves are very praiseworthy. Through them, the world became a better place, more receptive to Godliness and spirituality. Because of the forefathers, and especially because of Avraham, who was the "vehicle" for

—— CHASSIDIC INSIGHTS ——

(continued from p. 287)

the extent to which we capitalize on these opportunities depends upon us, upon our talents and our inclinations. Our parents provide the opportunity, but whether we actualize it depends on us. Similarly, in reference to our spiritual level, the *Kriat Shema* brings down a very high light with great potential. However, if we do not utilize it, that light remains transcendent and "extraneous" to our lives.

It is during the *Shemonah Esreh* that we seize the infinite light of the *Kriat Shema* and we make use of it. Each blessing of the

(continued on p. 292)

Between Rosh Hashana and Yom Kippur add:
Remember us for life, King Who desires life,
and inscribe us in the book of life, for Your sake, living God.

The King who assists and saves and shields; Blessed are You, Lord, the shield of Abraham.

Transcendent within Immanent
Cleaving to Godliness
Higher Fear – Awe
Haya and *Yechida*
World of Atzilut

---

chesed, the world became uplifted. God became known as *Elokim* — spirituality concealed within nature. So, in a very real sense we can say that it is Avraham who made God praiseworthy, by causing people to recognize Him in the lower physical world.

We would normally want to organize our praises of God before praying, but here in the *Shemonah Esreh* we reverse the order. We first mention the forefathers, and then we mention God's praises — "the great, the mighty and the awesome." However, the truth is that God is praiseworthy precisely because such a great man as Avraham found Him and worshipped Him. Just as a king is not a king unless he has subjects over whom he rules, so God is not "our God" until we recognize and worship him. And that is precisely what happened when Avraham found God and publicized Him among men. In this context, it makes sense to first mention Avraham's name, and then proceed to praise God.

📖 Within the Words

The advice of our sages, as we begin the *pesukei dezimra*, is to "first organize our praises, and then pray to God." After issuing praises, we make our requests. The first half of our prayers is a process of ascent, from below to above. However, when we reach the twelve intermediary blessings, of the *Shemonah Esreh*, we stand at the pinnacle of the ladder of prayer. Now is the time to make our requests. From our newfound "heights," we beseech God to bring down divine energy from above to below. As it descends, the new level of Godliness uplifts creation and improves our lot in the lower worlds. Here, it makes sense to make our requests, and then praise God because, through our requests, the world becomes a better place.

אַתָּה גִּבּוֹר לְעוֹלָם אֲדֹנָי,
מְחַיֵּה מֵתִים אַתָּה רַב לְהוֹשִׁיעַ:

קיץ: מוֹרִיד הַטָּל

חורף: מַשִּׁיב הָרוּחַ וּמוֹרִיד הַגֶּשֶׁם:

מְכַלְכֵּל חַיִּים בְּחֶסֶד, מְחַיֵּה מֵתִים בְּרַחֲמִים רַבִּים, סוֹמֵךְ נוֹפְלִים, וְרוֹפֵא חוֹלִים, וּמַתִּיר אֲסוּרִים, וּמְקַיֵּם אֱמוּנָתוֹ לִישֵׁנֵי עָפָר.

סובב בתוך ממלא
דביקות באלקות
יראה עילאה
חיה-יחידה
עולם האצילות

> [It is written in the Book of Isaiah:] "And Hezekiah turned his face to the wall and prayed…"[277] From this verse, our sages learned that, "when praying the *Shemonah Esreh*, there should be nothing between us and the wall." (*Talmud Berachot* 5B, *Shulchan Aruch HaRav* 90:20, *Torat Shmuel* 5627/1867, pp 182-86, *Torat Shmuel* 5630/1870, p. 347)[278]

From the Zohar, we learn that the word *kir* which means "wall" in Hebrew means "lord" in Greek, while "lord" is *adon* in Hebrew. This alludes to the name *Ado-nay*. If the world was created through His name *Havaya* alone, it would be an infinite unlimited world. Instead the name *Havaya* illuminates the world refracted through the name *Ado-nay* (equivalent to *Elokim*), and the result is a limited creation in which there is nonetheless some room for Godly revelation. Another word for "wall" is *kotel,* which breaks down into *ko* (kaf-vav) and *tel* (tof-lamed); *ko* has the *gematria* of 26 which is the same as the *gematria* of the name *Havaya*, and *tel* has the *gematria* of 430, which is five times the *gematria* of the name *Elokim*. A *kotel*, just as a *kir*, hides Godliness but leaves room for spiritual revelation.[279]

There is another kind of "wall," and that is the "wall of iron" that is associated with Amalek, the quintessential enemy of the Jewish people. The *gematria* of *barzel* ("iron") is 240 and it is the same as that of Amalek. Thus we learn that the iron wall of Amalek

Transcendent within Immanent
Cleaving to Godliness
Higher Fear – Awe
Haya and *Yechida*
World of *Atzilut*

> You are forever mighty, Lord,
> You enliven the dead, very able to save.
>
> During summer: You bring down the dew.
>
> During winter: You cause the wind to blow and the rain to fall.
>
> He Who in His goodness provides life, in great mercy enlivens the dead, supports the fallen and heals the sick and frees the imprisoned, and fulfills His promise to those [already] sleeping in the dust.

completely hides and conceals Godliness. For that reason, no object made of iron was allowed into the holy Temple, and if iron came into contact with a stone, that stone was rendered unsuitable for use in the Temple. When the Temple was destroyed, the sages said that "a wall of iron separates the Jews from their Father in Heaven."[280]

📖 Within the Words

Our task is to create cracks and openings in the "wall of iron" (as in the verse in the Song of Songs, "peeking from the cracks and peering through the windows…"), in order to "let the Godliness in." We create cracks and openings in the "iron wall" with our meditation and prayers. That is the true meaning of "And Hizkiyahu turned his face to the wall and prayed…" — he drew down Godly revelation, as in the Priestly Blessing, "May Hashem cause His countenance to illuminate" within the *kir* — that is, within the name *Ado-nay*. In our prayers, we achieve this during *Shemonah Esreh*, as we say the word *Baruch*, drawing Godly illumination down to illuminate the "wall." That is why there should not be anything between us and "the wall" as we pray.

מִי כָמֽוֹךָ בַּֽעַל גְּבוּרוֹת וּמִי דֽוֹמֶה לָּךְ, מֶֽלֶךְ מֵמִית וּמְחַיֶּה וּמַצְמִֽיחַ יְשׁוּעָה:

סובב בתוך ממלא
דביקות באלקות
יראה עילאה
חיה-ויחידה
עולם האצילות

❝ The continuity at the beginning of *Shemonah Esreh* proceeds as follows, "Who is like You, Master of mighty deeds, Who takes away life (by "breaking the vessels") and Who grants life (by rectifying the "shattered vessels"), and sprouts salvation from below to Above with much additional vitality..." (Alter Rebbe's Siddur with Chasidut, Page 176)

This section of *Shemonah Esreh* alludes to the primordial process of "shattering of the vessels" (*shvirat hakelim*). The initial illumination with which God created the universe was too intense for the world to tolerate, and the "vessels" meant to contain such high divine light "shattered," scattering sparks of holiness throughout creation. Our task in *shemona esreh* is to retrieve the scattered sparks and return them to their rightful level in creation. When we do so, we also receive a spiritual elevation, while participating in the *tikun* ("rectification") of the world.

The "fallen sparks" of Godly illumination also affect our ability to meditate and pray. Since the world that we inhabit has fallen from a much higher spiritual level, it is difficult for us to achieve those high levels during prayer and meditation and return the sparks to their source. In the world of *Asiya* (the lowest world of "action"), we are called *asirim* ("prisoners"). In the next world up, *Yetzira* (the world of general templates of creation, or "angels"), we are called *cholim* (those who are "sick," referring to the unquenchable lust for Godliness that we experience, making us "love-sick"). Finally in

─── **CHASSIDIC INSIGHTS** ───

(continued from p. 288)

Shemonah Esreh serves as a channel and conduit for a specific task. As we say the first blessing (*chonen hada'at*) our goal is to bring down wisdom into the world. As we say *refaeinu*, we seek to bring healing to the world. As we say *mevarech hashanim*, we seek to bring down

(continued on p. 294)

> Transcendent within Immanent
> Cleaving to Godliness
> Higher Fear – Awe
> *Haya* and *Yechida*
> World of *Atzilut*

Who is like You, master of mighty deeds, and Who is comparable to You, King Who takes away life and Who gives life and germinates salvation…

the next higher world of *Bria* ("creation," the world of *neshamot*, or "souls"), we are called *noflim*, or "the fallen."

> **Within the Words**
>
> During *Shemonah Esreh*, as we say, *somech noflim* ("support the fallen"), we consider how the souls in the world of *Bria* wish to return to their original spiritual level in *Atzilut* and beyond. They have merely "fallen," and therefore it is relatively easy to support and elevate them to their source. As we say, *rofeh cholim*, we consider the angels and sparks of *yetzirah*. They are "sick" with love of God that they are unable to satiate because of the great distance between them and their true spiritual level. Finally as we say *matir asirim* ("free the imprisoned"), we think of ourselves, "imprisoned" in the world of *Asiya* with little ability to free ourselves and ascend to our true spiritual level. About all of these levels, we continue, "Who is like You, Master of mighty deeds," because it required great "might" for God to "lower" Himself to these low spiritual levels and enable us to elevate and uplift the fallen sparks of the lower three worlds. In fact, it was "against the nature" of God to create such low worlds, but He did so in order to give us an opportunity to ascend and discover Him and experience the spirituality of *Atzilut* and beyond. That is why the words of the *Shemonah Esreh* continue, "King Who takes away life," even before mentioning that He "enlivens." He allowed the "shattering of the vessels" (a form of "death") to take place, and then prompted us to uplift the holy sparks in an act of "enlivening." Our words during *Shemonah Esreh* allude to this process of shattering followed by rectification. And when we achieve the rectification, we experience the words of the prayer, *matzmiach yeshua* ("germinate salvation").

בעש״ת יש להוסיף:

מִי כָמוֹךָ אַב הָרַחֲמָן זוֹכֵר יְצוּרָיו לְחַיִּים בְּרַחֲמִים:

וְנֶאֱמָן אַתָּה לְהַחֲיוֹת מֵתִים.

בָּרוּךְ אַתָּה יְיָ, מְחַיֵּה הַמֵּתִים:

קדושה

קהל, ואחר כך חזן:

נַקְדִּישָׁךְ וְנַעֲרִיצָךְ כְּנֹעַם שִׂיחַ סוֹד שַׂרְפֵי קֹדֶשׁ הַמְשַׁלְּשִׁים לְךָ קְדֻשָּׁה, כַּכָּתוּב עַל יַד נְבִיאֶךָ, וְקָרָא זֶה אֶל זֶה וְאָמַר:

קהל, ואחר כך חזן:

קָדוֹשׁ, קָדוֹשׁ, קָדוֹשׁ יְיָ צְבָאוֹת, מְלֹא כָל הָאָרֶץ כְּבוֹדוֹ:

חזן: לְעֻמָּתָם מְשַׁבְּחִים וְאוֹמְרִים:

קהל, ואחר כך חזן: בָּרוּךְ כְּבוֹד יְיָ מִמְּקוֹמוֹ:

חזן: וּבְדִבְרֵי קָדְשְׁךָ כָּתוּב לֵאמֹר:

קהל, ואחר כך חזן: יִמְלֹךְ יְיָ לְעוֹלָם, אֱלֹהַיִךְ צִיּוֹן לְדֹר וָדֹר הַלְלוּיָהּ:

CHASSIDIC INSIGHTS

(continued from p. 292)

parnassa ("income"). In other words, we seek to bring down the infinite light, available since *Kriat Shema*, and apply it to our specific needs as well as the needs of the world. The sages called this process *yichud z'un* the "unity of the male and female." It is the unity of male and female that brings offspring to the world. This is the unity that bears fruit, in terms of our everyday experience and achievements. While the unity of the *Kriat Shema* makes the infinite light accessible, it is during the *Shemonah Esreh* that we actually put the light to use.

Another way to understand the difference between *Kriat Shema* and the *Shemonah Esreh* is through the instruction given to us by our

(continued on p. 295)

Transcendent within Immanent
Cleaving to Godliness
Higher Fear – Awe
Haya and *Yechida*
World of Atzilut

Between Rosh Hashana and Yom Kippur add:

Who is like You, merciful Father,
Who recalls His creations for life with mercy.

And You are entrusted to enliven the dead.
Blessed are You, Lord, Who enlivens the dead.

KEDUSHAH

Congregation, followed by the cantor:

We sanctify You and we revere You, as in the pleasant, hidden conversation of the holy seraphim, who thrice-mention You in holiness, as written by Your prophets, 'And they called to one another and said':

Congregation, followed by the cantor:

Holy, holy, holy is the Lord of Hosts, the entire earth is full of His glory.

Cantor: And facing them, they praise [God] and say…

Congregation, followed by the cantor: Blessed be the glory of the Lord from His place.

Cantor: And in Your holy words, it is written, saying:

Congregation, followed by the cantor: May the Lord reign forever, Your God of Zion from one generation to the next, Halleluyah!

CHASSIDIC INSIGHTS

(continued from p. 294)

sages, who say that we should pray "to God, and not to His attributes." That is, we should always direct our requests and attention to God as He exists in essence and not to His mere attributes. If that is the case, though, then why does God possess various names, and why do we

(continued on p. 296)

אַתָּה קָדוֹשׁ וְשִׁמְךָ קָדוֹשׁ, וּקְדוֹשִׁים בְּכָל יוֹם יְהַלְלוּךָ סֶּלָה. בָּרוּךְ אַתָּה יְיָ, (בעשי״ת: הַמֶּלֶךְ הַקָּדוֹשׁ:) הָאֵל הַקָּדוֹשׁ:

סובב בתוך ממלא
ספירת הכתר
קמץ (ָ)
עולם האצילות

" The eighteen blessings of the *Shemonah Esreh* correspond to the eighteen vertebrae of the backbone through which is drawn the spinal cord." (*Likutei Torah* of the Alter Rebbe, *parshat Balak*, p. 140)[281]

While reciting the *Shema*, we perform *yichud av v'aim* — "unity of the father and mother" (*chochma* and *bina*). That is, with intense dedication while meditating on the word *echad*, we access the infinite light that transcends the spiritual chain of creation. Our *kavana* ("intention") is to ascend from below to above. However, during *Shemonah Esreh*, we perform *yichud zu'n* — "unity of the male and female" (*Z"a* and *malchut*). That is, we channel the holy light of *chochma* and *bina* (*mochin*) into the vessels (*kelim*) of the ten *sephirot* of *Atzilut*, from above to below. This occurs as we concentrate on the vowels of the name *Havaya* that are specific to each blessing, bringing Godly illumination down to the *sephirot*.[282]

Even though the *Shemonah Esreh* is not among the 613 mitzvot of the Torah, it connects and unites all of the mitzvot together. Each mitzvah is associated with a limb or organ of the body; the 248 positive mitzvot are associated with the organs, while the 365 negative mitzvot are associated with connective tissue. The spinal cord is not counted as one of the organs or limbs of the body. Nevertheless, it connects and unites all of them together. The same is true of the *Shemonah Esreh*. It is not a mitzvah from the Torah, but it provides the spiritual infrastructure that brings unity to our *avodat*

— CHASSIDIC INSIGHTS —

(continued from p. 295)

employ different names and different forms of the same name of God when praying to Him?

One of the answers is that the directive to pray "to Him, and not to His attributes" applies to the *Kriat Shema*. That is, as we recite the

(continued on p. 297)

Transcendent within
Immanent
Sephira of *Keter*
Vowelization: *Kametz*
World of *Atzilut*

YOU ARE HOLY, AND YOUR NAME IS HOLY, AND HOLY creatures praise You every day, forever. Blessed are You, Lord the holy God.

(Between Rosh Hashana and Yom Kippur:

Blessed are You, Lord, the holy King)

Hashem ("divine service"). That is why, during the *Shemonah Esreh*, we must maintain our intention as we say the specific blessings.

> *Within the Words*
>
> The sages were more stringent regarding our focus and intention during the *Shemonah Esreh* than they were regarding the recitation of the *Shema*. This is curious, because while the *Shema* is a mitzvah from the Torah (and should therefore merit greater stringency), the *Shemonah Esreh* was mandated by the rabbis. The likely explanation is that, during the *Shema*, we transcend the "system" of *seder hishtalshelut* (the "spiritual chain of creation") and therefore we require only general awareness that we are doing a mitzvah.[283] However, during *Shemonah Esreh*, we bring the divine illumination down into the "system" (*seder hishtalshelut*). Even though our words flow spontaneously and automatically, they need focus in order to direct the spiritual flow to the correct "address" (*sephira*) in the system of *seder hishtalshelut,* and to achieve the specific goal of each blessing.

Word Sparks
"You are holy' — alludes to chochma, the beginning of divine revelation. "Your name is holy" alludes to concealed bina..." (Torat Shmuel 5637/1877, V 2, p. 649)

CHASSIDIC INSIGHTS

(continued from p. 296)

Kriat Shema with full devotion and dedication, we direct our attention to God in His very essence. But during the *Shemonah Esreh*, when we wish to pray for our specific needs and desires, we use specific names of God as we pray. We can do that because at this point in prayer, during the *Shemonah Esreh*, we have totally nullified

(continued on p. 298)

אַתָּה חוֹנֵן לְאָדָם דַּעַת, וּמְלַמֵּד לֶאֱנוֹשׁ בִּינָה. חָנֵּנוּ מֵאִתְּךָ חָכְמָה בִּינָה וָדָעַת. בָּרוּךְ אַתָּה יְיָ (לכון: יַהֲוַה), חוֹנֵן הַדָּעַת:

סובב בתוך ממלא
ספירת החכמה
פתח (ְ)
עולם האצילות

> The *Sifri* quotes the verse, "Who is like our God [who is near to us] whenever we call upon Him?"[284] and comments, "but not to His attributes." That is, we do not "call upon" (pray to) His divine attributes, but only to God Himself. (The Alter Rebbe's Siddur with Chasidut, p. 85 [פ"ה])[285]

The early Kabbalists pointed out a difficulty: How is it possible to pray to God Himself? As the Zohar says, "No thought can grasp Him whatsoever…" They resolved this difficulty by suggesting that as we pray to God, we remain aware of His infinite illumination. During the *Shemonah Esreh*, we focus our attention on His infinite light and "direct" it so that it descends to illuminate the universe. The divine illumination descends via His name *Havaya*, which exists on two levels: 1) as undifferentiated light that transcends creation, and 2) as light that descends to illuminate the world. Our task is to focus on His infinite light with intention to bring it down to illuminate the trait associated with each blessing — to bring wisdom down to us while saying *chonen hada'at* ("grace us with knowledge"), to bring down wealth during *mevarech hashanim* ("blessed the yearly [crop]"), and health during *refaeinu* ("heal us"), etc.[286]

─── **CHASSIDIC INSIGHTS** ───

(continued from p. 297)

ourselves and can address God from the best possible position — in which we acknowledge that we are nothing, and that He is everything. This is the power of the *Shemonah Esreh* — we have no existence of our own — and that is why we are able to access His infinite light and direct it to His attributes. At no point do we pray "to His attributes" (the *sephirot*) themselves. We pray to God, asking Him to direct His infinite light into His *sephirot* so that it may affect us in the physical world below. After the long path of prayer, progressing through the "great wind" of the *pesukei dezimra*, traversing the "great noise" of the *Birchot Kriat Shema* and navigating the "great fire" of

(continued on p. 299)

Transcendent within Immanent
Sephira of *Chochma*
Vowelization: *P'tach*
World of *Atzilut*

YOU GRACE MAN WITH KNOWLEDGE, AND TEACH man understanding, grace us with wisdom, understanding and knowledge from You. Blessed are You, Lord, Who grants knowledge.

Nevertheless, the original question remains, because the *Sifri* states that we should call upon (pray to) God directly, and not to His attributes. If the answer is that we should cling to the infinite light as it becomes enclothed in His *sephirot*, why does the *Sifri* not say so openly, rather than instructing us to pray "to Him?" The true answer, which is also mentioned in the *Sifri*, is that the instruction to pray directly to God applies to the first verse of the *Kriat Shema*, when we uplift and devote our soul directly to the One above. That is what is meant by "to Him." This prayer is necessary before we begin the *Shemonah Esreh*, during which our *kavana* is to bring down and direct God's infinite light into each of the ten *sephirot*.

Within the Words

During *Shemonah Esreh*, we focus on His name *Havaya* with specific vowelization that guides His infinite light to the right address within the ten *sephirot*. In that manner, our requests may be answered more efficiently. This is comparable to requesting the King to instruct his appointees. It is important for the King to send our request to the appropriate "ministers." Failure to do so may result in delays and disruptions. Requests for medicine should go to the health department, requests for a loans should go to the treasury, etc… In order to direct our prayers to the correct "appointee," we should know what vowellization to use during the *Shemonah Esreh*.[287]

CHASSIDIC INSIGHTS

(continued from p. 298)

the *Shema* itself, in none of which we found the very essence of Godliness, we ultimately find our voice. It turns out to be a "still small voice" within. And that, the Zohar tells us, is where God is found… This is the attitude of ultimate "awe" in front of the supreme One

(continued on p. 300)

הֲשִׁיבֵנוּ אָבִינוּ לְתוֹרָתֶךָ, וְקָרְבֵנוּ מַלְכֵּנוּ לַעֲבוֹדָתֶךָ, וְהַחֲזִירֵנוּ בִּתְשׁוּבָה שְׁלֵמָה לְפָנֶיךָ. בָּרוּךְ אַתָּה יְיָ (לכון: יֱהֱוֵה), הָרוֹצֶה בִּתְשׁוּבָה:

סובב בתוך ממלא
ספירת בינה
צירי (..)
עולם האצילות

❝ **The sages asked, 'Why do the Jews call upon God and fail to receive answers?' Because when they call out to Him, they do not know how to focus properly on His name…"** (*Imrei Bina* of the Mittler Rebbe, ch. 17 in the introduction)[288]

> The four letters of God's holy name *Havaya* correspond to four levels of contraction that occur as His infinite light descends to the creation. But His name *Havaya* exists on two levels: 1) His essential name above creation, about which the Torah (in Exodus 6:3) says, "And by My essential name *Havaya*, I did not make Myself known [to the forefathers]" and 2) His "active" name within creation, associated with the *kelim* of the World of *Atzilut*. Our task is to bring the attribute from its state of potential in His infinite light down into the *kelim* of *Atzilut*. This occurs as we mention His name *Havaya* during the blessings of the *Shemonah Esreh*. Every time that we say a blessing, we focus upon the appropriate vowelization of His name that will bring His infinite light from above into the *kelim* of the *sephirot* of *Atzilut*.[289]

CHASSIDIC INSIGHTS

(continued from p. 299)

above. It is associated with the world of *Atzilut*, the state of mind of *yirah ila'ah*, and the soul-level of *chaya* (Chasidut tells us that when we say *modim anachnu lach* ("we acknowledge You") during *Shemonah Esreh*, we achieve the soul level of *yechida* as well).

The question that remains, though, is how to meditate during the *Shemonah Esreh*. During *Kriat Shema*, our meditation demands tremendous concentration and devotion to transcend our own personal awareness, and achieve *mesirut nefesh* ("self sacrifice") as we proclaim His oneness and unity. However, how can we meditate when we are in a state of abject *bitul* ("nullification") during the *Shemonah Esreh*? If we have parted with our ego, who is left to think and meditate? The answer, though, is that it is precisely because of the state of

(continued on p. 302)

Transcendent within Immanent
Sephira of Bina
Vowelization: Tziri
World of Atzilut

BRING US BACK, OUR FATHER TO YOUR TORAH, and draw us, our King, to Your service, and return us in total repentance before You.
Blessed be You, Lord, Who desires repentance.

During the blessing *chonen hada'at* ("grace us with knowledge"), we focus on His infinite light with the intention of bringing it down to the attribute of wisdom, which corresponds to the *keli* ("vessel") of *chochma*. We do this by focusing upon the name *Havaya* vowelized with a *patach* (written as an underline). The *patach* (from the word *liftoach* meaning "to open") symbolizes the "opening" of divine illumination as it becomes revealed in our intellect. During the next blessing, *hashiveinu* ("Bring us back"), we seek to bring His infinite light down to the *keli* of *bina* (the process of *teshuva* requires that we analyze our behavior utilizing our power of *bina*). We do this by focusing on the name *Havaya* vowelized with a *tzeiri* (two horizontal dots). During the blessing *selach lanu* ("forgive us"), we seek to bring His infinite light down to the *keli* of *chesed* (the act of forgiving is an act of kindness). We do this by focusing on the name *Havaya* vowelized with a *segol* (three dots in a triangle), symbolizing His infinite kindness. Via the blessing *refaeinu* ("Heal us"), we seek healing by requesting that His infinite light descend to the *keli* of *tiferet* in the form of His name *Havaya* vowelized with a *cholem* (straight vertical line with a dot above it).

Within the Words

By way of illustration, when we want something from the king, we go to the minister who has been appointed over that matter. If we were to go to another minister who had no responsibility for that matter, we would not be successful, since the king appointed each minister over his specific task alone. The *kelim* of the ten *sephirot* are like notes placed in the hands of the ministers, and therefore our job is to ask the king to place the notes in the hands of the correct ministers by focusing on His infinite light and bringing it down to the *sephirot*, using the proper vowelization of His name *Havaya* for each of the eighteen blessings of the *Shemonah Esreh*.[290]

סְלַח לָנוּ אָבִינוּ, כִּי חָטָאנוּ, מְחַל לָנוּ מַלְכֵּנוּ, כִּי פָשָׁעְנוּ, כִּי אֵל טוֹב וְסַלָּח אָתָּה.

בָּרוּךְ אַתָּה יְיָ (לכון: יְהֹוָה), חַנּוּן הַמַּרְבֶּה לִסְלֹחַ:

סובב בתוך ממלא
ספירת חסד
סגול (ֶ)
עולם האצילות

❝ Since we are commanded to call upon God, meaning to His very essence which is not defined or categorized in any manner or form, why does it matter if we are unable to 'focus on His name'? …All Jews call upon His essence…" (*Derech Mitzvotecha* of the *Tzemach Tzedek*, *Shoresh Mitzvat Tefila*, ch. 7, p. 117 קי"ז)[291]

There is a big difference between God's attributes and His names. His attributes (the *sephirot*) are divine emanations, united and one with God, but not associated with His essence. His names, however, are indicative of His very essence. Although they are not His essence, nevertheless, His names are the intermediaries through which His infinite light is channeled to the ten *sephirot*. They enable the divine energy to become enclothed within His *sephirot*, so that He may be called "wise" or "kind", or "powerful", etc. Even so, His essence remains unchanged as previously, simple and complete, without any variation.

The recommendation of the sages to "focus on His name" by using the appropriate vowelization of the name *Havaya* does not constitute praying to His divine "attributes." Rather, we pray directly to God, to His very essence. If our goal is to reveal divine wisdom, for example, the correct address is via the *sephira* of *chochma*. Therefore, we mention His name *Havaya* while mentally focusing on a *patach*

──────── **CHASSIDIC INSIGHTS** ────────

(continued from p. 300)

nullification that we achieve during *Shemonah Esreh* that we are able to channel His infinite light to the appropriate destination. Because we are so nullified, we ask for nothing for ourselves. We therefore become conduits, or channels for His holy light to descend to our lower worlds. We become like a lightning rod, which is a mere piece of metal that, placed in the right location, attracts lightning from

(continued on p. 303)

Transcendent within Immanent
Sephira of Chesed
Vowelization: Segol
World of Atzilut

FORGIVE US, OUR FATHER, FOR WE HAVE SINNED, pardon us our King, for we have transgressed, for You are a kind and forgiving God.

Blessed are You, Lord, gracious One, Who abundantly forgives.

when we wish for His divine light to descend to *chochma*. In this process the attribute of *chochma* is but a tool in the service of His infinite illumination. It emerges, then, that when we utter the blessing, *Baruch Atah Ha*vaya, *chonen hada'at*, while focusing upon His name *Havaya* vowelized with a *patach*, we are truly calling upon God as He is enclothed in the vessel of *chochma*. This is also true of the other vowelizations of His name in relationship to the appropriate *sephirot*.

📖 Within the Words

By way of illustration, if what we request from the king is within reach at the time of our request — for example, if he is in his treasury surrounded by gold and silver — it is easier for him to fulfill our requests than if he were involved in something else at that time. If he is elsewhere, even though we may succeed in diverting his attention in order to grant us a gift from his treasury, it requires a greater degree of merit and prayer, and only then might he turn to our request and respond. But if our request arrives as he is in his treasury, it is easier for him to respond.[292]

─────── CHASSIDIC INSIGHTS ───────

(continued from p. 302)

the atmosphere and passes it on to the ground. Because of our great level of nullification during the *Shemonah Esreh*, we attract His infinite light and conduct it to the appropriate "location" within the ten *sephirot*. However, because we are human beings, blessed with intelligence, we can do better than an inert piece of metal. We can actually choose the "location" to where His holy influx should be directed.

Our sages asked, "Why do the Jews scream to God without receiving answers? Because they do not know how to call Him by His

(continued on p. 306)

רְאֵה נָא בְעָנְיֵנוּ וְרִיבָה רִיבֵנוּ, וּגְאָלֵנוּ מְהֵרָה לְמַעַן שְׁמֶךָ, כִּי אֵל גּוֹאֵל חָזָק אָתָּה. בָּרוּךְ אַתָּה יְיָ (לכוון: יְהוָה), גּוֹאֵל יִשְׂרָאֵל:

סובב בתוך ממלא
ספירת הגבורה
שווה (.)
עולם האצילות

בתענית ציבור בחזרת הש"ץ חזן אומר:

עֲנֵנוּ יְיָ עֲנֵנוּ בְּיוֹם צוֹם תַּעֲנִיתֵנוּ, כִּי בְצָרָה גְדוֹלָה אֲנַחְנוּ, אַל תֵּפֶן אֶל רִשְׁעֵנוּ, וְאַל תַּסְתֵּר פָּנֶיךָ מִמֶּנּוּ, וְאַל תִּתְעַלַּם מִתְּחִנָּתֵנוּ, הֱיֵה נָא קָרוֹב לְשַׁוְעָתֵנוּ, יְהִי נָא חַסְדְּךָ לְנַחֲמֵנוּ, טֶרֶם נִקְרָא אֵלֶיךָ עֲנֵנוּ, כַּדָּבָר שֶׁנֶּאֱמַר: וְהָיָה טֶרֶם יִקְרָאוּ וַאֲנִי אֶעֱנֶה, עוֹד הֵם מְדַבְּרִים וַאֲנִי אֶשְׁמָע, כִּי אַתָּה יְיָ הָעוֹנֶה בְּעֵת צָרָה, פּוֹדֶה וּמַצִּיל בְּכָל עֵת צָרָה וְצוּקָה: בָּרוּךְ אַתָּה יְיָ, הָעוֹנֶה לְעַמּוֹ יִשְׂרָאֵל בְּעֵת צָרָה:

> **The sages asked, 'Why do the Jews call upon God and fail to receive answers? Because when they call out to Him, they do not know how to focus properly on His name. But in the future, 'when they know My name, they will call Me and I will answer them.' From this we deduce that it is necessary to focus properly on His name [and only in this way are we answered].**" (*Torat Shmuel* of the Rebbe Maharash, 5639/1879, vol. 1, p. 32)[293]

> According to Kaballah, the names of God are associated with divine illumination (*orot*), while His attributes are associated with the divine vessels (*kelim*) that contain the illumination. Therefore, "when we call out to Him" (and not to His attributes) in prayer, we focus on the divine illumination that is enclothed in the vessels. Even though the vessels themselves are holy, the source of infinite illumination is higher than the vessels, and qualitatively different. The vessels are associated with the "potential for limitation" that is inherent in the infinite light of God, while the illumination comes from the infinite light that is beyond limitation.

> The infinite light is the "soul" of His attribute of kindness. We refer to the infinite light by the name *El* or *Eloka* when it descends to the attribute of *chesed*. We don't apply God's names to the attribute itself, God forbid, since the attribute is merely a vessel to

Transcendent within Immanent
Sephira of *Gevura*
Vowelization: *She'va*
World of *Atzilut*

SEE, PLEASE, OUR POVERTY, AND FIGHT OUR BATTLES, and quickly redeem us for the sake of Your name, for You, God are a powerful Redeemer. Blessed are You, God, Redeemer of Israel.

On a Public Fast Day the following is said by the chazzan during the repetition of the Amidah:

Answer us, Lord, answer us on our fast day, for we are in great distress; Turn not toward our wickedness, do not conceal Your countenance from us, nor hide from our pleas. Be near to our cries, let Your kindness comfort us. Answer us before we call upon You, as in the verse, "And it will be that even before they call, I will answer, even while they speak, I will hear." For, You are the Lord Who answers in times of distress, [Who] redeems and rescues from every season of trouble and crisis. Blessed are You, Lord, Who answers His people Israel in times of distress.

contain the "soul." The same applies to the name *Elokim* in relation to the attribute of *gevura*. The same is true of all of the divine names; even though each applies to a specific divine attribute, our focus is on the infinite light that is the soul of the attributes, as we pray. However, such a high infinite illumination needs an intermediary in order to descend and become enclothed in His attributes. The intermediary is called *Erech Apayim* (*Erech Anpin*). It includes His infinite light, while it is also the source of His attributes.[294]

📖 *Within the Words*

By way of illustration, the king may choose to give a gift with his right hand, or his left hand. They are two separate hands, but it is the king who gives, and not his hands. The overall vitality of his body is also invested in his hands. Similarly, we focus on the infinite light of the King above when we make our requests. The infinite light is simple and undifferentiated, but it must descend and become invested in His attributes in order to achieve our aims, such as to heal, or provide income, etc...[295]

רְפָאֵנוּ יְיָ וְנֵרָפֵא, הוֹשִׁיעֵנוּ וְנִוָּשֵׁעָה כִּי תְהִלָּתֵנוּ אָתָּה, וְהַעֲלֵה אֲרוּכָה וּרְפוּאָה שְׁלֵמָה לְכָל מַכּוֹתֵינוּ. כִּי אֵל מֶלֶךְ רוֹפֵא נֶאֱמָן וְרַחֲמָן אָתָּה.

בָּרוּךְ אַתָּה יְיָ (לכוון: יהוה), רוֹפֵא חוֹלֵי עַמּוֹ יִשְׂרָאֵל:

סוֹבב בְּתוֹךְ מְמַלֵּא
סְפִירַת הַתִּפְאֶרֶת
חוֹלָם (׳)
עוֹלָם הָאֲצִילוּת

> **The theme of 'whenever we call upon Him'** applies to the selfless devotion that we experience during the *Kriat Shema*, when we must dedicate ourselves to God alone and not to His attributes but rather to His divine essence. The theme of 'focusing on His name' applies to the *Shemonah Esreh*, during which we must focus on His name during the blessings. (*Sefer Maamorim* 5654/1894 of the Rebbe Rashab, p. 117)[296]

There are several names of God associated with every divine attribute (*sephira*). For example, we find the name *Kel* is associated with the *sephira* of *chesed*, and that the name *Havaya* vowelized with a *segol* is also associated with *chesed*. Regarding *gevura*, we find the name *Elokim* as well as the name *Havaya* vowelized with a *sh'va*. The difference between the vowelized *Havaya* of each *sephira* and the other name associated with the *sephira* is the distinction between the inner dimension (*pnimiyut*) of the *keli* ("vessel") and the external aspect of the *keli*. The vowelized name *Havaya* is associated with the inner dimensions of the vessel of the *sephira*, while the other name is associated with the external dimensions.[297]

The name *Havaya* is associated with the Godly light (*ohr*) that illuminates the vessel of *chesed*. Before it enters the vessel, the light is simple and undefined. Since it is undifferentiated, it is

─────── **CHASSIDIC INSIGHTS** ───────

(continued from p. 303)

name." Although the high priest used to announce the name of God as he exited the Holy of holies once every year on Yom Kippur, the proper pronunciation was promptly forgotten by all who heard it. The world was not and is not yet a proper receptacle for such a high level of spirituality and therefore we simply forgot how to say His name

(continued on p. 309)

Transcendent within Immanent
Sephira of Tiferet
Vowelization: Cholem
World of Atzilut

Heal us, Lord, and we will be healed, rescue us and we will be saved, for You are our Praise, and bring complete cure and healing to all of our wounds, for You God are King, a trustworthy and merciful healer.

Blessed are You, Lord,
Who heals the sick of His people, Israel.

---

represented by the name *Havaya* without vowelization at all. The name *Havaya* takes on vowelization only when it becomes associated with the inner dimensions of the vessel. It then unites the undifferentiated illumination with the inner dimensions of the vessel, which is why it retains the name *Havaya* as it takes on a vowelization. Aside from their divine names, the *sephirot* also have several "nicknames," such as "merciful" and "beneficent" for the *sephira* of *chesed*, and "strong" and "capable" for the *sephira* of *gevura*. The "nicknames" are associated with the external aspects of the *sephirot*, of which there are several levels.[298]

> 📖 *Within the Words*
>
> The process of "having intention" as we mention His name *Havaya* and apply the appropriate vowelization, occurs *bederech ma'avar* ("in passing"). That is, although we have in mind the final "target" of the divine illumination, we remain aware of its ultimate source in God's infinite light. To illustrate, when we petition the mortal king, we do so through the particular minister who is appointed over the matter with which we are concerned. Nevertheless, the fulfillment of our request comes from the king himself, even though it goes through his minister. The minister does not fulfill our request of his own volition; the response merely passes "through" him from the king. Similarly, our request from the King above is addressed to Him — His transcendent illumination (infinite light) — but it descends to us through the ten *sephirot* of *Atzilut*, "in passing," until it reaches us.[299]

בָּרֵךְ עָלֵינוּ יְיָ אֱלֹהֵינוּ אֶת הַשָּׁנָה הַזֹּאת וְאֶת כָּל מִינֵי תְבוּאָתָהּ לְטוֹבָה,

קיץ: וְתֵן בְּרָכָה   חורף: טַל וּמָטָר לִבְרָכָה

עַל פְּנֵי הָאֲדָמָה, וְשַׂבְּעֵנוּ מִטּוּבֶךָ, וּבָרֵךְ שְׁנָתֵנוּ כַּשָּׁנִים הַטּוֹבוֹת לִבְרָכָה, כִּי אֵל טוֹב וּמֵטִיב אַתָּה וּמְבָרֵךְ הַשָּׁנִים:

בָּרוּךְ אַתָּה יְיָ (לכוון: יְהוָה), מְבָרֵךְ הַשָּׁנִים:

סובב בתוך ממלא
ספירת הנצח
חיריק (.)
עולם האצילות

> "God is holy and removed altogether, way beyond the origin and source of the spiritual evolution of the worlds *ABY"A*. He is not in the category of 'worlds' at all, and it is not even appropriate to say about Him that He is transcendent, beyond the spiritual chain of *ABY"A*… He is holy and exalted in and of Himself." (*Yom Tov shel Rosh Hashana 5666/1906* of the Rebbe Rashab, p. 182, or p. 242 in the new edition)[300]

When we say (in the first blessing of *Shemonah Esreh*, which requires focus and intention), "You are holy, and Your name is holy," why do we separate God and His name into two different levels? Why not just say, "You and Your name are holy"? When we mention "You," it is as if we are addressing God Himself, in His very essence. On that level, He is completely holy and removed, without any connection with creation. However, the purpose of His name is to relate to creation, so even though His name is holy and removed, it bears a relation to creation. That is why we separate the phrases: "You" are completely holy and removed, but Your "name," while holy and removed is still associated with creation.

During the blessing, *selach lanu* ("forgive us…"), we might ask: Why do we say this blessing during the highest point of prayer, during the twelve middle blessings of the *Shemonah Esreh*? Why do we ask forgiveness exactly when we reach the pinnacle of prayer? We should first ask forgiveness and then pray, because we should have a "clean slate" before we approach God with our personal requests. But, the explanation is that as we pray — progressing through *hoda'ah* ("admission/thankfulness") and then *pesukei dezimra* ("Songs of Praise"), and

Transcendent within Immanent
Sephira of *Netzach*
Vowelization: *Chirik*
World of *Atzilut*

OUR LORD, OUR GOD, BLESS THIS YEAR FOR US, AS well as all its produce for good, and grant

(during the summer) blessing

(during the winter) dew and rain for blessing

upon the face of the earth, and satisfy us out of Your Goodness, and bless our year like other good years of blessing, since You a good and beneficial God and You bless the years.

Bless are you, Lord, Who blesses the years.

Birchot Kriat Shema and finally the *Shema* — we become more sensitized and aware of our faults and deficiencies. We become more aware of our traits that are in need of rectification as we ascend the ladder of prayer. And that is why precisely in the middle of *Shemonah Esreh* is the appropriate time to ask for forgiveness.[301] Furthermore, the three initial blessings (of the intermediate twelve) take us through a process of meditation (during *chonen hadaa't*), followed by *teshuva* (during *hashiveinu*) and finally to asking forgiveness (during *selach lanu*).[302]

> 📖 *Within the Words*
>
> During the twelve intermediate blessings that we say during the *Shemonah Esreh*, we do not really request anything "new." All of our requests are for renewal of spiritual or physical levels that were already present. For example, during *refaeinu* ("heal us…"), we request that God restore that state of health that we previously enjoyed. And during *bareich aleinu* ("bless this year for us…"), we pray that God provide the same level of blessing in our physical sustenance as we enjoyed in the past. The only time that we bring a truly new light into the world is while studying Torah.[303]

SHEMONAH ESREH — THE AMIDAH

CHASSIDIC INSIGHTS

(continued from p. 306)

properly. The proper pronunciation will become revealed only when the *mashiach* (Jewish messiah) arrives. Nevertheless, we do know what God's name is — the essential name of four letters, the name

(continued on p. 310)

סובב בתוך ממלא

(תקע וכו')
ספירת ההוד
קובוץ (ֻ)

(השיבה וכו')
ספירת היסוד
שורוק (וּ)

(ולמלשינים וכו')
ספירת הכתר
קמץ (ָ)

תְּקַע בְּשׁוֹפָר גָּדוֹל לְחֵרוּתֵנוּ, וְשָׂא נֵס לְקַבֵּץ גָּלֻיּוֹתֵינוּ, וְקַבְּצֵנוּ יַחַד מֵאַרְבַּע כַּנְפוֹת הָאָרֶץ לְאַרְצֵנוּ: בָּרוּךְ אַתָּה יְיָ (לכון: יְהֹוָה), מְקַבֵּץ נִדְחֵי עַמּוֹ יִשְׂרָאֵל:

הָשִׁיבָה שׁוֹפְטֵינוּ כְּבָרִאשׁוֹנָה, וְיוֹעֲצֵינוּ כְּבַתְּחִלָּה, וְהָסֵר מִמֶּנּוּ יָגוֹן וַאֲנָחָה, וּמְלוֹךְ עָלֵינוּ אַתָּה יְיָ לְבַדְּךָ בְּחֶסֶד וּבְרַחֲמִים, בְּצֶדֶק וּבְמִשְׁפָּט. בָּרוּךְ אַתָּה יְיָ (לכון: יֻהוֻוּהֻ), מֶלֶךְ אוֹהֵב צְדָקָה וּמִשְׁפָּט:
(בעשי"ת: הַמֶּלֶךְ הַמִּשְׁפָּט:)

וְלַמַּלְשִׁינִים אַל תְּהִי תִקְוָה, וְכָל הַמִּינִים וְכָל הַזֵּדִים כְּרֶגַע יֹאבֵדוּ, וְכָל אוֹיְבֵי עַמְּךָ מְהֵרָה יִכָּרֵתוּ, וּמַלְכוּת הָרִשְׁעָה מְהֵרָה תְעַקֵּר וּתְשַׁבֵּר וּתְמַגֵּר, וְתַכְנִיעַ בִּמְהֵרָה בְיָמֵינוּ. בָּרוּךְ אַתָּה יְיָ (לכון: יָהֳוָה), שֹׁבֵר אֹיְבִים וּמַכְנִיעַ זֵדִים:

עַל הַצַּדִּיקִים וְעַל הַחֲסִידִים, וְעַל זִקְנֵי עַמְּךָ בֵּית יִשְׂרָאֵל, וְעַל פְּלֵיטַת בֵּית סוֹפְרֵיהֶם וְעַל גֵּרֵי הַצֶּדֶק וְעָלֵינוּ, יֶהֱמוּ נָא רַחֲמֶיךָ יְיָ אֱלֹהֵינוּ, וְתֵן שָׂכָר

CHASSIDIC INSIGHTS

(continued from p. 309)

Havaya, and we do use His name *Havaya* every time that we recite a blessing during the *Shemonah Esreh.* (We substitute the pronunciation of His name with the name *Ado noy,* meaning "Lord"). So, why did the sages claim that we do not know how to call Him by His name?

The sages of kaballah and the Chassidic masters gave us an answer. They revealed details of His name that lend us more precision as we pray the *Shemonah Esreh.* They advised us to mentally concentrate not

(continued on p. 312)

> Transcendent within Immanent
>
> (Blow...)
> *Sephira* of *Hod*
> Vowelization: *Kubutz*
>
> (Restore...)
> *Sephira* of *Yesod*
> Vowelization: *Shuruk*
>
> (And let...)
> *Sephira* of *Keter*
> Vowelization: *Komotz*

Blow the great shofar for our freedom, and raise a flag to gather our exiles, and gather us together from all four corners of the earth to our land.

Blessed are You, Lord, Who gathers the scattered remnants of His people, Israel.

Restore our judges to their original status, and our advisors as in the beginning and remove from us all misery and sighing, and reign over us — You alone, Lord — in kindness and mercy, in righteousness and justice.

Blessed are You, Lord,
King Who loves righteousness and justice.
(Between Rosh Hashana and Yom Kippur: the just King)

And let the informers have no hope, and all the heretics and the wicked be immediately destroyed, and all the enemies of Your people quickly excised, and may You quickly uproot, break, crush — and subdue the kingdom of evil swiftly in our days.

Blessed are You, Lord, Who shatters enemies and subdues the wicked.

Regarding the righteous and the pious, and regarding the elders of Your people, the house of Israel, and regarding the remnants of their sages, and regarding the righteous proselytes and regarding us, please arouse Your mercy, Lord our God, and grant goodly reward to all those who

טוֹב לְכָל הַבּוֹטְחִים בְּשִׁמְךָ בֶּאֱמֶת, וְשִׂים חֶלְקֵנוּ עִמָּהֶם, וּלְעוֹלָם לֹא נֵבוֹשׁ כִּי בְךָ בָּטָחְנוּ.
בָּרוּךְ אַתָּה יְיָ (לכון: יֻהְוַוֻהוּ),
מִשְׁעָן וּמִבְטָח לַצַּדִּיקִים:

וְלִירוּשָׁלַיִם עִירְךָ בְּרַחֲמִים תָּשׁוּב, וְתִשְׁכּוֹן בְּתוֹכָהּ כַּאֲשֶׁר דִּבַּרְתָּ, וְכִסֵּא דָוִד עַבְדְּךָ מְהֵרָה לְתוֹכָהּ תָּכִין, וּבְנֵה אוֹתָהּ בְּקָרוֹב בְּיָמֵינוּ בִּנְיַן עוֹלָם.
בָּרוּךְ אַתָּה יְיָ (לכון: יְהֹוָה), בּוֹנֵה יְרוּשָׁלָיִם:

אֶת צֶמַח דָּוִד עַבְדְּךָ מְהֵרָה תַצְמִיחַ, וְקַרְנוֹ תָּרוּם בִּישׁוּעָתֶךָ, כִּי לִישׁוּעָתְךָ קִוִּינוּ כָּל הַיּוֹם.
בָּרוּךְ אַתָּה יְיָ (לכון: יהוה), מַצְמִיחַ קֶרֶן יְשׁוּעָה:

סובב בתוך ממלא

(על הצדיקים וכו' מעמוד הקודם)
ספירת היסוד
שורוק (וּ)

עולם האצילות
(ולירושלים וכו')
ספירת ההוד
קובוץ (ֻ)

(את צמח וכו')
ספירת הנצח
חיריק (ִ)

CHASSIDIC INSIGHTS

(continued from p. 310)

only upon the letters of His name, but also on the vowels. They revealed that for every *sephira*, there is a special vowellization of His four-letter name that should be applied. Each of the blessings corresponds to one of the ten *sephirot*, and it is to that *sephira* that we must direct His infinite light as we pray the *Shemonah Esreh*. For example, during the blessing *chonen hada'at*, we wish to bring "wisdom" down into the world, through the *sephira* of *chochma*. During *hashiveinu*, we wish to arouse *tshuva* via the *sephira* of *bina*. During *selach lanu*, we wish to bring down forgiveness through the *sephira* of *chesed*. During the blessing, *goel Yisrael*, we wish to bring redemption to the world via the *sephira* of *gevura*. And during *refa'einu*, we wish to bring down healing via the *sephira* of *tiferet*, and sustenance during the blessing *Bareich aleinu* via the *sephira* of *netzach*. In other words, all of the blessings correspond to one of the *sephirot*. And it is by applying the correct vowellizations to His name during each blessing that we are able to

(continued on p. 313)

Transcendent within Immanent

(Regarding...
from prev. page)
Sephira of *Yesod*
Vowelization: *Shuruk*
World of *Atzilut*

(And return...)
Sephira of *Hod*
Vowelization: *Kubutz*

(Speedily grow...)
Sephira of *Netzach*
Vowelization: *Chirik*

truly trust in Your name, and place our portion among them, and let us never be disgraced, for in You we trust.

Blessed are You, Lord, the support and fortress for the righteous.

AND RETURN IN COMPASSION TO YOUR CITY, Jerusalem, and dwell in it as You once spoke, and speedily establish the throne of Your servant, David within it, and build it soon in our days, as an eternal edifice.

Blessed are You, Lord, Builder of Jerusalem.

SPEEDILY GROW THE SPROUT OF DAVID, YOUR servant, and raise his profile of Your salvation, for it is Your salvation that we long for all day.

Blessed are You, Lord, Who grows the profile of salvation.

CHASSIDIC INSIGHTS

(continued from p. 312)

direct the holy influx to its source in the *sephirot*. And then, ultimately His holy influx will descend to us and have a positive influence in the world. (See *Derech Mitzvotecha* of the *Tzemach Tzedek, Shoresh Mitzvat Tefila,* Chapters 16-17, pp 123-124)

The source of the vowelization of the name *Havaya* within the *Shemonah Esreh* is the *Sha'ar Hakavanot* ("Gate of Intentions") authored by Rabbi Chaim Vital from the teachings of the Ari.[x] Here are a few excerpts:

- The blessing that begins *Chonen hada'at* ("You grant wisdom to man...") corresponds to the *sephira* of *chochma* ... now it is already known[xi] that each and every *sephira* contains a specific name *Havaya* with its own vowelization. And they are as follows: the name

(continued on p. 315)

שְׁמַע קוֹלֵנוּ יְיָ אֱלֹהֵינוּ, אָב הָרַחֲמָן, רַחֵם עָלֵינוּ, וְקַבֵּל בְּרַחֲמִים וּבְרָצוֹן אֶת תְּפִלָּתֵנוּ, כִּי אֵל שׁוֹמֵעַ תְּפִלּוֹת וְתַחֲנוּנִים אָתָּה, וּמִלְּפָנֶיךָ מַלְכֵּנוּ רֵיקָם אַל תְּשִׁיבֵנוּ. כִּי אַתָּה שׁוֹמֵעַ תְּפִלַּת כָּל פֶּה.

בָּרוּךְ אַתָּה יְיָ (לכון: יוּהוּוּוּהוּ יְהֹוָה), שׁוֹמֵעַ תְּפִלָּה:

סובב בתוך ממלא
ספירת התפארת
חשק (חולם-שוא-קמץ)

❝ **When the matter touches the very essence of our soul, it bears no relation to our conscious faculties, and we lack even the ability to cry out loud. All that we are capable of doing is standing still like a rock, totally nullified within. This is the inaudible scream of the heart that transcends the audible cry of a voice. In general, it is the voice of prayer…"** (*Sefer Maamorim* 5669/1909 of the Rebbe Rashab, pp. 99-101)[304]

> Throughout Jewish history, we have experienced different "styles" of prayer. While the Temples stood, we came to "see" Godliness as well as to be seen (by God). We had the power to gaze upon the spiritual source of creation and how it "is, was and will be," simultaneously. This is the illumination of the name *Havaya*, shining from above creation into our souls. Likewise, in the Temple, the High Priest would pronounce God's name as it is written and that would produce an experience of *yichuda ila'ah* ("higher consciousness") within us in which God is the foreground and creation is in the background. This occurred during the three festivals and the revelation remained with us for the entire year. Another effect of hearing the essential name of God was to produce an awareness of how God renews and refreshes the creation at every instant.[305]

> With the destruction of the Temple and the advent of *galut* ("exile"), the power of spiritual vision disappeared, and our style of prayer switched to "hearing." We now serve God by using our intellect to understand spiritual concepts and to meditate upon Godliness. This takes place from "afar," since intellectual pursuit occurs from an "objective distance." Rather than experience the essence of Godliness, we merely become aware of God's existence. The result is that rather than "clinging" and "cleaving" to God, we suffice with intellectual

Transcendent within Immanent
Sephira of *Tiferet*
Vowel: Chashak
(*Cholem-Sh'va-Komotz*)

LISTEN TO OUR VOICE, LORD OUR GOD; MERCIFUL Father have mercy upon us, and accept our prayer in compassion and goodwill, for You are God Who hears prayers and supplications. From before You, our King, do not turn us away empty-handed, for You hear the prayers of every mouth.

Blessed are You, Lord, Who hears prayer.

---

stimulation that filters down to our emotions, stimulating love and fear of God.

> *Within the Words*
>
> These days, we lack even the power of spiritual hearing. All that is left is the "power of imagination" (*koach hamedameh*), which is the lowest rung of "hearing." We are compared to "dreamers," since we are so lacking in conscious ability to apprehend Godliness that we are capable of imagining two totally incongruent topics at one time. That is why we are capable of praying and then acting in a manner that is totally incongruent to our prayers. Still, the inaudible voice of prayer that emerges from the walls of our heart and the essence of our soul brings down a new light and revelation that changes the world, and this is the main expression of prayer.

CHASSIDIC INSIGHTS

(continued from p. 313)

Havaya with a *kometz* corresponds to *keter*; the name *Havaya* with a *patach* corresponds to *chochma*; *Havyaya* with *tziri* corresponds to *bina*. And, therefore, as you say the words *Baruch Atah Havaya chonen hada'at*, you should focus on this name *Havaya* entirely vowelized with a *patach*, since it is associated with *chochma*, as mentioned.

- The blessing beginning with *Hashiveinu* ("Return us...") corresponds to *bina*, but one must focus on the *chesed* within *bina* ... and therefore one should focus on the name *Havaya* vowelized with a *segol* [and not *tziri*] while reciting *Hashiveinu avinu leToratecha* ... And while reciting the name *Havaya* that concludes this blessing,

(continued on p. 317)

❝ Every generation, we are obligated to see ourselves as if we emerged from Egypt. Not merely every generation, but each and every day, we are obligated to see ourselves as if that very day, we emerged from Egypt…And our daily prayers are arranged accordingly❞ (*Torat Shmuel* 5631/1871 of the Rebbe Maharash, vol. 1, pp. 275-277)

סובב בתוך ממלא
דביקות באלקות
יראה עילאה
חיה-ויחידה
עולם האצילות

When asleep, we are as if in prison. Our soul temporarily vacates our body, leaving nothing more than an impression of life in our body, and only when we begin praying in the morning does our soul return to our body to provide vitality and spiritual sustenance. At that point, we begin to pray, saying *Hodu* — "We acknowledge/thank the Lord…" Our prayers begin with acknowledgment alone, similar to simple faith in God. We acknowledge that He is the King, even before we are aware that it is true. We then launch into praises of God, lauding Him in every possible way, such as, "He lowers the wicked down to the ground," "He takes revenge," etc. These phrases are similar to the ten plagues with which God afflicted the Egyptians. Then, before reading of the splitting of the Reed Sea (during *pesukei dezimra*), we recite passages recording the lead-up up to the exodus, and then finally we recite the "Song of the Sea," which itself is a model for the exodus from Egypt. That enables us to say *Barchu* and begin to recite the *Birchot Kriat Shema*, which is the refinement of the animal soul. Our goal is that the animal soul should also agree to nullify itself before God. This part of prayers parallels the counting of the *omer* during which we purify and uplift our animal soul. That process leads us to the giving of the Torah during the *Kriat Shema*. *Shema Yisrael* is parallel to the first commandment of "I am the Lord your God," and "the Lord is one" is parallel to the commandment of "You shall not have other Gods…"

In the second paragraph of the *Kriat Shema*, we mention the "anger" of God, which seems to have no place in our prayers. The *Kriat Shema* is all about nullification to God and His oneness, so why mention anger? But in reality, the "anger" is directed at whatever prevents us from developing *bitul* and recognizing the oneness and unity of God. When we meditate well and deeply on His unity, we may become filled with anger and frustration over the opposite of Godliness in the world. It is toward those opposing forces that the anger in the second paragraph of the *Kriat Shema* is directed. There is an inner battle taking place, and the "anger" that we mention in

Transcendent within Immanent
Cleaving to Godliness
Higher Fear – Awe
Haya and Yechida
World of Atzilut

the second paragraph help us to focus on our battle against the *yetzer harah*, or "evil inclination" that is inside of us. The war against the *yetzer harah* is equivalent to the war against Amalek that the Jews waged after the exodus, but before receiving the Torah.

📖 Within the Words

However, there is a difference between the war within us, and the war that took place historically between the Jews and Amalek. The historic war took place after the exodus from Egypt, but before the Jews received the Torah. We, however, recite the second paragraph of the *Shema* (alluding to the war with Amalek) after receiving the Torah. The reason is that the historical war was fought by Moshe and Yehoshua. However, we have a spark of Moshe and Yehoshua within us, that is already part of our constitution, and we have already received the Torah, so our "struggle" with Amalek comes at a later stage, represented by the second paragraph of the *Kriat Shema*, after *matan Torah*. Furthermore, we are instructed to go into the *amidah*, or *Shemonah Esreh*, and not to interrupt our prayer, even if a "snake is wrapped around our heel." The "snake" is the *yetzer harah*, or evil inclination. The snake has already been defeated, since during the second paragraph of the *Kriat Shema* we fought against it with the powers of Moshe and Yehoshua that we have at our disposal. And just as Yehoshua "weakened" Amalek, so the *yetzer harah* is weakened after the *Kriat Shema* (the "war on Amalek"), and all the "snake" can do is to wrap itself around our heel (our lower extremities) — it cannot affect our intellect or emotion in any way. And therefore, we are instructed to continue our prayers "even if a snake is wrapped around our foot," because the snake (the *yetzer harah*) has already been neutralized and nothing seriously negative can come from it.

CHASSIDIC INSIGHTS

(continued from p. 315)

one should focus on the vowel *tziri*, since it corresponds to *bina* as it descends to *malchut*.

- *Selach lanu avinu* ("Forgive us, our Father...") corresponds to *chesed*, and therefore the name *Havaya* at the conclusion of the blessing takes on the *segol*.

(continued on p. 323)

רְצֵה יְיָ אֱלֹהֵינוּ בְּעַמְּךָ יִשְׂרָאֵל וְלִתְפִלָּתָם שְׁעֵה, וְהָשֵׁב הָעֲבוֹדָה לִדְבִיר בֵּיתֶךָ, וְאִשֵּׁי יִשְׂרָאֵל וּתְפִלָּתָם בְּאַהֲבָה תְקַבֵּל בְּרָצוֹן, וּתְהִי לְרָצוֹן תָּמִיד עֲבוֹדַת יִשְׂרָאֵל עַמֶּךָ:

סובב בתוך ממלא
דביקות באלקות
יראה עילאה
ויחידה
עולם האצילות

בראש חודש וחול המועד מוסיפים:

אֱלֹהֵינוּ וֵאלֹהֵי אֲבוֹתֵינוּ, יַעֲלֶה וְיָבֹא וְיַגִּיעַ, וְיֵרָאֶה וְיֵרָצֶה וְיִשָּׁמַע, וְיִפָּקֵד וְיִזָּכֵר זִכְרוֹנֵנוּ וּפִקְדוֹנֵנוּ וְזִכְרוֹן אֲבוֹתֵינוּ, וְזִכְרוֹן מָשִׁיחַ בֶּן דָּוִד עַבְדֶּךָ, וְזִכְרוֹן יְרוּשָׁלַיִם עִיר קָדְשֶׁךָ, וְזִכְרוֹן כָּל עַמְּךָ בֵּית יִשְׂרָאֵל לְפָנֶיךָ, לִפְלֵיטָה לְטוֹבָה, לְחֵן וּלְחֶסֶד וּלְרַחֲמִים לְחַיִּים טוֹבִים וּלְשָׁלוֹם בְּיוֹם

רֹאשׁ הַחֹדֶשׁ / חַג הַמַּצּוֹת / חַג הַסֻּכּוֹת הַזֶּה.

זָכְרֵנוּ יְיָ אֱלֹהֵינוּ בּוֹ לְטוֹבָה וּפָקְדֵנוּ בוֹ לִבְרָכָה וְהוֹשִׁיעֵנוּ בוֹ לְחַיִּים טוֹבִים וּבִדְבַר יְשׁוּעָה וְרַחֲמִים חוּס וְחָנֵּנוּ וְרַחֵם עָלֵינוּ וְהוֹשִׁיעֵנוּ, כִּי אֵלֶיךָ עֵינֵינוּ, כִּי אֵל מֶלֶךְ חַנּוּן וְרַחוּם אָתָּה:

❝ The thoughts of man in this lower world flow constantly, without interruption, forever. And the letters of supernal Godly thought also flow, as written (in Genesis 2:10), 'And a river emerged from Eden…'"
(Alter Rebbe's Siddur with Chassidut p. 606/ש"ג)306

> The verse, "And a river emerged from Eden…" alludes to the two sephirot of chochma and bina, which are called in the Zohar, "two fast friends who never part company." That is, the process of renewal of the creation from nothing (ayn, within chochma) to something (yesh, in bina) is a constant process that is ongoing and occurs beyond time. And since Jewish souls themselves come from the same level that is beyond time and space, they are very aware of the constant renewal of creation from nothing to something.

> Our awareness of hitchadshut, the ongoing renewal and re-creation of the universe, comes from our Godly soul, that transcends time and space. However, when the Godly soul descends to become enclothed in our animal soul, we lose our conscious awareness of the ongoing renewal of creation. Instead, we perceive a physical world without spiritual input. Therefore, all we can do is admit or acknowledge (modeh) that He does indeed create and enliven the world from nothing to something at all times. We do not see or perceive the process, but we know that it takes place.

Transcendent within Immanent
Cleaving to Godliness
Higher Fear — Awe
Yechida
Atzilut World of

FIND FAVOR, LORD OUR GOD IN YOUR PEOPLE, ISRAEL, and turn to their prayers, and restore the service to Your glorious house, and lovingly accept the offerings and prayers of Israel, and let the service of Your people Israel always find favor.

On Rosh Hodesh and Chol Hamoed add:

Our God and God of our forefathers, may there ascend and come and arrive, be seen and accepted and heard, recalled and remembered before You our remembrances and our recollection, and the remembrance of our forefathers, and the remembrance of Mashiach, son of David Your servant, and the remembrance of Jerusalem, Your holy city, and the remembrance of Your entire people, the house of Israel, before You, for positive deliverance, for grace and kindness and compassion and good life and for peace, on this day of

Rosh Hodesh / Festival of Matzot / Festival of Succot

Remember us, Lord our God for the good, and recall us for blessing, and help us for good life. With promise of salvation and mercy, have compassion upon us, and be merciful with us and save us, for our eyes are directed to You, since your God are a merciful and compassionate King.

📖 *Within the Words*

As we say *modim anachnu lach* ("we acknowledge You") during the *Shemonah Esreh*, we bow from the waist and actualize the highest level of our soul — the *yechida sh'b'nefesh*. This is curious, because the sages said that this section of the prayers corresponds *to hoda'ah sh'b'hoda'ah* — "admission within acknowledgment." That is, our awareness of spirituality at this point is so low that all we can do is admit that we must acknowledge God's presence. If we had some intellectual awareness, we would be able to admit that God is the omniscient Creator. But, when we lack even basic awareness, all we can do is "admit" that we really should understand and know Him better. This is called *hoda'ah sh'b'hoda'ah* — "admission within acknowledgment" — and it occurs at the highest point of

וְתֶחֱזֶינָה עֵינֵינוּ בְּשׁוּבְךָ לְצִיּוֹן בְּרַחֲמִים. בָּרוּךְ אַתָּה יְיָ, הַמַּחֲזִיר שְׁכִינָתוֹ לְצִיּוֹן:

מוֹדִים אֲנַחְנוּ לָךְ, שָׁאַתָּה הוּא יְיָ אֱלֹהֵינוּ וֵאלֹהֵי אֲבוֹתֵינוּ לְעוֹלָם וָעֶד צוּר חַיֵּינוּ, מָגֵן יִשְׁעֵנוּ, אַתָּה הוּא לְדוֹר וָדוֹר נוֹדֶה לְּךָ וּנְסַפֵּר תְּהִלָּתֶךָ, עַל חַיֵּינוּ הַמְּסוּרִים בְּיָדֶךָ, וְעַל נִשְׁמוֹתֵינוּ הַפְּקוּדוֹת לָךְ, וְעַל נִסֶּיךָ שֶׁבְּכָל יוֹם עִמָּנוּ, וְעַל נִפְלְאוֹתֶיךָ וְטוֹבוֹתֶיךָ שֶׁבְּכָל עֵת, עֶרֶב וָבֹקֶר וְצָהֳרָיִם, הַטּוֹב, כִּי לֹא כָלוּ רַחֲמֶיךָ, הַמְרַחֵם, כִּי לֹא תַמּוּ חֲסָדֶיךָ, כִּי מֵעוֹלָם קִוִּינוּ לָךְ:

📖 *Within the Words*

our prayers. As At the moment we admit that we should know and understand God even though we don't, we become a vessel for revelation of the highest levels of Godliness. When we admit that we should have more Godly awareness but we are incapable, that's when the unlimited, undefinable light from above penetrates our soul.

❝ We say, "You are the good, for Your mercy is unceasing, the merciful, for Your kindness is unending..." At first glance, this appears like a case of "mixed adjectives," and we should rather say, "You are the Good, for your kindness is unending, the merciful for Your mercy is unceasing..."
(Torat Shmuel 5637/1877 of the Rebbe Maharash, V 1, pp. 168-70).

The source of all divine influence is *Tov* ("good"), and it comes in a variety of forms (as alluded in the verse, "Remembrance of Your many goodnesses" — Psalms 145:7). *Tov* — "good" — is associated with Yoseph the *tzaddik*, who is the symbol of "good" and beneficence in the Torah, since he provided "good" to his family and to the people of Egypt. The Torah tells us that *tzaddikim* in general are associated with the *sephira* of *yesod*, which channels divine influence (*tov*) from the higher *sephirot* into the creation. There are five *partzufim*, or "structures" of *sephirot* in the world of Atzilut. They are, *keter*, *chochma*, *bina*, the six *sephirot* of *z'a* (*chesed* through *yesod*), and *malchut*. With each *partzuf*, or structure, are associated three 'vectors,' or channels of influence (according to *Mishnat Chasidim*, *Masechta leil*

Transcendent within Immanent
Cleaving to Godliness
Higher Fear – Awe
Haya and *Yechida*

AND MAY OUR EYES BEHOLD YOUR RETURN TO ZION IN mercy. Blessed are You, Lord, Who returns His Divine Presence to Zion.

WE GIVE THANKS TO YOU, SINCE YOU ARE THE LORD our God and the God of our forefathers forever, the rock of our lives, shield of our salvation, in every generation. We acknowledge You and narrate Your praises, for our lives that are placed in Your hands, and for our souls that are entrusted to You, and for Your miracles that occur every day among us, and for the wonders and kindnesses that occur every moment; evening and morning and noon. You are the Good, for Your mercy is unceasing, the compassionate One, for Your kindness does not stop, forever we have hope in You.

Pesach 12:2, the three are "external, middle, and internal" to each *partzuf*). Since there are five *partzufim*, each with three 'vectors,' the result is a total of fifteen channels of "good," that we mention on the night of Pesach when reciting, "How many degrees of goodness."

The motivation to be "good" to His world goes all the way to the essence of God, since it is the "nature of the Good to do good." Therefore, His ultimate, essential *tov* is the source of all the good and mercy in the world. Specifically, His essential *tov* is the source of the thirteen attributes of mercy, which are contractions of His goodness in order to bring it down from its supremely high state in His essence, to the worlds, both spiritual and physical. When His mercy descends to this world, it becomes the source of good and blessing in the world. What we see here are two kinds of "good." To begin with, His good descends indiscriminately, to the entire creation. That is the good that we refer to with the words, "You are the good…" After His good has descended via the contractions of the thirteen attributes of mercy, it becomes "good" for specific recipients. The purpose of the contraction is to become more specific, and therefore it is those who specifically "search" for and look for His beneficence, and transform themselves into vessels, who receive the second, more "internal" level of His good, in this world. About that level of good, we say, "Your kindness is unending."

מודים דרבנן

מוֹדִים אֲנַחְנוּ לָךְ, שָׁאַתָּה הוּא יְיָ אֱלֹהֵינוּ וֵאלֹהֵי אֲבוֹתֵינוּ, אֱלֹהֵי כָל בָּשָׂר, יוֹצְרֵנוּ, יוֹצֵר בְּרֵאשִׁית, בְּרָכוֹת וְהוֹדָאוֹת לְשִׁמְךָ הַגָּדוֹל וְהַקָּדוֹשׁ, עַל שֶׁהֶחֱיִיתָנוּ וְקִיַּמְתָּנוּ, כֵּן תְּחַיֵּנוּ וּתְקַיְּמֵנוּ, וְתֶאֱסוֹף גָּלֻיּוֹתֵינוּ לְחַצְרוֹת קָדְשֶׁךָ, וְנָשׁוּב אֵלֶיךָ לִשְׁמוֹר חֻקֶּיךָ, וְלַעֲשׂוֹת רְצוֹנֶךָ, וּלְעָבְדְּךָ בְּלֵבָב שָׁלֵם, עַל שֶׁאָנוּ מוֹדִים לָךְ, בָּרוּךְ אֵל הַהוֹדָאוֹת:

בחנוכה ופורים מוסיפים:

וְעַל הַנִּסִּים וְעַל הַפֻּרְקָן וְעַל הַגְּבוּרוֹת וְעַל הַתְּשׁוּעוֹת וְעַל הַנִּפְלָאוֹת שֶׁעָשִׂיתָ לַאֲבוֹתֵינוּ בַּיָּמִים הָהֵם בַּזְּמַן הַזֶּה:

בחנוכה:

בִּימֵי מַתִּתְיָהוּ בֶּן יוֹחָנָן כֹּהֵן גָּדוֹל, חַשְׁמוֹנָאִי וּבָנָיו, כְּשֶׁעָמְדָה מַלְכוּת יָוָן הָרְשָׁעָה, עַל עַמְּךָ יִשְׂרָאֵל, לְהַשְׁכִּיחָם תּוֹרָתֶךָ וּלְהַעֲבִירָם מֵחֻקֵּי רְצוֹנֶךָ, וְאַתָּה בְּרַחֲמֶיךָ הָרַבִּים, עָמַדְתָּ לָהֶם בְּעֵת צָרָתָם, רַבְתָּ אֶת רִיבָם, דַּנְתָּ אֶת דִּינָם, נָקַמְתָּ אֶת נִקְמָתָם,

---

📖 *Within the Words*

"When he waters the field, he provides water for every plant. When he hoes the field, he hoes only the good (strong) plants." The phrase during *modim*, "You are the good, for Your mercy…" is an inversion from "good" to two different levels of "mercy" and finally back to "good" again. The initial "good" is His essential nature to be good to all. When He contracts His good through the thirteen levels of mercy in order to descend to creation, His good becomes "mercy" that includes not only *chesed* ("kindness"), but also the *din* ("judgment, contraction") that is necessary to contract and descend. Finally, those who fulfill mitzvoth, learn Torah and pray, becomes the recipients of His ultimate good, in this world. That is why we first mention His good, followed by His mercy and finally by His good once more.

MODIM D'RABBANAN

Transcendent within Immanent
Cleaving to Godliness
Higher Fear – Awe
Haya and Yechida

We give thanks to You, since You are the Lord our God and the God of our forefathers, the God of all flesh, the One Who formed us, and Who formed all creation. We offer blessings and acknowledgement to Your great and holy name, for You have enlivened and sustained us, so may You continue to enliven and sustain us, and gather our exiles to the courts of Your holy Temple. And we will return to You, to keep Your laws and to do Your will, and to serve You whole-heartedly, for which we thank You, blessed is the God of acknowledgements.

On Purim and Chanukah:

For the miracles and for the salvation and for the mighty deeds and for the acts of salvation and for the wonders that You did for our forefathers in those days, at this time:

On Chanuka:

In the days of Matitiyahu, son of Yochanan the High Priest, the Hasmonean and his sons, when the wicked kingdom of Greece rose up against Your people, Israel, in order to make them forget Your Torah and to make them forsake the laws that are Your will, and You in Your great mercy stood up for them in the time of their

--- CHASSIDIC INSIGHTS ---

(continued from p. 317)

- *Re'eh na be'eineinu* ("See now our poverty...") corresponds to *gevura* and therefore the concluding name *Havaya* is vowelized with a *sheva*.
- *Refaeinu* ("Heal us...") is associated with *tiferet* and therefore the concluding *Havaya* is vowelized with a *cholem*.
- *Barcheinu avinu* ("Bless us, our Father...") corresponds to *netzach*, and therefore the concluding *Havaya* is vowelized with a *chirik*.
- *Tekah beshofar* ("Sound the great *shofar*...") corresponds to *hod* and therefore the concluding *Havaya* is vowelized with a *kubutz*.
- *Hashiva shofteinu* ("Return our judges...") corresponds to *yesod* and therefore the concluding *Havaya* is vowelized with a *shuruk*.

(continued on p. 323)

מָסַרְתָּ גִבּוֹרִים בְּיַד חַלָּשִׁים, וְרַבִּים בְּיַד מְעַטִּים, וּטְמֵאִים בְּיַד טְהוֹרִים, וּרְשָׁעִים בְּיַד צַדִּיקִים, וְזֵדִים בְּיַד עוֹסְקֵי תוֹרָתֶךָ. וּלְךָ עָשִׂיתָ שֵׁם גָּדוֹל וְקָדוֹשׁ בְּעוֹלָמֶךָ, וּלְעַמְּךָ יִשְׂרָאֵל עָשִׂיתָ תְּשׁוּעָה גְדוֹלָה וּפֻרְקָן כְּהַיּוֹם הַזֶּה: וְאַחַר כַּךְ בָּאוּ בָנֶיךָ לִדְבִיר בֵּיתֶךָ, וּפִנּוּ אֶת הֵיכָלֶךָ, וְטִהֲרוּ אֶת מִקְדָּשֶׁךָ, וְהִדְלִיקוּ נֵרוֹת בְּחַצְרוֹת קָדְשֶׁךָ. וְקָבְעוּ שְׁמוֹנַת יְמֵי חֲנֻכָּה אֵלּוּ, לְהוֹדוֹת וּלְהַלֵּל לְשִׁמְךָ הַגָּדוֹל:

פורים:

בִּימֵי מָרְדְּכַי וְאֶסְתֵּר בְּשׁוּשַׁן הַבִּירָה, כְּשֶׁעָמַד עֲלֵיהֶם הָמָן הָרָשָׁע, בִּקֵּשׁ לְהַשְׁמִיד לַהֲרוֹג וּלְאַבֵּד אֶת כָּל הַיְּהוּדִים, מִנַּעַר וְעַד זָקֵן, טַף וְנָשִׁים, בְּיוֹם אֶחָד, בִּשְׁלֹשָׁה עָשָׂר לְחֹדֶשׁ שְׁנֵים עָשָׂר, הוּא חֹדֶשׁ אֲדָר וּשְׁלָלָם לָבוֹז. וְאַתָּה בְּרַחֲמֶיךָ הָרַבִּים הֵפַרְתָּ אֶת עֲצָתוֹ, וְקִלְקַלְתָּ אֶת מַחֲשַׁבְתּוֹ, וַהֲשֵׁבוֹתָ לּוֹ גְּמוּלוֹ בְרֹאשׁוֹ. וְתָלוּ אוֹתוֹ וְאֶת בָּנָיו עַל הָעֵץ.

וְעַל כֻּלָּם יִתְבָּרַךְ וְיִתְרוֹמֵם וְיִתְנַשֵּׂא שִׁמְךָ מַלְכֵּנוּ תָּמִיד לְעוֹלָם וָעֶד:

בעשי"ת: וּכְתוֹב לְחַיִּים טוֹבִים כָּל בְּנֵי בְרִיתֶךָ:

CHASSIDIC INSIGHTS

(continued from p. 323)

- *Velamalshinim* ("And regarding the informers...") corresponds to *keter* ... and therefore the *Havaya* of the concluding blessing is vowelized with a *kamatz*.
- *Ve'al hatzaddikim* ("And regarding the righteous...") and the succeeding blessings follow a different order. Until now, all of the ten *sephirot* mentioned were those that are emanated and rectified within *malchut* [of *Atzilut*]. However, from now on, they are the *sephirot* that are within the [lower third of *Atzilut*], in *netzach*, *hod* and *yesod* and the lower two thirds of *tiferet* of *Zeir Anpin* [of *Atzilut*] itself. They illuminate from within *Z"A*, and now their order is from below to above. The blessing *Ve'al hatzadikim* is within the *yesod* of *Z"A* because the righteous are the foundation of the universe

(continued on p. 325)

Transcendent within Immanent
Cleaving to Godliness
Higher Fear – Awe
Haya and *Yechida*

troubles. You fought their fights, judged their judgments, exacted their revenge. You delivered the strong in the hands of the weak, the many in the hands of the few, and the impure into the hands of the pure, and the wicked into the hands of the righteous, and the iniquitous in the hands of those keeping Your Torah. And as for You, You made a good and holy name for Yourself in Your world, and for Your people Israel You provided a great salvation and rescue to this very day. And afterward, Your children entered the shrine of Your holy house, and emptied out Your chambers, and purified Your dwelling place, and kindled candles in Your holy courtyards, and established these eight days of Chanuka, in order to give thanks and to praise Your great Name.

On Purim:

In the days of Mordecai and Esther in Shushan the capital, when Haman the wicked rose up against them, seeking to destroy, to kill and to eradicate all of the Jews, from youth to elders, children and women in one day, the thirteenth day of the twelfth month, which is the month of Adar, and to plunder their property. And You in Your great mercy, foiled his plan and You frustrated his counsel, and repaid his just deserts on his own head, hanging him and his sons on the tree.

And for all of these things, Your name is blessed,
exalted and uplifted, our King forever and ever.

Between Rosh Hashana and Yom Kippur add:
And inscribe all of the members of
Your covenant for a good life.

--- CHASSIDIC INSIGHTS ---

(continued from p. 324)

and the *tzadik* is called *yesod*. And if so, we must focus on the name *Havaya* in the conclusion of this blessing with the vowelization of a *shuruk*.

(continued on p. 327)

וְכָל הַחַיִּים יוֹדוּךָ סֶּלָה וִיהַלְלוּ שִׁמְךָ הַגָּדוֹל לְעוֹלָם כִּי טוֹב, הָאֵל יְשׁוּעָתֵנוּ וְעֶזְרָתֵנוּ סֶלָה. הָאֵל הַטּוֹב.

בָּרוּךְ אַתָּה יְיָ, הַטּוֹב שִׁמְךָ וּלְךָ נָאֶה לְהוֹדוֹת:

סוֹבב בתוך ממלא
דביקות באלקות
יראה עילאה
חיה-ויחידה

> **'One should always pass through two doorways before praying,'** [*Berachot* 8a]... Although the spirituality that we access with our prayers comes from the very essence of God's infinite light, we must make ourselves into vessels in order to receive it. That is why we must pass through two doorways..." (*Sefer Maamorim 5678* (1918) of the Rebbe Rashab, pp. 244-245)[307]

> The two sides of the first entrance correspond to the *sephirot* of *netzach* and *hod,* the two "advisors." The doorway represents transition to a new realm, and *netzach* and *hod* advise us during the transition. The overhead lintel corresponds to *tiferet*. The three together correspond to Torah, prayer and mitzvot. The two sides of the second entrance correspond to *chesed* and *gevura,* which are the love and fear of God that we develop during meditation. The second overhead lintel corresponds to *bina,* or the meditation that precedes prayer. The three together (of the second entrance) correspond to the three kinds of love: *bechol levavcha, bechol nafshecah* and *bechol meodecha*.

> The first stage of prayer — *hoda'ah* — lays the foundation of Godly service. *Hoda'ah* is the self-effacing acknowledgment with which we enter into a relationship with God. As we pass through the first entrance, we acknowledge Him and also resolve to maintain the connection with Him even after prayers. The acknowledgment and resolution are associated with *hod* and *netzach*. All of this requires mercy (*tiferet*) on our soul which is entrapped in a physical body; this mercy imparted from above by the first lintel. We then pass through the second door, the sides of which impart *chesed* (love of God) and *gevura* (fear of God) that descend so that we may grasp them with our own limited faculties. Both have a source in *bina* (the intellect) which is imparted by the second lintel during meditation.

Transcendent within Immanent
Cleaving to Godliness
Higher Fear – Awe
Haya and *Yechida*

AND ALL LIFE ACKNOWLEDGES YOU FOREVER, AND praises Your great Name eternally, for You are good. Almighty God, You are our salvation and our assistance forever, Almighty God.

Blessed are You, Lord, Magnanimous is Your name, and to You it is pleasant to give thanks.

📖 *Within the Words*

The highest form of *hoda'ah* ("acknowledgment") during prayers occurs as we say within the *Shemonah Esreh, modim anachnu lach* ("we acknowledge You"). But why mention *hoda'ah* during the *Shemonah Esreh* when we already mentioned it during the beginning of our prayers, saying *Hodu Lashem*? The answer is that during the *Shemonah Esreh*, our *hoda'ah* is of a much higher caliber. We do not merely admit that God exists; at this point, we know and acknowledge that His is the only true and real existence — *ayn od milvado* ("there is none other than Him"). That is, after much meditation and contemplation, we conclude that He is beyond our intellectual grasp, and that all we can do is tacitly acknowledge His existence. (This is the intention of *modim anachnu lach* during the *Shemonah Esreh*.) The two doorways through which we enter into prayers are more than merely symbolic — they actually perform the task of transforming us into *kelim* ("vessels") to absorb His infinite light.

--- CHASSIDIC INSIGHTS ---

(continued from p. 325)

- *U'vnei Yerushalayim* ("And Your city Jerusalem...") corresponds to *hod* and the concluding *Havaya* is vocalized with a *kubutz*. And since this blessing is within *hod*, the left side, therefore mentioned within it is the building of Jerusalem, since Jerusalem is associated with the left [*gevura*], as is known. And as we say the words *Vechisei David avdecha meheirah* ("And speedily establish the throne of Your servant David"), we should focus upon what Shamaya and Avtalyon explained to my master [the Ari] one day as he walked to

(continued on p. 328)

ברכת כהנים

הכהנים מברכים את הקהל בחזרת הש"ץ; הקהל עונה אמן

אֱלֹהֵינוּ וֵאלֹהֵי אֲבוֹתֵינוּ, בָּרְכֵנוּ בַבְּרָכָה הַמְשֻׁלֶּשֶׁת, בַּתּוֹרָה הַכְּתוּבָה עַל יְדֵי מֹשֶׁה עַבְדֶּךָ, הָאֲמוּרָה מִפִּי אַהֲרֹן וּבָנָיו כֹּהֲנִים עַם קְדוֹשֶׁךָ כָּאָמוּר:

יְבָרֶכְךָ יְיָ וְיִשְׁמְרֶךָ: (אָמֵן)

יָאֵר יְיָ פָּנָיו אֵלֶיךָ וִיחֻנֶּךָּ: (אָמֵן)

יִשָּׂא יְיָ פָּנָיו אֵלֶיךָ וְיָשֵׂם לְךָ שָׁלוֹם: (אָמֵן)

שִׂים שָׁלוֹם, טוֹבָה וּבְרָכָה, חַיִּים חֵן וָחֶסֶד וְרַחֲמִים, עָלֵינוּ וְעַל כָּל יִשְׂרָאֵל עַמֶּךָ, בָּרְכֵנוּ אָבִינוּ כֻּלָּנוּ כְּאֶחָד בְּאוֹר פָּנֶיךָ, כִּי בְאוֹר פָּנֶיךָ נָתַתָּ לָּנוּ יְיָ אֱלֹהֵינוּ תּוֹרַת חַיִּים וְאַהֲבַת חֶסֶד, וּצְדָקָה וּבְרָכָה וְרַחֲמִים וְחַיִּים וְשָׁלוֹם, וְטוֹב בְּעֵינֶיךָ לְבָרֵךְ אֶת עַמְּךָ יִשְׂרָאֵל בְּכָל עֵת וּבְכָל שָׁעָה בִּשְׁלוֹמֶךָ:

בעש"ת: וּבְסֵפֶר חַיִּים בְּרָכָה וְשָׁלוֹם וּפַרְנָסָה טוֹבָה, יְשׁוּעָה וְנֶחָמָה וּגְזֵרוֹת טוֹבוֹת נִזָּכֵר וְנִכָּתֵב לְפָנֶיךָ, אֲנַחְנוּ וְכָל עַמְּךָ בֵּית יִשְׂרָאֵל, לְחַיִּים טוֹבִים וּלְשָׁלוֹם:

בָּרוּךְ אַתָּה יְיָ, הַמְבָרֵךְ אֶת עַמּוֹ יִשְׂרָאֵל בַּשָּׁלוֹם:

סובב בתוך ממלא
דביקות באלקות
יראה עילאה
חיה-יחידה

CHASSIDIC INSIGHTS

(continued from p. 327)

Gush Chalav to pray at their graves. And there, they themselves said that we must have in mind that when we pronounce these words three time a day, we should pray to God about [the precursor to the Messiah] Mashiach ben Yosef that he will live and not be killed by Armelius the Wicked ... It is known from the *Zohar*[xii] that Moses

(continued on p. 330)

PRIESTLY BLESSING

Transcendent within Immanent
Cleaving to Godliness
Higher Fear – Awe
Haya and Yechida

This blessing is added during the chazzan's repetition of the Amidah, the congregation responds Amen where indicated:

Our God and the God of our forefathers, bless us with the three-part blessing written in Your Torah by Moses, Your servant, uttered from the mouths of Aaron and his sons, the priests of Your holy people, as stated:

"May the Lord bless you and keep you. (Amen)

May the Lord shine His countenance to You and grace you. (Amen)

May the Lord turn His countenance to You and grant you peace." (Amen)

PLACE PEACE, GOOD AND BLESSING, LIFE, HARMONY and kindness and compassion on us and on all of Israel, Your people. Bless us, our Father, all of us as one in the light of Your countenance, for in the light of Your countenance, You gave us, Lord our God, the Torah of life and love of kindness, and justice and blessing and mercy and life and peace. Let it be good in Your eyes to bless Your people Israel at all times and all hours, with Your peace.

Between Rosh Hashana and Yom Kippur add:

And recall and inscribe before You, in the book of life, blessing and peace and prosperity, salvation and comfort and good decrees, we and all of Your people, the House of Israel, for good life and for peace.

Blessed are You, Lord,
Who blesses His people in peace.

סוֹבֵב בְּתוֹךְ מְמַלֵּא
דְּבֵקוּת בֶּאֱלֹקוּת
יִרְאָה עִילָּאָה
חַיָּה-יְחִידָה

יִהְיוּ לְרָצוֹן אִמְרֵי פִי וְהֶגְיוֹן לִבִּי
לְפָנֶיךָ יְיָ צוּרִי וְגוֹאֲלִי:

אֱלֹהַי, נְצֹר לְשׁוֹנִי מֵרָע וּשְׂפָתַי מִדַּבֵּר מִרְמָה וְלִמְקַלְלַי, נַפְשִׁי תִדּוֹם, וְנַפְשִׁי כֶּעָפָר לַכֹּל תִּהְיֶה, פְּתַח לִבִּי בְּתוֹרָתֶךָ, וּבְמִצְוֹתֶיךָ תִּרְדּוֹף נַפְשִׁי, וְכָל הַחוֹשְׁבִים עָלַי רָעָה, מְהֵרָה הָפֵר עֲצָתָם וְקַלְקֵל מַחֲשַׁבְתָּם. יִהְיוּ כְּמוֹץ לִפְנֵי רוּחַ וּמַלְאַךְ יְיָ דּוֹחֶה. לְמַעַן יֵחָלְצוּן יְדִידֶיךָ, הוֹשִׁיעָה יְמִינְךָ וַעֲנֵנִי. עֲשֵׂה לְמַעַן שְׁמֶךָ, עֲשֵׂה לְמַעַן יְמִינֶךָ, עֲשֵׂה לְמַעַן תּוֹרָתֶךָ, עֲשֵׂה לְמַעַן קְדֻשָּׁתֶךָ. יִהְיוּ לְרָצוֹן אִמְרֵי פִי וְהֶגְיוֹן לִבִּי, לְפָנֶיךָ, יְיָ צוּרִי וְגוֹאֲלִי:

עֹשֶׂה שָׁלוֹם (בעשי״ת: הַשָּׁלוֹם) בִּמְרוֹמָיו,
הוּא יַעֲשֶׂה שָׁלוֹם עָלֵינוּ, וְעַל כָּל יִשְׂרָאֵל,
וְאִמְרוּ, אָמֵן:

יְהִי רָצוֹן מִלְּפָנֶיךָ, יְיָ אֱלֹהֵינוּ וֵאלֹהֵי אֲבוֹתֵינוּ,
שֶׁיִּבָּנֶה בֵּית הַמִּקְדָּשׁ בִּמְהֵרָה בְיָמֵינוּ,
וְתֵן חֶלְקֵנוּ בְּתוֹרָתֶךָ:

CHASSIDIC INSIGHTS

(continued from p. 328)

suffered greatly in order to prevent the death of Mashiach ben Yosef ... and about him we should pray that "the throne of David, Your servant, should be speedily re-established."
- *Et Zemach David* ("Speedily grow the sprout of David...") corresponds to *netzach*, with the concluding name of *Havaya* vowelized with a *chirik*.
- *Shema koleinu* ("Listen to our voice...") corresponds to *tiferet* of *Z"A*, from which *keter* is made ... and the name *Havaya* that concludes this blessing is vowelized with a *chashak* — a *cholem-sheva-kometz* on the first three letters, while the final *hey* is without vowelization. These three vowels are the secret of the three forefathers; the *cholem*

(continued on p. 332)

Transcendent within Immanent
Cleaving to Godliness
Higher Fear – Awe
Haya and *Yechida*

May the words of my mouth and the thoughts of my heart find favor before You, Lord, my Rock and my Redeemer

My God, guard my tongue from evil, and my lips from speaking deceitfully, and let my soul be still before all those who curse me, and make my soul like dust before all that may occur. Open my heart to Your Torah, and may my soul pursue Your commandments. And all those who plot against me, speedily foil their plans and ruin their thoughts. Let them be as chaff in the wind, let an angel of the Lord deflect them. In order to release your dear ones, let Your right hand save and respond to me. Do this for the sake of Your Name, do this for the sake of Your right hand, do this for the sake of Your Torah, do this for the sake of Your Holiness. May the words of my mouth and the thoughts of my heart find favor before You, Lord, my Rock and my Redeemer.

He Who establishes peace
(between Rosh Hashana and Yom Kippur, "the peace")
in His heavens, may He establish
peace over us and over all of Israel,
and let it be said, Amen.

May it be Your will,
Lord our God and the God of our fathers,
to build the holy Temple speedily in our days,
and grant us our portion in Your Torah.

CHASSIDIC INSIGHTS

(continued from p. 330)

is in *tiferet*, the *sheva* in *gevura* and the *kometz* in *chesed* ... and this is the secret meaning of the verse, "Only your forefathers desired (*chashak*) God" from all humankind.

The following table summarizes the above information:

BLESSING	SEPHIRA	VOWELIZATION
Chonen hada'at	Chochma	Patach
Hashiveinu	Bina	Segol, Tziri
Selach lanu	Chesed	Segol
Re'eh na be'eineinu	Gevura	Sheva
Refaeinu	Tiferet	Cholem
Barcheinu avinu	Netzach	Chirik
Teka beshofar	Hod	Kubutz
Hashiva softeinu	Yesod	Shuruk
Velamalsinim	Keter	Kometz
Ve'al hatzadikim	Yesod of Zeir Anpin	Shuruk
U'bnei Yeruahalayim	Hod of Zeir Anpin	Kubutz
Et Zemach David	Netzach of Zeir Anpin	Chirik
Shema Koleinu	Tiferet of Zeir Anpin	Chashak — cholem-sheva-kometz

These are the vowelizations that enable us, according to the sages and Chasidic masters, to more effectively receive answers to our requests during the *Shemonah Esreh*. As during the meditation of the *Shema*, this meditation requires us to maintain focus upon more than one element at a time. While reciting the *Shema*, we must focus on the meaning of the words and the number of words in the paragraph. During the *Shemonah Esreh*, we must envision both the four-letter name of God and the correct vowels of His name for each blessing. Simultaneously, we must maintain our focus on the infinite light of

(continued on p. 333)

CHASSIDIC INSIGHTS

(continued from p. 332)

the One Above, and then our *kavana* (from the word *kivun*, meaning "direction") will guide the infinite light to its correct address in the corresponding *sephira*. Unlike the *Shema*, though, the *Shemonah Esreh* demands that we be in a state of utter nullification, as if we do not exist. Of course, this is not an easy task; it demands a supple mind and subtle intellect. It is not really even a "meditation" in the traditional sense, because it demands a state of being rather than a state of mind, in order that we become able to act as a conduit for His infinite light. Obviously, this is not a practice for a beginner or even a veteran, unless they have refined and worked upon themselves to the point that they think not about themselves, but upon the state of the world. But like everything else, the practice evolves with time and effort.

The remainder of our morning prayers follows a path that is the inverse of the first half of our prayers. Now that we have reached the pinnacle of our prayers during the *Shemonah Esreh*, we want to bring our newfound level of spirituality down to the lower worlds of *Bria*, *Yetzira* and *Asiya*. This occurs during the prayers following the *Shemonah Esreh*. First, we ask for forgiveness during the *tachanun*, which follows *Shemonah Esreh*. We ask for forgiveness at this point in prayer because the *Shemonah Esreh* has elevated us to a position from which we can recognize our personal strengths and weaknesses clearly. That allows us to utilize our strengths to correct our weaknesses as we ask for forgiveness. Following *tachanun*, we begin the path of descent, bringing Godly influence down to bear on the lower worlds.

We begin the descent with the prayer *Ashrei* (Psalm 145), followed by Psalm 20 and then the prayer, *U'Va LeTzion*. Within *U'Va LeTzion*, we find the same angels who made an appearance during the *Birchot Kriat Shema*. They once more say *kadosh* three times, and *baruch*. This indicates that this section of prayers is associated with the world of *Bria*.

We then move on to recite the *Shir shel Yom* — the "song of the day." The "days" represent the six emotional attributes, with which the world was created. Although these attributes exist in all the worlds, they are most prominent in the world of *Yetzira*. Furthermore, the concept of *shir* — "song" — recalls the *pesukei dezimra*, the "verses of praise" earlier in our prayers, which are associated with the world of

(continued on p. 334)

תחנון

ודוי

עוֹלָם הָאֲצִילוּת
עַצְמוּת אוֹר אֵין סוֹף
בִּטּוּל בִּמְצִיאוּת
יְחִידָה שֶׁבַּנֶּפֶשׁ
כֶּתֶר דַּאֲצִילוּת

אֱלֹהֵינוּ וֵאלֹהֵי אֲבוֹתֵינוּ, תָּבֹא לְפָנֶיךָ תְּפִלָּתֵנוּ, וְאַל תִּתְעַלַּם מִתְּחִנָּתֵנוּ, שֶׁאֵין אָנוּ עַזֵּי פָנִים וּקְשֵׁי עֹרֶף, לוֹמַר לְפָנֶיךָ יְיָ אֱלֹהֵינוּ וֵאלֹהֵי אֲבוֹתֵינוּ, צַדִּיקִים אֲנַחְנוּ וְלֹא חָטָאנוּ, אֲבָל אֲנַחְנוּ וַאֲבוֹתֵינוּ חָטָאנוּ:

אָשַׁמְנוּ, בָּגַדְנוּ, גָּזַלְנוּ, דִּבַּרְנוּ דֹּפִי. הֶעֱוִינוּ, וְהִרְשַׁעְנוּ, זַדְנוּ, חָמַסְנוּ, טָפַלְנוּ שֶׁקֶר. יָעַצְנוּ רָע, כִּזַּבְנוּ, לַצְנוּ, מָרַדְנוּ, נִאַצְנוּ, סָרַרְנוּ, עָוִינוּ, פָּשַׁעְנוּ, צָרַרְנוּ, קִשִּׁינוּ עֹרֶף. רָשַׁעְנוּ, שִׁחַתְנוּ, תִּעַבְנוּ, תָּעִינוּ, תִּעְתָּעְנוּ:

סַרְנוּ מִמִּצְוֹתֶיךָ וּמִמִּשְׁפָּטֶיךָ הַטּוֹבִים וְלֹא שָׁוָה לָנוּ. וְאַתָּה צַדִּיק עַל כָּל הַבָּא עָלֵינוּ, כִּי אֱמֶת עָשִׂיתָ וַאֲנַחְנוּ הִרְשָׁעְנוּ:

אֵל אֶרֶךְ אַפַּיִם אַתָּה וּבַעַל הָרַחֲמִים נִקְרֵאתָ, וְדֶרֶךְ תְּשׁוּבָה הוֹרֵיתָ. גְּדֻלַּת רַחֲמֶיךָ וַחֲסָדֶיךָ, תִּזְכֹּר הַיּוֹם

CHASSIDIC INSIGHTS

(continued from p. 333)

Yetzira. So, at this point, we bring the "daily dose" of spirituality down to the world of *Yetzira*.

Next, we recite *Ein Kelokeinu*, followed by the "incense," which lists the physical ingredients that go into the incense that was offered

(continued on p. 338)

TACHANUN

World of Atzilut
Essential Infinite Godly Illumination
Absolute self-annulment
Yechida shb'nefesh
Keter of Atzilut

Viduy

OUR GOD AND THE GOD OF OUR FOREFATHERS, LET our prayer come before You, and hide not from our pleas, for we are not so bold-faced and stubborn as to claim before You, our God and the God of our forefathers, that we are righteous and have not sinned; rather we and our forefathers have transgressed…

We are guilty, we have betrayed, we have robbed, we have spoken evil: We have acted perversely, we have done wrong, we have purposely sinned, we have acted violently, we have accused falsely: We have given bad advice, we have fooled others, we have scoffed, we have rebelled. We have provoked, we have disobeyed, we have deviated, we have acted criminally, we have oppressed, we have been obstinate: We have been wicked, we have destroyed, we acted abominably, we have strayed, we have forced others astray.

We have turned away from Your commandments and from Your good laws, and it has not been worthwhile. And You are righteous regarding all that has occurred to us, for You act only in truth, and we have acted wickedly.

You are a patient God, and You are called the Master of Mercy. And You educate in the path of

וּבְכָל יוֹם לְזֶרַע יְדִידֶיךָ. תֵּפֶן אֵלֵינוּ בְּרַחֲמִים, כִּי אַתָּה הוּא בַּעַל הָרַחֲמִים. בְּתַחֲנוּן וּבִתְפִלָּה פָּנֶיךָ נְקַדֵּם, כְּהוֹדַעְתָּ לֶעָנָו מִקֶּדֶם. מֵחֲרוֹן אַפְּךָ שׁוּב, כְּמוֹ בְּתוֹרָתְךָ כָּתוּב. וּבְצֵל כְּנָפֶיךָ נֶחֱסֶה וְנִתְלוֹנָן, כְּיוֹם וַיֵּרֶד יְיָ בֶּעָנָן. תַּעֲבוֹר עַל פֶּשַׁע וְתִמְחֶה אָשָׁם, כְּיוֹם וַיִּתְיַצֵּב עִמּוֹ שָׁם. תַּאֲזִין שַׁוְעָתֵנוּ וְתַקְשִׁיב מֶנּוּ מַאֲמָר, כְּיוֹם וַיִּקְרָא בְשֵׁם יְיָ וְשָׁם נֶאֱמַר:

עולם האצילות
עצמות אור אין סוף
ביטול במציאות
יחידה שבנפש
כתר דאצילות

❝ If a man sins by failing to fulfill one of the positive mitzvot, or by transgressing one of the negative commandments, he creates a blemish. He diminishes the flow of Godly energy to the [particular attribute or *sephira* associated with that mitzvah]. Moreover, he syphons the spiritual energy away from the Godly attributes into the depths of the *klipot* to a far greater degree than what they were meant to receive." (*Derech Mitzvotecha* of the *Tzemach Tzedek, Mitzvat vidui v'tshuva,* p. ל"ח)308

The 613 commandments are called *Mitzvot Havaya* ("Commandments of God") since they facilitate the descent and revelation of God's infinite light via His holy name *Havaya*. There are mitzvot that correspond to the letter *yud* of His name, and to the letter *hey*, etc., and those that also correspond to the ten *sephirot*. The mitzvot are also called the "limbs of the King," since the ten *sephirot*, with which the mitzvot are associated, are like a body in relation to the Godly light that flows into them whenever the mitzvot are fulfilled. However, when we transgress, the opposite occurs — by failing to fulfill a positive command we fail to drawn down His holy light, and by transgressing a negative command, we cause His holy illumination to flow in the wrong direction, toward the forces that hide and conceal Godliness and create darkness in the world.

Our sins cause a "leak" of holy light that diminishes the amount of illumination that flows into the ten *sephirot*. Therefore, we must operate on two fronts in order to rectify the problem: 1) we must repair the blemish and to patch the leak, and 2) we must

World of Atzilut
Essential Infinite Godly Illumination
Absolute self-annulment
Yechida shb'nefesh
Keter of Atzilut

tshuva ("return to Him"). Great is Your mercy and Your kindness, remember today as well as every day the descendants of Your intimate ones. Turn to us in compassion, for You are the Master of Mercy. We approach Your countenance in pleading and in prayer, as You once informed Your humble one. Retract Your fiery anger, as is written in Your Torah, and in the shade of Your wings we will take cover and lodge, as on the day that "The Lord descended in the cloud." Pass over iniquity and erase guilt, as on the day that we stood with Him there. Take heed of our cry, and listen to our statement, as on the day that he called in the name of the Lord: And there it was said:

---

staunch the flow of Godly energy to the unholy forces. The latter also divides into two efforts: a) the unholy forces should cease to receive extra flow of Godly energy, and b) we should retrieve whatever flowed to them wrongfully because of our sins.

> 📖 *Within the Words*
>
> When we do proper *teshuva* — expressing honest regret over our misdeeds — we bring down a higher level of spiritual energy that transcends our previous behavior. This transcendent light "blinds" the negative forces, repairing the breach that we caused and patching the leak. However, retrieving the lost energy from the "other side" involves more effort. Our sins create a "bad angel" with a "body" and a "soul." The regret that we express "kills" the soul of the "bad angel," and our *Vidui* (verbal "confession") kills the "body" of the angel. The *Vidui* is composed of words utilizing all of the letters of the *aleph-beit*, and the movement of our lips while reciting these words is the action that eliminates the bodies of the negative forces.

TACHANUN

וַיַּעֲבֹר יְיָ עַל פָּנָיו וַיִּקְרָא:

יְיָ יְיָ אֵל רַחוּם וְחַנּוּן אֶרֶךְ אַפַּיִם וְרַב חֶסֶד וֶאֱמֶת: נֹצֵר חֶסֶד לָאֲלָפִים נֹשֵׂא עָוֹן וָפֶשַׁע וְחַטָּאָה וְנַקֵּה:

רַחוּם וְחַנּוּן חָטָאתִי לְפָנֶיךָ רַחֵם עָלֵינוּ וְהוֹשִׁיעֵנוּ:

עולם האצילות
עצמות אור אין סוף
ביטול במציאות
יחידה שבנפש
כתר דאצילות

נפילת אפים

לְדָוִד אֵלֶיךָ יְיָ נַפְשִׁי אֶשָּׂא:

אֱלֹהַי בְּךָ בָטַחְתִּי אַל אֵבוֹשָׁה, אַל יַעַלְצוּ אוֹיְבַי לִי:

גַּם כָּל קֹוֶיךָ לֹא יֵבֹשׁוּ, יֵבֹשׁוּ הַבּוֹגְדִים רֵיקָם:

דְּרָכֶיךָ יְיָ הוֹדִיעֵנִי, אֹרְחוֹתֶיךָ לַמְּדֵנִי:

הַדְרִיכֵנִי בַאֲמִתֶּךָ וְלַמְּדֵנִי כִּי אַתָּה אֱלֹהֵי יִשְׁעִי, אוֹתְךָ קִוִּיתִי כָּל הַיּוֹם:

זְכֹר רַחֲמֶיךָ יְיָ וַחֲסָדֶיךָ כִּי מֵעוֹלָם הֵמָּה:

חַטֹּאות נְעוּרַי וּפְשָׁעַי אַל תִּזְכֹּר כְּחַסְדְּךָ זְכָר לִי אַתָּה, לְמַעַן טוּבְךָ יְיָ:

טוֹב וְיָשָׁר יְיָ עַל כֵּן יוֹרֶה חַטָּאִים בַּדָּרֶךְ:

CHASSIDIC INSIGHTS

(continued from p. 334)

in the Temple. Of course, these are the same ingredients that we mentioned before prayers, as we recited the section on *korbanot*. So, like the section on *korbanot*, *Ein Kelokeinu* is associated with the world of *Asiya*.

(continued on p. 340)

World of Atzilut
Essential Infinite Godly Illumination
Absolute self-annulment
Yechida shb'nefesh
Keter of *Atzilut*

And the Lord passed before him and declared:

Lord, Lord, God of mercy and grace, patient and of much kindness and truth. He preserves kindness for thousands of generations, forgiving sin and iniquity and transgression — and He cleanses.

Oh, Merciful and Gracious One, we have sinned before You, have mercy upon us and save us!

Putting Down the Head

For David…To You, Lord, I lift up my soul

My God, in You I placed my trust, let me not be embarrassed, let my enemies not gloat over me.

And neither should those who place their hope in You be embarrassed — let the traitors be embarrassed in their emptiness.

Inform me of Your ways, Lord, and teach me Your paths.

Guide me in Your truth and teach me, for You are the God of my salvation, it is for You that I yearn all the day.

Recall Your mercy, Lord, for Your kindnesses are eternal.

Remember not the sins of my youth, nor my transgressions; in Your mercy remember me, for the sake of Your goodness, Lord.

Good and straight-forward is the Lord, therefore He informs sinners of the path.

TACHANUN

יַדְרֵךְ עֲנָוִים בַּמִּשְׁפָּט וִילַמֵּד עֲנָוִים דַּרְכּוֹ:

כָּל אָרְחוֹת יְיָ חֶסֶד וֶאֱמֶת, לְנֹצְרֵי בְרִיתוֹ וְעֵדֹתָיו:

לְמַעַן שִׁמְךָ יְיָ וְסָלַחְתָּ לַעֲוֹנִי כִּי רַב הוּא:

מִי זֶה הָאִישׁ יְרֵא יְיָ יוֹרֶנּוּ בְּדֶרֶךְ יִבְחָר:

נַפְשׁוֹ בְּטוֹב תָּלִין וְזַרְעוֹ יִירַשׁ אָרֶץ:

סוֹד יְיָ לִירֵאָיו, וּבְרִיתוֹ לְהוֹדִיעָם:

עֵינַי תָּמִיד אֶל יְיָ, כִּי הוּא יוֹצִיא מֵרֶשֶׁת רַגְלָי:

פְּנֵה אֵלַי וְחָנֵּנִי, כִּי יָחִיד וְעָנִי אָנִי:

צָרוֹת לְבָבִי הִרְחִיבוּ, מִמְּצוּקוֹתַי הוֹצִיאֵנִי:

רְאֵה עָנְיִי וַעֲמָלִי, וְשָׂא לְכָל חַטֹּאותָי:

רְאֵה אֹיְבַי כִּי רָבּוּ וְשִׂנְאַת חָמָס שְׂנֵאוּנִי:

שָׁמְרָה נַפְשִׁי וְהַצִּילֵנִי אַל אֵבוֹשׁ כִּי חָסִיתִי בָךְ:

תֹּם וָיֹשֶׁר יִצְּרוּנִי, כִּי קִוִּיתִיךָ:

פְּדֵה אֱלֹהִים אֶת יִשְׂרָאֵל מִכֹּל צָרוֹתָיו:

וְהוּא יִפְדֶּה אֶת יִשְׂרָאֵל מִכֹּל, עֲוֹנֹתָיו:

עולם האצילות
עצמות אור אין סוף
ביטול במציאות
יחידה שבנפש
כתר דאצילות

--- CHASSIDIC INSIGHTS ---

(continued from p. 338)

Finally, we close our prayers with *Aleinu*, and the journey that we took, ascending the ladder of prayers brings us back full circle as we descend to our own physical world with added spiritual meaning and determination to refine and elevate the world.

(endnotes on p. 432)

World of Atzilut
Essential Infinite Godly Illumination
Absolute self-annulment
Yechida shb'nefesh
Keter of *Atzilut*

TACHANUN

He guides the humble in justice, and teaches the humble His way.

All the paths of the Lord are kind and true, for those who keep His covenant and testimonies.

For the sake of Your Name, Lord, forgive my iniquities, for they are many.

Who is the man who fears the Lord, show him which way to choose.

His soul will dwell in goodness, and his descendants will inherit the land.

The secret of the Lord is for those who fear Him; they will be informed of His covenant.

My eyes are fastened always upon the Lord, for He who extracts my legs from the net.

Turn to me and grant me grace, for I am alone and poor.

The sorrows of my heart have expanded, extract me from my distress.

See my poverty and my efforts, and put up with all my sins.

See, my enemies have multiplied, and with terrible hatred they detest me.

Guard my soul and save me; do not let me be ashamed for I have taken refuge in You.

Integrity and honesty will guard me, for I have hope in You.

Redeem Yisrael, God, from all of its troubles.

And He will redeem Israel from all his iniquities.

תחנון לשני וחמישי

וְהוּא רַחוּם, יְכַפֵּר עָוֹן וְלֹא יַשְׁחִית,
וְהִרְבָּה לְהָשִׁיב אַפּוֹ, וְלֹא יָעִיר כָּל חֲמָתוֹ.

אַתָּה יְיָ לֹא תִכְלָא רַחֲמֶיךָ מִמֶּנּוּ,
חַסְדְּךָ וַאֲמִתְּךָ תָּמִיד יִצְּרוּנוּ.

הוֹשִׁיעֵנוּ יְיָ אֱלֹהֵינוּ, וְקַבְּצֵנוּ מִן הַגּוֹיִם,
לְהוֹדוֹת לְשֵׁם קָדְשֶׁךָ, לְהִשְׁתַּבֵּחַ בִּתְהִלָּתֶךָ.

אִם עֲוֹנוֹת תִּשְׁמָר יָהּ, אֲדֹנָי מִי יַעֲמֹד.

כִּי עִמְּךָ הַסְּלִיחָה, לְמַעַן תִּוָּרֵא.

לֹא כַחֲטָאֵינוּ תַּעֲשֶׂה לָּנוּ,
וְלֹא כַעֲוֹנֹתֵינוּ תִּגְמֹל עָלֵינוּ.

אִם עֲוֹנֵינוּ עָנוּ בָנוּ, יְיָ, עֲשֵׂה לְמַעַן שְׁמֶךָ.

זְכֹר רַחֲמֶיךָ יְיָ, וַחֲסָדֶיךָ, כִּי מֵעוֹלָם הֵמָּה.

יַעַנְךָ יְיָ בְּיוֹם צָרָה, יְשַׂגֶּבְךָ שֵׁם אֱלֹהֵי יַעֲקֹב:

יְיָ הוֹשִׁיעָה, הַמֶּלֶךְ יַעֲנֵנוּ בְיוֹם קָרְאֵנוּ.

אָבִינוּ מַלְכֵּנוּ חָנֵּנוּ וַעֲנֵנוּ, כִּי אֵין בָּנוּ מַעֲשִׂים,
עֲשֵׂה עִמָּנוּ צְדָקָה לְמַעַן שְׁמֶךָ.

וְעַתָּה אֲדֹנָי אֱלֹהֵינוּ, אֲשֶׁר הוֹצֵאתָ
אֶת עַמְּךָ מֵאֶרֶץ מִצְרַיִם בְּיָד חֲזָקָה,
וַתַּעַשׂ לְךָ שֵׁם כַּיּוֹם הַזֶּה, חָטָאנוּ רָשָׁעְנוּ.

עוֹלָם הָאֲצִילוּת
עַצְמוּת אוֹר אֵין סוֹף
בִּיטוּל בִּמְצִיאוּת
יְחִידָה שֶׁבַּנֶּפֶשׁ
כֶּתֶר דַּאֲצִילוּת

World of Atzilut
Essential Infinite Godly Illumination
Absolute self-annulment
Yechida shb'nefesh
Keter of Atzilut

TACHANUN

Additional Prayers for Monday and Thursday

And He, being merciful, atones for our sins and refrains from destroying us, He repeatedly quashes His anger, and avoids arousing all of His wrath.

Lord, do not withhold Your mercy from us, may Your kindness and truth always guard us.

Save us, Lord, our God, and gather us from among the nations, in order to acknowledge Your holy Name, and to be extolled in Your praises.

God, if You were to preserve sins, my Lord, who could survive?

For, with You resides forgiveness, so You will be feared.

Do not deal with us according to our sins, nor recompense us according to our transgressions.

If our sins speak for us, Lord then deal with us [kindly] for the sake of Your Name.

Remember Your mercy, Lord, and Your kindness, since they are forever.

May the Lord answer us on our day of distress, may the name of the God of Jacob protect us.

Lord, help us, may the King answer on the day we call!

Our Father, our King, grace us and answer us, for we have no [good] deeds, deal with us justly for the sake of Your Name.

And now, Lord our God, who took Your people out of the land of Egypt with a strong arm, and made for Yourself a name as of today; we have sinned and we have transgressed.

אֲדֹנָי כְּכָל צִדְקֹתֶיךָ, יָשָׁב נָא אַפְּךָ וַחֲמָתְךָ מֵעִירְךָ יְרוּשָׁלַיִם הַר קָדְשֶׁךָ, כִּי בַחֲטָאֵינוּ וּבַעֲוֹנוֹת אֲבֹתֵינוּ, יְרוּשָׁלַיִם וְעַמְּךָ לְחֶרְפָּה לְכָל סְבִיבֹתֵינוּ.

וְעַתָּה, שְׁמַע אֱלֹהֵינוּ אֶל תְּפִלַּת עַבְדְּךָ וְאֶל תַּחֲנוּנָיו וְהָאֵר פָּנֶיךָ עַל מִקְדָּשְׁךָ הַשָּׁמֵם, לְמַעַן אֲדֹנָי:

הַטֵּה אֱלֹהַי אָזְנְךָ וּשֲׁמָע, פְּקַח עֵינֶיךָ וּרְאֵה שֹׁמְמֹתֵינוּ, וְהָעִיר אֲשֶׁר נִקְרָא שִׁמְךָ עָלֶיהָ, כִּי לֹא עַל צִדְקֹתֵינוּ אֲנַחְנוּ מַפִּילִים תַּחֲנוּנֵינוּ לְפָנֶיךָ, כִּי עַל רַחֲמֶיךָ הָרַבִּים.

אֲדֹנָי שְׁמָעָה, אֲדֹנָי סְלָחָה, אֲדֹנָי הַקְשִׁיבָה, וַעֲשֵׂה אַל תְּאַחַר, לְמַעַנְךָ אֱלֹהַי, כִּי שִׁמְךָ נִקְרָא עַל עִירְךָ וְעַל עַמֶּךָ:

אָבִינוּ אָב הָרַחֲמָן, הַרְאֵנוּ אוֹת לְטוֹבָה וְקַבֵּץ נְפוּצוֹתֵינוּ מֵאַרְבַּע כַּנְפוֹת הָאָרֶץ, יַכִּירוּ וְיֵדְעוּ כָּל הַגּוֹיִם, כִּי אַתָּה יְיָ אֱלֹהֵינוּ. וְעַתָּה יְיָ אָבִינוּ אָתָּה, אֲנַחְנוּ הַחֹמֶר וְאַתָּה יֹצְרֵנוּ, וּמַעֲשֵׂה יָדְךָ כֻּלָּנוּ.

אָבִינוּ מַלְכֵּנוּ צוּרֵנוּ וְגוֹאֲלֵנוּ. חוּסָה יְיָ עַל עַמֶּךָ, וְאַל תִּתֵּן נַחֲלָתְךָ לְחֶרְפָּה לִמְשָׁל בָּם גּוֹיִם, לָמָּה יֹאמְרוּ בָעַמִּים אַיֵּה אֱלֹהֵיהֶם.

עוֹלָם הָאֲצִילוּת
עַצְמוּת אוֹר אֵין סוֹף
בִּיטוּל בַּמְּצִיאוּת
יְחִידָה שֶׁבַּנֶּפֶשׁ
כֶּתֶר דַּאֲצִילוּת

World of Atzilut
Essential Infinite Godly Illumination
Absolute self-annulment
Yechida shb'nefesh
Keter of *Atzilut*

My Lord, in accordance with all of Your righteousness, hold back Your anger and your wrath, from Your city Jerusalem, Your holy mountain, for through our sins and the sins of our fathers, Jerusalem and Your nation are held in contempt among all who surround us.

And now, our God, heed the prayers of Your servant and his pleading, and shine Your countenance on Your devastated Temple, for Your sake, my Lord.

Incline Your ear, my God and listen, open Your eyes and observe our desolation, and the city upon which Your Name is called, for not on account of our righteousness do we issue our pleas before You, but on account of Your great mercy.

My Lord, hear, My Lord, forgive, my Lord, pay attention and act, do not delay, for Your sake, My God, for Your name is declared over Your city and over Your nation.

Our Father, merciful Father, show us a positive sign and gather our scattered remnants for the four corners of the earth, so that the nations will know and recognize, that you are the Lord our God. And now, Lord our God, You are our Father, we are the raw material and Your are [the Craftsman] Who forms us, and we are all the work of Your hand.

Our Father, our King, our Rock and our Redeemer. Have mercy, Lord upon Your people, refrain from letting Your inheritance become a disgrace that the nations govern over, [for] why should the nations say, 'where is their God?'

TACHANUN

יָדַעְנוּ יְיָ כִּי חָטָאנוּ, וְאֵין מִי יַעֲמֹד בַּעֲדֵנוּ, אֶלָּא שִׁמְךָ הַגָּדוֹל יַעֲמָד לָנוּ בְּעֵת צָרָה.

כְּרַחֵם אָב עַל בָּנִים, כֵּן תְּרַחֵם יְיָ עָלֵינוּ וְהוֹשִׁיעֵנוּ לְמַעַן שְׁמֶךָ.

חֲמוֹל עַל עַמֶּךָ, רַחֵם עַל נַחֲלָתֶךָ, חוּסָה נָּא כְּרֹב רַחֲמֶיךָ, חָנֵּנוּ וַעֲנֵנוּ, כִּי לְךָ יְיָ הַצְּדָקָה. עֹשֵׂה נִפְלָאוֹת בְּכָל עֵת:

הַבֵּט נָא, וְהוֹשִׁיעָה צֹאן מַרְעִיתֶךָ. וְאַל יִמְשָׁל בָּנוּ קֶצֶף, כִּי לְךָ יְיָ הַיְשׁוּעָה, בְּךָ תוֹחַלְתֵּנוּ, אֱלוֹהַּ סְלִיחוֹת. אָנָּא, סְלַח נָא, כִּי אֵל טוֹב וְסַלָּח אָתָּה:

אָנָּא מֶלֶךְ חַנּוּן וְרַחוּם, זְכוֹר וְהַבֵּט לִבְרִית בֵּין הַבְּתָרִים, וְתֵרָאֶה לְפָנֶיךָ עֲקֵדַת יָחִד וּלְמַעַן יִשְׂרָאֵל אָבִינוּ. אַל תַּעַזְבֵנוּ אָבִינוּ, וְאַל תִּטְּשֵׁנוּ מַלְכֵּנוּ, וְאַל תִּשְׁכָּחֵנוּ יוֹצְרֵנוּ, וְאַל תַּעַשׂ עִמָּנוּ כָלָה כְּחַטֹּאתֵינוּ, בְּגָלוּתֵנוּ, כִּי אֵל מֶלֶךְ חַנּוּן וְרַחוּם אָתָּה:

אֵין כָּמוֹךָ חַנּוּן וְרַחוּם יְיָ אֱלֹהֵינוּ, אֵין כָּמוֹךָ אֵל אֶרֶךְ אַפַּיִם וְרַב חֶסֶד וֶאֱמֶת, הוֹשִׁיעֵנוּ וְרַחֲמֵנוּ, מֵרַעַשׁ וּמֵרֹגֶז הַצִּילֵנוּ. זְכֹר לַעֲבָדֶיךָ לְאַבְרָהָם לְיִצְחָק וּלְיַעֲקֹב, אַל תֵּפֶן אֶל קְשִׁינוּ וְאֶל רִשְׁעֵנוּ וְאֶל חַטָּאתֵנוּ. שׁוּב מֵחֲרוֹן אַפֶּךָ וְהִנָּחֵם עַל הָרָעָה לְעַמֶּךָ.

וְהָסֵר מִמֶּנּוּ מַכַּת הַמָּוֶת כִּי רַחוּם אָתָּה, כִּי כֵן דַּרְכֶּךָ עֹשֵׂה חֶסֶד חִנָּם בְּכָל דּוֹר וָדוֹר.

World of Atzilut
Essential Infinite Godly Illumination
Absolute self-annulment
Yechida shb'nefesh
Keter of *Atzilut*

TACHANUN

We know that we sinned, and there is no-one to stand up for us, let Your great Name to stand up for us at the time of distress.

As a father has compassion on his children, so have mercy, Lord, upon us and save us for the sake of Your name.

Have mercy on Your nation, be compassionate over Your inheritance, spare us in Your abundant benevolences, be gracious and answer us, for righteousness is Yours Lord, [He Who] performs wonders at all times.

Gaze [over us], please and save the sheep of Your pastures.

Let not anger overwhelm us, for salvation is Yours, it is You we yearn for, God of forgiveness. Please, forgive us now, since You are a good and forgiving God.

Please, gracious and merciful King, recall and look back upon the covenant [with Abraham] between the pieces, and visualize before Yourself the binding of [Isaac], and for the sake of Israel our father, do not forsake us, our Father, and do not leave us, our King, and do not forget us, our Maker, and do not bring destruction upon us in accordance with our sins in exile, for Your are God, King Who is gracious and merciful.

There is none like You, gracious and merciful Lord, our God, there is none like You, God of patience and abundant kindness and truth, save us and have mercy upon us, rescue us from violence and rage! Recall Your servants, Abraham, Isaac and Jacob, do not turn to our obstinacy and to our wickedness and to our sins. Refrain from Your fiery anger, and retract the evil intended for Your people.

And remove from us the plague of death, since You are merciful, for so is Your way, to perform gratuitous kindness in every generation.

אָנָּא יְיָ הוֹשִׁיעָה נָּא. אָנָּא יְיָ הַצְלִיחָה נָּא. אָנָּא יְיָ עֲנֵנוּ בְיוֹם קָרְאֵנוּ. לְךָ יְיָ קִוִּינוּ, לְךָ יְיָ חִכִּינוּ, לְךָ יְיָ נְיַחֵל, אַל תֶּחֱשֶׁה וּתְעַנֵּנוּ, כִּי נָאֵמוּ גוֹיִם אָבְדָה תִקְוָתָם, כָּל בֶּרֶךְ לְךָ תִכְרַע וְכָל קוֹמָה לְפָנֶיךָ תִשְׁתַּחֲוֶה:

הַפּוֹתֵחַ יָד בִּתְשׁוּבָה לְקַבֵּל פּוֹשְׁעִים וְחַטָּאִים, נִבְהֲלָה נַפְשֵׁנוּ מֵרוֹב עִצְּבוֹנֵנוּ, אַל תִּשְׁכָּחֵנוּ נֶצַח, קוּמָה וְהוֹשִׁיעֵנוּ. וְאַל תִּשְׁפֹּךְ חֲרוֹנְךָ עָלֵינוּ, כִּי אֲנַחְנוּ עַמְּךָ בְּנֵי בְרִיתֶךָ.

עוֹרְרָה גְבוּרָתְךָ וְהוֹשִׁיעֵנוּ לְמַעַן שְׁמֶךָ, וְאַל יִמְעֲטוּ לְפָנֶיךָ תְלָאוֹתֵינוּ. מַהֵר יְקַדְּמוּנוּ רַחֲמֶיךָ בְּעֵת צָרוֹתֵינוּ לֹא לְמַעֲנֵנוּ אֶלָּא לְמַעַנְךָ פְּעַל, וְאַל תַּשְׁחִית אֶת זֵכֶר שְׁאֵרִיתֵנוּ, כִּי לְךָ מְיַחֲלוֹת עֵינֵינוּ, כִּי אֵל מֶלֶךְ חַנּוּן וְרַחוּם אָתָּה,

וּזְכֹר עֵדוּתֵנוּ בְּכָל יוֹם תָּמִיד אוֹמְרִים פַּעֲמַיִם בְּאַהֲבָה:

שְׁמַע יִשְׂרָאֵל יְיָ אֱלֹהֵינוּ. יְיָ אֶחָד:

יְיָ אֱלֹהֵי יִשְׂרָאֵל, שׁוּב מֵחֲרוֹן אַפֶּךָ, וְהִנָּחֵם עַל הָרָעָה לְעַמֶּךָ:

הַבֵּט מִשָּׁמַיִם וּרְאֵה, כִּי הָיִינוּ לַעַג וָקֶלֶס בַּגּוֹיִם, נֶחְשַׁבְנוּ כַּצֹּאן לַטֶּבַח יוּבָל, לַהֲרוֹג וּלְאַבֵּד וּלְמַכָּה וּלְחֶרְפָּה. וּבְכָל זֹאת שִׁמְךָ לֹא שָׁכָחְנוּ, נָא, אַל תִּשְׁכָּחֵנוּ:

עולם האצילות
עצמות אור אין סוף
ביטול במציאות
יחידה שבנפש
כתר דאצילות

World of Atzilut
Essential Infinite Godly Illumination
Absolute self-annulment
Yechida shb'nefesh
Keter of Atzilut

Please, Lord, save us, please Lord grant us success, please Lord answer us on the day that we call. With You, Lord is our hope, for You Lord we are waiting, for You, Lord we yearn, do not be silent and allow us to suffer, for the nations declare, "all their hope is lost." Let every knee bend to You, and every upright person prostrate himself to You.

You Who opens His hand to receive those who return in tshuva — and accepts wrong-doers and sinners — our soul is troubled by deep sorrow; do not forget us forever, rise up and save us.

And do not pour out Your wrath upon us, since we are Your people, members of Your covenant.

Arouse your might and save us for the sake of Your Name, and do not trivialize our suffering before You.

Quickly advance Your clemency at the time of our travails, not for our sake, but for Your sake act, and do not destroy the remembrance of our remnant, for to You our eyes yearn, since Your are God, King Who is gracious and merciful. Recall our testimony, lovingly proclaimed twice every day:

Hear of Israel, the Lord is our God, the Lord is One.

Lord, God of Israel, refrain from Your fiery anger, and retract the evil intended for Your people.

Peer from the heavens and see, that we have become scorned and disdained among the nations, we are thought of as sheep for slaughter and obliteration, to be killed and destroyed, and beaten and disgraced. And nevertheless, we have not forgotten Your Name; please do not forget us!

TACHANUN

יְיָ אֱלֹהֵי יִשְׂרָאֵל, שׁוּב מֵחֲרוֹן אַפֶּךָ,
וְהִנָּחֵם עַל הָרָעָה לְעַמֶּךָ:

זָרִים אוֹמְרִים אֵין תּוֹחֶלֶת וְתִקְוָה, חוֹן אוֹם לְשִׁמְךָ
מְקַוָּה, טָהוֹר, יְשׁוּעָתֵנוּ קָרְבָה, יָגַעְנוּ וְלֹא הוּנַח לָנוּ,
רַחֲמֶיךָ יִכְבְּשׁוּ אֶת כַּעַסְךָ מֵעָלֵינוּ: אָנָּא שׁוּב
מֵחֲרוֹנְךָ, וְרַחֵם סְגֻלָּה אֲשֶׁר בָּחָרְתָּ:

יְיָ אֱלֹהֵי יִשְׂרָאֵל, שׁוּב מֵחֲרוֹן אַפֶּךָ,
וְהִנָּחֵם עַל הָרָעָה לְעַמֶּךָ:

חוּסָה יְיָ עָלֵינוּ בְּרַחֲמֶיךָ, וְאַל תִּתְּנֵנוּ בִּידֵי אַכְזָרִים,
לָמָּה יֹאמְרוּ הַגּוֹיִם אַיֵּה נָא אֱלֹהֵיהֶם, לְמַעַנְךָ עֲשֵׂה
עִמָּנוּ חֶסֶד וְאַל תְּאַחַר: אָנָּא שׁוּב מֵחֲרוֹנְךָ
וְרַחֵם סְגֻלָּה אֲשֶׁר בָּחָרְתָּ:

יְיָ אֱלֹהֵי יִשְׂרָאֵל, שׁוּב מֵחֲרוֹן אַפֶּךָ,
וְהִנָּחֵם עַל הָרָעָה לְעַמֶּךָ:

קוֹלֵנוּ תִשְׁמַע וְתָחוֹן, וְאַל תִּטְּשֵׁנוּ בְּיַד אֹיְבֵינוּ
לִמְחוֹת אֶת שְׁמֵנוּ, זְכֹר אֲשֶׁר נִשְׁבַּעְתָּ לַאֲבוֹתֵינוּ,
כְּכוֹכְבֵי הַשָּׁמַיִם אַרְבֶּה אֶת זַרְעֲכֶם, וְעַתָּה
נִשְׁאַרְנוּ מְעַט מֵהַרְבֵּה. וּבְכָל זֹאת שִׁמְךָ
לֹא שָׁכָחְנוּ, נָא אַל תִּשְׁכָּחֵנוּ:

יְיָ אֱלֹהֵי יִשְׂרָאֵל, שׁוּב מֵחֲרוֹן אַפֶּךָ,
וְהִנָּחֵם עַל הָרָעָה לְעַמֶּךָ:

עָזְרֵנוּ אֱלֹהֵי יִשְׁעֵנוּ עַל דְּבַר כְּבוֹד שְׁמֶךָ, וְהַצִּילֵנוּ
וְכַפֵּר עַל חַטֹּאתֵינוּ לְמַעַן שְׁמֶךָ:

World of Atzilut
Essential Infinite Godly Illumination
Absolute self-annulment
Yechida shb'nefesh
Keter of *Atzilut*

Lord, God of Israel, refrain from Your fiery wrath, and retract the evil intended for Your people.

Strangers say there is no expectation or hope [for us]. Be gracious to the nation that desires Your Name. Pure One, bring our salvation near; we have became weary and there is no relief for us. Let Your mercy overwhelm Your anger from upon us. Please, back off from Your wrath, have mercy on the treasured people which You chose.

Lord, God of Israel, refrain from Your fiery wrath, and retract any evil intended for Your people.

In Your compassion, Lord, have mercy upon us, and do not put us in cruel hands, for why should the nations say, 'where is their God?' For Your sake, do for us kindness without delay; please refrain from Your wrath, have mercy upon the treasured people whom Your chose.

Lord, God of Israel refrain from Your fiery anger, and retract any evil intended for Your people.

Hear our voices and be gracious, do not forsake us in the hands of our enemies, to erase our names. Remember what You swore to our forefathers, "I will make your descendants as numerous as the stars of the heavens," and yet now we remain only a few among many. And nevertheless, we have not forgotten Your Name, please, do not forget us.

Lord, God of Israel, refrain from Your fiery wrath, and retract the evil intended for Your people.

Our help, God of our salvation, for the sake of the glory of Your Name, rescue us and atone for our sins, for the sake of Your Name.

TACHANUN

יְיָ אֱלֹהֵי יִשְׂרָאֵל, שׁוּב מֵחֲרוֹן אַפֶּךָ, וְהִנָּחֵם עַל הָרָעָה לְעַמֶּךָ:

אם צום גדליה נופל ביום שני או חמישי,
מוסיפים סליחות לצום גדליה

שׁוֹמֵר יִשְׂרָאֵל, שְׁמוֹר שְׁאֵרִית יִשְׂרָאֵל, וְאַל יֹאבַד יִשְׂרָאֵל, הָאוֹמְרִים שְׁמַע יִשְׂרָאֵל:

שׁוֹמֵר גּוֹי אֶחָד, שְׁמוֹר שְׁאֵרִית עַם אֶחָד, וְאַל יֹאבַד גּוֹי אֶחָד, הַמְיַחֲדִים שִׁמְךָ יְיָ אֱלֹהֵינוּ יְיָ אֶחָד:

שׁוֹמֵר גּוֹי קָדוֹשׁ, שְׁמוֹר שְׁאֵרִית עַם קָדוֹשׁ. וְאַל יֹאבַד גּוֹי קָדוֹשׁ, הַמְשַׁלְּשִׁים שָׁלוֹשׁ קְדֻשּׁוֹת לְקָדוֹשׁ:

מִתְרַצֶּה בְרַחֲמִים, וּמִתְפַּיֵּס בְּתַחֲנוּנִים, הִתְרַצֵּה וְהִתְפַּיֵּס לְדוֹר עָנִי כִּי אֵין עוֹזֵר:

נגמר כאן התוספות ליומי שני וחמישי

אָבִינוּ מַלְכֵּנוּ אָבִינוּ אָתָּה.
אָבִינוּ מַלְכֵּנוּ אֵין לָנוּ מֶלֶךְ אֶלָּא אָתָּה.
אָבִינוּ מַלְכֵּנוּ רַחֵם עָלֵינוּ.
אָבִינוּ מַלְכֵּנוּ חָנֵּנוּ וַעֲנֵנוּ כִּי אֵין בָּנוּ מַעֲשִׂים עֲשֵׂה עִמָּנוּ צְדָקָה וָחֶסֶד לְמַעַן שִׁמְךָ הַגָּדוֹל וְהוֹשִׁיעֵנוּ:

וַאֲנַחְנוּ לֹא נֵדַע מַה נַּעֲשֶׂה, כִּי עָלֶיךָ עֵינֵינוּ.
זְכֹר רַחֲמֶיךָ יְיָ וַחֲסָדֶיךָ, כִּי מֵעוֹלָם הֵמָּה.

עולם האצילות
עצמות אור אין סוף
ביטול במציאות
יחידה שבנפש
כתר דאצילות

World of Atzilut
Essential Infinite Godly Illumination
Absolute self-annulment
Yechida shb'nefesh
Keter of Atzilut

Lord, God of Israel, refrain from Your fiery wrath, and retract the evil intended for Your people.

When the Fast of Gedaliah occurs on a Monday or Thursday, Selichot for Tzom Gedaliah are recited at this point

Guardian of Israel, guard over the remnants of Israel, do not destroy Israel, who say 'Hear O Israel.'

Guardian of the one people, guard the remnants of the one people, and refrain from destroying the one people, who unite Your Name, 'the Lord Our God, the Lord is One.'

Guardian of the holy people, guard the remnants of the holy people, and refrain from destroying the holy people, who three times mention the three-part sanctification of the Holy One.

He Who accepts us in compassion, and is appeased in grace, accept and be conciliated over the this poor generation, for there is none to help.

Here ends the tachanun prayer for Monday and Thursday, the following is pertinent to every day of the week:

Our Father, our King, You are our Father.

Our Father our King, we have no King other than You.

Our Father, our King, have mercy upon us.

Our Father, our King, grace us and answer us, for we have no good deeds, perform with us justice and kindness for the sake of Your great Name, and save us.

And we do not know what we will do, for our eyes are upon You.

Recall Your mercy, Lord, and Your kindness, for they are forever.

יְהִי חַסְדְּךָ יְיָ עָלֵינוּ, כַּאֲשֶׁר יִחַלְנוּ לָךְ.

אַל תִּזְכָּר לָנוּ עֲוֹנוֹת רִאשֹׁנִים, מַהֵר יְקַדְּמוּנוּ רַחֲמֶיךָ כִּי דַלּוֹנוּ מְאֹד.

חָנֵּנוּ יְיָ חָנֵּנוּ, כִּי רַב שָׂבַעְנוּ בוּז.

בְּרֹגֶז רַחֵם תִּזְכּוֹר, בְּרֹגֶז עֲקֵדָה תִּזְכּוֹר, בְּרֹגֶז תְּמִימוֹת תִּזְכּוֹר, בְּרֹגֶז אַהֲבָה תִּזְכָּר:

יְיָ הוֹשִׁיעָה הַמֶּלֶךְ יַעֲנֵנוּ בְיוֹם קָרְאֵנוּ.

כִּי הוּא יָדַע יִצְרֵנוּ, זָכוּר כִּי עָפָר אֲנָחְנוּ.

עָזְרֵנוּ אֱלֹהֵי יִשְׁעֵנוּ עַל דְּבַר כְּבוֹד שְׁמֶךָ, וְהַצִּילֵנוּ וְכַפֵּר עַל חַטֹּאתֵינוּ לְמַעַן שְׁמֶךָ.

יִתְגַּדַּל וְיִתְקַדַּשׁ שְׁמֵהּ רַבָּא. (קהל: אָמֵן) בְּעָלְמָא דִי בְרָא כִרְעוּתֵהּ וְיַמְלִיךְ מַלְכוּתֵהּ, וְיַצְמַח פֻּרְקָנֵהּ וִיקָרֵב מְשִׁיחֵהּ. (קהל: אָמֵן) בְּחַיֵּיכוֹן וּבְיוֹמֵיכוֹן וּבְחַיֵּי דְכָל בֵּית יִשְׂרָאֵל, בַּעֲגָלָא וּבִזְמַן קָרִיב. וְאִמְרוּ אָמֵן: (קהל: אָמֵן. יְהֵא שְׁמֵהּ רַבָּא מְבָרַךְ לְעָלַם וּלְעָלְמֵי עָלְמַיָּא, יִתְבָּרֵךְ:) יְהֵא שְׁמֵהּ רַבָּא מְבָרַךְ לְעָלַם וּלְעָלְמֵי עָלְמַיָּא, יִתְבָּרֵךְ, וְיִשְׁתַּבַּח, וְיִתְפָּאֵר, וְיִתְרוֹמָם, וְיִתְנַשֵּׂא, וְיִתְהַדָּר, וְיִתְעַלֶּה, וְיִתְהַלָּל, שְׁמֵהּ דְּקֻדְשָׁא בְּרִיךְ הוּא. (קהל: אָמֵן) לְעֵלָּא מִן כָּל בִּרְכָתָא וְשִׁירָתָא, תֻּשְׁבְּחָתָא וְנֶחֱמָתָא, דַּאֲמִירָן בְּעָלְמָא, וְאִמְרוּ אָמֵן: (קהל: אָמֵן)

בימים שאין קריאת התורה ממשיכים עם אשרי

עולם האצילות
עצמות אור אין סוף
ביטול במציאות
יחידה שבנפש
כתר דאצילות

World of Atzilut
Essential Infinite Godly Illumination
Absolute self-annulment
Yechida shb'nefesh
Keter of Atzilut

May Your kindness, God be upon us, as You are our Hope.

Do not recall our former sins, rapidly bring forward Your mercy, since we are very impoverished.

Be gracious, Lord, be gracious, for we are filled with disgrace.

In anger, recall the mercy [of Abraham], in anger recall the binding [of Isaac], in anger recall the perfection [of Jacob], in anger remember the love [of David].

Lord, save us; King, answer us on the day that we call.

For He knows our natural inclination,
He well knows that we are but dust.

Help us, God of our salvation, for the sake of the glory of Your Name, save us and atone for our sins, for the sake of Your Name.

Exalted and sanctified is His great Name. (cong: "Amen") In the universe that He created according to His Will, May He establish His reign, and sprout forth His redemption, and quickly bring His mashiach. (cong: "Amen") In your life and during your days and in the life of the entire house of Israel, speedily and soon, and say Amen! (the congregation here says, "Amen, may His great Name be blessed forever and for eternity") May His great Name be blessed forever and for eternity. (cong: "Amen") May He be blessed, may He be extolled, may He be glorified, may He be exalted, may He be elevated, may He be honored, may He be lauded, and may he be praised, the Name of the holy One, blessed be He. (cong: "Amen") Beyond all the blessings and the hymns, the praises and the consolations that are recited in the world, and let us say Amen.

On days when The Torah is not read continue with Ashrei.

TACHANUN

פרט לימים שלא אומרים תחנון, בימי שני וחמישי מוסיפים:

אֵל אֶרֶךְ אַפַּיִם וְרַב חֶסֶד וֶאֱמֶת, אַל בְּאַפְּךָ תוֹכִיחֵנוּ, חוּסָה יְיָ עַל עַמֶּךָ, וְהוֹשִׁיעֵנוּ מִכָּל רָע, חָטָאנוּ לְךָ אָדוֹן, סְלַח נָא כְּרוֹב רַחֲמֶיךָ אֵל:

סדר קריאת התורה

קוראים את התורה בימי שני, חמישי, ראש חודש, חנוכה, ותעניות ציבור.

וַיְהִי בִּנְסֹעַ הָאָרֹן וַיֹּאמֶר מֹשֶׁה, קוּמָה יְיָ וְיָפֻצוּ אֹיְבֶיךָ וְיָנֻסוּ מְשַׂנְאֶיךָ מִפָּנֶיךָ. כִּי מִצִּיּוֹן תֵּצֵא תוֹרָה וּדְבַר יְיָ מִירוּשָׁלָיִם. בָּרוּךְ שֶׁנָּתַן תּוֹרָה לְעַמּוֹ יִשְׂרָאֵל בִּקְדֻשָּׁתוֹ:

בְּרִיךְ שְׁמֵהּ דְּמָרֵא עָלְמָא, בְּרִיךְ כִּתְרָךְ וְאַתְרָךְ, יְהֵא רְעוּתָךְ עִם עַמָּךְ יִשְׂרָאֵל לְעָלַם, וּפֻרְקַן יְמִינָךְ אַחֲזֵי לְעַמָּךְ בְּבֵית מַקְדְּשָׁךְ, וּלְאַמְטוּיֵי לָנָא מִטּוּב נְהוֹרָךְ וּלְקַבֵּל צְלוֹתָנָא בְּרַחֲמִין. יְהֵא רַעֲוָא קֳדָמָךְ דְּתוֹרִיךְ לָן חַיִּין בְּטִיבוּ, וְלֶהֱוֵי אֲנָא פְקִידָא בְּגוֹ צַדִּיקַיָּא, לְמִרְחַם עָלַי וּלְמִנְטַר יָתִי וְיָת כָּל דִּי לִי, וְדִי לְעַמָּךְ יִשְׂרָאֵל. אַנְתְּ הוּא זָן לְכֹלָּא וּמְפַרְנֵס לְכֹלָּא, אַנְתְּ הוּא שַׁלִּיט עַל כֹּלָּא. אַנְתְּ הוּא דְשַׁלִּיט עַל מַלְכַיָּא. וּמַלְכוּתָא דִּילָךְ הִיא. אֲנָא עַבְדָּא

> World of *Atzilut*
> Essential Infinite Godly Illumination
> Absolute self-annulment
> *Yechida shb'nefesh*
> *Keter* of *Atzilut*

The following paragraph is said on Mondays and Thursdays, except when Tachanun is not said:

Almighty God Who is patient, abounding in kindness and truth, do not rebuke us in anger. Lord, have mercy on Your nation, and save us from anything bad. We have sinned before You, Master, please forgive us in Your great mercy, God.

TORAH READING

At this point the Torah is read on Mondays, Thursdays, Rosh Chodesh, Chanukah, public fast days and Chol haMoed.

And when the ark would journey, Moshe would say, "Rise, O Lord, and Your enemies will scatter, and those who hate you will run away from you. For, the Torah goes out from Zion, and the word of God from Jerusalem. Blessed be He Who gave Torah to His people, in sanctity.

Blessed is the Name of the Master of the universe. Blessed is Your crown and the place [of Your glory]. May Your will be forever with Your people Israel, and with the deliverance of Your right hand, show [re-build] Your people the holy Temple. And may goodness of Your light should reach us and our prayers be accepted in compassion. May it be Your will before You to lengthen our lives in goodness. May I be considered among Your righteous, so that You will have mercy on me and protect me and all that is mine, and that belongs to Your people, Israel. It is You Who sustains everyone and feeds everyone. You govern over everything. You are the One

דְקֻדְשָׁא בְּרִיךְ הוּא, דְסָגִידְנָא קַמֵּהּ וּמִקַּמֵּי דִיקַר אוֹרַיְתֵהּ. בְּכָל עִדָּן וְעִדָּן לָא עַל אֱנָשׁ רָחִיצְנָא וְלָא עַל בַּר אֱלָהִין סָמִיכְנָא. אֶלָּא בֶּאֱלָהָא דִשְׁמַיָּא, דְּהוּא אֱלָהָא קְשׁוֹט, וְאוֹרַיְתֵהּ קְשׁוֹט, וּנְבִיאוֹהִי קְשׁוֹט, וּמַסְגֵּא לְמֶעְבַּד טַבְוָן וּקְשׁוֹט. בֵּהּ אֲנָא רָחִיץ. וְלִשְׁמֵהּ קַדִּישָׁא יַקִּירָא אֲנָא אֵמַר תֻּשְׁבְּחָן. יְהֵא רַעֲוָא קֳדָמָךְ דְּתִפְתַּח לִבָּאִי בְּאוֹרַיְתָא, וְתַשְׁלִים מִשְׁאֲלִין דְּלִבָּאִי, וְלִבָּא דְכָל עַמָּךְ יִשְׂרָאֵל, לְטַב וּלְחַיִּין וְלִשְׁלָם:

החזן מגביה את הספר תורה ואמר:

גַּדְּלוּ לַיְיָ אִתִּי, וּנְרוֹמְמָה שְׁמוֹ יַחְדָּו:

כשנושאים את התורה לבמה כולם אומרים:

לְךָ יְיָ הַגְּדֻלָּה וְהַגְּבוּרָה וְהַתִּפְאֶרֶת וְהַנֵּצַח וְהַהוֹד, כִּי כֹל בַּשָּׁמַיִם וּבָאָרֶץ. לְךָ יְיָ הַמַּמְלָכָה וְהַמִּתְנַשֵּׂא לְכֹל לְרֹאשׁ. רוֹמְמוּ יְיָ אֱלֹהֵינוּ, וְהִשְׁתַּחֲווּ לַהֲדֹם רַגְלָיו, קָדוֹשׁ הוּא. רוֹמְמוּ יְיָ אֱלֹהֵינוּ וְהִשְׁתַּחֲווּ לְהַר קָדְשׁוֹ, כִּי קָדוֹשׁ יְיָ אֱלֹהֵינוּ:

אַב הָרַחֲמִים הוּא יְרַחֵם עַם עֲמוּסִים וְיִזְכּוֹר בְּרִית אֵיתָנִים וְיַצִּיל נַפְשׁוֹתֵינוּ מִן הַשָּׁעוֹת הָרָעוֹת וְיִגְעַר בְּיֵצֶר הָרָע מִן הַנְּשׂוּאִים וְיָחוֹן עָלֵינוּ לִפְלֵיטַת עוֹלָמִים. וִימַלֵּא מִשְׁאֲלוֹתֵינוּ בְּמִדָּה טוֹבָה יְשׁוּעָה וְרַחֲמִים:

Who governs over Your Kingdom, and the Kingdom is Yours. I am the servant of the Holy One, may He be blessed before Whom and before Whose holy Torah I bow. At no time do I place my trust in man, nor do I ever rely upon an angel. Rather, I trust in the God of the heavens, for He is the true God, and His Torah is true and His prophets are true, and He performs multiple deeds of truth and goodness. In Him I trust, and it is His holy and dear Name that I praise. May it be Your will to open our hearts to Torah, and to fulfill the requests of our heart, and the heart of all of Your people, Israel, for the good and for life and for peace.

The chazzan takes the Torah, lifts it slightly, and says:

Exalt the Lord with me,
and let us elevate His Name together.

As the Torah is being carried towards the Bimah the following is recited:

Yours, Lord, is the greatness, and the might and the glory, and the victory, and the splendor, as all that is in the heavens and on the earth. Yours, Lord is the sovereignty and You are elevated, over all. Exalt the Lord our God, and bow down to His footrest, for He is holy. Exalt the Lord our God and bow down at His holy mountain, for holy is the Lord, our God.

May the merciful Father demonstrate mercy with the nation that is borne [by Him], and recall the ancient covenant and shield our souls from evil times, and repulse the evil inclination from those who are carried [by Him]. May He graciously grant us eternal survival and fulfill our requests in generous measure, with salvation and compassion.

החזן קורא לכהן לעלות לתורה.
אם אין כהן אז לוי או ישראל עולה:

וְתִגָּלֶה וְתֵרָאֶה מַלְכוּתוֹ עָלֵינוּ בִּזְמַן קָרוֹב, וְיָחוֹן פְּלֵטָתֵנוּ וּפְלֵטַת עַמּוֹ בֵּית יִשְׂרָאֵל לְחֵן וּלְחֶסֶד וּלְרַחֲמִים וּלְרָצוֹן וְנֹאמַר אָמֵן. הַכֹּל הָבוּ גֹדֶל לֵאלֹהֵינוּ וּתְנוּ כָבוֹד לַתּוֹרָה, כֹּהֵן קְרָב יַעֲמוֹד (פלוני) בֶּן (אלמוני) הַכֹּהֵן, בָּרוּךְ שֶׁנָּתַן תּוֹרָה לְעַמּוֹ יִשְׂרָאֵל בִּקְדֻשָּׁתוֹ:

הקהל עונה וגם החזן:

וְאַתֶּם הַדְּבֵקִים בַּיְיָ אֱלֹהֵיכֶם,
חַיִּים כֻּלְּכֶם הַיּוֹם:

ברכות קריאת התורה

בָּרְכוּ אֶת יְיָ הַמְבֹרָךְ:

בָּרוּךְ יְיָ הַמְבֹרָךְ לְעוֹלָם וָעֶד:

בָּרוּךְ אַתָּה יְיָ אֱלֹהֵינוּ מֶלֶךְ הָעוֹלָם, אֲשֶׁר בָּחַר בָּנוּ מִכָּל הָעַמִּים, וְנָתַן לָנוּ אֶת תּוֹרָתוֹ. בָּרוּךְ אַתָּה יְיָ נוֹתֵן הַתּוֹרָה: (קהל: אָמֵן)

בָּרוּךְ אַתָּה יְיָ אֱלֹהֵינוּ מֶלֶךְ הָעוֹלָם, אֲשֶׁר נָתַן לָנוּ תּוֹרַת אֱמֶת, וְחַיֵּי עוֹלָם נָטַע בְּתוֹכֵנוּ. בָּרוּךְ אַתָּה יְיָ, נוֹתֵן הַתּוֹרָה:
(קהל: אָמֵן)

The Gabbai recites the following to call a Kohen to the Torah. If a Kohen is not present a Levite or Israelite is called up to the Torah instead:

May His reign over us soon be revealed and made visible, and may He deal graciously with our remnant as well as with the remainder of His people, the House of Israel, with harmony and kindness and compassion and goodwill and let us say, Amen. Let us all express the greatness of our God and give honor to the Torah. Let a Cohen approach. Stand forth (call the Hebrew name of the person called up to the Torah, together with his father's name), HaCohen. Blessed be He Who in His holiness gave the Torah to His people, the Jews.

Congregation, followed by the gabbai responds:
And you who cleave to the Lord your God, are alive, all of you, today!

Blessings for the Torah Reading

Blessed be the Lord, Who is blessed

Bless the Lord, Who is blessed forever and ever

Blessed are You, Lord, our God, King of the universe, Who has chosen us from amongst all the nations and given us His Torah. Blessed are You, Lord, Giver of the Torah.

Blessed are You, Lord, our God, King of the universe, Who has given us the true Torah, and planted eternal life amongst us. Blessed be You, Lord, Giver of the Torah.

ברכת הגומל

בָּרוּךְ אַתָּה יְיָ אֱלֹהֵינוּ מֶלֶךְ הָעוֹלָם, הַגּוֹמֵל לְחַיָּבִים טוֹבוֹת, שֶׁגְּמָלַנִי טוֹב:

הקהל עונה:

אָמֵן. מִי שֶׁגְּמָלְךָ טוֹב, הוּא יִגְמָלְךָ כָּל טוֹב סֶלָה:

ברוך שפטרני

אחרי העליה הראשונה של חתן בר מצוה אביו אומר הברכה (אנחנו נוהגים לא להגיד את המילים בסוגריים):

בָּרוּךְ (אַתָּה יְיָ אֱלֹהֵינוּ מֶלֶךְ הָעוֹלָם) שֶׁפְּטָרַנִי מֵעָנְשׁוֹ שֶׁלָּזֶה:

חצי קדיש

יִתְגַּדַּל וְיִתְקַדַּשׁ שְׁמֵהּ רַבָּא. (קהל: אָמֵן) בְּעָלְמָא דִּי בְרָא כִרְעוּתֵהּ וְיַמְלִיךְ מַלְכוּתֵהּ, וְיַצְמַח פֻּרְקָנֵהּ וִיקָרֵב מְשִׁיחֵהּ. (קהל: אָמֵן) בְּחַיֵּיכוֹן וּבְיוֹמֵיכוֹן וּבְחַיֵּי דְכָל בֵּית יִשְׂרָאֵל, בַּעֲגָלָא וּבִזְמַן קָרִיב. וְאִמְרוּ אָמֵן: (קהל: אָמֵן. יְהֵא שְׁמֵהּ רַבָּא מְבָרַךְ לְעָלַם וּלְעָלְמֵי עָלְמַיָּא, יִתְבָּרַךְ:) יְהֵא שְׁמֵהּ רַבָּא מְבָרַךְ לְעָלַם וּלְעָלְמֵי עָלְמַיָּא, יִתְבָּרַךְ, וְיִשְׁתַּבַּח, וְיִתְפָּאַר, וְיִתְרוֹמַם, וְיִתְנַשֵּׂא, וְיִתְהַדָּר, וְיִתְעַלֶּה, וְיִתְהַלָּל, שְׁמֵהּ דְּקֻדְשָׁא בְּרִיךְ הוּא. (קהל: אָמֵן) לְעֵלָּא מִן כָּל בִּרְכָתָא וְשִׁירָתָא, תֻּשְׁבְּחָתָא וְנֶחֱמָתָא, דַּאֲמִירָן בְּעָלְמָא, וְאִמְרוּ אָמֵן: (קהל: אָמֵן)

Thanksgiving Blessing

Blessed be You, Lord our God, King of the Universe, Who grants goodness to the culpable, Who has granted good to me.

Congregation responds:
Amen. He Who has granted good to you, should grant you all good forever!

Bar Mitzvah Blessing

After a bar mitzvah boy's first aliyah his father recites the following blessing (it is our custom to not recite the words in brackets):

Blessed be He who has absolved me from punishment [resulting from] this [boy].

Half Kaddish

Exalted and sanctified is His great Name. (cong: "Amen") In the universe that He created according to His Will, May He establish His reign, and sprout forth His redemption, and quickly bring His mashiach. (cong: "Amen") In your life and during your days and in the life of the entire house of Israel, speedily and soon, and say Amen! (the congregation here says, "Amen, may His great Name be blessed forever and for eternity") May His great Name be blessed forever and for eternity. (cong: "Amen") May He be blessed, may He be extolled, may He be glorified, may He be exalted, may He be elevated, may He be honored, may He be lauded, and may he be praised, the Name of the holy One, blessed be He. (cong: "Amen") Beyond all the blessings and the hymns, the praises and the consolations that are recited in the world, and let us say Amen.

שמחזירים את התורה לארון:

וְזֹאת הַתּוֹרָה אֲשֶׁר שָׂם מֹשֶׁה לִפְנֵי בְּנֵי יִשְׂרָאֵל:

עֵץ חַיִּים הִיא לַמַּחֲזִיקִים בָּהּ, וְתֹמְכֶיהָ מְאֻשָּׁר. דְּרָכֶיהָ דַרְכֵי נֹעַם, וְכָל נְתִיבוֹתֶיהָ שָׁלוֹם. אֹרֶךְ יָמִים בִּימִינָהּ, בִּשְׂמֹאלָהּ עֹשֶׁר וְכָבוֹד. יְיָ חָפֵץ לְמַעַן צִדְקוֹ, יַגְדִּיל תּוֹרָה וְיַאְדִּיר:

אשרי

אַשְׁרֵי יוֹשְׁבֵי בֵיתֶךָ, עוֹד יְהַלְלוּךָ סֶּלָה:

אַשְׁרֵי הָעָם שֶׁכָּכָה לּוֹ,
אַשְׁרֵי הָעָם שֶׁיְיָ אֱלֹהָיו:

תְּהִלָּה לְדָוִד,

אֲרוֹמִמְךָ אֱלוֹהַי הַמֶּלֶךְ,
וַאֲבָרְכָה שִׁמְךָ לְעוֹלָם וָעֶד:

בְּכָל יוֹם אֲבָרְכֶךָּ, וַאֲהַלְלָה שִׁמְךָ לְעוֹלָם וָעֶד:

גָּדוֹל יְיָ וּמְהֻלָּל מְאֹד, וְלִגְדֻלָּתוֹ אֵין חֵקֶר:

דּוֹר לְדוֹר יְשַׁבַּח מַעֲשֶׂיךָ. וּגְבוּרֹתֶיךָ יַגִּידוּ:

הֲדַר כְּבוֹד הוֹדֶךָ, וְדִבְרֵי נִפְלְאֹתֶיךָ אָשִׂיחָה:

וֶעֱזוּז נוֹרְאֹתֶיךָ יֹאמֵרוּ, וּגְדֻלָּתְךָ אֲסַפְּרֶנָּה:

> Soul level of *Neshama*
> World of *Bria*
> Bringing Godliness down to lower worlds

Upon returning the Torah scroll to the Ark:

And this is the Torah that Moshe placed before the children of Israel.

It is a tree of life for those who grasp it, and its supporters are most happy. Its ways are pleasant, and all of its paths are peace. On its right side is long life, at its left side are wealth and honor. The Lord desires to aggrandize and endear the Torah, for the sake of His people's honor.

Ashrei (Psalm 145)

Happy are those who dwell in Your house, they will yet praise You forever.

Happy is the nation for whom this is their lot, happy is the nation whose God is the Lord.

A psalm of praise from David;

I will exalt You, my God the King, and I will bless Your name forever.

Every day, I will bless you, and I will praise Your name forever.

Great is the Lord, and very praiseworthy, there is no limit to His greatness.

One generation to the next praises Your works, and tells of Your might.

Your majesty is glorious, and words of Your wonders I will speak.

They will talk of the boldness of Your awesome acts and of Your greatness I will tell.

זֵכֶר רַב טוּבְךָ יַבִּיעוּ, וְצִדְקָתְךָ יְרַנֵּנוּ:
חַנּוּן וְרַחוּם יְיָ, אֶרֶךְ אַפַּיִם וּגְדָל חָסֶד:
טוֹב יְיָ לַכֹּל, וְרַחֲמָיו עַל כָּל מַעֲשָׂיו:
יוֹדוּךָ יְיָ כָּל מַעֲשֶׂיךָ, וַחֲסִידֶיךָ יְבָרְכוּכָה:
כְּבוֹד מַלְכוּתְךָ יֹאמֵרוּ, וּגְבוּרָתְךָ יְדַבֵּרוּ:
לְהוֹדִיעַ לִבְנֵי הָאָדָם גְּבוּרֹתָיו,
וּכְבוֹד הֲדַר מַלְכוּתוֹ:
מַלְכוּתְךָ, מַלְכוּת כָּל עוֹלָמִים,
וּמֶמְשַׁלְתְּךָ בְּכָל דּוֹר וָדֹר:
סוֹמֵךְ יְיָ לְכָל הַנֹּפְלִים, וְזוֹקֵף לְכָל הַכְּפוּפִים:
עֵינֵי כֹל אֵלֶיךָ יְשַׂבֵּרוּ,
וְאַתָּה נוֹתֵן לָהֶם אֶת אָכְלָם בְּעִתּוֹ:
פּוֹתֵחַ אֶת יָדֶךָ, וּמַשְׂבִּיעַ לְכָל חַי רָצוֹן:
צַדִּיק יְיָ בְּכָל דְּרָכָיו, וְחָסִיד בְּכָל מַעֲשָׂיו:
קָרוֹב יְיָ לְכָל קֹרְאָיו, לְכֹל אֲשֶׁר יִקְרָאֻהוּ בֶאֱמֶת:
רְצוֹן יְרֵאָיו יַעֲשֶׂה, וְאֶת שַׁוְעָתָם יִשְׁמַע וְיוֹשִׁיעֵם:
שׁוֹמֵר יְיָ אֶת כָּל אֹהֲבָיו,
וְאֵת כָּל הָרְשָׁעִים יַשְׁמִיד:
תְּהִלַּת יְיָ יְדַבֶּר פִּי,
וִיבָרֵךְ כָּל בָּשָׂר שֵׁם קָדְשׁוֹ לְעוֹלָם וָעֶד:
וַאֲנַחְנוּ נְבָרֵךְ יָהּ, מֵעַתָּה וְעַד עוֹלָם, הַלְלוּיָהּ:

> Soul level of *Neshama*
> World of *Bria*
> Bringing Godliness down to lower worlds

Remembrance of Your great goodness will be expressed,
and Your righteousness will be sung.
The Lord is harmonious and compassionate,
He is patient, and of great kindness.
The Lord is good to all, and
compassionate over all of His works.
Lord, all of Your works are grateful to You,
and they bless You for Your kindness.
They narrate the honor of Your reign, and speak of Your might.
In order to inform men of His might,
and the honor of His glorious reign.
Your reign is the Kingship of all worlds,
and Your dominion over all generations.
The Lord raises all who have fallen,
and straightens all who are stooped.
The eyes of all gaze at You longingly,
and You grant them their sustenance at the right time.
You open Your hands, and satisfy the
desire of all living creatures.
The Lord is righteous in all of His paths,
and kind in all His deeds.
The Lord is near to all who call Him,
to all who call upon Him in truth.
He fulfills the will of those who fear Him,
hears their cry and saves them.
The Lord guards over all who love Him,
and destroys the wicked.
My mouth speaks the praises of the Lord,
and all flesh blesses His holy name forever.
And we bless God, from now and forever, Halleluyah!

בפורים קוראים כאן את המגילה. בתשעה באב מחזירים את הספר תורה לארון ואומרים קינות. בימים שלא אומרים תחנון מדלגים על הקטע הבא אבל אומרים את זה לפני פרקי תהילים.

לַמְנַצֵּחַ מִזְמוֹר לְדָוִד:

יַעַנְךָ יְיָ בְּיוֹם צָרָה,
יְשַׂגֶּבְךָ שֵׁם אֱלֹהֵי יַעֲקֹב:

יִשְׁלַח עֶזְרְךָ מִקֹּדֶשׁ,
וּמִצִּיּוֹן יִסְעָדֶךָּ:

יִזְכֹּר כָּל מִנְחֹתֶךָ,
וְעוֹלָתְךָ יְדַשְּׁנֶה סֶלָה:

יִתֶּן לְךָ כִלְבָבֶךָ וְכָל עֲצָתְךָ יְמַלֵּא:

נְרַנְּנָה בִּישׁוּעָתֶךָ וּבְשֵׁם אֱלֹהֵינוּ נִדְגֹּל,
יְמַלֵּא יְיָ כָּל מִשְׁאֲלוֹתֶיךָ:

עַתָּה יָדַעְתִּי, כִּי הוֹשִׁיעַ יְיָ מְשִׁיחוֹ,
יַעֲנֵהוּ מִשְּׁמֵי קָדְשׁוֹ,
בִּגְבוּרוֹת יֵשַׁע יְמִינוֹ:

אֵלֶּה בָרֶכֶב וְאֵלֶּה בַסּוּסִים,
וַאֲנַחְנוּ בְּשֵׁם יְיָ אֱלֹהֵינוּ נַזְכִּיר:

הֵמָּה כָּרְעוּ וְנָפָלוּ,
וַאֲנַחְנוּ קַּמְנוּ וַנִּתְעוֹדָד:

יְיָ הוֹשִׁיעָה הַמֶּלֶךְ
יַעֲנֵנוּ בְיוֹם קָרְאֵנוּ:

Soul level of Neshama
World of Bria
Bringing Godliness down to lower worlds

On Purim the Megillah is read at this point. On Tisha b'Av the Sefer Torah is returned to the Ark and the Kinot are said. On days when Tachanun is not said the following paragraph is omitted, however it should be recited before the daily reading of Psalms:

FOR THE CONDUCTOR, A SONG BY DAVID. The Lord will answer you on your day of distress, the Name of the God of Jacob will fortify you.

He will send Your help from His holiness, and from Zion He will support you.

He will recall all of Your offerings, and Your accept Your sacrifices forever.

May He grant you all of your heart's wishes, and fulfill all of your counsel.

We will revel in Your salvation, and be glorified in the Name of Our God, may the Lord fulfill all of your desires.

Now I know, that the Lord saved His anointed one, answering him from His holy heavens, with the might of salvation of His right hand.

There are those who arrive in a chariot, and those on horses, our way is to mention the name of the Lord, our God.

They stumbled and fell, and we arose reinforced.

The Lord is our salvation, the King will answer us on the day we call out.

ובא לציון

וּבָא לְצִיּוֹן גּוֹאֵל וּלְשָׁבֵי פֶשַׁע בְּיַעֲקֹב, נְאֻם יְיָ:

וַאֲנִי זֹאת בְּרִיתִי אוֹתָם אָמַר יְיָ,

רוּחִי אֲשֶׁר עָלֶיךָ, וּדְבָרַי אֲשֶׁר שַׂמְתִּי בְּפִיךָ, לֹא יָמוּשׁוּ מִפִּיךָ וּמִפִּי זַרְעֲךָ וּמִפִּי זֶרַע זַרְעֲךָ, אָמַר יְיָ מֵעַתָּה וְעַד עוֹלָם.

וְאַתָּה קָדוֹשׁ, יוֹשֵׁב תְּהִלּוֹת יִשְׂרָאֵל. וְקָרָא זֶה אֶל זֶה וְאָמַר,

קָדוֹשׁ, קָדוֹשׁ, קָדוֹשׁ, יְיָ צְבָאוֹת, מְלֹא כָל הָאָרֶץ כְּבוֹדוֹ. וּמְקַבְּלִין דֵּין מִן דֵּין וְאָמְרִין: קַדִּישׁ בִּשְׁמֵי מְרוֹמָא עִלָּאָה בֵּית שְׁכִינְתֵּהּ, קַדִּישׁ עַל אַרְעָא עוֹבַד גְּבוּרְתֵּהּ, קַדִּישׁ לְעָלַם וּלְעָלְמֵי עָלְמַיָּא: יְיָ צְבָאוֹת מַלְיָא כָל אַרְעָא זִיו יְקָרֵהּ.

וַתִּשָּׂאֵנִי רוּחַ, וָאֶשְׁמַע אַחֲרַי קוֹל רַעַשׁ גָּדוֹל,

בָּרוּךְ כְּבוֹד יְיָ מִמְּקוֹמוֹ:

וּנְטָלַתְנִי רוּחָא וּשְׁמָעִית בַּתְרַי קָל זִיעַ סַגִּיא דִּמְשַׁבְּחִין וְאָמְרִין בְּרִיךְ יְקָרָא דַיְיָ מֵאֲתַר בֵּית שְׁכִינְתֵּהּ.

יְיָ יִמְלֹךְ לְעֹלָם וָעֶד.

יְיָ מַלְכוּתֵהּ קָאֵים לְעָלַם וּלְעָלְמֵי עָלְמַיָּא.

Soul level of Neshama
World of Bria
Bringing Godliness down to lower worlds

U'Va LeTzion

And a redeemer will come to Zion, and to the repentant sinners of Jacob, says the Lord.

And as for Me, this is my covenant with them, says the Lord.

My spirit that is upon you, and my words that I have placed in your mouth, will not depart from your mouth, or from the mouths of your descendants, nor from the mouths of your descendants' offspring, says the Lord, from now and forever.

And You are holy, ensconced upon the praises of Israel.

Holy, holy, holy, is the Lord of Hosts, His glory fills the earth. And they receive each from the other, saying: He is holy in the supernal heights where His Divine Presence dwells, He is holy on the land, his mighty work, He is holy forever and ever, the Lord of Hosts, a ray of His glory fills the entire land.

And a spirit uplifted me, and I heard the sound of a great noise behind me,

"Blessed be the glory of the Lord, from its place."

And the spirit overtook me and I heard a mighty voice moving behind me, praising and saying, "Blessed be the glory of the Lord, from where it dwells."

The Lord reigns forever and ever.

The sovereignty of the Lord is established for all eternity.

יְיָ אֱלֹהֵי אַבְרָהָם יִצְחָק וְיִשְׂרָאֵל אֲבוֹתֵינוּ,

שָׁמְרָה זֹאת לְעוֹלָם, לְיֵצֶר מַחְשְׁבוֹת לְבַב עַמֶּךְ, וְהָכֵן לְבָבָם אֵלֶיךָ

וְהוּא רַחוּם יְכַפֵּר עָוֹן וְלֹא יַשְׁחִית, וְהִרְבָּה לְהָשִׁיב אַפּוֹ, וְלֹא יָעִיר כָּל חֲמָתוֹ.

כִּי אַתָּה אֲדֹנָי טוֹב וְסַלָּח, וְרַב חֶסֶד לְכָל קֹרְאֶיךָ.

צִדְקָתְךָ צֶדֶק לְעוֹלָם, וְתוֹרָתְךָ אֱמֶת.

> [Following *Kriat Shema* and *Shemonah Esreh*], Godly influence descends to the lower worlds of *BY"A*. The World of *Bria* receives its portion during the prayer *U'va LeTzion*, the World of *Yetzira* receives during the *Shir shel Yom* ('Song of the Day'), and the World of *Asiya* receives during *pitum haketoret* (the incense following *Ein Kelokeinu*). A new revelation from the infinite light of God, from the very source, descends every day and permeates every detail of the creatures of these worlds, renewing their vitality every day..." (*Derech Mitzvotecha* of the *Tzemach Tzedek, Shoresh Mitzvat Tefila*, ch. 11, p. ק"כ)[309]

> The three times that we say *Kadosh* within *U'va LeTzion* correspond to the three paragraphs of the *Kriat Shema*. The first paragraph, containing 42 words, corresponds to the holy name of God (*Ana B'koach*) that is associated with ascent from below to above. The second paragraph, containing seventy-two words (until the word *vesamtem*) corresponds to the name of God which has the *gematria* of 72, and which is associated with the descent of kindness to the world. And the third paragraph, containing the command to wear *tzitzit*, corresponds to the Torah, which imparts both ascent and descent.[310]

> It is the Torah which imparts the power that we possess to bring down the holy infinite light of God. Although the infinite revelation within us becomes revealed as we penetrate the concealments

Soul level of Neshama
World of Bria
Bringing Godliness down to lower worlds

Lord, God of Abraham, of Isaac
and of Israel our fathers;

keep this forever, as the desire and the thoughts
of the heart of Your people, and incline
their hearts toward You.

And He, being merciful, atones for our sins and
refrains from destroying us, He repeatedly
quashes His anger, and avoids arousing all
of His wrath. The Lord saves, the King
answers us on the day that we call [Him].

For, You, Lord are good and forgiving, abounding
in kindness to all those who call upon You.

Your righteousness is forever just,
and your Torah is truth.

---

of the physical body, the power to break through concealment comes from the Torah. Spoken words of Torah impart the ability to bring down light, while our Torah thoughts impart the ability to ascend spiritually. Similarly, the written Torah acts from above to below, while our labor in the oral Torah takes place from below to above.

U'VA LETZION

> 📖 *Within the Words*
>
> The *Targum* (Aramaic translation) of the first word *Kadosh* ("holy") within *U'va LeTzion* is, "Holy in the heights of the heavens above, wherein resides His divine presence…" This indicates elevation from below to above. The *Targum* of the second word *Kadosh* is, "Holy on the earth, expressing His might." This represents descent from above to below. The third word *Kadosh* is translated, "Holy forever and ever." This is an allusion to the holiness of the Torah, which imparts both dynamics, from above to below and below to above. The Torah imparts the power to the Jews to ascend spiritually and to bring holiness down with them from above.

תִּתֵּן אֱמֶת לְיַעֲקֹב, חֶסֶד לְאַבְרָהָם, אֲשֶׁר נִשְׁבַּעְתָּ לַאֲבֹתֵינוּ מִימֵי קֶדֶם.

בָּרוּךְ אֲדֹנָי יוֹם יוֹם יַעֲמָס לָנוּ. הָאֵל יְשׁוּעָתֵנוּ סֶלָה.

יְיָ צְבָאוֹת עִמָּנוּ, מִשְׂגָּב לָנוּ אֱלֹהֵי יַעֲקֹב סֶלָה.

יְיָ צְבָאוֹת, אַשְׁרֵי אָדָם בֹּטֵחַ בָּךְ:

יְיָ הוֹשִׁיעָה, הַמֶּלֶךְ יַעֲנֵנוּ בְיוֹם קָרְאֵנוּ:

❝ There are those who possess a more forceful and revealed element of Godly fire in their heart, comparable to fiery coals. And there are others in whom the Godly spark is concealed within, similar to hot embers. The spark may be small and concealed within but, in any case, it is always present inside the soul of each and every Jew…It is necessary only to blow upon it forcefully and it bursts into flames of fire…" (*Venikdashti* from *Likutei Torah* of the Alter Rebbe, *Parshat Emor*, p. ל"א)[311]

The soul is enclothed within the body on three levels — the head (intellect), the heart (emotions) and the lower body (instincts). In contrast, the energy with which God creates the world is beyond divisions. It is transcendent and beyond our grasp, holy and removed. The limited vitality that enlivens us is called *memalle kol olmin* ("immanent spirituality"). The unlimited light of creation is called *sovev kol olmin* ("transcendent light"). The *Seraphim*, angels of the World of *Bria*, are holy creatures with very high intellectual grasp. Because they sense the holiness that is beyond them, they are in a state of perpetual yearning for transcendent Godliness. They long to "gaze upon the glory of the King" — upon His transcendent holiness in the World of *Atzilut*.

Like the *Seraphim*, man also burns with desire for Godliness. The animal soul of man is composed of the four physical elements: earth, fire, water and air. Within the divine soul of every Jew, there is also fire. The level of fire varies from person to person, but it is present within each and every one of us. There are those within whom the fire burns brightly and intensely like flaming coals, and there are

Soul level of Neshama
World of Bria
Bringing Godliness down to lower worlds

Grant truth to Jacob, kindness to Abraham, as you swore to our forefathers in former days.

Blessed is the master, who loads us up [with goodness] from day to day, the almighty God is our salvation forever.

The Lord of Hosts is with us, the God of Jacob is our fortress forever.

The Lord of hosts, happy is the man who relies upon Him.

The Lord saves, the King answers us when we call to Him."

---

others within whom the fire is concealed, like glowing embers. When the spark is low and concealed, it is necessary to "blow upon it" in order to reveal the fire within. This is called *v'nikdashti* — "and I will be sanctified."

> 📖 *Within the Words*
>
> The way we "blow" upon the fire inside is through prayer. We meditate with focus and persistence as we say the *Shema*, and this actualizes the love that we feel within, "with all of your heart(s)." This also happens when we say the first *Kadosh*; then we become like the angels — the *Seraphim* — who burn with love of God and say the words *Kadosh* once, since they burn with a singular desire to gaze upon the holy transcendent light of Godliness. As we say *Kadosh* a second time, we consider the second group of angels (the *Chayot* of the World of *Yetzirah*), who say *Kadosh* twice because they wish not only to ascend, but also to bring the holy Godliness down with them from above to below. And finally we say *Kadosh* a third time, corresponding to the *Ofanim*, or angels of the World of *Asiya*. Their love of God is *bechol meodecha* ("with all your might") since they throw themselves completely into love of God in order to fulfill His mitzvot properly.

U'VA LETZION

בָּרוּךְ הוּא אֱלֹהֵינוּ שֶׁבְּרָאָנוּ לִכְבוֹדוֹ, וְהִבְדִּילָנוּ מִן הַתּוֹעִים. וְנָתַן לָנוּ תּוֹרַת אֱמֶת, וְחַיֵּי עוֹלָם נָטַע בְּתוֹכֵנוּ, הוּא יִפְתַּח לִבֵּנוּ בְּתוֹרָתוֹ, וְיָשִׂים בְּלִבֵּנוּ אַהֲבָתוֹ וְיִרְאָתוֹ, לַעֲשׂוֹת רְצוֹנוֹ וּלְעָבְדוֹ בְּלֵבָב שָׁלֵם, לֹא נִיגַע לָרִיק וְלֹא נֵלֵד לַבֶּהָלָה.

וּבְכֵן יְהִי רָצוֹן מִלְּפָנֶיךָ יְיָ אֱלֹהֵינוּ
וֵאלֹהֵי אֲבוֹתֵינוּ, שֶׁנִּשְׁמוֹר חֻקֶּיךָ בָּעוֹלָם הַזֶּה,
וְנִזְכֶּה וְנִחְיֶה וְנִרְאֶה, וְנִירַשׁ טוֹבָה וּבְרָכָה,
לִשְׁנֵי, יְמוֹת הַמָּשִׁיחַ וּלְחַיֵּי הָעוֹלָם הַבָּא.

לְמַעַן יְזַמֶּרְךָ כָבוֹד וְלֹא יִדֹּם,
יְיָ אֱלֹהַי לְעוֹלָם אוֹדֶךָּ:

בָּרוּךְ הַגֶּבֶר אֲשֶׁר יִבְטַח בַּיְיָ; וְהָיָה יְיָ, מִבְטַחוֹ.

בִּטְחוּ בַּיְיָ עֲדֵי עַד, כִּי בְּיָהּ יְיָ,
צוּר עוֹלָמִים. וְיִבְטְחוּ בְךָ יוֹדְעֵי שְׁמֶךָ,
כִּי לֹא עָזַבְתָּ דֹּרְשֶׁיךָ יְיָ.

יְיָ חָפֵץ לְמַעַן צִדְקוֹ,
יַגְדִּיל תּוֹרָה וְיַאְדִּיר:

קדיש שלם

יִתְגַּדַּל וְיִתְקַדַּשׁ שְׁמֵהּ רַבָּא. (קהל: אָמֵן)

בְּעָלְמָא דִּי בְרָא כִרְעוּתֵהּ וְיַמְלִיךְ מַלְכוּתֵהּ,
וְיַצְמַח פֻּרְקָנֵהּ וִיקָרֵב מְשִׁיחֵהּ. (קהל: אָמֵן)

> Soul level of *Neshama*
> World of *Bria*
> Bringing Godliness down to lower worlds

BLESSED IS HE, OUR GOD, WHO HAS CREATED IN HIS Honor, and has distinguished us from those who err, and given us His true Torah, and planted everlasting life within us. May He open our hearts to His Torah, and place in our hearts love and fear of Him, [in order] to do His will and to serve Him wholeheartedly, rather than serve Him for naught, nor become confounded.

And so may it be Your will before You, our God and God of our forefathers, that we fulfill Your laws in this world, and merit to live and observe, and inherit the good and the blessing, of the Messianic years and the life of the world to come.

Therefore, I shall sing to You and not be silent, Lord my God, I will forever thank and acknowledge you.

Blessed is the man who trusts in the Lord, and the Lord will be His fortress.

Trust in the Lord forever, for in God the Lord is the strength of worlds. And those who know Your name trust You, for You do not forsake those who seek You, Lord.

The Lord desires for the sake of his [Israel's] righteousness, to aggrandize and glorify the Torah.

Full Kaddish

Exalted and sanctified is His great Name. (cong: "Amen")

In the universe that He created according to His Will, May He establish His reign, and sprout forth His redemption, and quickly bring His mashiach. (cong: "Amen")

בְּחַיֵּיכוֹן וּבְיוֹמֵיכוֹן וּבְחַיֵּי דְכָל בֵּית יִשְׂרָאֵל, בַּעֲגָלָא וּבִזְמַן קָרִיב. וְאִמְרוּ אָמֵן: (קהל: אָמֵן. יְהֵא שְׁמֵהּ רַבָּא מְבָרַךְ לְעָלַם וּלְעָלְמֵי עָלְמַיָּא:)

יְהֵא שְׁמֵהּ רַבָּא מְבָרַךְ לְעָלַם וּלְעָלְמֵי עָלְמַיָּא, יִתְבָּרַךְ, וְיִשְׁתַּבַּח, וְיִתְפָּאַר, וְיִתְרוֹמַם, וְיִתְנַשֵּׂא, וְיִתְהַדָּר, וְיִתְעַלֶּה, וְיִתְהַלָּל, שְׁמֵהּ דְּקֻדְשָׁא בְּרִיךְ הוּא. (קהל: אָמֵן)

לְעֵלָּא מִן כָּל בִּרְכָתָא וְשִׁירָתָא, תֻּשְׁבְּחָתָא וְנֶחֱמָתָא, דַּאֲמִירָן בְּעָלְמָא, וְאִמְרוּ אָמֵן: (קהל: אָמֵן)

תִּתְקַבֵּל צְלוֹתְהוֹן וּבָעוּתְהוֹן דְּכָל בֵּית יִשְׂרָאֵל, קֳדָם אֲבוּהוֹן דִּי בִשְׁמַיָּא, וְאִמְרוּ אָמֵן: (קהל: אָמֵן)

יְהֵא שְׁלָמָא רַבָּא מִן שְׁמַיָּא וְחַיִּים טוֹבִים עָלֵינוּ וְעַל כָּל יִשְׂרָאֵל, וְאִמְרוּ אָמֵן: (קהל: אָמֵן)

עֹשֶׂה שָׁלוֹם (בעשי"ת: הַשָּׁלוֹם) בִּמְרוֹמָיו, הוּא יַעֲשֶׂה שָׁלוֹם עָלֵינוּ, וְעַל כָּל יִשְׂרָאֵל, וְאִמְרוּ אָמֵן: (קהל: אָמֵן)

כשמחזירים את התורה לארון החזן אומר:

יְהַלְלוּ אֶת שֵׁם יְיָ, כִּי נִשְׂגָּב שְׁמוֹ לְבַדּוֹ:

(הקהל עונה:) הוֹדוֹ, עַל אֶרֶץ וְשָׁמָיִם: וַיָּרֶם קֶרֶן לְעַמּוֹ, תְּהִלָּה לְכָל חֲסִידָיו, לִבְנֵי יִשְׂרָאֵל עַם קְרֹבוֹ, הַלְלוּיָהּ:

**Soul level of *Neshama*
World of *Bria*
Bringing Godliness down to lower worlds**

In your life and during your days and in the life of the entire house of Israel, speedily and soon, and say Amen! (the congregation here says, "Amen, may His great Name be blessed forever and for eternity")

May His great Name be blessed forever and for eternity. May He be blessed, may He be extolled, may He be glorified, may He be exalted, may He be elevated, may He be honored, may He be lauded, and may he be praised, the Name of the holy One, blessed be He. (cong: "Amen")

Beyond all the blessings and the hymns, the praises and the consolations that are recited in the world, and let us say Amen. (cong: "Amen")

May the prayers and requests of all of the house of Israel be accepted before their father in Heaven, and let us say Amen (cong: "Amen").

May there be plentiful peace from Heaven and a good life for all of us and for all of Israel, and let us say, Amen (cong: "Amen").

He Who makes peace (during ten days of repentance: "the peace") on high, may He create peace for us and for all of Israel, and let us say Amen (cong: "Amen").

FULL KADDISH

As the Torah is returned to the Ark the following is recited by the chazzan:
Let the Name of the Lord be praised, for His Name alone is exalted.

(Congregation responds:) His glory is over the earth and the heavens. He will elevate the prestige of His people, praise to all of His pious ones, to the children of Israel, His intimate nation, Halleluyah.

בימים שלא אומרים תחנון מדלגים על הבא
וממשיכים עם בֵּית יַעֲקֹב:

תְּפִלָּה לְדָוִד: הַטֵּה יְיָ אָזְנְךָ עֲנֵנִי, כִּי עָנִי, וְאֶבְיוֹן אָנִי: שָׁמְרָה נַפְשִׁי כִּי חָסִיד אָנִי, הוֹשַׁע עַבְדְּךָ אַתָּה אֱלֹהַי, הַבּוֹטֵחַ אֵלֶיךָ: חָנֵּנִי אֲדֹנָי, כִּי אֵלֶיךָ אֶקְרָא כָּל הַיּוֹם: שַׂמֵּחַ נֶפֶשׁ עַבְדֶּךָ, כִּי אֵלֶיךָ אֲדֹנָי נַפְשִׁי אֶשָּׂא: כִּי אַתָּה אֲדֹנָי טוֹב וְסַלָּח, וְרַב חֶסֶד, לְכָל קֹרְאֶיךָ: הַאֲזִינָה יְיָ, תְּפִלָּתִי, וְהַקְשִׁיבָה בְּקוֹל תַּחֲנוּנוֹתָי: הַאֲזִינָה יְיָ, תְּפִלָּתִי, וְהַקְשִׁיבָה, בְּקוֹל תַּחֲנוּנוֹתָי: בְּיוֹם צָרָתִי אֶקְרָאֶךָּ כִּי תַעֲנֵנִי: אֵין כָּמוֹךָ בָאֱלֹהִים אֲדֹנָי, וְאֵין כְּמַעֲשֶׂיךָ: כָּל גּוֹיִם אֲשֶׁר עָשִׂיתָ יָבוֹאוּ וְיִשְׁתַּחֲווּ לְפָנֶיךָ אֲדֹנָי, וִיכַבְּדוּ לִשְׁמֶךָ: כִּי גָדוֹל אַתָּה וְעֹשֵׂה נִפְלָאוֹת אַתָּה אֱלֹהִים לְבַדֶּךָ: הוֹרֵנִי יְיָ, דַּרְכֶּךָ אֲהַלֵּךְ בַּאֲמִתֶּךָ, יַחֵד לְבָבִי לְיִרְאָה שְׁמֶךָ: אוֹדְךָ אֲדֹנָי אֱלֹהַי בְּכָל-לְבָבִי, וַאֲכַבְּדָה שִׁמְךָ לְעוֹלָם: כִּי חַסְדְּךָ גָּדוֹל עָלָי, וְהִצַּלְתָּ נַפְשִׁי מִשְּׁאוֹל תַּחְתִּיָּה: אֱלֹהִים, זֵדִים קָמוּ עָלַי, וַעֲדַת עָרִיצִים בִּקְשׁוּ נַפְשִׁי, וְלֹא שָׂמוּךָ לְנֶגְדָּם: וְאַתָּה אֲדֹנָי אֵל רַחוּם וְחַנּוּן, אֶרֶךְ אַפַּיִם, וְרַב חֶסֶד וֶאֱמֶת: פְּנֵה אֵלַי וְחָנֵּנִי, תְּנָה עֻזְּךָ לְעַבְדֶּךָ, וְהוֹשִׁיעָה לְבֶן אֲמָתֶךָ: עֲשֵׂה עִמִּי אוֹת לְטוֹבָה וְיִרְאוּ שֹׂנְאַי וְיֵבֹשׁוּ, כִּי אַתָּה יְיָ עֲזַרְתַּנִי וְנִחַמְתָּנִי:

בֵּית יַעֲקֹב, לְכוּ וְנֵלְכָה בְּאוֹר יְיָ: כִּי כָּל הָעַמִּים יֵלְכוּ אִישׁ בְּשֵׁם אֱלֹהָיו, וַאֲנַחְנוּ נֵלֵךְ בְּשֵׁם יְיָ אֱלֹהֵינוּ לְעוֹלָם וָעֶד:

יְהִי יְיָ אֱלֹהֵינוּ עִמָּנוּ, כַּאֲשֶׁר הָיָה עִם אֲבֹתֵינוּ, אַל יַעַזְבֵנוּ וְאַל יִטְּשֵׁנוּ:

> Soul level of *Ruach*
> World of *Yetzira*
> Bringing Godliness down to lower worlds

On days when Tachanun is not said the following Psalm is omitted. Continue with "Beit Yaakov":

A psalm for David; Lord, incline Your ear and answer me, for I am a pauper and a poor man. Preserve my soul, for I am pious, deliver Your servant, for You are My God, in Whom I place my trust. Be gracious to me, Lord, for to You I call every day. Make the soul of Your servant joyous, for to You, Lord, I lift my soul. For You, Lord are good and forgiving, abundantly kind to all who call to You. Listen, Lord to my prayer, and heed the voice of my pleas. On the day of my distress, I call to You, for You will answer me. There is none like You, God, among the celestial creatures, my Lord, and nothing like Your works. All of the nations whom You made will come and bow down before You, Lord, and they will honor Your Name. For Your are Great, and You perform wonders, You alone are God. Teach me, Lord, Your ways, that I may walk in Your Truth; unify my heart to fear Your Name. I thank You, Master, my God, will all of my heart, and I honor Your Name forever. For Your kindness overwhelms me, and You delivered my soul from the depths of the grave. God, wrongdoers rise up against me, and a band of malicious men seeks my soul; and they have not taken You into consideration. And You, Master, are a good and gracious God, patient and abounding in kindness and truth. Turn to me and be gracious, give of Your strength to Your servant, and save the son of Your maidservant. Show me a favorable sign, so that those who hate You may see and be ashamed, for You, Lord, have helped me and consoled me.

> House of Jacob, let us go and make progress in the light of the Lord. For, all of the nations walk, each man in the name of his God, and we walk in the name of the Lord, our God, for all eternity.
>
> May the Lord, our God be with us, as He was with our fathers, may He not leave us or forsake us.

FULL KADDISH

לְהַטּוֹת לְבָבֵנוּ אֵלָיו, לָלֶכֶת בְּכָל דְּרָכָיו וְלִשְׁמֹר מִצְוֹתָיו וְחֻקָּיו וּמִשְׁפָּטָיו, אֲשֶׁר צִוָּה, אֶת אֲבֹתֵינוּ:

וְיִהְיוּ דְבָרַי אֵלֶּה אֲשֶׁר הִתְחַנַּנְתִּי לִפְנֵי יְיָ, קְרֹבִים אֶל יְיָ אֱלֹהֵינוּ יוֹמָם וָלָיְלָה, לַעֲשׂוֹת מִשְׁפַּט עַבְדּוֹ, וּמִשְׁפַּט עַמּוֹ יִשְׂרָאֵל דְּבַר יוֹם בְּיוֹמוֹ:

לְמַעַן דַּעַת כָּל עַמֵּי הָאָרֶץ כִּי יְיָ, הוּא הָאֱלֹהִים, אֵין עוֹד:

שִׁיר הַמַּעֲלוֹת לְדָוִד: לוּלֵי יְיָ, שֶׁהָיָה לָנוּ, יֹאמַר נָא יִשְׂרָאֵל:

לוּלֵי יְיָ, שֶׁהָיָה לָנוּ, בְּקוּם עָלֵינוּ אָדָם:

אֲזַי חַיִּים בְּלָעוּנוּ, בַּחֲרוֹת אַפָּם בָּנוּ:

אֲזַי, הַמַּיִם שְׁטָפוּנוּ נַחְלָה עָבַר עַל נַפְשֵׁנוּ:

אֲזַי עָבַר עַל נַפְשֵׁנוּ, הַמַּיִם הַזֵּידוֹנִים:

בָּרוּךְ יְיָ, שֶׁלֹּא נְתָנָנוּ טֶרֶף לְשִׁנֵּיהֶם:

נַפְשֵׁנוּ כְּצִפּוֹר נִמְלְטָה מִפַּח יוֹקְשִׁים, הַפַּח נִשְׁבָּר, וַאֲנַחְנוּ נִמְלָטְנוּ:

עֶזְרֵנוּ בְּשֵׁם יְיָ, עֹשֵׂה שָׁמַיִם וָאָרֶץ:

Soul level of Ruach
World of Yetzira
Bringing Godliness down to lower worlds

That He may incline our hearts to Him, to walk in all of His ways and to keep His commandments and His statutes and laws, that He commanded our fathers.

And may these words of mine that I have pleaded before the Lord, be close to the Lord our God, day and night, that He may fulfill the needs of His servant and the needs of His people Israel, according to their daily requirements.

So that all of the nations of the earth may know that the Lord is our God, there is no other.

A song of ascents for David: Were it not for the Lord Who was with us — so says Israel —

Were it not for the Lord Who was with us, when man rose up against us.

Then they would have swallowed us alive, in their burning rage against us.

Then the waters would have drowned us, the deluge would have swept us away.

Then, the torrential waters would have inundated our souls.

Blessed is the Lord, Who did not let us become fodder in their teeth.

Our soul is like an escaped bird, from the snare of the trapper; the snare broke, and we escaped.

Our help is in the Name of the Lord, Creator of heavens and earth.

FULL KADDISH

שיר של יום

יום ראשון

הַיּוֹם, יוֹם רִאשׁוֹן בְּשַׁבָּת, שֶׁבּוֹ הָיוּ הַלְוִיִּים אוֹמְרִים בְּבֵית הַמִּקְדָּשׁ:

לְדָוִד מִזְמוֹר, לַיְיָ הָאָרֶץ וּמְלוֹאָהּ, תֵּבֵל וְיֹשְׁבֵי בָהּ:

כִּי הוּא עַל יַמִּים יְסָדָהּ, וְעַל נְהָרוֹת יְכוֹנְנֶהָ:

מִי יַעֲלֶה בְהַר יְיָ, וּמִי יָקוּם בִּמְקוֹם קָדְשׁוֹ:

נְקִי כַפַּיִם וּבַר לֵבָב,
אֲשֶׁר לֹא נָשָׂא לַשָּׁוְא נַפְשִׁי,
וְלֹא נִשְׁבַּע לְמִרְמָה:

יִשָּׂא בְרָכָה מֵאֵת יְיָ, וּצְדָקָה מֵאֱלֹהֵי יִשְׁעוֹ:

זֶה דּוֹר דֹּרְשָׁו, מְבַקְשֵׁי פָנֶיךָ יַעֲקֹב סֶלָה:

שְׂאוּ שְׁעָרִים רָאשֵׁיכֶם,
וְהִנָּשְׂאוּ פִּתְחֵי עוֹלָם וְיָבוֹא מֶלֶךְ הַכָּבוֹד:

מִי זֶה מֶלֶךְ הַכָּבוֹד:
יְיָ עִזּוּז וְגִבּוֹר, יְיָ גִּבּוֹר מִלְחָמָה:

שְׂאוּ שְׁעָרִים רָאשֵׁיכֶם וּשְׂאוּ פִּתְחֵי עוֹלָם,
וְיָבֹא מֶלֶךְ הַכָּבוֹד:

מִי הוּא זֶה מֶלֶךְ הַכָּבוֹד,
יְיָ צְבָאוֹת הוּא מֶלֶךְ הַכָּבוֹד סֶלָה:

Song of the Day

Soul level of Ruach
World of Yetzira
Bringing Godliness down to lower worlds

On Sundays, we recite Psalm 24:

TODAY IS THE FIRST DAY OF THE WEEK, ON WHICH THE Levites said the following in the holy Temple:

For David, a Psalm, for the earth and all that fills it is the Lord's, the globe and all who dwell upon it.

For, on the seas, He founded it, and upon the rivers he established it.

Who is allowed to ascend the mountain of the Lord, and who may stand in His holy place?

[He who possesses] clean hands and a pure heart, who has not brought Me up [taken My name] in vain, nor sworn falsely.

He will receive a blessing from the Lord, and justice from the God of his salvation.

This is the generation of seekers of Him, who forever search for the countenance of Jacob.

Lift up your heads, gates, and elevate the entrances of the universe, and let the King of honor arrive.

Who is this King of honor, the Lord, strong and heroic, the Lord is a hero of war.

Lift up your heads, gates, and elevate the entrances of the universe, and let the King of honor arrive.

Who is this King of honor, the Lord of Hosts, is the King of honor forever.

אחרי כל שיר אומרים:

הוֹשִׁיעֵנוּ יְיָ אֱלֹהֵינוּ וְקַבְּצֵנוּ מִן הַגּוֹיִם לְהֹדוֹת לְשֵׁם קָדְשֶׁךָ, לְהִשְׁתַּבֵּחַ בִּתְהִלָּתֶךָ:

בָּרוּךְ יְיָ אֱלֹהֵי יִשְׂרָאֵל מִן הָעוֹלָם וְעַד הָעוֹלָם וְאָמַר כָּל הָעָם אָמֵן הַלְלוּיָהּ:

בָּרוּךְ יְיָ מִצִּיּוֹן שֹׁכֵן יְרוּשָׁלָיִם הַלְלוּיָהּ:

בָּרוּךְ יְיָ אֱלֹהִים אֱלֹהֵי יִשְׂרָאֵל, עֹשֵׂה נִפְלָאוֹת לְבַדּוֹ:

וּבָרוּךְ שֵׁם כְּבוֹדוֹ לְעוֹלָם, וְיִמָּלֵא כְבוֹדוֹ אֶת כָּל הָאָרֶץ, אָמֵן וְאָמֵן: קדיש יתום

יום שני

הַיּוֹם, יוֹם שֵׁנִי בְּשַׁבָּת, שֶׁבּוֹ הָיוּ הַלְוִיִּים אוֹמְרִים בְּבֵית הַמִּקְדָּשׁ:

שִׁיר מִזְמוֹר לִבְנֵי קֹרַח:

גָּדוֹל יְיָ וּמְהֻלָּל מְאֹד, בְּעִיר אֱלֹהֵינוּ הַר קָדְשׁוֹ:

יְפֵה נוֹף מְשׂוֹשׂ כָּל הָאָרֶץ הַר צִיּוֹן, יַרְכְּתֵי צָפוֹן קִרְיַת מֶלֶךְ רָב:

אֱלֹהִים בְּאַרְמְנוֹתֶיהָ נוֹדַע לְמִשְׂגָּב:

כִּי הִנֵּה הַמְּלָכִים נוֹעֲדוּ, עָבְרוּ יַחְדָּו:

הֵמָּה רָאוּ כֵּן תָּמָהוּ, נִבְהֲלוּ נֶחְפָּזוּ:

רְעָדָה, אֲחָזָתַם שָׁם, חִיל כַּיּוֹלֵדָה:

Soul level of *Ruach*
World of *Yetzira*
Bringing Godliness down to lower worlds

After each song of the day, we recite the following:

Save us, Lord our God, and gather us from among the nations, to thank Your holy name, and to revel in Your praises.

Blessed is the Lord, God of Israel from this world to the next world, and the entire nation said Amen, halleluyah!

Blessed is the Lord from Zion, dwelling in Jerusalem, halleluyah.

Blessed is the Lord, God Who is God of Israel, Who alone works wonders.

And blessed is His glorious Name forever, and let the entire earth be full of His glory, amen and amen.

On Mondays, we recite Psalm 48:

THIS IS THE SECOND DAY OF THE WEEK, ON WHICH the Levites said the following in the holy Temple:

A song, a psalm for the children of Korach.

The Lord is great and very praiseworthy, in the city of our God, the mountain of His sanctuary.

Of beautiful scenery, the joy of the whole earth is Mt. Zion, on the northern slopes, the city of the great King.

In its palaces, God became known as a tower of strength.

For here, the kings assembled, they joined forces [to attack Jerusalem].

They beheld [the wonders of the Almighty] and were astonished; they were awe-struck and quickly scattered.

They were seized by trembling there, like a woman in the pangs of labor.

SONG OF THE DAY

בְּרוּחַ קָדִים, תְּשַׁבֵּר אֳנִיּוֹת תַּרְשִׁישׁ:

כַּאֲשֶׁר שָׁמַעְנוּ כֵּן רָאִינוּ בְּעִיר יְיָ צְבָאוֹת, בְּעִיר אֱלֹהֵינוּ, אֱלֹהִים יְכוֹנְנֶהָ עַד עוֹלָם סֶלָה:

דִּמִּינוּ אֱלֹהִים חַסְדֶּךָ, בְּקֶרֶב הֵיכָלֶךָ:

כְּשִׁמְךָ אֱלֹהִים כֵּן תְּהִלָּתְךָ עַל קַצְוֵי אֶרֶץ, צֶדֶק מָלְאָה יְמִינֶךָ:

יִשְׂמַח הַר צִיּוֹן תָּגֵלְנָה בְּנוֹת יְהוּדָה, לְמַעַן מִשְׁפָּטֶיךָ:

סֹבּוּ צִיּוֹן וְהַקִּיפוּהָ, סִפְרוּ מִגְדָּלֶיהָ:

שִׁיתוּ לִבְּכֶם לְחֵילָה פַּסְּגוּ אַרְמְנוֹתֶיהָ, לְמַעַן תְּסַפְּרוּ לְדוֹר אַחֲרוֹן:

כִּי זֶה אֱלֹהִים אֱלֹהֵינוּ עוֹלָם וָעֶד, הוּא יְנַהֲגֵנוּ עַל מוּת:

הוֹשִׁיעֵנוּ וכו' קדיש יתום

יום שלישי

הַיּוֹם, יוֹם שְׁלִישִׁי בְּשַׁבָּת, שֶׁבּוֹ הָיוּ הַלְוִיִּם אוֹמְרִים בְּבֵית הַמִּקְדָּשׁ:

מִזְמוֹר לְאָסָף, אֱלֹהִים נִצָּב בַּעֲדַת אֵל, בְּקֶרֶב אֱלֹהִים יִשְׁפֹּט:

עַד מָתַי תִּשְׁפְּטוּ עָוֶל, וּפְנֵי רְשָׁעִים תִּשְׂאוּ סֶלָה:

שִׁפְטוּ דַל וְיָתוֹם, עָנִי וָרָשׁ הַצְדִּיקוּ:

פַּלְּטוּ דַל וְאֶבְיוֹן, מִיַּד רְשָׁעִים הַצִּילוּ:

> Soul level of *Ruach*
> World of *Yetzira*
> Bringing Godliness down to lower worlds

[Like] an east wind that shatters the ships of Tarshish.

As we have heard, so we saw in the city of the Lord of Hosts, in the city of our God; may God establish it for all eternity.

We imagined, God, Your kindness [as revealed] within Your Sanctuary.

As Your Name, O God [is great], so is Your praise to the ends of the earth; Your right hand is full of righteousness.

Let Mt. Zion rejoice, let the towns of Judah exult, because of Your judgments.

Walk around Zion, encircle her, count her towers.

Consider well her ramparts, behold her lofty citadels, that you may recount it to later generations.

For this God is our God forever and ever; He will lead us eternally.

Save us… (found after the song for Sunday)

On Tuesdays, we recite Psalm 82:

TODAY IS THE THIRD DAY OF THE WEEK, ON WHICH the Levites said the following in the holy Temple:

A psalm for Asaf; God stands in the assembly of the Almighty, amongst the judges He renders judgment.

How long will you render crooked judgments; and show permanent bias toward the wicked!

Judge the poor and the orphans, justify the impoverished and the destitute.

Rescue the poor and the destitute, save them from the hands of the wicked.

לֹא יָדְעוּ וְלֹא יָבִינוּ בַּחֲשֵׁכָה יִתְהַלָּכוּ,
יִמּוֹטוּ כָּל מוֹסְדֵי אָרֶץ:

אֲנִי אָמַרְתִּי אֱלֹהִים אַתֶּם, וּבְנֵי עֶלְיוֹן כֻּלְּכֶם:

אָכֵן כְּאָדָם תְּמוּתוּן, וּכְאַחַד הַשָּׂרִים תִּפֹּלוּ:

קוּמָה אֱלֹהִים שָׁפְטָה הָאָרֶץ,
כִּי אַתָּה תִנְחַל בְּכָל הַגּוֹיִם:

הוֹשִׁיעֵנוּ וכו' קדיש יתום

יום רביעי

הַיּוֹם, יוֹם רְבִיעִי בְּשַׁבָּת, שֶׁבּוֹ הָיוּ הַלְוִיִּם אוֹמְרִים בְּבֵית הַמִּקְדָּשׁ:

אֵל נְקָמוֹת יְיָ, אֵל נְקָמוֹת הוֹפִיעַ:

הִנָּשֵׂא שֹׁפֵט הָאָרֶץ, הָשֵׁב גְּמוּל עַל גֵּאִים:

עַד מָתַי רְשָׁעִים יְיָ, עַד מָתַי רְשָׁעִים יַעֲלֹזוּ:

יַבִּיעוּ יְדַבְּרוּ עָתָק, יִתְאַמְּרוּ כָּל פֹּעֲלֵי אָוֶן:

עַמְּךָ יְיָ יְדַכְּאוּ, וְנַחֲלָתְךָ יְעַנּוּ:

אַלְמָנָה וְגֵר יַהֲרֹגוּ, וִיתוֹמִים יְרַצֵּחוּ:

וַיֹּאמְרוּ, לֹא יִרְאֶה יָּהּ, וְלֹא יָבִין אֱלֹהֵי יַעֲקֹב:

בִּינוּ, בֹּעֲרִים בָּעָם, וּכְסִילִים, מָתַי תַּשְׂכִּילוּ:

Soul level of Ruach
World of Yetzira
Bringing Godliness down to lower worlds

They know not, nor do they understand,
they walk in darkness, they stumble,
the foundations of the earth all tremble.
I said to them, 'You are angels — all of you —
and supernal beings.'
However, like any man you will die,
and like a prince you will fall.
Rise, God and judge the land,
for You will bequeath among all of the nations.
Save us... (found after the song for Sunday)

On Wednesdays, we recite Psalm 94, followed by Psalm 95:1-3

TODAY IS THE FOURTH DAY OF THE WEEK, ON WHICH the Levites said the following in the holy Temple:

The Lord is a God of revenge:
God of revenge, reveal Yourself!
Judge of the earth, arise,
repay the arrogant their just desserts.
How long shall the wicked, Lord,
how long shall the wicked exult?
They express, speaking insolently;
all of the evildoers boast.
They crush Your people, Lord,
and oppress Your heritage.
They kill the widow and the stranger,
and murder the orphans.
And they say, 'The Lord does not see,
the God of Jacob does not grasp.'
Understand, you boors among people;
you fools, when will you wise up?

SONG OF THE DAY

הֲנֹטַע אֹזֶן הֲלֹא יִשְׁמָע, אִם יֹצֵר עַיִן הֲלֹא יַבִּיט:

הֲיֹסֵר גּוֹיִם הֲלֹא יוֹכִיחַ, הַמְלַמֵּד אָדָם דָּעַת:

יְיָ יֹדֵעַ מַחְשְׁבוֹת אָדָם, כִּי הֵמָּה הָבֶל:

אַשְׁרֵי הַגֶּבֶר אֲשֶׁר תְּיַסְּרֶנּוּ יָּה,
וּמִתּוֹרָתְךָ תְלַמְּדֶנּוּ:

לְהַשְׁקִיט לוֹ מִימֵי רָע,
עַד יִכָּרֶה לָרָשָׁע שָׁחַת:

כִּי לֹא יִטֹּשׁ יְיָ עַמּוֹ, וְנַחֲלָתוֹ לֹא יַעֲזֹב:

כִּי עַד צֶדֶק יָשׁוּב מִשְׁפָּט,
וְאַחֲרָיו כָּל יִשְׁרֵי לֵב:

מִי יָקוּם לִי עִם מְרֵעִים,
מִי יִתְיַצֵּב לִי עִם פֹּעֲלֵי אָוֶן:

לוּלֵי יְיָ עֶזְרָתָה לִּי,
כִּמְעַט שָׁכְנָה דוּמָה נַפְשִׁי:

אִם אָמַרְתִּי מָטָה רַגְלִי, חַסְדְּךָ יְיָ יִסְעָדֵנִי:

בְּרֹב שַׂרְעַפַּי בְּקִרְבִּי,
תַּנְחוּמֶיךָ יְשַׁעַשְׁעוּ נַפְשִׁי:

הַיְחָבְרְךָ כִּסֵּא הַוּוֹת, יֹצֵר עָמָל עֲלֵי חֹק:

יָגוֹדּוּ עַל נֶפֶשׁ צַדִּיק, וְדָם נָקִי יַרְשִׁיעוּ:

וַיְהִי יְיָ לִי לְמִשְׂגָּב, וֵאלֹהַי לְצוּר מַחְסִי:

Soul level of Ruach
World of Yetzira
Bringing Godliness down to lower worlds

He who implants the ear — does He not hear,
He who forms the eye — does He not see?

He who chastises nations — does He not rebuke? —
He who imparts knowledge to man —
[does He not know]?

The Lord knows the thoughts of man,
that they are naught.

Fortunate is the man whom You chastise, Lord,
and whom You instruct in Your Torah.

In order to calm him down in times of adversity,
until the pit is dug for the wicked.

For the Lord will not abandon His people,
nor forsake His heritage.

Until judgment matches [corresponds to] justice,
and all the upright of heart pursue it.

Who would rise up for me against the wicked ones,
who would stand up for me against the evildoers?

Had the Lord not helped me, my soul would soon
have dwelt in the silence [of the grave].

When I thought that my foot was slipping,
Your kindness, Lord supported me.

When [worrisome] thoughts multiply within me,
Your consolation delights my soul.

Can the seat of evil, which turns iniquity into law,
consort with You?

They band together against the life of the righteous,
and condemn innocent blood.

The Lord has been my stronghold;
my God, the Rock of my refuge.

SONG OF THE DAY

PRAYING LIKE FIRE AND WATER

וַיֵּשֶׁב עֲלֵיהֶם אֶת אוֹנָם, וּבְרָעָתָם יַצְמִיתֵם,
יַצְמִיתֵם יְיָ אֱלֹהֵינוּ:

לְכוּ נְרַנְּנָה לַיְיָ, נָרִיעָה לְצוּר יִשְׁעֵנוּ:

נְקַדְּמָה פָנָיו בְּתוֹדָה, בִּזְמִרוֹת נָרִיעַ לוֹ:

כִּי אֵל גָּדוֹל יְיָ,
וּמֶלֶךְ גָּדוֹל עַל כָּל אֱלֹהִים:

הוֹשִׁיעֵנוּ וְכוּ' קדיש יתום

יום חמישי

הַיּוֹם, יוֹם חֲמִישִׁי בְּשַׁבָּת, שֶׁבּוֹ הָיוּ הַלְוִיִּם אוֹמְרִים בְּבֵית הַמִּקְדָּשׁ:

לַמְנַצֵּחַ עַל הַגִּתִּית לְאָסָף:

הַרְנִינוּ, לֵאלֹהִים עוּזֵּנוּ,
הָרִיעוּ לֵאלֹהֵי יַעֲקֹב:

שְׂאוּ זִמְרָה וּתְנוּ תֹף, כִּנּוֹר נָעִים עִם נָבֶל:

תִּקְעוּ בַחֹדֶשׁ שׁוֹפָר, בַּכֵּסֶה לְיוֹם חַגֵּנוּ:

כִּי חֹק לְיִשְׂרָאֵל הוּא,
מִשְׁפָּט לֵאלֹהֵי יַעֲקֹב:

עֵדוּת, בִּיהוֹסֵף שָׂמוֹ בְּצֵאתוֹ עַל אֶרֶץ מִצְרָיִם,
שְׂפַת לֹא יָדַעְתִּי אֶשְׁמָע:

הֲסִירוֹתִי מִסֵּבֶל שִׁכְמוֹ, כַּפָּיו מִדּוּד תַּעֲבֹרְנָה:

Soul level of Ruach
World of Yetzira
Bringing Godliness down to lower worlds

He will turn their violence against them and
destroy them through their own wickedness;
the Lord our God will destroy them.

Come, let us sing to the Lord; let us raise our voices
in jubilation to the Rock of our deliverance.

Let us approach Him with thanksgiving;
let us raise our voices to Him in song.

For the Lord is a great God,
and a great King over all supernal beings.

Save us ... (found after the song for Sunday)

On Thursdays, we recite Psalm 81:

O**N THE FIFTH DAY OF THE WEEK, THE LEVITES** would say in the holy Temple:

For the conductor, a psalm sung on the Gitit
[a musical instrument], for Asaf.

Sing joyously to God, our strength;
sound the shofar to the God of Jacob.

Raise your voice in song: sound the drum,
the pleasant harp and the lyre.

Blow the shofar on the new moon,
on the designated day of our festival.

For it is a decree for Israel, a ruling of the God of Jacob.

He established it as a testimony for Yehoseph
when he went forth over the land of Egypt;
I heard a language I did not know.

I relieved his shoulders of their burden;
his hands from the cauldron.

בַּצָּרָה קָרָאתָ וָאֲחַלְּצֶךָּ אֶעֶנְךָ בְּסֵתֶר רַעַם, אֶבְחָנְךָ עַל מֵי מְרִיבָה סֶלָה:

שְׁמַע עַמִּי וְאָעִידָה בָּךְ, יִשְׂרָאֵל אִם תִּשְׁמַע לִי:

לֹא-יִהְיֶה בְךָ, אֵל זָר, וְלֹא תִשְׁתַּחֲוֶה לְאֵל נֵכָר:

אָנֹכִי יְיָ אֱלֹהֶיךָ הַמַּעַלְךָ מֵאֶרֶץ מִצְרָיִם, הַרְחֶב פִּיךָ וַאֲמַלְאֵהוּ:

וְלֹא שָׁמַע עַמִּי לְקוֹלִי, וְיִשְׂרָאֵל לֹא אָבָה לִי:

וָאֲשַׁלְּחֵהוּ בִּשְׁרִירוּת לִבָּם, יֵלְכוּ בְּמוֹעֲצוֹתֵיהֶם:

לוּ עַמִּי שֹׁמֵעַ לִי, יִשְׂרָאֵל בִּדְרָכַי יְהַלֵּכוּ:

כִּמְעַט אוֹיְבֵיהֶם אַכְנִיעַ, וְעַל צָרֵיהֶם אָשִׁיב יָדִי:

מְשַׂנְאֵי יְיָ יְכַחֲשׁוּ לוֹ, וִיהִי עִתָּם לְעוֹלָם:

וַיַּאֲכִילֵהוּ מֵחֵלֶב חִטָּה, וּמִצּוּר דְּבַשׁ אַשְׂבִּיעֶךָ:

הוֹשִׁיעֵנוּ וכו' קדיש יתום

יום שישי

הַ**יּוֹם**, יוֹם שִׁשִּׁי בְּשַׁבָּת, שֶׁבּוֹ הָיוּ הַלְוִיִּים אוֹמְרִים בְּבֵית הַמִּקְדָּשׁ:

יְיָ מָלָךְ גֵּאוּת לָבֵשׁ, לָבֵשׁ יְיָ, עֹז הִתְאַזָּר, אַף תִּכּוֹן תֵּבֵל בַּל תִּמּוֹט:

Soul level of Ruach
World of Yetzira
Bringing Godliness down to lower worlds

In distress you called and I delivered you; [you called] in secret, and I answered you with thunderous wonders; I tested you at the waters of Merivah, Selah.

Hear, my people, and I will testify on your behalf; Israel, if you would only listen to Me!

You shall have no alien god within you, nor shall you bow down to a foreign deity.

I am the Lord your God who brought you up from the land of Egypt; open your mouth wide [state all of your desires], and I will fill it.

But, My people did not heed My voice; Israel did not want [to listen to] Me.

So, I sent them away in the stubbornness of their heart, that they should follow their own [evil] design.

If only My people would listen to Me, if Israel would only walk in My ways.

I would speedily subdue their enemies, and turn My hand against their oppressors. Those who hate the Lord would shrivel before Him, and the time [of the retribution] shall be forever.

And He would feed him [Israel] with the finest of wheat, and satisfy him with honey from the rock.

Save us... (found after the song for Sunday)

On Friday's, we say Psalm 93

SONG OF THE DAY

ON THE SIXTH DAY OF THE WEEK, THE LEVITES would say the following in the Holy Temple:

The Lord reigns; He is garbed in majesty, the Lord is enclothed, He is girded with strength, and He has firmly established the globe so that it will not falter.

נָכוֹן כִּסְאֲךָ מֵאָז, מֵעוֹלָם אָתָּה:

נָשְׂאוּ נְהָרוֹת יְיָ, נָשְׂאוּ נְהָרוֹת קוֹלָם,
יִשְׂאוּ נְהָרוֹת דָּכְיָם:

מִקֹּלוֹת מַיִם רַבִּים אַדִּירִים מִשְׁבְּרֵי יָם,
אַדִּיר בַּמָּרוֹם יְיָ:

עֵדֹתֶיךָ נֶאֶמְנוּ מְאֹד,
לְבֵיתְךָ נַאֲוָה קֹדֶשׁ, יְיָ, לְאֹרֶךְ יָמִים:

הוֹשִׁיעֵנוּ וכו' קדיש יתום

בראש חודש אומרים:

בָּרְכִי נַפְשִׁי אֶת יְיָ, יְיָ אֱלֹהַי גָּדַלְתָּ מְאֹד,
הוֹד וְהָדָר לָבָשְׁתָּ:

עֹטֶה אוֹר כַּשַּׂלְמָה, נוֹטֶה שָׁמַיִם כַּיְרִיעָה:

הַמְקָרֶה בַמַּיִם עֲלִיּוֹתָיו, הַשָּׂם עָבִים רְכוּבוֹ,
הַמְהַלֵּךְ, עַל כַּנְפֵי רוּחַ:

עֹשֶׂה מַלְאָכָיו רוּחוֹת, מְשָׁרְתָיו אֵשׁ לֹהֵט:

יָסַד אֶרֶץ עַל מְכוֹנֶיהָ, בַּל תִּמּוֹט עוֹלָם וָעֶד:

תְּהוֹם כַּלְּבוּשׁ כִּסִּיתוֹ, עַל הָרִים יַעַמְדוּ מָיִם:

מִן גַּעֲרָתְךָ יְנוּסוּן,
מִן קוֹל רַעַמְךָ יֵחָפֵזוּן:

יַעֲלוּ הָרִים יֵרְדוּ בְקָעוֹת,
אֶל מְקוֹם זֶה יָסַדְתָּ לָהֶם:

Soul level of Ruach
World of Yetzira
Bringing Godliness down to lower worlds

Your throne is firmly established from of old,
You are from eternity.

The rivers raise, Lord, the rivers raise their voices,
the rivers uplift their waves.

More than the sound of mighty waters, and the [sound of] ocean breakers, is the might of the Lord above.

Your testimony is very trustworthy, Your house will be magnificent in holiness, Lord, forever.

Save us … (found after the song for Sunday)

On Rosh Chodesh (the beginning of the new month, which may be either one or two days), we recite the following after the song of the day:

My soul, bless the Lord; Lord my God,
You are greatly exalted, You

have garbed yourself with majesty and splendor.

You enwrap [Yourself] with light as with a garment:
You spread the heavens as a curtain.

He roofs His heavens with water; He makes the clouds His chariot, He causes [them] to move on the wings of the wind.

He makes the wind His messengers,
the blazing fire His servants.

He established the earth on its foundations,
that it shall never falter.

The depths covered it like a garment;
the waters stood above the mountains.

At Your exhortation they fled; at the sound of
Your thunder they rushed away.

They ascended mountains, they flowed down valleys,
to the place which You assigned to them.

SONG OF THE DAY

גְּבוּל שַׂמְתָּ בַּל יַעֲבֹרוּן, בַּל יְשׁוּבוּן, לְכַסּוֹת הָאָרֶץ:

הַמְשַׁלֵּחַ מַעְיָנִים בַּנְּחָלִים, בֵּין הָרִים יְהַלֵּכוּן:

יַשְׁקוּ כָּל חַיְתוֹ שָׂדָי, יִשְׁבְּרוּ פְרָאִים צְמָאָם:

עֲלֵיהֶם עוֹף הַשָּׁמַיִם יִשְׁכּוֹן, מִבֵּין עֳפָאיִם יִתְּנוּ קוֹל:

מַשְׁקֶה הָרִים מֵעֲלִיּוֹתָיו, מִפְּרִי מַעֲשֶׂיךָ תִּשְׂבַּע הָאָרֶץ:

מַצְמִיחַ חָצִיר לַבְּהֵמָה, וְעֵשֶׂב לַעֲבֹדַת הָאָדָם, לְהוֹצִיא לֶחֶם מִן הָאָרֶץ:

וְיַיִן יְשַׂמַּח לְבַב אֱנוֹשׁ, לְהַצְהִיל פָּנִים מִשָּׁמֶן, וְלֶחֶם, לְבַב אֱנוֹשׁ יִסְעָד:

יִשְׂבְּעוּ עֲצֵי יְיָ, אַרְזֵי לְבָנוֹן אֲשֶׁר נָטָע:

אֲשֶׁר שָׁם צִפֳּרִים יְקַנֵּנוּ, חֲסִידָה בְּרוֹשִׁים בֵּיתָהּ:

הָרִים הַגְּבֹהִים לַיְּעֵלִים, סְלָעִים מַחְסֶה לַשְׁפַנִּים:

עָשָׂה יָרֵחַ לְמוֹעֲדִים, שֶׁמֶשׁ יָדַע מְבוֹאוֹ:

תָּשֶׁת חֹשֶׁךְ וִיהִי לָיְלָה, בּוֹ תִרְמֹשׂ כָּל חַיְתוֹ יָעַר:

הַכְּפִירִים שֹׁאֲגִים לַטָּרֶף, וּלְבַקֵּשׁ מֵאֵל אָכְלָם:

תִּזְרַח הַשֶּׁמֶשׁ יֵאָסֵפוּן, וְאֶל מְעוֹנֹתָם יִרְבָּצוּן:

יֵצֵא אָדָם לְפָעֳלוֹ, וְלַעֲבֹדָתוֹ עֲדֵי עָרֶב:

מָה רַבּוּ מַעֲשֶׂיךָ יְיָ, כֻּלָּם בְּחָכְמָה עָשִׂיתָ, מָלְאָה הָאָרֶץ קִנְיָנֶךָ:

Soul level of Ruach
World of Yetzira
Bringing Godliness down to lower worlds

You set a boundary which they may not cross, so that they should not return to engulf the earth.

He sends forth springs into streams; they flow between the mountains.

They water all the beasts of the field; the wild animals quench their thirst.

Above them dwell the birds of the heaven; they raise their voices from among the foliage.

He irrigates the mountains from His clouds above; the earth is satiated from the fruit of Your works.

He causes grass to grow for the cattle; and vegetation for the labor of man, to bring forth food from the earth.

Wine that gladdens man's heart, oil that makes the face shine, and bread that sustains man's heart.

The trees of the Lord drink their fill, the cedars of Lebanon which He planted.

Wherein birds build their nests; the stork has her home in the cypress.

The high mountains are for the wild goats; the rocks are a refuge for the rabbits.

He made the moon to calculate the festivals; the sun knows its place of setting.

You bring on darkness and it is night, when all the beasts of the forest creep forth.

The young lions roar for prey, and seek their food from God.

When the sun rises, they return and lie down in their dens.

Then, man goes out to his work, to his labor until evening.

How manifold are Your works, Lord, You have made them all with wisdom, the earth is full of Your possessions.

זֶה הַיָּם גָּדוֹל וּרְחַב יָדָיִם, שָׁם רֶמֶשׂ וְאֵין מִסְפָּר, חַיּוֹת קְטַנּוֹת עִם גְּדֹלוֹת:

שָׁם אֳנִיּוֹת יְהַלֵּכוּן, לִוְיָתָן זֶה יָצַרְתָּ לְשַׂחֶק בּוֹ:

כֻּלָּם אֵלֶיךָ יְשַׂבֵּרוּן, לָתֵת אָכְלָם בְּעִתּוֹ:

תִּתֵּן לָהֶם יִלְקֹטוּן, תִּפְתַּח יָדְךָ יִשְׂבְּעוּן טוֹב:

תַּסְתִּיר פָּנֶיךָ יִבָּהֵלוּן, תֹּסֵף רוּחָם יִגְוָעוּן, וְאֶל עֲפָרָם יְשׁוּבוּן:

תְּשַׁלַּח רוּחֲךָ יִבָּרֵאוּן, וּתְחַדֵּשׁ פְּנֵי אֲדָמָה:

יְהִי כְבוֹד יְיָ לְעוֹלָם, יִשְׂמַח יְיָ בְּמַעֲשָׂיו:

הַמַּבִּיט לָאָרֶץ וַתִּרְעָד, יִגַּע בֶּהָרִים וְיֶעֱשָׁנוּ:

אָשִׁירָה לַיְיָ בְּחַיָּי, אֲזַמְּרָה לֵאלֹהַי בְּעוֹדִי:

יֶעֱרַב עָלָיו שִׂיחִי, אָנֹכִי אֶשְׂמַח בַּיְיָ:

יִתַּמּוּ חַטָּאִים מִן הָאָרֶץ וּרְשָׁעִים עוֹד אֵינָם,

בָּרְכִי נַפְשִׁי אֶת יְיָ, הַלְלוּיָהּ:

<small>מראש חודש אלול עד הושענא רבא אומרים תהילים פרק כ"ז:</small>

לְדָוִד, יְיָ אוֹרִי וְיִשְׁעִי מִמִּי אִירָא, יְיָ מָעוֹז חַיַּי מִמִּי אֶפְחָד:

בִּקְרֹב עָלַי מְרֵעִים לֶאֱכֹל אֶת בְּשָׂרִי צָרַי וְאֹיְבַי לִי, הֵמָּה כָּשְׁלוּ וְנָפָלוּ:

> Soul level of *Ruach*
> World of *Yetzira*
> Bringing Godliness down to lower worlds

This sea, vast and wide, where there are countless
creeping creatures, living things small and great.
There ships travel, there is the Leviatan
that Your created to frolic therein.
They all look expectantly to You to give them
their food at the proper time.
When You give it to them, they gather it; when
You open Your hand, they are satiated with goodness.
When you conceal Your countenance, they are
terrified; when you take back their spirit,
they perish and return to their dust.
When You send forth Your spirit they are created anew,
and you renew the face of the earth.
May the glory of the Lord endure forever;
may the Lord find delight in His works.
He gazes upon the earth and it trembles;
he touches the mountains and they erupt.
I sing to the Lord with my life:
I chant praise to my God with my [entire] being.
May my prayer be pleasant to Him; I will rejoice in the Lord.
May sin be excised from the earth,
and the wicked be no more.
Bless the Lord, my soul, Halleluyah!

SONG OF THE DAY

From the first day of Rosh Chodesh Elul through Hoshana Rabba, Psalm 27, is recited:

For David; the Lord is my light and my salvation —
whom shall I fear? The Lord is the strength of
my life — whom shall I dread?
When evildoers approached me to devour my flesh, my
oppressors and my foes, they stumbled and fell.

אִם תַּחֲנֶה עָלַי מַחֲנֶה לֹא יִירָא לִבִּי, אִם תָּקוּם עָלַי מִלְחָמָה, בְּזֹאת אֲנִי בוֹטֵחַ:

אַחַת שָׁאַלְתִּי מֵאֵת יְיָ אוֹתָהּ אֲבַקֵּשׁ, שִׁבְתִּי בְּבֵית יְיָ, כָּל יְמֵי חַיַּי, לַחֲזוֹת בְּנֹעַם יְיָ וּלְבַקֵּר בְּהֵיכָלוֹ:

כִּי יִצְפְּנֵנִי בְּסֻכֹּה בְּיוֹם רָעָה יַסְתִּרֵנִי בְּסֵתֶר אָהֳלוֹ, בְּצוּר יְרוֹמְמֵנִי:

וְעַתָּה יָרוּם רֹאשִׁי עַל אֹיְבַי סְבִיבוֹתַי, וְאֶזְבְּחָה בְאָהֳלוֹ זִבְחֵי תְרוּעָה, אָשִׁירָה וַאֲזַמְּרָה לַיְיָ:

שְׁמַע יְיָ קוֹלִי אֶקְרָא, וְחָנֵּנִי וַעֲנֵנִי:

לְךָ אָמַר לִבִּי, בַּקְּשׁוּ פָנָי, אֶת פָּנֶיךָ יְיָ אֲבַקֵּשׁ:

אַל תַּסְתֵּר פָּנֶיךָ מִמֶּנִּי, אַל תַּט בְּאַף עַבְדֶּךָ עֶזְרָתִי הָיִיתָ, אַל תִּטְּשֵׁנִי וְאַל תַּעַזְבֵנִי אֱלֹהֵי יִשְׁעִי:

כִּי אָבִי וְאִמִּי עֲזָבוּנִי, וַיְיָ יַאַסְפֵנִי:

הוֹרֵנִי יְיָ דַּרְכֶּךָ וּנְחֵנִי בְּאֹרַח מִישׁוֹר, לְמַעַן שֹׁרְרָי:

אַל תִּתְּנֵנִי בְּנֶפֶשׁ צָרָי, כִּי קָמוּ בִי עֵדֵי שֶׁקֶר וִיפֵחַ חָמָס:

לוּלֵא הֶאֱמַנְתִּי לִרְאוֹת בְּטוּב יְיָ בְּאֶרֶץ חַיִּים:

קַוֵּה אֶל יְיָ חֲזַק וְיַאֲמֵץ לִבֶּךָ וְקַוֵּה אֶל יְיָ:

Soul level of Ruach
World of Yetzira
Bringing Godliness down to lower worlds

If an army were to beleaguer me, my heart would not fear; if war were to arise against me, in this I trust.

One thing I have asked of the Lord, this I seek; that I may dwell in the House of the Lord all the days of my life, to behold the pleasantness of the Lord and to meditate in His Sanctuary.

For He will hide me in His tabernacle on the day of adversity; He will conceal me in the nooks of His tent; He will lift me upon a rock.

And now, my head will be raised above my enemies surrounding me, and I will offer sacrifices of jubilation in His tabernacle; I will sing and chant to the Lord.

Lord, hear my voice as I call; be gracious to me and answer me.

On Your behalf my heart says, "Seek My countenance," Your countenance, Lord I will seek.

Do not conceal your countenance from me, nor cast aside Your servant in wrath; You have been my help; do not abandon me nor forsake me, God of my deliverance.

Though my father and mother have forsaken me, the Lord has taken me in.

Lord, teach me Your way and lead me in the path of righteousness because of my watchful enemies.

Do not give me over to the will of my oppressors, for there have risen against me false witnesses and they speak evil.

[They would have crushed me] had I not believed that I would see the goodness of the Lord in the land of the living.

Hope in the Lord, be strong, and He will give your heart courage, and hope in the Lord.

קדיש יתום

יִתְגַּדַּל וְיִתְקַדַּשׁ שְׁמֵהּ רַבָּא. (קהל: אָמֵן)

בְּעָלְמָא דִּי בְרָא כִרְעוּתֵהּ וְיַמְלִיךְ מַלְכוּתֵהּ, וְיַצְמַח פֻּרְקָנֵהּ וִיקָרֵב מְשִׁיחֵהּ.
(קהל: אָמֵן)

בְּחַיֵּיכוֹן וּבְיוֹמֵיכוֹן וּבְחַיֵּי דְכָל בֵּית יִשְׂרָאֵל, בַּעֲגָלָא וּבִזְמַן קָרִיב. וְאִמְרוּ אָמֵן:

(קהל: אָמֵן. יְהֵא שְׁמֵהּ רַבָּא מְבָרַךְ לְעָלַם וּלְעָלְמֵי עָלְמַיָּא, יִתְבָּרַךְ:)

יְהֵא שְׁמֵהּ רַבָּא מְבָרַךְ לְעָלַם וּלְעָלְמֵי עָלְמַיָּא, יִתְבָּרַךְ, וְיִשְׁתַּבַּח, וְיִתְפָּאַר, וְיִתְרוֹמַם, וְיִתְנַשֵּׂא, וְיִתְהַדָּר, וְיִתְעַלֶּה, וְיִתְהַלָּל, שְׁמֵהּ דְּקֻדְשָׁא בְּרִיךְ הוּא.
(קהל: אָמֵן)

לְעֵלָּא מִן כָּל בִּרְכָתָא וְשִׁירָתָא, תֻּשְׁבְּחָתָא וְנֶחֱמָתָא, דַּאֲמִירָן בְּעָלְמָא, וְאִמְרוּ אָמֵן:
(קהל: אָמֵן)

יְהֵא שְׁלָמָא רַבָּא מִן שְׁמַיָּא וְחַיִּים טוֹבִים עָלֵינוּ וְעַל כָּל יִשְׂרָאֵל, וְאִמְרוּ אָמֵן:

עֹשֶׂה שָׁלוֹם (בעשי"ת: הַשָּׁלוֹם) בִּמְרוֹמָיו הוּא יַעֲשֶׂה שָׁלוֹם עָלֵינוּ וְעַל כָּל יִשְׂרָאֵל, וְאִמְרוּ אָמֵן:

The Mourners Kaddish

<small>Soul level of *Ruach*
World of *Yetzira*
Bringing Godliness down to lower worlds</small>

Exalted and sanctified is His great Name. (cong: "Amen")

In the universe that He created according to His Will,
May He establish His reign, and sprout forth
His redemption, and quickly bring His mashiach.
(cong: "Amen")

In your life and during your days and in the life of the
entire house of Israel, speedily and soon,
and say Amen!

(the congregation here says: "Amen, may His great Name
be blessed forever and for eternity")

May His great Name be blessed forever and for eternity.
May He be blessed, may He be extolled, may He be
glorified, may He be exalted, may He be elevated,
may He be honored, may He be lauded, and may he
be praised, the Name of the holy One, blessed be He.
(cong: "Amen")

Beyond all the blessings and the hymns, the praises and
the consolations that are recited in the world,
and let us say Amen.

May there be plentiful peace from Heaven and
a good life for all of us and for all of Israel,
and let us say, Amen (cong: "Amen").

He Who makes peace (during ten days of repentance: "the
peace") on high, may He create peace
for us and for all of Israel, and
let us say Amen (cong: "Amen").

אין כאלקינו

קַוֵּה אֶל יְיָ, חֲזַק וְיַאֲמֵץ לִבֶּךָ וְקַוֵּה אֶל יְיָ: אֵין קָדוֹשׁ כַּיְיָ, כִּי אֵין בִּלְתֶּךָ, וְאֵין צוּר כֵּאלֹהֵינוּ: כִּי מִי אֱלוֹהַּ מִבַּלְעֲדֵי יְיָ; וּמִי צוּר זוּלָתִי אֱלֹהֵינוּ:

אֵין כֵּאלֹהֵינוּ, אֵין כַּאדוֹנֵינוּ,
אֵין כְּמַלְכֵּנוּ, אֵין כְּמוֹשִׁיעֵנוּ:

מִי כֵאלֹהֵינוּ, מִי כַאדוֹנֵינוּ,
מִי כְמַלְכֵּנוּ, מִי כְמוֹשִׁיעֵנוּ:

נוֹדֶה לֵאלֹהֵינוּ, נוֹדֶה לַאדוֹנֵינוּ,
נוֹדֶה לְמַלְכֵּנוּ, נוֹדֶה לְמוֹשִׁיעֵנוּ:

בָּרוּךְ אֱלֹהֵינוּ, בָּרוּךְ אֲדוֹנֵינוּ,
בָּרוּךְ מַלְכֵּנוּ, בָּרוּךְ מוֹשִׁיעֵנוּ:

אַתָּה הוּא אֱלֹהֵינוּ, אַתָּה הוּא אֲדוֹנֵינוּ, אַתָּה הוּא מַלְכֵּנוּ, אַתָּה הוּא מוֹשִׁיעֵנוּ, אַתָּה תוֹשִׁיעֵנוּ:

אַתָּה תָקוּם תְּרַחֵם צִיּוֹן כִּי עֵת לְחֶנְנָהּ, כִּי בָא מוֹעֵד:

אַתָּה הוּא יְיָ אֱלֹהֵינוּ וֵאלֹהֵי אֲבוֹתֵינוּ, שֶׁהִקְטִירוּ אֲבוֹתֵינוּ לְפָנֶיךָ אֶת קְטֹרֶת הַסַּמִּים:

פִּטּוּם הַקְּטֹרֶת, הַצֳּרִי, וְהַצִּפֹּרֶן, הַחֶלְבְּנָה, וְהַלְּבוֹנָה, מִשְׁקַל שִׁבְעִים מָנֶה, מוֹר, וּקְצִיעָה, שִׁבֹּלֶת נֵרְדְּ, וְכַרְכֹּם, מִשְׁקַל שִׁשָּׁה עָשָׂר שִׁשָּׁה עָשָׂר מָנֶה, הַקֹּשְׁטְ שְׁנֵים עָשָׂר, קִלּוּפָה שְׁלֹשָׁה, קִנָּמוֹן תִּשְׁעָה, בֹּרִית

Ein Kelokeinu

Soul level of Nefesh
World of Asiya
Bringing Godliness down to lower worlds

Hope in the Lord, be strong, and He will give your heart courage, and hope in the Lord. None is holy like the Lord, for there is none other than You, and there is no fortress like our God. For, Who is God aside from the Lord, and Who is a fortress aside from our God.

There is none like our God, there is none like our Lord, there is none like our King,
there is none like our Deliverer

Who is like our God, who is like our Lord,
who is like our King, who is like our Deliverer?

We acknowledge our God, we acknowledge our Lord,
we acknowledge our King,
we acknowledge our Deliverer.

Blessed is our God, blessed is our Lord,
blessed is our King, blessed is our Deliverer!

You are our God, You are our Lord, You are our King,
Your are our Deliverer! You will save us!

You will arise, comfort Zion, for the time to be gracious to her has arrived, for the season is upon us!

It is You, Lord, our God and the God of our fathers, before Whom our fathers burned the smoke of the incense.

The composition of the incense includes, balm, onycha, galanum, frankincense — each of which weighed seventy units; there was myrrh, cassia, spikenard, and saffron, each of which weighed sixteen units. There was costus, weighing twelve units, and aromatic bark weighing three units, and cinnamon, which weighed nine units.

כַּרְשִׁינָה תִּשְׁעָה קַבִּין, יֵין קַפְרִיסִין סְאִין תְּלָתָא וְקַבִּין תְּלָתָא, וְאִם אֵין לוֹ יֵין קַפְרִיסִין סְאִין תְּלָתָא וְקַבִּין תְּלָתָא, וְאִם אֵין לוֹ יֵין קַפְרִיסִין מֵבִיא חֲמַר חִוַּרְיָן עַתִּיק, מֶלַח סְדוֹמִית רוֹבַע, מַעֲלֶה עָשָׁן, כָּל שֶׁהוּא.

רַבִּי נָתָן הַבַּבְלִי אוֹמֵר, אַף כִּפַּת הַיַּרְדֵּן כָּל שֶׁהִיא, וְאִם נָתַן בָּהּ דְּבַשׁ פְּסָלָהּ, וְאִם חִסַּר אֶחָד מִכָּל סַמְמָנֶיהָ חַיָּב מִיתָה:

רַבָּן שִׁמְעוֹן בֶּן גַּמְלִיאֵל אוֹמֵר, הַצֳּרִי אֵינוֹ אֶלָּא שְׂרָף הַנּוֹטֵף מֵעֲצֵי הַקְּטָף, בֹּרִית כַּרְשִׁינָה שֶׁשָּׁפִין בָּהּ אֶת הַצִּפֹּרֶן, כְּדֵי שֶׁתְּהֵא נָאָה; יֵין קַפְרִיסִין שֶׁשּׁוֹרִין בּוֹ אֶת הַצִּפֹּרֶן, כְּדֵי שֶׁתְּהֵא עַזָּה. וַהֲלֹא מֵי רַגְלַיִם יָפִין לָהּ, אֶלָּא שֶׁאֵין מַכְנִיסִין מֵי רַגְלַיִם בַּמִּקְדָּשׁ מִפְּנֵי הַכָּבוֹד:

תָּנָא דְּבֵי אֵלִיָּהוּ כָּל הַשּׁוֹנֶה הֲלָכוֹת בְּכָל יוֹם מֻבְטָח לוֹ שֶׁהוּא בֶּן עוֹלָם הַבָּא שֶׁנֶּאֱמַר הֲלִיכוֹת עוֹלָם לוֹ, אַל תִּקְרֵי הֲלִיכוֹת אֶלָּא הֲלָכוֹת:

אָמַר רַבִּי אֶלְעָזָר אָמַר רַבִּי חֲנִינָא, תַּלְמִידֵי חֲכָמִים מַרְבִּים שָׁלוֹם בָּעוֹלָם, שֶׁנֶּאֱמַר וְכָל בָּנַיִךְ לִמּוּדֵי יְיָ, וְרַב שְׁלוֹם בָּנָיִךְ: אַל תִּקְרֵי בָּנָיִךְ, אֶלָּא בּוֹנָיִךְ:

שָׁלוֹם רָב לְאֹהֲבֵי תוֹרָתֶךָ, וְאֵין לָמוֹ מִכְשׁוֹל:

יְהִי שָׁלוֹם בְּחֵילֵךְ, שַׁלְוָה בְּאַרְמְנוֹתָיִךְ:

> Soul level of *Nefesh*
> World of *Asiya*
> Bringing Godliness down to lower worlds

There were nine kavin of lye from Carshina used in the preparation, as well as three kavin and three se'in of Cypriot wine, and if there was no wine from Cyprus available, strong, white wine could be used instead. A quarter kab of sodomite salt went into the preparation, as well as a tiny bit of a herb for smoking.

R' Natan the Babylonian said that a small amount of Jordan amber was used as well. If any honey was added, [the mixture] became invalid, and if any one of these spices were missing, the [person making the mixture] was liable for capital punishment.

Raban Shimon ben Gamliel says, balm is nothing more than sap that exudes from balsam trees. Lye of Carshina is used to massage the onycha and make it look nice, and Cypriot wine is used to marinate the onycha and make it stronger. Now, uric acid would also be good for this job, but we do not bring uric acid into the Temple out of respect.

The House of Eliyahu said, "Those who review Jewish law every day, are certain to attain the world to come, as it is said, 'Eternal ways (*halichot*) are His': Do not say ways (*halichot*), but rather Torah laws (*halachot*)."

Rebi Elazar said in the name of Rebi Chanina, "Torah scholars increase peace in the world, as it says, 'And all of your children (*banayich*) are students of the Lord, and great will be the peace of your children.' Do not say "your children" (*banayich*), but rather "your builders" (*bonayich*)."

There is great peace among those who love Your Torah, and they do not stumble:

Let there be peace within your walls, serenity in your palaces.

לְמַעַן אַחַי וְרֵעָי אֲדַבְּרָה נָּא שָׁלוֹם בָּךְ:
לְמַעַן בֵּית יְיָ אֱלֹהֵינוּ, אֲבַקְשָׁה טוֹב לָךְ:
יְיָ עֹז לְעַמּוֹ יִתֵּן, יְיָ יְבָרֵךְ אֶת עַמּוֹ בַשָּׁלוֹם:

קדיש דרבנן

יִתְגַּדַּל וְיִתְקַדַּשׁ שְׁמֵהּ רַבָּא. (קהל: אָמֵן)

בְּעָלְמָא דִּי בְרָא כִרְעוּתֵהּ וְיַמְלִיךְ מַלְכוּתֵהּ, וְיַצְמַח פֻּרְקָנֵהּ וִיקָרֵב מְשִׁיחֵהּ. (קהל: אָמֵן)

בְּחַיֵּיכוֹן וּבְיוֹמֵיכוֹן וּבְחַיֵּי דְכָל בֵּית יִשְׂרָאֵל, בַּעֲגָלָא וּבִזְמַן קָרִיב. וְאִמְרוּ אָמֵן:

(קהל: יְהֵא שְׁמֵהּ רַבָּא מְבָרַךְ לְעָלַם וּלְעָלְמֵי עָלְמַיָּא, יִתְבָּרַךְ:)

יְהֵא שְׁמֵהּ רַבָּא מְבָרַךְ לְעָלַם וּלְעָלְמֵי עָלְמַיָּא, יִתְבָּרַךְ, וְיִשְׁתַּבַּח, וְיִתְפָּאַר, וְיִתְרוֹמַם, וְיִתְנַשֵּׂא, וְיִתְהַדָּר, וְיִתְעַלֶּה, וְיִתְהַלָּל, שְׁמֵהּ דְּקֻדְשָׁא בְּרִיךְ הוּא. (קהל: אָמֵן) לְעֵלָּא מִן כָּל בִּרְכָתָא וְשִׁירָתָא, תֻּשְׁבְּחָתָא וְנֶחֱמָתָא, דַּאֲמִירָן בְּעָלְמָא, וְאִמְרוּ אָמֵן: (קהל: אָמֵן)

עַל יִשְׂרָאֵל וְעַל רַבָּנָן. וְעַל תַּלְמִידֵיהוֹן וְעַל כָּל תַּלְמִידֵי תַלְמִידֵיהוֹן. וְעַל כָּל מָאן דְּעָסְקִין בְּאוֹרַיְתָא דִּי בְאַתְרָא הָדֵין וְדִי בְכָל אֲתַר וַאֲתַר. יְהֵא לְהוֹן וּלְכוֹן שְׁלָמָא רַבָּא חִנָּא וְחִסְדָּא וְרַחֲמִין וְחַיִּין אֲרִיכִין וּמְזוֹנָא רְוִיחָא וּפוּרְקָנָא מִן קֳדָם אֲבוּהוֹן דְּבִשְׁמַיָּא וְאִמְרוּ אָמֵן:

Soul level of Nefesh
World of Asiya
Bringing Godliness down to lower worlds

For the sake of my brothers and my friends,
I speak of peace among You.

For the sake of the House of the Lord,
our God, I seek your welfare.

The Lord shall give strength to His people,
the Lord will bless His people with peace.

The Rabbis' Kaddish

Exalted and sanctified is His great Name. (cong: "Amen")

In the universe that He created according to His Will, May He establish His reign, and sprout forth His redemption, and quickly bring His mashiach. (cong: "Amen")

In your life and during your days and in the life of the entire house of Israel, speedily and soon, and say Amen!

(the congregation here says: "Amen, may His great Name be blessed forever and for eternity")

May His great Name be blessed forever and for eternity. (cong: "Amen") May He be blessed, may He be extolled, may He be glorified, may He be exalted, may He be elevated, may He be honored, may He be lauded, and may he be praised, the Name of the holy One, blessed be He. (cong: "Amen") Beyond all the blessings and the hymns, the praises and the consolations that are recited in the world, and let us say Amen.

Upon Israel, and upon the rabbis, and upon their students and upon all the students of their students, and upon all those who are involved in Torah, whether in this place or whether in any other place, they and you should experience much peace, harmony and kindness and mercy and long life and plentiful sustenance and salvation from before their King in the heavens, and let us say, Amen.

יְהֵא שְׁלָמָה רַבָּא מִן שְׁמַיָּא וְחַיִּים טוֹבִים עָלֵינוּ וְעַל כָּל יִשְׂרָאֵל, וְאִמְרוּ אָמֵן:

עֹשֶׂה שָׁלוֹם (בעשי״ת: הַשָּׁלוֹם) בִּמְרוֹמָיו הוּא יַעֲשֶׂה שָׁלוֹם עָלֵינוּ וְעַל כָּל יִשְׂרָאֵל, וְאִמְרוּ אָמֵן (קהל: אָמֵן):

עלינו

עָלֵינוּ לְשַׁבֵּחַ לַאֲדוֹן הַכֹּל, לָתֵת גְּדֻלָּה לְיוֹצֵר בְּרֵאשִׁית,

שֶׁלֹּא עָשָׂנוּ כְּגוֹיֵי הָאֲרָצוֹת, וְלֹא שָׂמָנוּ כְּמִשְׁפְּחוֹת הָאֲדָמָה, שֶׁלֹּא שָׂם חֶלְקֵנוּ כָּהֶם, וְגוֹרָלֵנוּ כְּכָל הֲמוֹנָם.

שֶׁהֵם מִשְׁתַּחֲוִים לְהֶבֶל וְלָרִיק.

וַאֲנַחְנוּ כּוֹרְעִים וּמִשְׁתַּחֲוִים וּמוֹדִים, לִפְנֵי מֶלֶךְ, מַלְכֵי הַמְּלָכִים, הַקָּדוֹשׁ, בָּרוּךְ הוּא:

שֶׁהוּא נוֹטֶה שָׁמַיִם וְיוֹסֵד אָרֶץ, וּמוֹשַׁב יְקָרוֹ בַּשָּׁמַיִם מִמַּעַל, וּשְׁכִינַת עֻזּוֹ בְּגָבְהֵי מְרוֹמִים,

הוּא אֱלֹהֵינוּ אֵין עוֹד.
אֱמֶת מַלְכֵּנוּ, אֶפֶס זוּלָתוֹ, כַּכָּתוּב בְּתוֹרָתוֹ:

וְיָדַעְתָּ הַיּוֹם וַהֲשֵׁבֹתָ אֶל לְבָבֶךָ, כִּי יְיָ הוּא הָאֱלֹהִים בַּשָּׁמַיִם מִמַּעַל, וְעַל הָאָרֶץ מִתָּחַת, אֵין עוֹד:

Soul level of Nefesh
World of Asiya
Bringing Godliness down to lower worlds

May there be plentiful peace from Heaven and a good life for all of us and for all of Israel, and let us say, Amen (cong: "Amen").

He Who makes peace (during ten days of repentance: "the peace") on high, may He create peace for us and for all of Israel, and let us say Amen (cong: "Amen").

Aleinu

It is incumbent upon us to praise the Master of all, to glorify the Maker of creation,

For He did not make us like the nations of the earth, nor did He place us among the families of the land; He has not assigned us a portion like theirs, nor placed our lot among all of their masses.

For they bow down to vanity and emptiness.

And we bend at the knee, bow down and concede before the King, King of Kings, the Holy One, blessed is He.

For He stretches out the heavens and establishes the earth, and His throne of glory is in the heavens above, and the abode of His mighty presence is in the loftiest heights.

He is our God, there is no other; in truth He is our King, and there is none beside Him, as written in His Torah:

"And you shall know this today, and place it on your heart, that the Lord is God, in the heavens above and on the earth below, there is no other."

וְעַל כֵּן נְקַוֶּה לְךָ יְיָ אֱלֹהֵינוּ, לִרְאוֹת מְהֵרָה בְּתִפְאֶרֶת עֻזֶּךָ, לְהַעֲבִיר גִּלּוּלִים מִן הָאָרֶץ וְהָאֱלִילִים כָּרוֹת יִכָּרֵתוּן, לְתַקֵּן עוֹלָם בְּמַלְכוּת שַׁדַּי;

וְכָל בְּנֵי בָשָׂר יִקְרְאוּ בִשְׁמֶךָ, לְהַפְנוֹת אֵלֶיךָ כָּל רִשְׁעֵי אָרֶץ.

יַכִּירוּ וְיֵדְעוּ כָּל יוֹשְׁבֵי תֵבֵל, כִּי לְךָ תִּכְרַע כָּל בֶּרֶךְ, תִּשָּׁבַע כָּל לָשׁוֹן.

לְפָנֶיךָ יְיָ אֱלֹהֵינוּ יִכְרְעוּ וְיִפֹּלוּ, וְלִכְבוֹד שִׁמְךָ יְקָר יִתֵּנוּ

> **Full-fledged emotions of the heart do not emerge spontaneously from our mind. Such emotions emerge only after the intellect undergoes a series of contractions and interruptions. And this is why the verse states, 'And you should know today and place it upon your heart…'"**
> (*Sefer Maamorim* 5665/1905 of the Rebbe Rashab, pp. 247-249)[312]

The place of contraction and interruption is within the throat. It is there that the emotional tendency within our mind descends and undergoes transformation. However, for this to occur, we must make a conscious effort to "place the emotions on our heart." We must prepare ourselves for prayer with the goal of achieving arousal of the heart. Then, the expansion and expression of our intellect, together with the depth of knowledge that we achieve through meditation, leads to emotions which emerge spontaneously. The initial illumination of intellect disappears, temporarily interrupted, and then re-appears in a more distant, transcendent form. We become pre-occupied with our new grasp of Godliness, and then, spontaneously, it "drops down" to become an emotion in our heart.

When we approach prayer without the proper preparation — that is, lacking a conscious decision to "feel" the prayers in our heart as well as without learning Chassidut before *tefila* — then our meditation does not have the same effect. We are forced to pay much more conscious attention to the emotions within our mind, and work

Soul level of Nefesh
World of Asiya
Bringing Godliness down to lower worlds

And therefore, we place our hope in You, Lord our God, to soon behold Your glorious might, to wipe away idols from the earth, and to surely excise false gods, in order to rectify the world for the kingdom of God.

And all beings of flesh will invoke Your Name, and all the wicked of the world will turn to You.

All who dwell on the globe will know and recognize You, for every knee will bow to You, and every language swear in Your Name.

Before You, Lord, our God, they will bow and they will fall down (prostrate themselves), and in honor of Your Name, they will express respect.

---

harder to become aware of them. As a result, our emotions are not truly real. We may experience some form of arousal and illumination, but it does not filter down to our heart spontaneously as it does when we prepare ourselves properly for prayers. As a result, it is much more difficult for the intellect to become transformed into emotion.

📖 Within the Words

At times, even after meditation, the intellectual concepts in our mind do not filter down to our heart. Proper preparation includes contriteness in the heart as well as learning Chassidut before prayers. However, sometimes even this does not suffice. At such times, it is a good idea to sing, since "the voice arouses intention" in the heart.[313] A quiet melody has more power to arouse our emotions than does quiet meditation. And that is also included in the injunction to "place it upon your heart." Another commandment — "You shall love the Lord your God…" — compels us to meditate on Godly concepts. But when even that does not help to produce the emotion of love in our heart, then we are enjoined to "place it upon our heart" through proper preparation and song. Without this, it may be impossible for the intellect to descend from the mind to the heart.

ALEINU

וִיקַבְּלוּ כֻלָּם עֲלֵיהֶם אֶת עוֹל מַלְכוּתֶךָ,
וְתִמְלֹךְ עֲלֵיהֶם מְהֵרָה לְעוֹלָם וָעֶד,

כִּי הַמַּלְכוּת שֶׁלְּךָ הִיא,
וּלְעוֹלְמֵי עַד תִּמְלוֹךְ בְּכָבוֹד, כַּכָּתוּב בְּתוֹרָתֶךָ:

יְיָ יִמְלֹךְ לְעוֹלָם וָעֶד.

וְנֶאֱמַר: וְהָיָה יְיָ לְמֶלֶךְ עַל כָּל הָאָרֶץ,
בַּיּוֹם הַהוּא יִהְיֶה יְיָ אֶחָד וּשְׁמוֹ אֶחָד:

קדיש יתום

יִתְגַּדַּל וְיִתְקַדַּשׁ שְׁמֵהּ רַבָּא. (קהל: אָמֵן)

בְּעָלְמָא דִּי בְרָא כִרְעוּתֵהּ וְיַמְלִיךְ מַלְכוּתֵהּ, וְיַצְמַח פֻּרְקָנֵהּ וִיקָרֵב מְשִׁיחֵהּ. (קהל: אָמֵן)

בְּחַיֵּיכוֹן וּבְיוֹמֵיכוֹן וּבְחַיֵּי דְכָל בֵּית יִשְׂרָאֵל, בַּעֲגָלָא וּבִזְמַן קָרִיב. וְאִמְרוּ אָמֵן:

(קהל: אָמֵן. יְהֵא שְׁמֵהּ רַבָּא מְבָרַךְ לְעָלַם וּלְעָלְמֵי עָלְמַיָּא, יִתְבָּרַךְ:)

יְהֵא שְׁמֵהּ רַבָּא מְבָרַךְ לְעָלַם וּלְעָלְמֵי עָלְמַיָּא, יִתְבָּרַךְ, וְיִשְׁתַּבַּח, וְיִתְפָּאַר, וְיִתְרוֹמַם, וְיִתְנַשֵּׂא, וְיִתְהַדָּר, וְיִתְעַלֶּה, וְיִתְהַלָּל, שְׁמֵהּ דְּקֻדְשָׁא בְּרִיךְ הוּא. (קהל: אָמֵן) לְעֵלָּא מִן כָּל בִּרְכָתָא וְשִׁירָתָא, תֻּשְׁבְּחָתָא וְנֶחֱמָתָא, דַּאֲמִירָן בְּעָלְמָא, וְאִמְרוּ אָמֵן: (קהל: אָמֵן) יְהֵא שְׁלָמָא רַבָּא מִן שְׁמַיָּא וְחַיִּים טוֹבִים עָלֵינוּ וְעַל כָּל יִשְׂרָאֵל, וְאִמְרוּ אָמֵן:

Soul level of Nefesh
World of Asiya
Bringing Godliness down to lower worlds

And all of them will accept upon themselves the yoke of Your reign, and You will reign over them soon, forever and ever.

For Kingship is Yours, forever and for all eternity You will reign in glory, as written in your Torah,

"The Lord will reign forever and ever."

And it says, "And the Lord will be the King over all the earth, on that day, the Lord will be one and His Name one."

The Mourners Kaddish

Exalted and sanctified is His great Name. (cong: "Amen")

In the universe that He created according to His Will, May He establish His reign, and sprout forth His redemption, and quickly bring His mashiach. (cong: "Amen")

In your life and during your days and in the life of the entire house of Israel, speedily and soon, and say Amen!

(the congregation here says: "Amen, may His great Name be blessed forever and for eternity")

May His great Name be blessed forever and for eternity. May He be blessed, may He be extolled, may He be glorified, may He be exalted, may He be elevated, may He be honored, may He be lauded, and may he be praised, the Name of the holy One, blessed be He. (cong: "Amen") Beyond all the blessings and the hymns, the praises and the consolations that are recited in the world, and let us say Amen. (cong: "Amen") May there be plentiful peace from Heaven and a good life for all of us and for all of Israel, and let us say, Amen.

עֹשֶׂה שָׁלוֹם (בעשי"ת: הַשָּׁלוֹם) בִּמְרוֹמָיו הוּא
יַעֲשֶׂה שָׁלוֹם עָלֵינוּ וְעַל כָּל יִשְׂרָאֵל,
וְאִמְרוּ אָמֵן:

אַל תִּירָא מִפַּחַד פִּתְאֹם,
וּמִשֹּׁאַת רְשָׁעִים כִּי תָבֹא:

עֻצוּ עֵצָה וְתֻפָר,
דַּבְּרוּ דָבָר וְלֹא יָקוּם כִּי עִמָּנוּ אֵל:

וְעַד זִקְנָה אֲנִי הוּא,
וְעַד שֵׂיבָה אֲנִי אֶסְבֹּל;
אֲנִי עָשִׂיתִי וַאֲנִי אֶשָּׂא וַאֲנִי אֶסְבֹּל וַאֲמַלֵּט:

אַךְ צַדִּיקִים יוֹדוּ לִשְׁמֶךָ יֵשְׁבוּ יְשָׁרִים אֶת פָּנֶיךָ:

סדר הנחת תפילין
של רבינו תם

בסוף תפילת שחרית יש נוהגים להניח תפילין של רבינו תם בלא ברכה. אומרים קריאת שמע ויש אלו שנוהגים להגיד גם את הפסוקים הבאים:

וַיְדַבֵּר יְיָ אֶל מֹשֶׁה לֵּאמֹר:

קַדֶּשׁ לִי כָל בְּכוֹר פֶּטֶר כָּל רֶחֶם בִּבְנֵי יִשְׂרָאֵל
בָּאָדָם וּבַבְּהֵמָה לִי הוּא:

וַיֹּאמֶר מֹשֶׁה אֶל הָעָם זָכוֹר אֶת הַיּוֹם הַזֶּה אֲשֶׁר
יְצָאתֶם מִמִּצְרַיִם מִבֵּית עֲבָדִים כִּי בְּחֹזֶק יָד
הוֹצִיא יְיָ אֶתְכֶם מִזֶּה וְלֹא יֵאָכֵל חָמֵץ:
הַיּוֹם אַתֶּם יֹצְאִים בְּחֹדֶשׁ הָאָבִיב:

> Soul level of *Nefesh*
> World of *Asiya*
> Bringing Godliness down to lower worlds

He Who makes peace (during ten days of repentance: "the peace") on high, may He create peace for us and for all of Israel, and let us say Amen (cong: "Amen").

Have no fear of sudden fright, nor of destruction of the wicked if it occurs.

Come up with a plan, it will be foiled; think of a scheme and it will fail, for God is with us.

Until old age, I am [with You]; until you have white hairs, I will accompany you.

I made you, and I will carry you, and I will accompany you, and I will deliver you.

Indeed, the righteous will acknowledge Your Name, the Upright will revel in Your countenance.

Rabbeinu Tam's Tefillin

Those who don a second pair of tefillin after the morning prayers (Shacharit) first recite the first three paragraphs of the Kriat Shema, as it appears in the siddur above, and then say the following (from Ex. 13:1-16), as well as the six remembrances:

And the Lord spoke to Moshe, saying,

Sanctify every firstborn to Me, the first to open every womb among the Jews, whether of people or of animals — it is Mine.

And Moshe said to the nation, remember this day on which you went out of Egypt, from the house of slavery, for with a strong arm the Lord brought You out of it, and no leavened bread shall be eaten. Today, you are leaving, during the Spring month.

וְהָיָה כִּי יְבִיאֲךָ יְיָ אֶל אֶרֶץ הַכְּנַעֲנִי וְהַחִתִּי וְהָאֱמֹרִי וְהַחִוִּי וְהַיְבוּסִי אֲשֶׁר נִשְׁבַּע לַאֲבֹתֶיךָ לָתֶת לָךְ אֶרֶץ זָבַת חָלָב וּדְבָשׁ וְעָבַדְתָּ אֶת הָעֲבֹדָה הַזֹּאת בַּחֹדֶשׁ הַזֶּה:

שִׁבְעַת יָמִים תֹּאכַל מַצֹּת וּבַיּוֹם הַשְּׁבִיעִי חַג לַיְיָ:

מַצּוֹת יֵאָכֵל אֵת שִׁבְעַת הַיָּמִים וְלֹא יֵרָאֶה לְךָ חָמֵץ וְלֹא יֵרָאֶה לְךָ שְׂאֹר בְּכָל גְּבֻלֶךָ:

וְהִגַּדְתָּ לְבִנְךָ בַּיּוֹם הַהוּא לֵאמֹר בַּעֲבוּר זֶה עָשָׂה יְיָ לִי בְּצֵאתִי מִמִּצְרָיִם:

וְהָיָה לְךָ לְאוֹת עַל יָדְךָ וּלְזִכָּרוֹן בֵּין עֵינֶיךָ לְמַעַן תִּהְיֶה תּוֹרַת יְיָ בְּפִיךָ כִּי בְּיָד חֲזָקָה הוֹצִאֲךָ יְיָ מִמִּצְרָיִם:

וְשָׁמַרְתָּ אֶת הַחֻקָּה הַזֹּאת לְמוֹעֲדָהּ מִיָּמִים יָמִימָה:

וְהָיָה כִּי יְבִאֲךָ יְיָ אֶל אֶרֶץ הַכְּנַעֲנִי כַּאֲשֶׁר נִשְׁבַּע לְךָ וְלַאֲבֹתֶיךָ וּנְתָנָהּ לָךְ:

וְהַעֲבַרְתָּ כָל פֶּטֶר רֶחֶם לַיְיָ וְכָל פֶּטֶר שֶׁגֶר בְּהֵמָה אֲשֶׁר יִהְיֶה לְךָ הַזְּכָרִים לַיְיָ:

וְכָל פֶּטֶר חֲמֹר תִּפְדֶּה בְשֶׂה וְאִם לֹא תִפְדֶּה וַעֲרַפְתּוֹ וְכֹל בְּכוֹר אָדָם בְּבָנֶיךָ תִּפְדֶּה:

> Soul level of *Nefesh*
> World of *Asiya*
> Bringing Godliness down to lower worlds

And it shall be that when the Lord brings you to the land of the Canaanites, the Hittites, the Emorites, the Hivites, the Yebusites, that He swore to your fathers to give you, a land flowing with milk and honey, then you should perform this service, this month.

For seven days, you should eat unleavened bread and the seventh day is a festival for the Lord.

Unleavened bread should be eaten during the seven days, and you should not see any leavened bread, nor should you see any leavening in all of your borders.

And you should tell your son on that day, saying, "this is on account of what the Lord did for me, as I left Egypt."

And it shall be a sign for you upon your hand and a reminder between your eyes, so that the Torah of God will constantly be in your mouth, for with a strong arm, the Lord brought you out of Egypt.

And you should observe this law at its appointed season, from year to year.

And it shall be that when the Lord brings you to the land of the Canaanites as He swore to you and to your fathers, and gives it to you.

You should transfer every [offspring] that first opens the womb to the Lord, and of the cattle, every male that first opens the womb is for the Lord.

Every [male] that first opens the womb among donkeys should be redeemed with a lamb, and if you do not redeem it, then you must break its neck from behind, and every firstborn among men, among your sons, you must redeem.

> **RABBEINU TAM'S TEFILLIN**

וְהָיָה כִּי יִשְׁאָלְךָ בִנְךָ מָחָר לֵאמֹר מַה זֹּאת וְאָמַרְתָּ אֵלָיו בְּחֹזֶק יָד הוֹצִיאָנוּ יְיָ מִמִּצְרַיִם מִבֵּית עֲבָדִים:

וַיְהִי כִּי הִקְשָׁה פַרְעֹה לְשַׁלְּחֵנוּ וַיַּהֲרֹג יְיָ כָּל בְּכוֹר בְּאֶרֶץ מִצְרַיִם מִבְּכֹר אָדָם וְעַד בְּכוֹר בְּהֵמָה עַל כֵּן אֲנִי זֹבֵחַ לַיְיָ כָּל פֶּטֶר רֶחֶם הַזְּכָרִים וְכָל בְּכוֹר בָּנַי אֶפְדֶּה:

וְהָיָה לְאוֹת עַל יָדְכָה וּלְטוֹטָפֹת בֵּין עֵינֶיךָ כִּי בְּחֹזֶק יָד הוֹצִיאָנוּ יְיָ מִמִּצְרָיִם:

שש זכירות

(1) לְמַעַן תִּזְכֹּר אֶת יוֹם צֵאתְךָ מֵאֶרֶץ מִצְרַיִם כֹּל יְמֵי חַיֶּיךָ:

(2) רַק הִשָּׁמֶר, לְךָ וּשְׁמֹר נַפְשְׁךָ מְאֹד פֶּן תִּשְׁכַּח אֶת הַדְּבָרִים אֲשֶׁר רָאוּ עֵינֶיךָ וּפֶן יָסוּרוּ מִלְּבָבְךָ כֹּל יְמֵי חַיֶּיךָ וְהוֹדַעְתָּם לְבָנֶיךָ, וְלִבְנֵי בָנֶיךָ: יוֹם אֲשֶׁר עָמַדְתָּ לִפְנֵי יְיָ אֱלֹהֶיךָ בְּחֹרֵב:

(3) זָכוֹר אֵת אֲשֶׁר עָשָׂה לְךָ עֲמָלֵק בַּדֶּרֶךְ בְּצֵאתְכֶם מִמִּצְרָיִם: אֲשֶׁר קָרְךָ בַּדֶּרֶךְ וַיְזַנֵּב בְּךָ כָּל הַנֶּחֱשָׁלִים אַחֲרֶיךָ וְאַתָּה עָיֵף וְיָגֵעַ וְלֹא יָרֵא אֱלֹהִים: וְהָיָה

Soul level of Nefesh
World of Asiya
Bringing Godliness down to lower worlds

And if your son shall ask you tomorrow (after time), saying, "what is this?" you should say to him, "With a strong hand, the Lord brought us out of Egypt, from the house of slavery.

And it happened that when Pharaoh obstinately refused to send us, the Lord killed every firstborn in the land of Egypt, from the firstborn of man to the firstborn of animals; therefore I slaughter every male animal that opens the womb to the Lord, and every firstborn of my sons, I redeem."

And it should be as a sign on your hand and for compartments between your eyes, for with a strong hand, the Lord brought us out of Egypt.

The Six Remembrances

(1) In order that you remember the day on which you left the land of Egypt, all the days of your life (Deut. 16:3)

(2) But, guard yourself and guard your soul scrupulously, lest you forget the events that your eyes have seen, and lest they turn [empty out] from your heart, all the days of your life, and inform your children and your children's children of these events. Of [what you saw on] the day that you stood before the Lord your God on Mt. Horev (Deut. 4:9-10).

(3) Remember what Amalek did to you as you were on the road during your exit from Egypt; how he met you on the way, and attacked all of the weak who straggled behind you, and you were tired and weary, and he was not God fearing. And when the Lord

בְּהָנִיחַ יְיָ אֱלֹהֶיךָ לְךָ מִכָּל אֹיְבֶיךָ מִסָּבִיב בָּאָרֶץ אֲשֶׁר יְיָ אֱלֹהֶיךָ נֹתֵן לְךָ נַחֲלָה לְרִשְׁתָּהּ תִּמְחֶה אֶת זֵכֶר עֲמָלֵק מִתַּחַת הַשָּׁמָיִם לֹא, תִּשְׁכָּח:

(4) זְכֹר אַל תִּשְׁכַּח אֵת אֲשֶׁר הִקְצַפְתָּ אֶת יְיָ אֱלֹהֶיךָ בַּמִּדְבָּר:

(5) זָכוֹר אֵת אֲשֶׁר עָשָׂה יְיָ אֱלֹהֶיךָ לְמִרְיָם בַּדֶּרֶךְ בְּצֵאתְכֶם מִמִּצְרָיִם:

(6) זָכוֹר אֶת יוֹם הַשַּׁבָּת לְקַדְּשׁוֹ:

Soul level of Nefesh
World of Asiya
Bringing Godliness down to lower worlds

your God will relieve you of your enemies around you, in the land that the Lord your God gives to you as a portion to inherit, erase the memory of Amalek from under the heavens, do not forget! (Deut. 25:17-19)

(4) Remember, do not forget how you provoked the Lord your God to anger in the desert. (Deut 9:7)

(5) Remember what the Lord your God did to Miriam on the way, as you exited Egypt (Deut. 24:9)

(6) Remember the day of Shabbat, to sanctify it. (Ex. 20:8)

THE SIX REMEMBRANCES

הערות
Endnotes

1. Genesis 28:12
2. *Besha'ah Shehikdimu* 5672/1912 of the Rebbe Rashab, vol. 1, p. 619, *Kuntres Ha'Avoda* of the Rebbe Rashab, p. 1
3. *Shulchan Aruch HaRav, Orach Chaim* 1:5 — *Mahadura Basra* (1:6 in the *Mahadura Kama*)
4. *Besha'ah Shehikdimu* 5672/1912 of the Rebbe Rashab, vol. 1, p. 619
5. "On the Essence of Chassidut," pp. 43-44, 63-65 (Page 79 in the Chasidic Heritage Series)
6. "On the Essence of Chassidut," pp. 42-43 (Page 58 in the Chasidic Heritage Series)
7. *Shulchan Aruch HaRav* — *Mahadura Basra* 1:7 and *Mishnah Berurah* 1:1
8. *Besha'ah Shehikdimu* 5672/1912 of the Rebbe Rashab, vol. 2, pp. 737-738
9. *Derech Mitzvotecha* of the Tzemach Tzedek, p. 127 (ס"ד)
10. *Shulchan Aruch HaRav* — *Mahadura Basra* 4:1
11. *Shulchan Aruch HaRav* — *Siman* 5
12. *Shulchan Aruch HaRav* — *Mahadura Basra* 4:1. The Rebbe Maharash (In *Torat Shmuel 5630* (1870), page 127-129), finds this reason "forced." He points out that according to Kaballah and Chasidut, the reason to wash is in order to remove the impurity, or *klipah* that resides on on the hands. He suggests that the word *netila* in this regard means "to remove," as in removing the impurity. He brings a verse from Isaiah 63 — *Vayinatlem vayinasem* ("And He removed them and raised them up"), in support.
13. *Tos R' Yitzchak* and the *Rif* on *Berachot*, ch. 3. The *Chesed l'Avraham* (R' Avraham Azulai ztz"l) explains that the *klipah* attached to the body takes on the form of "air" (*ruach*), which cannot remain attached to the body when it is immersed in the waters of the *mikveh* (*Mayan* 2, *Nahar* 59)
14. *Sefer Maamorim* 5672-6/1912-6 of the Rebbe Rashab, p. 137
15. *Imrei Bina* of the Mittler Rebbe, *Sha'ar Kriat Shema*, ch. 42, "On the Essence of Chassidut," p. 83 (Page 100-101 in the Chasidic Heritage Series)
16. *Sefer Maamorim* 5688/1928 of the Rebbe *Rayatz*, pp. 168-170
17. *Kovetz Meah She'arim*, letters of the *Tzemach Tzedek*, p. 90, *Ohr HaTorah, Inyanim*, p. 304
18. R' Chaim Vital in *Sha'arei Kedusha*, cited *in Likutei Amarim Tanya*, ch. 1
19. *Torat Chaim* of the Mittler Rebbe, *Shemot* p. 108 or p. 148 in the new edition
20. *Behar* 107, *Shalach* 171
21. Quoted in *Torat Chaim* of the Mittler Rebbe
22. *Yoma* 20a
23. *Sefer Maamorim* 5672-5676/1912-1916 of the Rebbe Rashab, p. 46
24. *Shulchan Aruch HaRav* 1:3 (*Mahadura Kama*)

25. *Besha'ah Shehikdimu* 5672/1912, vol. 2, pp. 737-738
26. Psalms 115:5, *Kovetz Meah Shearim*, from the *Tzemach Tzedek*, p. 90, *Ohr HaTorah, Inyanim*, p. 306
27. *Kovetz Meah Shearim*, from the *Tzemach Tzedek*, p. 90, as well as *Ohr HaTorah, Inyanim*, p. 306
28. *Kovetz Meah Shearim*, from the *Tzemach Tzedek*, pp. 91-92, *Ohr HaTorah, Inyanim*, pp. 306-307
29. From the Siddur, quoted in *Torat Shmuel* of the Rebbe Maharash, 5629/1869, pp. 71-72. See also *Ohr HaTorah* of the *Tzemach Tzedek*, *parshat Mishpatim*, P. 1156
30. *Pirkei d'R'Eliezer*, ch. 31
31. *Beshaah Shehikdimu* 5672/1912 of the Rebbe Rashab, vol. 1, p. 116
32. *Talmud Yerushalmi, Taanit*, ch. 2, halacha 1
33. See *Likutei Sichot* of the Lubavitcher Rebbe, vol. 25, p. 131
34. Zohar, Genesis 6:9
35. *Shulchan Aruch HaRav, Mahadura* Batra 1:10, from the *Beit Yoseph* on the *Tur*
36. *Sefer Maamorim* 5656/1896 of the Rebbe Rashab, p. 292
37. *Likutei Amaraim Tanya*, ch. 1 and 2
38. *Kuntres Hit Paalut* of the Mittler Rebbe
39. *Ramah* in *Shulchan Aruch, Orach Chaim* 98:1, *Shulchan Aruch HaRav* 98:1
40. Zohar III 168A, quoted in *Tanya, Likutei Amarim* Ch. 29
41. *Tanya, Likutei Amarim*, Ch 29
42. *Shulchan Aruch HaRav — Mahadura Kama* 1:5
43. Talmud, *Berachot* 32, *Shulchan Aruch, Orach Chaim* 93:2
44. *Sefer Maamorim* 5758/1898 of the Rebbe Rashab, pp. 147-151
45. Alter Rebbe's Siddur with Chassidut, p ל"א
46. *Tanya, Igeret Hakodesh* Ch. 15, p. קכ"א
47. *Torat Shmuel* 5629/1869, p. 262
48. Alter Rebbe's Siddur with Chassidut, p. ל"ג
49. *Torat Shmuel* 5630/1870 of the Rebbe Maharash, p. 126. The cow (oxe) represents *ohl malchut shamayim* (the ability to accept the "yoke of heaven" upon ourselves), the sheep is a *tikun* ("rectification") for lack of mercy in our service of God, and the goat is a *tikun* for being over-confident and bold (from *Torat Shmuel* 5631/1871 of the Rebbe Maharash, vol 1, p. 283.
50. Alter Rebbe's Siddur with Chassidut, p. 33a
51. *Besha'ah Shehikdimu* 5672/1912 of the Rebbe Rashab, Vol. 1, pp. 429-430. This is also alluded to in the phrase, *am segula* ("special nation") — the vowel *segol* contains three points in the shape of a triangle.
52. *Sefer Maamorim* 5643/1883, p. 105, and *Sefer Maamorim* 5658/1898, pp. 48 and 57 of the Rebbe Rashab
53. *Kuntres Ha'Avoda* of the Rebbe Rashab, first page
54. The Alter Rebbe's Siddur with Chassidut, p. 606, 303c

55. *Reshimot* #158 of the Rebbe ממ"ש
56. *Midrash Rabba Vayera* 54
57. *Torat Shmuel 5627*/1867 of the Rebbe Maharash, p. 47
58. *Torat Shmuel 5627*/1867 of the Rebbe Maharash, p. 41
59. *Zohar Vayakhel*
60. *Megaleh Amukot* (R' Nosson Nata Shapira *ztz"l*) on *Parshat Korach*
61. Psalms 42:9
62. *Talmud Hagiga* 12B
63. *Torat Shmuel 5635*/1875 of the Rebbe Maharash, pp. 178-182
64. *Torat Shmuel 5635*/1875 of the Rebbe Maharash, p. 338
65. Letter of the Mitteler Rebbe in *Kovetz Meah Shearim*, p. 22
66. *Sefer Maamorim 5659*/1899 of the Rebbe Rashab, pp. 5-6
67. *Sefer Maamorim 5659*/1899 of the Rebbe Rashab, p. 106. See also *Torat Shmuel 5630* of the Rebbe Maharsh, p. 140
68. *Sha'arei Kedusha* of R' Chaim Vital, mentioned in ch. 2 of *Likutei Amarim* of the *Tanya*
69. *Likutei Amarim* ch. 3
70. *Sefer Maamorim 5658*/1898 of the Rebbe Rashab, p. 151
71. *Shulchan Aruch HaRav* 93:1-2
72. *Sefer Maamorim 5655*/1895 of the Rebbe Rashab, pp. 105-107
73. *Shulchan Aruch HaRav* 98:1
74. *Sefer Hasichot 5706-10*/1946-50 of the *Rebbe Rayatz*, pp. 143-145
75. 1 *Melachim* 19:11-12
76. *Sefer Maamorim 5668*/1908 of the Rebbe Rashab, pp. 116-117, *Besha'ah Shehikdimu 5672*/1912 of the Rebbe Rashab, Vol 2, P.819 (Ch 398)
77. *Maamorei Admor Hazaken* on *Maamorei rz"l*, p. 349
78. *Derech Mitzvotecha* of the *Tzemach Tzedek, Shoresh Mitzvat Tefila*. See also *Sha'ar Hayichud* ("*Kuntres Hahitbonenut*") of the Mitteler Rebbe, Ch. 4, 7, 10
79. *Shulchan Aruch HaRav* 51:2
80. *Pirush Hamilot* of the Mitteler Rebbe, ch. 98, p. 62c
81. Alter Rebbe's Siddur with Chassidut, Page 78
82. *Likutei Torah* of the Alter Rebbe, *Ve'etchanan* 2a
83. *Sefer Maamorim 5673* in the book *Maamorim 5672-6*/1912-6 of the Rebbe Rashab, pp. 80-81
84. *Likutei Torah* of the Alter Rebbe, *Shir HaShirim* 41d
85. *Sha'ar Hatefila*, within *Sha'arei Tshuva* of the Mitteler Rebbe, p. 53, sec. 9
86. *Sefer Maamorim 5679*/1919 of the Rebbe Rashab, pp. 231-232. The Rebbe Maharash in *Torat Shmuel 5632*/1872 (pp. 80-81) gives an illustration to help us understand *ohr chozer*. Comparing the prophecy of Moshe Rabeinu, who prophesied "through a shining lense" to the other prophets, who prophesied through a "lense that does not shine," the Maharash suggests that this distinction was the same as that between *ohr yashar* ("direct illumination") and *ohr chozer* ("reflected illumination"). While the "shining light"

of a telescope or binoculars allows us to see the object itself, that otherwise may be invisible, the "non-shining light" of a mirror allows us only to see an "image" of the object, not the object itself. The prophecy of the other prophets was comparable to a mirror in which we can only detect the image, but not the object itself. However, there is a benefit to the mirror, that allows us to view ourselves and even what is "behind" us — and that is the benefit of *ohr chozer* as well. It allows us to look inside and find our own blockages and resistances, and to deal with them, helping us to improve and refine our character.

87. *Sefer Maamorim 5679/1919* of the Rebbe Rashab, p. 232
88. *Besha'ah Shehikdimu 5672/1912* of the Rebbe Rashab, vol. 1, pp. 129-132, 293
89. *Ohel Yoseph Yitzchak* on *Tehilim*, from the *Tzemach Tzedek*, p. 652
90. *Torat Shmuel 5629/1869* of the Rebbe Maharash, pp. 327-328
91. *Shulchan Aruch HaRav* 51:1
92. *Torat Menachem* of the Rebbe, vol. 12, p. 166
93. *Pirush Hamilot* of the Mitteler Rebbe, ch. 108, p. 69a
94. *Pirush Hamilot* of the Mitteler Rebbe, ch. 117, p. 75c
95. *Besha'ah Shehikdimu 5672/1912* of the Rebbe Rashab, vol.1, p. 136
96. *Sefer Maamorim 5672-5676/1912-1916* of the Rebbe Rashab, p. 139
97. *Sefer Maamorim 5671/1911* of the Rebbe Rashab, pp. 69-70
98. *Besha'ah Shehikdimu 5672/1912* of the Rebbe Rashab, vol.1, p. 238
99. *Likutei Torah* of the Alter Rebbe, *Beha'alotcha* p. 32d (64)
100. *Torat Shmuel 5629/1869*, p. 285
101. *Berachot* 34a
102. *Likutei Torah* of the Alter Rebbe, *Shir HaShirim* P. ל"ט and P. 82, *Sefer Maamorim 5662/1902* of the Rebbe Rashab, pp. 247-249
103. *Sefer Maamorim 5657/1897* of the Rebbe Rashab, p. 122. See also *Torat Shmuel 5630/1870* of the Rebbe Maharash, p. 151
104. *Besha'ah shehikdimu 5672/1912* of the Rebbe Rashab, vol. 2, ch. 392 (Page 806)
105. Psalm 33:9
106. Psalm 147:5
107. *Sefer Maamorim 5679/1919* of the Rebbe Rashab, p. 315
108. *Yalkut*
109. *Sefer Maamorim 5679/1919* of the Rebbe Rashab, pp. 315-317
110. *Yahel Ohr*, the *Tzemach Tzedek* on Psalms, p. 369, *ot beit*
111. *Megaleh Amukot* of R' Natan Nata Shapira on *Ve'etchanan, ofen* 239
112. *Siddur* of the Alter Rebbe with Chassidut, p. *mem-dalet*
113. Saying of the sages from *Chulin* p. 60a, quoted in *Torat Shmuel 5626/1866* of the Rebbe Maharash, p. 219
114. Psalms 37:25
115. *Chulin* 60a

116. *Pirush Hamilot* of the Mitteler Rebbe, ch. 158, p. *kuf*
117. *Pirush Hamilot* of the Mitteler Rebbe, ch. 159
118. *Torat Shmuel 5627/1867* of the Rebbe Maharash, pp. 179-180
119. *Torah Ohr* of the Alter Rebbe, מ"ז , col. 2
120. *Shulchan Aruch HaRav* 51:8
121. *Torah Ohr* of the Alter Rebbe, p. 94, col 1
122. *Maamorei Admor Hazake (Maamorei R'zl) n* on *Tefila*, pp. 381-382
123. *Torat Chaim* of the Mitteler Rebbe, *Parshat Vayechi*, p. 100c, or p. 241a in the new printing
124. *Sefer Maamorim 5665/1905* of the Rebbe Rashab, p. 84
125. *Torat Shmuel 5629/1869* of the Rebbe Maharash, p. 321
126. Alter Rebbe's Siddur, p. 112
127. Psalm 145:14, Alter Rebbe's Siddur with Chasidut, P. 114
128. Alter Rebbe's Siddur with Chassidut, P. נ"ח
129. Alter Rebbe's Siddur with Chassidut, P. נ"ח, col 2
130. *Torat Shmuel 5630/1870* of the Rebbe Maharash, P. 232
131. Alter Rebbe's Siddur with Chasidut P. נ"ז, col. 2
132. Alter Rebbe's Siddur with Chasidut, P. נ"ט, col 1
133. *Maamorei Admor Hazaken (Maamorei R'zl)* on *Tefila*, p. 389
134. *Torat Shmuel 5627/1867* of the Rebbe Maharash, pp. 423-425. See also *Torat Shmuel 5630/1870*, p. 135, *Zion* is *sadeh* ("field"), since the field is where harvesting takes place. "Harvesting" alludes to transcendent spiritual revelation, such as *ahavah rabba*
135. *Sefer Maamorim 5659/1899* of the Rebbe Rashab, p. 114
136. Daniel 7:9
137. *Sefer Maamorim 5655/1895* of the Rebbe Rashab, p. 3
138. Rashi on *Shabbat* 118b
139. *Torat Shmuel 5627/1867* of the Rebbe Maharash, p. 169
140. Alter Rebbe's Siddur with Chassidut, P. ס"ז
141. *Torat Shmuel 5627/1867* of the Rebbe Maharash, p. 176. In *Torat Shmuel 5634/1874* (page 177), the Rebbe Maharash tells us that "when Hashem chose Yaakov and his sons, is equivalent to *vayarem keren le'amo Yisrael*.
142. *Torat Shmuel 5629/1869*, p. 293. In *Torat Shmuel 5632/1872*, vol 2 page 552, in a *hanacha*, the Rebbe Maharash adds that the three definitions of קרן — corner, horn, and light — correspond to *malchut, bina*, and *keter*, respectively. He adds that they correspond as well to the three levels mentioned in *Shir Hashirim*: "daughter, sister and mother" which are symbolic of the elevations of *malchut*."
143. Alter Rebbe's Siddur with Chassidut, P. ס"ז
144. *Maamorei Admor Hazaken (Maamorei R'zl)* on *Tefila*, p. 415
145. Alter Rebbe's Siddur with Chassidut, p. 70D (140)
146. *Sefer Maamorim 5655/1895* of the Rebbe Rashab, p. 126
147. *Sefer Maamorim 5680/1920* of the Rebbe Rashab, pp. 291-292. In *Torat Shmuel 5633/1873*, vol 2 page 398. the Rebbe Maharash explains that *vTakem et D'varecha*

("and You fulfilled Your word") means that there occurs revelation of the ten creative utterances within the physical world when we pray and and speak words of Torah.

148. *Likutei Torah* of the Alter Rebbe, *Parshat Tzav*, p. 14b
149. *Zohar, Parshat Ve'etchanan* 267b. "Hashem, who is like You, rescuer of the poor" is part of the prayer *Nishmat*, recited on Shabbat as part of *pesukei dezimra*, preceding *Barchu*
150. *Chulin Perek Gid Hanasheh, Daf* 91-92
151. From the *Sefer HaIkarim, Maamer* 2, ch. 23
152. *Torat Shmuel* 5627/1867 of the Rebbe Maharash, pp. 487-493
153. *Bereishit Rabba* 153, *Ovadia* 1:21, *Talmud Yerushalmi, Avoda Zara*, beginning of *Ein Ma'amidim*
154. *Torat Shmuel* 5627/1867 of the Rebbe Maharash, pp. 493-499
155. *Sha'ar HaTefila* within *Sha'arei Teshuva* of the Mitteler Rebbe, Page ל"א. "When we say *Yachid chey haolamim melech* during *Baruch She'Amar*, the phrase indicates enmeshing of the name *Havaya* within *Adni* (from Above to below, with the letters of the name *Havaya* preceding those of *Adny* [see *Lehavin shoresh inyan* Yom Kippur תקע"ז of the Mitteler Rebbe under שמו]). When we say *Melech yachid chey ha'olamim*, the phrase indicates enmeshing of the name *Adni* within *Havaya* (from below to Above, with the letters of *Adny* preceding the letters of *Havaya*.) — from *Torat Shmuel* 5630/1870 of the Rebbe Maharash, p. 46. See also *Torah Ohr* of the Alter Rebbe, *parshat Mikeitz* page 80, column 1, and *Torat Shmuel* of the Rebbe Maharash 5633/1873, vol 1 p. 80 as well as p. 278. *Sefer Maamorim* 5678/1918 of the Rebbe Rashab, p. 115
156. *Sefer Maamorim* 5662/1902 of the Rebbe Rashab, p. 354
157. *Sefer Maamorim* 5680/1920 of the Rebbe Rashab, p. 134. See note 155 above
158. *Torat Shmuel* 5627/1867, p. 18. The Rebbe (M.M.Schneerson) explains in the *maamer* "*Lehavin Hahefresh*" of the year 5719 (1969), "We might understand the difference between these two dynamics, using the illustration of a Rav who seeks to convey a new concept to his students. There are two ways in which he might do this. The first occurs when the student is intellectually inclined and has the potential to understand the concept, but is not yet on the level of the Rav. He own level is far below that of his teacher. In such a case, the teacher contracts and limits his own intellect to bring the concept in range of the student. By accepting and internalizing the concept as taught by the Rav, the intellect of the student becomes refined and elevated. So, the student's intellect becomes elevated so that eventually he becomes capable of understanding and internalizing the intellect of the Rav. The is the path "from below to Above." The second path occurs when the student is not at all capable of understanding what the Rav would like to convey to him. His own intellectual ability is not within the range of the intellect of the Rav. In such a case, the teaching dynamic occurs from Above to below. The Rav teaches the concept "as it is," without any effort to bring it within range of the student. For, the nature of illumination is that it may descend to the lowest place, since it is precisely the highest spiritual level that is capable of descending to the lowest. This path is unlike the first path, from below to Above, during which the student's intellect becomes refined and ascends. Rather the illumination — as it is — descends to the place of the recipient. The advantage of this dynamic is that the very essence and innermost

meaning of the intellectual concept descends. For since the dynamic does not take into account the potential and the capabilities of the recipient, but rather of the illumination itself, therefore what descends to the student is the very essence and inner meaning of the concept."

159. *Sefer Maamorim 5666* /1906 of the Rebbe Rashab, p. 300 and p. 399 of the new printing
160. *Sefer Maamorim 5655*/1895 of the Rebbe Rashab, p. 141
161. *Sefer Maamorim 5656*/1896 of the Rebbe Rashab, pp. 293-294
162. *Sefer Maamorim 5666*/1906 of the Rebbe Rashab, p. 136, (Page 180 in the new printing)
163. *Tanya, Igeret Hakodesh* #6
164. *Pirkei d'R'Eliezer*, ch.3
165. *Besha'ah Shehikdimu 5672*/1912 of the Rebbe Rashab, vol. 1, p. 49
166. *Sha'ar Hatefila* within *Sha'arei Teshuva* of the Mitteler Rebbe, p. 54
167. *Sha'ar Hatefila* within *Sha'arei Teshuva* of the Mitteler Rebbe, p. 54
168. *Besha'ah Shehikdimu 5672*/1912 of the Rebbe Rashab, vol. 1, p. 129 (Ch. 69)
169. *Tanya, Igeret Hakodesh* ch. 6, p. 220
170. *Sefer Maamorim 5650*/1890 of the Rebbe Rashab, p. 297
171. Alter Rebbe's Siddur, *Tefilot Rosh Hashana* p. 472
172. Daniel 7:10
173. *Likutei Torah* of the Alter Rebbe, *Parshat Re'eh*, p. 38 (bottom left column)
174. *Besha'ah Shehikdimu 5672*/1912 of the Rebbe Rashab, vol. 3, p. 1453
175. *Sefer Maamorim 5665* (1905) of the Rebbe Rashab, p. 261
176. *Sefer Maamorim 5655* (1895) of the Rebbe Rashab, pp 13, 16-17
177. *Besha'ah Shehikdimu 5672*/1912 of the Rebbe Rashab, vol. 2, p. 684, (Ch. 333)
178. *Likutei Torah* of the Alter Rebbe, *parshat Re'eh* p. 98, column A in name of the Ramban, *Torat Shmuel 5635*/1875 of the Rebbe Maharash, pp. 178-182
179. *Torat Shmuel 5627*/1867 of the Rebbe Maharash, p. 118
180. *Besha'ah Shehikdimu 5672*/1912 of the Rebbe Rashab, vol. 1, p. 288.
181. Psalm 104:14
182. *Torat Shmuel 5630*/1870 of the Rebbe Maharash, p. 175. In *Torat Shmuel 5634*/1874 (page 176), the Rebbe Maharash tells us that the purpose of meditation on the *merkava* before *kriat shema* is so that, "even though we meditate, we will not become non-existent." In other words, the meditation on *merkava* topics give us the power to withstand very high spiritual revelation.
183. *Sefer Maamorim 5666*/1906 of the Rebbe Rashab, pp. 137-138 (pp. 182-3 in the new printing)
184. *Sefer Maamorim 5655*/1905 of the Rebbe Rashab, pp. 16-17
185. *Tanya*, ch. 49. In a series of discourses, the Rebbe Maharash describes the importance of the seven blessings preceding *Kriat Shema* — three of which we say in the morning and the other four at night, based on the verse, "I will praise You seven times..." (Psalms 119:164) and mentioned in the fourth mishnah of tractate *Berachot*. Their

importance, according to the Maharash is that they prepare us for the *Shemonah Esreh*, during which we receive "seven supernal levels." The seven supernal levels correspond to the six *midot* drawn down into *malchut*, which is equivalent to drawing *"yachid"* into *"melech,"* via the *"chei olamim"* — the 18 *berachot* of the *Shemonah Esreh. Torat Shmuel 5633* (1873) vol 1 pp. 276-309

186. *Likutei Torah* of the Alter Rebbe, *Parshat Emor* p. 31a, quoting *Chulin* 91b
187. *Berachot* 10a
188. *Sefer Maamorim 5655*/1895 of the Rebbe Rashaba, p. 223
189. *Pri Eitz Chaim*, quoted in *Sefer Maamorim 5677*/1917 of the Rebbe Rashab, p. 173 and in *Likutei Torah* of the Alter Rebbe, *Parshat Emor*
190. *Sefer Maamorim 5677*/1917 of the Rebbe Rashab, p. 85
191. *Sefer Maamorim 5678*/1918 of the Rebbe Rashab, pp. 278-279, as well as *Sefer Maamorim 5679*/1919, p. 241
192. *Likutei Torah, Parshat Emor* and also *Sefer Maamorim 5678*/1918 of the Rebbe Rashab, pp. 278-279, *Sefer Maamorim 5654*/1894 of the Rebbe Rashab, Pp 300-301
193. *Sefer Maamorim 5678*/1918 of the Rebbe Rashab, pp. 214-215
194. *Likutei Torah* of the Alter Rebbe, *Shir HaShirim*, p. 5, col 2
195. *Sefer Maamorim 5661*/1901 of the Rebbe Rashab, p. 198
196. *Torat Shmuel 5630*/1870 of the Rebbe Maharash, page 272-273.
197. *Sefer Maamorim 5663*/1903 (vol. 2) of the Rebbe Rashab, pp. 314-316
198. *Sefer Maamorim 5654*/1894 of the Rebbe Rashab, p. 300
199. *Ohr HaTorah* of the *Tzemach Tzedek*, *Shemot*, vol. 8 (*Parshat Bo*), p. 2937
200. *Pardes Rimonim* of the *Ramak, Erchei Hakinuim*, gate 23, ch.1
201. *Torat Shmuel 5639*/1879 of the Rebbe Maharash, vol. 1, pp. 141-142
202. *Megaleh Amukot* of R' Nosson Nata Shapira (1585-1633), *Parshat Kedoshim*. R' Shapira cites verses in support of this correspondence.
203. *Sefer Maamorim 5679*/1919 of the Rebbe Rashab, p. 375
204. *Sefer Maamorim 5658*/1898 of the Rebbe Rashab, p. 167
205. *Sefer Maamorim 5658*/1918, p. 167
206. *Sefer Maamorim 5679*/1919, pp. 257-259
207. *Sefer Maamorim 5669*/1909, pp. 98-99 and *Sefer Maamorim 5680* (1920), pp. 145-146. But see *Torat Shmuel 5631*/1871 of the Rebbe Maharash, vol 1, P.544-545: If the ongoing creation of the world is dependent upon Torah and mitzvot, then what occurred before *Matan Torah*? On this and previous pages, the Rebbe Maharash engages in investigation of *hitzonius* ("external") and *pnimiyus* ("internal") manifestations of *hamechdesh b'tuvo b'kol yom*...that we say twice during the *Birchot Kriat Shema*. And in truth there are resolutions of this matter suggesting that the creation and maintenance of the universe is not dependent upon Torah and mitzvot, but this *drasha* (*maamar*) is based upon earlier discourses by the Alter Rebbe and the Mitteler Rebbe suggesting that creation is dependent upon Torah and mitzvot. Accordingly, the Maharash suggests that the creation of the world occurring on the 25 of Ellul is dependent upon Torah and mitzvot, and yet the Torah and mitzvot associated with Rosh

Hashana bring down a higher more essential light that is associated with the creation of man, "in a manner that is similar to God." See pages 540-548 for a fascinating *chakira*. See also footnote #1 on Page 539

208. *Sefer Maamorim 5680*/1920, pp. 145-146, *Sefer Maamorim 5669*/1909, p. 92, *Sefer Maamorim 5655*/1895, pp. 43-44

209. *Tanya, Likutei Amarim* ch. 49, also found in *Rishonim*.

210. *Torat Shmuel 5626*/1866, p. 217. According to the Rebbe Maharash, the blessing beginning "*Ahavat olam*" alludes to the highest, most sublime level of divine love, called "love with delights" (*ahava beta'anugim*). However, how could it be that the *ahavat olam* mentioned refers to such a high level, when we know that elsewhere, *ahavat olam* refers to divine love derived from the world, from creation? But the answer is that the word *olam* has two connotations. One is "world," and the other is "eternal." According to the Rebbe Maharash, the word *olam* in our blessing carries the connotation of "eternal," and therefore it can legitimately refer to the highest form of divine love, *ahava beta'anugim*. In his series of discourses from the year תשל"ז (1877), the Maharash quotes from the *Tana d'bei Eliyhahu* (section 1, 1), "If you think think that this love lasts three years, or ten years, or one hundred years - that is not the case, for God says, 'I love you (the Jewish people) forever. The Maharash goes on to interpret "three years" as three worlds of *BY"A*, and the "ten years" as the ten *sephirot* of *Atzilut*, and finally the one hundred years as an allusion to *Keter*, above *Atzilut*.

211. *Sefer Maamorim 5656*/1896 of the Rebbe Rashab, pp. 297-298

212. *Sefer Maamorim 5663*/1903 of the Rebbe Rashab, vol. 2, pp. 305, 309

213. *Gemora Berachot* 50a, quoted in *Derech Mitzvotecha* of the Tzemach Tzedek p. קכ"ד

214. *Derech Mitzvotecha* of the Tzemach Tzedek, p קכ"ד

215. *Derech Mitzvotecha* of the Tzemach Tzedek, p. קכ"ד

216. Exodus 33:21. The Rebbe Maharash adds two alternative interpretations: The "א" symbolizes the unity of the creation and its nullification to God, the "ח" symbolizes the seven heavens and the earth, and the "ד" represents the four facets of the *merkava* ("chariot") in the visions of Yehezkel and Isaiah (*Torat Shmuel 5633* (1877) vol 1 p. 136). The Maharash also suggests to understand the word אחד ("one") as אח ("brother" or "joining") — an allusion to God — with the ד being the souls of the Jewish people (*Torat Shmuel 5633* (1873) vol 1, page 289

217. *Derech Mitzvotecha* of the Tzemach Tzedek, p. 248 at the bottom

218. *Sefer Maamorim 5655*/1895 of the Rebbe Rashab, p. 42

219. *Sefer Maamorim 5678*/1918 of the Rebbe Rashab, pp. 386-395

220. *Derech Mitzvotecha* of the Tzemach Tzedek, p. 272

221. Job 33:33

222. Numbers 15:24

223. *Derech Mitzvotecha* of the Tzemach Tzedek, p. קכ"ז

224. *Sefer Maamorim 5680*/1920 of the Rebbe Rashab, p. 266

225. *Sefer Maamorim 5655*/1895, pp. 124-125

226. *Talmud Yoma* 86a discussed in *Torat Shmuel 5631*/1871, vol. 1, p. 70 of the Rebbe Maharash, and *Sefer Maamorim 5678*/1918 of the Rebbe Rashab, p. 70

227. Leviticus 16:1
228. *Shnei Ham'orot*, vol. 2, p. 30
229. *Torat Shmuel* 5630/1870 of the Rebbe Maharash, p. 121, as well as pp. 140-44. *Sefer Maamorim* 5657/1897 of the Rebbe Rashab, pp. 101-102
230. *Berachot* 13b
231. The Rebbe Maharash points out that before the Flood in the time of Noach, people lived for hundreds of years. It was only after the Flood that people's lives were shortened. Before the Flood, there was a transcendent level of Godliness (*sovev kol olmin*), associated with the soul level of *ruach*, that illuminated the world. However, after the Flood this transcendent level was no longer available ("My spirit — *ruchi* — will not abide with man forever..." Genesis 6:3). Nevertheless, with profound meditation and desire for Godliness, we may still access the higher level of *ruach*. About this, Scripture says, "Whomever dedicates his heart, spirit and soul will be gathered to Him" (Job 34). The implication is that with proper Transcendent Godliness during the *Kriat Shema*, we may even access the level of *ruach* that was available before the Flood, thus adding to our days and years, literally! (*Torat Shmuel* 5627 of the Rebbe Maharash, pp. 433-434)
232. *Torat Chaim* of the Mittler Rebbe, *Parshat Tezaveh*, p. 364, col. 3
233. *Maamorim Kuntresim Beit* of the Rebbe Rayatz, p. 776. From *Torat Shmuel* 5630/1870 of the Rebbe Maharash, page 241, we find that the three levels of love correspond to the three worlds of *Bria*, *Yetzira* and *Asiya*, as well as to the three "pillars" of prayer, Torah and good deeds. Prayer stems from the *korbanot*, which require steady thought, associated with *Bria* and with "love with all your soul." Torah requires speech, associated with *Yetzira* and with "love with all your heart." And *gemilut chasadim* is action, associated with *Asiya* and with "love with all your might."
234. *Torat Menachem* of the Lubavitcher Rebbe, vol. 1, p. 92
235. *Torah Shmuel* 5630/1870 of the Rebbe Maharash, p. 40
236. Tanya, sec. 2, *Shaar hayichud ve'haemuna*, ch. 2
237. *Sefer Maamorim* 5664/1904 of the Rebbe Rashab, p. 191
238. R' Chaim Vital in *Sha'arei Kedusha*, quoted in *Likutei Amarim Tanya*, ch. 1
239. *Remzei Torah* of the Mezricher Maggid, #166
240. *Sefer Maamorim* 5679/1919 of the Rebbe Rashab, pp. 104-107, *Torat Shmuel* of the Rebbe Maharash 5634/1874, pp. 61-62
241. *Likutei Torah* of the Alter Rebbe, *Parshat V'etchanan*, p. *yud-gimmel*, column 2. See also *Likutei Torah*, Parshat *Masei*, Page *Tzadik-Beit*, column 2
242. Alter Rebbe in the Siddur, *Sha'ar Kriat Shema*, p. *eyn-dalet*, column 2. This explanation is the opposite of the above explanation of the Alter Rebbe in his *Likutei Torah* — see next footnote.
243. *Derech Mitzvotecha* of the *Tzemach Tzedek*, in *Shoresh Mitzvat Tefila*, ch. 12, p. 120. Here the *Tzemach Tzedek* agrees with the explanation of the Alter Rebbe in *Likutei Torah*, that the first paragraph of the *Shema* presents a vessel of *chesed*, with illumination of *gevura*. The Mitteler Rebbe also mentions this explanation in *Imrei Bina*, Page 49A-B. However, the *Tzemach Tzedek* (in *Derech Mitzvotecha* p. 120) acknowledges that there is another, opposite explanation: "And if one should look in the Alter Rebbe's

siddur and find the opposite explanation, that the first paragraph presents the illumination of *chesed* in a vessel of *gevura*, then in truth both are the "living words of God." The explanation that I offer here is what I heard from his holy mouth when the Alter Rebbe spoke on the night of Shabbat Noach in the year 5565 (1805) as the emissaries of the holy R' Aharon of Totiav, grandson of the Ba'al Shem Tov *ztz"l* visited with the Alter Rebbe. And together with them, I heard this explanation. Regarding what is written in the siddur, it seems to me that the Alter Rebbe mentioned it on another occasion, and the truth is that both explanations are true, because the divine names are intermediaries between the illumination and the vessels, as we have mentioned elsewhere regarding the verse, *et Shabetotai tishmoru*...)

244. *Torat Shmuel* of the Rebbe Maharash, 5629/1859, p. 245, and from *Sefer Maamorim 5660*/1900 of the Rebbe Rashab, p. 382

245. *Imrei Bina* of the Mitteler Rebbe, ch. 58, p. *nun-hey*

246. *Sefer Maamorim 5665* /1905 of the Rebbe Rashab, p. 272

247. *Imrei Bina* of the Mitteler Rebbe, ch. 60, p. *nun-vav*. See also *Torat Shmuel 5630*/1870 of the Rebbe Maharash, p. 137: *Degancha* alludes to the revealed halachic dimension of the Torah, *Tiroshcha* refers to *Agadetah,* and *Yitzharecha* alludes to the secrets of the Torah.

248. *Likutei Torah* of the Alter Rebbe, *Parshat Re'eh*, p. 66 (33b)

249. *Torat Shmuel 5629*/1869 of the Rebbe Maharash, pp. 271-272

250. *Imrei Bina* of the Mitteler Rebbe, ch. 61, p. 57. The Rebbe Maharash points out that Reuven found *"Dudaim"* in the field that he brought to his mother (*parshat Vayeitzei*). The simple understanding is that the *dudaim* were plants that contained a substance that enables fertility. However, the Maharash explains that the *Dudaim* allude to the angels, Sandal and Metat (and ultimately the *Cheruvim* of the *mishkan* and Temple), who elevate the prayers of the Jews and also convey holy influence down to the world from Above. Reuven wished to remain on the far side of the Jordan River because there he could maintain his *avoda* of "immanent Godliness," which is "food for the animals" because such *avoda* calms and uplifts the animal soul. However, the limitation of such *avoda* is that it does not "transform" the animal soul, which only occurs with the *avoda* of *Eretz Yisrael* itself, which is an *avoda* of "transcendent Godliness," far beyond "fodder for the animal." (*Torat Shmuel 5633*/1873 vol 1, page 37)

251. *Sefer Maamorim 5661*/1901 of the Rebbe Rashab, p. 208

252. *Imrei Bina* of the Mitteler Rebbe, ch. 61, p. *nun-zayin*

253. *Torah Shmuel 5630*/1870 of the Rebbe Maharash, p 359. An additional explanation of *Tzitzit* from the Alter Rebbe in *Likutei Torah, parshat Shalach*, p. 92: "The *talit* represents *ohr makif* ("transcendent light") and the threads of the *tzitzit* represent a mere contracted spiritual descent, similar to "hairs," that are not within range or comparison to the essential transcendent light." In other words, the garment (*talit*) represents *ohr makif*, while the *tzitzit* represent *ohr pnimi*. And thus in the following *parsha*, Korach takes issue with Moshe Rabeinu by saying, "if one wears the *talit* (transcendent light), why does he need *tzitzit* (immanent illumination)?" His theory was that it was possible to "live" and be "nourished" by the transcendent light of *ohr makif* alone. It took the answer of Moshe to make it clear to the Jews that the proper path to the *makif*, determined by God Himself, is through the *ohr pnimi*, or step by step organized *avodat Hashem* in study and meditation.

254. *Sefer Maamorim* 5679/1919 of the Rebbe Rashab, p. 639
255. *Sefer Maamorim* 5665/1905 or the Rebbe Rashab, pp. 135
256. *Besha'ah Shehikdimu* 5672/1912 of the Rebbe Rashab, vol. 1, p. 161
257. Genesis 29:35
258. *Sefer Maamorim* 5680/1920 of the Rebbe Rashab, p. 220
259. *Baba Kama* 85b
260. *Baba Batra* 12a
261. Genesis 29:35
262. *Yom Tov shel Rosh Hashana* 5666/1906 of the Rebbe Rashab, p. 145 or p. 191 in the new version
263. *Sefer Maamorim* 5679/1919 of the Rebbe Rashab, pp. 349-350
264. *Yom Tov shel Rosh Hashana* 5666/1906 of the Rebbe Rashab, p. 145 (pp. 191-192 in the new printing)
265. *Tzemach Tzedek* in *Kovetz Meah Shearim*, p. 99
266. *Besha'ah Sh'hikdimu* 5672/1912 of the Rebbe Rashab, vol. 2, p. 1031
267. *Sefer Maamorim* 5654/1894 of the Rebbe Rashab, pp. 110 and 116
268. *Micha* 6:15
269. *Sefer Maamorim* 5658/1898 of the Rebbe Rashab, pp. 87, 93
270. *Job* 28:27
271. *Sefer Maamorim* 5680/1920 of the Rebbe Rashab, pp. 153, 155. The Rebbe Maharash explains that the proximity of *Kriat Shema* to *Shemonah Esreh* occurs so that the *mesiras nefesh* ("devotion") that we develop during the *Kriat Shema* will carry over into the *Shemonah Esreh*. When that occurs, our words of *tefila* are called *avanim tovot* ("precious stones"), which the angel Sandal elevates above. This elevation occurs during the first three blessings of the *Shemonah Esreh*, and during the twelve middle blessings, we bring down the *tov* ("good") that is intended for us in response to our prayers. Similarly, there were twelve stones in the breast plate of the high priest, and three letters in each one, alluding to the first three blessings of the *Shemonah Esreh*. (*Torat Shmuel* 5633/1873, vol 1 p. 163). In *Torah Shmuel* 5634/1874 (page 152), the Rebbe Maharash explains that it is the final words of the *Kriat Shema* (*Tehilot L'Kel Elyon...*) that "give power to draw down from Above during the *Shemonah Esreh*" and are thus comparable to *smicha* prior to *tefila*.
272. *Berachot* 42a
273. *Sefer Maamorim* 5659/1899 of the Rebbe Rashab, p. 200
274. *Torat Shmuel* 5631/1871 of the Rebbe Maharash, p. 70, *Sefer Maamorim* 5678/1918 of the Rebbe Rashab, p. 70
275. *Torat Shmuel* 5631/1870 of the Rebbe Maharash, p. 37
276. *Maamorei Admor Hazaken* (*Maamorei R'zl*) on *Tefila*, page 443. The Rebbe Maharash adds that the word *magen* ("shield") in the blessing *magen Avraham*, is an acrostic for the three angels, Michael, Gavriel and Nuriel (from the *Pardess*). Why do we say "God of Avraham, God of Yitzhak and God of Yaakov"? Why not "Creator of the heavens and the earth"? But the forefathers brought revealed Godliness down to the world, which

was a greater feat than creation from nothing to something." (*Kuzari*, *Torah Shmuel 5630*/1870, p. 71).

277. Isaiah 38:2
278. *Talmud Berachot* 5B, *Shulchan Aruch HaRav* 90:20
279. *Torat Shmuel 5627*/1867 of the Rebbe Maharash, pp. 182-186. See also *Torat Shmuel 5630*/1870, p. 192: "*Tel* refers to the *tzadik*, foundation of the creation, to whom all mouths turn because through him all spiritual influence comes into the world." And *telem* is the channel through which Godliness flows to the world, and therefore, "every cow [souls of the lower worlds *BY"A*] must learn to plow [uplift] in its own *telem*, in its own path of ascent to the world of Atzilut." There is a *kotel* in the world of *Bria*, where the amount of "evil" is so minimal that it can be separated from the good by a wall, or *kotel*. When the King (God) looks for the *matronita* (the *shechina*) and her son (the Jews), He "climbs on the roofs, descends the stairs, and climbs on the walls (the *kotel*)," peering through the cracks to find them (*Torat Shmuel 5630*/1870 of the Rebbe Maharash, p. 347)
280. *Talmud Berachot* 32b (see also *Talmud Sota* 38b)
281. *Likutei Torah* of the Alter Rebbe, *parshat Balak*, p. 140
282. *Derech Mitzvotecha* of the Tzemach Tzedek, *shoresh mitzvah tefila* Ch 13 and 17
283. *Shulchan Aruch Orach Chaim siman* 60, *Talmud Berachot* 6b, 16a
284. *Devarim* (Deut) 4:7
285. The Alter Rebbe's Siddur with Chasidut, p. 85 (*Pey-hey*)
286. Alter Rebbe's Siddur, *Sha'ar Kriat Shema*, p. 170
287. Alter Rebbe in his Siddur, *Sha'ar Kriat Shema*, p. 170
288. *Imrei Bina* of the Mittler Rebbe, ch. 17 in the introduction
289. Mitteler Rebbe in the introduction to *Imrei Bina*, ch. 17
290. *Imrei Bina* of the Mitteler Rebbe, *Petach sha'ar*, ch. 17
291. *Derech Mitzvotecha* of the Tzemach Tzedek, *Shoresh Mitzvat Tefila*, ch. 7, p. קי״ז (117)
292. *Derech Mitzvotecha* of the Tzemach Tzedek, *Shoresh Mitzvat Tefila*, ch. 7, p. 234
293. *Torat Shmuel* of the Rebbe Maharash, *5639*/1879, vol. 1, p. 32. *Torat Shmuel* of the Rebbe Maharash, *5633*/1873, vol. 1 page 197
294. See also *Torat Shmuel* of the Rebbe Maharash, 5630/1870, p. 98.
295. Rabbi Adin Steinsaltz on *Shoresh Mitzvat Tefila* of the Tzemach Tzedek adds the following illustration: When we enter the *Shemonah Esreh*, it as if we are entering a "supermarket," with tens of thousands of items available to purchase. If we have no idea where the item is located, it is difficult to locate it. But, if we have an "address," such as an aisle number and row, then we can easily locate the item that we wish to buy. Similarly, proper intention while mentioning God's name during the *Shemonah Esreh* provides a pathway and vessel for our request.
296. *Sefer Maamorim 5654*/1894 of the Rebbe Rashab, p. 117
297. *Sefer Maamorim 5663*/1903, vol. 2 of the Rebbe Rashab, p. 233
298. *Sefer Maamorim 5663*/1903, vol. 2 of the Rebbe Rashab, p. 233. Before it enters the *kelim* ("vessels") of the *sephirot* of *Atzilut*, the *ohr* ("divine illumination") is completely simple and undivided. Once it enters the *kelim*, it takes on some of the nature of the *kelim*. There are three levels associated with the *kelim*: *pnimiyut hakelim* (the "inner

dimensions of the vessels"), *emtzait hakelim* (the "intermediate level") and *chitzoniut hakelim* (the "external levels of the vessels"). These *kelim* may be likened to physical vessels that have three components: the internal receptacle of the vessel (*pnimiyut hakeli*), the body of the vessel (*emtzait hakeli*), and the handle with which we grasp the vessel (*chitzoniyut hakeli*). As it enters the vessels, the simple undivided light of the name *Havaya* (without vowels) "fills" the receptacle of the vessel, uniting with the *pnimiyut* of the *keli*. Here, it takes on the vowels that we must focus on during the *Shemonah Esreh*. The *keli* itself (*emtzait hakeli*) is described by the other names of God, such as *Kel* in *chesed*, *Elokim* in *gevura*, etc. Finally, the nicknames with which we describe the *sephirot* ("merciful," "strong," etc.) are associated with the external dimensions (the "handle") of the *sephirot*. Our task during the *Shemonah Esreh* is to focus on the undivided simple light of *Havaya* and "direct" it to the inner dimensions of the *kelim* of *Atzilut*, where it takes on vowelization. We do so by focusing upon the vowelization, which "channels" the light of *Havaya* to the *sephira* which is appropriate for that blessing.

299. *Sefer Maamorim 5669*/1909, p. 92
300. *Yom Tov shel Rosh Hashana 5666*/1906 of the Rebbe Rashab, p. 182, or p. 242 in the new edition
301. *Sefer Maamorim 5654*/1894 of the Rebbe Rashab, p. 186
302. *Torat Shmuel 5629*/1869 of the Rebbe Maharash, p. 348 (p. 302 in the older edition)
303. *Sefer Maamorim 5680*/1920 of the Rebbe Rashab, pp. 145-146. See also *Sefer Maamorim 5663*/1903, vol. 2, p. 234 — "Torah is a mere garment while prayer is internal…" See also *Sefer Maamorim 5655*/1895, pp. 40-49 and *Sefer Maamorim 5679*/1919, pp. 114-116, where it is implied that the *Shemonah Esreh* brings down true "new light."
304. *Sefer Maamorim 5669*/1909 of the Rebbe Rashab, pp. 99-101
305. *Torat Shmuel 5629*/1869 of the Rebbe Maharash, p. 216 (pp. 236-7 in the older edition)
306. Alter Rebbe's Siddur with Chassidut p. ש"ג/606
307. *Sefer Maamorim 5678* (1918) of the Rebbe Rashab, pp 244-245
308. *Derech Mitzvotecha* of the *Tzemach Tzedek*, *Mitzvat vidui v'tshuva*, p. ח"ל
309. *Derech Mitzvotecha* of the *Tzemach Tzedek*, *Shoresh Mitzvat Tefila*, ch. 11, p. כ"ק
310. *Sefer Maamorim 5654*/1894 of the Rebbe Rashab, p. 251
311. *Venikdashti* from *Likutei Torah* of the Alter Rebbe, *Parshat Emor*, p. א"ל
312. *Sefer Maamorim 5665*/1905 of the Rebbe Rashab, pp. 247-249
313. *Tur* and *Shulchan Aruch, Orach Chaim* 61:4

ENDNOTES FOR CHASSIDIC INSIGHTS

i. Three reasons are given for this section of the prayers, preceding the *Kriat Shema*. 1) Tanya (Ch. 49) tells us that we say the blessings in order to prepare ourselves for the *mesiras nefesh*, or "self-sacrifice" that we experience during the *Kriat Shema*. By reviewing and reciting how the angels are willing to be subsumed in Godliness, we ourselves develop the necessary emotions of self sacrifice in order to be ready for the *mesiras nefesh* of the *Kriat Shema* 2) In *Likutei Torah* of the Alter Rebbe, we are taught that the animal soul has its source in the angels of the *merkava*, or "chariot" that is the source of

creation in the worlds of *Bria* and *Yetzira*. By focusing our attention on these levels, we are able to "teach" our animal soul about its own source in the spiritual worlds, and then it is transformed and desires Godliness. This is the "fire from below" that the animal soul brings to the prayers, which are answered by the "fire from above" from the angels
3) In *Torat Shmuel 5627/1867*, the Rebbe Maharash tells us that in the time of Yehezkel, the Godly influx began to descend to the world via the *malachim*, or angels, and that is when the *rabonim* decreed that we should add the *Birchot Kriat Shema* (mentioning the angels) to our prayers.

ii. Approaching *Birchot Kriat Shema*, we encounter an apparent contradiction. Our previous meditation on the spiritual origins of creation was focused upon *memalle kol olmin* — "immanent spirituality" that is embedded in the universe in order to create from nothing to something. Our goal during *Birchot Kriat Shema* is to delve even deeper into the Godliness that enlivens creation, and to strip away the "shrouding" and "packaging" in order to discover the Godly spark that is the real essence of creation. This process and state of mind is called *pnimiyut bina* ("inner dimensions of *bina*"), and it obviously demands the ability to meditate deeply on the Godliness within creation — *memalle kol olmin*. Yet, the Rebbe's instructions (as well as the *nusach* of *tefila*) for this section of prayer are to focus on *sovev kol olmin*, or Godliness that transcends creation. How can we reconcile these two seemingly opposite directions and paths in meditation?

Perhaps the resolution comes from the Chasidut of the Rebbe Rashab, in which he breaks down *bina* into two components: "In *bina* we find two components; one which is immanent (*pnimi*), and one that is transcendent (*makif*). For, the birth of emotions occurs from the intellect; that is, our intellect obligates us to either love or detest something. If we love the item, we develop closeness to it. If we detest the matter, then quite the opposite — we distance ourselves completely. Nevertheless, we are capable of meditating upon and considering the matter [objectively] even though we detest it. This is called *gadlut hamochim*, or "mature mindfulness." That which emerges from *bina* in a manner of "immanent light" (*ohr pnimi*) is contracted and limited and does not permit us to tolerate whatever we may hate or detest. But, the essential nature of *bina* is to remain transcendent and aloof, without becoming contracted to invest itself in any matter. For that reason, essential *bina* is capable of tolerating even that which is hateful to it. That is the transcendent nature of *bina*..." (From *Sefer Maamorim 5678/1918* of the Rebbe Rashab, p. 289).

Elsewhere, the Rebbe Rashab explains how this dual nature of *bina* is applicable to meditation and prayer: "As we meditate, using our capacity of intellect to attain grasp of Godly concepts, and we contemplate the depth of the topic, our contemplation has no influence upon our emotions whatsoever. Even the external, more superficial aspects of our intellect, which do bear a connection to emotions, have little influence upon them — our intellect remains aloof. This is comparable to one who hears or understands something that has nothing to do with him. Similarly, our meditation does not touch us emotionally within, even as we achieve full comprehension of the topic....Only with our faculty of *da'at* ("visceral knowledge") do we begin to experience the concept inside, and even then we feel only an offshoot of the intellect…even during meditation, the concept remains aloof." (from *Sefer Maamorim* 5679/1919 of the Rebbe Rashab, pp. 396-7).

In practical terms, this means that the meditator, while practicing the technique of *pnimiyut hamochin* and achieving awareness of the Godly spark at the essence of creation will be captivated and enthralled by his discovery. This will produce the awareness of *neshama* described in *Kuntres Ha'avoda*, in which he loses all contact with his surroundings. On the other hand, he will retain focus on a higher "truth" that is the objective awareness of the source of creation — God Himself. In other words, even as he penetrates to the essential depths of creation and finds Godliness, he simultaneously remains aware that "this cannot be all there is to it." God is also beyond and as much as the meditator is enthralled with his new discovery, he remains aware that there are higher levels of spirituality waiting for him to achieve. Thus, during *Birchot Kriat Shema*, we may be both "within the meditation" of *memalle kol olmin*, and also beyond the details of creation and retain cognizance of God's higher transcendent Presence.

iii. In his teachings, the Rebbe also emphasizes that our meditation upon the transcendent light of *ohr makif* is associated with the verse, *Ain kadosh k'Havaya* — "there is no holiness like that of *Havaya*" (*Shmuel* 1, 2:2). *Havaya* is the holy name that transcends creation, and as the Zohar explains, "there are many levels of holiness, but none of them are as holy as His holy name *Havaya*." And yet, in the *Kuntres Ha'avoda*, the Rebbe Rashab associates this level with the divine illumination that bursts through the *parsa* ("curtain" separating *Atzilut* from *Bria*) in order to create and enliven the lower worlds of *Bria, Yetzira* and *Asiya*. This would place it in the category of *ohr p'nimi*, or the same inner permeating illumination that we meditated upon during the *pesukei dezimra*. As the Rebbe Rashab writes there, "...we can say that there are two kinds of Godly energy invested in the creation of the lower worlds of *BY'A: Koach* ("power") and *ohr* ("light"). *Koach* is associated with the *kelim*, or "vessels" of *BY'A*, and *ohr* is associated with *neshama*, or "soul" of creation as well as beyond...and about them, it is said, "There is no holiness like that of *Havaya*,"...since it is holy and removed and yet it is en-clothed..." (Page 174 of "Love like Fire and Water"). At first glance, this seems to contradict what the Rebbe says in the *sicha*, that the illumination of "There Is no holiness like *Havaya*" applies to the transcendent illumination of *ohr makif*?

However, the Rebbe answers this apparent contradiction in a footnote to the *Kuntres Ha'avoda*: There (on p. 296 of "Love like Fire and Water"), he refers us to *Shir HaShirim* within *Likutei Torah* of the Alter Rebbe: "The name *Havaya* indicates that He creates everything and even though He creates everything, He is nevertheless holy and removed from them. He is *sovev kol olmin* — "Transcendent illumination of the worlds" — unlike the soul [which fills the body and which is therefore *memalle kol olmin* — "immanent illumination"]. And for that reason, this category of holiness is not to be found among all the other expressions of holiness that exist above. Regarding the other levels of *seder histalshelut* ("spiritual chain of creation"), whatever is called "holy" — meaning that it is somehow "removed" — does not imply the following two opposites. One, it permeates and penetrates, and two, it is holy and removed. Above, though, the infinite light of *sovev kol olmin*, which is holy and removed, nevertheless descends to create all of the worlds. The main impetus for creation comes from the *makif* ('transcendent light"), as written in Tanya end of Ch. 23 and the end of Ch 48...And that is why "there is no holiness like that of *Havaya.*" The special holiness of *Havaya* is that it is simultaneously transcendent, above creation, yet also immanent, permeating creation.

iv. Incidentally, this may be what Tanya alludes to in Ch. 44, when it says, "Furthermore, these two distinctions of love (intellectual and natural love)...contain a quality of love which is greater and more sublime than the intelligent fear and love, termed above *Ahavat olam...*" Possibly the reference is to *Ahava b'ta'anugim*, which is a form of "love like water" that overwhelms us and also motivates us toward action).

v. *Ahava rabba* is distinguished from "*ahavah betaanugim* in the following subtle manner: While we may prepare for *ahavah rabba* via our meditation on the infinite light of God (utilizing *avodat hashlilah*), we may or may not experience it. The preparation is a necessary but not sufficient condition to achieve *ahavah rabba* Only one who is complete in his *avodat Hashem*, both in love like water and love like fire, may experience *ahavah rabba*. But even if he is complete in his meditation, there is no guarantee that he will achieve it. However, there is nothing that we can do whatsoever to prepare for *ahavah betaanugim* — it is purely a gift from Above (See *Yom Tov shel Rosh Hashana 5666* of the Rebbe Rashab, p. 132)

vi. In this case, the fire from below of the Godly soul is brought during the *pesukei dezimra* (perhaps during the process described above as "Gazing on the glory of the King." However fire from above and below of the animal soul occurs during the *Birchot Kriat Shema* during the declarations of the angels, as described above in the text.

vii. (In *Yom Tov shel Rosh Hashana 5666*, p. 150, the Rebbe Rashab distinguishes between *reiya b'eyn hasechel* ("seeing in the mind's eye") that occurs during meditation on *ohr pnimi*, which brings us to awareness of the kernel of Godliness within the worlds (*memalle kol olmin*), and between *avodat hashlilah* on a more transcendent level, leading to awareness of *sovev kol olmin*, or transcendent Godliness).

viii. With "seeing in the mind's eye" is associated another spiritual experience, called *yichuda ila'ah* ("supernal awareness"). During our normal awareness, the physical creation is in the foreground of our consciousness, while God and spirituality are in the background. Usually, the physical creation is much more "real" to us than is spirituality, and all the moreso, than God Himself. We are generally aware of our physical environment, but we have to strive mightily to experience anything that is Godly or spiritual. That all changes when we meditate properly going into the *Kriat Shema*. All of a sudden, a transition takes place as we say the word *echad* ('one') and we realize the God is the true reality, and His creation is secondary. He is the real "existence," since He will never blink out of existence and He will always be present. But, the world upon which we have meditated so assiduously in order to detect Godliness, is temporary and limited — it only exists as long as He desires that it should exist. When we say the *Shema*, we are uplifted to this new "Godly" point of view in which He is the true reality and the physical world is of questionable existence. This is the experience of *yichuda ila'ah*, or "supernal awareness." It lasts as long as we meditate upon the first verse of the *Shema* (*Shema Yisrael*...). Upon saying the next verse, *Baruch shem*...we revert to our "normal" state of awareness, in which the physical creation is in the forefront of our consciousness, and God is in the background. This consciousness is also called, *yichuda tata'ah*, or "lower awareness."

ix. See *Torat Shmuel* 5629 (1867), pp. 270-271, 286

x. In the section called *Inyan cavanat ha'amida, drosh vav*.

xi. As it is written in the *Tikunim*, no. 70, p. 128a.

xii. *Raya Mehemna, Parshat Teitzei*, p. 276b.

APPENDIX 1

Free translation of notes from the Rebbe Rayatz, based on his studies with his father, the Rebbe Rashab in the year תרע"ב (1912)

Three Levels of Divine Love[1]

Explanations given by the Rebbe Rashab regarding his Chassidic discourses for the year תרס"ו (1906), as recorded by his son, the Rebbe Rayatz.

In the introduction to the 1971 edition of תרס"ו (from Kehos Publishing Co.), there appears a note: "According to Chassidic lore, the Rebbe Rashab studied with his son, Rabbi Yoseph Yitzhak Schneersohn (the Rayatz), the series of Chassidic discourses for the year תרס"ו (1906), with added explanations. The Rayatz recorded the explanations and added his own. The dates appearing on the recorded notes and explanations are the dates on which the Rayatz heard the explanations or when he wrote them down."

In *Torat Menachem*, the diary entry on page 182, the Rebbe (Rabbi Menachem Mendel Schneerson, son-in-law of the Rayatz) writes: "He [the Rayatz] told me that when they studied the series תרס"ו, the schedule was as follows: 'We learned on Mondays, Wednesdays and Motzei Shabbat, using the Rashab's handwritten manuscript. He [the Rashab] would hold the manuscript, as would I, and so we learned. We also studied the introductory words to each *parsha* — each and every one. After learning, I created summaries of all that we learned during the session.' [Accordingly, the dates that do not correspond to Monday, Wednesday or

---

1. It is instructive to compare this treatment of the three levels of divine love (*ahavat olam, ahava rabba*, and *ahava bet'anugim*) with the treatment that the Rebbe Rayatz gives to the same topic in a letter printed at the end of *Kuntres Ha'avoda* of the Rebbe Rashab, and appearing at the end of our translation, "Love like Fire and Water." The two treatments are very different from one another.

Motzei Shabbat would seem to be the dates on which the Rayatz wrote his summary.]²

The following notes, currently in the publisher's possession, are from *Tishrei* through *Kislev*, תרע"ג (roughly October through December, 1912).

1

רעותא דליבא (*reuta deliba* — "will or desire of the heart") — and תשובה (*teshuva*, or "return to God") — both result from internal arousal of the soul, but they are nevertheless distinct in their nature. Following is a summary of what we learned, based upon both study and reason…

The difference between the arousal of *reuta deliba* and the arousal of *teshuva*: *Reuta deliba* occurs in proximity, during which the meditator "sees," but does not experience ("taste") Godly illumination. The experience occurs during *ahava betaanugim*. The arousal of *teshuva* occurs from afar, from a distance, which is not the case during *ahava betaanugim* when he "tastes" and very much experiences [Godliness] from nearby.

Questions:

1) Does the concept of "nearness and distance" that applies to *reuta deliba* and *teshuva* also apply to *ahava rabba* ("great love") and *ahava betaanugim* ("love with delight")?

---

2. Apparently the custom of the Rebbe learning with his son three times a week went back previous generations, until at least the generation of the *Tzemach Tzedek*. The Frierdiker Rebbe (the Rayatz) records (in *Sefer Maamorim* 5708/1948, page 175, also mentioned in *Sefer Maamorim* 5631/1871 of the Maharash, v.2, page 689) that,"The *Tzemach Tzedek* fixed a time three times per week to tell his son, the Rebbe Maharash about various matters in private. No other person was allowed to know about these meetings, so that there would be no jealousy among the brothers [the *Tzemach Tzedek* had six sons, among whom the *Maharash* was the youngest]. And from the year 5631/1871, the Rebbe *Maharash* established three times a week to learn with his son, the Rebbe *Rashab*, in absolute secrecy, and to tell him various stories. The *Rashab* wrote them down and explained them at length, with instructions and teachings in regard to rectification of character traits and *tefila* (prayer)."

2) Does *ahava betaanugim* occur after *reuta deliba*, just as *reuta deliba* occurs after love according to reason and logic, or is *ahava betaanugim* a separate and distinct level, on its own?

3) Is *ahava betaanugim* of a lower world on the same level as *ahava rabba* of the world above it, since they are of one essence?

4) The spiritual elevation associated with divine love that results from reason and logic, as well as of *ahavah rabba*, is commensurate with the level of the person. That is, the person's abilities influence the spiritual level that he attains. Is the same true of *ahava betaanugim*? Do the person's individual abilities affect the level of love that he attains, or not?

5) Clearly, those who place more emphasis on refining their character traits and developing love and fear of God (עובדים) achieve a deeper grasp of divine concepts than do those who merely seek to understand the same concepts (משכילים). This is true despite the fact that those who place emphasis on understanding are faster to grasp the subtleties of the concept, at least at the beginning. At what point does the transformation occur, when the concept is "felt" by the עובדים and "grasped" by the משכילים?

Introduction #1: Whenever we reveal Godly illumination in the world — whether via speech (such as saying blessings or reciting prayers) or by action (by fulfilling the mitzvot of the Torah) — the quality of illumination will be higher when it comes down through our actions, than through our words, assuming all other factors to be equal. As is implied by the phrase, "There is no wiser man than the man of action," our deeds do more to express our very essence than do our thoughts and intentions. Furthermore, our deeds are associated with "reflected illumination" which may not directly reveal who we are, but which, nevertheless, sheds true light on our motivation and desires.[3]

---

3. For example, we may not say what we are really thinking, but with a simple gesture, we may reveal some of our deepest emotions. As of this writing, Jews are allowed to ascend the *Har Habayit* ("Temple Mount") in Jerusalem, but are not allowed to pray. There are some Jews who ascend the Temple Mount and make a gesture with their upturned palms indicating their deep desire to change the status quo. That one gesture does more to reveal their aspirations than would their prayers.

Introduction #2: There are some matters that cannot be expressed in speech at all, and action is the primary mode through which they come into expression. This may occur for two reasons: 1) either because the essence of the matter itself is best expressed in action; or 2) because our egos are suppressed, and we become *kelim* ("vessels") for revelation of essential Godliness while working through the medium of action. When that occurs, it becomes clear that there is "no wiser man than the man of action," for what he reveals with his "action" is far beyond expectations, and beyond of the normal revelation of Godliness in the world…

Summary: "Intellect" (השכלה) results in the grasp of a concept, while the personal "work" that we do on ourselves (עבודה) culminates in emotion. By way of explanation, all spiritual levels are mutually inclusive — each level includes all others. For example, even though intellectual grasp (in חכמה) and faith (in כתר) are opposites of one another, nevertheless they complement each other. Knowledge (דעת) and recognition (הכרה) are also two very distinct attributes. They are nearly separate from one another, and yet they are part of the same personal attribute (recognition is a deep, visceral dimension of knowledge[4]). While *da'at* is knowledge and *hacara* is similar to trust, the two traits go together. A student must first trust his mentor before he can learn from him, for two reasons. First, it is the trust that he places in his teacher that prevents him from becoming confused. And second, it is his trust in his mentor that enables him to grow and flourish in his studies. So, trust is an integral component of knowledge that makes it possible for us to "envision" matters in our soul.

The same is true of spiritual proximity and distance. At the very moment that we experience proximity to a spiritual level, we immediately feel a need to "back off" and distance ourselves. Yet, as soon as

---

4. When we say that we "know" something, we are expected to back up our knowledge with facts and logic. However, when we "recognize" something, we do not necessarily have the ability to explain "why" we recognize, because recognition is based upon past experience leaving an indelible impression on our memory and sensory organs. Thus, conscious experience leads to "knowledge," which with repetition becomes "recognition." They are very different, but yet closely related.

we distance ourselves, we feel a need to return and approach the matter.[5] What we must do in such situations is identify the main trend (the "closeness" of love of God, or the "distance" associated with fear of God). By way of illustration, the stories of the Torah are transmitted not only through the letters and words of the Torah, but also through the "crowns" (*tagin*) on the letters, the vowels (*nekudot*) that tell us how to pronounce the letters, and the cantillations (*ta'amim*) that tell us how to chant the words. (Collectively, these four elements are called *Tanta* — (טנת״א) — which is an acrostic for "*ta'amim* ("cantillations"), *nekudot* ("vowels"), *tagin* ("crowns") and *otiot* ("letters"). The crowns, vowels and cantillations may tell a very different story than what appears in the letters and words of the Torah, or they may offer a sub-text that illuminates and may even contradict the main narrative as it emerges from the letters. Important information that is not imparted by the letters may find expression in the crowns, vowels or chants of the Torah verses. Nevertheless, the "main" narrative is the one told by the letters, and that's why they are "close" to us (easiest to decipher). The narratives imparted by the other elements (the crowns, vowels and cantillations) are secondary, and in that sense they are "distant."

Something of a similar nature occurs among *ovdim* — among those who attempt to get close to God by working on themselves to internalize Torah concepts and emotions. The concepts that they study form the main narrative that they then internalize. Yet, during the process of integration of the "main" concept, which brings them "nearer" to God, they also experience contradictions, secondary "narratives" that may contradict the main story, and sub-texts that illuminate and shed tangential light on the main narrative. These "secondary narratives" may seem to work against getting closer to God, but ultimately they illuminate the path in a higher manner as the *oved* remains focused on the love of God. The seeming contradictions are an example of *ohr chozer* ("reflected illumination") that appears to block the path, but when resolved and integrated, actually brings the *oved* closer to God. Similarly among "wise men of action," it is action which activates their emotions in a process of

---

5. See *Rambam Hilchot Yesodei Hatorah* 2:2 as well as *Tanya Likutei Amarim* Ch 3.

ohr chozer but, like "back-lighting," it highlights our true love of God and indicates our true essence, since "none is as wise as the man of action." (The "man of action" does not express or feel his love for God through his intellect, but rather through his actions. Paradoxically, though, his actions arouse the highest emotions of love of God, since, "there is no wise man like the man of action").

Summary: *Ahava* ("love") is a feeling in the heart, and as such, it cannot be commanded. Nevertheless, via meditation and contemplation — which can be commanded — we can achieve love of God. We experience such love after meditating correctly on Godly concepts. If we have meditated correctly, the experience of love follows our meditation as a confirmation that we have correctly grasped the concept. Such love is a revealed, conscious emotion that occurs even as we meditate, using our intellect. There is order within the emotion we feel (even though that order is not the same as during the intellectual phase). While in the throes of the Godly emotion (love of God), the meditator experiences something "high" and "removed," but only incidentally ("by the way," as if to say, "I wasn't looking for this"). The meditator remains aware of his intellect and of the concept upon which he was focused, since even an intellectual concept "exists," and as a result, the emotion remains at full strength. This is true even when the meditation leads to action (performance of a mitzvah). Even then, the feeling remains at full strength just as it did when he was meditating. The emotion fulfills the function of joining the intellect with the action, so that even in the midst of his action, the meditator experiences the full power of his meditation.

From all of the above, it should be clear that the goal of a Chassid is not mere exercise of his intellect. Even the most basic form of intellect, predicated upon straight-forward reason and logic, is meant to provide us with experience of love of God. This comes about through the work (meditation and soul searching) that we do within, refining ourselves to the point that we experience Godliness. Intellect and understanding is a preface to such experience, but it is not its ultimate goal. Those who depend on the intellect alone, stay at that level. But, those who work upon themselves in order to add a layer of feeling and emotion — which translate into deed and action — create a vessel within themselves to receive essential illumination from Above. Their power of intellectual grasp is felt and experienced below, in their emotions and actions, and that is the true explanation of, "there is no wiser man than the man of action."

Solutions to the above questions:

1) Within *ahava rabba* and *ahava betaanugim* are also found the concept of "nearness" and "distance."
2) It is not certain that *ahava betaanugim* will follow upon *ahava rabba*. However, *ahavah rabba* removes any resistance and obstacles to revelation of *ahava betaanugim*.
3) *Ahava betaanugim* in lower worlds consists of enjoyment of the essence of the concept, but on a lower level [than *ahavah betaanugim* in the higher worlds].
4) Even during *ahava betaanugim*, our senses and abilities influence our experience, similar to the principle that "a full vessel contains."
5) Those who work upon themselves experience divine emotions, and as a result of their emotions, their intellectual grasp takes place on a different plane altogether.

2

This section is the conclusion of the Rayatz's summary from 25 Tishrei, תשנ"ז. A summary of the entire theme appears above in Introduction #1.

The main theme of *ahava rabba* is "distance."[6] That is because, while in the throes of *ahava rabba*, we experience our distance from God. (We "see" divine illumination, but we do not experience it directly). Nevertheless, there is a sub-text of nearness and proximity within *ahava rabba* that comes from the "feeling of infinite illumination that we

---

6. The theme of distance may be connected with the technique of meditation that is used to achieve *ahava rabba*. As the Rebbe Rayatz writes later in his notes, the technique to achieve *ahava rabba* is "negative grasp," during which one negates his previously held concepts of Godliness in order to achieve a new, higher level of awareness and Godly understanding. While the net effect is elevation to a higher, more sublime spiritual level, the accompanying feeling is that one really does not grasp Godliness — hence the main theme of *ahava rabba* is "distance."

experience in our soul"[7] as a result of peering intently.[8] For this, we make use of our power of spiritual vision (*chochma*), which penetrates to the unity of creation. Thus, *ahava rabba* is associated with unity.[9] The feeling of distance never departs during *ahavah rabba*, but there are also elements of nearness, even if sub-conscious.

However, the main dynamic of *ahava betaanugim* ("love with delights") is nearness and proximity to God. Nevertheless, even this experience (which is very real, as in "taste and see" — Psalms 34:10) contains elements of "distance." The distance is the internal "brokenness" (צוא בראכינקאייט) that we experience, which is imparted by very high spiritual illumination.[10] This is not the same distance that we experience during *teshuva* (desire to "return" to God). The distance of *teshuva* is associated with bitterness over our situation, which is not positive, and is, in fact, the opposite of good. This dynamic does not exist during *ahava betaanugim*. Yet, in the very heart of proximity and nearness to God, we discover this "distance" as a feeling of "lowliness" and "forlornness" (און דיא צוברכן קייט אראפגיפאלין-קאייט) as well as brokenness that comes in the wake of high, elevated divine illumination. However, while the general dynamic of *ahava rabba* is "distance," the general trend of *ahava betaanugim* is closeness and proximity.

We should not become confused and think — because in the midst of *ahava rabba* we also experience closeness to God (that has a "feeling" similar to *ahava betaanugim*) — that there is a "ray" of *ahava betaanugim* shining into our service of *ahava rabba*. Nor should we think the opposite — because during *ahava betaanugim* we also experience the distance from God that is associated with *ahava rabba* — that that this

---

7. *Yom Tov shel Rosh Hashana 5666* /1906 of the Rebbe Rashab, page 2.
8. Meditating at length, with great focus — this may be the experience of "gazing upon the glory of the King" described in *Kuntres Ha'avoda* and elsewhere in the Chassidut of the Rebbe Rashab.
9. Which is why *ahava rabba* occurs during the *Kriat Shema*, when we declare the unity of Hashem.
10. Certainly, there is a feeling of "what did I do to deserve this — I am not deserving of this love and proximity." Perhaps this is the feeling of "brokenness and forlornness" that accompanies *ahava betaanugim* which provides of backdrop of "distance" as well as closeness.

feeling is an expression of *ahava rabba* that "draws down" and causes *ahava betaanugim* to descend to us. This is certainly not the case. *Ahava betaanugim* is a far higher level, far beyond *ahava rabba*, and is not at all within range to be drawn down and revealed by *ahava rabba*. It is not at all necessary for this to occur (this is the solution to the second question above).

In any case, it is clear that, without working on ourselves in addition to meditation and introspection, no revelation or Godly illumination will occur. Intellect alone achieves nothing. The goal must be to refine ourselves with *avoda* in order to draw down divine revelation. And then even our intellectual grasp will occur on a higher level. What an *oved* (one who works on himself with meditation and introspection) knows he grasps on a far higher level than the top *maskil* (one who relies on intellect alone). This is because the *oved* focuses upon the "divine feeling" of the concept, rather than the intellect behind it alone. It may be that intellectual activity takes place on a higher level, while attaining a "feel" for the concept takes place on the [lower] emotional level. And, therefore, there is no change in the *maskil* as he meditates and understands a concept intellectually. But, the approach of an *oved* is to "create vessels" in his psyche in order to experience divine revelation. He does this even in order to experience "external" matters, such as action, in accordance with his intellectual understanding. However, this does not apply to "action" in the supernal realm. There, it is the action itself (the mitzvah) that creates a vessel for emotional experience [as opposed to any work that the *oved* does upon himself]. (This is the solution to question 5 above.)[11]

It is possible that, as we refine our emotions after achieving the spiritual experience of *ahava rabba*, we may further attain the level of *ahava*

---

11. Here, it seems as if the Rebbe Rayatz wants to differentiate between actions that the *oved* takes upon himself, in order to cultivate Godly "feeling," and actions that are decreed from Above, such as mitzvot. A *minhag* or custom that the *oved* accepts upon himself will maintain the continuum from intellect to action that began with the *oved's* meditation upon a given concept. Then, when he fulfills the related custom or *minhag*, he will not only feel the emotion but also bring down additional spiritual illumination. However, when fulfilling a mitzvah, the *oved* need not "prepare" such a mental vessel, since it is the mitzvah itself that will bring down the Godly illumination and emotion.

betaanugim. However, this will not necessarily occur. There is no causal relationship between the two levels that "forces" *ahava betaanugim* to become revealed to us — *ahava rabba* does not influence or draw down the higher level of *ahava betaanugim*. It may be that, in the course of time, the higher level will become revealed, but it does not occur as a causal relation wherein stimulation from below facilitates a spiritual response from Above.

The dynamic of "feeling" is far more pronounced among *ovdim* that it is among *maskilim*, since *ovdim* have a greater "feel" for the concept than do *maskilim*, and also because the nature of emotions is to descend and become enclothed in lower spiritual levels, as mentioned already. All the levels of love mentioned above are to be found in every person, each according to his individual level and nature. Even one who exists in essence on a lower level, such the *nefesh* of the World of *Asiya*, may also experience all of the above-mentioned spiritual levels. He, on his own individual level of "love with all his might" (בכל מאדיך), may also experience true *ahava betaanugim*, even if on a lower spiritual level that someone else. Someone on a higher level may experience the same level of love, but for him it will be *ahava rabba*, or even the lowest form of love predicated on reason and logic alone, but he will experience it in a settled, natural manner. However, such love remains *ahava betaanugim* for the person on the lower level. While it is a low level of *ahava betaanugim*, it is nevertheless *ahava betaanugim*. (This is the solution to the third question.) All levels of elevation associated with *ahava betaanugim* become manifest as emotion. But, since *ahava betaanugim* comes from the very essence of the soul, even the lowest levels of Godly illumination, coming from the essence of the soul, reflect essential Godliness.

Based on all of the above, it should be clear that the ultimate heights of spiritual elevation that we achieve, including all levels of love, are based upon a foundation of logic and reasoning. Everything begins with logic and reason, and then, in proportion to our intellect, we develop a feeling of the heart. This is true of *ahava rabba* as well; our love evolves from the intellect.

In truth, our personal faculties and aptitudes affect the purity and refinement of the "vessels" that we develop in order to contain and experience spiritual light (עבודת ההרג), all the way up to the highest levels. [At first, this may seem paradoxical, since] during *ahava betaanugim*, there are no "vessels" with which to draw down divine illumination, because this is not a level that is drawn down by "vessels," [at least not in the standard sense]. Nevertheless, on this level, it is the absence of vessels that "creates" a "container" for divine revelation. Without the preface of love based upon reason and logic, followed by *ahava rabba* (love that is beyond reason and logic), we cannot achieve *ahava betaanugim* [the highest level of divine love]. It is nullification (in the sense of a "full vessel that contains" — *Succah* 46a)[12] of the intellectual vessels containing the lower levels of love that transforms those vessels into illumination. And then, the light itself becomes a "vessel" for revelation. So it is understood that we are speaking of very high spiritual levels. Since this is so, it is understood that the nature of the "vessels" that we develop is indeed of vital importance. (This is the answer to question 4.) However, these vessels are not "containers" which draw down and contain illumination; rather, here the term "vessels" refers to the nullification and transformation [of the psychic "vessels" formed during "positive grasp"][13] so that they do not obstruct the subtle

---

12. "R' Zera, and some say R' Hanina bar Papa, said, 'Come observe the nature of *Hakadosh Baruch Hu*. The way of man is that his vessel, when empty, is able to contain something, but when it is full, it is unable to contain anything more. But the nature of *Hakadosh Baruch Hu* is that a full vessel contains while an empty vessel fails to contain...as the Torah says, "If you listen now, you will continue to listen..." implying that if not, you will not continue to listen.'" (*Succah* 46a) The meaning of this statement is, as Rashi explains, that "if you accustomed yourself to 'hear' (to learn), you will continue to learn and to add to your learning." Applied to our context, this means that one who is accustomed to meditating on certain spiritual levels will continue to do so, and even add to the levels that he already achieved. If , through *hasagat hashlilah*, he was able to achieve *ahavah rabbah*, he will continue on to negate the "vessels" of his intellectual grasp and possibly achieve *ahava betaanugim* as well.

13. "Vessels" are needed when there is great distance between the meditator and the divine concept upon which he is meditating. Since the concept is infinite and the meditator is finite, the meditator must develop mental constructs, or "vessels" to grasp and contain the infinite spiritual light. This generally occurs on the first level of meditation, that takes place according to logic and reason. It is at that point that we need vessels that "hold" light when they are "empty" (devoid of ego). However, as the meditator increases in awareness and refinement, the same "vessels" that initially

revelation of divine emotion, leading to the highest spiritual elevation.[14]

In this case, it is not the purpose of this emotion to express anything "new." Rather, the purpose is only to experience the ultimate depth and purpose of the divine concept [upon which the *oved* was meditating]. And since each and every spiritual level includes all others, by way of experiencing illumination on one level, we experience all the others as well. Ultimately then, the intellectual concept becomes grasped on the highest levels of refinement.

A further advantage of the emotional experience ("feeling") [of the *oved*] is that it is not restricted to any particular spiritual level. It permeates all levels, right down to the World of *Asiya*, as already mentioned.

---

helped him grasp the light, may actually conceal some of that light from him. The very tool that enabled us to grasp divine light can become an obstacle as we approach the full power of the divine concept, and want to face the illumination directly. At that point, we are ready for the second level of meditation, called *ahavah rabba* ("great love"), which requires that we use "negative grasp" to sunder and remove the "vessels," enabling us to apprehend His infinite light on a much higher and more subtle spiritual level. At this stage, it is appropriate to mention vessels that "contain," even though they are "full" (since they have received the infinite illumination resulting from meditation on the first level). That is, even though we have already attained grasp of some illumination, there is room for more illumination if we utilize "negative grasp" to "remove" these vessels and receive the full power of Godly illumination. These are the vessels mentioned in the *gemora* (*Succah* 46a) — that contain even though they are already full. And that is what the Rebbe means by "it is the absence of vessels that creates a container." It is still appropriate to mention "vessels" in regard to *ahavah rabba*, since it was necessary to negate vessels in order to achieve the desired understanding and love. However, regarding the final level of love — *ahava betaanugim* — we are "face to face" with the divine concept on which we meditated, and there is no separation whatsoever — neither positive nor negative, and therefore "vessels" are not needed because there is only illumination (as in R' Akiva's statement, "when you reach the marble slabs..."). And in fact any form whatsoever of "vessels" is only a construction of the human psyche which at that point obstructs the divine illumination, rather than illuminates it. At that point, as the Rebbe writes, "the light itself becomes a vessel..."

14. This description of "lack of vessels" dovetails well with the Rebbe Rashab's interpretation (in *B'Sha'ah sh'hikdimu* 5672/1912, Vol 2 Page 964-5) of R' Akiva's mystical statement in the Gemara (*Chagiga* 14b): "When you arrive at the slabs of pure marble, do not cry, 'water, water.'" The Rebbe Rashab describes this as an experience of *ahava betaanugim* during which there is no real blockage or resistance between the meditator and the highest most sublime spiritual levels.

In fact, the emotion may be more evident as the concept comes to fruition in the physical fulfillment of the mitzvah than during meditation on the concept itself. That is why, as we fulfill the mitzvah, we may experience the very essence of the concept in its original pristine form. (That is, we experience the transcendent nature of the concept, as explained above, to the extent that it becomes revealed in our intellect. It may be that the high transcendent feeling is the cause of the concept, but that by no means guarantees that we will understand and grasp the concept. And yet, we may grasp the concept as a real "feeling" when we actually perform the mitzvah.[15]) This is because the quality of "feeling" is connected with the very essence, and as explained previously, *Asiya* ("the World of Action") is a vessel for "containing" essence. And, therefore, the feeling (whether because of its own essential nature or because of the innate advantage of "action" as explained previously) occurs precisely in the World of *Asiya*. From all of the above, it should be clear that *avoda* takes place on the level of feeling and experience, since *avoda* takes place mainly in the World of *Asiya*. This explains the advantage of *ovdim* [over *maskilim*].

3

Monday 26 Tishrei, תשע״ג (1912)

We need to understand the three kinds of love mentioned above: Love predicated on reason and logic [elsewhere called *ahavat olam* — *olam* in the sense of "world" since this level of love is the result of meditation on Godliness embedded in creation], *ahava rabba* ("great love"), and *ahava betaanugim* ("love with delights"). We need to understand their respective qualities and levels. Why does *ahava rabba* develop after we achieve love based upon reason and logic [*ahavat olam*], implying that love based upon reason and logic is a prelude to *ahava rabba*,

---

15. This expression recalls the statement of the Zohar, that "Even though no thought can grasp Him, He is grasped in *the reuta deliba*" — referring, to the "will of the heart." The inner core of emotion in the heart grasps spiritual realities that are beyond our intellectual grasp.

and yet *ahava betaanugim*, which is so much higher than [either *ahavat olam* or *ahava rabba*], is not [necessarily drawn down] by these two forms of love? The answer is that *ahava betaanugim* is an essential love that need not descend and become revealed. Yet, after the introduction of love based on logic and reason, it may become revealed. That is, without the labor [of *ahavat olam* and *ahava rabba*], there are obstacles and impediments that prevent revelation of *ahava betaanugim*, while after such labor, there is nothing to block its descent and revelation. But, even though there is no obstacle and impediment, there is also no obligation for it to become revealed.

By way of explanation, using our soul-powers to illustrate: There are three levels of knowledge and intellectual grasp. 1) We may directly grasp a concept by using logical reasoning (השגת החיוב), 2) we may grasp a concept by negating a previously-existing concept (השגת השלילה), or 3) we may grasp the essential nature of a concept. This final level is far above the previous two.

For example, when we wish to study a subject, both [of the first two] processes mentioned above are useful. We may employ the positive approach, activating the conscious intellect to gain direct knowledge of the subject, with all of its details. To illustrate, the subject of love includes several details, such as that love occurs in proximity and closeness, that it is an emotion, and that there is no reason or cause that forces us to love. Love emerges from the very essence of our being. (It is understood that there is also love that is "dependent upon something," but in that case, "love" is merely a borrowed term which does not accurately depict the psychic process. When the reason for it disappears, this love also disappears.) Since love is defined by proximity and emotion, it necessarily adopts a specific form of "existence." Proximity and emotion require us to approach and unite with the object of our affection, and in fact, that is the very essence of love. One might think that if there is a cause and reason leading to love, then the love that results from the reason is essential on its own level. However, this is not the case. The result [that emerges from the "reason"] is only the "existence" of love [but not the essence of love]. And on the scale of "existence," there are a number of distinct rungs. Indeed, regarding every matter, there are aspects that define its true essence (even the lowest levels of this are of this essence), and there are aspects that are only "borrowed." The nature and quality of love is that its very essence and foundation is defined by proximity and emotion. That is when the word *ahava* ("love") truly applies (lit: "becomes its real name") and is not merely a borrowed term.

Much explanation and clarification is needed, in order to grasp the true process, and to avoid doubts and questions regarding the essence of intellectual pursuit. It is also necessary to avoid contradictions and inconsistencies emerging from the concept itself, as well as our understanding of it. Our intellect imposes limitations and forms images of the concept, specifying that it is "like this" or "like that." That is why this level of intellect is described as "obligatory" (חיוב), or "positive intellect." Utilizing this process, [we arrive at] unavoidable conclusions that become obligatory [according the laws of logic]. This intellectual process determines a particular מציאות, or "mental construct," that is both necessary and unavoidable. It is analogous to one who "owes" (חוב, or חיוב, means "debt") something to his friend, because the friend did him a favor, and therefore, he is naturally obligated to return the favor. In like manner, when operating on this level of intellect, we naturally arrive at concepts with specific parameters that shape their "existence." For example, utilizing the subject of "love," mentioned above — once the person grasps and understands [that love entails] proximity and emotion, this "forces" his love to come into existence in a manner that unites him with the object of his love. It follows, then, that unity with the object of his love does not occur on the same level as the essential [emotion] of love [in his mind and heart] itself. It is [even] possible that his love [as it exists in his mind and heart] will never come to fruition. That is, he may decide that the object of his love is totally out of his range, and he is totally unprepared to become united with it. Or, even if he decides that it is appropriate to approach and, as a result of his feeling of love, he tries to do so, [he finds that] his love adopts a different image entirely (which leads him to experience the emotion of closeness, as described above regarding "distance" as an internal element of proximity[16]).

---

16. Apparently the "distance" here refers to the "change" that the person experienced

And that brings us to the second level of intellect, called השגת השלילה, or "negative grasp." During this process, the person concludes that the concept which he has been contemplating and investigating transcends the categories that he initially applied in order to understand it. And even though here as well, the contemplator experiences closeness to God and emotion, the nearness is not real proximity. Rather, it is the internal dimension of proximity. (As noted above, within our topic itself — distance within proximity — there are two categories. One is the "distance" of *teshuva*, in which the emphasis is upon "not good" aspects of the person's situation. The other is the distance experienced during *ahavah betaanugim*, which is distance of forlornness [over his distance from God]. And within the latter category (distance within proximity experienced during *ahavah betaanugim*), there are also two levels. First, there is distance as a dynamic of *teshuva*, wherein the divine illumination causes nullification [of the ego]. And the second is a dynamic of proximity during *ahava betaanugim*, as a result of its high spiritual elevation, as will be explained, God willing.) This "internal dimension" of proximity is distinct from the closeness experienced during love predicated on reason and logic. During both experiences of divine love, there is feeling and emotion, but the emotion of the second level [employing "negative grasp"] is more elevated than the emotion that develops during love based upon reason and logic (חיוב). From this [negative grasp] emerges a mental construct that is completely beyond that which emerged when he employed the tools of love based on reason and logic (חיוב).

Regarding intellectual pursuit, we may understand this process in the following manner. Let us say, for example, that one is studying the topic of "four zones" (ארבע רשויות — private zone, public zone, semi-private zone and free zone, with regard to carrying objects on Shabbat).[17]

---

as he approached the object of his love. The fact that achievement of his goal gave him a "different" result than what he expected, is referred to as "distance," compared to his expectations.

17. The subject of "four zones" is the focus of the first chapter of Tractate Shabbat in the Talmud. A "private zone" is one that is dedicated to a particular person, family or group, and one may carry freely within this zone on Shabbat, but may not either receive objects from outside of this zone, or remove objects from this zone. The "public zone" is even more restricted — one may not carry more than four cubits (roughly 2

He understands and grasps this topic with all of its attendant details and intertwining categories. He is also aware of the questions that arise from other areas of study regarding this topic. Upon gaining full understanding, he forms a ציור, or "mental construct," of what the *halacha* ("Jewish law") is in this situation. And that is, that one who transgresses this law is guilty of a חטאת — a Torah based transgression for which he must bring a sin-offering to the Temple to achieve atonement. This construct is called a "necessary outcome," since the result — the final *halachic* decision — emerges unavoidably from the details, legal categories and intellectual understanding of the case. There are two components to this process: The first is that the "packaging" [the physical details] of the study and knowledge of the "four zones," is vital to the scholar. He may not compare this case to another case involving, for example, *tefillin*, etc. He may compare this case only to a similar case. (He must bring proofs or raise questions only from a case whose details — in their physical expression — are similar to the case that he is considering. For example, it would be acceptable to ask questions from the *halachic* category of "two removals on Shabbat that become four"[18] or from "two oaths," or "two experiences of impurity," or "appearances of plague."[19]) And the second component is that while learning, he may anticipate deciphering the *halachic* outcome. That is, since the "mental picture" that develops is based on the specifics of the case that he is studying, therefore, he may already foresee the outcome that will emerge from them (since the mental image of the subject requires certain details, therefore the same details must come to expression in the physical manifestation of the case). All of this takes place on the level of "required grasp" (השגת החיוב) in which the understanding that we achieve is the natural outcome of the particular situation.

---

meters) within the public zone on Shabbat, except under particular circumstances. The "semi-private zone" is a compromise between a public and private zone, and the "free zone" is as it sounds; there are no restrictions on carrying or traveling within the "free zone." The "four zones" are a major *halachic* topic with regard to Sabbath observance, and it requires a lot of study and application in order to master it.

18. Tractate *Shabbat* 2a.
19. Tractate *Shabbat* 2a, 2b.

The above categories of reasoning do not apply to *hasagat hashlila* — "negative" or "circumscribed" reasoning. The categories and details [that are required for "positive reasoning"] are not applicable [during "negative reasoning"]. On the contrary, "negative grasp" strips away and abstracts the concept from the categories that characterize "positive grasp." For example, the Talmud will sometimes state, "according to R' Meir and his line of reasoning,"[20] or name another sage and state "according to his reasoning."[21] These are oblique references to the "negative reasoning" that these sages employed.[22] They are not similar to the categories of "positive grasp" that include supporting details, such as we find in the Gemara: "…when a scholar gives a ruling, he should also indicate his reason so that, whenever he is reminded of it, he will recall it."[23] In such a case, the Gemara refers to the reason for a particular opinion, and by recalling the reason, the scholar will also recall the details. However, during "negative grasp," the "reason" is equivalent to general overall knowledge of the topic, without [the accompanying details] and "packaging," [physical representations] such as "the four zones," or *tefillin* for

---

20. Tractate *Shabbat* 125a, *Chulin* 72b, and elsewhere.
21. Tractate *Berachot* 13b, 36b and elsewhere.
22. This seems to be a *chiddush*, or novel insight of the Rebbe Rayatz. His father, the Rebbe Rashab, quoted from the Gemara (*Beitza* 6a), regarding one of the sages, Rav, who during a halachic discussion, gave his opinion without backing it up. Even though the other sage(s) disagreed with him and gave reasons for their disagreement, Rav stood by his opinion, as the Gemara reports, *shatik Rav* — "Rav was silent." Most *poskim* nevertheless agreed with Rav and the *halacha* is according to his opinion in this matter even though he could not explain himself. The Rebbe Rashab explains (in *Yomtov shel Rosh Hashana* 5666/1906, page 150 (112 in the older version) that Rav was unable to explain his position only because he needed to ascend to the source of his intellect in order to "retrieve" the explanation (see also *Likutei Torah* of the Alter Rebbe, *parshat Bechukotai* Page 92). That is, his silence was not due to lack of an explanation, but because his understanding of the matter was on a higher level that he himself was able to put into words. This suggests that the source of intellect is a higher level that does not always descend to conscious awareness, and sometimes it is necessary to ascend to that source in order to put our ideas into words. The Rebbe Rayatz's *chiddush* here may be that when the Gemara mentions the name of a sage and then says, "according to," without specifying the reason, it is because the reason exists on a higher intellectual level that is described here as "negative grasp," or השגת השלילה.
23. Tractate *Nidah* 24b.

example, wherein the same reason applies to all of them. For that reason, at the time that he is involved in the thought process of "negative grasp," he is far from any halachic decision. That is, he is far from forming a mental construct of the matter [as it exists in physical reality] since, in his mind, the concept is not consciously based upon any of the categories which are characteristic of "positive reasoning." Yet, nevertheless, there is some sort of mental construct present, which will eventually adopt an intellectual form, though not the same form as exists within the categories of "positive reasoning."

We may similarly understand love. Our knowledge of love covers two levels: "positive [required] grasp" and "negative grasp." They are [forms of knowledge that are] distinct from one another, even though their names ("intellectual grasp") are the same. Nevertheless, it is understood that "positive grasp" must precede "negative grasp." Furthermore, the deeper that we delve into the topic utilizing "positive grasp," the deeper will be our understanding when employing "negative grasp." This indicates that our "negative grasp" is proportional to the level of our "positive grasp." (This is true even though they utilize completely different techniques, as noted above regarding proximity vs. distance and knowledge vs. recognition.) The technique of "negative grasp," if employed during "positive grasp," will result in total confusion and the meditator will never succeed in grasping the main point of the matter (as noted above regarding the necessary trust that the student must have in his teacher, without which the student will be confused). The concept will remain completely beyond him. The same applies if the meditator did the opposite, trying to grasp the concept directly using the technique of "positive grasp" regarding matters that require "negative grasp," (in which case, the meditator will be far from understanding the true nature of the concept) since the techniques are very different from one another. And yet, one approach is predicated upon the other; the more one delves into the topic using "positive grasp," the higher he will ascend when utilizing "negative grasp." (Yiddish: As he digs deeper, he arrives to an intellectual point at which positive categories are no longer appropriate.) These are two approaches to intellectual grasp.

However, there is yet a third process that is beyond "negative grasp." And that occurs when we grasp the very essence of the concept.

During "negative grasp," we enjoy a more subtle awareness of the concept under consideration. We experience its transcendent nature, and this uplifts our sense of intellect so that we feel elevation of the soul. For, all intellectual activity and examination unites us with our intellect, while the intellect uplifts us with its elevated and exalted nature. Consequently, "negative grasp" also has an uplifting effect upon us as we meditate, and in this elevated state we attains great breadth of awareness (unlike during "positive grasp" which puts us in a state of intellectual contraction). And this elevation results from the transcendent nature of our grasp. Nevertheless, this elevated awareness does not yet constitute grasp of the very essence of the concept, but only of an expression thereof. On the third level, we grasp the very essence of the concept, beyond the process of "negative grasp." That is, we no longer have it within our power to negate our thoughts, just as we are no longer able to activate our "positive" (required) thought processes. The categories of negative and positive grasp are inoperative (they "don't exist").

Even in this sublime state, the divine illumination has an influence on the meditator [he still "feels" something]. He experiences an emotion of forlornness, [distance from God]. He regrets his own existence. During "negative grasp," his heightened awareness also produces an uplifting experience, but he still experiences his own self, and this uplifted awareness is very much a part of how he experiences himself. It is "he" who is exalted and uplifted. But, on this third level, "he" does not "exist." There is merely a flow of intellect, as brief intellectual bullet-points, revealing amazing concepts, which are corroborated and correct in all aspects. Following the experience, the meditator has no "entry" [is unable to fathom] the concept [that he just experienced]. He has no access to it whatsoever, and as much as he "circles" around the concept, he is unable to get ["a handle on"] it. Even as the experience occurs, he is confused by what he perceives; his confusion is a mixture of knowing (as in "positive grasp" and recognition) and not knowing ("negative grasp" and faith) the ultimate truth. All is one — his forlornness and spiritual elevation (the distance and proximity mentioned above) all occur simultaneously, which is what completely confuses him. And he is totally unable [to return] and replicate the experience. Nevertheless, since the experience contained an intellectual core, it is possible that in the course of time it will become revealed to him. (This will not necessarily occur, but there is nothing to prevent it from occurring, as mentioned previously; however, the absence of obstructions or obstacles does not guarantee that the desired outcome will occur.) And if it does become revealed, it will do so within his conscious awareness, within the confines of "positive grasp" (as mentioned above in the discussion of the two categories of "intellect" and "experience/emotion"). In the realm of "feeling," the experience [*ahava bettanugim*] is very real, as explained previously; it lies at the core of the intellect. But in the realm of "intellect," while we may experience the "existence" of the core concept, it does not necessarily become revealed. If it does so, it becomes fully revealed within one's conscious intellect, and the corresponding feeling may also become revealed. But the grasp will take place in a different manner entirely.

This [experience] is comparable to a statement of the Talmud, "Just as everyone benefits from a pile of wheat, so everyone derives benefit from the reasoning of the Sanhedrin."[24] The reasoning and logic of the sages of the Sanhedrin is acceptable to those who hear it, because of the astounding, transcendent nature of their great wisdom. Their intellectual grasp takes place on a different plane altogether (possibly because of the influence of "negative grasp" over "positive grasp"). Nevertheless their logic enters our conscious awareness as "positive grasp," which reflects the very essence of the concept with all of its depth, as during the third level [*ahava betaanugim*] of intellectual grasp. This [experience] corresponds to the statement of the sages based on the verse [in the Book of Kings], "and both of them were alone in the field..."[25] — meaning, that "all the reasoning of the Torah was revealed to them like in a field."[26] This is an astonishing level of transcendent intellect that encompasses everything in its purview. [And yet], the elevated illumination of this third level of intellect is possible to grasp in our conscious

---

24. Tractate *Sanhedrin* 37a.
25. *Melachim* 1, 11:29
26. Tractate *Sanhedrin* 102a

minds, while we [simultaneously] remain aware that the essential intellectual revelation occurred in a different manner completely.

Accordingly, we may understand the three levels of love: 1) love according to reason and logic [called *ahavat olam*], 2) "great love" (*ahavah rabba*), and 3) "love with delights" (*ahavah betaanugim*). Love according to logic and reasoning is associated with "positive grasp" (as previously explained at length). However, logic and reasoning are not the essence of love; the essence of love, as explained, is a "feeling" or emotion. The second level, *ahavah rabba* is a higher love that is not at all in the same category. [That is because] love according to reason and logic has a goal. That goal is intellectual grasp in order to understand and come to grips with the concept according to our soul level. This is not the case regarding *ahavah rabba*, during which we experience a great feeling of elevation, similar to "negative grasp," which is not associated with any "positive" categories or definitions at all. In fact, it is a completely different experience — an experience of proximity to illumination, during which the meditator "sees" the divine light. Quite possibly this is *reiya d'chochma* — "vision associated with *chochma*." However, it is not the experience of "recognition," during which the meditator recognizes the very essence of the light ("recognition" — *hacara* — combines with reason, as in the verse from Psalms 34:9, "taste and see"). Here, he only "sees the light," which is the internal dimension of intellectual grasp. If so, then the two [*reiya* and *hacara*] are within range of each other, even though *reiya* — "seeing" — is a greater spiritual level. In fact, *reiya* is a form of unity [that occurs] when we unite with the object of our "vision," even though we does not become one with it in essence. And, therefore, the greater our positive grasp of a concept [with *hacara* during *ahavat olam*], the stronger will be our "vision" [during *ahava rabba*]. That is, [the better we grasp the topic using positive knowledge and recognition, the greater will be our ability to "see"] the internal dimensions of the concept. In any case, these two spiritual levels [*hacara* and *reiya* — "recognition" and "seeing"] are in range of one another (as mentioned above in relation to *daa't* and *emunah* — "recognition" and "faith").

However, *ahava betaanugim* is associated with the third level of intellect cited previously, during which all is revealed to the meditator, and nothing concealed. Our ego is completely nullified during this experience. That is, it is as if we do not exist at all, and the sign of that occurring (during *avoda* — meditation and prayer) is that we experience true expiry of the soul while in a state of *ahavah betaanugim*.

Now, it is possible that the two dynamics of "distance" (remorse or broken-heartedness) and "elevation," are two aspects of *ahava betaanugim* itself. For, it was already explained that during every intellectual investigation, the concept under consideration has an influence upon the meditator (and that is its main purpose), and it was explained that grasp of the essence of the concept, which is the third level of intellect mentioned previously, of necessity also has an effect upon the meditator. Perhaps, it might be suggested that the effect [on the meditator] takes place with both "positive grasp" and "negative grasp," working together. Neither are "within range" of *ahavah betaanugim*; both merely remove the obstacles that prevent its revelation. And, therefore, the experience and *avoda* of *ahava betaanugim* is completely beyond the range of both love according to logic and reason, and of *ahavah rabba*. The parameters of "range" [in this case] are space and spiritual level, which need to be commensurate (in this case, above being a *keli*, or vessel) in order to draw down the appropriate level of spirituality.[27] But, [mere] removal of obstacles and impediments does not constitute the "range"

---

27. Here, the Rebbe Rayatz discusses why no preparation or meditation can reliably draw down the level of *ahava betaanugim*. He tells us that in order for any preparation for a spiritual level to be successful, we must create a "vessel" that is within range of the level. "Range," the Rebbe tells us, is defined by two parameters — מקום ומדריגה — "space and spiritual level." By "spiritual level" is meant how refined the person is — how much he has refined and elevated his intellectual and emotional abilities to allow himself to receive spiritual revelation. By "space," it is less clear what the Rebbe meant. Perhaps he is referring to the physical/spiritual environment in which the person finds himself. For, even the most refined person, in an un-refined environment (for example, an environment that is not friendly to Torah and mitzvot, or an environment that is not physically appropriate) is unlikely to receive spiritual revelation. Alternatively, "space" may refer to the Chassidic interpretation in which "space" is the source of the six divine emotions (*chesed* through *yesod*). Moreover, *HaMakom* ("The Space") alludes to the *Beit Hamikdash*, or "Holy Temple" in Jerusalem. Whatever the intention of the Rebbe with these words, he concludes that since *ahavah betaanugim* occurs with revelation of the very essence of the divine concept under consideration, there is no spiritual level (מדריגה) or environment (מקום) that is can enable or facilitate it to occur. As we say in the vernacular, "It is what it is."

that will later facilitate revelation to occur from "out of range." (This is added explanation to the answer to question #2.)

In general, revelation of *ahava betaanugim* occurs in accordance with each person's essential nature. One whose soul level is from *malchut* of *malchut* of *Asiya* is not at all comparable to one from the level of *neshama* of *Yetzira* or *Bria*, and all the more so, to one who is a *neshama* of *Atzilut*. While all levels of love vary and not only *ahava betaanugim* differs from soul level to level, but even love based upon logic and reason. [What one person develops] may be completely beyond [the grasp of another person], the difference between them being accentuated on the higher soul levels. (This is an answer to question #4.)

It is not at all out of the question that *ahava betaanugim* experienced by one on the soul-level of *malchut* of *malchut* of *Asiya* will be equivalent to the experience of love based on logic and reason of one who is a soul of *Atzilut*. Nevertheless [on whatever spiritual level he happens to be], *ahava betaanugim* will be beyond his normal "settled" experience. After all, his *avoda* (meditation and prayer) is on the level of [*ahavah betaanugim*]. And since *ahava betaanugim* is an experience of "essence," and even a portion of the essence is essential, therefore, his *avoda* also takes place on this essential level. (This is a solution to question #3.) The difference is that his experience is on a lower level of *ahava betaanugim* itself, even though it is the level of [*ahava betaanugim*]. The same cannot be said of love based upon logic and reason. One may be a *neshama* of *Atzilut*, whose knowledge and intellectual grasp is on a higher level entirely but, nevertheless, he uses the same tools of reason and logic [as a soul of *Asiyah*] while applying them to the World of *Atzilut*. Yet, when he is involved in the *avoda* (meditation and prayer) of *ahava betaanugim*, then he is operating in the realm of *ahava betaanugim* [on whatever spiritual level he might be holding]. It might be on a lesser and lower level but, nevertheless, it is [an experience] of the essence.

[Summary:] Explanation of the three levels of love: Love according to reason and logic, *ahava rabba* and *ahavat olam* [usually called *ahava betaanugim*].[28] Within intellectual grasp, there are also three levels —

---

28. The word *olam* may take on multiple meanings (see the letter from the Frierdiker

"positive grasp," "negative grasp," and grasp of the very essence of the intellectual concept beyond the two preceding levels. And they correspond to the three levels of love, according to previous explanations...

4

"The nature of *ratzoh* ("desire for Godliness") is also proximity [the "experience of infinite light that the meditator feels in the soul"], since the meditator seeks to become subsumed [included in a higher level]..." (From *Yom Tov shel Rosh Hashana 5666/1906* of the Rebbe Rashab, page 2)

Reuta d'liba (the "will of the heart") is the *avoda* (meditation and prayer) corresponding to *ahava rabba* ("great love" based upon "negative grasp" as described above). It takes place with proximity [to Godliness]. However, the proximity is not true proximity, since it is only the nearness that is borne of visualizing [Godliness] but does not include actually "tasting" (experiencing) Godliness. The meditator does not actually experience ("taste") the divine light in his soul, and that is why the entire approach of *ahava rabba* is one of ongoing "will" to be subsumed ("included") in a higher spiritual level. This fits in well with what was previously mentioned regarding the *avoda* of *ahava rabba*, which is that it still includes elements of love based upon logic and reason. And (as explained earlier), love based upon logic and reason includes elements of both proximity and emotion that "obligate" the meditator to unite with the object of his love. So, even though in order to achieve *ahava rabba* it is necessary to forsake the categories of love based upon reason and logic, nevertheless, an impression of love according to reason

---

Rebbe at the end of "Love Like Fire and Water" for a completely different treatment of the three levels of divine love. There, he mentions that *olam* may take on the connotation of "world or universe," in which case *ahavat olam* is the divine love that derives from contemplation of Godliness in the creation. Or, *olam* may take on the connotation of "forever," in which case *ahavat olam* is a much higher form of divine love that is beyond the creation). The Frierdiker Rebbe's grandfather, the Rebbe Maharash, says that that *ahavat olam* in the sense of "forever," is actually *ahava betaanugim* (*Torat Shmuel 5626/1866*, page 217)

and logic remains. And that impression is what motivates the meditator, during *ahava rabba*, to become subsumed [in Godliness]. There are two factors here: 1) a desire for closeness [to God], and 2) that closeness leads to unity. That is why during *ahava rabba*, the main desire is to become included within Godliness.

5

"Which is not the case regarding *teshuva* … during which he is very troubled over his distance." (From *Yom Tov shel R'H*, page 2)

The main dynamic of *teshuva* is a desire to forsake our initial position. That is, the only issue that pre-occupies us. We are not concerned with thoughts of approaching and achieving proximity to Godly illumination. We finds no room within ourselves to achieve closeness to God. Our only concern is to escape the "place" that we previously occupied and to uproot all of our previous desires. In general, *teshuva* is an emotional dynamic, defined by a feeling of distance [from Godliness].

6

"And there is also, within this [dynamic], a Godly emotion" [in Yiddish, "He feels a divine illumination"], but it is regarding matters that are negative and bitter. What touches him in the innermost chambers of his heart is the feeling of distance, and that is what provides the impetus … [to do *teshuva*]" (From *Yom tov shel R"H 5666/1906*, page 2)

The general trend of *teshuva* is distance. A feeling for God's transcendent infinite light, leading to excitement, is not applicable, because 1) the meditator does not feel the illumination, and 2) and if he were to experience it, the dominant dynamic of *teshuva* would cause him to feel even greater distance. [It would induce him to] place even more emphasis on his negative situation, [causing him even more] bitterness and distress.

For example, when we say *tachanun*, mentioning על חטא ("expressing remorse"), there are two themes. One is the sense of distance, the awareness that we have drifted away from God, about which we express remorse: "for the sin that we have transgressed before You," meaning our transgressions before God. This generates overall distress over the fact that we sinned before Him. And then, we follow that up with the particular details of how we sinned. The initial general expression of mentioning "our sins" brings the details of the sin into stark relief, and then we feel our distance from God with even greater intensity. All this is because the basic dynamic of *teshuva* compels us to experience distance (within this distance there is also a dynamic of proximity, which gives us a "taste" of Godliness, but we experience it as something "negative" and bitter). Nevertheless, there is something that descends to us as a result of this state. And that is, as a consequence of our sadness and distress, we automatically wish to draw closer to God. This is the experience of *ratzoh* (desire for Godliness). However, it is not a desire for proximity to Godliness. Rather it is rooted in the dynamic of distance, as will be explained. And since this *ratzoh* is not about proximity, there is no desire to become included [subsumed in a higher level]. For when the level and situation of the *ratzoh* is proximity to God, then the desire is to become included (subsumed), as explained above regarding the *ratzoh* of *reuta deliba*. The desire to attain a higher level is the goal. But this is not the case during *teshuva*, when there is no desire to become included in a higher level. The desire for proximity to Godliness is merely a function of our decision not to be far from God. Our entire purpose is to "run away" from our initial [negative] situation. We does not desire to ascend and attain a specific spiritual level, but only to abandon our initial status and to approach Godliness. Our *ratzoh* is expressed as devotion and dedication, as we surrender ourselves to Godliness, without any desire or purpose to attain any spiritual level. The general theme of Godliness is enough for us. The benefit that we derive from this is twofold; first, we are no longer distant, and second, we become dedicated and devoted to Godliness, meaning to whatever falls in the category of "Godly." But even then, our experience remains one of *teshuva*, which implies distance.

Summary: The dynamic of *teshuva* revolves around two concerns: our transgression "before God," and what that transgression consisted of. Both concerns produce an effect of "distance."

7

"And therefore during *reuta d'liba* that is caused by proximity, its condition is also [described by] proximity." (From *Yom Tov shel R"H 5666/1906* of the Rebbe Rashab, page 2)

For that reason, [*reuta d'liba*] only occurs silently. The implication is not that *reuta d'liba* occurs silently because silence is a part of [the condition of] being close to God. Rather, it occurs silently as a result of proximity to God. Therefore, we need to differentiate between the reason (motivating factor) and the condition. A reason is a cause, but the "condition" describes the essential status [of *reuta deliba*]. (In the terminology of "cause and effect," we could describe the "condition" as an effect, but then, if the condition is "caused," [there are circumstances in which] the cause and its effect may no longer be present at this particular moment. However, if we use the word "condition," we are referring to the state in which we find ourselves.)

As explained previously regarding proximity and distance, "proximity" leads to unity with the object of the meditator's love, and this is its true dynamic. (This is unlike the proximity of *ahava rabba* mentioned earlier, which is *reiya* or "seeing" Godliness, aside from the fact that *reiya* is also a form of unity.) This "proximity," in which the meditator truly approaches [Godliness], is the reason for his silence. His silence in this situation connotes *bitul*, or "nullification." For this reason, the Rebbe was precise with his words, saying that the "cause" [of *reuta deliba*] is proximity, and therefore it occurs silently. That is, the reason for the silence is the result of another cause, and not that the silence is part of the essential nature of *reuta dliba*. Rather, the silence comes as a result of the meditator's proximity [to Godliness]. If [the Rebbe] had said that *reuta deliba* occurs silently because its nature is proximity [to Godliness], then silence would itself be an essential attribute [of *reuta deliba*], and it would not be possible to apply this description [of *reuta deliba*] to *ahavah rabbah*, but only to *ahavah betaanugim*. And therefore, the Rebbe was precise with his words, saying that the silence is "caused" by the meditator's proximity.

As for what he writes, that "the condition is also one of proximity," so it truly is. In general, *reuta deliba* occurs silently, but that is not the "reason" for the silence.

Summary: *Reuta deliba* occurs in proximity to Godliness, and therefore it occurs silently. There is a distinction between a "reason" and a "condition." And it is explained that proximity occurs with "vision" of *chochma* and, therefore, it is accompanied by silence which also signifies nullification.

8

"And this is the topic of the shofar blasts known as *shevarim* and *truah*, which express the inner voice which goes unheard…" (Source?)

It emerges that *teshuva* in general is also an internal arousal of the soul. However, it is distinguished from the internal arousal of the soul that occurs during *ahava rabba*. There, the internal arousal is a completely different dynamic, since *ahava rabba* occurs in proximity, while the dynamic of *teshuva* is distance. Distance induces commotion and excitement [in the soul], while proximity causes clinging and occurs silently. At any rate, according to what was explained previously regarding proximity and distance — that they are mutually inclusive — therefore, even during *ahavah rabba* that occurs in proximity [to Godliness], the accompanying silence is not part of the essential nature of [of *ahavah rabba* or *reuta deliba*], but is rather a result. [29] And even though *teshuva* is

---

29. With this sentence, the Rebbe Rayatz ties up and concludes this section of learning with his father, the Rebbe Rashab. One of the main elements of this learning was to come to an understanding that all spiritual levels are related to one another, and that there is an element of both proximity (feeling the infinite light of God) and distance (feeling our distance from God) present on all spiritual levels. Earlier in the learning, the Rebbe Rayatz emphasized the element of "distance" that is present during *ahava rabba*, but said little about the proximity. In this final section, he establishes that there is also an element of proximity during our experience of *ahava rabba*. In fact, it is our proximity that results in one of the major characteristics of *ahava rabba* — that it takes place in silence. It is proximity to Godliness that produces the silence (*bitul* — "self nullification") that overcomes us as we experience *ahava rabba* (and *reuta deliba*). However, it is necessary to emphasize that the silence is not a part of the essential condition of *ahava rabba*. As the Rebbe explained earlier, if we attributed our silence to the essential condition of *ahava rabba*, then what would we be able to say about silence during *ahava betaanugim*, during which we are totally one and united with Godliness? Of course, while one and united, we are quiet (since it is as if we don't exist). Under those circumstances our quiet IS a part of the condition of *ahava betaanugim*. Therefore, we

generally a dynamic of distance, nevertheless on that level it contains an element of silence — the inner voice that goes unheard. For this reflects the true nature of Godliness, that every spiritual level includes all other spiritual levels. And even more-so — the completion and perfection of every level comes only from the other levels, as mentioned.

Summary: *Teshuva* occurs with distance but nevertheless it also contains elements of silence, of the "inner voice that is not heard."

---

have to say that our silence during *ahava rabba* is not part of the essential condition. Rather, during *ahava rabba*, our silence is only the result of another factor — that we are close to God. And therefore, we find within *ahava rabba* both factors — proximity (expressed by our silence) and distance (expressed by our becoming "love sick" for Godliness).

APPENDIX 2

Novel Themes
in the *Chassidut* of the Rebbe Maharash

In the Chassidut of the Rebbe Maharash (R' Shmuel, fourth Rebbe of Chabad, from 1866 until 1882), are found novel ideas that do not appear (as far as the author has been able to ascertain) in the Chassidut of the previous Rebbeim of Chabad (the Alter Rebbe, the Mitteler Rebbe and the Tzemach Tzedek). There are also themes that receive more emphasis in the Chassidut of the Maharash, than they do either before or after his lifetime as the Rebbe. It is worth mentioning and discussing these themes because they have a direct bearing on *avodat Hashem* (our divine worship) through meditation and meditative prayer.

The novel themes are the following: The way that the Rebbe Maharash discusses prayer in general, his treatment of *ahavat olam*, his emphasis on the *merkava* ("chariot" of angelic archetypes and its role in meditation) and his treatment of the Hebrew letters. While none of these topics are unique in Chabad Chassidut, they receive novel treatment in the Chassidut of the Maharash that is unusual in Chabad Chassidut.

First of all, the need for meditation. It is a *halacha* (Code of Jewish law, *Orach Chaim, Siman 98*) that we must contemplate the "greatness of God and the lowliness of man" before prayers, and the *Ramah* there notes that the early "Hasidim" used to meditate at length, reaching states of abstraction and holiness that were "close to prophecy." Nevertheless most Jews do not practice meditation these days. Either we don't have the time, or we do not know how to go about Jewish meditation, or both. But in the early days of Chassidut (late 1700's to mid-1800's), meditative practice was part of the fabric of Jewish life and prayers, and continued to be part of Jewish practice for generations afterward that as well. Four stories from that era will suffice to demonstrate just how widespread and important the practice was among Chasidim. Two of them are stories of R' Yekutiel Leppler, a Chassid of the Alter Rebbe (founder of the Chabad movement of Chassidut) and later of his son the Mitteler Rebbe. This R' Yekutiel Leppler was not known as a *maskil*, or particularly intellectual individual, but in his thirst for Chassidut, he developed the *kelim* ("tools") to understand the most complicated and spiritually deep Chassidic discourses delivered by the Rebbe. In fact, some of the Mitteler Rebbe's discourses were written expressly for R' Yekutiel As a result, his *avodat Hashem* — his divine service in prayer — was heavily influenced by Chassidut and like many of the Chassidim of his day, he prayed at length in meditative prayer based on the complicated discourses that he studied.[1]

1. R' Yekutiel prayed all day long; he made no separation between *shacharit, mincha* and *ma'arviv*. It was not uncommon for R' Yekutiel, after a significant amount of time (an hour or more) of contemplation and meditation, to begin davening (praying), only to cease in the middle and say, "no that's not it." He would say *Hodu*... (the first few words of morning prayers) and then stop. This could take place two or three times until he continued with his prayers (sometimes he would begin and continue without interruption). Each time, he ceased praying, returned to his contemplation, and then tried again, *Hodu*...until he felt himself ready and then continued with his prayers.

2. Rav Vilshanky's grandfather (in the town of Herson) knew a hoary old Chasid who was from the town of Lepel, where R' Yeutiel lived. R' Vilshansky's grandfather asked him if he had met R' Yekutiel. He said, "No, but my grandmother did know R' Yekutiel." He asked the grandmother if she remembered him, and she replied, "Yes, he was a *meshuganeh*." That is, "He was crazy." So of course he asked his grandmother, "Why do you say about R' Yekutiel that he was "crazy"? She replied that he sat in his tallit and tefillin all day long, and "anyone who sits in tallit and tefilin all day long was definitely crazy."

3. Such stories were not unique to R' Yekutiel, though he was indeed a special figure in Chassidic lore. R' Vilshanksy tells another story

---

1. These stories were all heard from R Yoseph Yitzhak (שיח') Vilshansky, Rosh Yeshiva of Tomchei Timim, Tzfas, who heard them from his grandfather.

from his grandfather, who was not sure if the story was from the Alter Rebbe or the Mitteler Rebbe: "A certain Jewish wheat merchant was known far and wide as a very straight and honest man. Not only Jews but also non-Jews from the area would come to buy from him. Once the local *paritz* ("duke," or landowner) heard of the honorable Jew and wanted to buy from him. However, when he entered the store, he found the Jew in the midst of prayer. In place of the storeowner, his wife was running the store and she offered to help the *paritz,* saying that she could do whatever her husband could have done for him. But, since the *paritz* had come to see and do business with her husband, he said, "So let your husband stop praying for two minutes so I can speak with him." The wife answered, "But, he won't hear you." But being the *paritz,* he wasn't satisfied, until she said to him, "Come you can see for yourself, he won't hear you." The *paritz* pulled out his pistol and shot at somewhere nearby her husband. The Chasid didn't move, did not as much as flinch at the sound of the pistol shot. At that point, the *paritz* realized that this was not going to work and went on his way. Once he had finished davening, his wife told the Chassid what had transpired while he was praying, including the amount of the business that the *paritz* had intended to send his way. The wheat merchant asked his wife, so why didn't you sell to him? She answered, because he only wanted to deal with you. His response was, "If so, he'll certainly return…(God will help)"

4. Yet another story occurred with R' Aharon, grandson of the Mitteler Rebbe, from his daughter Freyda. He lived in Kremenchug (Ukraine). After the Mitteler Rebbe passed away, there was discussion about who should become the next Rebbe. The Tzemach Tzedek (grandson of the Alter Rebbe) at first did not want to take on the awesome responsibility (later, he did so), and suggested that R' Aharon should take on the leadership. On one occasion, this R' Aharon was praying in the shul when it caught on fire. Unable to attract R' Aharon's attention because he was so deep within his thoughts and his *d'veikut* (clinging and cleaving to God), the local folks picked him up and brought him to safety in another building. After he finished davening and observed his surroundings, R'

Aharon of course didn't recognize where he was and asked, "Why am I standing here in this house and not in my own house?"

These stories and other similar stories are characteristic of the early period of Chabad Chassidut, from the time of the Alter Rebbe (founder of Chabad) through his grandson, the Tzemach Tzedek. After the Tzemach Tzedek's youngest son, R' Shmuel (known as the "Rebbe Maharash") became the Rebbe in 1866, there are less stories of Chasidim davening at length and reaching such high states of devotion that they were detached from their surroundings (to some extent, the phenomena recurred during the later years of the Rebbe Rashab, son of the Maharash in the early 1900's). Instead, the Rebbe Maharash had "simple Chasidim," known in the Chasidic terminology as *balabatim* — "homeowners," "workers" — who while observant and devoted, were better known for their simple faith and good deeds than for their piety and prayers. The following story[2] serves to illustrate the point: Once, a group of his Chasidim came to the Rebbe Maharash and complained to him that, "We are unable to connect the various concepts of the Rebbe's *maamorim* ("Chasidic discourses")." The Rebbe answered them with an illustrative example: "Once a merchant went to the fair to buy some merchandise. When it came time to pay, he did not have the required funds, so he requested "credit" from the sellers to pay them back in due course. They granted him credit so that he could take the merchandise and repay them later, but he then found that he had no cord to tie his purchase together and take it home. When he asked them for some rope, they responded, "What kind of merchant are you? If we give you credit, that's one matter, but you also want us to give you rope?" In other words, the Maharash was telling his Chasidim, "work it out yourselves. I can give you the ideas, but a Chasid has to be clever enough to know how to put the ideas together and "take them home" — that is, to integrate them into his life and divine service. From this, we may infer that the Chasidim of the

---

2. Also heard from R' Vilshansky, who heard it from his father, R' Raphael Vilshansky (A"H) who was a student in *Tomchei Tmimim* in Russia during the early years (~1920's) of the Previous Rebbe's leadership.

Rebbe Maharash were not on the same high intellectual level as those of the earlier Rebbeim (the Alter Rebbe, the Mitteler Rebbe and the Tzemach Tzedek).

Perhaps in recognition of this fact that his Chasidim were not up to the intellectual challenge as much as they had been in previous generations, the chasidut of the Rebbe Maharash's contains some inspirational content that is subtly different in nature than the Chassidut that preceded him from the first three Rebbeim of Chabad. Rather than long and extended discourses, the Rebbe Maharash's Chassidut tends to be shorter, less explanatory and more "inspirational" (although it is known that the Rebbe Maharash went more into detail when he actually said the discourse than when he wrote it. This is evident in the *hanachos* ("records," "summaries") that his son, the Rebbe Rashab wrote of his father's Chassidut from the years 1876 and onward). The intellectual imprimatur of Chabad is definitely present in the Chassidut of the Maharash, but nevertheless his Chassidut also has a distinct character that is different than his predecessors. Regarding *hitbonenut,* or "meditation," the Maharash found it necessary to exhort his followers: "Man is obligated to think deeply (meditate with concentration and focus on Godly topics)…and he who does not delve deeply in meditation is like an animal" (*Torat Shmuel 5636/1876* of the Rebbe Maharash, P 411). It is difficult to imagine any of his predecessors having to exhort their Chassidim to engage in contemplation in a similar manner.

The *Merkava*, or "Chariot" in Meditation

Perhaps for similar reasons, the Chassidut of the Maharash is also more visual than that of his predecessors. One of the examples is the emphasis that he places on the role of the *merkava* (literally "chariot," the *merkava* refers to the divine revelation of the prophet Yehezkel, with its "face of the ox, face of the lion, face of the eagle and face of man," including wings, wheels and feet) during the process of meditation. The *merkava* concept makes appearances throughout Chabad Chassidut, and in almost all cases it is conceptualized in terms of the ten *sephirot* of Atzilut: the face of the lion represents the *sephira* of *chesed* ("kindness"), the face of the ox represents *gevurah* ("might," discipline), the face of the eagle represents *tiferet* ("harmony, mercy") and the face of the man represents man's animal soul or his intellectual soul. Furthermore, each of the archetypes (lion, ox, eagle, man) of the *merkava* serves as a spiritual source for the creations that stem from it: The lion is the spiritual source of wild beasts, the oxen is the spiritual source of domesticated animals, the eagle of fowl and the man is the source of all of our animal/intellectual souls. The *merkava* exists on all levels, from the lowest world of *asiya* to the *Ohr Ein Sof*, the "infinite light of God." Yet, the Maharash "promotes" the *merkava* in a manner that none of his predecessors did — as a focal point of meditation. For example, we "need" the *merkava* with its angels for purposes of meditation now during this period of Jewish history before the advent of Mashiach, but it will not be necessary in the future (*Torat Shmuel 5637/1877*, Vol 2, p. 389). We "need" the *merkava* in order to avoid being overcome and "nullified" from the high spiritual revelations that we achieve (*Torat Shmuel 5634/1874*, p. 176). We need angels and the *merkava* to support us in our ascent to our spiritual levels, and without such support, we cannot proceed in our *avodat Hashem* (*Torat Shmuel 5634/1874*, p. 357). Although certainly mentioned and discussed in the Chassidut of the other Chabad Rebbeim, it is rare to find the express emphasis and usage of the *merkava* as it is found in the Chassidut of the Rebbe Maharash.

It is legitimate to ask, "what does it mean to meditate upon the *merkava*"? If I want to incorporate this element of kaballah and Chassidut into my own personal *avodat Hashem*, how would I do so? Chassidut answers (in Tanya and elsewhere), that in the *merkava* is found the source of our animal and our intellectual soul. (The Maharash[3] mentions that the *seraphim* of the *merkava* illuminate our divine Godly soul, while the *ofanim* and *chayot* inspire our animal enlivening soul). One of the goals of detailed meditation upon how Hashem creates and enlivens the world, is to involve our animal soul so that it also becomes elevated in the process of prayers. If our animal soul "grasps" and understands

---

3. *Torat Shmuel 5633/1873*, Vol 1, p. 162

that its own spiritual source lies in this higher spiritual entity, it becomes "nullified" and seeks unity with its own spiritual source in the entity (the *merkava*). Thus, meditation on the vision of the *merkava* provides an elevation for the animal soul.

Moreover, the emotions of love and fear that we develop, that are essential to our *avodat Hashem*, are also connected to the *merkava*.[4] Our love of God is associated with the "face of the lion," which is to the right (*chesed*). Our fear of God is associated with the "face of the oxe," which is to the left (*gevura*). Our ability to arouse mercy on our soul and bring down transcendent Godly illumination is associated with the "face of the eagle." And our ability to develop visceral knowledge (*da'at*) of Godliness that even our animal soul can appreciate, is associated with the "face of the man." While this is a satisfying intellectual explanation, it still leaves the person wondering, "What am I supposed to meditate upon"? What am I supposed to do in order to "find" and meditate on the *merkava*?

In this case, we have to develop a whole new way of understanding the universe and the nature of creation in order to answer the question. The explanation is not only that the "angels" and the supernal beings of the *merkava* are the source of our animal soul. The angels of the *merkava* are the source of all of physical creation. The "face of the lion" is the source of all wild beasts. The "face of the ox" is the source of all domesticated animals. The "face of the eagle" is the source of all fowl. And the "face of man" is the source of all human beings (the faces together "carry" the "image of a man" who is above the *merkava* — this is the source of the divine soul). The vision is of animals and man because taken together, they are the pinnacle of creation. The four fundamental elements of mineral, vegetable, animal and man are also included in the *merkava*. Birds often consume mineral matter as part of their digestive process, so the inanimate mineral world receives elevation through the "face of the eagle." Domesticated animals (cows, sheep, goats, etc) consume vegetable matter, so the vegetable world receives elevation through the "face of the ox." And wild beasts consume other

---

4. *Torat Shmuel* 5642/1882, p. 184

animals, so the animal world receives elevation through the "face of the lion" (as well as through the "face of man," who consumes all of the elements of the physical world). Since these various "faces" include all of the creation, it means that all of the creations that we contemplate in our meditation, seeking their spiritual root, find their source in the *merkava*. Thus through the *merkava*, the entire universe achieves spiritual elevation. And the *merkava*, in turn, is a "vehicle" or conduit for the expression of Godliness in the world. It conducts divine influence into the creation, and elevates man and his prayers to the appropriate spiritual level. Since there are an infinite number of spiritual levels, there are an infinite number of *merkavot* (plural of *merkava*) as well.

In general, though, the *merkava* visions that appear in the prophets, correspond to important spiritual levels upon which we focus our meditation. The vision of Isaiah (*Yishayahu*, Ch 6), with its *seraphim*, corresponds to the world of *bria*. The vision of Yehezkel (Ch 1) with its *ofanim* and *chayot* corresponds to *yetzirah*, and the vision of Zecharia (Ch 6) with its horses corresponds to the world of *asiya*. As we contemplate creation, we want to first consider its source in the *merkava* of *asiya*, then of *yetzira* and finally of *bria*. Each level of meditation involves an elevation of the soul to that level. Each time that we meditate on an object, considering its physical properties and their source, we connect that item to the world of *asiya* and its *merkava*. When we elevate our meditation to consider how that object has a spiritual source in a general template or archetype of that kind of creation, we attach the object to the *merkava* in the world of *yetzira* (which is the world of archetypal and general templates of creation, also known as "angels"). And our own soul also achieves an elevation to the world of *yetzira*. When we contemplate how that general archetype and template has a spiritual source that is not a creation as such, but only the "possibility" or "potential" for creation, we attach that object to the *merkava* in the world of *bria* (which is the world of potential or possible creation), as well as raise our soul to that level as well. This is the meaning of *merkava* meditation, and obviously it is detailed and requires devotion and discipline.

It was at *matan Torah* (the "giving of the Torah) at Mt. Sinai, that all Jews first perceived the *merkava* of the world of *asiya*, which was a *merkava* of "horses."[5] Horses, according to Chassidic literature, allude to the Hebrew letters.[6] Just as a horse has the ability to transport us up the highest mountains and down again, so do the Hebrew letters allow us to ascend and descend spiritual levels. The ability to ascend and descend was granted at *matan Torah*, when the "decree that separated the upper realms from the lowers realms" was rescinded. Because the purpose of the *merkava* ("chariot") is to take us from one spiritual "location" to another, and that ability was granted at *Matan Torah*, that is when all the Jews as a nation first perceived the high spiritual levels that they could now attain. The horse obeys what its rider commands it to do, and the horse can carry us up the highest mountains, and down again. So, at *matan Torah* we gained the ability to transcend our own spiritual level and rise to higher spiritual levels. The ability was granted to us in the form of the letters of Torah and *tefila* ("prayer").[7]

However, in an amazing passage, the Rebbe Maharash informs us that in *galut*, in exile outside of our land, the *merkava* of horses is no longer sufficient.

> A *merkava* of horses was appropriate for *Matan Torah* on Mt. Sinai, when the world was in a state of *bitul*, or "nullification" to the One above. However, a *merkava* of horses will not suffice to bring Godliness down to the universe during the *galut* ("exile") in which we now find ourselves. In order to draw spirituality down to protect us during the *galut*, we need to consult the verse from Song of Songs (2:9), "My Lord resembles a

---

5. In a remarkable *sicha* of the Lubavitcher Rebbe, he tells us that the reason the haftorah for the festival of Shavuot is read from the prophet of Yehezkel (and not from Yishayahu, where a "higher" *merkava* is described) is because we are commanded to meditate on the lower levels of creation (as detailed in the vision of Yehezkel) in order to elevate them. See Likutei Sichot of the Lubavitcher Rebbe, Vol 33, Page 18. Available in English translation in "Torah like Fire and Water"

6. In Likutei Torah of the Alter Rebbe, *parshat Bechukotai*, we learn about letters. Among the things we learn is that the Hebrew words for "horse," — סוס (*sus*) — carries a gematria of 2 X 63=126. Each "63" is a name of *Hashem* (one of the ways in which His four letter Tetragrammaton may be spelled. This "name" helps us ascend and also descend, spiritually, as do letters.

7. Moreover, when we follow Jewish law, or *halacha*, we are enabled to make spiritual progress (*halicha* in Hebrew).

gazelle." A gazelle is light on its feet, and quickly traverses the terrain from one valley to another, and from a valley to a mountain and a mountain to a valley. There is nothing to stop the gazelle, unlike the horse, and therefore the gazelle is effective even during *galut*. The Supernal Man of the *merkava* is only a "likeness" of a man (of the ten *sephirot* of Atzilut), but a gazelle brings down Godliness from "You" (God Himself), who is above the likeness of man. In fact, the gazelle accesses a level that is expressly "not man," meaning from above man, from above *mamash*. A man cannot "ride" a gazelle, because it is a "vehicle" for levels that transcend man. Man only "resembles" the supernal man of the ten *sephirot* of Atzilut, and therefore the horse is a vehicle on which man can ride, but a gazelle which accesses spiritual levels beyond man, is not suitable for man to "ride upon." For that very reason, the "gazelle" can be a vehicle to bring Godliness down to us in *galut*, bringing down the *Shechina* ("God's presence") to dwell with us and "protect us." That is why the verses in Song of Songs tells us that, "You God are similar to a gazelle or to a young stag on the mountains of Bater." The "mountains of Bater" are the "peaks of separation" discussed in the Zohar, and even though the "peaks of separation" are not normally a place where spirituality is found, even they may become receptacles for Godliness. That is why the verse in Leviticus (26:44) states, "Even so, in the lands of their enemies, I will not destroy them nor abandon them to destruction." The verse uses the terminology "destroy" (which also carries the connotation of *calut*, or "spiritual expiry") because it is precisely during exile that Godliness of a higher level is drawn down to the Jews. (*Torat Shmuel* 5639/1879 of the Rebbe Maharash, V 1, p. 434)

The original *merkava* of *asiya* was a *merkava* of horses, which the Chasidic sources tell us are analogous to the letters of the Torah. By learning the Torah, we automatically mount the "horse" that takes us from one spiritual level to the next. However, what does this passage from the Maharash tell us about our *avodat Hashem* in *galut*? If it is no longer possible to access spiritual levels via meditation on the various levels of the *merkava*, and instead we must rely on the *merkava* of the "gazelle" that man cannot mount, so then what is left for us? Perhaps the idea is that even when we cannot manage to elevate ourselves spiritually, and our meditation does not take us to the spiritual places to which we want to go, we can still access levels of Godliness that are beyond us. The *merkava* of the gazelle does not allow us to ride it, but it nevertheless fulfills the role of a *merkava* by elevating our prayers and bringing Godliness down to guide and protect us even in exile.

OTIOT, or Hebrew Letters

Another topic that receives unique treatment and emphasis in the Chassidut of the Rebbe Maharash is the subject of *otiot*, or Hebrew letters as objects of meditation. In the final chapters of his *Shaar Hayichud vehaEmunah* (second section of Tanya), the Alter Rebbe not only touches upon, but presents detailed information about the letters of the Hebrew alphabet, in a manner that could very well lend itself to meditation. However, we do not find that his treatment of the letters as objects of meditation is repeated in his own Chassidut (*Torah Ohr, Likutei Torah* and his other discourses). Neither do we find it (as far as the author was able to ascertain) in the Chassidut of his successors (the MItteler Rebbe and the Tzemach Tzedek).[8] But, we do find that the Maharash not only mentions the letters, but writes of them in a manner that leaves no question that he expects his Chassidim to consider the letters a topic of *hitbonenut,* or "meditation" prior to prayers. The Maharash writes the following (in the series of discourses entitled *Mayim Rabim* of the year 5636/1876, Ch 28):

> Since every letter of the twenty-two letters represents a specific descent of divine vitality and influx that is distinct and separate from every other letter, therefore each letter possesses its own unique form. The shape of each written letter therefore also has its own particular form in writing that indicates the nature of the descent of Godliness that is associated with that letter. The shape of the letter reveals how the Godly influx is drawn down through that letter, from His holy attributes, His will and

---

8. See *Maamorei Admor Ha'emtzai* (the Mitteler Rebbe) on Shemot, V 1, P 29-30 — Here the Mitteler Rebbe does discuss the topic in a general manner: "The 22 letters draw down Godliness in the three general vectors of *chesed, din* and *rachamim* ("Kindness, Strictness and Mercy")." But the Mitteler Rebbe does not go into further detail.

His wisdom, all of which exist in total unity with Him, as explained above at length. And when we delve into this topic in depth, with great focus for an hour or two, a true impression of His unity and expansiveness will be engraved upon our mind and heart. It will be clear that in the heavens and on the earth, there is none other than He, even in space. [This meditation] is associated with the letter *hey* of His name (*Havaya*) and within the soul of man, that corresponds to meditation on the infinite light of God and His unity. It is especially associated with recital of the *shema*, including the two blessings that precede the *kriat shema* which refer to this topic. In each and every word of these prayers, we should feel the Godly illumination and vitality that is present, and in this manner we will be vitalized with a spiritual energy while experiencing the infinite light that enlivens us and creates us. And in this manner we will merit to become included in the infinite light above, which is the source of all life.

Thus, it is clear that the Rebbe Maharash intended meditation on the letters of the Hebrew alphabet to be part of the "repertoire" of a chassid, not only in theory, but also in practice. Yet, we do not find that Chassidim practice this sort of meditation as part of their preparation for prayers. The explanation may be as the Maharash himself explains elsewhere, that we simply do not have enough information. As he writes (in *Torat Shmuel* 5637/1877, Vol 1, page 40-41):

> There are four elements to the Torah: Incantations, vowels, crowns and letters. The incantations have not been revealed, meaning that they are not evident at this time. In truth, not only the incantations remain concealed, but all of the elements — the vowels, the crowns, and the letters remain concealed. All that is revealed is the *pshat* — or "simple meaning" — of the letters. The essence of letters is not revealed... For example, in the Talmud, we learn all of one chapter (*Hashoel*) in Gemorra *Baba Metzia* 95A from the letter *vov* of the word *veki yishal* ("When one borrows..." — Shemot 22:13). But this is only because the *vov* [which means "and"] adds to the initial topic. Or there may be extra letters or missing letters, as we see there. But we learn nothing about the letter itself, or its essence; for example, why does it take on this specific shape or form? Similarly, regarding R' Akiva, who produced many interpretations of the Torah based on nothing more than the 'point' of the letters — this is also

based only on superficial knowledge (*pshat*) of the letters, and not about the essence of the letters…And yet, when we learn Torah, it includes all of the four levels; the incantations, the vowels, the crowns and the letters…

From the above passage, it is clear that according to the Rebbe Maharash, we do not know enough about the shape of the letters (which he calls the "essence" of the letters), to meditate upon them. Yet elsewhere,[9] he informs us that we do know a little about the shapes from the book called *Sefer Hatemuna* ("The book of pictures"), but what little knowledge is possible to glean from the book is "a drop in the bucket." And if so, we are left to ask why he exhorts his followers to practice meditation on the letters as preparation for prayers? The same could be asked of the Alter Rebbe and his explanations of the letters in Tanya (*Shaar Hayichud* Ch 11-12). Although the Alter Rebbe did not explicitly encourage his Chassidim to contemplate or meditate on the letters, he did present the information. What we might answer, though, is that by focusing our attention on the letters as a means of preparation for prayers, we do achieve some elevation of the soul, even based on the limited knowledge that we possess. That is, since we know that it is the Hebrew letters that enliven creation, and we focus our meditation on the creative power of the letters even though we do not know exactly "how" they draw down Hashem's power to create, we nonetheless undergo some elevation of the soul and thus prepare ourselves for prayers.[10]

---

9. *Torat Shmuel* 5637/1877, Vol 1, P 45

10. The noted Rav/Mashpia, R' Chaim Shalom Deitsch שיח׳ (Rosh Kollel of the Tzemach Tzedek shul in Jerusalem), during a Tanya *shiur* on June 26, 2012 (the *shiur* can be viewed on video at www.chasidut.net) remarked on this very topic. He noted the emphasis on the letters in the Alter Rebbe's *Sha'ar Hayichud Vehaemuna*, and commented, "I have no *kabala* regarding this matter." That is, R' Deitsch did not receive any kind of instruction or tradition from his own mentor (R' Shlomo Chaim Kesselman A"H) about how to incorporate the letters into his own *avodat Hashem* in meditation and prayer. Nevertheless, R' Deitsch suggested (in his *shiurim* on *Kuntres Ha'avoda*) that meditation on any quality of the created object enhances our appreciation of the divine energy that enlivens it. For example, the taste, the color, the shape…are all qualities that are imparted to the created object by Hashem. And therefore, the letters as well, are among the qualities that we might consider in contemplating on the object. One might add that the Hebrew letters with which the object is created are not mere

Ahavat Olam, or "Everlasting Love"

The goal of all meditation, whether on the *merkava* or the Hebrew letters or any other topic of Chassidut, is to achieve greater love of Hashem. That much is clear from the *Kuntres Ha'avoda* and other sources: While fear of God is a necessary ingredient and foundation of divine service, the purpose of meditation and meditative prayer at length is to attain love of God. There are three levels of love of God described in Chassidic literature, in order of their spiritual level: *Ahavat Olam* ("Everlasting love"), *Ahava Rabah* ("Great love") and *Ahava B'taanugim* ("love with delights"). *Ahavat Olam* is love that is generated by meditation on the creation and God's presence in creation and His role as the Creator. This is the level on which we consider specific objects of creation and "look for" their spiritual source and how the object connects to successively higher spiritual levels (such as in the *merkava* meditation described above). *Ahavat olam* requires intense intellectual concentration and discipline, but it eventually results in the pleasurable realization that He is present in all of creation and that He is the source of creation. The Chassidic sources (*Kuntres Haavoda*) describe this as "love like water," because it has a soothing and calming effect on the psyche, not unlike the effect that bathing or swimming in water has on the body. This is how we begin our meditation and launch our prayers as well, during the *pesukei dezimra* ("songs of praise"). After a suitable amount of *hitbonenut* and achievement of *Ahavat olam*, we are elevated to another level of spiritual and intellectual endeavor. *Ahavat olam* demands of us to meditate on spiritual levels, and ascend through the *seder hishtalshelut* ("hierarchy of spiritual levels"), including the *sephirot* and worlds. Eventually, we reach a "stage" of understanding in which there are no more discernible "levels" to attain, and we are constrained by our intellect. We "know" that there is more to spirituality and that

---

"qualities" of the item. They are the spiritual source and essence of the created object. And therefore, contemplation on the letters that create the object is far deeper than meditation on the superficial physical qualities of the object. Meditation upon the letters touches upon the very essence and spiritual root of the object, which is why the Alter Rebbe mentions and the Rebbe Maharash recommends meditation based on the letters, even if we do not grasp the essence of the letters themselves.

God is not limited to what we are able to grasp with our feeble minds, and yet we lack the "tools" to continue our meditation.

When that occurs, Chassidut instructs us to employ another technique of *hitbonenut*, called *avodat hashlila*, or "negation of grasp." This technique, mentioned by the Rambam as the highest form of intellectual pursuit, requires that we negate our concepts of Godliness in order to reach a higher understanding of Godliness. When we realize that our limited grasp of Godliness is not sufficient, we negate it (mentally), while simultaneously declaring (to ourselves) that while God is not "limited to this concept," He is also not the "opposite" of the concept. In other words, whatever concept of God we have grasped, we recognize as correct, but as insufficient to grasp Him. As Rambam describes this process, we realize that 1) our concept is not sufficient to describe Him, and 2) Yet God, is not the opposite of our concept. For example, we may through our meditation arrive to an understanding of the *sephira* of *chochma* as the "interface" between God's infinity and our own limited grasp. And since it is the interface, *chochma* requires that we *mevatel* ("nullify") ourselves to His infinite light that is beyond us. At this point, we 1) grasp the nature of *chochma* and 2) acknowledge that He is not *chochma*, but he is also not the opposite of *chochma*: He is beyond *chochma*. This in turn catapults us to the natural conclusion that there is something beyond *chochma* (His infinite illumination). There is something beyond *chochma* that is "not *chochma*," and even though we do not grasp what it is, we know that it exists. In this manner, the *oved Hashem* (one who serve God by getting close to Him) will reason" to himself, "I understand *chochma*, but God is unlimited, therefore He is not limited to *Chochma*. At the same time, He is also not the opposite of *chochma*." The person engaged in this *hitbonenut* thus projects his awareness beyond *chochma*, to a level that in fact cannot be described by any affirmative adjective or definition. It is simply "not *chochma*."

Welcome to the world of *makifim*, or transcendent Godliness. By "negating" the positive concepts which we have developed, we project our awareness to infinite realms that are beyond the intellect. This is hard work, and is appropriate only for those who have already undertaken the long and arduous path of *ahavat olam*. Only one who thoroughly grasps all levels of Godliness that are associated with *seder hishtalshelut*, leading to *ahavat olam* (which is also described as "love like water"), may successfully strive for *Ahava rabah* (which is a form of "love like fire"). Only after meticulous meditation on the lower level leading to *Ahavat olam*, in a complete and thorough manner, do we become a *keli*, or "vessel" for the higher transcendent love of *Ahava rabah*.[11] The work that we do upon ourself to attain *ahavat olam* is a necessary condition in order to attain *Ahavah rabah*. Whether or not it is a sufficient condition is up to the One above.

The importance of this second level of *hitbonenut*, is that it lifts us to the awareness of Godliness that is called *sovev kol olamim* ("transcendent illumination"), or *makifim*, which is transcendent awareness. In the order of prayers, it is associated with the blessings preceding the *kriat shema* (after *Barchu*) and with the *kriat shema* itself. Since it brings us to awareness of matters that are beyond our normal awareness, it generates "love like fire." Unlike the soothing divine love of *Ahavat olam*, this "love like fire" is a strong and overwhelming need to be close to God, called *Ahavah rabah*, or "great love." It is not a love of the heart alone, but of the entire body. The Rebbeim tell us that "all Chassidim should strive to experience *Ahava rabah*."

Finally, there is a third level of divine love that far surpasses either *Ahavat olam* or *Ahavah rabah*. Known as *Ahavat beTaanugim* ("Love like Delights"), it is the love of the essence of the soul. Since the Jewish divine soul is a "piece of Godliness," when this level of love is activated, it is as if the soul comes "face to face" with its source, and there is no distance between the soul and the One above. This is the love of which R' Akiva spoke, when he said (*Hagiga* 14B), "When you arrive to the pure slabs of marble, do not cry 'water, water." Because it is a love borne of proximity and closeness to God, *Ahava BeTaanugim* bears more resemblance to love like water than it is to love like fire. Therefore while in the throes of this love, R' Akiva told us, we should not assume that there is any distance between ourselves and the One above. What

---

11. See *Kuntres Ha'avoda* of the Rebbe Rashab, Ch 4. In translation ("Love like Fire and Water" — p. 111)

we "see" is not "two waters" ("water, water") but only a reflection of ourselves.[12] It is regarding this level of love that the Rebbe Maharash makes new contributions to our understanding that (as far as the author can ascertain) do not appear in the Chassidut of his predecessors (except perhaps by way of implication, but not stated explicitly). Here are a few of his unique *chiddushim* ("novella") regarding *Ahava betaangim*…

1. Regarding R' Akiva's statement ("When you arrive to the pure marble slabs, do not say 'water, water'…), the Maharash says, "Do not say water, because what you perceive is actually 'light.'"[13] Although the Maharash does not explain this insight, perhaps it is understood in light of the Previous Rebbe's (the Rayatz) comments on the explanations of his father to his Chassidic discourses of the year 5666/1906. There,[14] the Rayatz explains that the *oved Hashem* makes *kelim* — 'vessels' — in order to contain and channel the Godly light that he perceives through his *hitbonenut* and *avodat Hashem*. As he ascends spiritual levels, though, the spiritual "vessels" that he creates for himself in order contain the light, become more and more refined and ethereal (since he becomes more and more able to experience direct perception of Godliness, without a need for *kelim*). The *kelim* are necessary on the level of *ahavat olam*, during which we need "filters" and "garments" in order to withstand and integrate Godly illumination. On the level of *Ahavah rabah*, the *oved Hashem* also needs *kelim* ("vessels") but they are the kind of

---

12. See the Rebbe Rashab in *Besha'ah Shehikdimu* 5672/1912, Vol 2, pp. 895 and 964. See also the notes of the Rebbe Rayatz from his study with his father the Rebbe Rashab, regarding the three levels of love (translated in this work, see Appendix 1, Parts 2 and 3).

13. See *Torat Shmuel* 5675/1875, V 2, p. 453. Here, the Maharash explains that R' Akiva's statement ("When you arrive near the pure marble slabs, do not say 'water, water'…") applies to experience of the highest level of the soul (the *yechida*). Therefore when he said, "Do not say water, water…" R' Akiva meant one should not identify the experience as "water" because really it is *ohr* ("light"). Elsewhere (p. 458), though, the Rebbe Maharash explains differently: "Do not differentiate between the supernal 'water' that lies beyond the heavens, and the waters below the heavens…" because really they are one, united by *da'at*.

14. Translated in Appendix 1 at the back of this siddur, Part 2 and 3.

vessels that he "negates" in order to achieve the higher perception associated with *makifim*, or "transcendent Godliness." So, the *kelim* associated with *Ahava rabah* are very refined. Ultimately, when meditating on the level of *Ahava beta'anugim*, the *Rayatz* tells us that there are no *kelim* per se. The *ohr*, or "light" is itself the *kelim*. In other words, the person has direct perception of the *ohr*, or light. He doesn't need *kelim*. This fits very well with the explanation that, "Do not say water, water," because it is really light.

2. The Rebbe Maharash tells us that Yoseph hid his silver (*kesef*, meaning both "silver" and also "yearning") cup in his brother Benyamin's sack for a very interesting reason.[15] The silver cup alludes to love of God on the highest level — *Ahava betaanugim*. And the reason that Yoseph hid the cup in Bejamin's sack was because he wanted to bring his younger brother up to this level of love of God. But if so, why did he not give his brother the cup outright, as a gift? The Maharash explains that since Benjamin was not on the same level of *tzaddik* ("righteous person") as Yoseph, who had no ego whatsoever, therefore Benyamin was subject to self-awareness. If he became aware that he experienced *Ahava be'taanugim*, it could have caused him to feel ego over his attainment of such a high spiritual level. Therefore, Yoseph hid the cup in Benyamin's belongings, so that Benjamin would not become conscious of his high spiritual level. There is much to be learned from this fascinating insight from the Rebbe Maharash, but one of the items to be learned is that *Ahavat betaanugim* may be experienced by everyone, including those who are not on the highest spiritual levels. Since it is an essential love, coming from the very essence of the soul, and every Jew possesses a Godly soul, every Jew may experience *Ahavah betaanugim*.

However, that does not mean that everyone will experience *Ahava betaanugim*. The Rebbe Rashab[16] explains that only one who has perfected his meditation leading to *Ahavat olam* may experience any levels

---

15. *Torat Shmuel* 5642/1882, Page 89
16. In *Kuntres Ha'avoda* Ch 4 and 5, as well as in the appendix to *Yomtov shel Rosh Hashana 5666* (edition published 2010), with the notes of the Rebbe Rayatz.

beyond that. Yet, perfection of *avoda* ("divine service") on the level of *Ahavat olam* by itself does not guarantee that he will experience either of the higher levels of divine love. Like *Ahava rabah,* there are requirements in order to achieve *Ahava betaanugim*. But unlike *Ahavah rabah*, one cannot "expect" to experience *Ahavah betaanugim* just because he has perfected his meditation and *avoda* on the lower level of *Ahavat olam*. Such perfection transforms him into a *keli* for *Ahava rabah* (even though it does not guarantee that he will experience *Ahavah rabah* either). However, there is no *keli* that can contain this highest level of divine love of *Ahava betaanugim*, and therefore even the perfection of our *avoda* on the lower level does not transform anyone into a "vessel" for such a sublime and essential level. *Ahavat olam* only fulfills a necessary condition for this very high level, but it does not automatically guarantee that he will attain it.

To understand better, the Previous Rebbe's illustration (appearing at the end of *Kuntres Haavoda* and translated in the appendix to "Love like Fire and Water") is useful. The previous Rebbe utilizes the parable of water deep underground in hidden reservoirs that never make it to the surface of the earth, and yet the earth is moist. There are underground reservoirs, there are subterranean springs that convey the water to the earth, and there are the bodies of water such as rivers and lakes and oceans that we see in front of us. The revealed love that we experience as a result of *ahavat olam* is comparable to the bodies of water that we see in front us. However, those bodies of water have a source; ultimately they are fed from the hidden reservoirs of water underneath the earth's surface. And we never see those bodies of water. Yet, they influence and moisten the earth's surface even in places that we do not detect any body of water. Occasionally we will find the location where an underground spring breaks the surface of the earth and becomes a river or stream. But in general, what is deep underground remains underground, even while it moistens the earth and provides irrigation for the crops. The same is true of divine love: Hidden deep within us are reservoirs of essential Godly love, for the very reason that the Godly soul within us is itself apart of the One above. Yet, for the most part, that essential love remains concealed and only emerges at times of its own choosing and for its own "reasons." Yet, when we meditate and make conscious attempts to find God in our own lives, that love deep within "feeds" and nourishes the conscious love that we develop through meditation, and brings it to life. So, in actual point of fact, the essential love within us remains concealed, while simultaneously it feeds the conscious and clear love that we develop through our meditation. If we are fortunate, we may occasionally experience the deep love rising to the surface from its concealed source within, and that would be an experience of the soul itself — of *Ahavah betaanugim*. We cannot decide when that might occur, nor can we prepare for it other than by removing all blockages that might prevent it. The soul itself decides if and when to make itself seen and heard; all we can do is make sure there is nothing to prevent its incursion in our daily life. But for the most, part, we only experience this essential love in the same way that we know about the soul — it must be there because otherwise we have no life. Similarly, because our meditation on the level of *Ahavat olam* leads to love of God, it must be that the deep reservoirs of love within us are what "feed" and nourish that love to develop, because otherwise, from where does it emerge "out of nowhere"?

Armed with this understanding, we can grasp another *chiddush* or novel insight of the Rebbe Maharash. He tells us that the *ahavat olam* mentioned in our prayers (during *birchot kriat shema*) is actually *ahavah betaanugim*.[17] Right smack in the middle of the blessings preceding *kriat shema*, appears the second blessing of this section, starting with the words, *Ahavat olam*. And the Rebbe Maharash tells us that this is an allusion, not to the "entry level" love that we attempt to develop during the previous section of prayers (*pesukei dezimra*), but to the highest, most developed divine love described above. How could this be? The Rebbe Maharash explains that the word *olam* may take on two different meanings. One is "world," and the other is "eternal and everlasting." When we initially begin preparing for prayers, we initiate our meditation with matters drawn from the creation and from the world, as described above. Because this "entry level" meditation requires hard work in focusing on specific items and created objects in an attempt to

---

17. *Torat Shmuel* 5626/1866, p. 217. See also *Torat Shmuel* 5636/1876, p. 445-449

find their divine spark and spiritual source, the resulting love is called *Ahavat olam*, or "love of the world" or "love derived from the world." On the other hand, this love is nourished and "fed" from afar by the very love of the soul that is deep within us, that is deep and everlasting since it is coming not only from out intellect but from the essence of our soul. And thus, *Ahava betaanugim* can also be referred to as *Ahavat olam* ("Everlasting love") as it is in the middle of the blessing preceding *kriat shema*. Why particularly here in the prayers is this *Ahavat olam* (which is *Ahava betaanugim*) mentioned? Since it is essential love, it could be mentioned anywhere in our prayers, since such essential love is not dependent upon anything that we might do (such as meditation). The only requirement is that there be nothing present to prevent it from making an appearance.

Nevertheless, there is some logic for this part of the prayers to allude to *Ahavah betaanugim*. In general, the prayers follow an ascending order, beginning with the *pesukei dezimra* and culminating in the *Shemonah Esreh*. *Hodu* and *pesukei dezimra* involve meditation on the level called *memalle kol olamim*, or Godliness as it "permeates and fills the worlds." Thus the love that results from such meditation derives from the "world" and creation and is called *Ahavat olam* ("world") as above. After *Barchu*, our attention is shifted to the higher level of Godliness that transcends the worlds, known as *sovev kol olamin* ("transcending the worlds"). It is at this point that we begin to utilize the tool of *avodat hashlila*, or "negative grasp" described above, in order to gain some kind of awareness of spiritual levels that are beyond us. The Rebbe Maharash tells us that the first blessing of the section following *Barchu* (*Birchot Kriat Shema*) is associated with the animal soul. By discovering and appreciating its own source in the spiritual archetypes that are associated with the *merkava*, the animal soul "gets on board," so to speak and undergoes an elevation. This elevation of the animal soul enables us to experience a higher level of sublime love called *Ahava rabah*, which is a fiery love and desire to connect with the One above. Then, following the blessing *yotzer hameorot* ("He who forms the luminaries"), the Maharash tells us that the blessing *Ahavat olam* is associated with the Godly soul. And if so, it is entirely logical that *Ahavat olam* (*olam* as in "everlasting" and "eternal") should be associated with *Ahava Betaanugim* as well, since that is the divine love that is associated with the essence of the Godly soul.

Moreover, *Ahava betaanugim* is the highest form of divine love that we may attain, so it makes sense that it would follow the *Ahava Rabah* that is associated with the blessing *yotzer hameorot* (in the *birchot kriat shema*). Although it is an essential love, not specifically associated with any particular spiritual level, and therefore it could theoretically appear anywhere in our prayers and it would not be "out of order," nevertheless as the highest expression of Godly love, it is logical that it should be associated with the section of the prayers that both follows *Ahavah Rabah* and is associated with the Godly soul.

Following this analysis of the unique contributions of the Rebbe Maharash to meditation before and during prayer, what remains to discuss are his suggestions and recommendations regarding prayer itself. It is one matter to discuss topics of meditation that, according to the Maharash allow us to prepare for prayers, such as the letters and upon the *merkava*. But what about the prayers themselves? Here again, we find a unique contribution from the Rebbe Maharash, that allows us to better appreciate the role and function of prayers in the life of a Chassid. If meditative prayer were a science or an orderly technique, then it would be necessary only to follow the prescribed steps and we would ascend from one spiritual level to the next. Everyone who applied themselves and followed the various stages of the technique would be guaranteed to attain the same results of love of God with the attendant effect on their everyday lives. However, it turns out that prayer (at least according to the Chabad Rebbeim) is far more of an art form than a technique. There are preparations that are recommended, such as learning a Chassidic discourse, immersion in a mikveh, and meditation (*hitbonenut*) before prayers, but the prayers themselves are more subjective and emotional (which is why prayer is called the "service of the heart") than they are technical.

Commonly, we divide those who take prayers seriously into three different categories. There are those who pray with attention to the simple meaning of the words; that is, with comprehension of what each word "means" on the simple textual level. Beyond this serious but elementary stage, are those who have learned Chassidut (Chassidic texts from the Chabad or other Chassidic rebbeim) and who understand the text from the perspective of Chassidut. They pray with their Chassidic understanding, which goes beyond the simple text and incorporates Chassidic concepts. Finally, there are those who *daven b'avoda* — who pray at length with introspection in order to not only understand but to internalize and utilize the Chassidic concepts that lie behind the words in their divine service, in an attempt to become closer to God.

However, the Rebbe Maharash, who lived and wrote his Chassidic discourses roughly 150 years ago, divided the serious prayers of his generation into four or five separate categories. The first category was those who were careful to pray with the precise pronunciation of the words. The second was those who prayed with the simple textual meaning of the words as well. Then there were those who could pray with kabalistic intention (unusual in our generation, though there are "pockets" of dedicated kaballists who pray according to the *kavanot* of the Ariz"l), and fourth were those who pray with Chassidic intention. Finally, the fifth and "highest" category were those who look "behind" the words of prayers, seeking to fathom the narrative underlying the prayers, or as the Maharash himself put it, "the story behind the words." About these five categories, the Maharash wrote the following:

> When praying with *kavana*, there are those who pray with the simple meaning of the words. Then, there are those who pray according to the *kavanot* of the *Ariz'l*, and there are those who pray with Chasidic intention, which is greater (the Rebbe Maharash reports in the name of his father, the *Tzemach Tzedek* that when the Alter Rebbe wanted to wanted to praise Chassidut, he would say, "*Kaballah* is merely 'names,' but Chassidut is נגילה ונשמחה בך — 'rejoicing and happy with You' — meaning with God's essential infinite illumination"). Finally, there are those who seek to know, "What is the story behind these words"? In general, what kind of story is Psalms trying to tell? For example, when reciting the psalm (148), "Praise be God in the heavens, praised be God in the heights," one person might seek to simply pronounce the words correctly. Another may seek to pray with the simple meaning of the words; for example, that "in the heights" means "high." Another may seek to pray with the *kavanot* of the *Ariz'l*, for example that "heavens" (*shamayim*) implies

"fire and water," meaning that the underlying vitality of the word differs from the surface meaning. But the highest form of prayers, higher than the others, is when the person delves into the "subject" of the prayers. He seeks to know, 'what is the story behind these words,' and he focuses his mind with great concentration and excitement on the words of prayer, as in the verse, "You cling to the Lord your God, all of you alive today," referring to cleaving to the infinite One, the source of all life. When we focus and concentrate in this manner, no "foreign thoughts" occur to us. Since our intellect is occupied, it cannot be distracted by a "foreign thought." (*Torat Shmuel 5638*/1878 of the Rebbe Maharash, pp. 452-3).

At first glance, it appears that those who pray with Chassidic intention are not in the same "category" as those who seek "…the story behind these words." The passage from the Maharash seems to divide them into two categories: "There are those who pray with Chassidic intention…" and "Finally, there are those who seek to know…" However, since the end of the quote does not mention praying with Chassidic intention, but only mentions those who pray by "looking for the story behind the words," it seems more likely that the Rebbe Maharash meant that they are one and the same thing. That is, those who pray with Chassidic intention are the same people as those who "look for the story behind the words." And if so, according to the Maharash, there is a whole new world of prayers that was opened up by the Chassidic movement. Rather than rote recitation of words, even when accompanied by understanding of the meaning of the words, and rather than memorization and visualization of kabalistic names, the Chassid "looks for the story" behind the word. This is why Chassidic davening can take hours and why it fixates the person who is praying. When we are searching for a "story," a hidden inner "narrative," the words come alive and captivate us. The process of prayer is no longer a "fixed" recitation of words. It becomes a live "search" that is joyful and absorbing ("rejoicing and happy with You") that can occupy the person for hours:

Since the 'early Hasidim' dedicated nine hours out of their day in order to prayer and meditation, their love and fear of God was lasting. This is the difference between *tzadikim* and *beinonim*; the *beinoni* must pray "like the nation escaping from Egypt." They had to escape the negative and evil influence of Egypt, in order to avoid strange and 'foreign' thoughts in their *avoda*. But the *tzadik*, in whom there is no evil whatsoever, is not afraid of "foreign thoughts." And therefore the "early Hasidim" took their time during prayers, allowing their love and fear of God to develop. In the future as well, it will not be necessary to "run away from evil," because there will be no evil at all. The process will be to shed the "outer aspects of the heart" (*chitzoniut halev*) and achieve "inner heart" (*pnimiyut halev*)…love 'with all your heart." (*Torat Shmuel* 5639/1879 of the Rebbe Maharash, p. 148)

The above passage deals with the "Hasidim" of the past as well as the "Tzadikim" of the present and the future. Nevertheless, the same applies to all of us:

In this manner, we may comprehend the verse that tells us, "Know the God of your father." This kind of knowledge is associated with contemplation. It requires focused meditation on Godliness, including concentration to the extent that the meditator becomes "moved." He then becomes generally careful to "avoid evil" and commited to doing good. In particular, the "movement" that results from focus and concentrating during meditation has an effect on his soul, causing him to be one who "progresses" from one level to the next. That is what is meant by "Know the God of your father, and serve Him with a full heart." As we know, the service of the heart is *tefila,* prayer. And in general prayer and meditation are one. The lengthy *pesukei dezimra* and *bircat Kriat Shema* are all about achieving the state of spiritual excitement and self nullification associated with *yichuda tata'ah* ("lower unity" in which it seems that the universe is real and God is in the background) and *yichuda ila'ah* ("supernal unity," in which it is evident that God is the true reality and the created universe is of questionable reality), each according to his own personal spiritual level. This is what is meant by *da'at*, which is intellectual "unity" that is so powerful that it influences the soul to free itself from the body, and to cleave to the infinite light of the One above, with great longing, cleaving and desire. (*Torat Shmuel* 5637/1877, V 1, pp. 105-6)

To a significant extent, this intellectual approach combined with meditation from the heart is what characterizes all of Chabad Chassidut, and the Rebbe Maharash added to the body of literature supporting meditative prayer as well as gave us hints how to put the meditative prayer into practice in our own lives.

OTHER BOOKS BY THE AUTHOR

Love Like Fire and Water — an essay on Jewish Meditation (translation and commentary of *Kuntres Ha'avoda* of the Rebbe Rashab) — published by Moznaim Press 2005

Inner Lights from Jerusalem — excerpts from the *Shem Mishmuel* — Moznaim Press 2007.

Meditation like Fire and Water — the Siddur with Chassidut (also known as Daven Chabad and Mind over Heart) — translated excerpts from Chabad Chassidus on prayer, including translations of virtually all that was written on the subject by the Rebbe Rashab) — 2012

Praying Like Fire and Water — a companion siddur to Love like Fire and Water, with a commentary designed to help the student apply the principles of Love like Fire and Water (*Kuntres Haavoda*) to prayer — 2017.

JERUSALEM CONNECTION

is a non-profit organization dedicated to Jewish outreach and education. It was created with the blessing of the Lubavitcher Rebbe in 1991 and has since flourished in the old city of Jerusalem. It is frequented by Jewish university students, tourists and new immigrants to Israel who seek spiritual guidance and connection with the One above and also instruction in the inner dimensions of Torah (Chassidic and Kaballistic literature).

For more information, visit us at www.jerusalemconnection.org or email jerconn1@ gmail.com